T0326530

From the Werner Plan to the EMU

In Search of a Political Economy for Europe

P.I.E.-Peter Lang

Bruxelles · Bern · Berlin · Frankfurt/M · New York · Oxford · Wien

SALTSA
A Joint Programme for Working Life Research in Europe

SALTSA is a programme of partnership in European working life research run by the Swedish National Institute for Working Life (NIWL/ALI) and the Swedish Confederations of Trade Unions (LO), Professional Employees (TCO) and Professional Associations (SACO).

The aim of SALTSA is to generate applicable research results of a high academic standard and relevance. Research is largely project-based.

Research is carried out in three areas:
* the labour market
* work organisation
* the work environment

The Labour Market Programme

Labour market research is predominantly based on projects in collaboration with European researchers and research institutes. The focus is on ongoing and/or social partner related processes in Europe.

Aims include providing a foundation for ongoing debate, current political issues and processes involving social partners in the European labour market.

Chairman of the Labour Market Programme Committee is Professor Lars Magnusson and programme secretary is Torbjörn Strandberg.

website: www.niwl.se/saltsa

Lars MAGNUSSON and Bo STRÅTH (eds.)

From the Werner Plan to the EMU

In Search of a Political Economy for Europe

Arbetslivsinstitutet

TCO SACO

SALTSA — JOINT PROGRAMME
FOR WORKING LIFE RESEARCH IN EUROPE
The National Institute for Working Life and The Swedish Trade Unions in Co-operation

"Work & Society"
No.29

© P.I.E.-Peter Lang s.a.
Presses Interuniversitaires Européennes
Brussels, 2001 – 2nd printing 2002
E-mail : info@peterlang.com
www.peterlang.net

ISSN 1376-0955
ISBN 90-5201-999-1
D/2001/5678/12

Die Deutsche Bibliothek – CIP-Einheitsaufnahme

From the Werner Plan to the EMU. In search of a political economy
for Europe / Lars Magnusson & Bo Stråth (ed.). – Bruxelles ; Bern ; Berlin ;
Frankfurt/M. ; New York ; Wien : PIE Lang, 2001
(Series Work & Society ; No.29)
ISBN 90-5201-948-7

*CIP available from the British Library, GB
and the Library of Congress, USA.*
ISBN   0-8204-4672-6

Contents

7

Preface

This book is the result of a cooperative project between the European University Institute in Florence and the SALSTA programme. At the EUI, the framework was provided by the European Forum 1999-2001 on Europeanization and the nation-state. The SALTSA programme studies working life in a European perspective and is a cooperative venture between the Swedish National Institute for Working Life and the three Swedish trade union confederations, LO, TCO and SACO.

The aim of the book is to discuss the preconditions of a European political economy in historical light, from the Werner Plan in 1970 – and, indeed, earlier – through until the implementation of the Maastricht EMU; and from this historical perspective to reflect on the future prospects of such a political economy. We have sought to do it in a way where we connect policy-making and politics with theory-building in economics and other social sciences, and long-term historical processes of structural change with social practices.

All the authors have stayed for varied lengths of time at the EUI, where they have presented ideas or drafts at a seminar series from the autumn of 1999 to the summer of 2000. At this seminar series the contours of the book, and its conceptualisation of the problem of a European political economy, took shape. In order to intensify the reflection, experts other than the contributors to this book were invited to present ideas. The seminar series has been supplemented with several half-day workshops on special topics. Further, the authors met twice at workshops over two days where drafts of the chapters were discussed in order to enhance the cohesion of the book and the links between the chapters.

We wish to thank Torbjörn Strandberg at the Working Life Institute/SALTSA for his very efficient coordination the project and Sylvie Pascucci at EUI for her equally efficient organisation of all the meetings, seminars and workshops in Florence. We also want to express our warm thanks to Paul Rouse who copy-edited this book in an excellent fashion. Finally we want to thank Philippe Pochet for his constructive suggestions at the final meeting with all the authors.

Lars Magnusson & Bo Stråth
Stockholm and Florence in May 2001

Abbreviations

AEFC	Association of European Financial Centres
BEPG	Broad Economic Policy Guidelines
CBI	Citizen's Basic Income
BIS	Bank for International Settlements
CAP	Common Agricultural Policy
CDEP	Centre of Decision for Economic Policy
CDU	Christian Democratic Union
CEEP	European Centre of Public Enterprise
CI	Citizen's Income
CRA	Community Reinvestment Act
DM	*Deutsche Mark*
EBRD	European Bank for Reconstruction and Development
EC	European Community
ECSC	European Coal and Steel Community
ECB	European Central Bank
ECU	European Currency Unit
EEC	European Economic Community
EMS	European Monetary System
EMU	Economic and Monetary Union
EP	European Parliament
EPC	European Political Cooperation
EPG	Employment Policy Guidelines
ERM	Exchange Rate Mechanism
ESC	Economic and Social Committee
ESCB	European System of Central Banks
ETUC	European Trade Union Confederation
EU	European Union
EUI	European University Institute
FRG	Federal Republic of Germany

13

FRW	Feasible Real Wage
GDP	Gross Domestic Product
IGC	Intergovernmental Conference
IMF	International Monetary Fund
MC	Monetary Committee (of the EC)
MOC	Method of Open Coordination
NATO	North Atlantic Treaty Organization
NCB	National Central Bank
NGO	Non-governmental Organisation
NIE	New Institutional Economics
NJL	Nickell-Jackman-Layard
OCA	Optimum Currency Areas
OECD	Organization for Economic Cooperation and Development
OEEC	Organization for European Economic Cooperation
OOPEC	Office for Official Publications of the EC
OPEC	Organization of Petroleum Exporting Countries
PES	Party of European Socialists
PS	*Parti Socialiste*
SDR	Special Drawing Rights
SEA	Single European Act
SGP	Stability and Growth Pact
SME	Small and Medium-sized Enterprises
SPD	*Sozialdemokratische Partei Deutschlands*
TCE	Transaction Cost Economics
TEU	Treaty on European Union
UK	United Kingdom
UNICE	Union of Industrial and Employers' Confederations of Europe
US	United States
USSR	Union of Soviet Socialist Republics

From the Werner Plan to the EMU:
A Chronology

1950

May

In a speech inspired by Jean Monnet, Robert Schuman, the French Foreign Minister, proposes in what becomes known as the "Schuman Declaration" that France and Germany – and any other European country wishing to join them – pool their Coal and Steel resources.

June

Belgium, Italy, the Netherlands, France, Luxembourg, and Germany all subscribe to the Schuman declaration.

August

The Council of Europe Assembly approves the Schuman plan.

September

The European Union of Payments is created.

1951

April

The Six (Belgium, France, Germany, Italy, Luxembourg, Netherlands) sign the Treaty of Paris to establish the European Coal and Steel Community (ECSC).

1957

March

The Treaties establishing the European Economic Community (EEC) and the European Atomic Energy Community (Euratom) are signed by the Six in Rome and become referred to as the "Treaties of Rome".

1958

January
The Treaties of Rome become operative.

July
A conference held in Stresa, Italy, sets out the basis of a common agricultural policy (CAP).

A formal liaison and collaboration agreement is signed between the EEC and the International labour Organisation (ILO).

December
The Governors of the newly-founded European Investment Bank (EIB) Council adopt the first directives regarding the credit policy of the Bank.

The European Monetary Agreement comes into force.

1960

January
The European Free Trade Association (EFTA) convention is signed in Stockholm and regroups Austria, Denmark, Norway, Portugal, Sweden, Switzerland and the United Kingdom.

1962

July
The regulations creating the CAP come into force.

1965

April
The Treaty merging the executives of the ECSC, the EEC and Euratom is signed in Brussels and later comes into force in July 1967.

1967

February
The EEC Council of Ministers decides to harmonise indirect taxes across the Community, to adopt the principle of the added-value tax system and to approve the first medium-term economic policy programme defining and setting the aims of the Community's economic policy for the years ahead.

1969

December

An EEC Summit at The Hague agrees to the establishment of EMU and EPU.

1970

March

The Commission submits a memorandum on the preparation of a plan for the establishment of economic and monetary union to the Council which assigns a committee of experts presided over by Pierre Werner, to formulate such proposals.

October

The Council issues a final report on the Commission memorandum on the establishment of economic and monetary union.

1971

March

The Council adopts the Werner Plan to improve the coordination of economic policies. The Member States must take measures to harmonise their budgetary policies and to reduce the margins of fluctuation between their respective currencies.

August

American President, Richard Nixon, terminates the gold-convertability of the dollar.

1972

March

The Council adopts a resolution based on a general conspectus by the Commission of the conditions for achieving the first stage of economic and monetary union.

April

The currency "snake" is established as the Six agree to limit the margin of fluctuation between their currencies to 2.25%.

September

The Ministers of Finance of the six and of the four countries that have applied for membership (Ireland, Britain, Norway and Denmark) meet in Rome and agree that, as the first stage of economic and monetary union, it is necessary to set up a European Monetary Cooperation Fund.

1973

January

Denmark, Ireland and the Britain join the EEC

1975

January

The International Monetary Fund (IMF) Interim Committee Board of Governors meets in Washington, USA and agrees to increase the total of member countries' quota, to abolish the official price of gold and to give the special drawing right the central place in the international monetary system.

1978

July

Agreement is reached on a strategy to achieve a higher rate of economic growth in order to reduce unemployment and to plan the establishment of a European Monetary System (EMS).

December

The European Council decides in Brussels to establish the European Monetary System based on a European currency unit (the ECU).

1979

March

The European Monetary System comes into operation.

1984

December

A European Council is held in Dublin where it is decided to reinforce the EMS and to give the ECU a more important role.

1985

June

The Committee of Governors of the Central Banks of the Member States adopts measures designed to strengthen the EMS.

Spain and Portugal sign treaties of accession to the community.

July

Ministers and Governors of Central Banks of the Member Sates adjust central rates within the EMS.

December

A European Council is held in Luxembourg. The Ten agree to amend the Treaty of Rome and to revitalise the process of European integration by drawing up a Single European Act.

1986

February

The Single European Act modifying the Treaty of Rome is signed.

1987

July

The Single European Act comes into force.

September

Measures are adopted to strengthen the EMS.

1989

April

The report on the economic and monetary union is presented by the Delors Committee.

June

Following the inclusion of the Spanish peseta and the Portuguese escudo, the composition of the ECU is adjusted. The peseta also enters the EMS.

The European Council adopts conclusions on economic and monetary union and emphasises the need for balance between social and economic aspects within a single market.

1990

June

The first phase of EMU becomes operative. Spain, Portugal, Greece and Ireland are granted special concessions on account of their insufficient progress towards financial integration.

December

Two Intergovernmental Conferences, one on Economic and Monetary Union, and the other on Political Union, are launched by the European Council meeting in Rome.

1992

February

The Treaty on the European Union is signed in Maastricht by the Foreign and Finance Ministers of the Member States.

1993

January

The Single European Market comes into being.

October

A European Council held in Brussels confirms that the second phase of economic and monetary union will come into operation on 1 January 1994.

November

With all ratification procedures now completed, the Treaty on the European Union comes into force.

The Commission adopts a Green Paper on European Social policy options for the Union.

December

A Brussels European Council draws up an action plan for the short and medium term, based on the Commission's White Paper on growth, competitiveness and employment. It also decides to convene a conference to conclude a stability pact for Central and Eastern Europe.

1994

January

The second stage of economic and monetary union begins, while the European Monetary Institute (EMI) is established.

December

The European Council held in Essen, Germany lays down proposed lines of action for strengthening the strategy of the White Paper on growth, competitiveness and employment. This includes special reference to measures to combat unemployment and to bring trans-European networks into operation. The Council also agrees on an overall plan to bring the associated countries of Central and Eastern Europe closer to the Community.

1995

March

The Stability Pact for Central and Eastern Europe is signed and adopted in Paris.

May

The Commission adopts a Green Paper regarding the practical arrangements for introducing the single currency.

December

At the European Council meeting in Madrid, 29 March 1996 is set as the starting date for the Intergovernmental Conference and 1 January 1999 is confirmed as the introduction date for the single currency: the euro.

1997

June

The European Council meets in Amsterdam and produces a draft Treaty. A variety of proposals facilitating the smooth passage to the third phase of the Economic and Monetary Union are approved and a resolution on growth and employment is adopted.

December

The European Council meets in Luxembourg and takes the necessary decisions to facilitate launching the enlargement process. A resolution on economic policy co-ordination is also adopted.

1998

March

The Commission adopts the convergence report and recommends that eleven Member States adopt the euro on 1 January 1999.

May

A special Council agrees that eleven Member States satisfy conditions for adopting the single currency on 1 January 1999. Following this decision, the Council adopts two regulations on technical specifications of euro coins and introduction of the euro, the ministers and Central Bank governors of Member States adopting the euro as their single currency. The Commission and the EMI set out the conditions for determining irrevocable conversion rates for the euro.

June

The European Central Bank is established.

A European Council is held in Cardiff and lays down essential elements of the EU strategy for economic reform to promote growth, prosperity, jobs and social inclusion.

December

The Council adopts fixed and irrevocable conversion rates between the euro and the national currencies of the eleven participating Member States.

1999

January

The euro is officially launched and Austria, Belgium, Finland, France, Germany, Ireland, Italy, Luxembourg, the Netherlands, Portugal and Spain adopt it as their official currency.

May

The Amsterdam Treaty comes into force.

2000

March

A special European Council is held in Lisbon, to decide on a new Union strategy to strengthen employment, economic reform and social cohesion as an element of a knowledge-based economy.

June

Greece's entry into the euro is approved.

2001

February

A new Treaty is signed which amends the Treaty on European Union and the Treaties establishing the European Communities (Treaty of Nice).

From the Werner Plan to the EMU: In Search of a European Political Economy. Historical Perspectives and Future Prospects

Lars MAGNUSSON and Bo STRÅTH

The aim of this book is to put the EMU process in a historical perspective and to discuss from this perspective the prospects for a new political economy for Europe. The establishment of monetary union and the European Central Bank constitutes without doubt a major step towards greater economic, social and political integration between the Member States of the European Union and is – as such – a momentous event in European history.

What do the historical preconditions, in practice and theory, of a European political economy mean in terms of future possibilities? What do Maastricht and EMU represent in this historical light? What does the trend in politics from the state towards civil society, and from central towards local and regional as heuristic points of reference mean? What does the parallel trend under the label of "globalisation" represent? What opportunities are there for social solidarity as a response to the trend towards social exclusion? This is understood, in this context, as a new kind of social solidarity without the bias in gender, or in other respects, manifested in the old class-based solidarity model of industrial society. These questions may seem a little distant from the more immediate and more technical questions concerning EMU, but they all underpin the search for a European political economy.

By "political economy" we understand the economy as polity: that is, a system of social relations, power and conflict, framed by institutions, rules and norms – themselves subject to challenge and change – in which economic, political and cultural processes are inseparably inter-twined. This conception diverges sharply from that shared by the majority of economists who proceed as if they were studying natural phenomena which can be understood without reference to history, law, politics or culture. The contributors to this volume, by contrast, treat history, economics and the other social sciences as equal partners in a collaborative enterprise.

In the nineteenth century, the nation-state became the primary unit of political life and, in the twentieth century, under the impact of war, the Great Depression and the disruption of international trade, the economic role of national governments was greatly extended. The effect was to transform nations from merely imagined communities into communities of fate. The Treaty of Rome and the early stages of European economic integration did not change this situation. Barriers to trade and cross-border mobility came down, but the nation and its state remained the point of departure for public policy, while systems of social protection and labour market regulation remained nationally entrenched. From the 1970s onwards, however, the pursuit of EMU opened up a distinctively European space within what had hitherto been almost exclusively national policy preserves. How are we to understand this development, both as a historical process and as an ongoing political project?

It is a common viewpoint to consider Maastricht EMU as a simple, logical consequence of neoliberal economic ideas which paradigmatically transformed economic theory in the 1980s. However, it seems more fruitful to regard EMU and the ECB in a longer historical perspective – from the Werner Plan to the Amsterdam Treaty and beyond. Such a longer view confronts the simplified notion of EMU as a closure created by neoliberal ideology. Rather, monetary union must be regarded as a very contested territory and as an open-ended process. In such a longer view, not only EMU but also its theoretical underpinning emerges as contested, as David Purdy convincingly demonstrates in Chapter 3. There was never a clean break between a Keynesian and a neo-liberal phase. In a certain sense, Keynes's attack on neoclassical theory failed. Indeed, in the 1930s and 1940s, his ideas were to a certain extent incorporated in neo-classical theory. From this merger followed the idea of discretionary counter-cyclical policy which is somewhat inaccurately called "Keynesian".

In fact, counter-cyclical measures to stimulate aggregate demand were little used in the 1950s and 1960s for the simple reason that, for the most part, they were not needed: the main macroeconomic problem for most governments during these years was to contain the underlying boom and prevent the economy from overheating. Conversely, in the late 1960s and early 1970s when expansionary fiscal and monetary policies were pursued, the preconditions for their success had disappeared and, with the failure of national governments to overcome "stagflation" by means of discretionary demand management, Keynesian ideas were discredited and the more rule-bound, market-oriented approach to economic and social policy generally known as neo-liberalism gained the ascendancy. This intellectual shift had a major impact on the meaning of EMU as a political project. Assessing the nature and magnitude of that impact is one of the themes of this book. One expression of the shifting entanglement between economic theory and economic politics is that the Werner Plan was aimed at an Economic and Monetary Union, while Maastricht EMU was termed a Monetary Union. The "economic" dimension, as opposed to the monetary dimension, was not as well developed as in the Werner Plan. The Maastricht Monetary Union can be referred to as an asymmetrical EMU[1]. However, the term, "economic", referring to fiscal policy as an element of the union, was restored in the 1990s through the Stability and Growth Pact, and was also there earlier in the form of the convergence criteria for the implementation of the Maastricht Treaty on EMU.

However, the impact of theoretical transformation does not mean that the market now rules and that the prospects for purposeful politics enlightened by a notion of a social Europe are gone for ever. This in fact builds on two misunderstandings, first, on what EMU really is and, secondly, on a serious misapprehension of the relationship between politics, institutions and the market. In this introduction we will deal briefly with both of these misunderstandings which at present feeds a sterile ideological lock-in which threatens the establishment of a new political economy for Europe which can cope with the dangers as well as the challenges of today and the future.

Since its inception the EMU process has been a contested territory and a project with a shifting content. Since the Werner Plan in the early 1970s the idea of an Economic and Monetary Union has undergone several important ideological shifts, from ideas of political management of the economy, which were about to develop into *dirigisme* when the Werner Plan was launched[2], to neoliberalism in the 1980s, and then to something more complex and ambiguous at the beginning of the twenty-first century. As already stated we believe that a historical reading of the establishment of EMU seriously challenges the idea that there are two separate and well demarcated rationalities, one political and one economic, with simple hierarchical relationships in terms of dominance and subordination. Politics and the economy are integrated and entangled. Politics means the setting of priorities under value deployment. Moreover, the market is not a non-value-based isolated sphere made up of rational maximisers. It is rather a social institution building on an intricate set of formal and informal rules, norms and values, and

---

[1]   Verdun, 1996, pp. 59-81.
[2]   Skidelsky, 1977; cf Stråth, 1987.

25

an entire set of scientific presuppositions about the nature of money, the market and the relationship between fiscal and monetary policy. Emerging as a historical outcome of both political and economic forces, it is unfruitful to label the "market" as the counterpart to politics[3]. Hence, the most certain division is not between politics and economy but rather that found on the level of values: the neo-liberal idea maintains that initiatives and responsibility should be located within the individual. The thrust of the new emphasis on the market was a shift from the state to the individual as vessels of social responsibility[4]. The old form of welfare capitalism, established in the 1930s as a response to the experiences of crisis after a century of social bargaining about the "social question", which was discursively shaped and put on the political agenda in the 1830s or earlier, rested on some kind of notion of collective responsibility and solidarity, in particular at the level of the state[5]. One main question, in historical light, is whether new forms of collective social responsibility can be re-established in view of persistent mass unemployment in some countries and social exclusion, given dramatically changed economic conditions. Certainly, the enlargement process will also highlight the question of social responsibility and European citizenship on a greater scale than perhaps ever before.

This question, in turn, can be reformulated as a search for value alternatives to the vulgarity of the new turbo economy. In the long run the credibility of any economic order is dependent on images of social utility and benefit beyond mere private profit. The solidarity language of the labour movement in the old order gave legitimacy to welfare capitalism. The value erosion of that solidarity rhetoric paved the way for a political economy of the American type. The US, in the 1980s, was used to replace Japan as a model to emulate in a situation when the old European order was shaken. Originally, as Zimmermann demonstrates in his chapter, the idea of a European economic polity emerged at the end of the 1960s under demarcation to the power of the dollar, and under attempts to create a European alternative to the American monetary hegemony. What is the best way to understand, against this backdrop of demarcation, the European underpinning of the American model in the 1980s? And what *was* the American model? Was it just the semblance of underpinning? Did not the ideas of a European alternative recur at the end of the 1990s when the implementation of the Maastricht EMU came closer? What was suggested in the 1980s as an American model was deprived of its history. In the new flexibility language and

---

[3]   Magnusson and Ottosson, 1997.
[4]   Stråth and Wagner, 2000.
[5]   Stråth, 2000b and 2000d.

adoration of the strong individual there was little place for social responsibility, as it had developed historically in its American form of the philanthropic tradition of Carnegie and Rockefeller. In the media world with short-lived icons like Tapie, Murdoch or Berlusconi there is little place for long-term thinking and values of human dignity irrespective of whether they are based on private philanthropy or public welfare capitalism[6]. What does EMU represent in this respect? Should it be seen as an alternative to or a confirmation of the general trend?

What is EMU today? Our belief is that this question can only be answered by referring to history. So what can be said of this wider historical context and for the future of political economy in Europe?

During a brief period of some twenty-five to thirty years after the Second World War economic theory legitimised the belief that economies could be politically governed. Key objectives of this governance were the political guarantee of welfare, with the guarantee of full employment as perhaps the most important instrument. This belief in political economic management experienced severe hardships in the 1970s. The international economic order (Bretton Woods), on which the belief was based, broke down (witness the dollar collapse in 1971 and the oil price shock in 1973). Somewhat later labour markets in the manufacturing industry sector experienced mass unemployment for the first time since the 1930s. Economic theory based on established connections between ("full") employment, investments and inflation did not fit anymore. The Fordist idea of mass consumption and mass production as mutually reinforcing entities could no longer provide popular support and legitimisation.

In this theoretical vacuum new economic ideas became predominating in the 1980s. The point of departure of these new ideas was that politicians should not try to manage the economy but economic forces should be given free rein, thus producing a new equilibrium. In the new theoretical and political language with key concepts like "market" and "flexibility", the responsibility for welfare shifted from the state to the individual. The theoretical solutions to the strains in the established order, *i.e.* that the politicians should keep their hands off the economy, and leave it to the "natural" equilibrium finding forces, did not result in a return to full employment, rather mass unemployment persisted and social marginalisation grew. The concept of full employment, which was a key concept in the old order, prevailed in the new conceptual embedding of "flexibility", "deregulation", "slimming-down", "laying off" and "out-sourcing[7]".

---

[6]   Hagtvet, 2000, p 13.
[7]   Stråth, 2000.

Simultaneously the concept of "globalisation" began to describe, in highly ideological terms, a "natural" economic process, which penetrated the nation-state. Globalisation was one of the key arguments when economic theory shifted from economy as subordinated to politics ("political management" of the economy) to politics as subordinated to economy. The background of the globalisation concept was the technological and organisational transformation of industrial society based on manufacturing (transformation not in terms of production output but in terms of manpower and employment) to the information society. The physical control of capital and labour by the nation-states, established through investments in manufacturing plants, which lasted over decades and tied wage labour to the factories, disappeared with severe effects on the financial power of the states. This development, in turn, had politically de-legitimising effects. Capital escaped political control. In the new globalisation language of politics and economics the main argument was that there was not much to do but to adjust to the requirements of the market. Global universalism went hand in hand with local individualism, and globalisation became glocalisation.

Keynes emphasised more than anybody else the social and psychological importance of expectations for the future and confidence in the performance of the economy. Economic theory creates a social belief in the future. Confidence is a social construct, with economic and social sciences as key producers. The social confidence created by Keynes and others after 1945 – with the experiences in the 1930s as a demarcation of "never more" – collapsed in the 1970s. As in the 1930s, confidence was transformed into fear. A search for a new point of confidence began, and in this process of construction new reliance was invested in the market and in the individual under demarcation to the earlier place of refuge for expectations: the state and collective solidarity.

Such oscillation between confidence, fear and new confidence is always contested where the outcome emerges through social bargaining and is the expression of social power relationships, and where representatives of economic and social sciences are key participants much more than external and neutral observers. The relationships between professional politicians and professional economists in the value production are crucial. The politicians in the 1980s and the 1990s connecting to the neo-liberal economic discourse have disempowered themselves not so much because of the disappearance of the goal of full employment but because of the loss of financial scope of manoeuvre in fiscal terms, which could be used for public redistribution in favour of employment and/or welfare politics, and, in turn, for the attraction of a *clientela* of voters. Politicians have lost legitimacy. The loss of control of resources has resulted in the loss of power. These changing preconditions concern

many more than the politicians, of course. The remoulding of governance and the model of democracy are at stake, which is a concern of
everybody.

Under still very little investigated circumstances the European Economic Community in the 1980s underpinned the process of construction
of a new confidence. This occurred through an adjustment to the new
market language with the Single European Act (SEA), at the same time
as the internal market was seen as a new regulative level to control
economic forces. Politics, which had been played down as powerless
and become de-legitimised at the nation-state level returned through the
backdoor at the European level. In this development it was not easy to
discern whether politics was seen as governing the economy or subjugated to it. There were contradictory views in this respect. However, the
intensified European market integration in the 1980s can hardly be
understood in terms of de-regulation, but rather as a great re-regulation
project, and there was much more continuity to the project for a
European political economy that collapsed in the 1970s than is assumed
in the frequent arguments for a clear break between the 1970s and the
1980s. It could be argued that Jacques Delors infused new confidence in
the European project.

The SEA, and the process initiated by Jacques Delors, continuing
with the Maastricht and the Amsterdam Treaties, can be seen both as a
confirmation of the neo-liberal market language, with its emphasis on
untied market transactions, and at the same time as an attempt to
regulate and control the unfettered Prometheus. The contours, or, better,
the potential of a social Europe emerged under these auspices. The
social protocol added to the Maastricht agreement (at this point not
included in the actual agreement due to the refusal of the conservative
British government to ratify any agreement which included general
social obligations levied on the Member States) implied a breakthrough
for a new European agenda. This was even more emphasised in the
Amsterdam Treaty of 1997, which included social priorities and obligations, and, for the first time, a commitment to employment as a main
political objective of European politics, although – it must be said – at
"as high a level as possible" instead of as earlier "full employment",
indicating a lowered ambition (we note that the Lisbon summit in 2000
once again introduced "full employment" as a prioritised political task).
In Luxembourg 1997 a fully developed European employment strategy
was established which, for instance, has made obligatory the construction of National Action Plans by each member state. So far the European employment strategy has started a process of bench-marking concerning policies combating unemployment and social exclusion. To
some extent it has furthermore lead to the creation of a common lan-

guage describing and identifying unemployment as a general European problem as well as finding common ways to combat it. Thus, by defining employment as an issue of common concern – and as such as important as economic stability and budget discipline – the Amsterdam Treaty opens the way to further coordination of national politics of the "soft" kind which means that the Member States are free to choose their own methods but are bound by common obligations to fulfil the general employment goals of the union which at the same time rule out "beggar-thy-neighbour" policies based on trade barriers, social or fiscal dumping etc., as a means to achieve this goal[8]. It is certainly debatable if this existence of a social dimension is enough or whether the way to tackle the social issue is the optimal one. Robert Salais takes a critical stand in this respect in his chapter.

Most certainly, the relationship between the social agenda introduced in the Amsterdam Treaty and the EMU is a complicated matter. However, from the Delors White Paper in 1993 (see the chapters by Diamond Ashiagbor and J. Peter Burgess and Bo Stråth), which was developed at the EU summits in Essen in 1994, Dublin in 1996, Amsterdam and Luxembourg in 1997, and Cologne in 1999, as well as in the development of the social dialogue between the partners, there was a slow emergence of a view which emphasises increased economic integration (SEA and EMU) as a precondition for economic growth, as well as for rising employment and a social Europe. This means that it is no longer possible to argue for monetary stability without looking at the social consequences for unemployment and social exclusion. This is most certainly the most important effect of Amsterdam, which without doubt sets a new framework for the ECB and Monetary Union to operate within. However, regarding the European policy agenda today, European integration is a contested battleground where different voices and interests put different emphasis on either macroeconomic stability or employment and social issues. As Burgess and Stråth emphasise in their chapter, the social dimension is embedded in budgetary rigidity through the SGP and the institutional framework is one of power migration from the Commission to the Member States. And as always in history the outcome of this struggle is by no means pre-determined.

Hence, rather than a sharp and frontal confrontation between two conflicting views, and sharp discontinuities in development since the 1970s, a pattern of coexisting and competing tendencies emerges. Their mutual challenge to one another entangles them in a bundle of continuities rather than separating them into distinct phases, where only one tendency exists. There was a continuous tussle under social bargain-

---

[8]   Foden and Magnusson, 1999 and 2000.

ing and redefinition of interests rather than sharp confrontation. In retrospect we can see how the mutual strength of the competing tendencies changed. In the 1980s the neo-liberal rhetoric dominated and in the 1990s – *as we have seen* – the approach emphasising the social dimension and some form of collective responsibility and solidarity became increasingly vociferous. One indication of this shift in the 1990s was Social Democratic governments in a number of West European countries. However, the point is that the two approaches all the time presupposed and constituted one another.

We are, in this historical light, interested in the question whether the EU with EMU can be an instrument to re-establish political management of the economy. When we talk about political control of the economy we want to break – as we already stated earlier – with the dichotomy between state and market, politics and economy, and the theoretical oscillation between these extremes. The market is not a natural force, not even in its most extreme *laissez faire* conceptualisations. The economy is always defined by politically created rules, which can go in very different directions, however. In this sense all economies are politically constructed and no one is "natural" and primordial. The political economy we want to refer to is a polity which emphasises social justice through political distribution, where market relations are politically regulated in socially acceptable forms rather than merely guaranteeing freedom of contract and transactions. Our main question is whether Europe can provide the framework of such a polity. This is exactly the same question as whether there can be such an entity as a "social Europe" or a specific European identity. Is there an alternative to politics based on the rule of "market forces" and can the EU provide for such an alternative path of political economy?

The Werner Plan for a European Economic and Monetary Union agreed upon in 1970 by the EEC heads of state and government had a clear social embedding with its emphasis on employment guarantee and social politics. This "EMU of 1970" was not only a monetary union but also an economic union including ideas of harmonised budget politics. What happened to this idea between the Werner Plan and the Maastricht Treaty, where the union was seen much more in strictly monetary terms than in the Werner Plan? What value does the Werner Plan have today? Could the realised "Maastricht EMU" be an instrument for employment politics? For social politics? What are the connections between employment and social politics given this new polity framework? These questions are central in the book.

The language of the Werner Plan seems in crucial respects to belong to another time. The fiscal policy and the political commitment to full employment was pronounced in the plan of 1970, as was the philosophy of political management of the economy. Today the emphasis is much more on monetary stability, stable currency rates, fiscal discipline and – eventually – a low rate of inflation. The focus is thus more on the role of the Central Bank. Crucial questions deal with the nature of the political full-employment commitment in 1970, how and more precisely when the change occurred between the two union drafts, how the process from Maastricht to Amsterdam and beyond, as described above, can be seen, and what these changes are worth today?

Any comparison of the two EMU plans and any discussion of the transformation from the one to the other must ask how the key problem was defined on the two occasions. What was the problem when the Werner Plan was drafted? Why was the plan launched at all? And the same goes for the series of steps which eventually lead to the formulation of the present EMU and ECB structures.

One important observation in the discussion of such questions is that the concept of "globalisation" did not exist in 1970. It became a key concept in the 1980s, when with high ideological charge it underpinned the idea that global markets for commodities and capital are good and necessary. Despite their argued goodness and necessity they posed considerable problems to political governance in established forms, however, and the speeding up of the European financial and monetary integration should be seen in this light. But was there any perception of an economic threat in 1970, and if so, what form did it take?

At the end of the 1960s the welfare model was based on the nation-state, Fordist production methods, and a certain basic belief in political governance of economies through fiscal and monetary politics, with many variations among countries, a belief, which cannot be deduced from a cohesive "Keynesian" theory, as already emphasised. The conflict level grew in the labour markets and the political language became radical and militant. Revolutionary language evoked memories of the 1930s. The European integration process had become stuck by De Gaulle's entrance to the scene. He resigned in 1969 as a consequence of political radicalisation. The tension with the US was obvious throughout 1960s, although it was dampened by the rhetoric of the Cold War. This tension can be connected to the processes of de-colonisation and, later, to the Vietnam War. The tension reflected concern about the control of the economy nationally and globally. The national welfare arrangements and full employment guarantees were dependent on the functioning of the international economic order, and this was not least a matter of political power and control. This order was very much built on beliefs and these beliefs became weaker at the end of the 1960s before they totally disappeared during the first half of the 1970s. Around 1970 the political leaders in Western Europe were on the retreat. They looked desperately for instruments with which they could take back the initiative. In this scenario the EEC summit in The Hague in December 1969 was crucial. With De Gaulle removed from the scene the meeting decided immediately both to enlarge the community by taking on board new members and to intensify integration. The heads of governments and states decided to establish both a European Economic and Monetary Union (the Werner Plan) and a European (Security) Political Union (the Davignon Plan).

The Werner Plan should not only be understood in terms of the economic rationality behind it, but also in its context of political power and prestige. The plan was an expression of the political attempt to take up the old European dream again and fill it with new content adjusted to a new historical situation. Europe has historically oscillated between dreams of eternal peace and dreams of military and political power. After the two world wars the pacifist version dominated, based more on self-contempt than on dreams. In the 1930s pacifist hopes were transformed to images of a military powerful Europe, and the same transformation occurred during a few years after 1945 in the wake of the emerging Cold War[9].

It is in the retrospective view of this oscillation between pacifist peace and military and political power worth reflecting somewhat on the fact that after 1945, in the European integration design, plans for intensified economic integration have been accompanied by plans for intensified security political and military cooperation. The Coal and Steel Community in 1951 went hand in hand with the plan for a European Defence Community in 1953, the Werner Plan around 1970 was entwined with the Davignon Plan and the economic pillar with the security political pillar in the Maastricht Agreement. The introduction of the euro was supported to the accompaniment of the bombs over Kosovo in a situation where the EU summit in Berlin had difficulties in agreeing on resource redistribution and budgetary politics in the wake of the enlargement talks.

In this view the connection of the Werner Plan and the Maastricht EMU to the idea of a European identity must be seen. The obsession with the concept of a European identity indicates a situation of a lack of identity. If one knows who one is, one does not need to persistently ask about it. The identity rhetoric began with the decision by the EEC summit in Copenhagen in December, 1973. The text that framed that decision is a clear allusion to the serious background of the collapsing international order following the dollar devaluation and the first oil price shock. As clear is the idea to use the concept of a European identity as

---

[9]   Orluc, 2000 and Stråth, 2000b.

an instrument to cope with this development and re-establish European strength at the global level[10]. The identity discourse began in a situation of experienced crisis.

In the 1970s the European identity concept was mobilised in the attempts to translate the collapsing national tripartite bargaining orders into a kind of Eurocorporatism. These attempts failed at the end of the 1970s, and in the 1980s the identity rhetoric was transformed under adjustment to the neo-liberal turn and began to connote individual rather than corporatist values. In this way the idea of a European identity is an illustrative element of the European dream, and its contradictory tension and oscillation between European peace and European power as action-orienting goals of the dream. Both the peace version and the power version have been derived from a rich historical heritage.

So, what is the exact content of the European dream for the future and what role does EMU play for the definition of a specific European identity? Surely, this dream can not be drawn up in purely market terms or be bogged down to concepts like "flexibility" and "deregulation". We argue instead that an European identity for the future must have a strong social dimension, a social Europe which combines sustainable growth and a restructuring of European economies which allows the know-ledge-based sectors of the economy to grow in relation to the old sectors with equal opportunities for men and women, a healthy work environment and social protection and which at the same time combats social exclusion.

A main problem with EMU in this context is its ambiguity. As we have argued, Maastricht EMU was launched at a time when neo-liberal attacks against the old regulated "Keynesian" type of political economy – including the welfare state – was especially intense. However, already in the Delors white book from 1993 and certainly after Amsterdam and Lisbon EMU, has surely been imbedded into a wider European agenda which includes not only further re-(rather than de-)regulation in Europe (the Cardiff process) but also social priorities (the Luxembourg process) and – ironically enough – from 2000 in Lisbon a commitment to full employment

Another important issue is also how far we shall go in looking for "Europeanisation"[11]. A much debated question – and a very heated one

---

[10] For the identity concept in general, see Niethammer 2000a. For the concept of a European identity, see Passerini 2000, White 2000, Niethammer 2000b, Burgess 2000 and Stråth 2000a and 2000b.

[11] The concept of Europeanization has been the subject of reflection in the European Forum, Robert Schuman Centre at the European University Institute in Florence. For the discussion of this concept at the Forum see www.iue.it/rsc.

– is how we shall find a sustainable power balance between the EU and the Member States. Certainly, EMU – we argue – will lead to further political economy convergence in a number of ways and the question is to what extent we want such convergence or not in order to boost an "European identity"? A radically different answer to this question – which certainly has its followers – is that such an "European identity" or spirit can only be found in Europe's variety, in its very different cultural and political forms and expressions.

Moreover according to such a view, Europeanisation is not teleologically bound to follow certain paths. It is when we look back into the past that we easily become Hegelians. A chain of historic events entail a concealed plan of history. A certain historical heritage gives the roots of a development, which becomes both very determinist and very essentialist with little scope for historic contingency. Things happened because they had to happen. What happened gets its *ex post* confirmation. The problem is how to incorporate into the analysis of past futures the same openness we experience when we look into our future. The European integration process is, as much as the community construction in the nation-states, a lengthy complicated learning process, including all the misunderstandings, polemics, reforms, and institutional and normative developments. Social and economic sciences are important players in this social learning – and un-learning.

Against this background we must also acknowledge that EMU as well as the whole process of Europeanisation means very different things to Europeans in the different Member States and must as such be interpreted against the backdrop of each Member States history. For example the French government operates in a historical heritage which since the French Revolution emphasises the (French) nation-state as a representative and instrument of the citizens. Democratic control of the economy is located in it. The historical preconditions of the German government are different: a fragile democracy after the First World War, hyper-inflation and lost legitimacy for the economy in the 1920s, mass mobilisation through identity politics in the 1930s provided quite different connections between the state and the question of democratic control. The central bank must in the French historical scenario stand under political, *i.e.* parliamentary control. In the German historical scenario there is always a risk if the monetary system is not independent of political mobilisation. In particular after 1968, Federal Germany settled this history with great inter-generational conflict. Not only the federal structure of the *Bundesrepublik*, through the *Bundesverfassung* and the *Verfassungspatriotismus*, was emphasised, but also the German embedment in a West European political and economic integration, whether federal or not.

Since the 1990s the German governments, whether CDU or SPD-Green, have in the new situation of the *Wiedervereinigung* after 1989 emphasised the German embedment in European integration and how important it is that this integration project keeps going. In the mid-1990s a Europe with various speeds or concentric circles was suggested in order to guarantee dynamics. In the spring of 2000 Green Foreign Minister Joschka Fischer proposed in this tradition a European federation, and so did Chancellor Gerhard Schröder, SPS, in May, 2001. The French tradition since De Gaulle emphasises the European project as a cooperation and coordination of politics and economies among autonomous nation-states. Similarly, the German government emphasises the autonomy of the ECB in order to guarantee monetary stability, whereas the French government wants political control in order to guarantee political stability. In many respects these alternative views are only seemingly alternative. The German Bundesbank might in a formal sense have operated independently from Parliament and government, but it had – and has – nevertheless to build its success on political and popular legitimacy. The French national bank might in a formal sense be under political control, but it must instruct the political institutions what can and has to be done. In both cases the point is not autonomy on the one or the other side of politics and economy, but on their entanglement and the capacity of this 'entanglement to gain legitimacy and popular acceptance. The issue at stake is rather legitimacy for both politics and economy rather than autonomy for the one or the other of them. The question is in other words whether the German and French histories can merge in a shared view on the ECB. The issue is also, as the chapter by Burgess and Ström argues, the new preconditions of the German-French dynamics through the change from DM to euro, and what these new preconditions mean for the future prospects of European integration.

One way of taking a step further in the current discussion on EMU and its consequences would be to acknowledge such important historical differences of the interpretation of EMU which surely exists and can not be wished away (see for example Ole Røste's chapter in this book on Norway and Sweden). On such a basis a more rational discussion might be developed which – most certainly – includes the kind of issues that we raise in our introduction: which is the present and future role of EMU? Which are its roles in the wider process of European integration? And against this backdrop: what is really the European identity we want to create which – also – include a common currency and common central bank?

***

The chapters of the book are organised in four clusters. The first one is more historically oriented, in order to discuss what assistance we can take today from the debate about the Werner Plan, and, in particular, how the ideas behind the Werner Plan and mainstream economic theory were transformed in the 1970s and the 1980s. We are not so much interested in the historical setting around the Werner Plan *per se*, but in the question of what can be used today, and what cannot, of the philosophy in the plan. The second cluster deals with financial structures and economic theory, and how their transformation affects the pre-conditions of EMU. The third cluster contains chapters on social practices and the legal framework. Finally the book ends with a cluster on future prospects.

The historically-oriented chapters by Hubert Zimmermann, Amy Verdun, David Purdy, J. Peter Burgess and Bo Stråth, and Lars Magnusson and Jan Ottosson all demonstrate the contingencies in operation when the European political economy took shape, and the crucial role of political decision-making in these processes. Two of these chapters compare the Werner Plan and the Maastricht EMU in terms of content, and similarities and differences. Zimmermann analyses the development since the 1950s of a growing tension between Western Europe and the US and the cracks in the Bretton Woods order from early on, leading up to the Werner Plan. Not only the tension between Western Europe and the US but also, within this Transatlantic scenario, the crucial connection between Germany and France, the role of Willy Brand's *Ostpolitik*, and the close connection between economic and military coordination are discussed in his chapter.

Amy Verdun analyses, in a comparative view, the political economies of the two projects and the problem formulations and bones of contention in the bargaining situations. Furthermore, she focuses on the composition of the committees that drafted the blueprints of both EMU projects, and seeks to find explanations for the similarities and differences between the two. Her core finding is that although there are significant similarities, the reason for the differences can be traced to the dominance of certain ideas as well as the experience with economic and monetary cooperation in the period prior to the drafting of EMU blueprints. In particular, the experience with the EMS in the 1980s and the focus on price stability in the 1980s compared to the lack of agreement over the road to EMU in the 1970s. She also highlights the difference in treatment of "economic government" as well as "social partners" in both periods. The 1989 blueprint did not include a developed role for these actors. However, she speculates that things may change in the years to come.

David Purdy offers a critical discussion of the conceptualisation of economic theory. He demonstrates in his eloquent analysis the continuous interaction between economic theory, ideological images and

37

political events. This insight is important in order to understand the economic exegetics around EMU based on convergence criteria and monetary operations.

J. Peter Burgess and Bo Stråth analyse the connections between the political, the economic, and the social in the two projects and the continuities between them. Their point of departure is money as a creator and carrier of value in a deeper social sense beyond mathematical transformation formulas. They find the conventional view problematical, where a social democratic, or Keynesian, phase, focusing on political management of the economy, with the Member State or the superstate EU as the key instrument, was replaced in the 1980s by a neo-liberal phase, focusing on the market, where everything changed and the social dimension disappeared. In this version Maastricht becomes very much a neo-liberal project. They emphasise continuities since the 1970s with a constant tension between the political and the economic when the social dimension took shape. The 1980s were much more complex in the European construction than what the label neo-liberal expresses. The long-term trend they discern is a migration of power from the Commission to the Member State governments in the 1990s.

Lars Magnusson and Jan Ottosson focus on the dynamic years between 1988 and 1991 when the Delors Report and the Maastricht Treaty were formulated. They emphasise the political contingency and the role of the political transaction costs when the European formula for the political economy emerged.

In the chapters on financial structures and economic theory Sheila Dow considers the connection between the monetary system in Europe and unemployment. She does it from a point of departure in an analysis of the banking sector from the over-expansion of credit in the 1970s and then the emerging plans for European monetary integration. These changes have affected the structure of European banking, and the place of banks in the wider financial sector. Dow rejects forcefully and convincingly the idea that the monetary system is neutral in relation to the "real" economy. As a rule social and labour market politics, and the whole problem complex of the welfare state, are, if at all connected to financial issues, seen in relation to fiscal politics but much less so in relation to the monetary issue[12]. A usual view in economic theory emphasised since the 1980s is that monetary policy has no consequences and is irrelevant for, *i.e.* unemployment politics. There is a strong field in neoclassical theory where the monetary issues are separated from the

---

[12]   A rather exceptional case so far is Lars Jonung's analyses of the Swedish welfare state and the credit politics imposed by the Bank of Sweden. Jonung, 1993.

38

"real". Barry Eichengreen's study of the Great Depression and of how politics mediate between financial markets and labour markets demonstrates how problematic such a view is. His analysis is of relevance not only for an understanding of the 1930s, but also for the ongoing debate over the EMU, however. Once the regulatory straitjacket of the Gold Standard was finally removed from the international scene, an economic recovery became possible. Recovery had been prevented by an overly-rigid monetary regime[13]. Eichengreen's detailed analysis of the connections between international financial politics and employment politics demonstrates that the employment issue must be considered alongside transnational financial movements and the monetary system. The idea that monetary and financial organisation was an instrument for the pursuit of wider welfare and employment goals was obvious in the Werner Plan but gradually disappeared from the forefront of debate during the 1970s. Sheila Dow, in her chapter, argues on this ground that political governance in the long run must build on this connection but that it is impossible through isolated monetary policy alone. Her concern is the question of a demand-deficient unemployment as a result of EMU, in which the flexibility language with its emphasis on budget rigidity opens up for monetary politics. This process is much further developed in the US and the UK but held back so far in continental Europe. The role of the EMU and the ECB must, according to her, be discussed in this light. The question of trust and legitimacy is important in her discussion of the emergence of a financial concentration in Europe, in the name of competition, and of what this development means for the EMU and for the prospects of a European political economy. Sheila Dow sees the large changes in the financial markets in the 1980s, and the connection to labour markets, in a long historical perspective, and asks how to understand the EMU and the ECB in this historical view. In her scenario there are other explanations for structural unemployment than capital substitution, notably the structural unemployment of immobile labour in the face of concentration of industry due to the single market's encouragement of firms to reap economics of scale. From this scenario there is a clear connection to Barbara MacLennan's chapter in the cluster on social practices and legal framework.

In a certain tension to the thesis brought forward by Sheila Dow, Roger Hammersland argues that monetary policy does not seem to have effects on the long-term interest rates, and thus on the "real" economy. In his view the effects of monetary policy have been severely over-estimated, and therefore he suggests a coordinated European fiscal policy as the feasible alternative. The ECB might be successful in the con-

---

[13]   Eichengreen, 1992.

trol of inflation but this does not mean a control of the "real" economy. Hammersland's evaluation of the relative importance of monetary and fiscal politics is based on an economic assessment of the structures in operation during the last decades. From this assessment he discerns future prospects. He problematises the common conviction that central banking has been the crux of the economic convergences within EU during the last decade. He argues that the role of the central banks has been overestimated in this respect, and looks for interpretation of the development – and for future recommendations – in the area of fiscal politics. He also draws attention to the effects of increased capital mobility, however, because of the implicit unacceptable social consequences. The alternative to monetary policy, given that there has been a significant setback in its potential to deal with real imbalances in the future, and to fiscal rigidity, that Hammersland discerns would be regional fiscal policies at a European level, which would be an instrument to bring back the social dimension onto the European policy agenda. In this respect there is a clear connection again to the chapter by Barbara MacLennan, although her focus is on financial and Hammersland's on fiscal policies.

Ole Røste discusses the preconditions of labour market politics in a currency area. He reflects critically on the role of stabilising monetary policy, *i.e.* devaluation. His point of departure for this critical reflection is the preconditions of Sweden and Norway remaining outside the eurozone. One problem, which restricts the freedom of action, is that currency areas are delimited not by economic but by administrative and political boundaries. Although his point of departure is the economic theory of Optimal Currency Areas, he emphasises the limits of economic theory in respect of consideration of cultural, historical and political factors. Such factors are crucial for decisions on changing a national currency area for the European. Such factors can explain why Sweden has not so far joined EMU and why Norway has not joined EU. However, Røste also discerns economic arguments for joining EMU. Or, rather, he critically scrutinises arguments for not joining. The report of the Swedish EMU commission concluded that the Swedish labour market was not flexible enough for EMU in 1995-1996 and highlighted the risks of high unemployment in joining EMU. Røste confronts this view with his own results from an in-depth analysis of regional labour markets in Norway. High regional diversity is compatible there with a common currency. The implicit message is that this should be valid also for EMU and thus make the rigidity argument by the Swedish EMU commission less relevant. His argument in this respect can also be related to the case of Italy mentioned in the chapter by Burgess and Stråth.

Barbara MacLennan takes as her point of departure the fault-line between monetary and financial policy, the former to be determined by the ECB while the latter is left with commercial banks, though subject to national, and some international, regulation. She regards access to finance as crucial for the implementation of investment decisions that determine not only future economic outcomes but also the quality of social and cultural life. Banks, both in granting personal loans to finance consumption and in providing business credit, have typically privileged private enterprise. The Stability and Growth Pact reinforces this privilege by setting limits on public sector borrowing (even for investment purposes) that do not apply to the private sector. If it disturbs this pattern of credit allocation, simply asking for a loan can constitute political action and contribute to the structural diversity of a mixed economy, including the voluntary sector of community associations and the domestic, or household, sector. Barbara MacLennan surveys the current state of play at national and European levels regarding the possibilities of securing bank finance for social investment. With an historical interpretation of the political economy of the post-war period, she tries to assess the prospects for redressing the gender imbalance in power to influence the future, having regard to the on-going reconfiguration of European politics.

Ulrike Liebert offers a political analysis of the widening gap in support of the European Union as monetary union became the dominant project of the 1980s and 1990s. She draws attention to the tension between the convergence criteria and the emphasis on mutual recognition of cultural particularity, which has put the EMU project under legitimacy pressure, in particular among women. Her point of departure is the term "permissive consensus" launched by Leon Lindberg and Stuart Scheingold in 1970 to argue that European integration is an elite undertaking, where the elites could reckon with the silent public support without political mass mobilisation[14]. The ratification process of the Maastricht Treaty overthrew their idea. The plan for EMU and other elements of the Treaty provoked protests and political mobilisation against the plan for intensified integration. The "permissive consensus" proved full with contingencies. In the context of EMU these contingencies have a particular gender bearing, which Ulrike Liebert sheds light upon by means of a rich analysis of European opinion polls. To the preconditions for a future Europe that she emphasises, the mobilisation of female citizens is a much more viable alternative to the idea of permissive consensus.

---

[14]   Lindberg and Scheingold, 1970.

Diamond Ashiagbor analyses in her chapter the shift from a social policy agenda in more general terms to a specific employment policy agenda in the EU, and connects this shift to EMU. She also discerns a shift from the idea of precise legal labour standards to the much vaguer policy concept. This shift is concomitant with the power migration from the Commission to the Member States. The issue at stake is the degree of inertia in normative orders. In West European countries, as well as in the US in the nineteenth century, a strong regulation of business operations in the industrial society emerged in the form of private law. As opposed to the US, a strong regulation of social conditions in general terms and labour market relations in particular emerged in Western Europe in the twentieth century in the form of public law in response to social protest. The labour movements were much stronger in Western Europe than in the US, and so was the pressure they exerted on the political and legislative order. This set of private and public laws in Western Europe as opposed to the US mutually supported each other and was inscribed in the national frameworks. It has proved difficult to expand these national regulations to a European level. European law has proved easier to develop in policy areas like competition and environment without strong national normative entrenchment. The question now is to what extent a European legislation in the labour market and welfare sphere is possible given the strong national interests there, in particular defended by trade unions and social democrats, where the question of a European standard so far has been secondary. Business has been much more interested in the development of a European (and global) rule coordination of competition conditions. Against this general backdrop, Ashiagbor discusses, from a legal viewpoint, the emergence of the Amsterdam Treaty, which has been seen as the social counterpart of EMU. Her main question is what preconditions for employment policies there are in the era of EMU from a legal point of view. She discusses the social question, including the employment problem, in the tension between such different market regulation principles as harmonisation and mutual recognition ("anything goes"). She refers in particular to Article 8 of the Amsterdam Treaty on employment, which is defined there as an objective. Data collection and an employment committee to promote coordination and monitoring under consultation of the 'social partners' are among the instruments.

In the more future-oriented cluster of chapters, based on analyses of the development in the 1990s, the focus is on the connections between investment, employment and financial and monetary markets, and on the relationships between employment and labour standards on the one side, and social standards ("welfare") on the other. Ton Notermans discusses critically whether the old Werner Plan can be seen – or be used – as a blueprint for the Maastricht EMU. He and Jos de Beus raise the provocative question whether Third Way Social Democrats are friends or enemies of European integration. Their point of departure is that while having been widely hailed as the solution to Europe's economic malaise in the 1980s, neo-liberal strategies, at the beginning of the twenty-first century rapidly seem to lose their popular appeal. As mass unemployment, sluggish growth, uncertain employment relations, welfare cutbacks and increasing income inequality continue to hold sway in a large majority of EU countries, European electorates call upon politicians to reassert the primacy of the political. The most salient manifestation of this change in ideological climate has been the spectacular recovery of European social democracy. Yet, at the same time extremist right-wing parties are gathering force with the promise to protect the electorate from an allegedly ruthless global capitalism by means of protectionist and xenophobic programmes. In this framework it will be crucial not only for the European economy but also for the future shape of democracy and social integration how the Social Democrats are going to employ their new strength to rearrange the relations between state and markets. Notermans and de Beus address three key questions:

- Is, in the age of global capitalism, a reassertion of the primacy of the political feasible at all, or has the growing geographical scope of markets irrevocably forced political management to become subservient to economics?

- Are the strategies of Third Way Social Democrats an adequate response to reassert the primacy of the political in a globalised economy, or, are they, as, for example, the French PS suggests, variants of neo-liberalism and hence unable to address the main concerns of the electorate?

- Is a reassertion of the political under the rule of Third Way Social Democrats compatible with further economic and political integration in Europe or is it likely to lead first of all to the reassertion of the role of the nation-state?

So what does a reassertion of the political mean in the twenty-first century? Ton Notermans talks about political management rather than political mobilisation and Jos de Beus about a tension between politics of management and politics of mobilisation at the national level, whereas Europe always was an arena for politics of management. It seems clear that the preconditions of mass mobilisation have changed considerably in comparison to the preconditions in industrial society. What are the preconditions of political engineering, or management, as an elite undertaking today? What relevance does the concept of "permissive consensus", criticised by Ulrike Liebert in her chapter, have? Is there anything to be regretted by the demise of mobilisation at the European level? Is there any risk that mobilisation comes back in through the back door as populist extremism in one form or the other?

For his part, David Purdy underlines the danger in competitive corporatism among the Member States. There is a risk of social dumping in the wake of the Stability and Growth Pact if every state is striving to keep ahead of the game, with no supranational rules to keep competition within bounds. An EU social code which regulates competitive relations, and lays down standards of social and environmental protection, could serve as an instrument to prevent social competition and accommodate economic disparities among Member States. Purdy discerns the contours of a European social citizenship based on the concept of "liberal workfare" defined as half-way between "welfare-to-work" and citizen's income. The focus in Purdy's chapter is on European employment politics compared to European social politics. Various views have emerged on the connections between monetary policies and investment policies, between social policies and employment policies. These various views are clustered along two alternative approaches. One emphasises work. The main aim is to bring people back into jobs through investment politics and work is the point of departure for social politics. Social security should be guaranteed in terms of income security. This is the full employment alternative, which could be labelled the North European Protestant employment alternative. The other alternative is emphasising the social dimension in a certain disconnection to employment. Everybody should be entitled to social security but rather at the subsistence level than the income level. The label for this approach would be the South European Social Catholic welfare alternative. What are the mutual relationships of strength between these alternatives? To what extent are they compatible? What do they mean for the possibilities to realise a European economic, employment and social polity? Is a social Europe workfare or welfare? Is there a way to combine workfare and welfare?

There is a close connection from Purdy's problem formulation to the concluding chapter by Robert Salais, although they set the focus somewhat differently. Robert Salais argues that there is an urgent need for new conceptualisation of economic and social policy in the construction of Europe. New European institutions must be designed with precedence over policies undertaken by the monetary system without trying to copy the nation-state arrangements in a new European super- (rather than supra-) state organisation. He argues that the Intergovernmental Conference leading up to the Maastricht Treaty was a missed opportunity in this respect. The failure was due less to the strength of neoliberal ideas than to the resurgence of social nationalism. On this point Salais comes close to Purdy's warning about downward competition in the social field. Diamond Ashiagbor confirms the critique of Salais. The social protocol and its continuity in the SGP are subordinated to macroeconomic priorities with a nation-state point of departure. There is a gap between the macroeconomic approach and (subordinated) employment politics, which must be filled. The flexibility language and wild liberalism cannot fill or bridge this gap. A more social set of rules of the game than the market language and its dictates is required. A harmonisation/coordination of labour standards at the European level would bridge the gap. Salais objects to views where economic growth is seen as the (independent) precondition of social standards. By tacit implication in such views social standards will follow more or less automatically on growth, which, of course, is an illusion. The relationship is more interactive. Social standards are fought for in a social contention, and improved social standards have feedback effects on productivity and economic growth. In his opinion, the productivity issue should be attacked from the social side as a more active and rule-making policy, Salais draws on Alain Supiot[15].

Historically social policy has been an instrument to *react ex post* in order to correct abuses and bad conditions. Salais is looking for a more *pro*active European approach to labour standards with positive long-term effects on economic performance. Once the proactive rule-making exists, the subsidiarity policy can be the point of departure for collective action in terms of implementation. In his scenario the transfer of power from the Commission towards the Member States by means of the Method of Open Coordination is unfortunate. The question could be added to his criticism whether the openness is greater in the intergovernmental bargaining process than in the policy-making in the Commission?

It is a truism to say that Salais's question, whether it is still possible to escape a future in which the European project risks dissolution in a market zone with states competing in social dumping, is important. The European project at the beginning of the twenty-first century is as open as it always was. Institutional change in the history of EC/EU has occurred in a number of ways, in a wide spectrum from founding acts and determined institution building to informal and gradual transformation of practices into formal and legal institutions. The emergence of institutional arrangements is contingent and malleable, although not

---

[15] For a demonstration of the positive correlation between social standards and economic efficiency, see Supiot, 1999, especially the chapter "Droit du travail et performance économique".

necessarily in a voluntary way[16]. The development could, as ever, go in very different directions. In this sense history does not provide us with certain trajectories or paths. They are discernible only in retrospect. The Europe of EMU is full of opportunities as well as risks, of contradictions and contention. This book wishes to demonstrate this sense of openness – in its past as well as into its future.

---

[16]   Olsen, 2001.

PART ONE

THE HISTORICAL
AND CONCEPTUAL SETTING

CHAPTER 1

The Fall of Bretton Woods and
the Emergence of the Werner Plan

Hubert ZIMMERMANN

In *The Fall of the House of Usher*, the famous novel by Edgar Allen Poe, a visitor to the House witnesses the decay of a once illustrious family and the collapse of the whole splendid building. "A sense of insufferable gloom pervaded the spirit" of this observer all through the inescapable disaster, until, in the end, he makes his narrow escape. A similar feeling must have pervaded the minds of monetary policy makers in the mid-1970s when they looked back at what had remained of the once proud Bretton Woods architecture of post-war international monetary cooperation. But whereas in Poe's novel, the visitor was able to leave the tragic scene, those observers of the 1970s had to try and rebuild a new framework for international economic policy. In Europe, they chose this new structure to be a decidedly European one, and the story of its rise from the ruins of Bretton Woods is the topic of this chapter.

The slow dissolution of the transatlantic post-war monetary order (the so-called Bretton Woods system) in the late 1960s and early 1970s was accompanied by an acute sense of crisis in the Western World. During this period, the political and ideological bases of international and national economic policies were challenged and profoundly transformed. The ideas and controversies which shaped these transitions continue to influence and inform the debate about the open-ended dynamics of European monetary union which is at issue in this book. This chapter seeks to elucidate in particular the shifting conceptions of monetary order which resulted in the first attempt to construct a European monetary union in the early 1970s. Special emphasis will be given to the increasingly divergent positions of the United States and European countries regarding international economic policy, the emergence of a fragile consensus in Europe regarding the legitimacy of monetary integration in regional terms, and the close correlation between developments in the Cold War security environment and international monetary

49

relations. The apotheosis of the "Keynesian" model (cf. Chapter 2 by David Purdy for the concept of "Keynesian") and the onset of its crisis in many Western economies – which was partly provoked by the effects of international monetary disorder and paralleled by increasing difficulties in the state-managed regulation of international monetary policy – provides the broader background to this analysis.

The public breakthrough of the idea of European monetary union came at the EC Hague Summit of December 1969. Based on a proposal by the German Chancellor, Willy Brandt, the six EC countries announced their intention to work out "a plan in stages [...] with a view to the creation of an economic and monetary union"[1]. This initiative signalled a clear challenge to the framework in which post-war monetary relations had been managed in the Western World: a transatlantic monetary order with the dollar at its centre, based on institutionalised as well as informal mutual cooperation. Like every social order, structures in the international realm are stabilised by three mechanisms: "coercion", "self-interest" and "shared beliefs in the legitimacy of a given order". Only rarely is just one of these mechanisms at work; usually we find a combination of them[2]. The Bretton Woods order was based on a mutually re-enforcing combination of self-interested calculations and strong beliefs in its legitimacy which were held by a majority of decision makers in all participating countries (with the partial exception of France). The element of coercion had only a negligible impact in preserving this order, mainly in the form of structural power exerted by the United States[3]. Accordingly, the prime motivations for the fall of Bretton Woods were, first, the perception by the participants that the monetary order more and more violated essential interests (above all state autonomy in setting domestic economic priorities) and, second, the de-legitimisation of core political elements of the existing order, combined with a rise of attractive contending conceptions. Which of these factors has a causal priority is left indeterminate on purpose. The historical record suggests an intricate web of mutual influence.

---

[1]   Final Communiqué of The Hague Summit, 2 Dec. 1969, in: *European Yearbook* XVII, 1971, p. 519.

[2]   The (essentially Weberian) conceptual framework of this chapter is based on: Hurd, 1999, pp. 379-408. For the use of a similar framework dealing with the legitimacy of EMU in the contemporary debate, see Patomäki, 1997, pp. 164-206.

[3]   This structural power, though important in shaping the form of the postwar order, accounted only marginally for its stability. Thus, it was not the decline of American power which led to the desintegration of Bretton Woods as some analysts such as Charles Kindleberger or Mancur Olson argued. For the concept of structural power and a critique of the "declinist" interpretation, see Strange, 1985, esp. pp. 10-13.

At the outset, the main features of the Bretton Woods order will be identified. Then, I will describe the progressive disintegration of the transatlantic consensus regarding this order and show how this strengthened already existing rival conceptions, above all the idea of European monetary integration. Finally, I will briefly survey the reasons for the breakdown of the state-managed regulation of monetary affairs on a worldwide level, symbolised by the August 1971 decision of President Nixon to terminate the gold-convertibility of the dollar. The parallel rise of a neoliberal language in economic discourse legitimised this step; its argument was greatly strengthened when the US escaped from the detrimental economic and political consequences of these events. Finally, this language also entered the European debate in the aftermath of the failure to reconstruct a comprehensive European political economy in the form of the Werner Plan (see the chapter by Burgess and Stråth in this volume). The conclusion will try to draw some inferences from this analysis which might be of relevance for the future development of EMU.

The Features of a Monetary Order

The post-war monetary system was named after the multilateral conference of 1944 in Bretton Woods (NY) which was to determine the shape of the international economic system for the post-war world. The conference was dominated by the American and British delegations (the latter was led by John Maynard Keynes), and their views shaped the resulting agreement. A series of new principles, rules and institutions, such as the IMF, was established. The term "Bretton Woods system" is a somewhat misleading label for the emerging order; the new institutions still had to find their role, the rules had to be implemented or, if considered inadequate, readjusted, and the consensus regarding the role of the state in the management of international financial markets had to be tested[4]. In the end, the features of the monetary system as it emerged after 1945 differed in important technical aspects from what had been envisaged, in particular concerning the role of the dollar as the world's principal reserve currency[5]. All major industrial countries linked the value of their currencies to the dollar. The dollar value was expressed in a fixed ratio to gold ($35 an ounce), and guaranteed by an American promise to exchange dollars on request to gold from the abundant reserves at Fort Knox. A system of fixed but adjustable exchange rates

---

[4] James, 1995, pp. 87-126.

[5] It is more accurate to speak of a fixed-rate dollar system which developed slowly in the course of the 1950s. However, for the sake of convenience, the term Bretton Woods system will be retained in this chapter. See McKinnon, 1993.

with a strong bias against parity changes emerged. The dollar-gold exchange guarantee provided the reserve currency with credibility; however, due to the core role of the American currency, the main condition on which the stability of the whole system rested was that the US managed its domestic economy and the effects of its external commitments in ways that were not detrimental to dollar stability.

Despite these variations to the Bretton Woods blueprint, its guiding principles remained intact during the post-war period. This included above all, closer cooperation among the industrial states in the management of international monetary affairs and a better surveillance of financial markets compared to what had existed prior to the Second World War. The post-war monetary order was to give political authorities tight control over foreign exchange markets with the triple intention of preventing the "beggar thy neighbour" policies which had characterised the foreign economic policies of the 1930s, of maintaining stable exchange rates in order to allow a smooth liberalisation of international trade, and – last but not least – of shielding their domestic economies from the impact of disruptive tendencies in international financial markets[6]. Supported by extensive capital controls, states closely monitored international financial movements in order to protect the newly created welfare state – the central element in legitimising post-war democracies – from eventual capital flight or currency speculation which might have easily undermined interventionist government policies[7]. Extensive state intervention in the international economy went hand in hand with the huge augmentation of the state's role in domestic economic management.

These objectives were furthermore closely related to the Cold War environment. The Bretton Woods idea of a cooperative monetary framework spanning the whole world was dead as soon as the superpower conflict began. The Communist countries would not participate. Monetary relations in the Western World became part of an overall strategy which was to shield Western democracies through economic stability and growth from the perceived threat from abroad and from within, especially in countries with strong Communist parties such as France and Italy. The United States became militarily and economically much more entangled in Europe and Asia than it had planned. In the immediate post-war period dollars streamed into Europe (and Japan) to finance reconstruction and the formidable military machinery of the

---

[6]   Ruggie, 1982, pp. 379-415. However, this label obscures the fact that the progressive liberalisation of international trade was supplemented by a close control of capital markets.

[7]   Helleiner, 1994.

Cold War, and the Europeans were building up their reserves with these dollars (which was more profitable than holding gold because dollars paid interest). In combination with the overwhelming superiority of the American economy, this was the major factor in making the dollar the world's most used currency. The US had not to worry about the balance of payments deficits resulting from its political and economic commitments as long as the bills were not presented at the US treasury for gold all at once. Thus, an informal bargain emerged: the US had the privilege of financing its huge external commitments by printing dollars accumulating in the system, the Europeans profited from this credit for investments and they acquired security against the East through the American military commitment. The essential thing to note is that political and economic aspects were very closely intertwined in this construction: the transatlantic monetary order was not only a set of economic arrangements. It was a highly political enterprise, based on a common outlook and language among the major participants in economic *and* political affairs. As long as the larger political and economic objectives of Europe and the US were in accordance, the Europeans would be content to allow the US call the tune in international monetary relations. In the 1960s, when dollar speculation threatened the stability of the system, it was the security partnership which was essential for the continued support most European countries lent to the Bretton Woods system[8]. This (unintended) transatlantic bargain was the political core of the post-war monetary system, which had as its normative base the combination of state-managed regulation of the international economy, the emerging Cold War political framework and the post-war welfare state.

Monetary decision makers on both sides of the Atlantic gradually acquired during the years of the common management of the system (particularly in institutions such as the IMF, the Bank for International Settlements, the OEEC/OECD etc.) a strong transatlantic identity regarding international monetary questions[9]. Alternative conceptions of monetary order were marginalised. The Rome Treaties of 1957 men-

---

[8]   Zimmermann, 2001.

[9]   This relatively restricted group of individuals formed a kind of epistemic community ("networks of knowledge based experts" acting on the basis of shared beliefs, expectations and ways of interpreting social reality. See Haas, 1992. In a field which required a rather special expertise, this epistemic community was able to exert a more than average influence on their peers who usually were elected politicians with little knowledge of financial matters. For these politicians, however, the link between the Bretton Woods system and the transatlantic security system was a dominant consideration and, thus, they generally agreed with the advice of the transatlantic monetary elite on the ways to preserve the existing system.

tioned European monetary cooperation only in passing and focussed on trade issues. Monetary policy was considered transatlantic business. The European Payments Union, which could have been the core of a European monetary order, was dissolved without discussion in 1959 when it had fulfilled its immediate task of regulating intra-European payments balances. Although this was regretted by many participants, there was no initiative to deepen and institutionalise European monetary cooperation.[10] Early proposals for a European currency policy, such as a resolution by the European parliament in 1959, were not taken seriously by the transatlantic elite managing international monetary policy[11].

However, cracks in the system appeared as early as the late 1950s, and this was not surprising. The fixed-rate dollar system was flawed, from a strictly economic point of view. Robert Triffin formulated the dilemma: the growing world economy necessitated a continuing supply of the reserve currency. However, as soon as the dollars accumulating in the system approached the value of the American gold reserves, doubts in the dollar-gold exchange pledge inevitably arose. The high dollar reserves in other countries cast a shadow on the future stability of the dollar[12]. Curbing the dollar outflow would result in a shortage of liquidity. To continue pumping dollars abroad, however, would cause increasing exchanges of dollars to gold, thereby undermining the base of the dollar even more. The American government felt particularly threatened by the possibility of a run on its gold reserves in case nervous holders began to cash in their dollars. From 1958 to 1961, the American gold stock declined from $20.6 billion to $16.9 billion. However, a devaluation of the dollar against gold was ruled out, partly for prestige reasons, partly because it would have made US investments and commitments abroad vastly more expensive. When President Kennedy asked his Secretary of Treasury to educate him on the actual advantages of a reserve currency, Douglas Dillon answered: "To date, foreign countries and their nationals have acquired nearly $20 billion in dollar accounts. This, in effect, is a demand loan to us of $20 billion which has allowed us to pursue policies over the years that would have been utterly impossible had not the dollar been a key currency[13]". Another reason against a dollar devaluation was the possibility of competitive devaluations by other countries, and that might have set in motion the unravelling of a post-war monetary order which had served all participants so

---

[10] Kaplan and Schleiminger, 1989, pp. 320-1.
[11] Tsoukalis, 1977, pp. 53-4.
[12] Triffin, 1960.
[13] Foreign Relations of the United States (thereafter: FRUS) 1961-63, IX, Memo Dillon to JFK, 11 Feb. 1963, p. 164.

well[14]. The possibility of cutting back on security commitments abroad was discussed extensively but Cold War objectives were overriding balance of payments concerns and only very small steps were taken[15]. Utterly inconceivable for the American government was the pursuit of a restrictive policy at home to stabilise the dollar, first, for electoral reasons, and, second, because it would have perverted the rationale of the fixed-rate dollar system which was to contain the disturbing influence of financial markets on domestic economic policies and to preserve national autonomy in economic policy making.

The consequence was that the US took a strong lead in forging a reaffirmation of the transatlantic bargain. Eisenhower and Kennedy called on the Europeans to help shore up the system. In the following years the leading industrial states devised an elaborate system of new rules and regimes which were to stabilise the monetary order (Goldpool, General Agreements to Borrow, Roosa-Bonds etc.)[16]. Germany (later joined by other countries such as Italy and Japan) agreed to transfer back the dollars it acquired from the huge American military machinery on its territory by buying American weapons – a clear sign for the close link between security and monetary system[17]. The American-led effort to stablilise the system glaringly exposed its political background. The European willingness to support the dollar rested upon the US promise to put their balance of payments in order and even more on the still intact common outlook regarding the political and economic bases of the transatlantic system.

Despite the re-enforcement of international cooperation, the American deficits did not disappear completely. However, the clearest sign for the continuing crisis of the transatlantic system was the plight of the holder of the second reserve currency, the United Kingdom. Sterling was widely considered the first line of defence for the dollar and its stability was seen by UK governments as a vital element in their attempts to preserve Britain's status as the second financial power in the world. However, the British reserves were woefully inadequate for this purpose and the relative slow growth of the economy suggested an overvaluation of the British currency. In addition, the promotion of London as the world's financial centre and the concomitant permission of the Eurodollar market by British authorities had the paradox effect that

---

[14] Odell, 1982.
[15] For these debates see the documents in FRUS 1961-63, volume IX.
[16] Strange, 1976.
[17] Zimmermann, 1999.

Britain itself created the conditions for increasing speculation[18]. The successive speculative waves against sterling were the most visible test cases for the transatlantic bargain. Time and again, Britain had to be bailed out by credit packages which were put together under the auspices of the IMF and multilaterally negotiated by American authorities. The single elements of the system were not fitting together anymore, at least not as well as they had done in the 1950s, and doubts whether it still served the interests of the participants multiplied. It was clear that the monetary system was in need of reform. Voices calling for a radical reform of the system became more influential among academic economists[19]. Even more ominous was the rise of alternative political conceptions of monetary order which would have radically transformed the system.

The Rise of Contending Conceptions

The emblematic figure in this context is the French President Charles De Gaulle. As soon as he assumed his post in 1958, he embarked on a mission of regaining national autonomy for France in what he considered the essential domains of state power. This was above all the field of military security, in which he challenged the legitimacy of the NATO security system. His actions culminated in the French withdrawal in 1966 from the military organisation of NATO. In parallel, France started to block all efforts regarding an extension of the supranational

---

[18] The Eurodollar market was a rapidly growing off-share market based in London which allowed dollar transactions with minimal state intervention. The US welcomed this because it provided an incentive for private financial operators to hold dollars and not cash them in for gold. Furthermore, US banks had felt constrained by various new government regulations which were to slow down the movement of dollar loans abroad. As a result they greatly expanded their European branches making heavy use of the Eurodollar market. For the UK, this market had the effect to bolster London's role as the world's financial centre without endangering the domestic economic policies of the government. If the London banks had continued to pursue all of their business in sterling (on the use of which the government had put in any case severe restrictions), sterling liabilities abroad would have increased uncontrollably, posing a threat to sterling stability. The Eurodollar market went against the spirit of the Bretton Woods compromise (regarding the close surveillance of markets by states) and was a first sign of its weakening. See: Helleiner, 1994, pp. 81-100.

[19] In addition to Triffin's proposals, Milton Friedman was the prominent representative of an alternative scheme based on flexible exchange rates and minimal state intervention. In 1964, the very influential German "Council of Economic Advisers" suggested in its Annual Report the introduction of a flexible exchange rate for the DM. The reaction of the German government was negative. It cited its international commitments, the danger of continuous DM revaluation, the necessity of international economic cooperation in order to harmonize economic policies and the importance of fixed exchange rates for the Common Market.

powers of European institutions and prevented a widening of the Common Market to include Britain. Soon, however, it became clear to De Gaulle that it was not enough to throw off the yoke of NATO or to rebuke European bureaucrats: as long as the dollar was the international reserve currency, France would not be free to determine its own fate. To the Gaullists, the Bretton Woods system symbolised a "Yalta monétaire fait à deux[20]", paralleling in importance the famous wartime conference of 1945 during which the Big Three allegedly had divided up Europe without regard to the concerns of smaller countries. The Gaullist critique of the dollar centred on two points: that an overvalued dollar (with respect to gold) helped the US to buy up European industries with cheap money, and that the key currency role of the dollar allowed the Americans to finance their expansive foreign policies by printing money[21]. By portraying the international monetary system as a structure which perpetuated American hegemony and from which defection was in French interest, De Gaulle tried to undermine the consensus underpinning the transatlantic order. In February 1965, the French President threw down the gauntlet: he announced that France from now on would exchange every dollar it earned immediately for gold in order to force the US to a radical change of the monetary system[22]. The healthy state of the franc in the mid-1960s provided De Gaulle with the necessary means for his challenge. This fundamentally different conception precluded in principle any French participation in attempts to reform the transatlantic system, notwithstanding the pressure exerted by France's partners. De Gaulle noted: "Le fameux isolement dont on nous menace n'a, dans l'espèce, aucune importance du moment que nous maintenons en bon ordre notre propre balance de paiements. D'ailleurs, nous nous sommes déjà 'isolés' nous-mêmes, et fort avantageusement, en convertissant automatiquement beaucoup de nos dollars en or."[23]

The Gaullist idea of national monetary autonomy, however, was not uncontested in France. French monetary authorities, for example, cooperated in the reform steps taken by the Western countries outlined above. France even remained in the gold pool (which was to stabilise the value of gold) until 1967, and it took part in talks about the reform of the transatlantic system. Thus, many officials in French monetary institutions obviously remained transatlantic in their outlook[24]. A third

---

[20] Testimony of Jean-Yves Haberer, Chef du Cabinet of French Foreign Minister M. Debré, in Institut De Gaulle, 1992.

[21] On French monetary policy in this period, see Bordo *et al.*, 1995.

[22] De Gaulle, 1969, pp. 330-4.

[23] De Gaulle, 1987, p. 245 (note to Pompidou, Couve de Murville, and Debré, 31 Jan. 1966).

[24] See Gavin and Mahan, 2000.

conception was represented by Finance Minister, Giscard d'Estaing, and pronounced by his deputy, André de Lattre, in January 1965: the idea of a European currency[25]. This was a surprising step. Previously, calls for a European currency had come mostly from European pressure groups, such as Monnet's Action Council for the United States of Europe. They had never been taken really seriously by the member countries. The same happened to the EEC Commission's ambitious Action Programme for the Second Stage of the Common Market, presented in 1962, which was formulated under the presidency of Walter Hallstein by Robert Marjolin. In this report, the Commission suggested joint economic planning on the Community level, fixed exchange rates among Member States and a common monetary policy leading finally to a single currency[26]. It argued that

> [The present international monetary system] makes for a certain fragility calling for constant action if undue strains are to be avoided. The Community will be all the more able to act effectively in this direction as it will function as a single unit; the emergence of a European reserve currency would considerably facilitate international monetary co-operation and a reform of the present system [...]. The establishment of the monetary union could become the objective of the third stage towards the Common Market.[27]

The explicitly "Keynesian" background of the programme was expressed in the introduction: "[A]n economic order based on freedom can only exist in the world of today at the price of constant state intervention in economic life."[28] In effect, this was a Bretton Woods programme without its transatlantic component.

The rebuff for the initiative was strong, particularly in Germany. Bundesbank president, Karl-Heinz Blessing, attacked the proposal as a pipe dream and insisted that monetary policies had to be dealt with on a larger basis, that is the transatlantic level. Furthermore, the economic policies of the member countries would have to converge much more before any discussion of monetary integration made sense[29]. This prefigured the "coronation theory" which later reappeared in the debate on the Werner Plan. Blessing's critique was echoed by his government

---

[25] Political Archive – Auswärtiges Amt (PA-AA), Dept. III A1, vol. 176, Botschaft Paris to AA, 19 Jan 1965.

[26] Memorandum of the Commission on the Action Programme of the Community for the Second Stage of August 1962. Full text in: *European Yearbook* X/1963, pp. 797-899.

[27] *Ibid.*, pp. 869, 871, 875.

[28] *Ibid.*, p. 799.

[29] Remarks of 27 Jan 1963, in: Deutsche Bundesbank, Auszüge aus Presseartikeln, 9/1963, pp.1-3.

and by the other member countries, particularly by De Gaulle. In 1963, the Action Programme was quietly shelved. Giscard's initiative, which came two years later, had a similar fate. It was greeted with silence in the EEC countries. The French president did not like the ideas of his minister either, and in January 1966 Giscard d'Estaing left the government, to be replaced by the Gaullist Debré. Later the same year, De Gaulle managed to remove Hallstein from his post as president of the Commission.

De Gaulle's intention of bringing down the transatlantic system failed, however, although the US gold reserves in Fort Knox shrank considerably. No other monetary power supported France. Germany immediately declared its solidarity with the US. To be sure, it shared with the rest of Europe some of the critique De Gaulle uttered against lax American monetary policies. The Germans complained that the system forced them to import inflation and thus undermined the domestic priority of price stability[30]. But the primacy of transatlantic cooperation in solving the monetary distortions remained dominant, not only in the Federal Republic but also in countries such as Britain, Italy or the Netherlands (as mentioned earlier, an important factor was the security partnership linking these states to the US). A clear indication of this was the case of the Italian exchange crisis of 1964. Rome turned to the United States for help, consulting in the process only with Bonn. This was strongly criticised by the European Commission which had repeatedly called for prior consultation among the Member States in the case of far-reaching economic measures[31].

Growing US Distance from the Transatlantic System

The crisis of the pound and the continuity of American deficits made clear that a small reform would be insufficient to save the transatlantic order. What was needed was a major adaptation of the system to the exigencies of the new economic situation, particularly regarding the regained strength of Europe and the increasing international mobility of capital, proffered mainly by the Eurodollar market. The American proposal for the introduction of Special Drawing Rights (an artificially created reserve medium which was to relieve the pressure on the dollar)

---

[30] Emminger, 1976.

[31] Strange, 1976, pp. 131-2. Later on, however, the Italian government accepted the Commission's recommendations for a restrictive policy; but this was mainly in the interest of providing external support for unpopular measures at home (*vincolo esterno*) – a parallel to the role the convergence criteria of Maastricht had for domestic reform in Italy.

in 1965 might have been the start of such a major undertaking[32]. Why did the great reform of the transatlantic order not come about?

One reason, of course, is that with France's actions, one core country was aiming at a radically different conception. But France would have been hardly able to resist, in the long term, a common front of the US and the other Europeans, if those were agreed on a managed transition towards a new form of transatlantic monetary cooperation. What was more important is that, from the mid-1960s onward, the Americans themselves, hit by societal unrest and the effects of Vietnam, increasingly came to question the central tenets of the transatlantic bargain. Over-extension and perceived lack of European helpfulness in South East Asia, but also in the monetary realm, became very prominent themes in US politics. This resulted in a much more assertive and confrontational American policy towards its allies, and in increasing de-legitimisation of a monetary system which appeared to place the burden of adjustment only on the shoulders of deficit countries. Vietnam put growing pressure on the American balance of payments and also on internal price stability, leading to inflation which, via the dollar, was transmitted to the international system. President Johnson refused to raise taxes in order to contain the inflation[33]. Domestic autonomy and the exigencies of the international monetary system increasingly appeared to contradict each other. The American government still defended the transatlantic order in the security field against vigorous attempts by Congress to cut the military commitment in Europe, and in the monetary realm against the critics of the dollar-gold-standard and increasing speculation. However, realising the difficulties of negotiating a major reform under these circumstances, the Secretary of Treasury, Henry Fowler, had the ingenious idea to suspend part of the fixed-rate dollar system until the Vietnam war was over:

> I propose that we give serious consideration to asking the key dollar-holding nations [...] to pledge *not to convert dollars they presently hold and not to convert any additional dollars* [emphasis in original] that may accrue to them as long as the Vietnam struggle continues. To accomplish this, we will have to state in the strongest possible terms that: 1. We most emphatically do intend to bring our balance of payments into equilibrium. 2. The Vietnam War, with its attendant direct and indirect balance of payments costs, has made it difficult for us to do this as soon as we hoped. But we will do it. 3. We are bearing virtually the entire burden of the Vietnam conflict. We view this as commitment on behalf of all free nations. We do not ask others

---

[32] The plan was announced by US Secretary of Treasury Fowler on 10 July 1965. See *American Foreign Policy. Current Documents* 1965, pp. 231ff. The ensuing complicated EEC-US negotiating process is analysed by Cohen, 1977.

[33] Zimmermann, 2001.

to see it this way, but we do ask that they not act in a manner that will prevent us from meeting our commitments and/or destroy the international financial institutions that are such a vital part of the world we are attempting to defend.[34]

This would have meant that Europe had to forego its principal element of control over America's management of its reserve currency and instead of that trust in an unbinding promise that Washington would do its best to behave responsibly in the future. Such a strategy could work only if the political and economic bases of the transatlantic system were intact. However, it was confidence in the wisdom and continuity of American policies which suffered most from the Vietnam fallout. The war provoked grave apprehensions in Europe whether the US would honour its side of the bargain and keep the dollar stable while preserving its security commitments in Europe. It also led to fundamental doubts in the general thrust of American policies. The charge that Europe was financing the Vietnam War by holding dollars derives from that. Another European worry was the American tendency to balance the problems in Asia with moves towards an accommodation with the Soviet Union, a process in which the allies were not sufficiently consulted[35]. The character of the transatlantic economic community as an anti-communist grouping was eroding. At the same time, the close link between a broad consensus among and within Western countries on security policy and continued support for the transatlantic monetary system was dissolving. Thus, American pressure to induce European countries to hold dollars (and thus extend credit to policies they would underwrite no more) in line with Fowler's proposal was deeply resented[36].

At the end of President Johnson's tenure in January 1969, the US government displayed a mixture of resignation and resentment against the Europeans who were not ready to completely break with De Gaulle

---

[34] FRUS 1964-8, VIII, Memorandum by Treasury Secretary Fowler to President Johnson, 10 May 1966, pp. 274–5.

[35] Examples for this tendency which began after the Cuban Missile Crisis are the Test Ban Treaty of 1963, the Non-proliferation Treaty of 1968, or Lyndon B. Johnson's bridge-building speech of October 1966.

[36] The only country which, after massive political pressure, would sign formally such a commitment was Germany in the form of the famous Blessing letter in 1967 (Text of the letter in: Hearings before the Combined Subcommittee of Foreign Relations and Armed Services Committees on the Subject of US Forces in Europe, US Senate, 90th Congress, 1st sess., 3 May 1967, Washington 1967, pp. 81ff.). This commitment was part of the acrimonious negotiations taking place in 1967 between the US, Britain, and Germany about the cost of Allied troops in Germany and the possibilities of Germany to offsetting this cost. The negotiations showed how strained the bargain had become. See: Zimmermann, 2001a.

and go along with the American proposals to reform the system. The quarrel about a veto right for the Europeans regarding the creation of new liquidity in the form of SDRs was one expression of this disenchantment. When the SDRs were finally agreed to, the result was far too unambitious to save the transatlantic system. The additional liquidity provided by the expansion of the American economy in the wake of both Vietnam and the attempt to construct a more comprehensive social network in the US (the "Great Society" programme) made clear that the core problem was not the lack of liquidity that Triffin had predicted. The various dollar and gold crises from 1966 to 1968 showed that the international monetary system rested upon the political will of the United States to keep the inflationary forces in the country under control and to accept at least some restrictions on its domestic autonomy for the sake of saving the transatlantic system – and this will was waning[37]. A last attempt in this sense was the restrictive balance of payments programme announced on New Years Day 1968 which imposed limits on investment abroad and foreign lending – to no avail, however[38].

These measures were strongly criticised by the business community which was a traditional supporter of the Republican Party. When Nixon came to power in 1969, the de-legitimisation of the transatlantic order in the US accelerated. The most important reason was the new emphasis Nixon placed on national autonomy. His admiration for De Gaulle was no accident. Like the general, Nixon had no *a priori* attachment to the institutionalised cooperation established by the Bretton Woods framework – particularly since the public debate suggested that its effects were damaging to American national interests. According to this discourse, the transatlantic system had led to a situation in which the European weight had grown so much that the US felt its policy autonomy threatened. The Nixon administration was not willing to agree to European demands for a domestic economic policy which would stabilise the external value of the dollar. In economic issues, Europe was seen as rival not as partner. Nixon's Secretary of Treasury, John Connally, wrote:

> I believe we must realise there is a strong element of thinking within Europe that would take advantage of weakness or clumsiness on our part to promote the Common Market not as a partner but as a rival economic bloc, competing vigorously with the dollar and reducing or shutting out, as best as it can, U.S. economic influence from a considerable portion of the world.[39]

---

[37] Nau, 1990, p. 152.
[38] Strange, 1976, pp. 288-9.
[39] Declassified Documents Reference System (thereafter: DDRS) 1999, Doc. 385, Connally to President Nixon, 8 June 1971.

In monetary relations, the Europeans became "the other", a feeling which was reciprocated on the other side of the Atlantic. Whereas in the post-1945 period the political background of the American support for the international monetary system had been the stabilisation of the European allies against the East, the Nixon administration was preoccupied by an alleged American decline and the need to find a reconciliation with the USSR and China. The language of American decline served to legitimise the non-compliance with previous rules. The danger that the disenchanted Europeans would be attracted by the East was now very tiny indeed (such a possibility would have changed the political background completely; this is suggested by the nervous reaction of Kissinger and Nixon to Brandt's *Ostpolitik*). A strategy of national autonomy was perfectly viable for the US, as long as the Cold War still kept the military Alliance together. However, the bipolar Cold War ideology which had been an important element in the US support for the monetary system was indirectly weakened by Nixon's détente policy.

This led to a situation in which the new government took no initiative to do anything about the monetary turmoil as long as it did not see its domestic priorities endangered by the "market". First, it tried to get domestic inflation under control by tightening macroeconomic policies and cutting government expenditure. When this policy failed and appeared to scare away voters, the government undertook a series of expansionary steps which struck the fatal blow to the Bretton Woods system[40]. Domestic expansion in the US went hand in hand with wage and price controls and a series of trade restrictions in the international field. The project of a mutual reform of the transatlantic order in accordance with the principles of Bretton Woods was dead. National autonomy was the new gospel, and in such a framework the transatlantic bargain had no place. The rise of neo-liberal thought in those years had the welcome function of legitimising this policy. The Americans continued to insist, however, that the Europeans should not rock the boat by transferring back the dollars which accrued to them. In June 1971, Connally advised Nixon to insist with Chancellor Brandt that "Germany's present policy of holding dollars and not buying gold is absolutely fundamental to US-FRG relations"[41]. As a result of the policy of "benign neglect", however, the US deficits rose out of all proportion. When dollar-holders desperately tried to cash in their reserves, Nixon acted and in August 1971, after years of precipitously increasing speculative crises, closed the gold window, imposing a ten percent surtax on all imports. As there was no alternative to the dollar, the world was set

---

[40]   Nau, 1990, pp. 154-6.
[41]   DDRS 1999, Doc. 378, Memorandum for the President, 12 June 1971.

on a virtual dollar standard. Thus, the burden of adjustment was shifted abroad, and America's autonomy regarding its domestic policies and the size of its external commitments was preserved. The Europeans, however, were left with two unpleasant options concerning the resulting dollar glut: either to re-value their currencies against the dollar or to try and neutralise the capital inflow by restrictive measures on the domestic market.

The Origins of the Werner Plan

What was the European reaction to these developments? The intensive battle in early 1967 in the German government about whether it should continue to hold dollars in order to preserve the American troop presence was an expression of growing irritation with American policies and a new phenomenon in the Federal Republic: increasing monetary nationalism, represented above all by Finance Minister Franz-Josef Strauss. This became very evident during the tempestuous Bonn *ad hoc* meeting of the Finance Ministers of the ten leading industrial states in November 1968 which had the purpose of finding a common response to a wave of huge capital movements into the DM. The main target of speculation were the French franc and sterling, and in a desperate attempt to defend the parities, the reserves of both France and Britain were soon brought close to exhaustion. Both governments put the blame for the crisis on the Federal Republic which refused to re-value an allegedly under-valued DM. Prior to the meeting, Prime Minister Harold Wilson had called the German ambassador in the middle of the night to demand immediate action by the German government; otherwise Britain would be forced to reconsider its NATO commitment on the continent which was costing it valuable foreign exchange[42]. The French government did not mince its words either. In a letter to the German Chancellor, Premier Ministre, Couve de Murville, warned: "Dans une question d'une telle gravité [...] le gouvernement français s'adresse donc au chancelier fédéral pour lui demander que son gouvernement prenne immédiatement les mesures ou les positions qui s'imposent pour éviter une nouvelle détérioration dramatique de la situation[43]". The unrest of May 1968 had resulted in a capital flight leading to a rapid decrease of French monetary reserves and to a period of prolonged difficulties for the franc. This was the reaction of the financial markets to the Grenelle Accords of May 1968 (which was intended to quell the social unrest by rising wages). It made obvious that

---

[42] AAPD 1968, II, Ambassador Blankenhorn to Foreign Minister Brandt, 20. Nov. 1968, pp. 1498-500.

[43] The letter is dated 9 Nov. 1969; PA-AA, Dept. III A 1, vol. 582.

the relatively undisturbed pursuit of domestic economic objectives was no more compatible with the idea of a strong and independent franc. De Gaulle's "splendid isolation" was an illusion.

Prior to the Bonn conference, the US joined the chorus of those requesting a DM revaluation. However, the German government did not bend although, at a meeting of the central bankers in Basle, the president of the Bundesbank had agreed with his French colleague on a concerted adjustment of the franc-DM parity. Subsequently, he tried in vain to convince his government of the benefits of such an arrangement[44]. Strauß and his colleague from the ministry of economics, Karl Schiller, declared that they would not act under pressure and devalue a solid currency just to bail out weak currencies. Doubts spread in Bonn on the franc parity ignited new speculation. When the conference ended in complete disagreement, everybody expected a huge franc devaluation. However, De Gaulle would not take the humiliation and decided to hold the parity by re-introducing severe exchange controls, cutting public expenditure and imposing a surcharge on imports coupled with subsidies for exports.

The clamorous Bonn conference was probably the key event in the process of dissolution of the transatlantic consensus and its substitution by a European conception in Western Europe. The Federal Republic's previous policy of stabilising the fixed rate dollar system finally led to very strong pressure on the German government to take measures which it considered adverse to core economic objectives, particularly the export interests of the German industry[45]. Unprecedented speculative funds streaming to the Federal Republic were to become a regular feature, undermining the domestic autonomy granted until then by the Bretton Woods system. The Bonn conference was a sign that the disillusionment of German politicians in currency matters was prevailing over the continued adherence of the financial elite to the transatlantic system.

The time was ripe for alternative conceptions and in early 1969 there was already one on the desks in European capitals: EC Commissioner Raymond Barre's report on European monetary integration[46]. The Barre report was a reaction to the Bonn conference and it reflected the deep concern of the Commission regarding the effects of monetary disunity

---

[44] Emminger, 1976, p. 518.

[45] The Federal Republic employed border adjustment taxes to make imports less and exports more expensive in order to reduce the extremely positive trade balance.

[46] Memorandum der Kommission an den Rat über die Koordinierung der Wirtschaftspolitik und die Zusammenarbeit in Währungsfragen; Bulletin der EG 3/1969, Sonderbeilage.

on the project of European integration. Barre appeared particularly worried about the prospect of possible changes in the exchange rates of major European currencies (which had been fixed since the DM revaluation of 1961). This would create grave dangers for the Common Market, particularly for the CAP, which was in economic terms the core project of the EC until then. Regarding the practical proposals of Barre, however, his memorandum was, compared to the 1962 Action Programme, very cautious. It suggested prior consultation among the member countries before they undertook important economic measures and the creation of a mechanism for short-term and medium-term assistance to help countries in balance of payments difficulties. Barre proposed neither a common currency, nor a European central bank nor a European reserve fond. He also argued that the planned monetary mechanism would not duplicate the work of transatlantic institutions. The reaction of the member countries during prior consultations ranged from mildly positive to indifferent[47]. In July 1969, the Finance Ministers met and endorsed the parts of the Barre plan related to consultation and short-term assistance[48]. Italy and the Netherlands still had reservations and warned of a duplication of transatlantic mechanisms by European structures.

The French government, however, welcomed the agreement and its Finance Minister called it "un premier pas important"[49]. His name was Giscard d'Estaing who had reassumed his post after De Gaulle was replaced by Georges Pompidou in April 1969[50]. Giscard lost no time to communicate to the German government that he still considered a European solution the best way to confront the monetary crisis, despite the silence which had greeted his earlier proposals[51]. It was obvious: during the months in which the member countries discussed Barre's memorandum, the French vision of monetary policy had changed. The outcome of the Bonn monetary conference was a severe blow for the Gaullist idea of French monetary autonomy. Instead of ending dollar hegemony, France had become dependent on German monetary policy and even had to accept American financial support. The huge speculative movements from franc to DM which continued regularly in 1969 convinced the non-Gaullist and non-Communist part of the French

---

[47] PA-AA, Dept. I A 2, vol. 1519, Telegram from the German EC-Embassy to Auswärtiges Amt, 6 December 1968.

[48] Apel, 1998, p. 31.

[49] *L'Année Politique* 1969, p. 273.

[50] The Social Catholic Chaban-Delmas became Prime Minister and he brought a young official with the name of Jacques Delors into his Cabinet.

[51] PA-AA, Dept. III A 1, vol. 612, Paris Embassy to Auswärtiges Amt: Future French Monetary Policy, 24 July 1969.

establishment that a strategy of national autonomy was illusory and that a European solution was the only possibility to avoid the franc, if ever free from dependence on the dollar, being subjugated to German monetary policy. To the long-term concern of avoiding monetary dependence on Germany came the urgent short-term business of saving the CAP which was thrown into havoc when France and the Federal Republic finally realigned their currencies (in August and October 1969 respectively)[52]. Remarks by the new German Foreign Minister Walter Scheel, to the end that the CAP was practically finished, deeply irritated Paris[53]. France left no doubt that the accomplishment of the common agricultural market was a precondition for any progress in the field of European integration. Thus, the de-legitimisation of Gaullist ideology and a mix of short- and long-term concerns opened the path for the French government's embrace of a European solution. However, this opening was fragile: Pompidou, for example, was not convinced that a European solution was preferable to the Gaullist conception[54].

Giscard's hints and the Commission proposals surprisingly struck a receptive chord in Germany, the country which had been the core supporter of the transatlantic system on the European side. How is this to be explained? The major reason is that the previous consensus in Germany on the priority of pursuing international monetary policy in a transatlantic framework was rapidly dissolving. Although important actors such as the Bundesbank, remained wedded to the Bretton Woods system[55], and although Strauss and Schiller flirted with a Gaullist conception of national autonomy, based on the success of Germany's anti-inflationary policies, it was the European option which ultimately prevailed at the EC Hague summit of December 1969. The central role in this decision fell to Willy Brandt who was elected Chancellor in September 1969. Brandt's core project was a reconciliation with the Eastern countries to enhance the Federal Republic's freedom of manoeuvre and to reduce its dependence on the Western allies in some of the most vital

---

52 The fixed agricultural prices in Europe were based on units of account equivalent to the dollar. The devaluation of the franc therefore led to a situation in which French producers got more money in franc for the same product (which was bought by the EC at the fixed price in units of account). Such a situation threatened to lead to overproduction and dumping in other EC countries. The reverse happened to German farmers.

53 AAPD 1969, II, Conversation of Scheel with French Foreign Minister, M. Schumann, 9 November 1969, pp. 1237-46.

54 Dyson and Featherstone, 1999, pp. 290-1.

55 See the memorandum by Bundesbank Vice-President Emminger to State Secretary Harkort (AA) on Monnet's proposal for European Monetary Cooperation 20 December 1968; PA-AA, Dept. III A 1, vol. 596.

fields of external relations[56]. At the same time, the Chancellor was acutely aware of the problem that this new *Ostpolitik* might provoke apprehensions from countries wary of greater German independence. The currency crisis of late 1968 had been a very good illustration of this fact. After the meeting, the British and French press speculated on how Germany would use its new power founded on the strength of its currency. A continuation of German policies of national autonomy at times of a disintegrating transatlantic order was bound to re-enforce these voices and increasingly undermine the achievements of Germany's *Westpolitik*. Brandt shared the analysis by the head of the Economic Division in the Federal Chancellory that "[a] consequent [...] German policy of stability inevitably would set in motion tendencies towards a dissolution of the EEC", because this would again and again undermine the other European currencies[57]. In his years as Foreign Minister since 1966 he had witnessed the progressive deterioration of relations with France, the procrastination in European institutions and the increasingly destructive influence of monetary conflicts on Germany's relations with its partners. Additionally, he was sympathetic to the critique levelled towards US policies by the European left and thus not particularly disposed to make a strong effort in order to save the transatlantic bargain. Thus, European integration became a crucial part of his foreign policy design. A symbolic and self-binding step by Germany would serve to provide a cover for the alarm Germany's partners might have felt regarding *Ostpolitik* and it would serve to repair the Franco-German relationship The situation prior to the EC summit of December 1969, which had been proposed in summer 1969 by Pompidou, was very suitable for such an initiative. France's "yes" for a start of the talks with the UK about EC membership in compensation for Bonn's support of the accomplishment of the CAP assured the success of the summit.

However, Brandt went a step further. During the heads of government meeting in The Hague, 1 December 1969, Brandt surprised the assembled group by endorsing the idea of a European reserve fund and calling for the accomplishment of an economic and monetary union in stages (based on a plan from the Economics Ministry)[58]. The reserve fund idea had been suggested by Monnet to Brandt prior to the summit: "[L'Allemagne] peut prendre une initiative constructive et pacifique et généreuse qui dépassera – je dirais presque effacera – les souvenirs du

---

[56] This is clearly reflected in the now available memoranda of Egon Bahr who was the main adviser of Brandt. See for example: AAPD 1969, II, Memorandum by Bahr on the Future Foreign Policy of the Federal Republic, 29 September 1969, pp. 1047-57.

[57] BA, B 136, Neyer (Dept. III A 1) to Chancellor, 8 January 1969.

[58] Brandt's statement is printed in *Bulletin des Presse- und Informationsamts der Bundesregierung*, 2 December 1969, pp. 1241-3.

passé[59]". On 7 November 1969, Brandt had told Monnet that such a step would still be premature[60]. Nonetheless, Monnet's argument that a German initiative in the monetary field might make a deep impression on the public and demonstrate leadership in Europe struck a receptive chord with Brandt. Despite the reservations of his officials, he decided therefore that a proposal for monetary union would have the necessary symbolic value and serve the series of important objectives outlined above. Like the 1989 agreement between Mitterrand and Kohl on the Intergovernmental Conference in Maastricht, Brandt's decision to table a plan for monetary union was taken in an extremely volatile international situation and in a very short-term and unpremeditated way. Retrospectively, Brandt wrote that he intended to give Europe renewed impetus with the reserve fund idea which was "encouraged by Jean Monnet, yet accompanied by the warnings of his ministries to employ the utmost diligence"[61]. This quote shows that Brandt's initiative rested on a very fragile base in the Federal Republic. Nonetheless, it was the first time that a German Chancellor publicly backed the idea of a European monetary order. Germany proposed to neutralise the instrument which in the months before appeared to demonstrate more than anything else the new weight of the Federal Republic. The proposal was presented at a moment when Germany embarked on a new policy which had at its core the intention to shed off many of the constraints imposed by its geo-strategic position. At a time when the security relationship with the United States weakened, suggesting less dependence, the government also took a step towards creating a rival zone *vis-à-vis* the dollar. The parallels to Maastricht are striking (see the chapter by Magnusson and Ottosson in this volume).

The EMU proposal was supported by the smaller countries; even Italy now emphasised the necessity of a European counterbalance to the US[62]. A working group, chaired by Luxembourg's Prime Minister, Pierre Werner, was charged with presenting a plan in respect of European Monetary Union. This assertion of a European "monetary personality" was accompanied by an attempt to achieve a closer coordination of European foreign policies in general, leading to the Davignon report (EPC). However, the process of constructing legitimacy in international politics is long and The Hague consensus was still very fragile. This accounts for the difficulties of the European project soon after it had

---

[59] BA, B 136, 6410, Monnet to Brandt, 21 October 1969.
[60] PA-AA, Dept. I A 2, vol. 1553.
[61] Brandt, 1976, p. 322.
[62] Tsoukalis, 1977, p. 89.

been started, although in the years after The Hague Summit the Bretton Woods consensus completely fell into pieces.

The Fall of Bretton Woods and the Contested Territory of Monetary Ideology

In 1970-71, international financial markets got increasingly out of control due to the fiscal expansion pursued by the Nixon administration and its indifference to the external balance. A quick implementation of the Werner Plan would have been a logical step in this situation, but the Europeans had wasted precious time during the 1960s. Given the views of General De Gaulle any move towards a supranational management of European currencies was out of the question in the 1960s, although the European economies boomed and although there was ample space to create a united position in the monetary talks with the US. In the 1970s, disruptive economic conditions made any ambitious project for monetary reform a very difficult enterprise. Equally detrimental to the European project were divergences among the Europeans regarding the implementation of The Hague proposals. In France, the Gaullists regained strength and this led to a re-nationalisation of French monetary policy. Giscard was unable to deliver what he had promised to his German interlocutors. Pompidou would not move towards a pooling of national sovereignty in monetary matters and he would not at all agree with the proposals of political union which the German government argued to be necessary for any prospective EMU. The French President was interested mainly in short-term monetary help[63].

Scepticism about the Brandt proposal soon emerged in the Federal Republic, too. On the one hand, proponents of an accommodation with the Americans were still very strong. On the other hand, the success of the German model in the economic turbulence of the early 1970s suggested that a strategy of national autonomy was the best viable option. Several unilateral monetary moves in the 1970s cast great doubts on Germany's readiness to fully support a European order. This feeling was intensified by the German negotiating stance in the Werner Group. The Germans from the start intended to impose the blueprint of the Bundesbank system on a prospective EMU. Against the "locomotive theory" of France and Belgium which saw monetary union as a first step towards economic union, the Germans insisted on a policy which required economic convergence as the precondition for monetary union, the so-called "coronation theory"[64]. The compromise which was finally

---

[63] Dyson and Featherstone, 1999, pp. 106-9.

[64] This cleavage becomes clear from the first memoranda of the Economics ministry already before The Hague Summit and it crystallised in the deliberations of the

found in the Werner report and which foresaw a parallelism in economic and monetary integration did resolve those differences only on the surface (see the chapter by Amy Verdun in this book). Thus, although after 1969 the final objective of European monetary policy had become consensus and slowly replaced the old transatlantic outlook, there was no agreement on the way to achieve it. The early 1970s became a period of ideological ferment with many different conceptions competing in Europe and it was to take time before the European monetary order inaugurated at government level in The Hague in 1969 gradually acquired the pre-eminence against all rival conceptions. In the 1970s and 1980s, European governments and central banks became less and less willing to make any sacrifices for the sake of transatlantic coopera-tion – in contrast with an increasing willingness to coordinate their monetary policies in the European context[65].

What lessons can we draw from the experience of the fall of Bretton Woods for the political economy of present day Europe? The essential nexus in this story has been the link between the preservation of domestic autonomy and the willingness of states to support the trans-atlantic order in which the monetary realm was but one, albeit very important, element. The international monetary crisis of the 1960s and 1970s was so threatening for Western governments because it had a deep impact on the autonomy of *domestic* economic policies. One of the most serious consequences of the resulting slow dissolution of the fixed-rate dollar system was that governments on both sides of the Atlantic progressively lost their ability to control the forces of the international market. During the late 1960s, states such as the US, Germany, France, Britain or Italy were all confronted with agonising episodes which made overtly clear that the control achieved after 1945 was once again slip-ping out of the hands of governments. Domestic economic objectives, whether it was full employment or low interest rates, had to be abandoned temporarily or for longer periods to meet external pressures. A mutual reform of the transatlantic system so as to allow the continued undisturbed pursuit of these policies was delayed due to discord across the ocean which eroded the political base of the monetary order. When this factor hit an international monetary order whose political framework was in serious disarray, a quick erosion of the previous pattern of monetary cooperation was set in motion.

Werner Group. See for example: PA-AA, Dept. I A 2, vol. 1553, *Deutsches Memorandum zur Wirtschafts- und Währungsunion auf der Konferenz der Staats- und Regierungschefs der EWG*, 11 November 1969; PA-AA, Dept. III A 1, vol. 590, Minutes of the 35th Meeting of EEC Finance Ministers, 29-30 May 1970.

[65] For this process, see Loedel, 1999.

In this analysis the Werner Plan has to be interpreted as a European attempt to reassert the primacy of the political, to (re-)legitimise governments in a changing economic and political environment, and to do this by implementing an alternative set of rules for a comprehensive political economy after the breakdown of the transatlantic consensus. The idea of monetary union as an element of a European ideology was to stay on the agenda. EMU gradually acquired a strong legitimacy based on European cooperation as an ordering principle in the international system, although its comprehensive character uniting the political and the economic was transformed later on, as the other chapters in this volume show.

CHAPTER 2

The Political Economy of the Werner and Delors Reports: Continuity amidst Change or Change amidst Continuity?

Amy VERDUN[1]

The Werner Report of 1970 and the Delors Report of 1989 have a lot in common, though they are significantly distinct from one another. They are similar in advocating a road to Economic and Monetary Union (EMU) for the European Community (EC) and identifying various stages in order to get there. They both also identify the need to have "economic" and "monetary" union as two parallel though distinct processes. In the Delors Report, however, less attention was paid to the need to have a fully developed "economic" union, insofar as an "economic government" might be required. Related to this, there was a different conception in the Delors Report about what would be the role of labour markets, social partners, tripartite relations etc.

This chapter offers a political economy perspective on the comparison of the Werner Report and the Delors Report. It asks the question, to what extent are the Werner and Delors Reports similar and different? What caused these similarities and differences? In order to answer these questions the chapter examines the historical context in which both reports emerged, the aims they had, the assumptions they made about the relationship between "economic" and "monetary" integration, between the state, social partners and labour markets. It also looks at the role of ideas, i.e. the idea about the role of monetary policy, and the role that EMU had in the broader European integration process. The chapter concludes by stating that one needs to look at the specific historical context in which each of these plans were written to understand some of the reasons for the similarities and differences

[1] An earlier version of this chapter was presented at a workshop held in February 2001 at the European University Institute in Florence, Italy. The author wishes to thank workshop participants for comments and feedback. Special thanks goes to Bo Stråth and Hubert Zimmerman for very useful detailed comments and suggestions.

between the two reports. In particular, it is necessary to consider the role of ideas and the overall economic development and the process of European integration to fully appreciate the changes and continuity in European economic and monetary unification.

The structure of this chapter is as follows. The next section offers a historical background. Section three compares the Werner Report with the Delors Report. The fourth section examines what the Werner and Delors Reports could do for macro-economic polities, labour markets and social issues. Finally the last section draws some conclusions.

Historical Background to the Werner Report and the Delors Report[2]

Werner Report

Economic and Monetary Union was not mentioned in the 1957 Rome Treaty. The first initiative to create an EMU was in the late 1960s in response to a number of factors. Most of the 1960s were characterised by high and stable economic growth, a system of fixed exchange rates (Bretton Woods), and steady progress towards completing the customs union in the European Community of six Member States.

By the late 1960s these circumstances all started to change. Revaluations and devaluations occurred among European currencies and between those currencies and the US dollar, leading to an exchange rate crisis. A number of events in 1968 (such as the May upheavals in France) also created a crisis-like atmosphere. Various people in national governments and in the European Commission (such as Pierre Werner from Luxembourg and the Frenchman, Raymond Barre) felt strongly that exchange rate stability in Europe should be maintained. This was considered important in particular to secure the feasibility of the Common Agricultural Policy (CAP). At the same time, by 1968 the EC Member States had managed to create a customs union ahead of schedule. They were looking for the next project of European integration. At The Hague summit in December 1969 the Heads of States and Governments formally agreed to explore the creation of an Economic and Monetary Union in the European Community "within the Council, on the basis of the memorandum presented by the Commission on 12 February 1969 and in close collaboration with the latter, a plan in stages (is to) be worked out during 1970 with a view to the creation of an economic and monetary union"[3].

---

[2] This section draws heavily on chapters 3 and 4 of Verdun, 2000a.
[3] The Hague Communiqué, 1969, para 8, quoted in Commission of the EEC 1970: 1.

In January 1970 the European Council adopted a resolution to establish an EMU in the Community. In February 1970 the EC Finance Ministers discussed a number of different plans but could not reach an agreement on the precise definition of, and road to, EMU[4]. Nevertheless, similar views were held on two areas: the need to give Europe some form of monetary organisation, and the wish to move further after the completion of the customs union, aiming for sustained and balanced growth, by progressing toward a single economic and currency area[5].

In March 1970, the Council of Ministers asked a seven-member working group to draft an EMU proposal. Pierre Werner, the Prime Minister and Finance Minister of Luxembourg, chaired a working group that studied the possible road to EMU. The Werner Group consisted of individuals who were chairmen of various economic and monetary EC committees. The individuals were Baron H. Ansiaux, (Chairman of the Committee of Central Bank Governors), Mr. G. Brouwers (Chairman of the Short-Term Economic Policy Committee), Mr. B. Clappier (Chairman of the Monetary Committee), Mr. U. Mosca (Director General of the Directorate General (DG) for Economic and Financial Affairs of the EC), Mr. J.B. Schöllhorn (Chairman of the Medium-Term Economic Policy Committee), Mr. G. Stammati (Chairman of the Budgetary Policy Committee). Each of these individuals was a national of one of the six Member States. Thus, this composition ensured that each member country was represented in the Werner Group. Virtually every committee member also had a high-ranking national position besides holding the official Community position mentioned above. They can be considered to have been part of an "economic and financial elite", which had been discussing European economic and monetary integration for more almost a decade[6].

The Werner Group succeeded in producing an interim report by the end of May, which dealt with the main aspects of establishing an EMU in stages. The first stage would start on 1 January 1971 and would last three years. In that first stage, measures would be taken to coordinate economic policies and taxation, liberalise capital markets, and reach monetary solidarity. It is noteworthy that at this time the Group considered the acceptance of EMU by the social partners to be of great

---

[4] See e.g. Political Archive –Auswärtigers Amt (PA-AA), Dept. III A1, Vol 589, 11 March 1970, report by Dr Robert, pp. 1-3).

[5] Kruse, 1980; Magnifico, 1973.

[6] Rosenthal 1975. Rosenthal stresses that the economic and financial experts had been getting together regularly since the end of the Second World War at meetings of the International Monetary Fund, the World Bank and the OECD. "The individuals responsible for policy proposals and decisions on economic and monetary matters [in the EEC] knew each other very well indeed by 1970", Rosenthal, 1970, p. 102.

importance. It advocated regular concertation between the Community institutions, on the one hand, and the unions, employers' federations and other representative bodies in particular economic and social sectors on the other[7]. The latter would be asked to state their views on the main lines to be followed in economic, fiscal and monetary matters, and on decisions of more direct interest to them[8].

How to reach EMU was stated very generally in the report and was open to numerous interpretations. The report indicated that there were two views on how to obtain exchange rate stability. One group was in favour of starting off with an autonomous exchange rate system and setting up an exchange stabilisation fund from the outset. Another group felt it not important to start with this in stage one, but rather to use this stage to focus on economic policy convergence prior to further monetary integration.

Thus, although the Group had reached considerable consensus on the contents of EMU, the rivalry between the two groups had dominated the discussions. This rivalry is often referred to as that of the so-called "economist" versus the so-called "monetarist" view of reaching economic and monetary union.

The Werner Interim Report was evaluated at the meeting of the Finance Ministers in Venice in late May 1970. The "economists" – the Federal Republic of Germany (FRG), and the Netherlands – insisted on the integration of national economic policies to precede monetary union[9]. The "monetarists" – Belgium, France, Luxembourg as well as the Commission – held the view that monetary solidarity would induce the necessary convergence of economic policies[10]. The Council "solved" the matter by giving the Werner Group a mandate to define the contents of the first stage by September 1970.

---

[7] See also Commission of the EEC (1970).

[8] Werner Interim Report, 1970.

[9] Italy did not really fit into one of the two camps. However, that country was often supportive of some of the proposals put forward by the FRG and the Netherlands. Upon his return to Rome from the meeting in February 1970, the Italian Minister of Finance stressed that the "Common Market would have to adopt a common economic policy before it could hope that a common currency would be created". See Rosenthal, 1970, p. 103. On the Italian position supporting the same parts of the German proposals see also Political Archive –Auswärtigers Ambt (PA-AA), Dept. III A1, Vol 590, 9 April 1970, report by Tietmeyer, pp. 5-6.

[10] Note that this use of the terms "economists" and "monetarists" is specific to the discussion about the division among the Member States regarding how to obtain EMU. Thus, in this context, the term "monetarist" does not refer to the "monetarist" views of Milton Friedman.

The Werner Group unanimously agreed to its final report on 8 October 1970. The Group had combined the wishes of the "economists" and the "monetarists", but by doing so, it had failed to commit the Member States to anything in the first two years. Only in 1973 would the amendment of the Rome Treaty, and hence the transfer of sovereignty, be on the agenda. The compromise package, often referred to as "parallelism", suggested that the "economist" and the "monetarist" paths to EMU could go hand in hand. However, because the two camps departed from opposite assumptions and priorities as to how EMU could be achieved, such a parallel approach could never work. Kruse notes: "Parallelism merely concealed the irreconcilable differences among the Member States"[11].

EMU had five aims: first, to create "an area within which goods and services, people and capital will circulate freely and without competitive distortions, without thereby giving rise to structural or regional disequilibrium"[12]. Second, to increase welfare, and reduce regional and social disparities. In order to achieve these aims the report envisaged the need for consultation with economic and social groups as well as the operation of market forces. Third, to create a monetary union, implying "a total and irreversible convertibility of currencies, the elimination of margins of fluctuation in exchange rates, the irrevocable fixing of parity rates and the complete liberation of movements of capital"[13]. Fourth, in EMU only the global balance of payments of the Community *vis-à-vis* the rest of the world would be of any importance. It was hoped that equilibrium would be achieved by the mobility of factors of production and financial transfers by public and private sectors, as is the case within a nation-state[14]. Finally, EMU would transfer responsibility from the national to the Community level. Monetary policy would be centralised, whereas economic policy-making would in part remain a national responsibility. The role of the European budget would need to increase gradually, but would fall short of the size of a national budget. The Group itself summarised the characteristics and most important consequences of EMU as follows:

- the Community currencies will be assured of total irreversible mutual convertibility free from fluctuations in rates and with immutable parity rates, or preferably they will be replaced by a sole Community currency;

---

[11] Kruse, 1980, p. 73.
[12] Werner Report, 1970, p. 9.
[13] Werner Report, 1970, p. 10.
[14] Werner Report, 1970, p. 10; *cf.* Baer and Padoa-Schioppa, 1989, p. 53.

- the creation of liquidity throughout the area and monetary and credit policy will be centralised;
- monetary policy in relation to the outside world will be within the jurisdiction of the Community;
- the policies of the Member States regarding the capital market will be unified;
- the essential features of the whole of the public budgets, and in particular variations in their volume, the size of balances and the methods of financing or utilising them, will be decided at the Community level;
- regional and structural policies will no longer be exclusively within the jurisdiction of the member countries;
- a systematic and continuous consultation between the social partners will be ensured at the Community level[15].

The Werner Plan consisted of a time-schedule in three stages to reach EMU by 1980. It was concrete about the first stage, which would last three years, but left the timetable for the last two stages completely open. Again, the vagueness was an indication of the compromise nature of the report. On the institutional side, in sharp contrast to what would be proposed nineteen years later, two main organs were envisaged. In addition to a "Community system for the central banks", a "Centre of Decision for Economic Policy" (CDEP) was to be created. Economic policies were to be coordinated, by carrying out at least three annual surveys of the economic situation in the Community, which would enable the adoption of common guidelines. Concerning budgetary policies, it was suggested that quantitative guidelines should be adopted on the principal elements of public budgets; that is, on global receipts and expenditure, the distribution of the latter between investment and consumption, and the directions and amount of balances. On the fiscal side, the Group voiced a progressive harmonisation of indirect taxes as well as those applicable to interest payments on fixed interest securities and dividends. A European Monetar·ʹ Fund was planned at the latest during the second stage. It would be the forerunner of the Community system of Central Banks to be set up in the third stage.

Throughout the autumn of 1970 proposals were being discussed. The Commission drafted a memorandum based on the Werner Report but had omitted reference to institutional arrangements for the eventual transfer of sovereignty, whereas it strengthened provisions for action in the structural and regional fields[16]. When the Council discussed the memorandum in November and in mid-December no agreement could

---

[15] Werner Report, 1970, p. 12
[16] *Bulletin of the EC*, Supplement 11, 1970, pp. 11-21.

be reached. The Dutch and West German delegations stressed that the supranational provisions needed to be installed, which was unacceptable for the French government officials.

In January, at a Franco-German meeting, the West German officials proposed a clause which would ensure "parallelism" between the economic and monetary provisions of the EMU arrangement. The first stage of both was to last four years; if there were failure to reach agreement on the transition to the second stage, the monetary mechanisms would cease to apply. On the basis of this compromise, agreement was reached on 9 February 1971[17]. The Council formally announced the EMU objective on 22 March 1971[18]. The process had begun, but the irreversible commitments were postponed for three years; a side-effect of the fact that the governmental representatives stood by their national positions until the very last moment, thus making far-reaching agreement very difficult.

Besides the stark division between the "economist" and the "monetarist" modes of thought about economic and monetary integration, the problems with coordination in 1971 stemmed from lack of solidarity among the Member States. National governments were reluctant to maintain an external balance, seeing that this had not worked in the 1960s. Therefore, the chances of success in coordinating them now, without a new supranational body, and without majority rule were small.

During the 1970s it became clear that the compromise solution clause did not work. Monetary integration proceeded slowly and followed mainly the scenario of the "monetarists" exchange rate agreements, the intervention mechanism and monetary support rather than the coordination of economic and monetary policies. This was no surprise as the aim of fixed exchange rates offered the public the most immediate benefits, and it was the only aim in the EMU plan to which all Member States agreed. Nevertheless, there are many reasons for the failure to achieve EMU during that decade.

As early as the first semester after 22 March 1971, it was apparent that the basis of common interests of the Member States was too narrow. It soon became clear that the gap that appeared at this time was the very same that had existed while drafting the EMU plan. The French were reluctant to accept any plans leading to the transfer of sovereignty to a European body. The powerful Gaullist groups in France strongly rejected the supranational element of the plans. Their opposition proved to be so strong that the French were obliged to change their policy on the

---

17   *Bulletin of the EC*, Supplement 3 and 4, 1971.
18   *Journal Officiel des Communautés européennes*, C 28 and L 73, 27 March 1971 and *Bulletin of the EC*, Supplement 4, 1971.

subject of EMU. Hence, the split between France, Belgium and Luxembourg on the one hand, and the FRG, the Netherlands, and to a lesser degree Italy on the other, was complete. Once again a plan for further integration failed to materialise. Again it was due to differences of opinion on which policies to coordinate or harmonise; that is, disagreement about how to proceed towards a "united Europe". In addition to the different interests among the EEC countries, international monetary events catalysed the breakdown of the EMU agreement. A major blow to the system came when the US president Richard Nixon announced on 15 August 1971 the suspension of the convertibility of the dollar into gold, together with import restriction measures to protect the American domestic economy. It signalled the end of the Bretton Woods system (see also Zimmerman in this volume). Unable to reach an agreement on joint action in response to the American policy change, the EEC countries and the Commission were left in a delicate situation. The result was that the EEC currencies were floating against each other, with the exception of the Benelux countries. As a result, a complicated system of border taxes and rebates, which was adjusted every week, was installed for the Common Agricultural Policy. Obviously, the EMU plan could not progress any further along the lines set up in March. The objective of EMU had quickly proven to be an unobtainable ideal.

What happened during the remainder of the decade is well known. The "snake" was set up, and it failed to stay connected to the US dollar (the "tunnel"). Moreover, not all EEC countries were able to keep the exchange rates fixed. With the rapidly changing external circumstances (*e.g.* deflation and rising oil prices) and the lack of common priorities and policy objectives, EMU failed to be relaunched during the course of the 1970s[19].

The Delors Report

Although by the late 1970s it was clear that the EMU plan had failed there still were final attempts to push for European monetary integration (Marjolin Report, Tindemans Report). One of these plans was the proposal to launch an EEC system of fixed but adjustable exchange rates, framed as the European Monetary System (EMS) launched in 1979. Though not at all as ambitious as the EMU plan, it was still very precarious to suggest the creation of an EEC exchange rate system, especially in light of the lack of success of the EEC countries in keeping their currencies in the snake arrangement.

At the turn of the decade some important changes happened to the ideas about policy-making in the area of monetary policy. West

---

[19]   For a detailed discussion see Verdun, 2000a, pp. 61-75.

Germany, the Netherlands, the UK, and Denmark decided that they should focus their monetary policy on safeguarding low inflation[20]. The West German monetary authorities pursued the most stringent policies. Many of the others started to shadow West German monetary policies. Countries such as Belgium and Luxembourg, France, and Italy came round a few years later. As a result the EMS turned out to be more of a success. The shadowing of Bundesbank policies had done the trick.

Another important lesson was learnt in this period. As the 1970s was coming to a close governments concluded that high inflation did not have positive effects on unemployment and growth. In other words, they came to the conclusion that there was no long-term trade off between inflation and unemployment. To the contrary, inflation meant that pensioners, wage earners and savers lost money. If inflation was high and if wages and prices were corrected for inflation, then the net benefit of inflation was zero, and if anything an interest rate premium had to be paid on the currency due to the inflationary risk.

Finally, a third important lesson was learned by both France, in the early 1980s, and by Italy, later in the mid-1980s. A country that is highly dependent on its neighbouring countries is unable to pursue a policy totally different from those in surrounding countries. An autonomous policy easily leads to speculative attacks on its national currency, capital flight, and the undermining of the policies pursued by the government of the day. "Socialism in one country", as had been envisaged by French President François Mitterrand in the early 1980s, had become an outdated concept.

These three changes in ideas about monetary policy-making and the role of inflation are crucial for understanding the relaunch of EMU in the EC. Two of these changes meant that monetary policy had become de-politicised. To a certain extent these changes meant that it had become more acceptable that a national or indeed a European central bank would have to be independent, as that would mean it would be better equipped to safeguard price stability. On the other hand the lesson about inflation meant that political struggles over the redistributive effects of the monetary policy regime would subside, as all had agreed that inflation was not desirable.

The EMS was not very successful in the early period (1979-1983) only moderately successful in the second period (1983-1987) but quite

---

[20]   The West German monetary authorities had decided earlier that it needed to refocus on price stability. Already towards the late 1960s, the West German government decided that inflation needed to be curbed. Yet, it was not really successful in obtaining this objective throughout the 1970s (see Giersch, Paqué and Schmieding, 1992 and Leaman, 1988, pp. 216-31).

successful in the last period, which was the period which witnessed the relaunch of EMU (1987-1992). Once it was decided that the success of the EMS was a symbol of successful European integration, Member State governments started to consider the exchange rates to be much more "fixed" than was economically desirable.

The immediate impulse that led to the relaunch of EMU in the late 1980s was the prospect of the completion of the Single Market. The Heads of State and Governments stated at the European Council meeting in Hanover on 27 and 28 June 1988 that "in adopting the Single Act, the Member States of the Community confirmed the objective of progressive realisation of economic and monetary union[21]". It was decided to set up a committee to study and propose, "concrete stages leading towards this union" to be on the agenda at the June 1989 summit in Madrid.

The committee was to be chaired by Jacques Delors and otherwise to comprise (i) the presidents or governors of member countries' central banks, (ii) another Commissioner (Frans Andriessen, DG I), and (iii) three experts, Niels Thygesen, professor of economics in Copenhagen, Alexandre Lamfalussy , Director General of the Bank for International Settlements in Basle and Miguel Boyer, President of the Banco Exterior de España.

Towards the end of the 1980s, the EC Member States had a variety of attitudes towards a possible Economic and Monetary Union in the EC. At the Hanover summit, the British Prime Minister, Margaret Thatcher, was strongly opposed to a monetary union. She declared that she did not share the "dream of a United States of Europe with a single European currency" and saw no possibility of a European central bank in her lifetime[22]. In West Germany Mr. Hans-Dietrich Genscher voiced the strongest support for a European central bank. As early as January 1988 he favoured the creation of a European central bank, when German Chancellor Helmut Kohl rejected further plans[23]. In a policy speech to the European Parliament on 16 June 1988 he called on the UK to "accept responsibilities" by joining the ERM. Although Kohl was more reserved, he said he would favour the creation of a European central bank if it resembled the Bundesbank by having a constitutionally independent position, and having price stability as its primary objective. The bank should, however, be set up only after the completion of the

---

[21]   Conclusions of the Hanover European Council, 27-28 June 1988, quoted in Delors Report (1989). It should be noted that no formal statement was made on the question of the possible establishment of a central bank.

[22]   Keesing's, 1988: 36003.

[23]   *Le Monde*, 16 and 22 January 1988.

Internal Market[24]. The French government was known to be committed to monetary union, openly so since January 1988, when it was reported to be in favour of creating a European central bank[25]. However, it favoured a European bank based on a "federal coordination between central bank governors[26]".

The Delors Report was published in April 1989[27]. It outlined in some detail three stages which would lead to the creation of an area with complete freedom of movement for persons, goods, services and capital, as well as irrevocably fixed exchange rates between national currencies and, finally, a single currency[28]. Each of the stages had specific characteristics.

Stage 1: Completion of the internal market and the reduction of existing disparities through coordination of fiscal and budgetary policies, and supported by more effective social and regional policies. Furthermore, the single financial area should be completed and, preferably, all Community currencies should be in the ERM and the same rules should apply for all participants. Also to prepare for the next stages, the Treaty of Rome should be amended to set up the future European System of Central Banks (ESCB). The mandate of the existing Committee of central bank governors would be amended so as to include the formal right of proposal or opinion to the Council of Ministers. The Committee was divided on the question of whether a European reserve fund, as a precursor to a European federal central bank, should be created at this or the next stage.

Stage 2: After the new Treaty has come into force the second stage can start, in which the basic organs and structure of Economic and Monetary Union would be set up. This includes the revision of existing institutions as well as the establishment of new ones. This stage would be very much a transition period, in which policies are evaluated and further coordinated and consolidated, and coordination should be strengthened. Most important in this stage would be the setting up of the ESCB – a federal body of national central banks with a separate new common bank – however ultimate decision-making on economic and monetary policy would still remain with national authorities.

---

[24] *Le Monde,* 28 January 1988.
[25] *Le Monde,* 12 January 1988.
[26] *The Times,* 25 June 1988, quoted in Keesing's, 36307.
[27] Committee for the Study of Economic and Monetary Union (1989) 'Report on economic and monetary union in the European Community' Hereafter referred to as 'Delors Committee' and 'Delors Report'.
[28] Delors Report, 1989, p. 17.

Stage 3: In this stage the exchange rates are "irrevocably locked" and convertible. National currencies would eventually be replaced by a single Community currency. Macroeconomic and budgetary rules would become binding; structural and regional policies would be evaluated and further strengthened. The ESCB would now take up all its responsibility as foreseen in the Treaty, including the formulation and implementation of monetary policy in the Community.

The Delors Report, like the 1970 Werner Report, made a subdivision between the "economic" union and the "monetary" union. As was the case in the 1970s this lack of clarity had its origins in the artificial distinction between what was considered the responsibility of the central bank ("monetary policy") and that of the national government ("economic policy"). It was further emphasised by the discord between the "economists" and the "monetarists"[29]. By stressing that Economic and Monetary Union should develop in parallel the report tried to settle the old dispute. The "economists", the Dutch and the Germans, still insisted on the need to have reached more economic convergence before locking the exchange rates. Belgium, France, Luxembourg and the Commission supported the "monetarist" approach which favoured a faster move to monetary integration whereby they assumed that the necessary convergence would automatically result from the operation of fixed exchange rates and a single monetary policy in the EEC. The British government wanted neither economic nor monetary integration, as far as a full EMU was concerned, proposing instead that a common currency be launched in parallel to the existing twelve currencies[30].

In the Delors Report the economic union is defined as consisting of four elements: a single market with the four freedoms (persons, goods, services, and capital), competition policy aiming at strengthening the market mechanism, common policies improving regional development and structural change and, lastly, macroeconomic policy coordination including binding rules for budgetary policies[31].

The monetary union is referred to as a currency area, with either irrevocably fixed exchange rates or, preferably, a single currency. As soon as the capital transactions are liberalised, financial markets were integrated and currencies locked and fully convertible, the national currencies would become increasingly close substitutes. As a result their interest rates would start to converge and would result in a *de facto* single monetary policy. Hence, fixed exchange rates require a common

---

[29] The debate between the "economists" and the "monetarists" refers to the specific question of in what order EMU ought to be obtained.

[30] HM Treasury, 1989; 1990; see also House of Lords 1989; 1990.

[31] Delors Report, 1989, p. 20.

monetary policy. The Delors Report thus calls for the setting up of a new institution in which monetary policy would be decided, that is, decisions on the level of the interest rates, money supply, inflation etc.[32]. The first stage would start on 1 July 1990, coinciding with the date set at the Hanover summit for the enforcement of full liberalisation of capital transactions in eight Member States[33]. The politically sensitive decision of the timetable for the following stages had been left to the politicians to decide upon.

The report was formally presented to the Council of (Finance) Ministers in Luxembourg on 17 April 1989. All but one of the European Member States agreed to the report. Nigel Lawson, the UK Chancellor of the Exchequer, was reported to have said that what EMU envisaged "would in effect require political union and a United States of Europe", which was "not on the agenda for now, or for the foreseeable future. [...] We cannot accept the transfer of sovereignty which is implied"[34]. In making these reservations the UK appeared to be completely isolated, as even Denmark's foreign minister had approved the report. Mr. Pöhl, president of the Bundesbank, even went as far as finding "Mr. Lawson's comments not entirely understandable"[35].

Hence, it can be concluded that the central bankers who until then had been conducting monetary policies, had put forward these monetary decisions to restructure monetary policy-making, and transfer it to a new European institution, a European Central Bank. They, however, left the political decision to the politicians. It soon became clear that the political debate on whether the political implications of EMU were acceptable had only just begun. The Delors Report was to be discussed at the European Council heads of government meeting in Madrid in June.

The Delors Report resembled the 1970 Werner Report in many aspects. It foresaw a parallel strategy, in three stages, of enforcing the "monetary" as well as the "economic" union; however, the new report

---

[32] Delors Report, 1989, pp. 18-19.
[33] On 13 June 1988 the Council of Ministers finally agreed after prolonged debate to remove all barriers to the free movement of capital within the EEC, effective from July 1990 (Greece, Ireland, Portugal and Spain being given until January 1992). However, in response to fears of France and the United Kingdom about a loss of fiscal sovereignty, the measure included provisions allowing member governments to impose special restraints on capital movements in times of emergency. The agreement added to the pressure on the UK to participate in the exchange rate mechanism of the EMS. During the meetings leading to the 13 June announcement the UK had insisted on the deletion of a clause which would have necessitated all Community currencies (thus also the pound) to enter the ERM by 1992.
[34] *Keesing's*, 1989: 36598.
[35] *Europe Bulletin*, No. 4999, 20 April 1989.

did not envisage a separate supranational institution ensuring economic coordination. It also stressed the need to create a central monetary authority – the ESCB – to pursue monetary policies in EMU. Member States would surrender their powers to formulate monetary policy to this new institution whose primary objective would be price stability[36].

As at the time of the drafting of the Werner Plan, the pressure for EMU was to increase after the realisation of other integration objectives. In 1968 the customs union had been completed, and the Common Agricultural Policy worked successfully, but was put under pressure by currency fluctuations. In comparison, EMU in the 1990s was to enjoy full benefit of the completed single European Market. Therefore, to eliminate transaction costs, there was a preference for a single currency, instead of just irrevocably fixed exchange rates, even though the latter was not excluded by the report if a single currency could not be agreed to politically.

The timing of the drafting of the Delors Report is also significant, for understanding some political motives. In 1989, when the Delors Report was being drafted the economic boom of the late 1980s was starting to wear out in Britain[37]. Business confidence had been accelerated by the prospect of the 1992 programme, and the hope was that this new project would keep expectations high, thereby stimulating economic growth[38]. The Delors Report therefore sought to continue rapidly with the integration process while the "Europhoria" still lasted. Also, the 1989-90 political events, the fall of Berlin Wall, German Reunification, the breaking up of the Soviet Union, and the end of Eastern European Communist regimes catalysed the revitalisation of EMU[39].

---

[36] The other tasks were: to support the general economic policy set at the Community level by the competent bodies; to be responsible for the formulation and implementation of monetary policy, exchange rate and reserve management and a properly functioning payment system; finally, to participate in the coordination of banking supervision policies of the supervisory authorities, Delors Report, 1989, p. 26.

[37] Due to its strong trading relationship with the US as well as the fact that its currency is a petro-currency, the United Kingdom is usually the first country to feel the changes in the business cycle. Other West-European countries tend to follow the trend shortly thereafter.

[38] See also Commission 1985; 1988a; 1988b.

[39] Authors differ about the role of German reunification and the end of the Cold War in determining the outcome of the EMU process. Some are convinced that the EMU negotiations were well underway, and most issues were settled even before the Berlin Wall came done, *cf.* Thiel, 1995. Others stress that German reunification provided Germany with the necessity to show the other EC/EU Member States that it was committed to Europe: Artis, 1994; Garrett, 1993; Sandholtz, 1993a. This author agrees with the latter argument.

In addition, the Community had, for several years, wanted to strengthen its position *vis-à-vis* the United States and Japan; in the late 1980s, before the Japanese bubble economy burst, that country seemed to manage its economy extremely well. In terms of economic growth, productivity, high technology development and the current account surplus, as well as the capacity to recover from the stock market crash of 1987[40], it was clear that Japan was outperforming Europe and the US.

These international factors were very important in attracting and maintaining the interest of the European Member States in creating EMU in the two-and-a-half year period from the Delors Report until the close at Maastricht of the Intergovernmental Conferences in December 1991. A major reason for trade unions, industry and monetary authorities to want to proceed with EMU is related to their perception of the limited freedom for policy-making and to their way of defining policy objectives. The interdependent, liberal, open world economy restricted the role political actors can play, in their home country, and the role a nation can play in Europe, and in the rest of the world. In other words, the prevailing concept in the late 1980s and early 1990s was the perception that there is only one way to answer the challenge posed by global change: identifying common objectives in the European framework. These were to strengthen the role of Europe and its currency in the global economy, and, internally, to maintain low inflation and to abolish exchange rate uncertainty.

Comparing the Werner and the Delors Reports

Let us now turn to a comparison of the Werner Report and the Delors Report. Let us examine a number of factors. First of all, the role of external factors. In both cases the external circumstances played an important role in triggering the launch of the EMU plan. In the case of the Werner Report the exchange rate fluctuations were part of the launch. Twenty years later exchange rate fluctuations played a smaller role. In the former the US was increasingly seen to be an unreliable partner. Yet, the Member States themselves were hopelessly divided as to how to solve problems. In the case of the Delors Report the context was that the EC was feeling it was becoming part of a third league after the US and the Pacific Basin.

European integration also played an important role. In the case of the Werner Report the customs union had been completed and the CAP really required stable exchange rates. Twenty years later the situation

---

[40]   Three months after the world-wide stock exchange crash, the Nikkei index was back to its pre-crash level, and an "all time high" was to follow shortly. The other OECD countries adjusted at a much slower pace.

87

was more or less similar. The prospect of completing the Single Market and the success of the EMS was making leaders more interested in relaunching EMU. The fact that the EC Member States had already decided to liberalise capital markets of course helped as well.

Thirdly, there were factors at stake involving experience with economic and monetary policy-making and the role of ideas. During the 1970s the various governments and the elites were still hopelessly divided between the "monetarists" and the "economists". It was unclear how governments would manage to decide what strategy to use to obtain EMU (either first fix exchange rates and then move to more economic convergence, or *vice versa*). By the late 1980s some of these problems had been dealt with. To start with the EMS worked well, and showed that some degree of exchange rate cooperation was possible even without there being full economic convergence. The planned completion of the "Internal Market" by 1992 meant that some market integration had moved ahead. On the other hand, in this period the rules about budgetary deficits and fiscal debts became more domineering in the debate. In part this came about because it was felt that a successful monetary union would require some convergence in the area of budgetary and fiscal policies. Another factor related to the role of ideas was the idea that at the time of the writing of the Werner Report there had not been the experience of the devastation of stagflation. By contrast, in the late 1980s the idea that inflation would be good for growth had been dropped. In the earlier period there also was a different belief about the role of the central bank versus the economic government and also fiscal policies. In the 1970s it was felt that an economic government and more coordination in the area of fiscal policies were necessary. In the late 1980s those ideas had been let go of. By this time the combating of low inflation had become the most important objective.

Fourth, it is worthwhile to look at the composition of the two Committees. The Werner Group was composed of experts in the monetary and financial field, who also happened to represent Member States and the European Commission. The same can more or less be said about the Delors Committee; it too could be considered an elite representing the Member States and the Commission. The main difference is that the Werner Group was composed of individuals who also held an important position in an EEC economic or monetary committee, whereas the Delors Committee was largely composed of central bankers the second time around.

Fifth, the actual blueprint looked alike in many ways but also differed on a number of important points. In both cases "parallelism" was being advocated, but in each case this meant different things. In the case of the Werner Report the "parallelism" hid the fact that there was no clear consensus about what should come first, economic convergence or the fixing of exchange rates. In the case of the Delors Report it meant that the completion of the Single Market and convergence on budgetary policies and public debt had to go hand in hand with exchange rate stability. The Delors Report did not discuss the necessity for *real* economic convergence (*e.g.* convergence in GDP per capita, levels of unemployment, economic growth rates etc.). The need for *real* economic convergence had been implicit in the view of the "economists" at the time of the Werner Report. In both cases they assumed the need to transfer sovereignty over monetary policy to a supranational European authority. In the case of the Werner Report the need was also felt to have a supranational European authority in the area of economic policy-making to flank the new supranational monetary authority (the European Central Bank). The monetary authority would also have to be responsible to the European Parliament (EP). No such economic government was perceived necessary in the late 1980s, nor was it felt that the ECB would need to be accountable to the EP[41]. In fact the ECB would need to be fully independent of political influence.

Sixth and finally, as regards the relationship of EMU and labour markets, social policies and the social partners, things had changed considerably over the two decades. In the early 1970s the neo-corporatist model was still dominant in most countries. The tripartite relationship of the national government, the employers' organisations and the trade unions were the legitimate bodies to decide macroeconomic policies regarding social and labour policies. They also collectively set wages. By the late 1980s these structures had lost much of their powers. Many of these decisions would by this time be determined by market forces. This change in view about the role of the social partners can be seen in the two reports. The Werner Report explicitly examines the role of the social partners and encourages them to take part. By contrast in the Delors Report the wording is such that it becomes clear that the social partners need to be aware that market forces will be strengthened by the creation of EMU and thus their room for manoeuvre limited. These differences and similarities between the two reports are illustrated in figure 1 below.

---

[41]   There currently is a provision for the President of the ECB to report to the European Parliament. However, this provision is merely to inform the EP. As such the provision cannot be considered implying that the ECB is "accountable" to the EP.

Figure 1: Differences and Similarities
between the Werner Report and the Delors Report

	Werner Report	Delors Report
External Conditions	Exchange Rate Turbulence	Exchange Rate Stability
	USA perceived to be an unreliable partner. European countries divided	Perceived competition from the US and the Pacific Basin
Development in European Integration	Customs Union completed ahead of time in 1968 and the need for a further project. The CAP together with exchange rate turbulence necessitate further integration in the area of exchange rates	The prospect of the Single Market being completed triggers the relaunch of EMU. Two other factors that help the relaunch is the success of the EMS and the decision in 1988 to liberalise capital markets in the EC
Ideas/ Experience	Split between the "monetarists" and the "economists"	Much less split between the "monetarists" and the "economists"
	Divergence on policy objectives regarding monetary policy	Convergence about policy objectives regarding monetary policy (*i.e.* need to maintain price stability)
	Role for both an Economic authority and a Monetary authority	No Role for the Economic authority, only for a monetary authority (that will be independent from national governments)
	Combating inflation is merely one of many objectives of the central bank	Low inflation is important
	There may be a trade-off between inflation and employment	There is no trade-off between inflation and unemployment
Composition of the Committee	Monetary and Financial experts representing all Member States and could be considered to have been part of a "Monetary and Financial Elite in the EC"	Central Bankers representing all Member States and few other experts that can be considered part of a "Monetary and Financial Elite in the EC"

	Werner Report	Delors Report
EMU Blueprint (the model)	Parallelism between "economic" and "monetary" union	Parallelism between "economic" and "monetary" union
	Parallelism means a equal development of both "economic" and "monetary" union	Parallelism means in the economic sphere the completion of the Single European Market, but no positive integration in this area. In the monetary sphere it means full transfer of sovereignty to the EC level
	European Central Bank	European Central Bank
	Creation of a Supranational Economic Authority to flank the European Central Bank	No "economic government" is envisaged
EMU and Social Partners and effects on Labour and Fiscal Policies	EMU requires regular consultation with social partners. Thus this consultation needs to be institutionalised	EMU requires cooperation from social partners. This will work via market principles
	Some degree of fiscal federalism is required	No fiscal federalism is required

Implications of the Werner and Delors Reports for Economic Policies, Labour Relations and Social Issues

As can be seen from the previous sections, the Werner and Delors Reports were similar and different in a number of ways. It is clear that the external factors provided the background against which the initiative to create EMU was placed and the European integration process provided a further impetus to the creation of a blueprint. It is the role of ideas and experience with monetary policy making that is perhaps most important for understanding the core differences between the two reports. Let us now turn to the implications of the Werner Report and the Delors Report for economic policies, labour relations and social issues.

As was noted above, the Werner Plan was drafted during a period in which tripartite relations were considered to be important for an effective governance of the economy. Also, the state-led, Keynesian model was still the dominant model in the early 1970s. However, the occurrence of stagflation in the 1970s, and the changes in ideas over monetary policy-making in the 1980s, made governments more hesitant to institutionalise social partners once the time came to draft another blueprint for EMU in the late 1980s. Yet, as we have seen, even the Delors Report mentions the importance of the role of social partners.

The reason social partners are mentioned in the Delors Report is that EMU will only be successful if there are not too many discrepancies between the participating countries in terms of economic growth, unemployment and the overall macroeconomic policy-making stance. There are a number of important restrictions on budgetary policy and public debt mentioned in the Delors Report (which were subsequently quantified and inserted in the Maastricht Treaty in the form of convergence criteria). For a fair spread of the pressures on the new single currency it is important that national governments have more or less the same levels of public debt and budgetary deficits. Differences could of course occur. However, if this happened it would mean that the higher premia on the euro (caused by higher exchange rates to support the euro) would have been caused by the heavy borrowing by one or more countries. For this reason, the Delors Report stated that budgetary deficits and public debt in the participating countries needed to be in line.

– Let us take a little side-step to discuss the convergence criteria. As was stated, they were not stated in the Delors Report. The Report merely stated the need for "binding rules and procedures for *budgetary policy*". This would include:

– effective upper limits on budget deficits of individual member countries; exclusion of access to direct central bank credit and other forms of monetary financing; limits on borrowing in non-Community currencies;

– the definition of the overall stance of fiscal policy over the medium term including the size and financing of the aggregate budgetary balance, comprising both the national and the Community positions[42].

The responsibility to determine the actual numbers of the convergence criteria was given to the Monetary Committee (MC) of the EC[43]. The MC is an influential committee which had been involved in many strategic decisions during its lifetime, for example the decisions for currency realignment in the Exchange Rate Mechanism (ERM) of the European Monetary System (EMS). The MC is comprised of two

---

[42] Delors Report, 1989, p. 28.
[43] See also Italianer, 1993.,

representatives of the European Commission and two from each EC Member States. One national representative is a top official from the national central bank; the other is a highly ranked official of the Ministry of Finance. In 1999, with the start of stage three of EMU the MC was renamed and became the "economic and financial committee". It will likely work very much like the MC[44].

The MC was divided over what the numbers of the convergence criteria should be. The countries with weaker economic performance in the area of budgetary deficits and public debts (*e.g.* Greece, Italy, Portugal, Spain) felt that the criteria should be more lenient. The countries that favoured strict criteria (*e.g.* the Netherlands and West Germany) were adamant that there should even be a differentiation between the figures for the budgetary deficit in case of recession or solid economic growth. They proposed that in the case of economic upturn the reference criteria should be one percent of Gross Domestic Product (GDP), whereas in a period of economic downturn it would be allowed to go up to three percent of GDP. Eventually a compromise was found, namely the three percent rule (which would apply regardless of the economic cycle). The figure of sixty percent of GDP for public debt was based on some kind of weighted average of the levels of public debt of the twelve EC Member States at the time[45].

The MC had done its work. It provided the criteria to the negotiators of the 1991 EMU-IGC. However, the countries with weaker economic and monetary performance on these criteria still were worried about these relatively arbitrary criteria[46]. Thus in the final bargaining about the text of the Treaty on European Union (Maastricht Treaty) two more compromises were made. The first was the way the convergence criteria were inserted in the Maastricht Treaty. Articles 104c and 109j state relevant passages on the excessive deficit procedure and the convergence criteria respectively. However, the actual figures – the budgetary deficit figure of three percent of GDP and the public debt figure of sixty percent of GDP – were not mentioned in the body of the text. Instead, two protocols were attached to the Treaty giving these details. The advantage of having the numbers in a protocol was that they could more easily be changed, if so desired. Had they been put in the Treaty, a change would imply an official Treaty change and hence ratification of all Member States.

---

[44] For further discussion of role and influence of the MC see Hanny and Wessels, 1999 and Verdun, 2000b.

[45] Interview of the author with a member of the Monetary Committee, October 1996.

[46] On the randomness of the criteria see *inter alia* Buiter, 1992.

The other compromise can be found if we examine the exact wording of articles 104c. Rather than referring to an absolute number (the "reference value") the Treaty allows for some laxity. Article 104c stipulates that Members States' performance in the area of excessive government deficits shall be judged on its progress. It allows for the government to meet this excessive deficit criterion if the budgetary deficit has "declined substantially and continuously and reached a level that comes close to the reference value[47]". Alternatively a government would be considered having met this criterion if "the excess over the reference value is only exceptional and temporary and the ratio remains close to the reference value[48]". For the ratio of government debt to GDP the Member States would meet the criteria if "the ratio is sufficiently diminishing and approaching the reference value at a satisfactory pace[49]".

In light of these observations it is remarkable that the national governments and the media has placed so much attention on meeting the absolute levels of the convergence criteria. True, as has often been pointed out by scholars, national governments sometimes use the EU stipulations as a way to "tie their hands" in order to push through domestic restructuring which they might have deemed necessary regardless of whether they were actually required as part of the convergence criteria[50]. However, for some analysts it was clear that whether Member States would eventually satisfy the criteria would remain a topic of political interpretation rather than economic calculation. To those analysts it was not surprising that in the end, by May 1998, the criteria were interpreted rather loosely. Yet, few would argue that they anticipated the EU Council to have been so blunt and daring so as to identify eleven Member States as having qualified for entry into the third stage of EMU in 1999. So, although the Delors Report did not spell-out the criteria, it had laid the ground for others to fill those in. It was clear that the Delors Report signalled the reduction in national sovereignty on these matters.

Given this context of limited room for manoeuvre by national governments to have excessive budgetary deficits and public debts, and given that monetary policy-making would be transferred to the European Central Bank, the logic of the Delors Report was that the role of the social partners would be to appreciate the importance of keeping wage demands under control, and set wages in line with competitiveness. By

---

[47] Article 104c of the *Treaty on European Union*, 1992, p. 27.
[48] *Ibid.*
[49] *Ibid.*
[50] See for example Dyson and Featherstone, 1999.

the late 1980s social partners were more than aware what was expected from them. With the change in policies in the 1970s and 1980s from inflationary to anti-inflationary this turnaround in policy had refocused the role of social partners. In most countries the power of trade unions had been reduced, as had tripartite bargaining. In countries where trade unions were seen to be a serious burden the government reduced their power (*e.g.* the United Kingdom). However, Delors, being a social democrat, felt it was important to keep the social partners involved.

In turn, the trade unions and employers' organisations felt it important to remain part of the policy-making process, now that the transfer of sovereignty over monetary policy would be transferred from the national level to the European level[51]. Many realised that this reduction in sovereignty over monetary policy, and macroeconomic policy making in general, had already *de facto* happened over the course of the 1980s with the decision of national monetary authorities to keep European exchange rates stable, and as a rule of thumb to follow German monetary policies. Moreover, in the design of the Delors Report envisaged a much smaller role for collective macroeconomic policy-making than in the Werner Report as in the former macroeconomic policy-making would not be transferred to the supranational level. Leaving it at the national level would not mean that Member State governments would have terribly much room for manoeuvre. The 1980s had shown that pursuing policies that were distinct from those pursued in neighbouring countries was not effective.

However, by not doing anything institutionally in the area of social and macroeconomic policies, the Community have kept open the question of how to deal with these matters in the context of EMU. The 1990s showed a renewed interest by social partners and governments to collectively deal with societal problems such as unemployment and sluggish economic growth. EMU, as such, cannot deal with these policies. It merely provides a framework within which economic activities should benefit. More structural problems in the labour market would have to be dealt with separately. Likewise, if EMU combined with the already existing pressures of globalisation lead to downward pressure on social provisions, it would clearly be up to Member States (and ideally social partners) to stop any undesirable trend. So far, however, there does not seem to be any evidence that EMU has led to either social dumping, tax competition or a massive reallocation of business. If this were to happen the EU would benefit from opening up the institutional framework of EMU to readdress the imbalance.

---

[51] Verdun, 2000a.

Conclusion

The Werner and Delors reports on how to create EMU offer a remarkably similar blueprint. They are also roughly reacting to similar pressures (a mixture of external factors and European integration achievements). It is remarkable that in both cases the report was drafted by a group of economic, financial, and monetary specialists each of whom had affinity with the EC integration process. The actual structure of the two reports was also quite similar (the wording, "economic and monetary union", the use of "parallelism" and the process of obtaining EMU in stages etc.). The differences between the two reports are mainly in the actual design of EMU, the underlying assumptions about the role of monetary and macroeconomic policy-making, and in particular whether it envisaged a need (or lack thereof) to have both a supranational *monetary* authority, as well as a supranational *economic* authority. The Werner Report advocated having both, whereas the Delors Report stated that there was no need for the latter.

This chapter has also indicated that the causes of these differences can be traced back to the changes in ideas and experience with economic and monetary policy-making in the period prior to the drafting of the respective blueprint. By the late 1980s consensus could be found on the aims of monetary policy-making, but in the area of economic policy-making no such consensus appeared. It was thought that each Member State could just continue to pursue national policies, provided it accepted restrictions on budgetary deficit and public debt. Another interesting difference is the envisaged role of social partners. Both reports mention them but in each there is a different view on what role they should play. In the 1970s this role was much more considerable than was the case by the late 1980s. However, it is possible that there is a slight reverse of this process, which has started in the late 1990s, if the social partners manage to keep on the agenda the importance of dealing with labour and social issues collectively. Given the importance of the role of experience with economic and monetary policy-making and the role of ideas it is more than possible that things will change. It is not unthinkable that labour market policies and social issues could be further incorporated within the framework of economic and monetary integration in the years to come.

CHAPTER 3

Economic Theory and Policy
from the Keynesian Revolution
to the Third Way[1]

David PURDY

This chapter examines the interplay of ideas, policy and events in the advanced capitalist democracies from the Great Depression of the 1930s to the end of the twentieth century. Its main focus is the evolution of economic theory, but since theory is always conditioned by events and always has *some* relationship to policy, however distant and indirect, it seems better to make these connections explicit and, on occasion, prominent than to leave them buried in the background. My main purpose is to map the principal currents of thought which have influenced economic policy over the period in question, paying particular attention to Keynes's *General Theory* and the way economists reacted to this work both at the time it was published and after.

I am mainly concerned with Britain and the US and pay only cursory attention to wider international comparisons. Ideally, the role of ideas in shaping policy and the role of policy in shaping events should be studied by a combination of comparative and historical methods, so as to bring out cross-national similarities and differences, as well as overall patterns of continuity and change. But that would require a team of researchers from different countries. The procedure I have adopted reflects the limitations of my own knowledge, though it can be justified on the grounds that Keynes was English and that, over the past fifty years, Anglo-American economics has largely supplanted competing traditions and schools[2].

The received view is that Keynes transformed the way economists think about their subject and gave governments the tools they needed to

---

[1]   I am grateful to Pat Devine, Phil Leeson, Barbara MacLennan and the editors of this volume for comments on earlier versions of this chapter.
[2]   For accounts of how and why this has happened, see Coates, 1999.

97

stabilise capitalism after the Second World War. This is certainly what Keynes himself *hoped* would happen. But it is not what actually happened, either in the realm of theory or in the sphere of policy. From the very beginning, the revolutionary aspects of the *General Theory* were obscured as economists sought to reconcile what Keynes was saying, or what they supposed he was saying, with the established body of economic doctrine. And although the long post-war boom in the advanced capitalist economies surely owed something to the prevailing belief that governments not only *could* prevent recessions from turning into depressions, but *should* and *would* do so, if necessary, the practice of counter-cyclical management turned out to be far more difficult, both technically and politically, than economists expected[3]. In any case, governments were never called upon to rescue capitalism from a catastrophic slump of 1930s proportions, which is just as well, since historical experience suggests that there are no panaceas for this kind of crisis, as Keynes – a policy pragmatist if ever there was one – never tired of pointing out.

Between the 1930s and the 1950s, a sanitised version of Keynes's theory was spliced on to the neoclassical tradition that had dominated Anglo-American economic thought since the last quarter of the nineteenth century. In the 1960s and 1970s, the "neoclassical synthesis", as it came to be known, was challenged on two fronts: by post-Keynesians seeking to retrieve the neglected insights of Keynes, the revolutionary theorist; and by followers of Piero Sraffa, one of Keynes's Cambridge colleagues, whose work in the *classical* tradition of political economy had exposed deep logical flaws in the heart of neoclassical theory. At the same time, the so-called "Keynesian" approach to macroeconomic policy, which by the mid-1960s had been adopted everywhere, was attacked by Milton Friedman (1968) for destabilising the economy and causing inflation.

Rising prices were, of course, a persistent feature of the long boom, but as long as the rate at which they rose remained low, on average, and did not vary much from year to year, they were more of an irritant than a threat to social stability. Indeed, it was widely believed that creeping inflation was good for business, helping to reduce uncertainty about future sales and profits and providing firms with more leeway in balancing costs and prices than the deflationary conditions of the Depression. In the late 1960s, however, inflation accelerated and there

---

[3] As Skidelsky, 2000 (p. 501) points out, the growth of public expenditure as a proportion of GDP due to the extension of public ownership and the expansion of the social services also helped to stabilize capitalist economies after the Second World War, but while the outcome was one that Keynes would have welcomed, this particular way of achieving it formed no part of his design.

ensued a period of "stagflation", when governments oscillated between allowing unemployment to rise in order to check inflation and allowing inflation to rise in order to check unemployment. These experiences destroyed faith in counter-cyclical demand management and, more generally, weakened public confidence in the power of government to solve social problems.

As the post-war Keynesian consensus was overwhelmed by the monetarist counter-revolution, the twin theoretical challenges to neo-classical hegemony were sidelined, not because of any inherent intellectual deficiencies, but because the dissident minorities who supported them offered no alternative policy or, at any rate, none capable of mobilising a broad social coalition. Yet monetarism itself, both as a school of macroeconomic thought and as a specialised technique for controlling inflation, was soon swept aside by rational expectations theory, which was more congenial to professional economists schooled in rational choice theory, and even more consonant with the neo-liberal view that government intervention in a market economy is either futile or pernicious. For exactly the same reasons, however, rational expectations theory was rejected by policy-makers. Thus, from the early 1980s onwards, macroeconomic theory and macroeconomic policy began to drift apart.

In the final section of the paper, I examine the idea, proposed by Heilbroner and Milberg (1995), that contemporary economic theory exhibits a "crisis of vision" and, while generally endorsing it, I suggest that "vision" in their sense is not everything. Neo-classical theory continues to provide psychic balm for true believers and, indeed, has a more general, common-sense appeal in a world dominated by commercialism. Moreover, contemporary capitalism can draw on other sources of legitimacy besides economics, and governments can draw on other sources of policy innovation besides economists. The advent of the Third Way as an alternative both to traditional social democracy and to free market liberalism illustrates these points. As yet, however, adherents of this emergent paradigm have made only limited headway in the struggle for hegemony: indeed, on key policy issues the rule of neo-liberalism has not even been challenged, much less overcome. From this point of view, while the age of Keynes has gone forever, there is much to be gained from studying the fate of the revolution to which he gave his name.

The *General Theory* and its Reception

The publication of *The General Theory of Employment, Interest and Money* in 1936 marked the high point of what Shackle (1967) called "The Years of High Theory", a period of deep crisis for the world capitalist system, which destroyed the Gold Standard, forced even the British government to abandon *laissez faire* and provoked a sustained revolt against neo-classical economics. In assessing the work that Keynes famously hoped would revolutionise the way we think about economic issues, two points need to be borne in mind. The first is his idiosyncratic use of the term "classical economics" to refer to *all* his mainstream predecessors, including not only Smith and Ricardo, to whom this epithet had originally been applied by Marx, but also Jevons, Walras, Menger, Marshall and other members of the marginalist or *neo-classical* school. The conventional distinction between these groups is intended to mark a major shift of theoretical focus: the classical economists were concerned with the macro dynamics of capitalism and the distribution of the social product among the classes which collaborate in producing it; the neo-classical school deals with the operation of the price mechanism and the process of resource allocation in a world where atomistic, self-interested agents, with predetermined tastes and preferences and with full knowledge of all relevant options, seek to maximise the satisfaction of their desires, subject to material and technological constraints.

From Keynes's standpoint, this difference was irrelevant: what mattered was that both schools were more interested in propounding deductive theorems about the long run than in analysing the interplay of expectations, action and experience in the short run; and both believed that the general or overall level of output and employment is limited only by the *supply* of available resources. The basis for this belief, generally known as "Say's Law", was the further belief that as long as all market prices, both for produced commodities and for original resources, are free to adjust up or down so as to remove temporary shortages or surpluses, the economy *will* operate at this limit: available resources will be fully utilised and there will be no problem in selling the resulting output due to a deficiency of aggregate *demand*. Keynes disagreed on both counts. His concern was with the short run when economic agents, poised between an irreversible past and uncertain future, have to make choices and take decisions; and his central contention was that in a capitalist economy, the proximate determinant of aggregate output and employment is aggregate spending. Businessmen, he maintained, will not produce more than they believe they can profitably sell and will not invest in new capacity, or even maintain existing capacity, unless they feel confident about future sales and profits.

Keynes's revisionary usage is understandable, but confusing. It also obscures the point on which his theory resembles that of the classical economists – and, indeed, that of Marx – for they were all concerned with the development of the economy as a whole and the dynamics of capital accumulation, not with the neoclassical problem of how scarce resources with alternative uses are allocated among different productive activities and how the resulting social product is distributed among resource-owning consumers. From this standpoint, Keynes might be described as the last of the classical economists. In the classical vision, as Milgate (1987) notes, the market mechanism confronts economic agents as an external force and serves to reproduce the capitalist system through time. Besides balancing supply and demand in each separate branch of production, market prices must also satisfy the *distributional* requirements of *reproduction*, ensuring that the owners of the means of production receive the customary rate of profit on the best practice techniques in whatever line of production they are employed, and that the real wage conforms to historically evolved social norms.

Keynes supplied not so much a complement as a corrective to this vision, focusing on the short run, recognising the importance of uncertainty about the future, particularly for those decisions whose consequences take years to unfold – foremost among them decisions to invest money in means of production – and accordingly emphasising that the critical variables in any capitalist economy are the expectations of business and financial interests and the degree of confidence with which they are held. Thus, Keynes's question: what determines the general level of output and employment in the short run? becomes: under what conditions will the existing level of aggregate output be reproduced in subsequent time periods (*i.e.* remain constant, be increased or be reduced)? This formulation makes it clear that Keynes's short-run theory of capacity utilisation deals with only one moment in an ongoing sequence and needs, therefore, to be set in a longer-run context of accumulation and development. A natural extension, for example, is Harrod's (1939) celebrated dynamic model analysing the interaction between short-term instability, long-run growth and employment trends.

The second point to be stressed is that the *General Theory* was written for professional economists. The book is full of brilliant passages and penetrating insights, but taken as whole, it is by no means easy to read: its laborious definitions and awkward presentation bear witness to what Keynes describes in the Preface as his long "struggle of escape from habitual modes of thought and expression". More is involved here than the rough edges to be expected in any path-breaking work. Indeed, as Tarshis (1987) and Pasinetti (1999) suggest, Keynes's first drafts for the *General Theory*, presented as lectures to students at Cambridge between 1932 and 1935[4], were in many ways clearer than the published version because they were more innocent and less encumbered by defences against anticipated criticism.

The fact is that for almost thirty years, ever since he had been persuaded to take up the study of economics by Marshall, Keynes had shared in the (neo-) classical orthodoxy he was now attacking, and his attitude to it remained ambivalent. As Joan Robinson[5] remarked: "[...] there were moments when we had some trouble getting Maynard to see what the point of his revolution really was". She hastened to add, however, that: "[...] when he came to sum it up after the book was published, he got it into focus". The reference here is to the article in the *Quarterly Journal of Economics* in which Keynes (1937), exasperated by the capacity of his reviewers to miss the wood for the trees, briefly restated his argument in clear and simple terms, roundly condemning traditional theory as a "pretty, polite technique" for concealing the fact that we know very little about the future.

These ambiguities and hesitations were typical of the economics profession at large. The idea that the government might give a boost to aggregate demand so as to restore business confidence and extricate the economy from a slump was not new: it had been contemplated, proposed and, in Sweden, actually implemented *before* Keynes wrote the *General Theory*. But two obstacles stood in the way of its widespread acceptance: one was the fear that, in practice, a policy of deficit finance might undermine business confidence, driving up interest rates, deterring investment and depressurising the pump rather than priming it; the other was that the idea lacked any elaborate grounding in economic theory, for as Salant points out, quoting a remark which Hansen (1938) attributed to James Conant: "It takes a theory to kill a theory"[6]. Keynes filled this gap, providing "policy heretics" with arguments against established orthodoxy. Moreover, to the extent that the case for gearing public finance to the state of the economy, rather than vainly struggling to balance the budget at every point in time, helped to change the climate of business opinion or could be presented in terms that were consonant with business interests, the danger of an adverse confidence effect was reduced.

These were major achievements. But whether, as Keynes hoped, they succeeded in displacing ideas which had dominated the minds of the

---

[4]   For the lecture notes of a "representative student", see Rymes (1989).
[5]   Robinson, 1975, p.125.
[6]   Salant, 1989, p. 37.

academic and governing classes for the previous century, is open to doubt. Apart from a small minority on the left, economists responded to the *General Theory* by seeking to reconcile its arguments with the received body of thought. Even some of Keynes's own disciples tended to minimise the extent of his break with neoclassical theory. James Meade, for example, was a prominent member of the "Circus", the coterie of young economists at Cambridge in the 1930s who pushed Keynes into embarking on the *General Theory* and provided him with intellectual stimulation, critical reactions and moral support. Later, as a Treasury official during the Second World War, Meade helped to perfect the techniques of national income measurement, economic forecasting and demand management. Yet the work for which he was subsequently awarded a Nobel Prize was thoroughly neoclassical in spirit, method and even, on occasion, in name.

In the case of Sir John Hicks, the intellectual trajectory ran in the opposite direction. In his famous paper, "Mr. Keynes and the Classics", Hicks (1937) sought to incorporate what he took to be the core elements of Keynes's theory – the marginal efficiency of capital (*sic*)[7], the consumption function and liquidity preference – into a Walrasian general equilibrium model with three markets – for goods, bonds and money. (The labour market is omitted because Hicks treats it as a "fix-price" market which fails to clear). This paper laid the foundations for what subsequently became known as the IS-LM model[8], faithfully reproduced in countless undergraduate textbooks and taught to students as the very essence of Keynesian theory. Yet towards the end of his career when it no longer really mattered, somewhat in the manner of an ex-NATO commander renouncing nuclear weapons, Hicks (1980) repudiated his youthful attempt to squeeze Keynes's full-bodied analysis of flux and uncertainty into the spectral, timeless world of Walrasian general equilibrium theory, concluding that there was little use for the IS-LM model "[...] as anything more than classroom gadget, to be superseded, later on, by something better".

Nothing better illustrates the confusion caused by this misbegotten "gadget" than Hicks's missing market. Hicks had two reasons for omitting the labour market from his model: one expository, the other

---

[7]   This term, devised by Keynes, is unfortunate: it conflates the rate of profit on capital received by capitalist firms with the benefits to society as a whole yielded by an increase in the capital stock.

[8]   So called because it depicts all the possible points at which: (1) aggregate planned investment (I) would equal aggregate planned saving (S): and (2) the public's liquidity preference or desire to hold their wealth in the form of money (L) would be exactly satisfied by the prevailing stock of money (M). If and when both these conditions are satisfied simultaneously, the economy as a whole is in equilibrium.

substantive. In a Walrasian system with n markets, only $n-1$ of the equations describing the conditions of equilibrium are independent: for the purpose of finding a solution, one equation is redundant and can be dropped. This meant that in a three-market model, the economy's general equilibrium state could be represented by means of a two-dimensional diagram. No such convenient visual aid would have been available to illustrate a four-market scheme. What enabled Hicks to work with three markets was that the labour market notoriously failed to clear: as everyone agreed, the persistence of mass unemployment was the outstanding fact that needed to be explained. But in a Walrasian world, when a market fails to clear, there can be only one explanation: the relevant price is above the equilibrium level and is prevented, for some reason, from falling. In other words, unemployment arises not because aggregate demand is too low, but because real wages are too high.

This is plainly not what Keynes either said or meant, but it was a conclusion that came naturally to economists steeped in the neoclassical tradition. As Brothwell (1988) argues, Keynes must bear some of the responsibility for failing to get his message across. At the beginning of his argument, he endorses what he calls the "first postulate of classical employment theory": that "the [real] wage is equal to the marginal product of labour[9]". This was widely taken to mean that Keynes had no quarrel with the concept of a "well-behaved" aggregate production function, according to which, with a given stock of capital equipment, aggregate output increases as employment rises, but at an ever-diminishing rate[10], or with the related idea that where competition prevails and employers seek to maximise profits, the aggregate marginal productivity curve can be identified with the aggregate labour demand curve, sloping conventionally downwards from left to right. This, in turn, allowed Keynes's critics to say that his attack on "classical" theory was confined to the *supply* side of the labour market and amounted to the assumption that workers suffer from money illusion, resulting in downward money (and real) wage rigidity. Thus, the *logic* of neoclassical theory was preserved intact and Keynes's entire argument was reduced to the empirical assertion that even without trade unions and collective bargaining, money wages are "sticky" in the presence of unemployment.

---

[9] Keynes, 1936, p. 5.

[10] This concept also gave rise to the regrettable habit of referring to aggregate output and employment as if they were interchangeable. With the level of output determined by aggregate spending, the associated level of employment could simply be read off from the aggregate production function, as if the translation of production plans into numbers of employees, hours of work and standards of effort involved nothing more than engineering calculations.

Keynes did, of course, believe this and it is, indeed, true, but it is not theoretically fundamental. What matters is the distinction between the money wage and the real wage. Micro-level wage setting determines the former, but the latter depends on the various forces affecting the general level of prices, and these lie outside the control of individual economic agents. An economy-wide cut in money wages would lower the aggregate supply curve, but it would also lead to a roughly proportionate fall in prices, lowering the aggregate demand curve and leaving the point of *effective* demand indeterminate. Keynes would have been on even stronger ground if he had pointed out that the labour market is not a market like any other because labour or, as Marx insisted on calling it, *labour power* is not a commodity like any other: the capacity for work cannot be separated from the person whose capacity it is; workers, unlike machines, care what happens to them when they are at work; and the employment contract is continually being adjusted and renegotiated in the process of production. But Keynes cared little for Marx, so the opportunity for clarification was lost.

The Neoclassical Synthesis

The difficulty of disentangling Keynes's thought from the neoclassical tradition together with the reluctance of economists to abandon that tradition gave rise, after the war, to what Samuelson christened the "grand neoclassical synthesis". This he defined as an amalgam of " [...] (1) the valid core of modern income determination theory with (2) the classical [*sic*] economic principles. Its basic tenet is this: solving the vital problems of monetary and fiscal policy by the tools of income analysis will validate and bring back into place the classical verities"[11]. What Samuelson meant by this last sentence was that full employment could be preserved and the economics of scarcity vindicated as long as government compensated for any tendency for private investment to fall below full employment saving, by increasing its own spending or cutting taxes so as to stimulate private consumption. Joan Robinson (1962) denounced this view as "bastard Keynesianism", the progeny of an illicit theoretical liaison. Parentage apart, it certainly ignored the *historical* problems of *reproducibility*. Would the econ-omy's relative *capacities* for producing consumption and investment goods match the ratio between consumption and investment *spending*? If private investment were deficient, how would compensatory public spending or tax cuts be financed and how would financial markets react? Would the process of capital accumulation be disrupted by

---

[11] Samuelson, 1955, p. vi.

conflicts between capitalists and workers over the distribution of income or by other unwelcome disturbances to business confidence?

In the long run, the neoclassical embrace proved fatal to Keynesian ideas, weakening their defences against external attack. A prime example is afforded by the history of the "Phillips Curve", the allegedly stable empirical relationship between the rate of change of money wages and the level of unemployment, which A. W. Phillips (1958) claimed to have identified in UK data extending over almost a hundred years from the 1860s to the 1950s. The validity of the data for the period before the First World War was dubious, as were the statistical methods by which Phillips sought to demonstrate that the relationship was inverse, non-linear and stable. His results were also consistent with more than one interpretation. Phillips himself maintained that money wages were set by employers in response to the state of the labour market, the tightness or looseness of which reflected the pressure of aggregate demand. But his findings could also be explained in terms of a cost-push theory of inflation in which workers' ability to secure money wage rises in excess of productivity growth depended on the ability of employers to shift increased unit costs forward on to their selling prices: given the degree of competition in the product market, this would also depend on the pressure of demand. Phillips did, however, note that the curve might become unstable in a period of endemic inflation when anticipated *future* price movements began to affect *current* wage decisions. It was also notable that his estimated regression curve flattened out at very high levels of unemployment, suggesting that even in a severe slump, workers were strongly resistant to cuts in money wages, as Keynes and other observers of the labour market had always maintained.

Despite these doubts and reservations, Phillips's work had a major impact on economists in the late 1950s and early 1960s. It was widely thought to have resolved the puzzle of how the "sticky" money wage – or, more precisely, how *changes* in the "sticky" money wage – were determined, and thus to have closed an outstanding gap in the neoclassical synthesis. Just as important, it was also believed to provide governments with a "menu" of policy choices: they could opt for low unemployment (or "high" full employment) and a correspondingly high rate of inflation or for higher unemployment ("low" full employment) and a lesser rate of inflation – possibly, if Phillips's estimates were to be believed, no inflation at all[12]. Yet a third option, advocated by

---

[12] The notion that governments could slide up and down the Phillips curve in the short run was inconsistent with the peculiar averaging procedure that Phillips had used to eliminate what he called "loops" in the data reflecting the influence of *cyclical fluctuations* in economic activity. The idea of a trade-off between the rate of *price* inflation and the level of unemployment a' o depended on a mark-up theory of price

economists who were sceptical about the Phillips curve, but found it expedient to suppress their doubts, was to try to improve the inflation-unemployment "trade-off", by instituting an incomes policy so as to lower the inflation cost associated with any given level of unemployment.

Rarely can such an imposing theoretical and political superstructure have been erected on such flimsy foundations. The whole episode reveals the self-delusion and hubris of economists who regarded the economy as a machine which could be manipulated at will once its laws of motion had been discovered and quantified. Nemesis was quick to follow. When inflation began to accelerate in the late 1960s and the word "stagflation" made its appearance in the economists' lexicon, the "breakdown" of the allegedly stable Phillips curve was greeted as a decisive setback for "Keynesian" theory and policy, and facilitated the rise of monetarism.

Not that the neoclassical synthesis was inherently conservative in its implications. During the early post-war period, for example, Alvin Hansen (1949), one of the leading expositors of Keynes in the US who helped to popularise the IS-LM model, argued strongly for an active fiscal policy on the grounds that private investment was insensitive to reductions in interest rates, especially when interest rates were historically low. And in a society characterised by "private affluence and public squalor", there was a stronger case for increased government spending than for tax cuts to stimulate private consumption. More generally, it might be argued, theoretical dilution was a price that had to be paid if Keynes's ideas were to exert an influence on economic policy, for hegemony is achieved not by eliminating rival positions, but by incorporating them into a common discourse. Thus, during the "golden age" of post-war capitalism, just as Keynesian social democracy provided the basis for a broad consensus between social democrats, collectivist liberals and "one nation" conservatives, so the neoclassical synthesis made possible a broad intellectual coalition between radical iconoclasts, cautious reformers and clever technocrats. And no doubt Keynes himself, had he lived, would have been happy to shift from one position to another in both sets of alliances.

There is, however, a distinction between theory and policy. The fact that, in the UK, social democrats, liberals and conservatives shared a

---

formation according to which firms set their selling prices by adding a fixed percentage profit margin to their costs per unit of output. This was a hypothesis which students of oligopolistic markets had entertained for some time, but it sat uneasily beside the more traditional theories of supply and demand favoured by those economists who believed that inflation was caused by "excess demand".

common approach to economic policy for twenty-five years after the war did not mean that their respective political traditions had become irrelevant. They continued to compete for votes and power and their reasons for supporting the post-war settlement diverged. Social democrats saw demand management, public enterprise and the welfare state as stepping-stones towards a more fully socialised economy, to be achieved through progressive taxation and a shift in the balance between public and private consumption. For collectivist liberals, the post-war policy consensus represented the best available compromise between individual freedom and the public good, while for "one-nation" conservatives, it offered a salve for class conflict and a safeguard against socialism. In the same way, a "popular front of the mind" based on a shared antipathy to the unfettered free market is perfectly compatible with maintenance of distinct theoretical frameworks and rival visions of the world.

At all events, the implication of the preceding argument is that in an important sense, there was no "Keynesian Revolution". In university departments, student textbooks and the minds of most professional economists, neoclassical theory *retained* the central position it had established over the period from the 1870s to the First World War. It was not displaced by a new scientific paradigm, (though this did not prevent post-war economists from trumpeting the "scientific" credentials of their discipline); rather, in a manner reminiscent of theological responses to Galileo or Darwin, economists contrived a *modus vivendi* between traditional doctrine and the challenge of Keynes.

In some ways, the position of neoclassical theory was strengthened, particularly in the US. Here, Keynesian ideas were quickly and enthusiastically embraced by professional economists during the 1930s, but lost ground after the war. During Roosevelt's first term, the New Deal was an exercise in public regulation rather than proto-Keynesian reflation. The government remained committed to balancing the budget and, indeed, as Salant argues[13], it was the *reduction* in the Federal budget deficit between 1936 and 1937 that was largely responsible for precipitating the steep recession of 1937-8, threatening the government's reputation and forcing it to change course. Not until the war years did Keynesians gain influence over economic policy. Thereafter, to varying degrees under different administrations, they remained influential until the 1970s. But their position in American universities was weakened by "academic McCarthyism" and the transformation of American economics. As Goodwin (1998) notes, the early Cold War period displayed many of the features of a holy war. American con-

---

[13]   Salant, 1989, pp. 42-5.

servatives regarded non-conformist ideas not just as apostasy, but as treachery and even treason. In the absence of any significant domestic support for Marxist ideas, Keynes and his US disciples became favourite targets for witch-hunters. Even Samuelson's introductory textbook was vilified as an insidious attempt to corrupt the minds of the young and provide the rationale for a strong state. In the face of such attacks, economists found it safer to conform by working within the neoclassical paradigm and taking refuge in mathematical models, which offered protection against persecution, a badge of political respectability and a hallmark of scientific status. As a result, argue Morgan and Rutherford (1998), American economics became a less diverse and tolerant, more formal and technical discipline than it had been in the inter-war period. Its exemplar was physics rather than biology, let alone history, and it sought impersonal guarantees of objectivity in formal mathematics and official statistics rather than in personal virtues such as honesty, integrity and fair-mindedness.

For twenty-five years after the war, the continued vitality of neo-classical economics seemed unimportant because Keynes's policy legacy seemed secure. But the allegiance of economists to Keynesian ideas was pragmatic and, in many cases, skin-deep. Consequently, when the "golden age" came to an end and economic performance began to deteriorate, resistance to monetarism and neoliberalism was weaker than it would have been had Keynes's theory been divested of its neoclassical residues at an earlier date and gained a stronger intellectual following. But not until the late 1960s did it become customary to draw a distinction between Keynesian economics and the economics of Keynes, and even then Leijonhufvud (1968) who used this distinction as the title of an influential work, reinterpreted the notion of "unemployment equilibrium" as a rhetorical device, treating Keynes as a disequilibrium theorist and arguing that recessions were the result of "co-ordination failures", as if the ideas from which Keynes had struggled to escape were those of Walras rather than Marshall. The long struggle waged by writers such as Shackle and Joan Robinson to release Keynes's revolutionary spirit from the orthodox body in which it had been imprisoned did not bear fruit until the 1970s when the newly founded post-Keynesian school and the followers of Sraffa declared war on neo-classical theory. By then, however, the post-war policy consensus was being assailed by the New Right and, with no time to mature in a stable environment, the fledgling movement soon found itself marginalised.

After Keynes and Sraffa

The period from the mid-1960s to the end of the 1970s was one of profound ideological ferment, in some ways comparable to the 1930s. Neo-classicism came under attack from two sides: post-Keynesians challenged the neoclassical synthesis; the followers of Sraffa challenged the theory's internal logic. Post-Keynesians such as Davidson (1972) insisted that Keynes had broken with neoclassical tradition on four key points: the distinction between calculable risk and genuine uncertainty; the importance of uncertainty in economic life, especially for business investment and financial speculation; the unique role of money as a store of wealth which offers a hedge against uncertainty; and the recognition that in a capitalist economy the real wage is not determined *ex ante* by microeconomic decision-making, but emerges *ex post* from the operation of the system as whole. As a corollary, the attempt to understand economic development by means of timeless equilibrium models must be abandoned. The analogy with Newtonian mechanics is fundamentally flawed: first, because whereas a pendulum swings to and fro in space, economies move through historical time where strictly one-way traffic is the rule; and second, because a pendulum, unlike a flying trapeze artiste, does not have expectations.

The rejection of physics as a model for the human sciences was coupled with a sharp critique of conventional economic policy. One of Keynes's lasting legacies was the idea that in a monetary economy, aggregate output, income and expenditure are linked in a circular flow which expands and contracts according to changes in the balance between *injections* – due to private investment, public expenditure and exports – and *leakages* – due to private saving, taxation and imports. But what one makes of this idea depends on one's wider conception of the economy. Someone who thinks of the economy as a gigantic machine independent of human consciousness and volition and who aspires to emulate the explanatory and predictive prowess of physics, will see nothing wrong in abstracting economic phenomena from the historical, institutional and cultural context in which they occur. Thus, in the 1950s, A. W. Phillips, an engineer-turned-economist, actually built a physical model of the circular flow, complete with transparent tubes and coloured liquids. It was probably this construction that Shackle[14] had in mind when he coined the term "hydraulics" to refer to mechanistic interpretations of Keynes's ideas. Certainly, from the mid-1950s onwards, economics textbooks began to include simple mathematical models of macroeconomic equilibrium, which made no reference to such key Keynesian concepts as uncertainty, fear, surprise and "animal

---

[14]   Shackle, 1967, p. 189.

spirits". This was a feature they shared in common with the larger and more sophisticated models that are still routinely used by governments, central banks and research institutes to forecast short-term changes in economic aggregates such as output, inflation, employment, consumption and investment.

Where post-Keynesians objected to the use of equilibrium models to analyse the process of capital accumulation, the followers of Sraffa (1960) challenged the internal logic of neoclassical equilibrium theory. Presciently subtitled "Prelude to a Critique of Economic Theory", Sraffa's book prompted a searching critique of the orthodox theory of capital, profits and income distribution. In a competitive capitalist economy in long run equilibrium, every branch of production would yield the same rate of profit. (In order for this to happen, the relative prices of different commodities would have to be proportioned accordingly. Thus, in general, prices and profits are *simultaneously* determined). Neoclassical theory sought to explain the *level* at which this uniform rate of profit would tend to settle – five percent, fifty percent or whatever – in terms of the supply and demand for "capital", conceived as an entity with a dual existence akin to the wave-like particles of quantum physics, being at once embodied in a heterogeneous collection of means of production designed for specific purposes, yet somehow remaining a homogenous fund of expansible value that merely happens to be lodged in a variety of temporary abodes.

Post-Keynesians emphasised that once funds have been committed to a particular project, they are effectively locked in and, even if all goes according to plan, will not be released until such time as the sum invested, together with associated interest costs (incurred or foregone), is recovered from sales proceeds or user charges. Only then will the original capital be available for re-investment, whether in the same field or in some other which is now expected to offer a better return. To elide the distinction between heterogeneous capital goods and homogeneous investible funds is to abstract from the fact that investment decisions are made in real historical time by agents who are perpetually poised between an irrevocable past and an uncertain future. This is equivalent to confining analysis to positions of long-run equilibrium where everything always goes according to plan and no one ever encounters any event that causes him to change his plans.

Disregarding this point, neoclassical writers treated "capital" as a "factor of production" exactly on a par with "labour" and "land", and sought to explain the distribution of income between wages, profits and land-rents in terms of a unified theory of market exchange. Sraffa undermined this theory by showing that, except in special conditions that were never likely to obtain in reality, the value of the aggregate capital stock employed in an economy that produces more than one commodity is not independent of the rate of profit and the real wage. In general, therefore, no sense can be attached to the notion of "capital-in-general" as a factor of production which, in competitive conditions, is rewarded in accordance with its marginal productivity. To be sure, *Walrasian* general equilibrium theory was left unscathed by Sraffa's critique because it treats each separately identified physical input as a source of income in its own right, avoiding the problem of aggregation. But such theoretical scrupulousness offered little comfort to neoclassical economists, for it left them unable to explain one of the central facts about any capitalist economy: the distribution of income between wages and profits.

For a time, the emergence of post-Keynesian theory, the rehabilitation of the classical tradition and revival of interest in Marxist political economy threatened the hegemony of neoclassical theory. Yet the critics had little lasting impact. At least Keynes had spawned the neoclassical synthesis and macroeconomic hydraulics, however much these distorted the spirit of his theory. Mainstream economists simply walked round the theoretical challenges of the 1960s and 1970s. Indeed, in the 1980s and 1990s, economics reached new heights of formalism, mathematical sophistication, remoteness from the other social sciences, inaccessibility to outsiders and sheer implausibility. How are we to explain this contrast?

The issue requires more detailed investigation than can be given here, but three considerations seem pertinent. First, the challenge to neoclassical economics was purely intellectual: neither post-Keynesians, Sraffians nor Marxists had anything important to say about *policy*, unlike Keynes in the 1930s or the monetarists in the 1970s. Sraffa and his followers were exclusively concerned with questions of high theory, while the post-Keynesians, as Skidelsky (1995) notes, show a marked preference for theorizing over policy prescription. Though sharply critical of the successive paradigms that have shaped macroeconomic policy over the years – Keynesian hydraulics, monetarist policy rules and the offshoots of rational expectations theory – they offer no agreed alternative of their own and shy away from questions such as: how likely are serious collapses such as that of the 1930s? Or what can actual, as opposed to idealised, governments do to improve economic performance?

Marxists might have been expected to have more to say about questions of policy, but since, for the most part, they continued to think of socialism as a form of society that lay wholly *beyond* capitalism and was, or would be when its time came, entirely distinct in its *modus operandi*, their conceptions of policy fluctuated between "transitional" programmes designed to destabilise capitalism and utopian visions of the future that took no account of experience under "actually existing socialism". What the "revisionist" Bernstein had once described as "evolutionary socialism" and what some latter-day admirers of Gramsci called "revolutionary reformism" was still very much a minority trend in the 1970s. This reluctance to take responsibility for trying to solve the problems thrown up by the development of capitalism was compounded by some egregious failures to keep up with what was happening. Steindl (1952), for example, sought to explain the gradual slowing down of accumulation from the late nineteenth century to the 1930s in terms of the rise of oligopoly. Unfortunately, his book appeared just as the post-war boom was getting under way and Steindl himself later regretted having failed to take account of waves of technological innovation. Similarly, Baran and Sweezy (1966) argued that Marxists had paid too little attention to monopoly, just as the degree of (national) monopoly was being reduced by the growth of international trade and direct overseas investment, and just before the share of profits in national income was severely squeezed by a combination of wage inflation, rising material and energy costs and intensified product market competition[15]. More generally, while individual Marxist scholars achieved eminence either for their lifetime *oeuvre* – Dobb, Hobsbawm, Sweezy – or for particular outstanding contributions – Baran, Bowles, Braverman, Cohen, Elster, Gordon, Steedman and Weisskopf – the Marxist camp as a whole could not be said to have produced either an agreed and coherent body of theory capable of challenging the dominant neoclassical paradigm or a cogent account of the contemporary world that reached out to the public at large.

Second, whereas Keynes was trying to restore faith in capitalism as an economic system after the worst crisis in its history, the critics of neoclassical theory were, for the most part, hostile to capitalism. Some sought structural reforms aimed at promoting economic democracy and socialising business investment. Others, as already noted, aspired towards an economy that was neither capitalist nor statist, though few had any clear idea what such a democratic socialist Third Way might look like or how it could be brought into existence[16]. Moreover, while

---

[15] The profits squeeze *was* spotted by Glyn and Sutcliffe (1972) in an innovative Marxist analysis which correctly identified its proximate causes as working class wage pressure and declining profit margins rather than the immanent logic of capital accumulation, but this sound diagnosis was still accompanied by an apocalyptic approach to policy based on the idea that capitalism and socialism are wholly incompatible.

[16] For a notable exception, at least as regards the *vision* of a post-capitalist, non-statist economy, see Devine (1988), though it is one thing to imagine a possible form of

the economic disarray of the 1970s was profound, there was no collapse on the scale of the 1930s. The last quarter of the twentieth century turned out to be more like the last quarter of the nineteenth century: the rate of economic growth slowed down, but periods of prosperity alternated with periods of recession and there was extensive technological innovation and structural change. The new feature was "stagflation" which proved much more intractable than most people, including the monetarists, anticipated.

Third, as already noted, Keynesian ideas, in some shape or form, attracted support from across the political spectrum and provided a platform around which political leaders could build broad social coalitions. After all, everyone stands to gain, including capitalists, if slumps can be avoided, the business cycle tamed and the economy operated closer to its maximum potential level of output, provided the measures adopted do not threaten the viability of capitalism as a system. The critics of neoclassical theory held out no such positive-sum prospect. If anything, the emphasis in Sraffa's work on the *inverse* relationship between real wages and the rate of profit, given the prevailing conditions of production, highlighted the *conflicting* interests of capitalists and workers, at any rate in the sphere of distribution. For good measure, those Marxists who took Sraffa seriously pointed out that the prevailing conditions of production themselves reflected the outcome of class struggle over the choice of technology and the control of the labour process[17].

Keynes's Policy Legacy

During the "golden age", Keynes's policy legacy seemed both substantial and secure. Nearly all economists accepted some version of Keynesian macroeconomics and believed that they could model the economy, diagnose its condition and devise appropriate fiscal or monetary interventions. Likewise, the *General Theory* provided the conceptual framework for the National Income and Product Accounts and gave a strong impetus to the collection of economic statistics and the development of econometric models, which were believed to provide a firm basis for economic forecasting, despite Keynes's well known misgivings on this score.

In retrospect, however, the "golden age" seems brief. It could not really be said to have begun before the end of the Korean War when the process of post-war reconstruction was complete and the conditions of

---

human society and quite another to devise socially acceptable and politically feasible remedies for pressing current problems.

[17]   See Rowthorn, 1974 and Steedman, 1981.

bipolar international conflict had been stabilised; and the period of crisis-free growth was effectively over by the mid-1960s. The more troubled phase that followed was marked by three new features: first, after a long period of conservative predominance, social democratic parties held office in most of the capitalist democracies; second, those countries which, after the war, had rejected demand management in favour of supply-side strategies of export-led growth – Germany, Italy and Japan – now began to make active use of fiscal policy in an attempt to *maintain* full employment; and third, fiscal policy itself became more ambitious. Hitherto, governments had merely sought to ensure that *existing* resources were fully utilised; now they deliberately stimulated demand in an attempt to boost the long-run rate of economic growth – a radical variant of hydraulic Keynesianism. The pursuit of faster growth, in turn, was a response to heightened popular aspirations. In a context where memories of the Depression were fading and full employment was taken for granted, workers were no longer content with maintaining the existing *level* of real wages, but expected to share in growing prosperity. Similarly, the general public wanted improved or extended social entitlements, and governments hoped that faster growth would provide a painless way of raising the tax revenue to pay for them. In principle, all these claims on available output could be accommodated without encroaching on profits, but because policy-makers were now pursuing three goals instead of one – faster growth and a shift of resources from private to public use, as well as "high" full employment – there was less policy "slack" than there had been previously.

"Growth Keynesianism" was soon in trouble. One problem was that despite much talk of "Verdoorn's Law" and "virtuous circles", no one really knew how to make the economy grow faster over time. This might not have mattered but for growing international turmoil and the intensification of distributional conflict. Under the post-war *Pax Americana*, the dollar was assigned a key role in the international monetary system as the only currency on the gold standard. The US government, in turn, was responsible for system management. Its tasks were to provide a secure anti-inflationary anchor and to supply sufficient international liquidity to avoid the deflationary bias of the classic gold standard. But the tax cuts and ambitious social programmes pursued by the Kennedy and Johnson administrations, together with the escalation of the war in Vietnam, gave rise to budget deficits and inflationary strains which destabilised the international economy.

At the same time, most countries began to experience the inflationary tug of war that Kalecki (1943) and other early Keynesians had always warned would emerge as the principal problem in an economy with "permanent" full employment. "Growth Keynesians" assumed that if the economy were run flat out, incomes policies could be used to restrain the growth of money wages. But this assumption concealed a serious and unacknowledged dilemma. In some countries, such as Britain, incomes policies followed an alternating, on-off sequence. Wage restraint would work for a while as an emergency stop-gap measure, but would then break down with a spectacular wages explosion, leading either to an upsurge in price inflation or a squeeze on profit margins, depending on the "softness" of product markets. The reason for this half-hearted, intermittent form of corporatism was the traditional preference of British trade unions and employers for "free collective bargaining" and their unwillingness to become partners of government in managing the national economy, attitudes that reinforced the British Treasury's enduring faith in arms-length macroeconomic "hydraulics", despite growing evidence of its shortcomings[18]. The consequences of this syndrome were not confined to short-term disruption, but extended to the effectiveness of counter-cyclical management itself, for as firms came to believe that a government-administered stimulus to aggregate demand would only impart a fresh twist to the wage-price spiral, they ceased to believe that expansion would be sustained and became reluctant to invest in new capacity.

Elsewhere, as in Sweden, where both trade unions and employers' associations were encompassing, unified, centralised and disciplined, corporatist policy bargaining became institutionalised and wage restraint was virtually permanent. Here, the problem was that trade unions would not agree to moderate their wage claims, nor would their members let them, without being offered concessions in return, whether in the form of tax cuts, additional individual or collective employment rights, improvements in the so-called "social wage" or advances in industrial democracy. But the first of these was at odds with the maintenance of a high-spending welfare state, while employers regarded the others with deep misgiving, for besides raising the costs of production or curtailing the "prerogatives" of management, they held out the prospect of creeping "socialisation" as the agenda of policy bargaining extended to more and more aspects of economic and social life and even corporate investment decisions had to be negotiated with civil servants and workers' representatives.

This, of course, is precisely what the anti-capitalist critics of neo-classical theory wanted. By the same token, it was what their pro-

---

[18] See, for example, the contemporary study by Dow (1964) which, from a standpoint broadly sympathetic to hydraulic Keynesianism, anticipated the arguments of Friedman and the monetarists that demand-management, as operated in the UK, had not been particularly successful in stabilising the economy.

capitalist opponents feared and what gave the policy controversies of the 1970s a sharp political and ideological edge. Though Friedman's monetarism had its technical aspects, it was always far more than a doctrine about the stability of the demand for money and the long-run "neutrality" of monetary policy, and far more than a proposal for replacing discretionary demand management by a predetermined and invariable monetary rule. Its wider significance was that it offered an alternative to the slow strangulation of free enterprise. For monetary policy did not have to be negotiated: it could be decided unilaterally by the government or, better still, entrusted to the central bank – or so, at any rate, it was believed in the mid-1970s, when monetarists were still defiant outsiders railing against Keynesian orthodoxy and had not yet had to face up to the problem of translating theoretical prescriptions into practical policies. More generally, monetarism fell into place as part of the broader intellectual and political movement which came to be known as neoliberalism. The other key components were public choice economics and Hayek's magisterial restatement of classical liberalism, published in three volumes from 1960 to 1973 under the title *The Constitution of Liberty*. And the ground in which this movement took root was fertile because, for a hundred years, it had been passionately guarded and carefully tended by neoclassical economists.

The Inward Turn

Economic policy is not *just* an instrument of ideological and political warfare any more than it is *just* a matter of applying technical expertise to the problems of the day: in varying proportions at different times and places, these elements are intertwined. Policy choices are also shaped by institutions and norms. While neoliberal ideas gained ground every-where in the 1980s, their influence was greatest in the UK, the US and the Antipodes. Even here, however, there were cross-cutting influences and pressures, notably in the US, where the increased military spending and tax cuts presided over by the Reagan administration gave rise to the largest budget deficit in the country's history and transformed the world's richest economy into a net external borrower. Elsewhere, governments were more dependent on regular collaboration with power-holders in civil society for managing the national economy – whether just with employers alone, as in Japan, or with both employers and trade unions, as in most Western European countries. They were, therefore, reluctant to embark on an abrupt and wholesale change of policy regime and instead sought to adapt their existing regimes to the new conditions.

To a remarkable extent, the monetarist counter-revolution was the work of one man. Like Keynes before him, Milton Friedman had previously been dismissed as a crank. In the crisis of the mid-1970s, he emerged as the new saviour. His expectations-augmented reformulation of the Phillips curve was widely believed to offer a ready-made explanation for "stagflation[19]", and his proposed remedy was seductively simple. Governments, he argued, should give up trying to manipulate aggregate demand. Attempts at "fine-tuning" only served to increase instability because of the long and variable time-lags involved. The best contribution government could make to preventing the alternation of rising inflation and rising unemployment was to make sure that the money supply grew at a steady rate, year in, year out, regardless of prevailing conditions. And the only rate consistent with stable prices was the trend rate of growth in real output.

In fact, the *k* percent rule was of little practical use. It showed how to *contain* inflation once it had been reduced, but said nothing about how to bring inflation down once it had taken hold. Should governments administer a short, sharp shock to inflation-expectations by instituting a tight credit squeeze? Or was it better to proceed gradually, perhaps even resorting to incomes policies so as to reduce the risk of monetary overkill? Worse still, as soon as governments began to set targets for its growth, they found it impossible to define the money supply, let alone control it. Even Friedman's moment of theoretical glory was short-lived. His account of the formation of inflation-expectations was soon challenged by rational expectations theory which, being grounded in the principles of rational choice rather than the psychology of human learning, was more congenial to orthodox economists and, with its message that no one – not even government – can "beat the market", was even more congruent with the conservative view that the best thing governments can do to revitalise capitalism is get out of the way.

Thus, monetarism did not survive the early 1980s either as a recipe for policy or as a body of doctrine. Since then, economic theory and policy have drifted apart. As Heilbroner and Milberg (1995) note, referring primarily to developments in the US, rational expectations theory was enthusiastically embraced by academic economists, but rejected by economists employed in government, business and research institutes. For economists who were already bewitched by neoclassical ideas, it offered powerful epistemic and psychic attractions. Like utility theory, it was beguilingly tautological: the market's movements could not have occurred had the expectations-guided actions of market

---

[19] Though monetarist writers never satisfactorily explained why it should have taken twenty-five years of persistent inflation before workers and employers started to anticipate *future* price movements in *current* money wage negotiations. As Rowthorn (1980) pointed out, there is a distinction between expecting prices to rise and taking action in advance to protect one's real income. Nor was it clear why workers and employers should hold the *same* expectations about the future.

participants, taken in their totality, not been what they were. This, in turn, enabled economists to perceive an otherwise invisible logic in events. In addition, the mathematical and statistical methods required to master the theory were formidably difficult and served to enhance the status and prestige of adepts. And the claim that neither fiscal nor monetary policy, if anticipated, can exert any real effects in the long run conveniently absolved economists from struggling to come up with any policy recommendations whatsoever.

For policy-makers, on the other hand, the message of rational expectations theory was distinctly uncongenial. Governments have little use for psychic balm: their business is to cope with events and maintain a reputation for competence. And it is not just galling, but positively disarming to be told that government is impotent or irrelevant, for if this is true, then there is no point in building macroeconomic models and no point in employing economists to manipulate and interpret them. (There might be some point in continuing to collect economic statistics, for the sake of the historical records, but these would have no more significance for contemporary policy than the accounts kept by the merchant kings of ancient Crete). Nor does rational expectations theory help to legitimise the social order, at any rate not in its "New Classical" guise. According to this school of thought, all markets, including the labour market, always clear. Thus, we are always in equilibrium and the results are always optimal. Recession, for example, is simply a "shock" to which the most beneficial adjustment is a reduction in output and employment. This is, to say the least, a difficult line to sell to voters. Governments prefer to avoid recessions if they possibly can. Otherwise, they apply the best gloss they can muster. "There is no alternative" was Mrs Thatcher's tough, but popular choice; "If it isn't hurting, it isn't working" was the ploy favoured by her less abrasive and less respected successor. But only a New Classical economist would try to prove that "It isn't hurting at all"!

The "New Keynesian" variant of rational expectations theory is less unworldly. It does not reduce government to impotence and does not assume that markets always clear, but allows that money wages and prices may be sticky. Thus, even in a Walrasian world, macroeconomic dysfunctions can still exist if there are "imperfections" or rigidities which prevent markets from clearing: efficiency wages, monopolistic competition, asymmetric information, "hysteresis" effects, and so on. This point is, of course, a direct response to the "New Classical" claim that involuntary unemployment is impossible in a free market economy composed of rational, profit-maximising firms and rational, utility-maximising consumers. But while "New Keynesian" theory is "new" in the sense that it incorporates rational expectations, its connection with

Keynes is tenuous and rests on an old misreading of what Keynes said about the labour market. In all other respects, its emphasis on the *supply* side of the economy is a complete reversal of traditional Keynesian perspectives, leading Davidson[20] to accuse it of "throwing out Keynes's baby with the New Classical bath water".

Heilbroner and Milberg (1995) argue that there is a crisis of vision in contemporary economic thought. It is not so much that the period since the demise of Keynesianism has been one of dissonance and disarray in economic thought – there is nothing new in that. Rather, the discipline has turned in upon itself and no longer provides non-economists with confidence in the economists' vision, the pre-analytic substratum of values and beliefs, present in all forms of social thought, about whether the prevailing social order is just, reasonable, benign, malleable and so on. Contemporary economics, to paraphrase these authors, offers neither a persuasive description of economic phenomena that makes sense of our individual and collective life-experience, nor guidance aimed at redressing specific economic problems.

Heilbroner and Milberg attribute this state of affairs to three broad reasons: the weaknesses of non-mainstream economics; the institutional characteristics of the economics profession; and the ahistorical, natural-istic conception of the economy that prevents economists from under-standing the phenomena they study. The first of these was touched on in the previous section. To discuss the second would take us too far afield. The third has been one the main themes of this chapter. Contemporary economists suffer from physics envy. They are obsessed with analytical technique, elevate rigour over relevance, prefer building models to interpreting them, refuse to take history seriously, including the history of their own subject, show no interest in or understanding of the other social sciences, and would never agree with Keynes that it is better to be roughly right than precisely wrong. The reason is that they conceive of economy and society as a machine governed by strict and mathemati-cally describable laws. This conception has a pedigree going back at least to Adam Smith who observed that: "Human society, when we contemplate it in a certain abstract and philosophical spirit, appears as a great, an immense machine, whose regular and harmonious movements produce a thousand agreeable effects"[21], though Smith's emphasis on *perspective* and on the *psychic* functions of social theory strikes a post-modern note that is far removed from the horizons of those who view the world not so much through a glass darkly as through "thickets of algebra".

---

[20] Davidson, 1992, p. 450.
[21] Smith, 1759, p. 316.

The Third Way

The crisis of vision diagnosed by Heilbroner and Milberg is real enough. Yet one should not exaggerate the seriousness of the consequences either for legitimizing the social order or for providing governments with a sense of where they are going and what needs to be done, the two other functions served by economic theory besides enabling its high priests to soothe their troubled brows. After all, when neo-classical theology is translated into the vernacular, it does make sense of the laity's experience of life in a society where almost everyone, including government, devotes a large proportion of their time and energy to the business of getting and spending. It finds expression, for example, in such homilies as "you can't buck the market", "the bottom line", "the customer is always right" and "there's no such thing as a free lunch". Furthermore, while the collapse of communism has created a general awareness that, for the foreseeable future, there is no practical alternative to *some* form of capitalism, the only issue being *what* form, the ongoing process of globalisation does not suggest a social order which is moribund, whatever the resulting dislocations and damage.

In the political realm, since the early 1990s, the period of unchallenged neo-liberal supremacy has come to an end. The market revolution of the 1980s has been widely blamed for causing or failing to prevent the growth of poverty, social inequality and social exclusion, for degrading the environment and for inflicting unacceptable levels of stress on workers, families and communities. To date, the most substantial response, which has found particular favour with the Democrats in the US and with New Labour in Britain, is the search for a Third Way, transcending both traditional social democracy and free market liberalism and seeking to reconcile economic dynamism with social cohesion.

This development owes little to economists. Robert Reich played a prominent role in providing a theoretical rationale for work-welfare activism in the US and served briefly as US Labor Secretary during Clinton's first term. Richard Layard played a similar role as economic guru and policy advisor to New Labour in Britain. But the chief exponent of "third way" thinking is Anthony Giddens (1998 and 2000), who is not exactly known for his contributions to economics. Moreover, what Giddens has to say about economics is explicitly addressed to the left: the subtitle of his first book, "The Renewal of Social Democracy", is meant to be taken seriously. In practice, he notes, the idea of "mixed economy" in which markets play a major role has long been accepted by the reformist left. Yet the left's characteristic mindset has remained hostile to markets. At the level of theory and principle, it still dreamed of a post-capitalist, non-market economy in which market forces would be replaced by government control, the price mechanism by central planning and the profit motive by the public good. This is not, he insists, a viable position. It fails to come to terms with the logic of 1989: the idea of a planned economy has been discredited by the communist experience. It also fails to acknowledge either the positive features of suitably regulated markets – for example, in securing peaceful exchange, encouraging personal responsibility and promoting economic growth – or the role of the price system in producing these benefits by providing a mechanism for coordinating economic activity and facilitating continuous adjustment to change that no command economy has been able to match. At the same time, Giddens recognises that market systems have certain characteristic defects: untrammelled commercialism threatens other human values; market-induced change generates social dislocation; markets are neither self-sustaining nor self-regulating; and if they are not properly regulated, they are liable to damage both the natural environment and the social fabric, for neither of these assets figures on the balance sheets of commodity-producing firms.

Giddens is not, however, simply restating the case for a mixed economy presided over by the sovereign nation state. On the contrary, he advocates wholesale reform of the public sector, arguing that the state should cease be a service provider and universal caretaker and instead play an enabling and facilitating role in building a strong and vibrant civil society. Equally, he emphasises that in a global economy the framework of governance needs to be correspondingly multi-tiered and outlines a programme of institutional reform designed to establish legitimate and effective systems of supranational regulation covering international finance, transnational corporations, the global environment, human rights and the settlement of international disputes.

Whatever one thinks of this approach, it is clearly neither mechanistic nor fatalistic and, to that extent, represents a welcome reassertion of the role of public policy in shaping human destiny. That said, there is a long way to go before the long shadow of neo-liberalism recedes. If one compares governments which claim to be following Third Way precepts with their neo-liberal predecessors, two main discontinuities in policy stand out. One is the acknowledgement that much more is required to tackle the backlog of poverty, unemployment, social exclusion and social disintegration inherited from twenty years of slow growth, technological innovation, structural change and fiscal retrenchment than a crude policy of labour market deregulation. The distinctive Third Way prescription is to combine flexible, lightly regulated labour markets with work-welfare activism, investment in human capital and programmes of civic renewal. The other novelty compared with the recent past, at any rate in Britain, is the recognition, however muted, that non-government organisations, including trade unions, have a role to play in those areas of economic and social policy where their intelligence and expertise can be harnessed to the public good.

In other respects, however, the Third Way signifies business as usual or, rather, business as we have been conditioned to accept it by twenty years of neo-liberal social engineering. A "mixed economy" could be construed as a system of *undominated diversity* in which the business, public, household and voluntary sectors all help to sustain each other, but none exerts a preponderant influence over the character of social life and the course of social development[22]. "Actually existing capitalism", to coin a phrase, is far from this ideal. Market forces have inundated spheres of social reproduction where, not so long ago, their presence was merely a trickle, from education, health care and public administration to childcare, sport and the arts. Similarly, public policy towards work remains narrowly focused on the labour market, oblivious to the role of unpaid household provisioning and caring in reproducing human beings, both from day to day and across the generations, or the role of voluntary activity in the formation and maintenance of social capital. Thus, when Third Way governments speak of reducing welfare dependency and combating social exclusion, what they mainly have in mind is increasing the employment rate and providing employers with a suitably skilled and motivated workforce, not helping to promote ways of living and working which would make people *less* dependent on waged labour and the vicissitudes of the market and give them more freedom in deciding how to spend their time and what to do with their lives.

On a wider front, the process of globalisation has *institutionalised* neo-liberal ideology and politics. Macroeconomic policy, in particular, is now hedged about by predetermined rules and commitments designed to reassure financial markets and business corporations that governments will maintain monetary discipline and fiscal prudence in pursuit of macroeconomic stability. This is understandable in a context where capital is footloose and financial markets mistrust deficit finance, even in conditions of recession. But it is disabling, for it means that fiscal policy is not available as an instrument of stabilisation policy, at least until such time as the markets are convinced that the "structural" budget deficits of the 1980s and 1990s have been eliminated. Meanwhile, the option of raising taxes to finance increased public

---

[22] In a four-sector scheme, what is here called the "voluntary" sector is a residual category covering all activities in civil society which are non-profit-seeking and are carried out by collective associations rather than individual households. Such associations, which vary greatly in purpose, size, form and longevity, employ both paid and unpaid labour.

spending is ruled out because it is judged to be unpopular with voters. But with fiscal policy thus boxed in, monetary policy may become overburdened if there is more than one policy objective. And what happens in a crisis: should governments stick to the rules or break them? So far, the resolve of Third Way governments has not been tested on this score. But it would be foolish to assume that the cherished goal of macroeconomic stability has been achieved and that from now on business cycles will be short-lived and shallow. The danger with rule-bound policies incorporating the presumed lessons of the past is that government will continue fighting old wars just when new ones are breaking out. As Keynes used to say: "When the facts change, I change my mind. What do you do?".

CHAPTER 4

Money and Political Economy:
From the Werner Plan
to the Delors Report and Beyond

J. Peter BURGESS and BO STRÅTH

Concepts are not timeless, ubiquitous categories given by nature. Their meaning is derived or constructed from the social, cultural and political context in which they are deployed and received. Nowhere is the contextual character of concepts more striking than in the evolution of the key notions of "market" and "money", "state", "nation," "Europe", "identity," in the post-war process of European construction. The concepts and ideas upon which the European project was founded and in the name of which its policies have sought legitimacy and political force are in a flux. They have been recreated, reformulated, discarded and rediscovered in conformity with changing scientific paradigms, political winds, social moods and moral temperaments. This chapter seeks to cast light on that conceptual history of the European Monetary Union by giving voice to the key concepts at the centre of the very economic thinking that tacitly assumed their silence.

From the first drafts of the Treaty of the European Coal and Steel Community in 1951 to the signing of the Treaty of the European Union at Maastricht in 1992, the *economic* agenda at the heart of the European project was openly connected to the *cultural*, *social*, and *security* consequences it might bring. Yet just as the validity of the notion of the European Community/Union ebbed and flowed throughout the second half of the twentieth century, the legitimacy of this connection was inconstant in both its nature and validity.

The fluid connection constitutes the framework of the European political economy. The conceptualisation of political economy in effect became a contested notion in the 1970s in the wake of the collapse of the Bretton Woods order, in contrast to its self-sufficiency and self-evidence during the post-war growth boom and emerging welfare capitalism. The collapse of the Bretton Woods provoked a redefinition of the international order and of Europe's role in it. Political economy became a wildcard, a concept built upon contention, some claiming that the economy was still to be politically managed, others arguing for a more economy-dependent understanding of European unity. In this sense the official proclamation of the concept of "European identity" by the European Commission in 1973 can be understood as an attempt to unify and steer the various discourses of political economy. First by reconstituting the European market in the world economy and in a new international order after the collapse of the Bretton Woods order, then by attempting to translate the dramatically eroding national tripartite bargaining order into a kind of tripartite Euro-corporatism with a view to stabilising the economic crisis.

The political road travelled between the publication of the Werner Plan in 1970 and that of the Delores Report in 1989 is a rocky one. The former builds upon a comprehensive system of values, relating European unity and monetary and economic policy in a single universe. The latter replies directly to the Werner Plan from a context in which economic theory and the social debate have revised the constellation of values all together. This value shift as a precondition of European construction means a paradigm shift of global scale in which ideas of political management of economies, dominant since the Second World War, reaches a kind of obsolescence as an interpretative model, giving way to neo-classical monetarism attached to American neo-liberal social philosophy.

It is the intention of this chapter to study this double transformation in economic theory and in European politics. It will focus not on the sociological systems of economic actors but rather on the changes in the conceptual fabric of its central operative notion: money. It will discuss the theoretical reflection on money and its connection to the social and the political, and the impact this changing theoretical reflection has had on political thinking and social debate. It will attempt to understand money in the framework of a larger system of meaning, involving the panoply of possibilities and limitations which such a system comprises. It will chart this understanding in light of the conceptual paradigm shift from politically managed economy ("Keynesianism"[1]) to monetarism. Next, it will attempt to incorporate this hermeneutic understanding of money in a parallel analysis of the conceptual retooling which takes place during the years between the Werner Plan and the Delors Report.

---

[1] For a critical discussion of the concept of Keynesianism as a term to generally describe the political economies of the 1950s and 1960s, see the previous chapter by David Purdy in this volume.

Our central hypothesis is that, in the period 1970-89 (from the release of the Werner Plan to that of the Delors Report), the conceptual foundations of European construction underwent a significant transformation associated with a transformation in the concept of money. We do not discern this transformation as two clear-cut phases where everything that was belonging to the old order disappeared and everything changed. Although less visible and less current, the idea of a kind of political management of the economy remained. These ideas were retrieved and resuscitated in particular in the 1990s, not the least because the long-term political legitimacy could not be maintained if politics were to be disconnected from economic processes. Such ideas were, however, rediscovered in a new form. Not only the dominant economic theories of the day, but also the very idea of political management of the economy went through immense changes between the 1970s and the 1990s.

In what follows we will try to plot this double transformation along three axes: (1) Money understood as a national and international system of meaning or network of reference based on a certain number of assumptions about value, collectivity, unity, exchange etc., (2) the shift from "Keynesian" to monetarist dominance in economic theory corresponding to a change in the dominant understanding of the nature of money on the macroeconomic level, and (3) the evolving discourse of EMU shifting from an understanding of European unity as a political economic problem based on socio-cultural parameters to European unity as a question of economic engineering and quantitative criteria[2].

The presentation is comprised of four sections. The first section explores the political, social and cultural meaning of money with special attention to the problem posed by the conglomerate of diverse national interests and historical traditions in both monetary considerations and social welfare policies. The second section analyses the historical background and concrete context of the Werner Plan. The third section turns to developments in the early 1980s up to the proposal of the Single European Act in 1985 and its implementation in 1987, and the subsequent Delors Report in 1989, analysing its conception of money and monetary policy in relation to both the economic horizon of the late 1980s and its deeper historical predecessor the Werner Plan. The fourth and final session connects the 1980s to the 1990s with the Third Way rhetoric and the Stability and Growth Pact.

---

[2] *Cf.* Dyson, 2000, McNamara, 1998, and Walsh, 2000.

The Social, Cultural and Political Meaning of Money

The Common European Currency

At the centre of the question of a European political-economic unity is the notion of a common European currency. The ambition to found a single European currency is already hinted at in the early 1950s, and clearly formulated in The Hague Communiqué of 1969. It then draws ever closer to the core of European development as economic and monetary union becomes the central discourse of European unity. Money and monetary considerations thus move to centre stage in the European theatre. The *meaning* of the role of money in the European political economy comes to the forefront, and in comparison to the earlier focus on the flow of commodities, money becomes the operative hinge-concept for European identity

National currency is a key symbol of the nation and one of the pillars of national legitimacy. The recognition of the validity of a currency as a medium of exchange is equivalent to recognising national sovereignty. The question facing the architects of the European Union is whether this equivalency is transferable to the European level. The symbolic power of currency poses a double-edged question. On the one hand, in conformity with neo-functionalist wisdom, something of the strategy involved in the development of a monetary union and the introduction of a common European currency is the ambition of creating a certain degree of social, cultural and political cohesion. On the other hand, this transfer of meaning poses a threat to the sovereignty of individual nations, by removing one of their tools and symbols of sovereignty. What's more, the transfer of monetary sovereignty has often been understood as a threat to traditional national framing of labour market and welfare politics. A new agenda and a new playground emerged with higher stakes, and the potential for more consequential responses to political crises such as the 1968 uprisings, the Vietnam protests, and later, the collapse of the dollar and the oil shock. A key question of this chapter is how this embryo of high symbolic politics was bogged down in the matter of economic processes and mathematical exegetics around phenomena like the convergence criteria in the 1990s, and how the common European currency from this process of de-symbolisation made a return to the political agenda and finally politically implemented in 2000.

The Concept of Money and the Notion of EMU

The "common scale of value" launched in the Treaty of Rome was a socio-cultural claim to solidarity, although without a specific scope for social policy. The convergence criteria for the Maastricht EMU involve

128

neither social nor employment criteria. Money at the beginning of the 1990s thus became the new European *mathesis universalis*, the new universal logic, the common denominator, which traverses all borders within the EU, all cultural divisions, all ideological dispositions[3].

This turned out to be an interlude that did not last very long. The 1990s brought a reaction to it, with attempts to retrieve and recreate lost connections between the political, the economic and the social. The point of departure for this retrieval was the idea of the economy as a polity and the nation as *the* polity. Understanding economy as a polity implies that economic processes are regulated and influenced by political rules and regulations, and that there is thus a connection to the question of political legitimacy and normative patterns. The polity as a value community (which, of course, does not mean that all share the same values) as the framework of the economic processes is a viewpoint that confronts the idea of the majority of economists that economic processes are "natural" processes, which follow their own inherent laws.

Despite its ambitions to cast the European Community as a value-based collectivity, the Treaty of Rome and the integration process that followed did not change the national point of departure of the polity. Barriers of trade, and so on decreased or disappeared, but, still, the nation was the point of departure. Social policy and labour market policy, for instance, was nationally entrenched. EMU as it was conceived in the 1970s was designed to transgress precisely this national entrenchment by re-casting it as a European project[4]. This design failed. In the 1980s, as part of an attempt to address the economic crisis leftover from the 1970s, financial operations were granted a growing role in the world economy. This meant increased difference between nations understood as polities and growing difficulties for national governments to control their polities. "Globalisation" emerged as a key concept to describe this development as necessary and natural.

---

[3] For a discussion of the scope for a European social policy in this development, see the chapter by Diamond Ashiagbor and David Purdy's Chapter 14 in this volume. See also Amy Verdun's chapter, where she compares the Werner Plan and the Maastricht EMU, and the chapter by Robert Salais, where he discusses the future prospects in the European political economy in terms of European labour market standards rather than social policy or employment policy.

[4] As Hubert Zimmerman's contribution to this volume shows, this attempt was made against the backdrop of growing tension between Europe and the US within the Bretton Woods order.

Economy as Polity

One response to the decline of the national polity was to take up the old idea of substituting the nation-as-polity with Europe-as-polity in the context of the monetary issue. This response was concretely initiated through the Single European Act's insistence on intensifying market integration and expanding the free movement of commodities to also encompass services, capital flows and persons. The nation, however, remained the polity in this re-design, now in terms of *fiscal* politics.

The European merger of monetary and fiscal politics envisaged in the Werner Plan was never to be seen again. The consequence in the Maastricht EMU of this "half copy" of the Werner Plan was a tension between the two policy areas and the two polity levels. Just how this residual tension effects institutional, legal, and normative frameworks in Europe is not very clear. The UK, Sweden and Denmark have tried to resolve this tension by declining to join EMU and thus maintain the idea of the nation as a polity in both fiscal and monetary terms. Thus the late twentieth century dilemma is the various and contradictory approaches between national and European regimes in terms of monetary, fiscal and employment policies where the preferences are picked *à la carte*.

Economic theory has from the beginning of European integration tried to comment on this tension. A key question has been what should come first, European fiscal policy or monetary policy, or whether they should be introduced simultaneously. Both the Ohlin Report – solicited by the negotiators of the Rome Treaty and issued in 1956 by an expert committee within the International Labour Organisation – as well as the parallellist approach in the Werner Report solved this Columbi egg by arguing that both policies would support one another in a self-sustaining circle[5]. Differences in productivity would decrease, and the European polity would become more homogeneous.

What value does such economic assertions about automatic equilibrium through "natural" market processes have today? Historical evidence, and cultural, normative and institutional factors suggest another scenario. In this alternative scenario means of production are not as mobile as assumed in economic theory. The expected equilibrium over the whole surface of the polity never occurs. The best illustration of this second scenario is perhaps Italy, with its clear North-South divide in a polity area where both fiscal and monetary politics have been the same. For another illustrative case, the regional differences in Norway, see, Ole Røste's chapter in this volume.

---

[5]   *Cf.* the contribution by Amy Verdun in this volume.

On the other hand the Italian illustration suggesting that economic processes do not conform to natural law or predictions by economic theory does not mean that historical and cultural heritages predetermine developments. Culture is always in a flux and under constant transformation and can always be changed. Only in retrospect do causal trajectories emerge. Here the political dimension comes in. Economies are not processes which behave according to natural law, and they do not follow trajectories predetermined by history. Economies are polities, politically framed in bargaining and with a focus oscillating between competition and coordination where the outcome and the future is open. They perform as they do because of political regulation and norms that shape what is allowed, desirable and good.

The European discourse on social policy is just such an instance. It was transformed into a more specific employment discourse after Maastricht, with the Green and White Papers in 1993, and the Essen Communiqué in 1994[6]. This transformation was a departure from macroeconomic considerations of how to promote growth, market "liberation" and competition . Instead of the convergence criteria came the Stability and Growth Pact. Employment did in the new scenario not come automatically through the market but required politics. However, the growing attention to employment politics went hand in hand with a softening of the idea of a European level of labour standards. The emphasis was on employment through growth, guaranteed by fiscal and monetary rigidity, rather than on the connection employment-labour standards. Expansion through a solid and stable currency was the key to growing employment levels, although the concept of full employment silently passed away from the vocabulary. The debate in Essen in December 1994 was heated and reflected a kind of traditional Left-Right opposition. This is the point where David Purdy (Chapter 14) and Robert Salais (Chapter 15) warn for the risk of employment creation through social nationalism.

We suggest to refine our understanding of this transformation by focusing on two of its major anchoring points: the Werner Plan and the Delors Report. The following reconstruction will attempt to focus on the conceptual terms and conditions, which have marked the evolution of the notion of a European Monetary Union, since its genesis in the 1950s to its most sophisticated form in the Maastricht Treaty, by plotting the conceptual topology of the central stations along the way to EMU.

---

[6]   As demonstrated by Diamond Ashiagbor in her contribution to this volume.

The Werner Plan

Pre-History I: The Inter-War Period

The old world economic order, which in the nineteenth century had the ambition of guaranteeing employment and economic growth, was based on the Gold Standard. Gold symbolised not only growth but also stability and solidity in the mythical underpinning of the global order. However, the stability became, in actual performance, instability. The long period of economic decline from the beginning of the 1870s to the 1890s produced the conceptual invention of depression to describe and analyse economic processes and brought the first steps towards cyclical theory as an attempt to interpret the outdrawn crisis. Nevertheless the belief in stability through gold prevailed until it came to an end with the outbreak of war in 1914.

Keynes, who was one of the most prominent advocates of a new approach in the peace negotiations in Versailles, criticised the peace settlement vehemently, claiming that it would lead to a new destruction of the international system rather than to security, order and balance. In his reflections on the peace negotiations he tried to incorporate Soviet Russia into the world community based on the idea of a "new world order", which was discussed at the World Economic Conference in 1922 in Genoa. His priority was the economic health of Europe. The territorial question – which was the main preoccupation of the diplomats at Versailles – could according to Keynes not be solved until the economic system was reconstructed. In his view a stable and prosperous international order went hand in hand with the employment issue and the questions of democracy and world peace. Keynes's imagined "new world order" bore a considerable resemblance to the plans for European unification proposed by the pan-European movement of Coudenhove-Kalergis and others. As we know, these dynamics failed in the wake of the worsening economic situation and increasing political instability. Big capital in the form of international price and production cartels took over the role of commercial and financial coordination from governments which had failed to maintain control. The highly explosive mix of inflation and unemployment led to the rise of political and economic nationalism.

Eichengreen's study of the Great Depression and of how politics mediate between financial markets and labour markets raises issues which are seen as analogous to those debated today around the question of the EMU[7]. Far from being synonymous with stability, the Gold Standard – briefly re-established in the 1920s after its first collapse

---

[7] Eichengreen, 1992.

when the First World War broke out – was the principal *threat* to financial stability and economic prosperity between the wars. Problems with the operation of the Gold Standard and the unprecedented rise in unemployment were two notable aspects of the interwar crisis. These were connected in ways that compounded and reinforced one another. The collapse of employment and output had gone so far by 1930 that the Gold Standard could no longer be supported for domestic political reasons. After the stock exchange and bank crash of 1929 the fixed exchange standard collapsed under the pressure of social protest against the breakdown of the financial order and its impact on labour markets. Once the regulatory straitjacket of the Gold Standard was finally removed from the international scene an economic recovery became possible. Previously recovery had been prevented by an overly rigid monetary regime. However, this recovery occurred through mobilisation of the nations under growing rivalry among them finally leading to a new world war. Those most concerned about the domestic consequences of international monetary policies had as yet acquired only limited political influence. In the long run the credibility of the commitment to Gold was undermined by the central bankers' insulation from political pressures, a growing number of analyses of the linkage between restrictive monetary policy and unemployment were articulated. The growing political influence of the working classes intensified pressure to adapt monetary policy towards employment targets.

Pre-History II: From the Second World War

After the Second World War Keynes insisted on the link between political structures and their economic foundations in his second programme for "a new world order" based on his conviction that the two World Wars had been the result of economic nationalism and the clash of uncontrolled economic and political interests. According to Keynes's view, the creation of a new international order to guarantee security and prosperity had to be based on new ideas and a radical shift away from the nineteenth century's focus on the balance of power and presumption of automatic economic progress sustained by liberal institutions. The future was to focus on maintaining a connection between order, security and prosperity through global governance of economic, financial and political institutions. These ideas provided an important intellectual setting for the negotiation of the Bretton Woods system. It was not difficult to see many of Keynes's ideas in the outline of the new order.

Bretton Woods functioned well for some two decades in the sense that it underpinned expectations of a better and more governable world and encouraged a faith that history is a linear progression towards ever-higher stages of civilisation. Admittedly, the relative degree of consensus over the distribution of incomes and allocation of resources delivered by national tripartite bargaining structures after the Second World War was achieved not the least because aspirations remained relatively modest. Such modest aspirations were due to memories of the 1930s, and by the fact that, thanks to the growing economy, there was a growing pie to be distributed politically. The spectre of the 1930s further reinforced the social responsibility convention, implying that the State guarantee full employment.

Economic theory provided interpretative frameworks and scientific legitimatisation for this guarantee. However, in institutional terms the new order had hardly been implemented when it began to erode. Currency convertibility and free trade were cornerstones in the architecture of the Bretton Woods scheme, though not introduced for implementation until much later. European currency convertibility, for instance, was introduced only in 1958 and free trade even later. Only in terms of full employment did the new order function at all times after the war, and it did so by riding piggyback on the general reconstruction boom. This boom lost momentum in the second half of the 1960s, just when it had begun to be regarded as a structurally permanent feature of the economy.

The strength of the Bretton Woods order was that it provided mobilising meaning and social confidence in the political guarantee of economic growth and full employment as well as political institutions for the structuring of world trade. Its weakness was that nobody controlled the key actor, the US government, and Federal Reserve provided the key instrument of the whole order, a stable dollar. The Dollar's stability was managed through its relationship to the gold reserve. President Johnson took advantage of this weakness in the control system after 1964, when he used inflation to pay for the Great Society programme and a few years later for the escalation of the Vietnam War. Nonetheless, tensions in the transatlantic order, with inflationary pressure, began well before that, and were deeply connected to the military issue, as Hubert Zimmermann demonstrates in his chapter. In the general bonanza mood in the mid-1960s, the resulting inflationary pressure was not given much attention outside a small circle of experts to whom few really listened[8]. In March 1968, Sweden hosted an informal conference on the theme of how the West should handle a situation in which the control mechanisms of the Bretton Woods order had been eliminated. However, the press reports from the meeting dealt more with police violence against Vietnam demonstrators greeting the American representatives than with the dollar problem.

---

[8]   *Cf.* Hubert Zimmermann's chapter in this volume.

Largely as a result of the flow of dollars required to finance the US war against communism in Vietnam the dollar's stability and its guarantee of free trade broke down in the summer of 1971. Oil prices fixed in terms of dollars fell as the value of the dollar fell against other currencies. When this price fall was reversed by OPEC's decision in 1973 to rise oil prices dramatically this signalled a change in the balance of global power and generated economic problems and a political challenge which the established doctrines of how to politically manage the economy failed to encompass. The worsening situation was emphasised by the collapse of key industries like steel, coal and shipbuilding slightly later. Experiences of crisis re-emerged for the first time since the 1930s.

The Horizon of Crisis

The Werner Plan was settled just a few months before the dollar collapsed in August 1971 bringing a complete shift in the whole framework of the discussion. Monetary problems began to be seen as exchange problems in their own right. The idea that monetary and financial organisation was an instrument for the pursuit of broader welfare and employment goals gradually disappeared from the forefront of debate. The Werner Plan was transformed into an attempt to compensate for the dollar's collapse, a strategy that ended up with the creation of the Exchange Rate Mechanism ("the snake"). This development was emphasised more and more in the wake of the oil crisis in 1973. Financial and monetary politics as a guarantee of full employment and as a tool for welfare politics were replaced by attempts to defend currency stability. Action became reaction. At the same time intensified attempts were made to keep the European project going. The decision on a European identity in 1973[9], and the connection of this identity to a Eurocorporatist order within the framework of the Werner Plan at the end of the 1970s in the wake of the collapse of key industries as well as the emergence of mass unemployment, should be seen in this light. The tension between new approaches to overcoming the situation through the establishment of a new kind of European polity through the Werner Plan, and dispirited reactions by national governments through inflation-driving subsidy packages was obvious.

In retrospect one can say that the outcome of this tension became visible. The Werner Plan, as it was adopted in a Council Decision of 22 March 1971, aimed at a step by step realisation of a European economic and monetary union. As a first step the economic politics of

---

[9] European Commission, "Declaration on European Identity," in General Report of the European Commission (Brussels, European Commission, 1973).

the Member States were to be coordinated. It was still the era of belief in economic management and structural and cyclical adjustments through political fiscal and monetary operations. This is made clear, for example, by the intention of promoting full employment in the framework of social policy through the creation of a European Social Fund. The Social Fund aimed at addressing what was seen as basically a technical problem through political interventions. A European equilibrium was to be created by raising the instruments of intervention to a European level. The need for regional structural policies in order to promote convergence in economic performance was also emphasised. This was an insight that deviated from the Ohlin Report in 1956, where convergence would emerge automatically through market mediation.

This broad idea of financial and monetary regulation through an economic and monetary union was no doubt embedded in general social policy considerations. Moreover, the anticipated progression from economic union, *i.e.* harmonisation of the national economic policies, towards monetary union and a common currency made the prospects of a European cyclical economic policy far more focused than it would turn out to be in post-Maastricht era of the 1990s, where monetary policy under conditions of fiscal rigidity were emphasised.

Under Werner the main economic policy decisions were to be taken at the Community level, which meant a transfer of decision-making from the national level. The budget policies of the Member States were to become Community objectives and a certain harmonisation was required in the fiscal area. Monetary and credit politics had to be strongly coordinated and the integration of financial markets regulated. Gradually the Community was to adopt common positions in monetary relations with third countries and international organisations. The final stage was to be a single currency that would, in turn, guarantee the irreversibility of the whole enterprise.

The Concept of Money and the Ambitions of the Werner Plan

What were the economic ambitions of the Werner Plan and what structural and conceptual tools did it deploy in order to achieve them? Under the Werner EMU common policies were to be subject to debate and control by the European Parliament. The coordination of the central banks were to be subject to politically determined growth and stability targets. The Council was to decide the *grandes lignes* of economic policy at Community level, after consultation with the *partenaires sociaux* in the Economic and Social Committee. Similarly the Werner Plan's project for an Economic and Monetary Union as formulated in March 1970 no doubt envisaged a clear political control over economic and monetary issues and a transfer of national power to the Community level.

In December 1969, in accordance with the plan outlined in the official communiqué from The Hague Summit, a memorandum was sent to the Commission detailing the objectives of the plan for monetary union to be set forth as the result of the work of the Werner Group. The memorandum, published in March 1970, seven months before the official Werner Plan, set forth the principles the Commission "feels should be borne in mind in the forthcoming discussions and the main aspects of the stages it considers could usefully be planned for the establishment of an economic and monetary union".

The objectives set out in the Plan are both internal and external. Internally the principle of free movement of goods, services and capital – the mantra of the 1980s – is already clear. Externally, the Community is envisaged as an "organic economic and monetary association having an individuality of its own[10]". The notion of "common interest" was to be the guiding light of the work toward formulation of a plan. Common interest would be best assured by economic coordination through an "economic union".

> While it is true that the monetary union, if it is to last, needs to be soundly based on economies evolving on compatible lines, with convergent economic policies, it is equally true that closer monetary solidarity enhances the prospects for both such compatibility and such convergence [...] Moreover, current international developments suggest that to delay overlong in giving the Community this greater monetary cohesion might eventually mean that the whole idea of monetary unification lost its point, economic unification was rendered largely irrelevant, and even the Community work already completed might be seriously undermined[11].

In this early document economic union is abstracted from monetary union. The two types of union are seen as separable though their linking is empirical, a question of performance or expeditiousness in the development of economic coordination. The *desirability* of economic coordination is taken for granted, while monetary coordination is considered as an "enhancement" of the "prospects" for counter-cyclical economic coordination. Monetary mechanisms are thus seen as incidental to the economic policies that are the true embodiment of national interests internally, and European interests externally. This priority of the "economic" over the "monetary" is precisely what one sees reversed

---

[10] European Commission. *Integral text of the final communiqué of the conference of the Heads of State or Government on 1 and 2 December 1969 at The Hague.* (*Hague Communiqué*). Annex 1 p. 3.

[11] *Hague Communiqué*, p. 3.

in the evolution between 1970 and 1988 when the counter-cyclical element had disappeared (*cf.* Verdun's chapter in this volume).

In the same way, the structural changes envisaged by the Commission Summit at The Hague hardly concerned the system of international European banking or monetary management. The object of the Werner initiative expresses the spirit of the traditional "Keynesian" mechanisms, to "even out the existing disparities, by measures relating primarily to employment and regional equilibrium, and [...] to prepare the way more effectively for future growth, more particularly by action in the fields of industry and technology"[12]. The most interesting available tools for coordination and community-building are typically "economic": the targeted administering of funds, the emphasis being on "offering incentives and guidance, and even practical demonstration[13]". The goal of the project is the "coordination of economic policies". The means, the *conditio sine qua non,* is monetary coordination. In other words, monetary structures are understood not as fundamental or essential, but as support for an already existing strategy for economic coordination.

In The Hague Memorandum the notion of a European currency lies on the distant horizon. Its symbolic function as a unifying medium of a wider European union is quite speculative. In the passage cited above it is evoked in the framework of Europe's external personality, as a means to emphasise the "individuality" of the European Community within the international monetary system, "without ceasing to belong and to contribute actively to that system"[14]. The monetary coordination of the Community thus takes a stance with respect to the IMF where the European governments already experienced strains[15]. Internally, the Community will be served "once and for all" by a fixed structure of exchange rates.

The Werner Plan thus takes as its point of departure the particular *economic* problems of the member countries, notably economic disequilibrium, the primary menace to "growth and stability" provoked by the crisis mood in the wake of the massive social critique and the strike wave at the end of the 1960s ("1968")[16]. Part of the political background was also the cracks in the transatlantic order, which, in turn, provoked severe tensions in the payment balances in France and the UK at the end of the 1960s, and fears grew in Europe that the ever stronger German economy would rush away alone. There was an awareness in the

---

[12] *Hague Communiqué*, p. 3.
[13] *Hague Communiqué*, p. 3.
[14] *Hague Communiqué*, p. 6
[15] *Cf.* the chapter by Hubert Zimmermann in this volume.
[16] Werner Plan, pp. 7-8.

German government that the strong DM potentially could destroy the whole European integration project (see Zimmermann's chapter). Growing uncertainty in France about how to interpret the *Ostpolitik* of the new (September 1969) German chancellor Willy Brand reinforced the French eagerness to control and contain the potential German *Alleingang*. The Werner Plan fit this purpose hand in glove.

The problem confronted by the authors of the Werner Plan concerns the particularity of national destinies and their interrelation with what is understood as the common or "universal" interests of the European Community in the context of a growing internationalisation of the individual European nations. The individual nations, notes the report, have suffered a "loss of autonomy" at the national level[17]. On the external horizon – that is in the matter of international monetary relations – the Community has failed to make its "personality" felt, "by reason as the case may be of divergences of policy or of concept"[18]. The burgeoning phenomenon of global capital, new market conditions, new economic agents, multinational companies, markets in Euro-currencies, speculative movement of capital in "enormous proportions", and the "constantly increasing interdependence of the industrialised economies" have all, according to the authors, underscored "the problem of individuality of the Community". The growing homogenisation of global finance created in their eyes the need to underscore the particularity of European reality and to develop a specific European response to and responsibility for this emerging problem.

Between National Values and European Currency

Thus we see the basic outline of the motivation for the economic and monetary project, such as it is formulated in Werner. The transparency of money, its ubiquity and universality, has flattened the global terrain, smoothed out differences, standardised and generalised criteria for *value*. This global force of standardisation has put "individuality" in peril, above all the individuality of the European Community of the late 1960s. And yet what is this individuality that the monetarisation of the global economy puts in peril? It is precisely that universe of European cultural values that *resist* monetarisation, those that are not immediately or naturally translated into the value equivalence of money. By "translating" the *interests* of the European continent into the "language" of global culture, Europe will be more capable of holding a dialogue with it and thereby more capable of advancing its interests in "terms" which are universally understandable. The individuality of the European

---

[17] Werner Plan, p. 8.
[18] Werner Plan, p. 8.

Community will be enhanced by its immersion in the global monetary system. The logic of IMF is a growing global monetary unity. The fixed dollar parity at the foundation of the Bretton Woods encourages – or indeed requires — transposition of Community, national and local concept of *value* into the common language of monetary equivalencies, *i.e.* the dollar. It thereby provokes increased and ever more nuanced interpenetration of the European *monetary* interests, which, in turn creates the need to accelerate "translation" of Europe into the discourse of money.

Indeed, experiences of a need to re-activate Europe came after De Gaulle had left the scene. He had blocked every attempt at such re-activation, which did not take the nation-state as the point of departure. However, there was one element in the approach of the General that continued after he had left the scene: his critical view on the US. The growing scepticism concerning the role of the US and the dollar as the world leader provoked action. Key elements of what De Gaulle had stood for could be politically canalised only after he had left the scene. The idea of a European currency as the final step in the implementation of the Werner Plan not only struck at the key symbol of the European nations, so strongly defended by De Gaulle, their national currency, but also the dollar, so despised by him.

The moment of both new-orientation (towards a European Monetary Union and the creation not of a European Bretton Woods, with the same weakness as this order had had, but a European "dollar") and continuity (the critical stance versus the US, underpinned by both the dollar collapse in 1971 and the radical anti-Vietnam critique in Western Europe) after De Gaulle did not last very long. Though it is clear that Edward Heath, who negotiated the British membership in the EC, and James Callaghan, who succeeded him, were committed to the European project, with the entrance of Margaret Thatcher on the scene in 1979 De Gaulle got his successor. The European project was a project of the nations. The difference between the General and Mrs Thatcher was her much more benevolent attitude to the US. With Ronald Reagan as a President from 1981 she found a kindred soul on the other side of the Atlantic much more so than with the European leaders. There was another important difference compared to Charles De Gaulle. She had much less authority to speak on behalf of Europe. This opened a scope of action for Jacques Delors as a President of the Commission where he managed to infuse new political energy in the European polity project.

The process of European integration was until then inseparable from the cultural and social particularity of individual nations. Though the free circulation of commodities within the EC certainly penetrated the other key symbol of national sovereignty – its borders – the physical check points remained. If implemented the Werner Plan would have transgressed this European focus on the nation. The "advantage" of the global monetary system inaugurated at Bretton Woods was that it was not burdened by the concrete situations of its participants. In principle, insertion into the communicative network of the International Monetary System presupposed on the contrary a *detachment* from but not dissolution of the culturally and socially conditioned national codes of communication, those that are organised within the framework of traditional economic thinking.

Monetary Value and Cultural Value

Thus the Werner Plan insisted that "economic and monetary union will make it possible to realise an area within which goods and services, people and capital will circulate freely and without competitive distortions, without thereby giving rise to structural or regional disequilibrium". This was coupled with the further aspiration that "the implementation of such a union will effect a lasting improvement in welfare in the Community and will reinforce the contribution of the Community to economic and monetary equilibrium in the world"[19]. The aim was not only economic political cooperation between sovereign nations but one step more, to transform them by going beyond one of their deepest cultural symbols.

Value is always partly cultural, partly social, nourished and supported by a system of social and cultural values, and cultivated by a certain synthesis of the national, regional and local economic systems from which they arise. Werner's conception of economic union was based on the supposition that by lowering the *resistance* to such transfers of value, general equilibrium would be enhanced, and collective viability increased with respect to the rest of the world. The "economic" systems, in their traditional sense, have always been formed and evolved in socio-cultural contexts, national, regional, or local, based on value equivalencies couched in culturally rooted traditions, forms of work, types of activities etc. The economic and monetary union envisaged by Werner supposed the possibility of Europeanising the socially and culturally rooted national values, then transposing them through the elimination of the exchange mechanisms.

Money in its most general sense is the ideal form for exchange. Indeed this is the hidden insight of the architects of Bretton Woods. (Moreover, in the colloquial, "dollar" and "money" are synonymous.) Money, in the ideal form supposed by the IMS, and courted by Werner as a European currency, is a resistance-free conduit of value. This long-

---

[19] Werner Plan, p. 9.

term implication was hardly fully realised when the Werner Plan was drafted. This is much easier visible in a global monetary system in which speculation in money itself has become a dominant industry. In this system the transfer of value has become the source of value, and, at the same time, as the other side of the coin, also the source of loss of value. For every winner there is a looser. Money is timeless and spaceless, a constant, detached from culture and the social. Or rather, it generates its own international cosmopolitan culture and social sphere, based on instantaneous communication and autonomous value under the hegemony of the dollar.

The Werner Plan was somewhat hesitant in seeing the economic and monetary controls given wholly over to the aegis of Community-level governance. Cohesion and coordination of economic and monetary policy were of course to be transferred "from the national to the Community" plane, but only "within the limits necessary". The Community would have at its disposal "a complete range of necessary instruments, the utilisation of which, however, may be different from country to country within certain limits"[20]. Budgetary and fiscal trends of the collective Community would be coordinated, but this too would have its limits, in that it was necessary to guard against "excessive centralisation". Thus transfer of powers from the local and national levels to the Community should take place to the extent necessary, but "allow for a differentiated budgetary structure operating at several levels, Community, national etc."[21] The need for a continuity of value was also expressed in Werner's emphasis on the collaboration of "social partners"[22]. National, regional, and local governance was taken as the foyer of value and importance. Werner remained irresolute about the monetarist conviction that monetary function is a mathematical and not a social, cultural or political one.

As we shall see, this point is one of the fundamental differences between the monetary-economic logic of Werner and that of the Delors Report. In the Werner Plan there is still an assumed – and perhaps real – interrelation between the economic and the monetary, between social and cultural agendas of traditional "Keynesian" political economy and the monetary policies undertaken as an attempt to position Europe in an expanding global economy, increasingly dominated by the logic of value of the IMS. Monetary policy is still seen primarily as a support for the economic, as one tool among others for coordinating the economic policies of national or European interests. The problem of the evolution

---

[20] Werner Plan, p. 10.
[21] Werner Plan, p. 10.
[22] Werner Plan, p. 11.

toward a European political economy is often cast as an opposition or alternative relationship between national economy and European economy. This tends to lose sight of the fact that the economic paradigm changed for both at the same time during the 1970s and the 1980s.

The Delors Report

Background: from the Werner Plan to the Delors Report

The 1970s saw the breakdown of an economic model based on mass consumption and mass production in a mutually reinforcing relationship, a model in which organised interests in most nations took part in some form of tripartite bargaining – with varying power relationships – that negotiated how to achieve high economic performance and how to share the fruits of growth in productivity. When examined more closely, the patterns of interest and identity were much more complex than any that can be described by a purely tripartite (the State, the employers and the trade unions) scheme, the broad basis of social bargaining was ideas of trade union or employee interests and a solidarity of workers against employers and capital. The promoter of a compromise formula between conflicting interests was the State and the idea of a national interest. When many firms in industries like coal, steel and shipbuilding faced bankruptcy in the 1970s these established solidarity and interest patterns changed. Local task forces of management and union leaders developed to fight against other local task forces in a struggle for survival.

In 1977 the MacDougall Report to the European Commission suggested a European corporatist strategy to bridge the economic crisis and the collapse of key industries. A serious attempt was made in 1977-1978 to translate national tripartite bargaining structures, which had functioned so well during the era of economic growth in the 1950s and 1960s, to a European level alongside a politics of de-industrialisation in industries like shipbuilding and steel. However, in the bargaining about capacity reduction and layoffs ties of solidarity between employers, trade unions and governments followed national lines rather than those of transnational sectoral interests[23]. The bargaining partners that the trade unions needed were missing. Business regarded its producers' interests well represented in national lobbying processes and did not see much sense in having to deal at the European level. The European project fell dormant for a while[24]. The proposals in the MacDougall Report were never realised and a European pattern of interest and solidarity ties never emerged.

---

[23]   Stråth, 1987 and 1996.

[24]   Stråth, 1987 and 1996.

In 1977 the OECD also published a report (the McCracken Report) recommending action to tackle the crisis. These recommendations proposed a quite different approach, offering solutions and hopes in the market. The OECD's suggestion won the support of the governments, which meant a general breakthrough for market liberal government approaches, and the MacDougall Report was forgotten[25]. The road was open for neo-liberal policies. The Werner Plan was stone dead even before all its stages were due for fulfilment. The "snake," the European Exchange Rate Mechanism, and other responses to the dollar's collapse absorbed the political energy.

The Re-Launch of European Integration

In January 1985 Jacques Delors began his term as the new President of the European Commission and embarked on a project of re-launching European integration. The European Council of December 1984 had mandated a reinforcement of the European Monetary System and Delors considered European nations ready to launch the notion of monetary integration, tabled since the early 1970s[26]. He did not waste time. Already in a speech to the European Parliament on 14 January he launched the notion of a "European social space" featuring the unusual but henceforth characteristic fusion of social solidarity and market liberalism[27]. Delors understood that there was a general consensus for economic union, and he chose that crusade not only because he saw it as the most pragmatic road toward the realisation of his social convictions. It was also a project which would serve as a means to reconstructing the legitimacy of the Commission, a legitimacy, which had decreased during the turmoil of the 1970s and the failure of the Werner Plan. In this spirit Delors appointed his social and political antithesis Lord Arthur Cockfield to take charge of the drafting of the Commission White Book *Completing the Internal Market*. Delors made the White Book the Commission's number one priority in the first months of his presidency[28]. Against the backdrop of years of stagnation after the failure to establish a tripartite Euro-corporatist order at the end of the 1970s and an atmosphere of growing political consensus, the new Commission got a running start. There was growing consensus for a European federation (Delors, famous for his federalist philosophies in the 1990s already

---

[25] Marcussen and Roscher, 2000.

[26] At the European Council held 3-4 December 1984 in Dublin, http://europa.eu.int/abc/history/1984/1984_en.htm.

[27] EP/1985, Drake, 2000, Grant, 1995, and Dyson and Featherstone, 1999.

[28] In less than six months since Delors took office the report was drafted, published, and presented to the Heads of State and Government at the Milan European Council of June 1985, Drake, 2000, p. 92.

evoked the notion in his first year as Commission president) and a general agreement that the time was in for general European social regulations and harmonisation of national differences in a number of polity areas. The Single European Act became the crowning glory of this movement.

The White Book listed 300 directives, finally reduced to 279, required for the establishment of the internal market: abolition of physical, technical and fiscal barriers of trade. The long-term goal was that eighty percent of the national regulations should have Community origin. The report's emphasis on the harmonising of norms for products and, in the long run, also production (environment, working-life standards, social legislation etc.) had clear and powerful consequences for the European economic interests.

It is difficult to describe this hectic agenda in terms of de-regulation, which became a key concept in the neo-liberal flexibility language of the 1980s[29]. It was far more a gigantic re-regulation project. Still, compared to the economic emphasis on market creation, the social dimension was not particularly pronounced in this approach. In this way the Commission could latch on to the neo-liberal rhetoric and thereby gain the impression of a new start in the same way as the neo-liberal economists marketed themselves as new thinkers and solvers of the crisis of stagnation wielding new concepts such as de-regulation and flexibility. The key question in this view is how neo-liberal the White Book design really was.

The Persistence of the Social

Quite obviously Delors was much more committed to a social philosophy of re-regulation than to the theory de-regulation as the neo-liberal economists would have it. The use of the discourse of the free-market was not unconditional. Rather it must be understood as reverence to the dominant European *Zeitgeist*. In the context of the expansive ideas of the European institutional setting it is also possible to discern a connection to the failed Euro-corporatist approach of the 1970s. Although less insistent under the neo-liberal rhetoric the continuity from the 1970s through the 1980s was represented by ideas of institutional expansion and re-regulation, as well as by the presence of a social dimension.

Reflection upon the question of social dialogue first began with the problem of how to reform Article 118 of the Treaty of Rome. The Parliament, which did what it could to keep the social question on the

---

[29]   Stråth, 2000.

agenda by recurring threats to stop the rule-making process for the internal market, put pressure on the Commission to pay due attention to the social dimension. In 1989 the declaration of the Social Charter by the European trade unions followed by a programme of action, half of which was formulated as directives, underpinned the social dimension in the European integration process.

Delors initiated a "social dialogue" with a plan for communication between employers and trade unions at the federal European level and a pilot study was made on the content and objectives of the European social dialogue. The aim was to relocate the social dialogue in the new institutional setting[30]. The European Council in Rome in 1990 emphasised the importance of the social dialogue. In October 1991 the project of revising Article 118 began in more operative terms. How in this light the agreement in December 1991 on a Social Protocol as an annex to the Maastricht Treaty should be interpreted is a contested issue, which Robert Salais deals with in his chapter in this volume. Irrespective of how the importance of the social protocol is evaluated, the protocol as such demonstrates that the social question was on the agenda.

In this scenario the 1980s were much more than the simple imposition of neo-liberal market "de-regulation". On the contrary, the intensified institution building must be seen as a continuation of the failed project begun by the Werner Plan and, later on in the 1970s, the Eurocorporatist ideas. By way of parallel Delors can be seen in his capacity as former French Minister of Finance against the backdrop of the French failure of economic governance through expansive politics in a national framework during 1981 and 1983, where he gained experience with the political preconditions of a world of ever more global financial markets. After these experiences the European level emerged as the level of political management of the economy in which the growing forces of transnational capital were to be canalised and integrated rather than confronted. Jacques Delors lead the Commission in a historical conjuncture full of contingencies in the wake of the collapse of the Bretton Woods order, the emergence of mass unemployment with the erosion of full employment as the basis of the welfare, the erosion of old solidarity patterns, and the emerging quasi-hegemonic neo-liberal prescription for healing suggested by the economists. Delors' response to these processes can not be described in terms of functional development or rational choice. The responses were the outcome of social contest, bargaining and compromises, where the responses emerged more in retrospect than *ex ante*. The answer was not

---

[30]   Pochet, 2001; Fajertag and Pochet (eds.), 2000.

only to the failure of the Werner Plan and the ideas of Eurocorporatism in the 1970s but also to the French economic political failure between 1981 and 1983. From these experiences a European future was designed under much more continuity than is normally discerned.

The Opposition between the Social and the Economic

The continuity between the Euro-corporatist failure at the end of the 1970s and the reinforced European institution building in the 1980s suggests an alternative view than the conventional historical one in which one phase replaces another and in which history is divided into a series of discontinuities. First was the crisis of the 1930s and then the Second World War, then came the era of welfare capitalism and national tripartite corporatism, then came a crisis because of a social democratic over-exploitation of the economy, and finally came the neo-liberal answer to the crisis. In some versions this answer was also the end of history.

What emerges in our alternative scenario to this periodisation and division in phases is both a more long-term *opposition* and a more long-term *entanglement* between capitalist expansion, and social/political ambitions to respond to and canalise the development of capitalism, to the extent that both were affected and – in the long term – transformed. The social democrats of the 1990s were not the social democrats of the 1960s or the 1970s, and those who represent capital in 2000 were not those who represent capital in the 1980s. The rejection of the idea of strong and decisive ruptures does not exclude temporary defeats and triumphs. (Such categories are, of course, dependent on the point of view.) There were certainly failures in the integration of the social dimension but such points of failure do not mean that one history stops and another and totally different one begins. Defeats and triumphs in specific points of time lead to new situations in terms of identification of problems, and to the emergence of new future horizons, where the experiences acquired in the past are part of the matrix that provides continuity.

Closing the Circle: European Unity and Political Economy in the Delors Report (1989)

The impetus of the 1985 White Book *Completing the Internal Market* was followed up 1988 by the organisation of a Committee on Economic and Monetary Union, chaired by the President of the Commission, Jacques Delors. The mandate of the committee was to deepen the proposals of the White Book and to make recommendations for setting up an economic and monetary union. The result of the com-

147

mittee's labours, published in April 1989, is at once more theoretically predisposed, more empirically anchored, and more conscious of its position in European economic history than the White Book. It represents the completion of a certain political ambition toward economic and monetary unity. The introductory comments of the report suggest that it clearly situates itself in the arc of *monetary history* beginning with the decline of the Bretton Woods order, considering the historical meaning of the Werner Report, the "snake" (1972), the EMCF (1973) and the EMS (1979). It explicitly takes its cue from the success of the EMS and the solid foundation provided by the adoption of the Single European Act. The focus of the success is clearly in the monetary sector. Indeed, the historical assessment contained in Chapter I of the report, "Past and present developments in economic and monetary integration in the Community" hardly stakes a claim for economic union or economic integration. The economic is only thematised in the ultimate section on "Problems and perspectives".

The jewel in the crown of the European Community is clearly the EMU. As the Delors Report underscores, the participants in its framework have succeeded in creating a zone of "increasing monetary stability", which has had as a consequence increased price stability in individual European countries and better exchange-rate stability. The Single European Act of 1985 added to this success by simplifying the requirements of harmonising national law (later on, in implementation, to a large extent by re-casting the concept of "harmonisation" as "mutual recognition"), by extending qualified majority voting, by expanding the role of the European Parliament, and by reaffirming the need to strengthen the Community's economic and social cohesion.

There are two sides to the Delorsian understanding of European Unity. On the one side, there is a concern for the particular destinies of individual European countries, regions, and local cultures. After attaining an economic and monetary union, the Community will clearly continue to consist of "individual nations with differing economic, social, cultural and political characteristics. The existence and preservation of this *plurality* would require a degree of autonomy in economic decision-making to remain with individual member countries and a balance to be struck between national and Community competencies"[31]. On the other side, there is a clear conviction that the success of the ambition to assure the economic, social, cultural and political viability of individual countries will depend upon the perfection of a monetary system capable of maintaining price and exchange stability. The realisation of the single market as it is set forth in the Single European Act,

---

[31] Delors Report, p. 17.

and operationalised in the Economic and Monetary Union to come, will bring with it deep economic integration entailing profound structural changes in the individual member countries. "These changes offer considerable opportunities for economic advancement, but many of the potential gains can only materialise if economic policy – at both national and Community levels – responds adequately to the structural changes." Clearly this "adequacy" is a one-way street, determined not by the "economic, social, cultural and political" viability of member countries, but by the logic, conditions, and givens of the monetary union alone. This is the (new) double-logic of Delors, and – by fiat – of the new European economic and monetary order. The question of economic, social, cultural and political viability returns, in proto-Keynesian clothing, under the sign of monetary prioritisation. The economic, social, cultural and political will follow implicitly from the instrumental presuppositions of monetary well-being. When the "economic" is evoked in the Delors Report it is automatically thematised as "perform-ance", or "convergence or "cooperative policy-making" where the "measure" of these concepts is quantitative or instrumentalised[32]. As a concept the "economic" is socially-culturally enriched, while at the same time being shrunk to the merely quantifiable.

The Tension between the Economic and the Monetary

The relationship between the realm of the economic and the realm of the monetary takes the form of a certain principle of parallelism between the discourses of the economic and the monetary. This parallelism develops into an explicit concept in the Delors Report, with all the inherent ambiguities this entails:

[...] monetary union without a sufficient degree of convergence of economic policies is unlikely to be durable and could be damaging to the Community. Parallel advancement in economic and monetary integration would be indispensable in order to avoid imbalances which could cause economic strains and loss of political support for developing the Community further into an economic and monetary union. Perfect parallelism at each and every point of time would be impossible and could even be counterproductive. Already in the past the advancement of the Community in certain areas has taken place with temporary standstill in others, so that parallelism has been only partial. Some temporary deviations from parallelism are part of the dynamic process of the Community. But bearing in mind the need to achieve a substantial degree of economic union if monetary union is to be successful, and given the degree of monetary coordination already achieved, it is clear that material progress on the

---

[32] Delors Report, p. 15f.

economic policy front would be necessary for further progress in the monetary policy front. Parallelism would have to be maintained in the medium term and also before proceeding from one stage to the next.[33]

Accordingly Delors goes on to outline the double ("parallel") process, which is intended to lead to the definitive form of economic and monetary union. There are two paths to be taken, the economic and monetary, two different (but "parallel") sets of givens, two different parallel goals, two different parallel means etc. This is the same attempt to build a bridge between two approaches as was undertaken in the discussions of the Werner Plan (see the chapter by Verdun).

The "principal steps in stage one", for example, aim at "greater convergence of economic performance through the strengthening of economic and monetary policy coordination within the existing institutional frameworks"[34]. This "convergence" of "performance" involves removal of "physical, technical and fiscal barriers" and the reform of "structural and regional policies". How is consistency between the economic domain and the monetary to be assured? By the participation of the Chairman of the Committee on Central Bank governors in "appropriate Council Meetings". In other words "convergence" of "performance" is the responsibility of the central figure of the monetary organisation. This conception of unilateral "coordination" is the same that structures the work of the Delors committee itself. The resolution of the Summit of Hanover in June, 1988 calling for the formation of the Delors committee also allows for the "president or Governor of the national central banks" to take part in "a personal capacity" in the proceedings of the Committee.

These reflections and the negotiations on how to speed up European integration through monetary unification gained unexpected momentum in November 1989 with the Fall of the Berlin Wall and the re-emergence in France of a perception of a German threat. The transformation of the *Deutsche Mark* into the euro under European supervision became a key instrument in order to control the perceived risks involved in the *Wiedervereinigung* at the EC Council in Strasbourg in December 1989 under French presidency. This French interest in containment of Germany was, as a matter of fact, an exact repeat of the scenario in 1969 when the German *Ostpolitik*, and the fears implicit in the strong DM at that time, was a factor that promoted the Werner Plan[35].

---

[33] Delors Report, p. 32.
[34] Delors Report, p. 34.
[35] Loedel, 1999.

The 1990s and the Third Way

The rest of the chapter is going to discuss how the social came back on the agenda in a more prominent way than during the 1980s, but how it did so under remaining requirements for economic discipline and budget rigidity. It is going to discuss how the development of the European integration project up to around 1990, as it has been analysed above, connected to the developments in the 1990s. It was not the old type of expansive social politics that recurred. At the same time, or somewhat later, as the social returned in a new economic entanglement, the institutional and regulative setting was transformed with a migration of power from the Commission to the Member State governments, from harmonisation to soft law. This migration of power occurred under growing strains between France and Germany, which will also be discussed on the remaining pages of the chapter. The French-German political coordination has from the very beginning been the generator of dynamics in the European post-1945 integration, which makes the strains between them more problematical. We will use our historical map to reflect on the present situation of the European integration.

Maastricht, the Social Protocol and the Treaty of Amsterdam are linked together through the White Paper in 1993 and the Essen Council in 1994. The Luxembourg agreement in 1997, the Employment Pact in Cologne in 1999, and Lisbon in 2000 with the emphasis on the quality of employment are continued indications of a social Europe as a kind of reverse of the monetary discourse, both presupposing and constituting one another. The social and the monetary discourses should not be seen as two parallel tracks but as an entanglement, where the two dimensions presuppose and use each other as critical corrections under mutual transformation. The continuous existence of a social dimension does not say anything about its strength and power or content, of course. Robert Salais is in his chapter critical with respect to the power of the social dimension. In retrospect, ten to twelve years after the social pacts around 1990, the outcome can be described mostly in terms of moderate wage agreements and limited labour market effects.

Moreover, the continuous existence of the social dimension was under permanent adjustment and transformation, as Diamond Ashiagbor so clearly demonstrates in her chapter. This adjustment and transformation was full of contingencies. The question of whether to include employment targets in the convergence criteria or not was discussed during the Inter-Governmental Conference preparing the Maastricht Treaty, but ultimately the insistence of the Member States on retaining employment policy as a national prerogative gained the upper hand. This insistence came particularly from those governments, which in

151

their self-understanding considered themselves as "progressive", and which fell back on well elaborated national welfare and labour market policy traditions.

Nevertheless, the referendum on the TEU in Denmark and France in 1992 and 1993 gave many European policy-makers second thoughts (see in particular the chapter by Ulrike Liebert for this development). A rhetoric of unemployment and a European employment policy emerged. Although social policy was included in the Maastricht approach through the Social Protocol, and thus had a much more solid treaty base than Article 118 in the Rome Treaty, the social dimension was quite subordinated to the macroeconomic dictates. In an attempt to show strength in the social and labour market field the Commission published a White Paper in December, 1993 with the brave and future-oriented title *The Challenges and Ways Forward into the 21st Century*. The framework was the fears that the European project was loosing popular support after the referendums on the Maastricht Treaty in France, in September 1992, and in Denmark, in May 1993. In the assertive White Paper the Commission proposed a massive employment programme through heavy European investments in communication and transport structures. This approach would have required more budget resources to the Commission. Its brave move was tacitly rejected by the governments under transformation of the employment rhetoric, which was set on an alternative track under alignment to the macroeconomic thinking so central in the convergence criteria. The contours of the Stability and Growth Pact took shape through the European Council in Essen in 1994, Dublin in 1996 and Amsterdam in 1997. The meeting in Luxembourg that year confirmed this development of not only employment policy alignment to macroeconomic politics but also of a migration of power from the Commission to the Council, *i.e.* the Member States. The Stability and Growth Pact was not the recurrence of counter-cyclical "Keynesian"/ neoclassical (see Chapter 3) ideas, as they possibly can be traced still in the White Paper in 1993, but the continuity and implementation of the convergence criteria. It must be emphasised that this development has, in particular, been promoted by those governments, which have understood themselves as being more "progressive" in terms of social and employment politics, in particular Germany. This development had very little to do with the implementation of EMU *per se*.

From the philosophy of the Treaty of Rome where the free trade instrument automatically was seen as levelling out differences in labour standards, and where remaining differences were seen as reflections of different degrees of productivity, via the philosophy in the 1970s and 1980s, in the wake of the Werner Plan, of a European labour standard, the arguments in the 1990s again went from European labour legislation to national employment policies coordinated at the European level. This is not to argue that the development had gone full circle back to the 1950s but that elements of the philosophy by then were taken up again. There was one important difference. In the 1950s the whole issue was tucked away in a remote corner, because unemployment was not a problem. In the 1990s the issue was much more centrally embedded in a forceful rhetoric with a pretension of an ability to take action.

Post-National Social Politics in the 1990s

The activation of the social issue before, and, in particular, after Maastricht, as a supplement to the negotiation of the formulation of the monetary and security policies, and as an instrument to integrate potential popular protests, provoked objections not only from the "progressive" governments. Philippe Pochet has demonstrated that the emergence of the concept of subsidiarity was a powerful instrument of such objections. An unholy alliance of British Conservatives, with a neo-liberal blend (Brittan: "[subsidiarity is] an ugly word but a useful concept") and German *Länder* lobbies incorporated a key concept from social catholic doctrines (*Quadragesima Anno 1931* in commemoration of *Rerum Novarum* in 1891) in their arguments against a European social policy[36]. In more secular, *i.e.* less Catholic readings the concept of subsidiarity connoted closely to "nearness", which was a key concept in the neo-liberal flexibility rhetoric.[37] The unholy alliance became even more unholy through the "progressive" opposition to a European regulation.

Was the continuous position of the social question on the European agenda only lip-service without substance? This would be a very biased view. In the 1970s the trade unions put national governments under pressure during the economic crisis, and the governments tried to coordinate their responses to the social pressure at the European level. This was the very meaning of the Eurocorporatist approach. The very fact that the social issue could be moved to the European level is an expression of the mood of crisis. Social politics were historically inscribed in national narrations after class performances and responses to them. This national entrenchment resulted in strong reluctance to giving them up to the European level. In this view the astonishing point is not that the Eurocorporatist efforts were pushed back, or that the Commission's first draft of the social protocol over ten years later were rejected, but that a social protocol could be agreed on at all. Another argument against the "lip-service" view is the emerging subsidiarity

---

[36]   Pochet, 2001.
[37]   Stråth, 2000a.

language, which hardly would have made the breakthrough it made if the threat had not been perceived as both real and dangerous from those who opposed a European social policy. The point here is, however, that the opponents came not only from the Right on a simple right-left schema but also from social democrats afraid of giving up what they perceived as more progressive national schemes. This joint opposition has so far constituted a significant barrier against a European social and employment approach understood in regulative and financial terms.

In the neo-liberal language the social issue more or less disappeared. However, the social issue remained all the time on the agenda, although subordinated to the dictates prescribed by the economists, and adjusted under impression of these dictates. The social problem was not identified in the same terms in 2000 as in the 1970s. Marginalisation and social exclusion emerged silently as social phenomena. For a short while these phenomena were expressed through concepts such as "two-thirds society", but this language disappeared very much under the transformation of the "social language" from "full employment" to "employment through growth and stability" and "quality in employment". The attempts to develop a language to cope with this situation ("two-thirds society") have so far not been very successful. These attempts were all attempts of national politics and they were never really imagined in European terms.

Economy and Social Politics go Separate Ways? The Post-Delors Decline of the European Commission's Legitimacy

The Maastricht process towards the implementation of EMU brought ever more macroeconomic dictates and subordination of the social issues under the convergence criteria. EcoFin and ECB enforced the trade unions to moderate their wage claims. The important long-term development is probably due less to the continuous trial of strength between the social and the monetary issues in European politics than it is to the migration of power from the Commission to the Council, however. After Delors' tenure as President the Commission became weak. Its enforced resignation in 1999 was exceptional but symbolic. Santer and Prodi are not Delors, but it would be a mistake to reduce the power erosion to personal factors. The migration of power must, in particular, be referred to the image of Europe in the Member States and the role Europe has in the perceptions of governments.

A historical case in point is De Gaulle's vision of Europe as nations in the mid-1960s, which clashed with the more post-national views in the Commission, in particular in agricultural politics, to the effect that the President Walter Hallstein was lead to resign. In Nice, in December, 2000 it was obvious that the Council had the full initiative. The arrogant and condescending treatment of Romano Prodi by the French Presidency during the chaotic negotiations is a good illustration of the development in the 1990s of the power relationships between the Council and the Commission. The Method of Open Coordination (MOC) is the new buzz-word for the heavy decision-making, where the governments in the ministerial meetings look for common denominators and agree on compromises which more often than not are at the mini level. The social policy does not represent a pillar like the monetary or the security policies and is not institutionalised and the object of directives to the same extent. What this means for the future prospects of a European social policy remains an open question.

The shift of power from the Commission to the Council was obvious in Luxembourg, but had already been indicated in the reactions to Delors' White Paper in 1993 and is a connection to the kind of European macroeconomic employment politics that failed as a response to the crisis of the 1970s. With Luxembourg in 1997, a political rather than institutional conceptualisation of the construction of Europe recurs. Agreements negotiated among the governments and the coordination of their politics are the condition *sine qua non* for any progress for Europe. This approach opposes the method Delors developed in relation to the ideas of Jean Monnet, where the production of rules precedes and sets the frames of politics. The Luxembourg approach has in fact incorporated the subsidiarity principle as the principle of governance, as Philippe Pochet has recently emphasised[38]. This institutional re-arrangement can be interpreted in two alternative ways:

1. This is what EC/EU has always been, namely a coordination among nation states, in which nobody was ever interested in giving up more competence than necessary to solve problems efficiently. This is the view most pronouncedly expressed by Alan Milward. The intensified use of the concept of integration in the 1950s and 1960s could shift neither the centres of political legitimacy, nor the basis of this legitimacy, mass production of welfare, from the national level. However, as Perry Anderson has eloquently argued in a critical review of Milward's thesis, this does not necessarily mean that there was no political commitment to institutional arrangements aimed at the transgressing of the national level, and there were other factors in the design of the European Community than the welfare concern[39]. Moreover, Milward builds his analysis on the period before the late 1970s and before Delors.

---

[38] Pochet, 2001.
[39] Milward, 1994 and Anderson, 1996a,b.

2. As a reaction to the institution building in the 1980s possible after the adjustment to the crisis in the 1970s, which had provoked a substantial pressure for Western European unification. The fact that EC/EU never really took over the legitimacy for political management of the economy, such as fiscal and social politics, from the nation-states was prevented by the introduction of the subsidiarity argument rather than by EU as basically a nation-state project. The subsidiarity approach contains the contours of a more fundamental shift from one institutional image to several: Europe with two or more speeds, Europe with a vanguard, Europe *à la carte* etc. Joschka Fischer's and Gerhard Schröder's proposals of a European federation (with a strong Commission) can in this scenario be seen as a counter-proposal, which provoked influential French politicians to emphasise "Europe of the nations", which, in turn, fits very well with the images of Europe in the UK and Scandinavia. The euro and the enlargement could possibly both underpin the Luxembourg approach, and promote the recreation of a strong and central European decision-making capacity with institutional expressions. The future is as always open.

Conclusion: Political Economy and European Identity

The roots of the new European identity policy lay in the fact that the political-economic linkage of full employment, budget manipulation and low inflation was replaced by a new regime of mass unemployment and high inflation (so called "stagflation"), which shifted the focus of discussion in the centenary long debate between market and state-oriented economists. A political economy paradigm based on the assumption that economies are nationally governable according to political priorities and management lost credibility. The conceptual topography was realigned towards market, small-scale enterprise, decentralisation, local and regional "networks," entrepreneurship, innovation, flexibility, deregulation, and so on. In this conceptual framework "the region" was identified as a new forum for remedy of economic performance. Compensation for the erosion of political legitimacy at the national level and the collapse of politically governed economics was simultaneously sought at the regional and European levels[40].

The principle of policy coordination through harmonisation was gradually reformulated as rules of mutual recognition. Anything which is permitted in one member State is automatically permitted everywhere in the European Union. This principle effectively destroys national sovereignty and undermines the idea of sovereignty in general, since it implicitly questions the legitimacy behind all political and administra-

---

[40] Burgess, 2001 and Burgess and Tunander, 2000.

tive regulation. However, EMU has changed the preconditions of the mutual recognition approach. The establishing of monetary union has rendered the old tension between national autonomy and EU authority increasingly visible. This tension can no longer be ignored. Monetary union implies a sacrifice of monetary prerogatives and the Maastricht Treaty further imposes restrictions on national fiscal policy[41]. These restrictions hit national symbols because aside from physical frontier lines and border controls and currency few things symbolise a country's sovereignty better than fiscal authority.

EMU means that the institutional preconditions for a *European* political redistribution to the benefit of a more solidaristic Europe becomes possible, and with it a restoration of political responsibility at the European level. The institutions exist but to what extent they can or will be used to achieve any such thing is a political question. It could perhaps be interpreted as a sign that a new attitude is emerging that the harmonisation of business taxation has become topical in Brussels. The ex-Internal Market Commissioner Mario Monti, for instance, has argued that low business taxes should be regarded as illegal state aids: as unfair subsidies to domestic firms at the expense of those based elsewhere in the EU[42]. The return to an old policy guideline, which was expressed by the concept of harmonisation, *could* mean that the contours of a European solution to the failure of the market to tackle unemployment are becoming apparent in EMU. Increasingly the concept of "co-ordination" is cited, in a rather obvious attempt to circumvent the now taboo vocabulary of harmonisation, but is there any difference between the two concepts?

When it is asked how identities and interest definitions have been changed as a consequence of the interaction between national and European bargaining processes, the focus is not so much on trans-national mobility of labour ("free movement of persons") as on the experience in labour markets, historically defined in national terms, in the increasingly competitive international sphere since the 1970s. How have these experiences affected the regulation and norms surrounding national labour markets? To what extent have European standards been developed? These questions indicate a trend towards coordination of labour standards, rather than a movement of labour to areas with most favourable standards, as the Single European Act idea of free movements would have it (without drawing attention to the fact that "most

---

[41] Eichengreen and Frieden (eds), 1998.
[42] *European Economic Perspectives*. Centre for Economic Policy Research, No. 21, February 1999.

favourable standard" is a very contested concept depending on whether it is seen from the viewpoint of the employees or the employers).

If a trend towards the development of a European standard is discernible (see, in particular, the chapter by Robert Salais for a discussion of that question), has this also resulted in the emergence of transnational European solidarity patterns, *i.e.* a kind of European identity? Has the American flexibility discourse been seen as a model to imitate, or does a European regulation rather reflect a resistance to this model? What do concepts like regulation, deregulation and re-regulation mean in this context?

Thus we come to the issue of the connection between the evolution of economic rhetoric, on the one side, and the idea of a European identity, on the other. The European identity, which in the early 1970s had been designed for another role than that it now plays, for a new definition of Europe's role after Bretton Woods, and, later, in support of a Euro-corporatist order, was reformulated to support the connection of the local/regional small-scale level and the large-scale European framework, a connection in which the nation was in some sense bypassed. In this reformulation the idea of a European identity was connected to the new concept of a European citizenship.

The changing framework of this policy means that the language of European identity has gained what it did not have when it was connected to the Euro-corporatist approach in the 1970s, namely an institutional framework. This means that the identity idea can be brought into action in pragmatic politics rather than merely ideologising rhetoric. Whether this institutional framework will promote the linkage of "identity" to politically guaranteed solidarity and social responsibility, or whether the linkage will in fact be to ideas of individual citizenship and individual responsibility is a matter of how the available institutional instruments are used, in other words whether the European Bank is placed under open political control or a disguised political control. (Compare on this point also the chapter by Barbara MacLennan in this volume where she discusses the broader and deeper potential for new perspectives in the wake of the institutional resetting of the European banking world). The open political control fashioned after the model of the *Banque de France*, would in some sense preserve the politicisation and ideologisation of European economic matters, thereby holding open a certain continuity between the economic technocracy and the social and cultural fabric of the continent. The politically detached model, fashioned after the model of the Bundesbank would be more apt to favour a more technical or technocratic, and less overtly political approach to the questions of economic policy. However, the decisive point is not this difference but the fact that the German policy tradition wants to anchor the "independence" of the ECB in a strong European economic policy confirmed by the German insistence on the convergence criteria. Through the economic policy and the convergence criteria the operative framework of the ECB is politically set in the direction of a strong Commission. The French tradition prefers a focus on monetary policy where the economic political dimension becomes less important and where the monitoring is more a matter under the control of the Council, *i.e.* the Member States.

Economic-political coordination (SGP) does not necessarily mean expansive and employment creative. The German emphasis on the convergence criteria and the SGP can rather be seen as an expression of the opposite dictated by the interest in a strong European currency as a substitute for the DM. The political control of the monetary regime does not necessarily mean a philosophy of monetary and fiscal rigidity. The French position can rather be seen as less rigid than the German. These differences between German and French priorities reflect deeper divergences concerning power and control, however, provoked by the introduction of the euro. The problem of this German-French competition is less whether the focus should be economic or monetary policy but whether there is institutional strength to control/coordinate at a European level in mutual interaction and in interaction with employment and social goals. The German-French competition can be seen as an illustration of what we said at the beginning of this chapter, that the transfer of meaning, in the wake of the introduction of the euro, can be experienced as a threat to the traditional sovereignty of individual nations. The fact that this experienced threat has a specific German-French touch can also be seen as an issue about the political control of Europe and its money. The control of the money requires political power.

How are in this scenario the varying perspectives of a variegated European cultural identity to be concretely applied to the politics of the European Central Bank regarding the question of work/employment? How can we understand the German-French competition historically?

Since the early 1950s the Commission has had three strong Presidents: Jean Monnet, Walter Hallstein and Jacques Delors. It is not by chance that they all were either French or German. Nor was it by chance that two of the presidents – the French – were successful while the third – the German – was forced by the French President De Gaulle to resign. The French-German axis has been the motor of the European integration from the very beginning. However, it has not been an axis between two equals. The German government has always had to demonstrate its European credibility whereas the French government has always had the pretension of representing Europe, to speak on behalf of

Europe. Germany has had to be European, while France has been Europe and told Germany what being European meant.

This opposition has been particularly palpable in two turbulent situations since 1945. The turbulence has meant among other things that German credibility was at stake. The German government had at these occasions to demonstrate its Europeanness. In 1969-1970 the German *Ostpolitik* provoked a German *Westpolitik* and the Werner Plan, as Hubert Zimmermann demonstrates in this volume. In a parallel fashion the German *Wiedervereinigung* in 1989 provoked the replacement of the *Deutsche Mark* by the euro and the establishment of EMU on French initiative.

The problem for Germany, France and for Europe is that through its response to this latter crisis Germany became too European. When it gave up its currency in exchange for a European currency Germany also became much more immediately interested in exerting control on European politics, *i.e.* in being or representing Europe rather than just demonstrating good Europeanness. This was the unintended and unforeseen consequence of the integration of the unified Germany into the European project. The same situation, seen from the French horizon, prevailed in the mid-1960s when a German President of the Commission became a threat as a representative of a stronger Europe. In the 1990s the German interest in controlling Europe and its new money was demonstrated through its interest in the Stability and Growth Pact as a kind of guarantee of the value of the new money. We have seen a demonstration of the old German interest in being good Europeans for the sake of credibility through offers of a tighter binding of Germany into the European project, as a kind of counter-weight to the fears that this German interest in control of the money might have provoked. On three occasions prominent German politicians have suggested steps for a federal Europe, in September 1994 the CDU-politicians Karl Lamers and Wolfgang Schäuble, in May 2000 the Green Foreign Minister Joschka Fischer and in May 2001 Chancellor Gerhard Schröder. More than anything else these suggestions have provoked French concern. The SGP and the German interest in controlling the euro have eroded the French self-understanding as the true representatives and spokesmen of Europe. The summit in Nice in December 2000 was a clear demonstration of this erosion. Now the French interest seems to be in stopping Germany from being too European, which no doubt is quite a change. The old basis of the European integration, the relationships between Germany and France, is in desperate need of new imagination in order to avoid a disintegrative spiral in the framework of the enlargement. The migration of power from the Commission to the Council has occurred simultaneously with the emergence of the SGP.

This migration can possibly be seen as an attempt to check the German interest in control of the European money. The outcome of this attempt to establish a counter-weight might well be the development of the EU into a kind of United Nations of Europe.

In the 1970s, in the debate about what should come first, the economic-political or monetary unification, the economists were represented by the Germans and the monetarists by the French[43]. This opposition continues in the views on the European Central Bank around 2000 expressed by the German and the French governments. However, the difference can also be related to a more general political-cultural opposition: the French view on Europe as a cooperation of the nation states and Germany's much stronger political interest in a European federation, which has been evident since the 1950s, and most recently demonstrated by the proposals by Joschka Fischer and Gerhard Schröder. It is in this field of opposed priorities that the development of the EMU will take place, where so far Germany and France have constituted the hub of the European dynamics. However, history does not mean all, and it does not give us much guidance to the question of whether the EMU will move in an economist or a monetarist, a federal or an interstate direction.

---

[43] *Cf.* Amy Verdun's chapter in this volume.

CHAPTER 5

The Political Transaction Costs of the Convergence Criteria – The EMU Compromise from the Delors Committee to Maastricht

Lars MAGNUSSON and Jan OTTOSSON

Introduction[1]

The role and function of the convergence criteria has been a much-discussed topic in the literature regarding the making of EMU. It has been suggested that the purpose of such criteria was to function as an instrument to punish small countries. We will in this chapter show the usefulness of using modern neo-institutional theory, especially political transaction costs, in further understanding the logic behind the convergence criteria, a process which started with the Delors committee and ended with the Maastricht Treaty document, outlining EMU and ECB from the perspective of political transaction cost theory. Also it is argued that the making and implementation of these criteria lowered the political transaction costs. We suggest that a discussion concerning the evolution of the political contract might be fruitful in order to further explore the mechanisms of the political economy of the EMU project. The complex making of the convergence criteria is a good example in interpreting the interplay between political and economic factors in policy outcome. Hence, it might be good reason to further discuss the subsequent structural changes in the economy, as well as the complex interplay between the international financial system and the EMU policy process.

---

[1] The authors would like to thank Bo Stråth, Amy Verdun, Hubert Zimmerman, Robert Salais and the other participants in the volume for helpful suggestions and comments. Our ongoing discussions with Torbjörn Strandberg have been of great value for us. Many thanks to Sylvie Pascucci in handling practical matters. Finally, thanks to Paul Rouse for helping us with the editing.

In the following we will first give a short historical account of the period between the Werner Plan and the making of the EMU. This is followed by some remarks on the political transaction cost approach to political economy, which is developed further by studying the convergence criteria from a political transaction cost perspective. There then follows some remarks to conclude the chapter.

The Background

After the golden years of economic growth, the new economic landscape of Western Europe in the 1970s and 1980s was accompanied by new monetary regimes. The era of stagflation also saw the Bretton Woods system of exchange rates being replaced by a free-floating managed exchange rate in Europe after the breakdown of Bretton Woods in 1971, and the first oil shock in 1973. This changed the conditions for the financial markets. It also changed the conditions for the national economies of the West European countries. The politicians faced high levels of unemployment, together with rising price levels. The economic policy measures of the "Keynesian era" were used but with rather dismal results. The problems of stagflation, at the time viewed only as temporary business cycle phenomena, were reflecting a changing industrial structure of the Western industrialised world. The restructuring of the industrial sector, from the traditional assembly line production towards an increasing tendency towards flexible production was at hand. One underlying force of this transformation was the increasing international competition, mirrored by a higher degree of international economic integration. The slowdown of the growth of the industrial sector continued, giving way for a rise of the service sector in several Western economies[2].

During the late 1970s and the early 1980s national political regimes were increasingly pressed from two sides. The expanding international financial markets and the deregulated national financial sectors pressed politicians towards a higher degree of international pressure. In the early 1980s several economies in Western Europe experienced increasing internal economic problems. This raised the question of the role of monetary regimes in relation to the need, as seen by the actors, of using the devaluation as a way of handling asymmetrical shocks. The traditional macroeconomic policy measures of handling a troublesome economic situation, *i.e.* taxation, rising public expenditures, and devaluation, resulting in high budget deficits were the main outcomes of national policy actions. These measures became more costly to use, due

---

[2]   See Magnusson, 2000, regarding the notion of a Third Industrial Revolution; Kitschelt *et al*, 2000.   ,

to the responses of the international capital market. Also, the national policy measures were suddenly inefficient, and could sometimes make a troublesome situation even worse. The expected result of increasing economic activity through, *e.g.* interest rate reduction often ended up in increasing capital flows[3]. Governments faced a larger degree of international pressure, while at the same time experiencing that the traditional policy measures were not sufficient[4].

The political uncertainty and the new economic climate paved the way for increasing political pressure from the voters. The political actors on the national level were therefore facing a higher degree of uncertainty. As a reaction and a response to the new problems, new policy regimes introduced neo-liberal measures. However, the trend towards neo-liberal convergence has by no means always been clear. Instead, the diversity of policy choices among European countries seems obvious[5].

The structural changes and the subsequent economic crises were also accompanied by new monetary regimes. The breakdown of the Bretton Woods system was followed by the European political initiative to introduce the "snake" in 1973[6]. The aim of the "snake" was to limit fluctuations between the exchange rates of the currencies within the EC at the time[7]. The European positive attitude toward pegged exchange rates has been attributed to negative historical experiences of free floating exchange rates, due to a higher degree of trade, and, thus, a high degree of sensitivity regarding the exchange rates[8]. Already during the 1960s an increasing suspicion toward the dominant American position

---

[3] The internationalisation and integration of the world financial market has been described as far more far-reaching since the 1970s compared with the integration of goods and services. For an overview of the arguments behind the capital market integration and the deregulation process, see further Simmons, 2000, p. 36.

[4] Jonung, 1999 and Kitschelt *et al* 2000.

[5] See Iversen and Pontusson, 2000, p. 2.

[6] Both economic and political factors were at hand when The Hague EC Summit discussed these questions in December 1969. The Werner Plan emanating from this summit suggested a plan for increasing economic policy coordination as well as monetary integration stage by stage, with the aim of forming a monetary union, see Zimmerman's chapter in this volume.

[7] Dyson, 1994 and Dyson and Featherstone, 1999, p. 2.

[8] Eichengreen suggests the experiences from the 1930s, the greater degree of trade, and the construction of the common agricultural policy, Eichengreen, 1998, p. 210. Eichengreen has also discussed the role of economic factors in the process leading to the EMU. He emphasises the process itself, claiming that the structure and the governance of the union will largely determine the success of the union. One important empirical finding by Eichengreen concludes that economic integration among European countries increased the potential for such countries being prepared for a monetary union, see Eichengreen, 1998 and Eichengreen, 1996, p. 152.

in the world economy was articulated in France especially. Also, a strong preference among several key EC states against free-floating exchange rates was also at hand[9]. The currencies within the "snake" should within certain limits follow the fluctuations of the dollar. The arrangement of the "snake" continued until 1979. After the English and the French decisions to step out of the "snake", their move was followed by other countries.

During the 1970s and the 1980s increasing problems with inflation and increasing unemployment in several European countries paved the way for new economic policy goals. Price stability, currency stability and a tendency to favour public finance being kept in balance started to be new keywords among politicians and economists as well. The German Bundesbank became a new economic-political model favouring the new "stability culture[10]". At the same time the economic integration of Europe gained new ground[11].

In the late 1970s, with the collapse of the dollar in 1977-78, a new political situation was at hand with new political leadership in Western Germany and France, respectively. A new mechanism, the EMS was introduced in 1979, initiated by the German and French political leaders[12]. The aim of the EMS was to introduce monetary stability to Europe. Once again, the timing coincided with external shocks to the system, due to the second oil crisis[13]. Also, unstable dynamics appeared due to the problematic balance between free trade and capital controls when the EMS was launched after the breakdown of the "snake". Since the European market integration was mobilised through increasing liberalisation, the control mechanisms of the exchange rates became less effective. The fast growing international financial markets were also important in this respect. The EMS was never fully implemented and experiencied severe problems during the first years. This statement applies of course somewhat differently regarding what time period is considered. The first period between 1979 and 1983 was turbulent. During the second period between 1983 and 1987, the EMS won greater confidence due to the French decision to stay within the EMS and the

---

[9]   See also Zimmerman's contribution in this volume.
[10] Dyson and Featherstone, 1999, p. 2, Verdun, 2000, Verdun and Christiansen, 2000 and Ungerer, 1999.
[11] Another important economic factor regarding the economic integration was the concern regarding the uncertainty of the economic impact of the Common Agricultural Policy in the late 1960s, see Dyson and Featherstone, 1999, p. 1, Eichengreen, 1996 and Verdun's contribution in this volume.
[12] The EMS was later agreed upon by all Member States, see Verdun, 2000.
[13] Ashworth, 1987, p. 312.

Basle-Nyborg agreement. A relatively better performance by the EMS was shown in the late 1980s[14].

The EMS was in some respects rather well functioning in the latter part of the 1980s[15]. The inflation was lower, and the exchange rates were beginning to be rather stable. On the other hand, there were signs of a growing political problem. Italy and France were uneasy with the German dominant asymmetry within the EMS. Also, another economic factor of growing importance was the emerging capital markets, meaning larger flows of capital, together with the political will to integrate the European capital markets into a single market. Both these factors were contributing to destabilise the EMS[16].

It was still an open question in the mid-1980s whether or not a new European monetary regime could have any chance being launched. There were economic arguments in favour of a monetary union. The political costs for small open economies might be very high if the country had to adjust to volatile exchange rate swings[17]. Therefore, there might be high political incentives to create monetary unions, despite the absence of traditional OCA criteria. There were, however, also examples of political hesitancy and resistance. Germany's official policy proclaimed that a monetary union had to be foregone by a slow process of integrating various markets paving the way for economic performance.

After one and a half decades with EMS (the "snake" etc.) the European nations were ready in 1988 to return to an idea which had already been launched in the form of the Werner Plan in the early 1970s but since then had remained in the backwater of European politics: the idea of creating an economic and monetary union in Europe. Most certainly, the content of the proposal which came out of the initiative by the Hanover European Council Meeting in June 1988 to form a Committee led ·by Jacques Delors, was designed quite differently than the

---

[14] See Szász, 1999, p. 178, who emphasises the important role of the complex relation between France and Germany during EMS. Gros & Thygesen, 1998, suggest that the EMS "was a succesful response [...] of the late 1970s".

[15] Szász, 1999, pp. 66-67.

[16] Padoa and Schioppa *et al.*, 1987, and see reference in Dyson and Featherstone, 1999, p. 3.

[17] Eichengreen's standpoint emphasises the economic factors at play mainly through increased European economic integration. Also, the interaction between the economic integration and the fast growing international financial markets limits the actual choices of national macroeconomic manoeuvring. By emphasising the making of the EMU as a process, Eichengreen points out the interplay between the integration process and the monetary unification. See Eichengreen, 1996, pp. 167, 195ff.

previous Werner Plan. The most important difference was without doubt the emphasis put by the Delors Committee – when its Report was launched in 1989 – on a strict monetary union and an independent European central bank. Moreover, in contrast to the Werner Plan, the Delors Report did not suggest a common European fiscal and invest-ment policy[18]. Further, there was no longer any mention of an all-European Monetary fund or any proposals for a collaborative European Keynesian-inspired demand and income policy. Another important difference was the discussion raised by the Delors report regarding the criteria to be fulfilled before entering the monetary union.

It has been discussed ever since why the debate on a monetary union opened again in 1988. It seemed at the time a defunct idea due to the increasing tensions between Western Germany and France regarding the value of the DM in the latter half of the 1980s[19]. We can also ponder the relative ease by which the monetary union was inserted into the Maastricht Treaty in 1991[20]. The suggestions made by the Delors committee as well as the final policy document to launch a number of steps – three as a matter of fact – to establish a European central bank and a common currency has mainly been regarded as a compromise between Germany and France-Italy.

Since the 1970s the Germans had pleaded for "the economist's" view which stated that a future monetary union – which everybody paid lip-service to – in Europe must be preceded by a significant period of economic integration. On the other side the French and Italians – who held the "the monetarist" view – had made it clear that they rather saw the creation of a monetary union as a push for further integration.

In early 1988 both the French and Italian finance ministers criticised the EMS. Soon enough the initiative taken by Italy and France was followed by German Foreign Minister Genscher, who, contrary to the earlier official German Bundesbank opinion, proposed to create a European Central Bank. Despite the traditional opinion expressed by German Finance Minister Stoltenberg, the political process was running. Based on the Genscher initiative, Mitterand and Kohl decided to move on with the question of finding a new base for a European Monetary Union. During the Hanover meeting (Hanover European Council) in June 1988 the Delors Committee was created *ad hoc*. The mission of the

---

[18] The Werner Plan was not fully clear on what kind of fiscal policy would be created. The authors would like to thank Amy Verdun for this remark.

[19] In the latter part of the 1980s, especially in 1987, the EMS was however rather well functioning, see Verdun, 2000 and Gros and Thygesen, 1998.

[20] Some scholars argue that one important factor in this respect was the relatively better performance of the EMS at the time, see Verdun, 2000.

committee was to study how the EMU could be formed. As Dyson and Featherstone note, this was of course an elegant way of bypassing the troubled question whether or not a European economic and monetary union was advantageous for the Member States.

At the Hanover meeting it was decided that all central bankers would constitute the committee, chaired by President Delors. Also, well-reputed economists, such as Thygesen, were appointed to the committee. The German position was that the central bankers would guarantee the legitimacy of the committee. However, the British un-official position was that the central bankers could be expected to block any further development towards a European Monetary Union. The British hope was in vain, however[21]. The Report was published in April 1989 and contained a plan made up by three stages on how to build a European Monetary Union. The Report was signed by all the bank governors of the European Community, and several parts of the Delors Report were also found in the Maastricht Treaty[22].

The reaction after the publication of the Delors Report in April 1989 was marked by critical reaction from England. There was some concern among the other EC states to proceed with the project, but on the other hand, with a very critical English attitude towards the EMU, it was considered to be a rather long-term process of implementing the EMU. Despite the agreement to discuss the EMU question further on, there was no fixed date for the planned intergovernmental conference (IGC).

The unforeseen rapid development during the autumn of 1989 in Germany speeded up the process. After the collapse of East Germany in November 1989 and the subsequent turmoil, there was French concern regarding the future position of a unified Germany. At the Strasbourg meeting in December 1989, a date of twelve months later was fixed for an IGC on EMU. Also, the future of a political union was also listed for discussion by an IGC[23]. These events were also based upon the concern regarding the future role of the new Germany[24]. During the Maastricht Council in December 1991, the EMU negotiations were finalised. It is clear that political matters were involved in the formulation of the EMU project, as it became included in the Maastricht Treaty. Pivotal to the

---

[21] Thatcher's position was criticised by several politicians in England, who opposed the idea of supporting the making of a committee at all.

[22] The main problem at this point was the position of England. Thatcher's view – as well as Nigel Lawson, the Chancellor – was very critical towards the question of a monetary union in Europe. The Governor of the Bank of England signed the Report, despite the criticism from the Prime Minister, see Dyson and Featherstone, 1999, p. 4; Scász, 1999.

[23] As shown by Dyson and Featherstone, 1999, p. 4.

[24] As noted by Dyson and Featherstone, 1999, p. 4

understanding of the German acceptance was also the Delors committee's stark commitment to price stability as an overreaching policy goal[25].

Political Transaction Costs

The background to the ideas of forming a monetary union in Europe, embodied in the the EMU project in general, and more specifically the EMU negotiations between 1988 and 1991, might be understood in terms of both economic and political dimensions. We will now go on to interpret the policy action in terms of the notion of political transaction costs, as developed by the late Mancur Olson, Oliver Williamson, and Avinash Dixit, respectively[26]. In recent years, the theoretical school labelled "New Institutional Economics" (NIE) regarding the role of institutions in the economy has become well known[27]. This approach has been influenced by, for example, contract theory which combines a more process-oriented and perhaps also a more realistic view of economic policy[28]. According to this approach, bounded rational actors try to cope with an uncertain and complex political world, where transaction costs are an important element of real world economies. In an important contribution drawing upon Williamson's model, Avinash Dixit has developed a set of analytical tools that can be used to discuss "political transaction costs"[29]. This is a welcome attempt to initiate a more formal discussion regarding the basis of political action which so far has been lacking in most new institutional economics[30].

Dixit applies the familiar "transaction cost" notions of uncertainty, complexity, information impact, opportunism, and asset specificity, within the field of political decision making in a dynamic context. By applying these notions also in the field of policy, Dixit shows conclusively that given such restraints, the analysis of policy measures necessarily needs to include the difference between policy aims and policy outcomes. The reason for this difference is constituted by the incompleteness of contracts.

A central theme is the complexity of the political contract, exemplified by the constitution. These contracts are less complete than eco-

---

[25] The process is described in great detail by Dyson and Featherstone, 1999.

[26] Williamson, 1996; Olson, 2000; Dixit, 1996.

[27] The argument regarding the political transaction cost approach is similar and in some respects quoted from the standpoint further developed in Magnusson and Ottosson, 2000.

[28] See Williamson, 1996 and Crocker, 1996.

[29] Dixit, 1996. See also Dugger, 1993.

[30] *Cf.* for example North, 1990.

nomic contracts, due to high transaction costs in the political environment. The consequence of such incomplete contracts is seen as more problematic in the political field, compared with economic transactions. The reason for this is the long-term character of constitutional arrangements. The incompleteness of such contracts also gives "large variations in the way a given rule operates. [...] In other words, an incomplete constitution can be manipulated by the participants to serve their own aims[31]".

Due to the differences between the economic and political fields of decision-making, it is more costly to enforce policy reforms, since monitoring and incentive contracts are more complicated to use in the political arena. The case with state agencies implementing various policy decisions illustrates further the complexity of the principal-agent problem. Since there are a multiplicity of agency relationships in public administration, this complicates the moral hazard problem.

One important aspect concerns the chosen paths of implementation. Implementation in this sense can be seen as a rather wide range of policy measures. One of the most important aspects of implementation is the making and the function of multi-purpose, multi-principal state agencies. In contrast with principal-agent relationships in the economic world, it is not always clear which of the parties in the political world are agents and principals. Instead, government agencies are often responsible towards several principals, sometimes with diverging interests, leading to a higher degree of incomplete contracts and unclear lines of authority[32]. These agencies are seen as crucial both regarding the timing and the content of political reforms.

Since such agencies implement policies in different ways, the outcome of these policies are not always predictable. Moreover, as political reforms will be implemented through state agencies, earlier lock-in events will affect the outcome of such policy measures in ways not always anticipated by the actors themselves. This is close to the view of Anne Krueger, who argues that regulatory systems after a while seem to live their own life[33]. This discussion illuminates the importance of taking account of the transaction costs in the political system, characterised by a higher degree of uncertainty, different rules of selection (voting systems etc.), and unclear principal-agent relationships. This also highlights the role of government agencies in a more pronounced way, allowing more nuances in the discussion of the actual function of

---

[31] Dixit, 1996, quote, pp. 20-21.
[32] Wilson, 1989, Chapter 17 and Dixit, 1996, p. 56.
[33] Krueger, 1996, pp. 169-218. For a pertinent discussion of regulations in a historical perspective, see Goldin and Libecap, 1994.

interest groups. Further, we argue, such a transaction cost analysis of the political system also allows us to further explore the actual role of history in explaining the initiating and the outcome of policy and regulatory processes. Since path-dependent organisational and political procedures will influence such implementation through various informal rules, routines, and the actors' mental models in a complex environment, the role of history will be of immense importance in understanding the way various policies are chosen and implemented.

This notion of the role of history is of course close to North's version of new institutional economics, where initial conditions together with various lock-in effects shape path dependent patterns. This may lead to sub-optimal institutional settings, enduring for long periods of time. In a broad sense this notion of path dependency challenges the neo-classical paradigm through its recognition of the importance of institutions and the role of history[34]. Thus, increasing returns, network externalities, and learning effects all reinforce the path chosen in the past. It is of course important to acknowledge the two major conditions that North emphasises. In order to apply the notion of path dependence within the analysis of institutions, both increasing returns and imperfect markets must exist. In the context of EMU and the convergence criteria, the notion of incomplete political contracts might be appropriate to study further[35].

Political Transaction Costs and the Convergence Criteria

In the following we will illustrate the notion of political transaction costs with regard to the case of the convergence criteria. It has been argued that the criteria only functioned as tool of punishment, and the small countries were suffering from the construction of such criteria. Some discussion – both political and scholarly – has been devoted to the convergence criteria that were already suggested by the Delors group and later on were included in the actual convergence criteria. The four convergence criteria required the states to fulfil four economic goals during phase three. In the timetable for EMU in the Maastricht Treaty, three stages together with four convergence criteria were involved[36]. Low inflation (defined as within a range of 1.5% compared with the three best performing states in the union), a maximum budget deficit of 3% of GDP, a debt level below 60% of GDP, no devaluation of the participants' currency in the ERM during the previous two years, and

---

[34] North, 1990; David, 1985, pp. 332–7; David, 1994, Setterfield, 1993, Magnusson and Ottosson, 1997.

[35] Dixit, 1996, pp. 93 and 107.

[36] Stage 2 started, as agreed, on 1 January 1994.

finally, stable interest rates, measured as a rate within 2% compared with the three best performing states. According to Gros and Thygesen it was in the formulation of these criteria that the "economist" or "fundamentalist" (German-Dutch) view found its main expression while the rapid timetable was an expression of the "telescopic" French-Italian view[37]. Hence, the argument from the German side won acceptance that the economies of the participating nations at least to some extent must have reached a certain stability – price and budget stability – before entering the union[38].

As the criteria only include formal macroeconomic entities these criteria seem illogical if a fuller integration between the economies was what was wanted. It is somewhat difficult to explain the specific features of the criteria only from a political actor perspective.

Instead it might be more appropriate to further discuss some key components of the political transaction cost model. Since the actors were experiencing a high degree of uncertainty during the process of modeling the EMU, and the possible outcomes of other actors in countries experiencing turbulent macroeconomic conditions, one key strategy according to the incompleteness of the political contract, both *ex ante* and *ex post*, was to try to handle the uncertainty by shaping contractual arrangements, which made it possible to keep the entry levels up. That made it possible to actually monitor the actors, keeping down monitor costs, it also helped to keep down information and search costs. The making of the complex, multiprincipal political contract of EMU was indeed a turbulent process. This made the dynamics of the political contract itself problematic in relation to the outcome. The making of rules and criteria regarding the entry of countries and the eventual reinforcements are central in this aspect. The multiplicities of principals with changing preferences in a dynamic setting have been of special interest. This may end up in low-powered incentives. However, as Dixit mentioned, the low-powered incentives may be the result of high political transaction costs, and thus the only way of coping with such specific transaction costs. We suggest that in order to cope with the radical uncertainty regarding the potential future action of countries applying for membership of the EMU, it could be argued that the bounded rational actors tried to deal with radical uncertainty through lowering some of the political transaction costs. It is more costly to enforce policy reforms, since monitoring and incentive contracts are more complicated to use in the political arena. This is also true when

---

[37] Gros and Thygesen, 1998.
[38] The debate of the convergence criteria is described in Walsh, 2000, pp. 97-98.

studying the EMU process. The notion of the bounded rational actors makes also the political actors' strategies more comprehensive.

However, the transaction cost theory explanation has been opposed mainly by political scientists. They have argued strongly against structural explanations, instead suggesting that policy games interprets the process of the EMU in a more refined way[39]. Some of the most common explanations within this field might be appropriate to mention here. The complementary intergovernmental bargaining type of explanation suggests that European integration might best be understood as a policy learning process. This learning process among politicians will lead to a convergence of policy preferences. The bargaining process is vital in the analysis, especially the process of finding mutual fields of interest[40]. The neo-functional explanation suggests a spill-over effect regarding integration from other policy sectors, further developed by national elites, with changing attitudes at the EC level as a result. Quite opposingly, the idea of the neo-federalist approach gives an important role to political ideas and visions empowered by elites and insightful politicians.

Dyson is critical of both economic theories rooted in new institutional economics, especially transaction cost theories, and theories suggesting that the role of the rise of financial markets and real economic change were important background factors in the EMU process. In contrast to some economists concerned with the EMU question, he argues that merely structural factors by themselves hardly explain the making of EMU[41]. Instead, policy actors are seen as crucial in every stage of the process. The economic conditions are merely seen as structuring the decisions made by policy actors. Neither the question of trade and economic integration of Europe seems to fulfil the necessary requirement in order to explain the outcome of the process. Further, the growing financial markets are not seen as the important underlying force, limiting political decisions to a narrow scope.

---

[39] Dyson discusses nine structural interpretations of monetary integration. They comprise both old and new approaches to structural explanations. The global structuralist explanation, as further developed by Susan Strange according to Dyson, emphasise the role of the United States and the rise of the financial markets. To sum up Dyson's own view, he suggests that a two-level policy game is rewarding in explaining the reasons behind the outcome of the EMU project.

[40] The policy learning approach, with Heclo, Weir and Skocpol as leading proponents, according to Dyson, has also been further developed by Swedish economist Lars Jonung (1999) in analysing politicians responses to asymmetric chocks in the Swedish economy.

[41] Dyson, 1994, p. 301ff.

Regarding the transaction cost explanation, as in the case of reducing transaction costs of economic exchange in European economic integration, the same arguments could be found also in the case of European Monetary Union. The implication of such an approach would suggest that policy actors would recognise the potential of reducing transaction costs further by a monetary union. However positive to several aspects of the transaction cost approach in this respect, Dyson argues that the will of the policy actors are not at hand in the transaction cost economics (TCE)-approach[42]. Also with reference to theories of path dependence, Dyson is highly critical, despite their "seductive power[43]". The main reason is once again the failure to take the will of the actors seriously. However, as we have argued above, Dyson's reference both to the TCE-approach, and the path dependence approach is somewhat limited. Instead we suggest that the TCE-approach should be complemented with the discussion regarding political transaction costs in this respect. The notion of political transaction costs opens up alternative analytic instruments. It points in a direction where both the political scene and the economic environment become more understandable. It makes more sense for policy-making rather than only functionalist arguments, or arguments emphasising only the role of ideology. It also makes changes in the economic environment of the political actors important.

We have argued elsewhere that there might be limitations in only using the concept of political transaction costs in the neoclassical inspired analysis. The transaction cost analysis must be discussed within a particular institutional framework and a specific incentive structure. We have also argued that there might be good reason also to include a path dependent factor using TCE in explaining dynamic processes in the market place[44]. This would mean that not only the transaction cost argument *per se* would be acknowledged. We suggest that the broader concept of political transaction costs might be fruitful in analysing the EMU process. The political transaction cost argument also permits a better understanding of the rationale and limitations behind policy actions. However, it should also be pointed out that an evolutionary process and a political search process makes it difficult to point out the most efficient policy solution in terms of political transaction costs. Rather, political transaction costs combined with the notion of path dependence might be more appropriate in order to better understand

---

[42] From an economist viewpoint, a critical argument in this respect is made by Barry Eichengreen, who argues that the benefits of economic integration in Europe are clear. But the potential of monetary union is less obvious, see Eichengreen, 1998.

[43] Dyson, 1994, p. 314.

[44] Magnusson and Ottosson, 1996, p. 353.

which historical factors in a given situation influences the actual policy. It makes it also possible to further study unintentional consequences, since the process of implementation becomes more transparent. The adaptive capacity and the learning process of bounded rational actors facing a situation of uncertainty thus remains central in explaining the outcome of the convergence criteria.

Conclusions

To sum up this discussion of political transaction costs in relation to explanations regarding the making of the EMU in general and the convergence criteria in particular, it seems to us that the role of transaction costs might be developed. In this context, we suggest that the notion of incomplete political contracts might be appropriate for further study. In the case of convergence criteria, several principals were involved in repeated games over the making of a common agency, the ECB and the making of rules and criteria regarding the entry of countries and the eventual reinforcements are central in this aspect. The multiplicities of principals with changing preferences in a dynamic setting have been of special interest. Our argument is that the bounded rational actors tried to cope with both an uncertain environment, and other actors with diverging interests. This may end up in low-powered incentives. However, as Dixit mentions, the low-powered incentives may be the result of high political transaction costs, and thus the only way of coping with such specific transaction costs. In the specific case with the convergence criteria, the action of introducing such criteria, might be understood in the light of such an uncertain environment, and the historical patterns of the opportunistic behaviour of other economies. The other option, free-floating exchange rate mechanisms, or a monetary union without power incentives, was not necessarily the best option available for politicians in countries with a high degree of trade, and a high degree of integration. One conclusion in this respect is that it makes it worthwhile to further study the interaction between economic and political factors determining political transaction costs and political constraints in the making of EMU.

PART II

FINANCIAL INSTITUTIONS AND ECONOMIC THEORY

CHAPTER 6

The ECB, Banking, Monetary Policy and Unemployment

Sheila C. Dow

The purpose of this chapter is to consider the implications for unemployment in Europe of the way in which the monetary system in Europe is developing. There have been dramatic changes in Europe, partly as a result of policy on European integration, partly due to market forces. These changes have affected the structure of European banking, the place of banks in the wider financial sector, and the role of the state in relation to banks, not only in terms of regulation but also in terms of monetary policy. Given the importance of finance for output and employment, and the importance of banks in this process, and monetary authorities for banks, this is an important dimension in considering the future political economy for Europe.

It is important to take a historical perspective on these forces operating within Europe. By considering the logic behind the evolution of the banking sector, we are able to understand the forces currently in operation, and to form a view about their future direction. I therefore consider the background to the over-expansion of credit in the 1970s alongside the emerging plans for European monetary integration. The consequences of this over-expansion are traced through the 1980s and 1990s alongside the emergence of plans for EMU. I then consider the current state of affairs, first in terms of the structure of banking in Europe and, then, in terms of EMU itself, before concluding with an assessment of future prospects.

But first I consider the underlying argument, that the structure of banking and the design of the monetary system in Europe have significance for the real side of the economy, *i.e.* output and employment.

179

Sheila C. Dow

Banking, Monetary Policy and Unemployment: What is the Connection?

As we shall see when we explore the development of ideas on European monetary integration, it is a substantive question, whether the financial system and monetary policy impact on the real economy, and if so what that impact is. There is an influential body of thought in economics – influential, we shall see, for the design of European Monetary Union – which sees money as being "neutral", *i.e.* having no impact on real variables such as output and employment, at least in the long run. Monetary policy is designed to influence the amount of money in the economic system either directly through direct controls, or more commonly indirectly by setting interest rates. The money supply and interest rates determine the level of demand in the economy; according to this view, the demand for money is stable. This means that any increase in its supply, relative to this stable demand, is spent, feeding through into an increase in the demand for goods and services. The supply of goods and services is determined by the supply of labour and (physical) capital and the state of technology. The supply of labour in turn is determined by conditions in the labour market, at the level of full employment if the market is competitive. So any change in demand for goods and services only impacts on prices; monetary policy is thus understood to be neutral. There may be some non-neutrality in the short run, if producers and workers do not predict correctly that monetary policy will only affect the general price level and therefore they temporarily adjust supply. The idea of transparency in monetary policy is to reduce the scope for confusion and thus for these real effects in the short run.

This simple textbook statement of affairs, however, does not include what are seen as the beneficial long term real effects of anti-inflationary policy, which derive from increased efficiency and stability of expectations. Both are seen as enhancing the supply side of the economy and thus promoting economic growth. The same rationale is applied to the financial sector. Growth is enhanced the more efficient is the financial sector in meeting the needs of borrowers and lenders alike; this seen as being achieved by greater freedom of movement of (financial) capital. Where there are barriers to entry to local financial markets, or regulatory impediments, the optimal growth rate will not be achieved.

However, there is another body of thought on which we will build in this chapter, and which sees monetary policy as being non-neutral. Monetary policy is thus seen as having real economic effects, even in the long run, and the removal of barriers to entry as well as deregulation in the banking sector are seen as having real effects which are not necessarily growth-enhancing. If it is the case that demand-deficient unemployment is a real possibility, then monetary policy, which influences demand, has the potential for altering the level of unemployment, for good or ill. For some this possibility only arises due to rigidities, notably in the labour market. But the Keynesian perspective understands the operation of the labour market differently; what are regarded by some as damaging rigidities may in fact be sources of stability which enhance economic performance. But what we are concerned about here is that, if there is demand-deficient unemployment, for whatever reason, then monetary policy, by acting on demand, will have real consequences[1].

Further the view outlined above, that growth is enhanced the more competitive the financial sector, has been challenged. The level and distribution of credit – by sector, by region, by type of borrower – differ depending on the structure of the banking system and its relationship with the rest of the financial sector, and with the state[2]. The importance of the financial sector lies in providing finance, both for working capital and for investment. Banks have a unique role given their capacity to create credit. Because bank deposits are used as a means of payment, and thus circulate within the banking system with minimal drain into cash, the banks can create credit as a multiple of reserves; this contrasts with the more limited capacities of other financial institutions as financial intermediaries – recycling existing finance. Availability of bank finance depends on the knowledge base of the financial institution with respect to different classes of borrowers; the nature of that knowledge base depends on the structure of the banking system. In particular, the more centralised the banking system, the more tenuous the knowledge held with respect to small borrowers and those located far from the centre. Further, the banking system as a whole determines the total volume of credit depending on their expectations as to asset prices, and thus default risk, in general. Regulation of the financial sector determines how much fragility can enter into the financial system. By creating a strong regulatory environment, the state can promote financial stability which in turn encourages, not only the supply of credit, but also the demand for it arising from more confident investment plans. Here also state policy with respect to interest rates plays a part. In what follows I will consider the changing structure of banking in Europe and thus its relationship with the "real" side of the economy, and the changing role of the state with the move towards EMU.

---

[1]   See, for example, Davidson, 1994, for an account of the Keynesian perspective relative to the neo-classical perspective outlined above.

[2]   See, for example, Dow, 1994.

The Credit Explosion of the 1970s

Banking in Europe in the 1970s was displaying a reaction to increasing competition in the market for financial services from non-bank financial intermediaries[3]. The development of the banking system thus far had successfully built up confidence in banks and the payments system. This had been achieved over centuries of experience, with banks developing mutually-supportive mechanisms – such as the inter-bank market – and the state developing mechanisms – such as reserve ratios, supervisory practices etc. – to promote systemic confidence. With central bank reserves at the apex of the inverted pyramid of the financial structure, and bank deposits providing a core of secure reserves for non-bank financial intermediaries, the latter had a strong foundation on which to build their market share.

The banks responded both by aggressively trying to recapture some market share and by putting pressure on governments to relax regulatory restrictions. Traditionally, banks had responded to demand for credit. But now there was pressure to seek out potential borrowers and at the same time ensure that deposit rates were competitive. Although banks were subject to reserve requirements, these no longer acted as a firm constraint on lending. By now, central banks had provided a lender-of-last-resort facility in order to further enhance confidence in the banking system; if banks could borrow reserves from the central bank, then the risk of bank failure became more remote. But this meant that they could expand credit first and borrow reserves second. The economic background to this was inflationary for a variety of well-rehearsed reasons, including rising oil prices. But the inflationary process was fuelled by the expansion of bank credit feeding expenditure on the one hand, and raising interest rates on the other. Banks were competing for deposits by raising deposit rates and borrowing firms were passing the cost on in higher prices[4]. Further, since much of the credit expansion did not come from demand from industry, it provided the fuel for speculation in asset markets, which drove up asset prices, further encouraging speculation. This was most clearly the case in the UK, where London hosted a range of major financial markets, and where the banks traditionally maintained an arm's length from industry – unlike, most notably, Germany.

Domestically, banks put governments under tremendous pressure to relax restrictions to allow them to compete directly with non-bank financial intermediaries, so that a process of structural deregulation was

---

[3]   The account which follows draws heavily on Chick's (1986, 1993) stages of banking development framework.

[4]   See Chick, 1986.

set in train. In the meantime the 1970s saw a massive increase also in international credit provision, much of which arose outside regulatory restrictions. The massive growth of the Euro-currency market illustrates the strength of market forces during that period. Bank for International Settlements (BIS) data show that the market grew to $1,300 billion by the end of 1980[5]. Much of the growth in this market in the 1970s also reflected the recycling of petro-dollars to developing countries, laying the foundation for the debt crisis of the 1980s.

The growth of this unregulated market sparked fears of international financial instability. It grew against a backdrop of general instability in international financial markets following the collapse of the Bretton Woods system in 1971[6]. The International Monetary Fund (IMF) had until then overseen a system of exchange rates tied to pegs which in theory were adjustable, but were rarely so in practice. But there was an internal contradiction in a system which relied on the US to provide reserves to governments and to international (financial and non-financial) companies on the one hand, and to run a balance of trade deficit to match the inflow of capital on the other. The result was a system of generalised floating of exchange rates, and a general climate of uncertainty which encouraged the banks to maintain much more liquid portfolios than previously[7]. Thus, while there was a massive expansion of international credit, much of it was short-to-medium term.

Meanwhile the international monetary instability which characterised the beginning of the 1970s encouraged the development of ideas within the European Economic Community for increasing European monetary integration. The Werner Group was set up in 1970 to devise a plan; a compromise was reached between the German "economists" approach and the French "monetarists" approach[8]. The most important difference of approach concerned the order in which steps were taken to approach monetary union. The economists' approach required convergence of member economies as the first step, on the grounds that monetary unification would otherwise be unworkable. But the monetarists saw convergence as the natural *outcome* of monetary unification, so that the emphasis was put on how to achieve monetary union, narrowing the scope for currency fluctuations and setting up a reserve fund for defending currencies.

---

[5] The size of the market stood at $11,000 billion by the end of 1999; of this almost one-third represents inter-bank borrowing and lending.

[6] See Akyüz, 1995.

[7] See Strange, 1986.

[8] See Coffey and Presley, 1971, and Verdun in this volume.

The 1970s saw a series of attempts to narrow exchange rate movements between European currencies, against a backdrop of increased policy coordination, in implementation of the Werner recommendations. First, in 1972, the EC currencies were restricted to fluctuation within narrower bands than with third-country currencies, first as a "snake in the tunnel" defined by the US dollar, then floating – still as a snake – along with other currencies from 1973. But the instability of the 1970s, fuelled by the expansion of credit, meant that some currencies could not be maintained in the snake. A further attempt was made in 1979 to move towards monetary union when the European Monetary System was set up, again with European currencies maintained, by central bank intervention, within narrow bands of each other, but with a more concerted attempt at policy coordination. Some members were allowed to have wider bands of fluctuation for their currencies to allow for expected instability in their currencies. The system was based on the Ecu, a new European currency valued on the basis of a weighted index of European currencies; this was a unit of account rather than a traded currency.

The 1980s Backlash

The credit expansion of the 1970s proved to be unsustainable, leading to popular support for efforts by the UK and US governments to control it. Demand-pull inflation due to credit expansion had been reinforced by monetary expansion to finance budgetary deficits. Cost-push inflation due to the competitive rise in interest rates was reinforced by rises in other key costs, notably oil and wage costs. There was a move towards monetary targeting – and fiscal tightening – in an effort to control this inflation. Contrary to the expectations of the "neutral money" theorists, the effect was a dramatic increase in unemployment. In order to control monetary growth, the only option, given the existence of the lender-of-last-resort facility, was to raise interest rates. Expenditure plans were curtailed, an effect exacerbated by a simultaneous fiscal tightening, and firms had to borrow working capital just to survive. Thus, for some time, distress borrowing ensured that credit growth continued, and the higher interest rates were passed on in higher prices.

The "neutral money" interpretation of this period was that the money supply had grown excessively due to lax monetary policy, in particular allowing a monetary financing of budgetary deficits. The oil price shock was accommodated by rising credit, whereas the appropriate response would have been a fall in real incomes of oil consumers. The unemployment of the 1980s was then a result of the delayed reaction of policy-makers who had instead allowed inflation to occur and only a short-run adjustment which was severe only because the delay had allowed inflation to take hold. This causal mechanism completely ignores the dynamic of banking developments in the 1970s and the inability of monetary policy to control the money stock in any case.

Traditional monetary policy was not effective in controlling the stock of money because reserve requirements no longer acted as an effective constraint on the banks. So the UK and the US introduced capital requirements and pushed for them to be applied to international banking as well, under the aegis of the BIS. Banks were required to hold capital in specified forms at a level no less than eight percent of assets, where these were weighted according to risk – government securities, for example, having a weight of zero. These capital adequacy ratios were later applied also to all domestic banking within the EU.

With the economic downturn induced to control inflation, many of the banks' assets had proved to be "bad debt", *i.e.* unlikely to be repaid. Taking this together with the need to raise capital to back assets, there was a tremendous incentive for the banks to off-load assets from their balance sheets. Simultaneously, markets had become aware of the seriousness of the bad debt problem, and were unwilling to supply the banks with additional capital. The outcome was a process of securitisation, whereby the banks turned loans into securities for sale – *i.e.* made them tradable to reduce their capital requirements. They had expanded their loan portfolios on the basis of knowledge which had proved to be inadequate or misleading. The banks now turned their attention away from their traditional role as providers of non-marketable loans, and focused on other activities: facilitating funding in securities markets by providing a range of services such as underwriting, as well as becoming increasingly engaged in activity derivatives markets which did not require capital backing[9].

Meanwhile, plans for European monetary integration were beginning to take effect. Within each country governments had been submitting to pressure for deregulation to improve the banks' competitiveness, leading to market diffusion as different types of financial institution competed in markets which were now common. This was further enhanced by efforts by the EU to create a single European market for financial services. Exchange controls within Europe were removed. Banks above a minimum size in the EU were now licensed to do business Europe-wide, so effectively there was increased competition across national markets as well as across categories of financial institution. But in practice the other barriers to entry in each other's national market proved to be substantial, so that there was very little cross-border activity until the

---

[9] Subsequently capital adequacy ratios were extended to apply to trading in derivatives.

late 1990s. These barriers range from differences in accounting conventions and differences in relationship with the central banks to differences in confidence in the retail market. Banks have developed to their current status, and with their current capacities, because they have built up confidence in their deposits as a means of payment. But this confidence is specific to the locale in which conventions and states of confidence are formed – this generally does not cross national boundaries. There was only significant cross-border activity by international banks. Nor was there a significant increase in cross-border trade in financial services. By the end of the 1980s, therefore, it could still not be said that there was a single European market in financial services.

But the single market was central to the EU's plans for monetary union. It was important for the financial sector to reap economies of scale in order to compete in world markets. Just as in other sectors, it was expected that increased competition in a single European market would increase efficiency, and also improve the availability of finance across Europe, at reduced cost. The Cecchini Report (1988) predicted significant cost savings in the financial sector – an estimated total of Ecu 22 billion. This prediction was based on the argument that competition would erode the high price differentials which were observed to apply between national markets in financial services. This conclusion was criticised, notably for paying inadequate attention to the process by which competition in financial services would affect the structure of the financial services sector and its cost profile; it was assumed that increased competition would lead to convergence at the lowest prices[10]. Indeed the research on which the EC was drawing for its analysis of the likely effects of EMU paid very little attention to the question of banking structure. The research summarised in the Commission's (1990) report makes brief mention of banking structure, by referring to the demise of local monopolies in banking in the Single Market. After noting the beneficial effects on the cost and availability of credit which will result for "lagging regions", the report notes the offsetting negative effects on credit availability as a result of entry by foreign banks crowding out the marginal borrowers in lagging regions. But the conclusion is sanguine: "Naturally, the situation will disappear once the local bank[s] ha[ve] recovered and adapted to new conditions"[11].

The implication was that the structure of European banking would settle back to a combination of international, national and regional banks, but in a more competitive environment, to the benefit of the user of financial services.

---

[10] See Gardener, 1993.
[11] Commission for the European Communities, 1990: 225.

But the single market in financial services was also important for balance of payments adjustment in individual countries to be facilitated by European capital flows once the exchange rate tool had been withdrawn. Further, a European central banking system could only work if there was a high degree of commonality between national banking systems. For monetary policy to be effective in a similar fashion throughout Europe, there must be a similar transmission mechanism through which the single European interest rate affects member economies. The single European market in financial services was thus central to plans for EMU.

Banking Structure in the 1990s and EMU

The benefits of the single European market in financial services were to arise from increased competition. Certainly if economies of scale were to be reaped there would be some consolidation. But there was an expectation that the banking sector would be highly competitive within the larger market, with scope for smaller regional banks to find a market niche alongside the larger banks. In fact, banking studies have thrown some doubt on the scope for economies of scale in the normal sense of the term. Nevertheless, the banking sector is peculiar because of the central importance of confidence, something which does enjoy economies of scale. Thus, in a turbulent market with many new entrants, it is the large, well-established banks which command most confidence[12] and which therefore attract more deposits and thus continue to maintain their dominance. In addition, in the face of increased competition, banks are justified in making a strategic choice to be pro-active in merger and acquisition activity in order to maintain and increase market share. Indeed banking history demonstrates that any period of increased competition, usually resulting from regulatory change, is almost inevitably followed by a period of consolidation and concentration[13]. Indeed, since banking relies on the confidence held in the system, it is in the nature of the sector that processes of fierce competition cannot be sustained.

The 1990s saw increasing merger and acquisition activity in European banking[14]. European Commission data suggest that most activity occurred among the large banks, and mostly within countries. This is consistent with the argument that the most significant economy of scale arises from confidence, which applies most strongly within national

---

[12] There are good reasons for such confidence, including the experience from history of large banks being regarded by government as being "too big to fail".

[13] See, for example, Dow and Smithin, 1992

[14] See Chick, 1998

borders. But there has also been a tremendous amount of consolidation among the smallest banks, which are not covered by the EC data. Thus, in Germany, in particular, there has been a significant exercise of consolidation among the small savings banks, with around 1,000 mergers in the period between 1990 and 1997[15]. There has been increasing incidence of cross-border merger and acquisition activity among the large banks, but significant barriers to entry to different national markets remain[16].

The Commission's (1990) report had implied that there might be some temporary crowding out of credit demand in lagging regions because new entrants into the local market might apply more stringent conditions than the local banks. But this would only be a temporary situation, as regional banks reasserted their market position. First, the evidence of a quickening pace of consolidation, particularly within national banking markets, does not support the view that any lack of competitiveness on the part of local banks will be corrected, so that they can reassert their market position. In any case, the process of consolidation seems to have more to do with preserving market share than with profitability.

But there is the larger question of the knowledge base on which credit supply decisions are based. If credit is being provided to regions remote from financial centres, then the knowledge base will be less sound than if it is being provided by local banks[17]. In a modern banking environment, banks are not significantly constrained in the total amount of credit they create. The effective constraint is the self-imposed constraint of perceived default risk, where this risk is not ultimately calculable, but based on expectations grounded in available knowledge. Superficial knowledge of a local economy may allow exaggerated expectations of growth as well as of decline, so the provision of credit to regions removed from the financial centre is likely to be highly volatile. This is compounded by capital outflows from such regions to assets issued in the financial centre. The outcome can thus be a general state of inadequate credit provision, creating a vicious cycle of low local asset prices, possibly punctuated by periods of inward investment followed by dramatic reversals[18].

---

[15] It should be noted however that this development is not peculiar to EU member countries; there have been similar developments in Switzerland and the US, for example.
[16] See Chick and Dow, 1997.
[17] See Dow, 1994, 1999.
[18] See Chick and Dow, 1988.

This pattern of credit availability, exacerbated by consolidation in European banking, will have real consequences for the pattern of economic development in Europe. In particular it creates forces for economic divergence in terms of output and employment. But in the meantime, the Maastricht Treaty of 1992 set out a programme, emanating from the German-led "economist" approach to EMU, which would require convergence among EU members as a precondition for EMU. But the convergence criteria were financial rather than "real", referring to inflation rates, interest rates and exchange rates; convergence to a low level of fiscal imbalance was required as a means of enforcing monetary controls. The achievement of a wide range of members in meeting the convergence criteria by the time the first wave of countries locked their currencies to the euro was won at the cost of significant real economic effects. In particular, the achievement of stable, low inflation together with a reduced fiscal deficit and stock of debt, were achieved by means of deflationary policies. The requirement to limit the size of fiscal deficits, and indeed to achieve a fiscal surplus in order to reduce national debt, ensures that there is an inherent deflationary bias in EMU.

Monetary policy in Europe is now implemented by the European Central Bank (ECB), with inputs from national central banks of euroland countries. The ECB is charged first and foremost with promoting price stability, by means of interest rate policy. The achievement of convergence prior to EMU, and the process of financial integration was intended to make euroland financially homogeneous, with the implication that European monetary policy would affect all member countries and their sub-regions equally. There is a significant problem in that member countries have not converged in terms of unemployment rates, and have lost both the exchange rate tool and, to any significant degree the fiscal tool, to address relatively high unemployment. But we focus here on the fact that meeting the convergence criteria has not ensured financial homogeneity in any case.

Restrictive monetary policy operates by discouraging credit creation, and thus expenditure, by means of high interest rates. But this effect is transmitted through several complex channels. First, there is the impact of high official discount rates on bank lending. Banking structure is still sufficiently different in Europe that this impact differs from country to country. Thus, for example, de Bondt (1999) shows ECB policy operating through different channels: directly discouraging demand for credit in Belgium, France and Italy where the banks raise loan rates in line with the discount rate, but restricting supply through adverse balance sheet implications in Germany and also Italy. This study also demonstrates the restriction of credit as a result of adverse balance sheet effects of high interest rates as hitting small banks hardest, because their balance sheets are relatively illiquid; there is therefore a disproportionate adverse impact on the borrowing capacity of small borrowers who make up the clientele of small banks.

This small bank effect also bears out the implication of the stages of banking development framework, that monetary control is more effective the earlier the stage of banking development. Small banks in a financially-advanced economy have the characteristics of the more constrained situation of the larger banks in earlier stages of development. But where we are considering enlargement, to include members with banking systems in the process of developing, the impact of European monetary policy will be relatively strong for the entire banking system. Thus curtailment of credit in Europe will fall disproportionately on small regional banks and banking systems at earlier stages of development, *i.e.* on the providers of credit to the less advanced economies of Europe. Restrictive monetary policy then may contribute to divergence in Europe, and not, as the French "monetarist" approach predicted, convergence.

But the impact of monetary policy is likely to differ across Europe also for reasons other than banking structure as such. Member States differ significantly according to both convention and regulations[19]. Thus for example a rise in the ECB rate would have a more direct effect on consumer expenditure in countries where variable rate mortgages are the norm than in those where they are not. Eventually competition will produce a single market where these differences are ironed out, but we are a long way off that stage. Thus, not only may monetary policy have real consequences at a European level, these real consequences may be unevenly distributed, contributing to economic divergence.

Future Prospects

Much of the argument developed above about the effect of the Single Market in general, and European monetary policy in particular, on the distribution of credit in Europe and thus on economic performance in different sub-economies of Europe, hinges on predicted changes in banking structure. Current sectoral developments suggest continued consolidation through merger and acquisition, with the emphasis possibly shifting from consolidation within national boundaries to consolidation across boundaries. Small banks find themselves under competitive threat and are themselves undergoing a process of consolidation, within regions.

---

[19] See Chick and Dow, 1997

Banks at a later stage of development have learnt, through a painful process of dealing with the fall-out of the 1970s, to structure their balance sheets in such a way as to limit their vulnerability. This includes limiting their vulnerability to restrictive monetary policy. So any banks, or banking systems, which have not reached this stage will bear a disproportionate burden of any monetary tightening to control inflation. However, it is not necessarily in the interests of economic development for the banking system to be so focused on preserving liquidity; commitment to financing industry is a major source of balance sheet illiquidity.

Further, it is still too early to predict what competition in European banking will produce in terms of banking structure. Barriers to entry in each others' markets have prevented homogenisation of European banking so far. But, while this has inhibited cross-border mergers and acquisitions to some extent, banking has become increasingly concentrated in national markets, with every sign that this will continue. Thus, the most clear outcome of increased competition in Europe has been a decline in competition in national markets.

One of the dominant predictions has been that larger banks will converge on the universal banking model; smaller banks will survive as a result of identifying a market niche[20]. But universal banking is not becoming the norm. For example, two major banks, the Royal Bank of Scotland and Deutsche Bank, are pursuing quite different strategies, the first emphasising retail banking and the second investment banking. Further, while small savings banks have been grouping together, particularly in Germany, the groupings, which are still relatively small banks, may retain a market niche in their local markets. The case for state support is enhanced by the fact that European regional banks have perceived their common interest by forming a group for lobbying and other joint activities; the Association of European Financial Centres (AEFC).

But market forces seem to be posing increasingly strong competitive threats to banks whose balance sheets reflect a commitment to industry, including small local banks. There needs to be some form of protection afforded to banks providing the necessary financial support to local business; these are the businesses which depend on banks for finance given the difficulties of accessing capital markets. The German banking system provides just one model of a state-supported network of small regional banks. But any action needs to take place at a European level, given the countervailing forces set in train by the setting up of EMU.

---

[20] See, for example, Canals, 1993, and Gardener and Molyneux, 1994.

CHAPTER 7

"We are arrogant because we are good[1]" –

A Critical Appraisal of Central Banking versus Fiscal Policy in Accomplishing the Community Wide Convergence of the 1980s and the 1990s[2]

Roger HAMMERSLAND

Introduction

During the last two decades the European community has witnessed two periods of convergence. The first as a result of the disciplinary effect implicitly imposed on Member States of the community by adherence to the EMS. The second period being a consequence of community countries pursuing a policy of commitment to meet the terms of the Treaty on European Union for creating EMU[3]. However, in both instances one gets the impression that monetary policy has been given the full credit for being the policy instrument through which this convergence was possible, without even taking as much as a glance at other possible explanations such as changed economic environments or the role played by fiscal authorities. For instance, as Lars Svensson (1999), a leading Swedish economist, firmly puts it:

---

[1] Statement made by Bundesbank representative, see Marsh 1992, p. 16.

[2] I am grateful for comments by Barbara MacLennan, Katarina Juselius, Michael Ehrmann, Andreas Beyer, Mike Artis and participants in the working group for the cooperation project between the Robert Schuman Centre, Florence and The Working Life Institute, Stocholm, called From the Werner Plan to the EMU. I would also like to thank Henrik Hansen and Gerdie Everaert. The first for an inspiring discussion with regard to interpretation of structural dynamic coefficients in structural VARS, the second for providing me with data on Primary Government balances for Europe.

[3] Both periods were characterised by a narrowing of interest differentials and a significant drop in the number of realignments as well as Inflation. However, as there are strong interderdependencies between these three quantities, I will by convergence in the following mainly refer to convergence in inflation.

193

There is little doubt that the decline of inflation has largely been due to the growing commitment on the part of monetary policy makers in the euro area to achieve and maintain low inflation. The gradual decline in inflation can therefore be interpreted as corresponding to a fall in the average (implicit) inflation objective of the central banks in the euro area.

These points of view are particularly strange as the two periods in addition to being characterised as one of tight monetary policy, precisely were periods of both structural change and fiscal consolidation, therefore potentially being both reasons for converging inflation rates within the community as much as strict monetary policy. For the last point I refer to Figure 1 and Figure 2 below, which give the graphs of the primary government balance for France and Germany, respectively. In the case of Germany the figures clearly identify the periods from about 1983 to 1988 and from 1994 and onwards as periods of considerable improvements in government balances, the periods coinciding almost fully with the two periods of convergence mentioned earlier on. The figures for France are less clear with regard to time intervals, but show the same pattern. Why focus in these matters has almost solely been on monetary policy and whether the conviction of Central Banking being the crux of convergence is well founded or could be regarded as a result of Central Bankers desire to ʒain influence and power in the process governing the Communiⅼy, are questions that need to be analysed.

A huge bulk of empirical literature (*e.g.* Cukierman (1992) and Alesina and Summers (1993)) has "established" that, in the case of industrialised countries, a higher degree of central bank independence goes hand in hand with lower inflation. A typical interpretation of this has been that monetary policy through independent central banks, seems to have provided the appropriate response to help promote a culture of monetary stability. Further, in the case of the US, two independent studies (Cohen and Wenninger (1994), Lee and Prasad (1994)) have shown that the correlation between policy rates and long-term interest rates in the US has increased. Typically, they interpret this as indicating gained control by central banks in the conduct of monetary policy. However, in making such kind of statements based on bi-variate correlations and non-stationary data, one typically embarks on a hazardous adventure where the possibility of making spurious or nonsensical correlations is imminent. The alleged ability of central bank policy to effectively control inflation is further reinforced by neoliberal theory, where a central message is precisely the necessity of getting control over the most serious threat to stable prices, namely the supply of money. This of course leaves Central Banks with an important role to play in both formulation and execution of a general policy stance at national levels and notwithstanding the empirical facts, may have contributed to the conviction of Central Banking being the main policy option through which one effectively controls inflation.

**Figure 1: Primary Government Balance for Germany
Cyclically Adjusted, % Potential GDP**

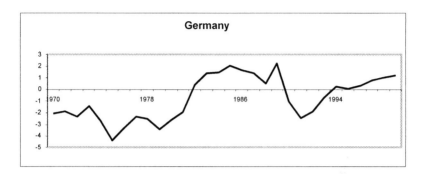

**Figure 2: Primary Government Balance for France,
Cyclically Adjusted, % Potential GDP**

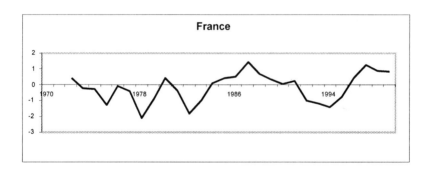

The recent contribution of New Keynesian ideas has shown that monetary policy by no means should be considered as the only effective measure of control. Also, within this framework the effectiveness of policies aimed at demand management heavily depends on whether we have a fixed exchange rate system and on the degree of mobility in capital and goods markets, the simultaneous appearance of which imply a total loss of money as a policy instrument. A more fundamental question is therefore whether monetary policy in a world close to perfect capital mobility, is at all effective. This suggests that even the common appreciation of monetary policy being a legitimate policy instrument through which administering real demand, may have been related to extrapolations based on historical structures that radically differ from the structure which prevails in the period we are looking at. That is, it may have been the case that the excellent post-war record of Germany in fighting inflation based on tight money under a regime that radically differed from one of perfect capital mobility, has been used to argue for the pursuit of a similar policy at the European level, but now in times where the structure of the economy is changed towards one of high capital mobility across borders. As already mentioned, a well known result in economic theory is that near perfect arbitrage in the capital market may totally undermine any possibility of control on behalf of monetary authorities, not only in real terms but also with regard to controlling a nominal quantity like inflation. This result hinges on the economy being one of fixed exchange rates. Whether one can consider EMS to have implied some kind of "fixedness" is therefore crucial for the argument. However, it is all too apparent that the EMS did not render realignments a thing of the past. In the period from 1979 to 1990 we had no less than twelve realignments within the members of the system. However, as pointed out by Swann (1996), the tendency was a declining one and compared with currencies such as Japanese yen and US dollar the scheme had the effect, of reducing day to day fluctuations between Member State currencies considerably. After the currency crisis of 1992 the currencies stabilised even more in the run up to the locking of national exchange rates. At best, we may therefore say that the two periods were two of a kind of fixed exchange rates, the more correct description perhaps being a very dirty float among the Member States. Even though national exchange rates of the Member States were floating against currencies outside the ERM area, the mere possibility of EMS and increased capital mobility having had a neutralising effect on monetary policy deserves attention. Especially since the process of hedging may have contributed to reducing the effective external exchange rate variation considerably.

New research based on time series analyses that takes into account both potential non stationarities and the typical multivariate simultaneity in macro economic data, persistently reveals exogeneity of long-term interest rates in the period after 1983 (*e.g.* Juselius (1996), (1998a) and (1998b)). In particular, long-term interest rates neither seem to have been much affected by domestic monetary policy nor inflation policy nor inflation to have been much affected by changes in money stock or the short-term interest rate as is usually believed. These results therefore constitute strong evidence of impotence with regard to monetary policy, and taken at face value could demonstrate the mutual inconsistency of an independent monetary policy with fixed exchange rates and near to perfect capital mobility. This suggests that long-term interest rates in some way is determined by a process that is beyond control of monetary authorities and is in sharp contrast to the boldly expressed goal of price stability by exerting influence on price inflation directly or indirectly through economic activity by affecting long-term interest rates. Further, such a finding implies that monetary policy by no means can have been the only central cause of convergence, suggesting other reasons such as, for example, fiscal policy and the abolishment of controls to capital and to free movement of goods and services. The aim of this chapter however, is more limited and is in the spirit of substantiating the first point more than making a serious attempt to look at alternative explanations for the convergence in the nineties. In doing so, I will heavily draw on the results of Juselius and MacDonald (2000) and confront their findings with the results of own ongoing research.

To sum up, this chapter addresses the relative importance of monetary *vs.* fiscal authorities in pursuing a general stance of policy within the European community. The perspective is retrospective as well as forward looking in that the chapter analyses historical structures governing the last two decades at the same time as it makes extrapolations with regard to the feasibility of alternative future policy stances. Based on econometric evidence, the chapter particularly aims at discussing the common conviction of Central Banking having been the crux of the observed convergences within the community during the last two decades. The results indicate that the role of Central Banks has been severely overrated in this respect and suggest looking also at other plausible reasons like fiscal policy and the effect of increased capital mobility. With regard to the making of a future policy stance where one of the most imperative tasks has to do with how to resolve the problem of unemployment in Europe, the chapter also strongly argues against the pursuit of "blind structuralism" in the sense of legitimating policies of *laissez faire* or policies geared towards a general abolishment of social security protection, most probably both leading to social distress and an ever-widening gap of social and economic differences in standards of living within the community. This leaves us of course with an important question to ask: if it is true that monetary policy is not as effective as we want to believe, and an extended use of structural measures is out of question due to its socially unacceptable consequences, is there anything at all we can do? The chapter seeks to answer this question by pointing to the need for regionally directed fiscal policies and policies geared towards regional stimulation of investment and growth, policies that most certainly will bring back the social dimension to the European policy agenda[4].

The chapter is organised as follows. To motivate and to be able to interpret the results of the econometric analysis, Section two discusses briefly the mechanism through which policy rates may affect the economy. In most Continental European countries bank lending is over-whelmingly linked to long interest rates, and the impact of monetary policy on the economy therefore depends crucially on how changes in policy rates are transmitted to the long end of the yield curve. Section two will therefore mainly deal with this part of the transmission mechanism, that is the mechanism through which policy rates affect long rates. Section three then presents and interprets the results of Juselius and MacDonald and compares these findings with the results in Hammersland (2000a). Based on the results of the preceding section, section four seeks to discuss the relative role played by monetary *vs.* fiscal policy in the future conduct of policy geared towards resolving the problem of unemployment in Europe. Section five contains concluding remarks.

The Monetary Transmission Mechanism and Stylised Facts

The link from monetary policy actions to the economy is far from trivial. Because bank lending in Continental Europe mainly is of a long-run character, however, the impact of monetary policy will depend crucially on how changes in policy rates are transmitted to the long end of the yield curve[5]. As pointed out in Buti *et al* (1999) this transmission depends heavily on how a hike in policy rates through interactions of future expectations with regard to inflation, exchange rates, the development of the real economy, and, as a function of these, future monetary policy, affects the long end of the market. Hence, a monetary contraction will in general not lead to an unambiguous effect on long rates, but will depend on how it is perceived to affect the expectations with regard to the future development of certain key economic variables.

---

[4]   For an interesting account of credit policy to reduce unemployment by stimulating social investment see MacLennan (this volume).

[5]   The policy rate refers to the policy instrument of the central bank and thus represents the discount rate. The short rates refer to interest rates in the money market for short-term assets. As Central Banks have a fairly tight control over the short end of the money market, I will in the following deliberately use these two concepts interchangeably, being aware that they are far from being equivalent. With long rates I mean interest rates on Government bonds with up to ten years to maturity. In the econometric analyses of Section 3 short- and long-term interest rates are represented by three month money market interest rates and interest rates on government bonds with ten years to maturity, respectively.

Depending on the political and economic situation a monetary contraction may therefore convey a different kind of information and thus potentially both lead to a fall and a rise in long term interest rates. However, that this link is not missing is of crucial importance for the argument that monetary policy had a central bearing on the convergence during the last two decades and for monetary policy to be effective in pursuing its goal of price stability, the sign of this relationship being of minor importance. To clarify matters further, I will bear on the classification made in the book referred to above and classify the effects on long rates into two categories, the effects from portfolio considerations and expectations, respectively.

The portfolio effect describes the effect of reallocation between assets of imperfect substitutability in the case of changes in their relative yields. This effect is unequivocally positive in the sense that a hike in the yield of one type of assets will lead to an increase also in the yield of the imperfect substitute. This effect goes through increased demand for the asset which have experienced a yield increase and reduced demand for the assets which has experienced a relative yield decline, the last effect leading to reduced prices and through fixed coupon dividend, an increased percentage return on the new value of the asset. Treating assets of different maturities as imperfect substitutes, this means that a hike in the short money market instrument through encouraging investors to redirect their funds from assets with a long maturity to the instrumental asset, will force yields on assets with a long maturity to increase as well.

The effects of expectations is based on two arbitrage conditions, the uncovered interest parity (UIP) and the expectation theory of the term structure[6] respectively. The first of these is a relationship between foreign and domestic interest rates on assets of the same maturity and says that in a steady state the return of investing one unit of domestic currency must be the same whether one invests domestically or abroad. The long rates should therefore be equal to the corresponding foreign long rates plus the expected rate of depreciation of the home currency against the foreign currency. The expectation theory of the term structure on the other hand is a relationship between interest rates of different degrees of maturity and says that long rates should be equal to a weighted average of current and expected future short-term interest rates. Thus, the impact on long-term interest rates from a change in current short-term interest rates depends on how expected future short-term interest rates are affected. A rise in current short-term interest rates that is regarded as permanent will lead to a full pass through from short-

---

[6]   Schiller, 1979.

term to long-term interest rates. On the other hand, if an increase in the current short-term interest rate leads to a significant reduction in inflation expectations, long-term interest rates may even decline.

A change in policy rates may affect the expectations with regard to future short rates and exchange rates in different ways. For instance as Buti *et al* point out, in the case of a central bank with a good anti-inflationary reputation and high credibility, a hike in the policy rate can be seen as signalling the determination of the central bank to fight inflation. Thus the hike could lead to expectations of an appreciating trend and a downward movement in future interest rates, both potentially leading to a decline in long-term interest rates. On the other hand, in the case of a central bank with a less good reputation, a hike in interest rates may be taken to signal the build up of an inflationary pressure, and thus most probably leading to increased expectations with regard to the necessity of undertaking upward adjustments in policy rates also in the future. In this case the hike will lead to an increase in long-term interest rates. Noteworthy, in the case of Germany the anti-inflationary reputation may have been so good that a hike may not have had an effect on either exchange rate expectations or expectations of future inflation. If so the only observable effect should be the portfolio effect implying an unambiguous positive effect on long rates.

Figure 3: Interest Spreads

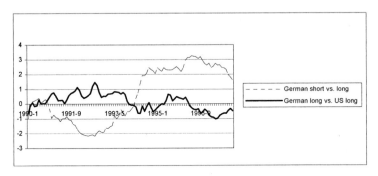

Looking at the stylised facts of Figure 3, the spread between German short- and long-term interest rates seems to be far from stationary in the sense of exhibiting a stable mean reverting process[7]. This implies that there does not seem to have been any long-run relationship at all

---

[7] An important caveat with regard to time-series being characterised as stationary or not is that these are sample sensitive and do not represent generic properties of the data.

between short and long rates in the sample interval we are looking at. On the other hand, looking at the spread between US and German long rates, data clearly reveals a stable long-run international interest rate relationship. This observation has implications far beyond the vague recognition made by Goodhart (1995) that increased capital mobility lately has led to a greater tension between international pressure (e.g. foreign long-term interest rates) and domestic factors (e.g. the expected time path of future short rates) in the determination of long-term interest rates. Taken at face value it implies that the long end of the yield curve has been almost totally dependent on what has been going on in international capital markets in the long run, the influence of domestic monetary policy in fact having been of minor importance. Figure 4, showing long German and US interest rates, further indicates that the direction of causality has been unidirectional in the sense that German long rates seem to be determined by US long rates.

Below, I will shed further light on these issues by referring to two independent papers analysing the determination of long-term interest rates in a simultaneous framework, the paper by Juselius and MacDonald and my own paper, from now on denoted Hammersland, respectively. Both papers use the cointegrating VAR methodology developed by Johansen (1988), but cover different sample periods and are based on different information sets. While Hammersland undertakes an analysis covering the period 1990 to 1998 based on a VAR of dimension 5 for long-and short-term interest rates in Germany and the US together with the bilateral exchange rate, Juselius and MacDonald also include nominal prices and money in an extended analysis which covers both periods of convergence.

Figure 4: Long interest rates of the US and Germany

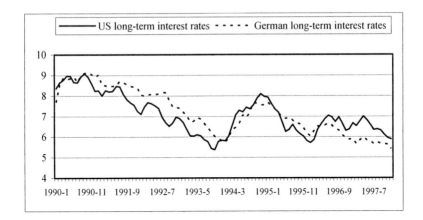

What Data Tells us: Two Independent Analyses of the Monetary Transmission Mechanism Based on the Cointegrating VAR

In their analysis Juselius and MacDonald use monthly data for the period 1975 to 1998. Thus, comprising both periods of convergence within the Community until the realisation of the EMU in the beginning of January 1999. In an information set comprising seven variables[8], they are able to identify no less than three long run relationships[9], out of which only one includes short rates. However, as neither of the two long-term interest rates show evidence of adjusting to any of the long-run relations and the structural model developed nor implies short-run effects from short to long rates, there is no evidence of a causal relationship implying that short rates feed long rates. Further, the lack of significant inflationary effects is evident in all four interest rate equations, ruling out the possibility that monetary policy might have had an important bearing on long rates through affecting these. These results are strong evidence against the expectation theory of the term-structure

---

[8]   The seven variables are respectively, long- and short-term interest rates in both Germany and the US, the bilateral real exchange rate and finally the two country specific inflation rates.

[9]   The three long-run relationships are respectively; a relationship between the real exchange rate and the real long-term interest spread, a relationship between German inflation, US inflation and domestic longterm interest rates and a relationship between real short interest rates and the long-term interest spread.

and indicate that an important channel through which monetary policy affects the economy does not seem to exist, neither directly nor through the channel of inflation expectations. One might expect that these results in some way are casual. However, as Juselius and MacDonald put it: "these are very strong results and have also been found in Danish, Spanish, and Italian data"[10]. Another aspect of their analysis is the lack of short rate effects on inflation in the case of Germany. Taken literally this finding undermines even the possibility of running a policy geared towards controlling inflation, the boldly expressed goal of the ECB.

As I have commented on, the results of Juselius and MacDonald are extremely strong and suggest not only that long-term interest rates in Germany are exogenous, but also that US long rates seem to be determined by factors outside the information set considered. This last point is especially surprising as there has been a common appraisal among economists that the FED in the conduct of monetary policy, has exerted a significant impact on the real economy through affecting long rates. However, in contrast to the results for Germany, Juselius and MacDonald do find that short rates play a significant role in the determination of inflation. Thus, the FED does at least seem to have a handle through which to manage inflation. Further, the stylised facts of Section two clearly suggest a long-run relationship between long American and German interest rates, thus questioning also the exogeneity status assigned to German long rates in the study by Juselius and MacDonald. As this result is controversial I will elaborate further on this by referring to research that diverges on this point.

In contrast to the analysis by Juselius and MacDonald, the analysis undertaken by Hammersland confirms that there is a long-run relationship between long rates in Germany and the US[11]. The results also indicate that the direction of causality is unidirectional in the sense that the latter ones seem to lead the first ones and not *vice versa*. Thus, the results in Hammersland seem to be totally in line with the stylised facts of section two. In the paper by Juselius and MacDonald this relationship is implicitly identified and categorised as spurious as they do not find support for an adjustment mechanism where the long spread functions as an attractor towards which the processes of long-term interest rates seek to move. However, even though the relationship identified by Hammersland may be identified as spurious in an extended information

---

[10]   Juselius, 1992, Juselius and Toro, 1999 and Juselius and Gennari, 2000.

[11]   The same data has been analysed in Hammersland, 2000b, using an altenative procedure to deal with time series data with a small cross sectional dimension. The results are totally in line with the findings referred to in the text and reveal both the lack of a long-run relationship between domestic short and long rates as the existence of a strong long-run relationship between German and US long-term interest rates.

set, the mere fact that Hammersland undertakes a clean analysis without falling back on measures to improve diagnostics together with the fact that the analysis confirms the striking evidence set out by Figure 4, should legitimate that the analysis deserves attention, if not from a statistical at least from a theoretical and practical point of view. Also, the argument of spuriousness is one that always can be addressed to partial economic analyses, the analysis by Juselius and MacDonald notwithstanding, and in general must be sought to be substantiated within the framework of prior beliefs and the reliability of results in conjunction with thoroughly testing for exogeneity in information sets extended in directions proposed by priors and theory. The analysis by Hammersland differs from the one by Juselius and MacDonald also by only focusing on the period after the reunification of Eastern and Western Germany, the argument being one of structural change and lack of credible long time series for unified Germany. However, like Juselius and MacDonald, Hammersland does not find any long-run relationship between short and long rates and long American rates are found to be exogenous with regard to the information set. In large measures therefore, the two analyses seem to be in line with each other, the main difference being that the long end of the German yield curve in the paper by Hammersland, directly is linked to the American bond market and thus is driven by a common underlying trend originating from international capital markets.

As Juselius and MacDonald, Hammersland develops a structural dynamic model based on the observed covariance structure of the residuals in the system consisting of all marginal processes in the information set. The short-run structure of this model shows that there are strong effects of short-term interest rates in the very short run. In fact the paper suggests that a one percent increase in the short-term interest rate will lead to an about 0.6 percentage increase in the long-term German rate after the first month[12]. Based on the fact that Hammersland

---

[12] Stochastic structural model builders are often confronted with the critique from statisticians that dynamic coefficients of structural models in general cannot be given the interpretation of *ceteris paribus* elasticities. This critique is based upon the recognition of marginal vector processes being the Data Generating Process (DGP) and that structural models represent deduced representations of these. In that case, unless the covariance matrix of the marginal vector process is diagonal, dynamic structural coefficients cannot be given a *ceteris paribus* interpretation as a shock to one of the processes in general will feed simultaneously into other variables through a non-diagonal reduced form covariance matrix. However, and this is a question appropriate to ask statisticians, what if the structure has the status of a data generating process and the marginal process itself thus being interpreted as a reduced form representation of the structure? In that case the marginal process will have a covariance matrix that only reflects the structure and thus being explained by it. If so,

is not able to identify any long-run relationship between long- and short-term interest rates, in either Germany or the US, this effect is only transitory. What is important, however, is to recognise that this could be indicative of monetary policy being effective through lowering expectations with regard to future interest rates and thus neutralising the effect of a hike in policy rates on long rates in the long run. Whether this interpretation is plausible, is partly dependent on what is said in the above footnote and the fact that Hammersland's structural model is not able to fully explain the observed correlation pattern in the marginal model. Also, the results of Juselius and MacDonald clearly indicate that inflation rates do not explain interest rates. This last point should indicate that expectations of future short rates are not very sensitive to inflation and is evidence against a channel through which changes in expectations of future short rates might neutralise the effect of a hike in policy rates in the long run.

Even though the analysis of Hammersland does not fully confirm the analysis of Juselius and MacDonald who find that long-term German interest rates are exogenous, the results clearly indicate that monetary policy through changes in short-term interest rates does not affect the long-term interest rate in the long-run. This result is of most importance as in most Continental European countries (particularly in Germany) bank lending is overwhelmingly linked to long interest rates, and the impact of monetary policy on the real economy depends crucially on how changes in policy rates are transmitted to the long end of the yield curve.

---

should not the interpretation of dynamic coefficients in a dynamic structural model as *ceteris paribus* structural elasticities then hinge on the assumption of a diagonal *structural* covariance matrix and a deduced non diagonal reduced form covariance matrix have no bearing on the interpretation of these, only reflect the inherent simultaneity of the structure itself? Shocks to one of the variables will in this case not be interpreted as a shock to its marginal process, but as a structural shock to the behavioural equation of the variable in the structural model. One may say that the issue is related to whether we choose the perspective of a marginal or a structural DGP as the underlying process governing the system of variables in an information set. In the first case a structural model is just another way to present the information contained in the system of marginal processes, while the latter gives the structural model the status of explaining these marginal processes. Anyhow, in the paper by Juselius and MacDonald the marginal perspective is used, and their structural model is therefore only another way to represent the results that better illustrates the economic content of their findings. The low degree of observed correlation between the residuals of the marginal model further allows them to interpret the structural coefficients as elasticities. The structural model in Hammersland, however, is based on a marginal model where the covariance matrix is far from triangular and the elasticity interpretation hinges on the interpretation of the structure being the DGP.

Some Remarks about the Future Role of Monetary vs. Fiscal Policy

EMU will have the effect of creating a huge currency area with an economic weight similar to that of the United States and with a large single and deep financial market. These characteristics should promote the development of the euro as an international currency and lead to increased influence in international capital markets with the possible effect of changing an eventual unidirectional link between US and European long-term interest rates[13]. The transmission of changes in policy interest rates to market interest rates may also be affected, and whether the ECB will gain or loose control with regard to the long end of the financial market, is an open question. However, taking the US as an example, Juselius and MacDonald's analysis suggests that EMU will not lead to gained control over the long end of the yield curve, only improving upon the possibility of inflationary control. Monetary policy might therefore attain importance as a measure of controlling inflation, but probably have a more limited effect in the conduct of policies geared towards managing real demand[14]. Notwithstanding, the mere possibility of the European Central Bank having to run a single-minded mandatory

---

[13]   In contrast to the positive exchange rate effect expected to originate from the promotion of the euro as an international currency, the euro exchange rate has experienced an almost continuous deterioration in its external value after the locking of national exchange rates on 1 January 1999. As late as in October 2000, several articles in the *Financial Times* rejected this as the result of speculation and adduced the role of the US dollar as an invoicing currency for international settlements as an alternative explanation. However, it is all too apparent that this cannot have been the whole story behind the decline in the euro exchange rate. The role of the US dollar as a safe heaven currency coupled with a widespread sceptism of the European project and the strong development of the US economy must have played a significant role as well. A more controversial issue is the impact of reallocations of private exchange rate portfolios. The prevailing view among economists has until today been that exchange rate effects of such portfolio movements cannot have played an important role in this respect as they have been a part of a diversification trend initiated already in the 1980s. However, the simple conversion of assets held in European currencies into euros meant that more than a third of the world portfolio was denominated in euros from 1 January 1999 and onwards. Notably a percentage close to the equivalence of what today is held in US dollars. Whether private investors wishing to maintain the degree of diversification of their portfolios, were willing to absorb such an amount of euros without a fall in the price of the currency is therefore not too obvious. Also, as pointed out by Notermans (this volume) the relatively lax stance of policy taken by the ECB in the wake of the continuous weakening of the euro exchange rate, may have been due to trade off considerations between output and exchange rate stability within the framework of low inflation.

[14]   For an extended list of reasons why the value of a stabilising monetary policy may be lesser than it is usual to assume, see Røste (this volume).

policy of price stability to establish its counter inflationary reputation, may severely undermine the possibility of the ECB to even run an offsetting policy in the wake of bad shocks. If it had not been for the Stability and Growth Pact, this would leave national fiscal policies with an important role to play, especially since EMU implies the loss of national exchange rates as a means of correcting real national imbalances. The criteria and procedures enshrined in the Stability and Growth Pact, however, may turn out to be too limited to bring about social cohesion and to cushion impacts of possible future shocks within the community through nationally conducted fiscal policies only. Also, as most unemployment in Europe recently has been characterised as natural, there has been an increasing acceptance that the scope for real demand management is small and that what is called for is policies geared towards the improved functioning of labour markets. However, to baptise the phenomenon of unemployment as structural or "natural" based on the concept of NAIRU may represent a huge disservice to the goal of understanding unemployment. Either one uses Elmeskov's procedure (Elmeskov (1993)) or alternative measures based on a univariate smoothing of the unemployment series, the different ways to measure the so-called NAIRU in my view are almost all severely biased towards giving unemployment a structural interpretation thus implying certainly the risk of throwing out the baby with the bath water. Notwithstanding the paradox of characterising unemployment rates in the range above ten percent as natural, the fact that unemployment rates generally show a high degree of persistence, implies that some of its natural part is heavily influenced by shocks to the economy. Not only shocks originating from the labour market and thus characterised as structural, but also shocks that are brought about from the demand side. This process is spelled out through shocks leaving a trace to the natural rate, the bigger the trace, the higher is the degree of persistence in unemployment, and is commonly denoted as hysteresis in the economic literature. Thus, even in the worst case of unemployment being completely characterised as structural, there is a channel through which real demand management not only works, but will be of most importance the higher the degree of persistence is. However, notwithstanding all that is said so far, the effects of structural policies are slow in coming and may turn out to be extremely costly both in terms of transitory output losses and increased unemployment as sociological and distributional changes needed to recover the economy when being confronted with huge real imbalances or bad shocks. Forgotten are perhaps the times when employers in their desire to maximise profits, unscrupulously exploited employees and more than half of the European population lived close to or under the subsistence level. However, structural policies geared towards reducing minimum wages and social protection in general could easily have the effect of reintroducing this *status quo ante* to some of the poorest members of the community. Especially since the lack of harmonisation in labour standards across countries may easily lead to, as Artis (1999) puts it, "a race to the bottom" in the level of social protection. However, not only the mere insufficiency of structural policy to solve the unemployment problem alone, but also the fact that unemployment in Europe is far from being exclusively structural, calls for instruments outside the structural sphere. That European unemployment is characterised by having a strong regional[15] dimension, further points to the need for instruments which affect regions without feeding into other parts of the economy. A pronounced regional policy is also imperative from the perspective of bringing about internal balance within the community. Without regional measures to bring about social cohesion by reducing disparities between regions and the backwardness of less favoured regions, EMU could easily end in a battle of national interests. A prerequisite for undertaking these kinds of policies however, is that there is a considerable budgetary slack. Due to unsustainable debt to GDP ratios, a revision of the criteria and procedures enshrined in the Stability and Growth Pact is probably not on the agenda. This leaves out the possibility of running additionally directed regional policies at national levels and in addition to an intensification of policies geared towards stimulating investment and growth through community banks like EIB and EBRD, calls either for a considerable strengthening of the Structural Funds of the community, notably through a significant increase of the community budget, or to undertake constitutional changes within the community giving rise to something like a federal common policy unit[16].

If not, the unaccommodating macroenvironment offered by the ECB in combination with the Stability and Growth Pact would probably merely promise a continuation of the unemployment problem and in the longer run also severely undermine solidarity within the community.

Summary and Conclusions

In this chapter I have discussed the role of monetary authorities in accomplishing the two periods of convergence observed during the mid-1980s and the seven years before the realisation of the EMU in January

---

[15] In this context regional is also taken to mean national.

[16] The structural funds of the community normally constitute respectively, the European Regional Development Fund (ERDF), the European Social Fund (ESF) and the guidance part of the European Agricultural Guidance and Guarantee Fund (EAGGF). In this context the concept is also taken to include the Cohesion Fund of the Maastricht Treaty.

1999. The chapter also addresses the issue of the future role of monetary *vs.* fiscal policy in the conduct of policies geared towards solving the problem of unemployment in Europe.

My findings indicate that during the 1990s, European Central Banks only to a certain extend can be said to have had control over the long end of the market and that this control eventually must have been of a very short-run character. This result stands in glaring contrast to the claimed position of central banking having been the main reason for the observed convergence and suggests that other sources must have had an important saying as well. In this respect the solemn commitment by national governments to pursue a policy of convergence enshrined in the Growth and Stability Pact, may have been one of the factors that played a significant role by tying the hands of national treasuries *vis-á-vis* the domestic public opinion. Based on the works of Juselius, the fact that also the mid-1980s was a period of fiscal contraction supports a similar point of view for this period. A point worth mentioning and which has not been discussed in the text, is whether the sole process of increased capital mobility independently in some way may have contributed to the convergence. This process is spelled out through strict inflationary control imposed by a regime of fixed exchange rates and the meeting of wage increases by laying off the least productive part of the labour force to uphold a constant profit share in the trading sector. This last point is given some support by the observed high degree of correlation between average productivity and unemployment rates in Europe and signals that the European wage bill to a large extend has been paid by higher unemployment.

The results of Juselius and MacDonald indicate that monetary policy may gain control in the conduct of future anti-inflationary policy. However, as a device to deal with real imbalances there is nothing to indicate a similar prosperity. US long-term interest rates are as exogenous as the German ones. Also, the fact that the ECB will have to pursue a policy geared towards establishing an anti-inflationary reputation will further impair the possibility of undertaking real demand management through the conduct of monetary policy. Structural policies on the other hand may turn out to have unwanted social consequences. Different ways of measuring the "natural" rate may in addition be severely biased in favour of assigning unemployment a structural interpretation. Together with the mere possibility of hysteresis this substantiates the imperative of a future fiscal policy stance, possibly regionally directed, to deal with the problem of unemployment in Europe. The criteria and procedures enshrined in the Stability and Growth Pact further implies that this probably will have to take place at a European level.

In all, this chapter strongly suggests that monetary policy by no means can have been the whole story behind the two periods of convergence. Fiscal policy and the inherent mechanism of high capital mobility are both factors that probably have had an important say as well. Furthermore, the reduced possibility of monetary policy to deal with future real imbalances combined with huge regional unemployment problems within Europe, leaves regional fiscal policy and policies geared towards stimulation of investment and growth as imperative policy measures dealing with real imbalances and unemployment in the future.

CHAPTER 8

Labour Markets and the EMU:
The Cases of Norway and Sweden[1]

Ole Bjørn RØSTE

Introduction

What would the macroeconomic implications be for Norway and Sweden if the countries joined the EMU? Should the two countries join EMU in the future? The standard economic frame of reference for addressing such issues is the theory of Optimum Currency Areas (OCAs), initiated by Robert Mundell[2]. The Swedish EMU Commission[3] provided a report along OCA lines for Sweden, emphasising in particular that an inflexible labour market could make it costly to adopt the euro. Similar, although hypothetical, arguments have been put forward in Norway. The debate has focused on the value of the ability to depreciate substantially outside the EMU, in the event of a large, adverse idiosyncratic real shock – *e.g.* a sharp drop in crude oil prices[4]. I hence focus on the exchange rate channel, one of two channels by which monetary policy can influence the real economy[5].

If we rule out substantial international fiscal transfers subject to national business cycles in the EMU, as I argue we can later in this

---

[1]   I thank Geir Bjønnes, Steinar Holden, Arne Jon Isachsen, Lars Jonung, the editors and conference participants at the *European University Institute* for comments and suggestions. I am grateful to Barry Eichengreen, Maurice Obstfeld, Haakon Solheim, Lasse Stambøl and Erling Steigum for discussions, and to Nils Martin Stølen for guiding my data collection. The usual disclaimer applies.
[2]   Mundell, 1961.
[3]   Calmfors *et al.*, 1997.
[4]   Implications for Norway of the EMU are discussed *e.g.* in Isachsen and Røste, 1999.
[5]   Monetary policy can affect the economy through the exchange rate and interest rate channels. The effects through the two channels are difficult to distinguish as they are dependent without a stable short run interaction pattern. To complicate matters further, monetary policy is known to work with long and variable lags.

chapter, economic adjustment will rely crucially on labour market flexibility, particularly wage flexibility and geographical mobility. I provide evidence on regional labour market adjustment in Norway by estimating the dynamic responses of the employment and participation rates to variations in employment growth (identified as labour demand shocks) in an autoregressive (VAR) system for seven regions and the nineteen counties. The results provide a measure of net geographical migration. I rely on a similar study for Sweden[6].

Intra-national geographical labour mobility is high in both Norway and Sweden. In Norway the regional adjustment processes following labour demand shocks appear quite diverse. The value of stabilisation of national aggregates would decline with increased regional shock or adjustment diversity. I therefore argue that the costs of adopting the euro could be lower for Norway than it is usual to believe. The argument is strengthened by tendencies towards decentralisation and increased transparency in the labour market, suggesting that wage compensation lags after depreciation will shorten in the future.

Enlargement of a given currency area is known to entail both macroeconomic stabilisation costs and microeconomic efficiency benefits, which should, according to the theory, be balanced to construct Optimum Currency Areas. There has been most focus on the macro-economic stabilisation costs, of which the degree of flexibility in the labour market is one particularly important aspect. Lack of flexibility in the labour market will slow down the macroeconomic adjustment process, and increase the value of the ability to pursue stabilising fiscal and monetary policies. The costs of abolishing a national currency to join the EMU would increase *ceteris paribus* if economic adjustment were slow due to inflexible labour or product markets.

Real shocks are either supply or demand disturbances. Supply, *i.e.* productivity or cost, shocks are typically more persistent than demand shocks, and perhaps the most relevant ones in relation to exchange rate adjustment[7]. On the other hand, it is easier to conceive of large asym-metrical demand shocks linked to particular raw materials. In Norway and Sweden, adverse price changes for crude oil and wood pulp could have such an effect. However, it remains controversial whether actual exchange rate changes in practice tend to address macroeconomic stabi-lisation needs. In fact, some asymmetric shocks are transmitted via monetary systems due to speculative transactions in financial markets – often associated with interest and exchange rate turmoil. Large devalua-

---

[6] Fredriksson, 1995.

[7] However, temporary shocks can have long-term real effects due to hysteresis mechanisms.

tions, banking crises and cross-border financial contagion, in several small countries in recent years, illustrate the dangers associated with monetary autonomy without sufficient low-inflation credibility. Nominal shocks of this type would disappear between the members of a currency union.

Needs for stabilising monetary or fiscal policy may arise because nominal rigidities delay the working of equilibrating mechanisms. Sticky nominal wages are perhaps the most important nominal rigidity. Money wages are usually rigid *downwards*. However, the effect of devaluation or depreciation depends largely on *upward* wage rigidity. Swift wage increases would reduce the stabilising effect of a devaluation. Voluntary wage restraint by labour unions could require acute crises and high crisis awareness[8].

The main argument for not joining the EMU seems to be linked to the possibility of large crises associated with unforeseen export shortfall. Under more normal circumstances, in "modern" societies with small, open economies, wage compensation in response to substantial depreciation is likely to be rapid – much more rapid than it was some decades ago. This can reduce the value of exchange rate policies. Collective wage bargaining will probably not suffice to delay wage compensation. First, substantial depreciation will be reflected quickly in consumer prices. Consumer price inflation is common knowledge and compensation claims by labour unions to protect their members' purchasing power can be expected sooner rather than later, also under centralised wage bargaining. Second, the work environment has become more transparent and employees often have good knowledge of their opportunity wages. Thus, labour unions that restrain wage compensation run the risk of losing the members whose skills are most highly valued by the market. Over time, a lower and less skilled membership could erode their political influence. This would reduce the labour unions' incentives to contribute to wage restraint, and thus also the value of a national monetary policy, other than, perhaps, in acute crisis situations.

Composition of real-world currency areas often does not reflect the predictions of the OCA literature[9]: currency areas are surprisingly large in view of this literature. The United States' currency union and the EMU are cases in point. Furthermore, currency areas are delimited not by economic, but by administrative and political boundaries. The former would have maximised macroeconomic stabilisation abilities. Domi-

---

[8] Acceptance by labour to reduce real wages to avoid unemployment is rare, but occurred in Sweden after the devaluation in 1982. See Calmfors and Forslund, 1990.

[9] The same applies for choices of exchange rate regimes within currency areas, as documented *e.g.* by Honkapohja and Pikkarainen, 1992.

nance of the latter suggests that in practice stabilisation is one concern amongst others. It is difficult to explain on OCA grounds why countries like Finland, Germany, Greece, Italy, Spain and Portugal want to participate in the EMU[10]. The Bundesbank could presumably have stabilised the German economy better than the European Central Bank (ECB), and the labour markets of Finland, Greece, Italy, Spain or Portugal are probably not much more flexible than the Norwegian and Swedish ones.

Germany may have consented to the launching of the EMU as a part of a larger bargain, the other side of which may have been the launching of the European Political Union or promises of future inclusion of Germany's neighbours to the East in the EU. Finland may participate in the EMU to demonstrate that this neutral country bordering Russia is firmly anchored in Western Europe[11]. Italy, a founder member of the EU, could loose in prestige if it did not participate in the EMU. It may also have been important to the governments of Italy and other Mediterranean countries to demonstrate their willingness and ability to participate fully in the European integration project. Neither for Denmark and Britain – the countries, other than Sweden, that have chosen not to take part – does the decision on whether or not to join EMU seem particularly related to OCA theory. Political prerogatives may thus overshadow economic arguments in decisions on currency area composition. With sufficient gains in other domains, even substantial OCA costs need not rule out monetary unification.

In the continuation I accept, for the sake of argument, that the costs of joining EMU would be particularly high for countries with rigid labour markets. Labour market flexibility, in terms of wage adjustment or geographic mobility in response to shocks then appears as a prerequisite for benefiting from participation in the EMU. I present the arguments related to my empirical investigation in a wide context that includes some history and institutional details.

The rest of the chapter is organised as follows: In the next section I discuss the macroeconomic policy tradition and practice in Norway and Sweden during the latest decades. Alternative exchange rate arrangements to EMU and the strong interlinkages in practice between stabilisation policy and redistribution, that reduce the possibility of countercyclical fiscal transfers between nations, are then addressed in successive sections. I go on to discuss some factors that limit the use of the exchange rate as a relative cost-competitiveness instrument. I further

---

[10] I discuss this in Røste, 1998 and 2000.

[11] Pekkarinen, 2001, argues that the economic arguments for Finland not to join EMU have been significantly stronger than for Sweden.

estimate a model of regional labour market dynamics in Norway and discuss the findings from this exercise in relation to possible labour market reform, before offering some concluding remarks.

Macroeconomic Policy in Norway and Sweden

Norway and Sweden are located close to the eurozone and are economically integrated with the EU common market. Both countries have traditions for ambitious demand management, aimed at securing high employment, and both have deregulated their economies since the 1980s. Deregulation seems to have been instigated by requirements of European integration, and a shift of the emphasis in economic policy, away from short-term demand management. Like in other countries, the policy establishment has developed close to consensus norms for the evaluation of economic policy, emphasising price stability and the long-term sustainability of public debts.

Although far from universally accepted, the schools of public choice, time inconsistency, and rational expectations, have been influential here as elsewhere in Europe. For example, the Maastricht and Amsterdam treaties on European monetary unification embody such policy norms[12]. In Norway and Sweden a shift in the same direction appears to have taken place since the mid-1980s, possibly as a lagged response to corresponding developments on the continent.

The late timing of this change may reflect the strong Keynesian influence in the two countries. Pekkarainen discusses the proliferation of Keynesian ideas, defined as activist macroeconomic policies, to Scandinavia, emphasising the role of the so-called *Stockholm* and *Oslo* schools of economic thought[13]. Keynes's views expressed in the *General Theory* were not new to Gunnar Myrdal or Ragnar Frisch. The two groups of economists developed Keynesian-style economic-policy views by themselves, which strengthened the Keynesian influence. Especially in Norway, economic policy-making has been tightly linked to the economics profession. Unlike in Sweden, there has been little conflict between policy makers and academic economists.

The new Swedish monetary and fiscal policy legislation of the 1990s can in part be understood against a background of disappointment with the economic outcomes produced by activist macroeconomic policies since the 1970s. The background documents[14] stressed the necessity to

---

[12] The appropriate degree of state intervention in the economy is an unresolved issue. For accounts that advocate a limited rule of the state, in contrast to the earlier practice in Norway and Sweden, see *e.g.* Tanzi, 1997 and Dhotier and Kapur, 1996.

[13] Pekkarainen, 1989.

[14] SOU 1993: 16; 1993: 90; 1996: 14.

avoid too lax monetary and fiscal policy, which had in the past led to higher inflation without higher output or lower unemployment[15]. Similar thinking has influenced policy-making in Norway. In this respect both countries appear to have become more "EMU compatible".

Since the recession of the early 1990s, Norway and Sweden have experienced low inflation, which could perhaps be locked in through EMU membership. However, the prospects for continued low inflation also appear good outside the EMU. One reason is the cited policy preference shift of the 1980s. A second reason is that the countries outside the EMU must convince financial markets that the decision not to join the union does not signal intentions to inflate and depreciate[16]. This point remains in spite of the weakening of the euro throughout 1999 and 2000: over time the euro will be the dominant currency in Europe. A third reason is that in the EU, exchange rate changes are seen as matters of common concern. In a common market ruling out the imposition of tariffs, the tolerance for exchange rate depreciation is likely to remain limited.

Moreover, credibility considerations reduce the scope for inflationary policies. The room for discretion in monetary and fiscal policy alike has arguably declined compared to the situation before the EMU was established. From the perspective of financial markets, the Maastricht and Amsterdam treaties not only establish a set of norms for responsible policies in the eurozone, but also establish a benchmark for the evaluation of economic policy in the EMU's vicinity. The "outs" may therefore find it in their own best interests to abide by the policy norms and regulations that were invented to secure price stability and fiscal policy sustainability within the EMU.

Like some other central banks, the Norwegian and Swedish ones have attained increased policy autonomy. Legally, this process has advanced most in Sweden, where the Riksbank has practised explicit inflation targeting since 1993, as codified in the Riksbank law in force from 1999. In Norway, the central bank has enjoyed considerable monetary policy discretion in its interpretation of a rather vague exchange rate regulation in recent years. The necessary conditions for maintaining exchange rate stability over time, not short term, were emphasised, and an inflation rate close to the one the ECB aims at was seen as a prerequisite. Thus, both central banks practice some sort of "inflation targeting". Norway formally introduced a 25% inflation target

---

[15] Jonung, 1999, pp. 225-230.
[16] Calmfors *et al.*, 1997. Even the governments of other Common Market countries may need to be convinced that a country's monetary arrangements do not imply risks of competitive devaluation.

in March 2001. The difference as EMU members would be the inability to pursue idiosyncratic monetary policy for national stabilisation purposes. This would be most costly in the event of large and frequent asymmetric shocks.

The Swedish Lindbeck commission[17] advised against the use of fiscal policy for the fine-tuning of aggregate demand. Fiscal activism was recommended only to achieve large adjustments, *i.e.* in crisis situations. By contrast, the Norwegian policy community emphasises the role of fiscal stabilisation within the so-called "Solidarity Alternative" (a three-component framework for macroeconomic management, where the two other components have been a fixed or stable nominal exchange rate and incomes' policy, meant to secure cost competitiveness). This optimism is perhaps understandable as regards stabilisation though fiscal expansion, in view of the large public sector surpluses. However, a fiscal contraction is particularly difficult to implement in Norway, as illustrated by the bi-annual budget processes during some recent years of strong growth. There has been a lasting problem of explaining to the public that one should refrain from domestic spending to avoid inflation. In my view, the obvious response to this problem would be to facilitate labour in-migration. This would make labour less scarce in the production of services and non-tradeable goods and dampen inflationary pressures. Membership of the EU and the EMU could contribute significantly, by reducing inflationary expectations and making it more attractive to migrate to Norway.

The Alternatives to EMU Membership

The defining real or nominal characteristics of a currency are (1) its yield curve across maturities (the interest rate) and (2) the exchange rate *vis-à-vis* any other currency. Monetary policy works through both channels. I focus here on the prospects for utilisation of the former, specifically the ability to devalue or depreciate substantially. This corresponds most closely with the concept of OCA costs. What menu could Norway and Sweden chose from as EMU "outs"?

Figure 1. Foreign-Exchange Regimes ranked by Exchange Rate Flexibility

|--------------------------x --------------x--------------------x----------------------x---------------------|

Monetary union Currency board ERM[18] Fixed, adjustable rate Crawling peg Floating rate

Figure 1 depicts some of the several possible monetary policy regimes, depending on the degree of restrictions on the exchange rate.

---

[17] SOU 1993: 16.

[18] ERM: The Exchange rate mechanism in the European Monetary System (EMS).

217

The possibility to realign will be associated with an option value that would vanish in a currency union, due to high political exit costs[19]. On the other hand, adjustable pegs and target zone arrangements facilitate realignment. More constrained arrangements like inflation-targeting regimes, could also allow instigation of exchange rate changes – though to a lesser extent. Such regimes aim at stabilising the economy through the anchoring of inflation expectations.

The ECB's monetary policy provides a benchmark that limits the feasibility of monetary expansion for the "outs". However, this is not to say that they cannot use monetary policy for economic stabilisation. For example, Britain and Sweden have addressed nation-specific stabilisation needs through monetary policy since the European currency turmoil in the fall of 1992. From the outset, independent monetary policies implied large nominal, but temporary, depreciation *vis-à-vis* the other pre-1992 ERM currencies. The results may appear better than the *ex ante* expectations. This has been possible due to the inflation-targeting regimes of Britain and Sweden that have been interpreted as strong commitments to low inflation. Another possible explanation is that the labour market reforms of the 1980s weakened the bargaining position of labour, particularly in Britain, and increased the wage compensation lags following depreciation. This might have made monetary policy more effective in stimulating aggregate demand.

The effect of a given policy can be expected to increase with its credibility. Monetary policy discretion for macroeconomic stabilisation will be limited under inflation-targeting, as the credibility of an inflation target might suffer if the economic policy stance is seen as too expansionary. Sharp depreciation usually means higher inflation that might jeopardise credibility unless there are prospects for very low inflation to begin with. On the other hand, a monetary policy seen as too restrictive can become less credible due to political opposition.

A credible commitment to keep inflation low, at a level not too different from the one the ECB aims at implies that any episodes of significant depreciation *vis-à-vis* the euro will be seen as temporary. By contrast, few would expect depreciation to be reversed if it reflects high domestic inflation and an eroded cost competitiveness position. Rather, the inflation expectations might rise and the depreciation continue, aggravating the inflation problem and leading to devaluation cycles, like in Norway and Sweden in the early 1980s.

---

[19] However, many currency unions have been broken up historically. The break-ups have been associated with large external shocks, such as World War One in the case of the gold standard, or the breaking up of large states like the Soviet Union. See Bordo and Jonung, 2000.

Because monetary authorities usually interact strategically with financial market players, the option to realign or depreciate is unlikely to be free. Investors will not hold claims in a currency that is expected to decrease in value unless they are compensated by higher yields. The costs of the option will thus materialise in risk premia on interest rates increasing with the expected likelihood of the option being exercised, and, possibly, influenced by risk aversion amongst investors. Consequently, the exchange rate and interest rates could become highly volatile or attain undesired levels due to the existence of an option to realign or depreciate. Worse still, the literature of self-fulfilling speculative attacks shows that financial market players can sometimes coordinate to force monetary authorities to exercise the realignment option even if they do not want to[20].

If the depreciation option is exercised, more depreciation will usually be expected. The price paid to retain the option, in terms of interest rate risk premia, will increase together with expected inflation. Policy credibility needs thus reduce the value of the option to devalue or depreciate. Following the large devaluations of the early 1980s, Holden and Vikøren[21] find empirical support for excess returns or a risk premium for the Norwegian but not for the Swedish krone. It was more costly for Norway to get away with several small devaluations than for Sweden to get away with a few large ones. The larger number of devaluations in Norway may have been detrimental to credibility.

One obvious way to address the credibility problem is the adoption of institutional designs that imply various degrees of "tying one's hands". However, actors who are capable of tying their hands are usually also able to untie them. Thus, to attain credibility, a sizeable political cost might be required to be associated with the reneging on the promises made not to depreciate. Political exit costs would further reduce the option value associated with devaluation or depreciation. Some of the institutional monetary and fiscal policy reforms in Norway and Sweden in the 1990s can probably be seen as attempts to enhance credibility by reducing flexibility.

High costs associated with retaining an option to depreciate substantially would *ceteris paribus* make adoption of the euro more attractive. The only viable alternative could be to adapt a policy framework made up by transparent and credible policies to keep inflation low. Thus far, the latter has been done by the central banks of both Norway

---

[20] An exchange rate peg that would survive indefinitely without an attack may be broken at once if attacked. Fundamentals may affect the likelihood of attacks. See *e.g.* Obstfeld, 1994.

[21] Holden and Vikøren, 1994.

and Sweden. However, it remains to be seen how robust and credible the new monetary policy will be in combination with the national fiscal policies. In Norway, a combination of low monetary policy credibility and oil-related fiscal expansion could entail monetary instability. In the event of this, EMU membership could imply a more stable monetary environment. This observation seems important in light of the political pressures to spend large revenues from abroad domestically.

Fiscal Co-Insurance: Stabilisation *vs.* Redistribution

National fiscal co-insurance schemes have entailed significant income redistribution between groups and regions. This would probably apply also for fiscal co-insurance between European nations[22]. It is difficult to maintain in practice a sharp distinction between insurance and redistribution, partly due to the difficulties of knowing the duration of shocks at early stages. A permanent negative real shock cannot be cushioned over the long term, due to the long-run budget constraint. If the currency is depreciated, the terms of trade worsen immediately. Residents of the affected will share the long-run income loss according to their exposure to foreign trade. In a small, open economy the loss may be widely shared amongst them – perhaps more so than losses due to high and persistent unemployment. This adjustment mechanism is not available in the EMU.

Within nations fiscal transfer provides an important adjustment mechanism. Obstfeld and Peri[23] point to the net transfers to the Atlantic Provinces and the *Mezzogiorno* of Canada and Italy. This pattern has remained intact for some time, and it has arguably been possible to predict the direction of future fiscal transfers. Also in Norway and Sweden, there have been predictable patterns in interregional transfers. For instance, the counties of the North of both countries have been net recipients. Redistribution thus appears an integral part of the national fiscal transfers systems. This renders such transfer schemes inefficient for insurance purposes. The potential moral hazard problems due to the possibility of behaviour aimed at securing continued fiscal transfers, could probably only be alleviated by inter-regional solidarity. This would be most easily achieved within small fiscal entities. Regional tensions within European nations have sometimes been seen as results of regional redistribution without the necessary solidarity. As the social cohesion that renders fiscal co-insurance schemes with regional redistribution possible in most nations seems to be missing in the EU, international fiscal co-insurance may not be available in the EMU.

---

[22] Fiscal transfer between countries subject to national business cycles.
[23] Obstfeld and Peri, 1998.

Schemes for international fiscal co-insurance in the EMU often suffer from serious potential moral hazard problems, entailing unattractive economic-efficiency properties. To address this concern, von Hagen and Hammond[24] have identified a rather complicated and non-transparent formula for the EU that satisfies the efficiency requirements (*i.e.* significant co-insurance without serious moral hazard problems). However, the simplifications that might be needed in practice would make it increasingly possible to forecast *ex ante* the direction and magnitude of the implied redistribution. This would worsen the insurance properties and/or the moral hazard problems[25].

Because workable fiscal co-insurance mechanisms seem to imply income transfers that will be predictable *ex ante*, strong feelings of community or solidarity could be a prerequisite. Ultimately, both the lack of an EU-wide fiscal policy and the highly independent ECB, could be attributed to a "solidarity deficit" at the EU level. Although the European elites may have good reasons to trust each other, they may have less reason to trust each other's electoral constituencies. The nation states may therefore dominate in fiscal policy for quite a while.

Macroeconomic Stabilisation through Monetary Policy

As discussed above, cost-competitiveness adjustment through the exchange rate may often be of limited value. First, the need to maintain monetary policy credibility limits the value of the depreciation option. Second, the reliance on exchange rate adjustment may be seen to entail unacceptable competitiveness shifts between the Common Market partners. The large fraction of intra-industry trade in Europe strengthens this argument. Third, the exchange rate is a very *macro*-oriented policy instrument. Exchange rate changes that satisfy the average needs of a national economy may entail costs for sectors or regions differing from that average. The more diverse one's production structure and trade, the less satisfied would one be even with exactly the desired impacts on the targeted aggregate relative prices. A correct macro-level adjustment could also be more difficult to assess and achieve in a highly diversified economy, due to insufficient or incomplete information on the state of the economy[26].

---

[24] Von Hagen and Hammond, 1998.
[25] The formula that the authors prefer on economic efficiency grounds would probably perform less well outside their sample due to the Lucas critique.
[26] Nonetheless, under centralised bargaining, wages tend to move together across sectors. It is thus not inconceivable that all exports may need price adjustment in the same direction.

Moreover, high capital mobility and developments of financial markets and information technology have implied fast market responses to economic policy. Potentially adverse reactions from global financial markets constrain economic policy aimed at national stabilisation. Globalisation implies that decisions of economic agents have effects in large geographical areas, and thus provides an argument for international policy coordination. Even policies that would in retrospect seem to have good effects on an isolated national economy may not suffice to secure the desired outcomes. There is probably a long-term trend for economies to become more diverse and for markets efficiency to increase. Such developments could over time limit the value and reduce the need for national stabilisation policies.

The Norwegian and Swedish devaluations of the 1970s and 1980s might have been successful in their historical context, in times of small capital flows and heavily regulated financial markets. Policy-makers and financial market participants have since learned, the capital flows have increased, and the financial markets have been deregulated. Today, policies that would entail devaluation cycles appear infeasible. Active demand-management has been discredited because of increased awareness of their attached costs, and due to dissatisfaction with the outcomes that such policies have produced.

The usual Keynesian argument for an active national stabilisation policy is nominal rigidities, particularly nominal wages that are rigid downwards, implying slow adjustment to adverse real shocks, possibly with protracted unemployment. The likely negative effects of significant depreciation or devaluation on the real economy, due to, for example, increased uncertainty and confusing price signals and the tendency for wages to be flexible upwards when the home currency weakens, have attracted less attention. Labour unions rarely accept lower relative wages as a *fait accompli*, and quick wage compensation could easily undo the intended stabilisation effects of a weaker currency.

The wage compensation lags have presumably decreased, and economies are probably less rigid than before[27]. Moreover, the remaining rigidities are likely to be unevenly distributed, reflecting that some groups are more able than others to secure compensation. This poses problems to the extent that one's aim is to strengthen the position of the relatively unfortunate. Short wage compensation lags across the board would make devaluation or depreciation useless. Fragmented wage

---

[27]   Holden, 1998, documents downward wage rigidity in the manufacturing sectors of Norway and Sweden in a switching regression model and estimates nominal wage floors of 2.6 and 3.9 % growth, respectively. The functional form of the wage setting process may however have biased positively the high Swedish figure.

bargaining could, however, entail quite long compensation lags for some. This would make devaluation or depreciation more effective as regards cost-competitiveness. However, legitimacy could suffer if the adjustment burden were increasingly to be placed on weak groups.

Successful devaluation or depreciation would thus require slow or incomplete wage compensation, preferably across the board. Under highly centralised bargaining the labour negotiators can internalise the negative inflationary and relative-cost-position consequences of high wage claims. However, this requires strong central labour organisations that are able to commit their members. Traditionally, the central labour organisations have been in this position in Norway and Sweden. Links to the oft-governing social democratic parties used to provide these organisations with considerable political clout. Today, however, social democratic parties govern more seldom and appear more conservative as regards economic policy.

As opportunity wages have become more transparent, employees who can secure better employment terms for themselves outside the unions tend to know of this. Labour unions that restrain wage increases thus risk eroding their membership. In line with this wage bargaining has recently been decentralised in Sweden, with the most important negotiations now taking place at the industry level. Similar tendencies could also entail less centralised wage bargaining in Norway, and reduce the feasibility of a national incomes policy. The central labour organisations can often not satisfy political demands for moderate wage claims across entire nations.

With employees who are sensitive to opportunity wages, labour will probably feel more affinity towards one organisation, the more homogenous it is with respect to member skills and productivity. This is supported by the observation that labour unions have been organised along the lines of functional sectors. The levels and specific types of human capital, as well as remuneration, have been more homogenous within than across sectors. With the development of the "new" economy based on advances in information and communication technology, the economic significance of different skill types and levels have increased[28]. Individuals differ in their abilities to utilise the new technologies. At a higher rate of technological innovation, productivity differences will probably increase, making it more difficult to maintain large

---

[28] The awareness of this has also increased. A manufacturing worker in the "old" economy was tied physically to the real capital and processes of his factory. A software-engineer in the "new" economy, however, could quit his job to sell consulting services, often with reliable information on the economic prospects from this choice and without heavy investments.

labour organisations constituted around collective agreements and remuneration principles. Decentralised bargaining with competition between labour unions could reduce the average wage compensation lags, and therefore diminish the costs of abolishing national exchange rate policies.

Regional Labour Market Adjustment

The evidence to be presented in this section suggests that it may be difficult to speak of one national adjustment pattern, at least in Norway. The approach followed is to estimate, first, for every county and region, and second for the counties pooled with region-specific effects, the dynamic responses to participation and employment rates from shocks to employment growth, identified as labour demand shocks. The Norwegian regional adjustment patterns appear diverse (in spite of statistical inference problems) suggesting that there may be significant economic costs from having a national exchange and interest rate in Norway rather than several regional ones.

Several currencies within Norway would clearly be unfeasible both economically and politically. Economically, scale economies and network externalities would be foregone, the national market for goods and services would become less transparent, and intra-national currency conversion would be too costly in terms of real resources. Regional sub-national monetary policies could also lack the credibility needed to be operational. The question is then whether the same argument applies in relation to adoption of the euro. Whether one should pursue monetary policy nationally or at the European level may not be obvious.

What would the adjustment process be like under EMU? There are good reasons to believe that wage bargaining could become less centralised in Norway, like it has in Sweden, so as to make real wage adjustment through incomes policies less realistic. One cannot either expect much help from substantial fiscal co-insurance at the EU level. Wage flexibility and, particularly, geographic mobility of labour could, however, become more important if Norway and Sweden were to join the EMU.

From the perspective of macroeconomic adjustment, it could be natural to favour wage and price flexibility, and perhaps international labour mobility, over public policy. Both mechanisms rely on market forces. Typically, price and wage flexibility is very limited and geographical mobility quite substantial, within countries. The social costs of migration may be lesser and more acceptable intra-nationally than internationally. Between countries, the real exchange rates have been flexible due to nominal exchange rate variations[29], but there has been little geographical mobility of labour.

Figure 2 illustrates that although there are many aspects of a "well-functioning" labour market, wage flexibility and geographic mobility of labour (or the lack thereof) are particularly important.

Figure 2. Some Aspects of Labour Market Flexibility

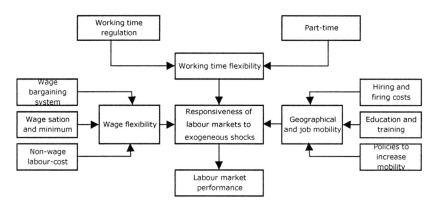

Source: Soltwedel *et al.*, 1999, p. 50.

In a low-inflation environment, nominal wage rigidity may correspond to rigid real wages. Mobility between jobs, locally and geographically, would reduce the stabilisation costs. The latter would however require that vacant positions could be filled elsewhere in the currency area, and limited barriers to relocation due to cultural and language diversity – which could render labour culture-specific with regard to productivity and remuneration – the availability of housing, and so on. Geographic mobility can be expected to decrease if the opportunity wage in another location decreases due to cultural factors, and/or there are significant welfare benefits for those that are unemployed or do not participate in the labour force without relocation. These two factors probably contribute significantly to the low degree of international labour mobility in Europe.

---

[29] This is not to say that nominal exchange rate variations reflect only, or even mainly, macroeconomic stabilisation needs. Rather, exchange rates have often moved for reasons that have appeared unrelated to adjustment needs in the short term, much like other asset prices. It has often been difficult even *ex post* to rationalise exchange rate changes with reference to macroeconomic stabilisation needs.

Wage Rigidity

Rigid nominal wages are well established empirically, yet poorly understood. In a commodity market, imbalances between supply and demand would be resolved by price changes. Analogously, one could imagine that unemployed workers would underbid the wage of the already employed under high unemployment. The labour markets work differently, however. Recent Swedish survey evidence suggests that the unemployed do in fact underbid wages, but that the employers reject underbidding that breaks the firms' internal rules for wage setting[30].

There are several reasons why market-conform adjustment may not be available for the labour market. First, to the employed insider, a stable wage may appear advantageous in the short to medium term. Planning for the near future is simplified, and relatively stable economic living conditions can be secured for a while. Insiders may also want to dampen fluctuations in wages due to risk aversion. However, the present pay will rarely carry much information about an individual's earning prospects in the distant future. Many factors could change, including the individual's productivity, output demand and prices and the technology with which a particular product is produced. If wages varied to reflect such changes, employment prospects would improve. However, labour market insiders would then lose to the unemployed or non-participating. This would be unlikely because the latter groups are rarely well organised. Second, human capital often accounts for a large portion of the wealth of employees, and labour income is more difficult to insure through financial markets than capital income. We can thus expect important political consequences to be associated with changes in labour market regulation.

The sources of wage rigidity remain disputed. To Keynes, nominal wage rigidity was a social fact of life, due to workers' concerns for relative wages and fairness that could not be changed by institutional reform. Others have emphasised the roles of the welfare state and labour unions, in which case institutional reforms could be used to reduce wage rigidity. Fairness considerations – that workers and managers view a cut in money wages as unfair – are also documented to be important for nominal wage rigidity[31].

---

[30] Agell and Lundborg, 1999. This finding conflicts with Solow's, 1990, claim that the absence of underbidding is a stylised fact that should be reflected in labour market models.

[31] Blinder and Choi, 1990, and Bewley, 1998.

226

Hicks[32] links the influence of workers' fairness concerns with the operation of Keynesian demand management policies. He observes that money wages in Britain, particularly in cyclical industries, were flexible before World War One. Since the early 1950s, public policy had made recessions less severe than before. In Hicks' view, this stimulated an increased emphasis on relative wage equalisation that led to more rigid money-wages. This argument appears interesting in relation to wage rigidity in the highly developed welfare states of Norway and Sweden[33]. Holden[34] shows that nominal wage rigidity is possible without fairness considerations, due to an important legal feature of many European labour markets: money wages are given in either collective agreements or individual employment contracts. Hence, employers cannot unilaterally cut nominal wages, even after the expiration of a collective agreement. Unless a work stoppage has been initiated, it is a well established practice that production continues under the terms of the old agreement until a new agreement is reached. Although there are circumstances where the union or employee will accept a wage cut, these circumstances are likely to be associated with higher unemployment than the situations where wage cuts are rejected.

To investigate how the mechanisms that create sticky wages are viewed by the relevant firm-level decision-makers, Agell and Lundborg[35] surveyed 157 Swedish firms in the years 1991 and 1998, before and after the recession of the early 1990s, asking about wage setting and personnel policy. Interestingly, they did not find evidence that the increase in unemployment had softened the mechanisms that generate wage rigidity. Rather, because nominal wages were seldom reduced, real wages had become more rigid in a period where inflation had been markedly reduced. The authors traced the nominal rigidities to both legal provisions of wage contracts and employees' concerns about relative income and fairness, and also conjectured that certain aspects of the social safety net provided by the Swedish welfare state have aggravated wage rigidity. This study confirms wages rigidity in Sweden, but does not provide clear answers on the relative strengths of the known sources for rigid wages. It documents that high unemployment has been insufficient to instigate nominal wage flexibility in Sweden. Unfortunately, this does not allow us to draw conclusions as to how

---

[32] Hicks, 1974.
[33] Nickell and Jackman, 1991 find flexible real wages in Norway and Sweden. This finding may, however, be due to frequent devaluations in the sample period – a policy option no longer available. More recent studies conclude that real wages in Norway and Sweden are rigid. See, *e.g.*, Holden, 1998.
[34] Holden, 1994; Holden, 2001.
[35] Agell and Lundborg, 1999.

EMU membership would influence wage formation, as Sweden is not a member of the EMU.

Agell and Lundborg's findings provide support for Tobin's "nominal wage floor"[36], which would make the labour market function less well when inflation is very low. Downward wage flexibility is very problematic in a low-inflation environment. Agell and Lundborg interpret their findings as *"prima facie* evidence that it will take more than several years of very high unemployment and very low inflation to create a hole in the Keynesian wage floor"[37]. However, others, including Berthold *et al.*[38], have argued that EMU is likely to lead to increased price and wage flexibility, because everyone will understand the need for this. This appears analogous to Thatcher's famous "there is no alternative": it is difficult to see that wage flexibility would follow automatically because it will be more needed. However, in the relatively closed eurozone economy, labour cannot be bailed out by currency depreciation if high real wages lead to increased unemployment. Many policy makers seem to believe in increased wage flexibility due to the EMU, and labour unions and others may increasingly find it in their own best interest to facilitate downward wages flexibility to avoid unemployment. Still whether or not the EMU will lead to wage flexibility and if so when, remain unresolved issues.

Labour Market Adjustment

Assume that an adverse trade shock leads to reduced labour demand and labour productivity stays constant. Equilibrium can in principle be restored by a combination of the following mechanisms:

1. Real wage reduction in the industry that is hit (reduced nominal wages);
2. Geographic mobility of workers to other labour markets, possibly abroad;
3. Reduced participation in the workforce;
4. Mobility of workers between firms in the local labour market.

The equilibrating process may work slowly. High wage and/or price flexibility would imply low OCA costs (*i.e.* low costs from giving up one's monetary autonomy). With limited flexibility in prices and/or wages, OCA costs could be significant. However, labour mobility, locally or geographically, could dampen the costs. Most relocation is

---

[36] Tobin, 1972.
[37] Agell and Lundborg, 1999, p. 6.
[38] Berthold *et al.*, 1999.

local. Micro-data studies confirm that local job mobility, which need not imply change of residence, is important in labour market adjustment. Geographical mobility is also important within some European nations. However, international labour mobility is very limited in Europe, in spite of the common labour market.

Blanchard and Katz[39] identify the changes in employment growth as labour demand shocks, which trigger transitory responses in wages and unemployment and lead to permanent changes in employment. The firms are assumed to be heterogeneous within regions[40]. Thus, the adjustment must take the form of a real wage reduction (due to reduced nominal wages, as higher prices is unrealistic following a negative shock), mobility of workers to other labour markets not affected by the shock, or by voluntary reduction of the participation rate. Empirical work indicates that the adjustment paths vary considerably across countries.

In the studies following Blanchard and Katz, a three-equation vector-autoregressive system is estimated[41]. The variables of interest are (1) the change in the log level of employment, (2) the log employment rate (ratio of employment to the labour force) and (3) the log participation rate (ratio of labour force to working age population). The employment series is usually differenced once because it contains a unit root (which appears to be true also for the data analysed here). The most crucial assumption is perhaps the identifying assumption – that changes in employment represent labour demand shocks. The innovations to the employment growth equation are thus interpreted as exogenous labour demand shocks.

By definition we have, (1) $N = E * P * Pop$,

where N is regional employment and E and P is the employment and participation rates and Pop denotes the working-age population. For percentage changes, and also for relative regional variables[42], this implies:

---

[39] Blanchard and Katz, 1992.

[40] Adjustment mechanism 4 above is thus not considered. It would be difficult to measure local labour-related relocation without access to register-based micro data. Such material is studied for Norway, Sweden and Finland by Stambøl *et al.*, 1999.

[41] Other studies in this tradition are Jimeno and Bentolila, 1998 (Spain, quarterly data), Decressin and Fatas, 1995 (Europe), Fredriksson, 1995 (Sweden), Obstfeld and Peri, 1998 (Europe and the United States), and Mauro and Spilimbergo, 1999 (Spain, workers by educational group).

[42] A relative regional variable is one particular regional variable minus the corresponding national variable. The relative regional variables can thus be interpreted as deviations from the national average.

(2) $\Delta N/N = \Delta E/E + \Delta P/P + \Delta Pop/Pop$.

Hence, a positive $\Delta Pop/Pop$ can be interpreted as inward migration, if regional demographic trends are shared by the entire nation, or if those trends evolve independently of the shocks to employment growth that are assumed to be exogenous labour demand shocks. Net migration can then be inferred from the behaviour of employment, the employment rate and the participation rate.

The Norwegian Data

The data are of the annual frequency from 1964 to 1998, and include the participation and employment rates, and the number of employed person for two aggregation levels – the nineteen counties and seven larger regions, comprised of two to four adjacent counties[43]. A data description with graphs is provided in appendix I. The unemployment rates have been high in the four northernmost counties (Nord Trøndelag, Nordland, Troms and Finnmark) and some rural counties of the South, and low in Oslo and Akershus. The participation rate has been particularly high (above 100%) for Oslo, as commuters from the surrounding counties make the number of labour market participants exceed the number of work-age residents. Graph 1 below shows developments in the national Norwegian labour market.

Graph 1: The National Variables

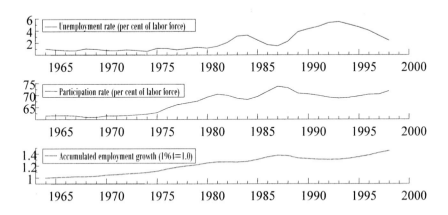

---

43 The regions are Oslo and Akershus, South Coast (Østfold, Buskerud, Vestfold and Telemark), South Central (Hedmark and Oppland), South West (Aust-Agder, Vest-Agder and Rogaland), West (Hordaland, Sogn og Fjordane and Møre og Romsdal), Central (Sør- and Nord-Trøndelag) and North (Nordland, Troms and Finnmark).

For the number of employed persons, there has been consistent growth with large regional variations. From 1964 to 1998, the national number has grown by on average 1.1% annually, multiplying by 1.45. Akershus County has experienced the highest growth, at an annual average of 3.1%, multiplying by 2.81. Also the South West, particularly Rogaland with the "oil capital" Stavanger has seen strong growth, at an annual average of about 2.0%. The opposite tendency is registered for the South Coast (except for Buskerud county which has grown like the national average), and the North (although Troms has grown at on average 1.8% annually, well above the national average). The growth has also been low in Telemark, Oppland and Hedmark – mainly agrarian counties of the South.

There is positive correlation for the averages of all variables, in both the counties and the regions, between the periods 1964-1968 and 1994-1998, suggesting persistency over time[44]. Unemployment has been most persistent at the highest aggregation level. This is consistent with more stable natural unemployment rates for the regions than for the counties. The data show strong auto-correlation, particularly for employment and participation rates[45]. The regional shocks are idiosyncratic by construction, as the relative regional variables are constructed by deducting the corresponding national variable from the regional one.

Results

The results indicate that intra-regional labour mobility is high. There appears to be large differences between the regions, as illustrated by the graphs in Appendix II. The estimated equations are:

$$\Delta N_{it} = \alpha_{i10} + \alpha_{i11}(L)\Delta N_{i,t-1} + \alpha_{i12}(L)E_{i,t-1} + \alpha_{i13}(L)P_{i,t-1} + \varepsilon_{iSt}$$

$$E_{it} = \alpha_{i20} + \alpha_{i21}(L)\,\Delta N_{i,t} + \alpha_{i22}(L)E_{i,t-1} + \alpha_{i23}(L)P_{i,t-1} + \varepsilon_{iE\,t}$$

$$P_{it} = \alpha_{i30} + \alpha_{i31}(L)\,\Delta N_{i,t} + \alpha_{i32}(L)E_{i,t-1} + \alpha_{i33}(L)P_{i,t-1} + \varepsilon_{iPt}$$

Employment growth (ΔN) is thus allowed to affect the employment (E) and participation (P) rates instantaneously, in period t, whereas the opposite is true only after one period's lag. The αs are the estimated coefficients on the lagged variables and the εs the error terms. The

---

[44] For the counties the positive correlation in relative regional variables is most marked for the participation and unemployment rates ($r = .86$ and $r = .60$), and lower for employment growth ($r = .40$). For the regions, the positive correlation is sharply lower for the participation rate ($r = .58$) and employment growth ($r = .14$). For the unemployment rate, however, correlation is sharply higher ($r = .95$).

[45] This is evident from both formal tests and estimates of univariate models.

equations allow for constants and trends, consistent with for example differing natural rates of unemployment, and differing levels of employment growth due to localisation preferences of employees and/or businesses. The estimation has been done with two and three lags, with very similar results. Henceforth I refer to the estimation with three lags, which seems to fit the data best.

I estimate dynamic responses to employment growth shocks in the individual counties and regions, and pooled for counties and regions[46]. The approach used here differs from previous studies following the Blanchard and Katz (1992) study by including in the pooled estimation a control variable for the distance of each county or region from Oslo (defined as road distance from the geographical centre of the region to Oslo).

Dynamic Responses to Employment Growth Shocks

The applied shock is a one-percent decrease in regional employment growth in year 1. Thus, migration is $(-.01 - \Delta E/E - \Delta P/P)$ in year one and $(\Delta N/N - \Delta E/E - \Delta P/P)$ in later years. The point estimates for regions and counties are inaccurate. However, the uncertainty may be reduced when results for individual counties and regions are compared and analyzed in the context of the results from pooled estimation.

Graph 3: Pooled Estimation for the Nineteen Norwegian Counties

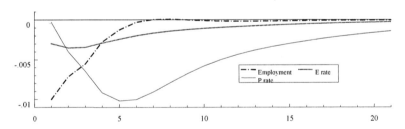

---

[46] The reliance on only two endogenous variables might instigate criticism that the model is too simple and severely misspecified, so that inferences based on the dynamic responses of the employment and participation rates based on equation (2) may be misleading. I have thus done the same estimations with a third endogenous variable included, wages costs per employee. This does not change the results a lot.

Graph 4: Pooled Estimation for the Seven Norwegian Regions

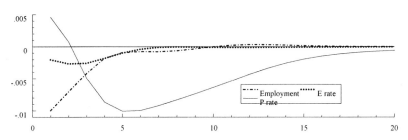

When regions and counties are pooled, net out-migration in response to the adverse shocks is initially very high, following a hump-shaped pattern. The out-migration then decreases rapidly, turns into in-migration in year 3, reaches its maximum in year 5, and tapers off to about zero in year 10. This pattern appears robust to specification (different lag lengths and inclusion of the variable wage costs per worker). The mobility between the regions is initially higher than between the counties. The impulse responses (in Appendix II) suggest a considerable variety in adjustment to labour demand shocks in the individual counties and regions. I interpret this as evidence of diverse adjustment processes although roughly the same stylised pattern emerges in the pooled estimation for counties and regions and even though the results are preliminary.

For the individual counties and regions, the diversity is particularly marked for the evolution of the participation rates, which in most instances decrease immediately. However, the participation rate is largely unchanged in the short run in the region South Coast and it increases in Akershus, Hedmark and Vestfold counties. There is relatively limited mobility out of the counties with the largest cities. The "regional capitals" may perhaps buffer strong flows of workers due to their large size and the relatively stable employment prospects they offer locally.

Fredriksson[47] found that Swedish regional labour market adjustment has been relatively rapid in an international perspective. Net inter-county labour mobility in response to labour demand shocks has been on par with mobility between the US states[48]. I find evidence of even higher net mobility between the Norwegian counties and regions.

---

[47] Fredriksson, 1995.
[48] Mobility between the US states is documented by Blanchard an Katz, 1992 and Obstfeld and Peri, 1998.

The focus on the typical region can in my view be a bit misleading, as there are often large regional differences[49]. For instance, there are essentially two Swedish labour markets: one in Stockholm with scarce labour, and one in the periphery with excess labour supply. The explanation of this dichotomy lies partly in the rent-regulated Stockholm housing market. Potential employees, who have not already been present, registered in a queue for subsidised housing for years, may not find housing. To buy housing would be very expensive for liquidity-constrained workers, and very risky for people with short time horizons. This situation probably entails large and persisting regional differences in labour market adjustment processes. A monetary policy well suited for Sweden on the aggregate might fit well neither for Stockholm nor for the periphery. The costs of refraining from monetary-policy-based stabilisation would be reduced due to such heterogeneity.

In Norway, there has been a tendency for Norwegian labour market segregation during periods with strong growth in the Oslo area. However, rent control for housing is being gradually phased out. Rental housing thus becomes available, providing an alternative for risk averse workers with short horizons to making the strong commitment of buying a home. However, most Norwegians own their own home and the rental market is small. Inflated rents thus dampen migration to Oslo during booms.

Workers from nations with high intra-national mobility could perhaps have a high propensity to be mobile internationally. If so, the high geographical mobility within Norway and Sweden might suggest that a high fraction of these countries' employees could be mobile internationally in the future, provided that they face suitable incentives. Following an adverse national shock, mobility would then be higher if there were many vacant positions elsewhere in Europe, if Norwegian and Swedish labour productivity were not closely tied to the national cultures, and if the welfare benefits favoured employment abroad over unemployment or non-participation in the labour force at home. The net gain from mobility would differ between age and education groups. Perhaps only the young and highly educated – with human capital to utilise and maintain – can sustain the costs of short-term relocation. However, with increased mobility expatriate networks of Norwegians and Swedes could develop. This could reduce the costs of mobility for other groups in the labour market and serve as a catalyst for migrations, even for short time horizons.

---

[49] In Sweden, Uppsala and Halland stand out as counties of dynamic growth in the sample period. The opposite tendency is found for the forest counties of the North.

Stambøl *et al.*[50] investigate labour market adjustment in Norway, Sweden and Finland during two periods marked by different cyclical conditions, using register-based micro data for ISIC 1-digit industries. Because the business cycles have been non-synchronous, they use different years to represent favourable and unfavourable cyclical conditions in Norway and Sweden[51]. Gross geographical mobility is highest under favourable business conditions, increases with education (a proxy for the level of human capital), and decreases with age except for among the highly educated. There are large differences across industries: workers of in the primary sectors and construction appear to be the least geographically mobile. (However, construction workers frequently commute to construction sites without change of residence.) The employees of the education-intensive sectors of public service provision and financial services were the most geographically mobile. Workers who left agriculture and manufacturing were frequently not employed in other industries. Labour mobility, made up of gross local and geographical mobility, was substantial in both countries but usually higher for Norway than for Sweden. Mostly, this was due to substantially higher geographical mobility in Norway. This fits well with my findings of higher net geographical mobility following labour demand shocks in Norway than in Sweden.

There has been substantial geographic mobility *intra-nationally* in Norway and Sweden, if not *internationally*. The relative number of foreign residents illustrates this for inward mobility. Although there was an increase from 1990 to 1998, the percentage of foreign residents was low in both countries[52]. It was higher for Sweden than for Norway, reflecting in part a substantial in-migration of Finns at a time when there was a large real-wage differential between Sweden and Finland[53]. Based on the small stock of foreign residents in Norway and Sweden, international labour-related mobility appears low, and lower for Norway than for Sweden.

---

[50] Stambøl *et al.*, 1999.

[51] The years representing weak cyclical conditions for Norway and Sweden are 1988-1989 and 1992-1993, respectively. The years that represent strong cyclical conditions are 1994-1995 in both countries.

[52] Between 1990 and 1998 the share of foreign residents in the population aged 15 to 70 years increased from 3.7 to 4.1% in Norway and from 5.9 to 6.4% in Sweden. In 1998, the Nordic and European share was 1.3 and 2.7% in Norway, compared to 2.1 and 4.3% for Sweden. The share of Norwegians in Sweden and Swedes in Norway were 0.6 and 0.4%, respectively.

[53] Lundborg, 1991.

To put the findings for Norway and Sweden into perspective, Obstfeld and Peri[54] report results for a number of countries with a similar methodology: the shock to employment is persistent for the first five years in all countries, both in Europe and the United States. Geographical mobility, however, is remarkably lower in Europe. Furthermore, in other European countries the participation rate typically moves sharply and temporarily to absorb the shock. Compared to this, the reaction in the participation rate in Norway appears to start later and be more persistent. Note, however, that international comparisons should be made with care as the geographical units usually differ in size.

There are typically large and persistent differences on labour market variables within countries. Soltwedel *et al.*[55] see the typical pattern in Europe as "regional non-adjustment to region-specific shocks". Regional adjustment seems to work better in Norway and Sweden. Still, the diverse regional adjustment pattern in Norway suggests that some regions could benefit from increased autonomy with regard to the national labour market regulations and institutions. The regional dimension of the labour market may thus deserve more attention. Focus on this could be a useful supplement to the selective regional fiscal measures used in Norway and Sweden.

Implications for Labour Market Reform?

In the EMU, an inflexible labour market can become costly due to high cyclical unemployment. The equilibrium or natural rate of unemployment might then increase if hysteresis effects are strong, due to for example skill degradation among the unemployed. We do not know that such problems would increase if Norway or Sweden joined the EMU. However, it is common to address needs for labour market reform in this perspective. Labour market reform can in principle come about through three channels:

- Endogenous labour market responses to a new monetary environment;

- Government reform of regulations and labour market institutions;

- Supply-side measures aimed at reducing equilibrium unemployment.

The labour market structure and institutions are important for economic stability, and it is often argued that this would be particularly important if participation in the EMU should become a reality. Some have argued that there is a need to promote nominal wage flexibility

---

[54]   Obstfeld and Peri 1998, p. 222.

[55]   Soltwedel *et al.*, 1999. .

through labour market reform. For instance, the Swedish EMU Commission suggested that it was important to enhance employer bargaining power through reduced unemployment benefit levels, reformed financing of unemployment benefits, reduced protection of employees against layoffs and a reformed framework for wage negotiations. These radical proposals must be understood in the context of the severe unemployment situation in 1995-96. It would be difficult politically to win acceptance for such far-reaching programmes, as easily identifiable, well-organised groups stand to lose. In spite of the costs for labour market outsiders if supply-side measures are not sufficiently addressed, one may thus have to consider alternatives.

Others have advocated that labour market reform should be addressed in a European framework. This approach would hardly be the best response to the unemployment problems in Norway and Sweden. First, the different problems and institutions in different countries may call for different policies. Second, as it is not clear how one should proceed to promote employment the co-existence of various institutions and regulations could be advantageous for learning. Some of the most severe unemployment problems appear to be regional. This suggests that increased leeway with regard to national regulations and institutions may be beneficial. I take the findings in this chapter to indicate that this may apply for Norway.

Minimum labour standards in the EU could be seen as an important symbol of political success for labour in a unified Europe. The fact that labour market regulation and institutions tend to be standardised and uniform within nations, in spite of diverse economic adjustment needs and regional structural problems, may suggest that EU-level labour market regulations and institutions will develop over time if the economic and political integration continues. If so, European labour standards should be created with a view to the needs for flexibility in the regional and national economies that constitute the EU. Too ambitious minimum standards could result in de-industrialisation and depopulation of some areas and aggravation of some severe national and regional unemployment problems.

Conclusions

The strongest argument for staying out of the EMU seems to be the value of the ability to depreciate the exchange rate substantially in the event of a large, adverse idiosyncratic shock. Recent years have seen events of far-reaching macro-economic consequences that could not easily be predicted, including the German reunification, the break-up of the Soviet Union and the wars in the Balkans. Unpredictable events can be expected also in the future. They may severely distort foreign trade, and may affect European nations differently, as Finland experienced when its exports to the Soviet Union abruptly ended in the early 1990s. The ability to depreciate one's currency *vis-à-vis* one's trading partners may in such instances be the best insurance available. Under more normal circumstances, however, the ability to depreciate may not be of much help.

The recession of the early 1990s illustrates the different exposure of Norway and Sweden to a large adverse shock. Sweden experienced the most severe downturn, partly becau Swedish public finances were weaker than the Norwegian ones[56]. Public debt levels constrained the room for fiscal expansion, but not to the extent implied by EMU-type constraints on public budget deficits and debts. Still, the weak public finances in Sweden may have blocked the option to counteract the downturn through job creation in public service provision, which played a role in Norway. Monetary policy became important. EMU membership at that time could have implied a tighter fiscal policy, which would have deepened the recession. It would not have been possible to get out of the crisis by currency depreciation. However, due to a firm anchoring of exchange rate and interest rate expectations, EMU membership might have stabilised nominal developments earlier, to make the crisis – and thus the stabilisation needs – less acute.

A second possible argument against EMU membership is that Norway and Sweden may have somewhat different preferences from other EMU members as regards the trade-off between GDP and price stabilisation. This could entail costs of monetary unification even without asymmetric real shocks. The strong consensus that has evolved among policy makers in recent years on what constitutes "good policy", suggests that preference divergence is unlikely to cause major problems soon. This common understanding and the logic of financial markets may suffice to convince governments that they should pursue low-inflation policies. It is perhaps more worrisome that the norms and rules for economic policy may change after one has become a member. EMU membership could then be costly if high exit costs made one accept otherwise unpalatable economic policy change.

Fiscal policy would be constrained by the Stability and Growth Pact and the *excessive deficit procedure*. However, the Stability Pact does not regulate the size of the public sector. Neither does it regulate public

---

[56] Between 1991 and 1993 the Swedish GDP fell by more than 5%. Total unemployment, including labour market programmes, increased from less than 4 to more than 12% of the work force. Negative economic growth combined with record unemployment severely drained public finances.

sector composition. The fiscal constraints would be more binding for Sweden than for Norway, at least for a while, due to the importance of extraction of oil and natural gas in Norway and the associated boost to public finances by conventional accounting rules[57]. To be able to cushion negative shocks through fiscal policy in the EMU, Sweden would need budget surpluses in periods of above-average growth. Given the large public sectors in the Nordic countries, and the strong effect of automatic fiscal stabilisers due to the large public sectors, one would need large surpluses in normal times.

If performance in terms of combinations of unemployment and inflation is best where wage negotiations are either very centralised, like in Norway, or very decentralised, like in the United States, the Norwegian wage bargaining system may seem better suited for EMU than the Swedish one[58]. However, we cannot know that the Norwegian central labour organisation will continue to restrain the wage claims of its members in the future, or that wage bargaining in Norway will stay centralised in spite of such restraints. This would be particularly uncertain if Norway joined the EMU, where labour unions face different incentives than they do nationally, due to their small size and a weak link between regional wage claims and eurozone inflation.

The report of the Swedish EMU Commission concluded that the Swedish labour market was not flexible enough for EMU in 1995-96, and highlighted the risks associated with joining the EMU with high unemployment. Labour market reform was needed, it was argued, irrespective of whether Sweden joined. In spite of some differences, the relevant labour market structures and institutions are quite similar in Norway and Sweden. Thus, the needs for labour market reform are likely to be similar. Wage rigidity would probably remain in the EMU, so labour market adjustment would to an increasing extent have to depend on geographical mobility *vis-à-vis* other eurozone countries. Whether this would be realistic remains an open question.

In assessments of the costs and benefits of adopting the euro, too little attention may have been given to the regional diversity behind nationally aggregated data. Asymmetries in adjustment processes between a set of nations would appear less dramatic if we knew of large asymmetries within the same nations. A national monetary policy could then be too loose in some regions and too restrictive in others. If so,

---

[57] Extraction of oil and gas counts as production in the national accounts, so increased extraction would increase GDP and thus provide some fiscal leeway in relation to the Stability and Growth Pact.

[58] EMU membership may, however, affect whether wage setting is coordinated, see Holden, 2000.

atypical regions would suffer, and the costs of monetary unification might be lower than it is usual to believe.

The other side of the coin would be microeconomic efficiency gains, positive network externalities, reduced needs for currency conversion services, and lower interest rates over the economic cycle. Furthermore, the literature on endogenous currency areas suggests that economic structures and price and wage formation can change to improve performance under a new monetary regime. Some expect the EMU to lead to lesser and less frequent asymmetric real shocks, so as to reduce the needs for national stabilisation policy. More efficient markets, that would increase the speed of economic adjustment, could also result from monetary unification. The positive effects of the euro would most likely increase, and the negative effects decrease, over time, with increasing transaction volumes and increased economic integration *vis-à-vis* the eurozone. Introduction of the euro could also be a particularly potent instrument for instigating increased integration.

The version of the EMU now in place is arguably the only one that was feasible in light of the difficult negotiations in 1995-1996, where North Europeans, particularly the Germans, were assured that they would found a low-inflation monetary area. Other countries were arguably granted a seat at the table for monetary policy decisions, in exchange for accepting "a monetary plan with a German accent[59]". The need to assure the Germans could account for the unique institutional independence of the ECB, unparalleled in national settings where politicians also could intervene directly to control their central banks should they feel the urge. While the ECB should not be expected to appear like its counterparts, with long-established track records and credibility in stable democracies, it could be reasonable to expect such developments over time. The worries voiced by some[60] that monetary policy in EMU is too tight due to the ECB's formal independence could thus be attributed to the logic of transition. Nonetheless, participation in the eurozone would perhaps appear more attractive for Norwegians and Swedes if the ECB were made more accountable, for instance through the national parliaments.

For Norway and Sweden the relevant question is how economic policy will change if the countries join the EMU. The room for policy discretion would be reduced. The critical question is how binding the restrictions would be. Independent monetary policies may be of less value today than before, particularly for small, open economies that are

---

[59] "The monetary plan with a German accent", *Financial Times*, 15 November 1995, p. 3.
[60] See *e.g.* Notermans' contribution to this volume.

highly integrated with their neighbours. In earlier times, aggregate demand management could be pursued with less regard to negative financial market reaction. The change in this domain coupled with the tendency of economic actors to become more sophisticated and markets to become more efficient has made it less important to pursue national policies. Simultaneously, increased economic integration and inter-dependence has made it more important to coordinate policy with one's neighbours. The costs of joining the EMU may thus have decreased.

APPENDIX I – The Norwegian Data

All data are at the annual frequency, from 1964 to 1998.

1. Labour market status for individuals

Unemployed persons. Source: *Historisk statistikk*, Arbeidsdirektoratet.

Labour force. Number of employed persons from the annual national accounts. Unemployed persons have been added on to this.

Working-age population. Data by age, category and county from Statistics Norway.

Employed persons: Aggregate national data redistributed regionally based on the regional national accounts for the years 1965, 1973, 1976, 1980, 1983, 1986 and 1993. The fractions are based on value added by seven sectors regionally. Interpolation is used for the years between the regional national accounts. Fractions for 1965 are used in 1962-1964, and fractions for 1992 are used after that year.

2. Wage data:

National data for nominal wage costs are obtained from the national accounts from 1962. Within industries wage differentials between counties are known to be small. Thus, the same regional distribution fractions are used as for employed persons under labour market status above. The regional wages are then divided by the number of employed persons in each region in each year.

Graph I.1: Relative Regional Variables for the Norwegian Counties

Unemployment (dash lines) and participation rates, relative variables for Norwegian counties 1964-1998

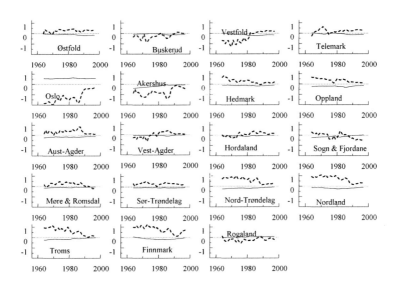

Employment growth, relative variables for the Norwegian counties 1964-1998

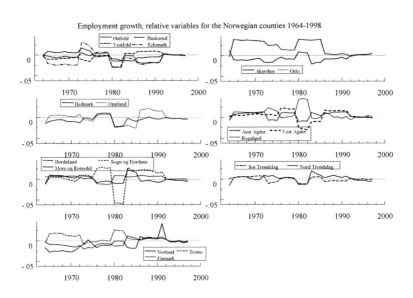

242

APPENDIX II – Results in Detail
Graph II.1 Results for the Individual Counties

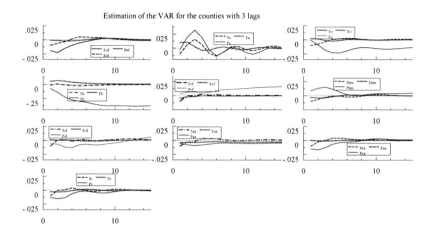

Estimation of the VAR for the counties with 3 lags

Symbols: Ei: Employment rate in county/region i
                  Pi: Participation rate in county/region i
                  Si: Employment Growth in county/region i

Counties: Of: Østfold   hm: Hedmark
                   a: Akershus   oc: Oppland
                   o: Oslo   aa: Aust-Agder
                   b: Buskerud   va: Vest-Agder
                   v: Vestfold   r: Rogaland

243

Graph II.2 Results for the Individual Regions

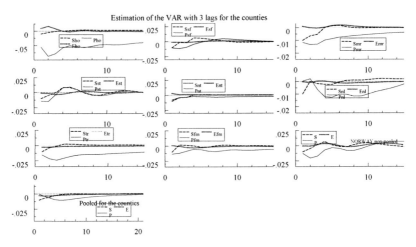

Counties

ho: Hordaland   nt: Nord- Trøndelag
sf: Sogn & Fjordane   nl: Nordland
mr: Møre & Romsdal   tr: Troms
st: Sør-Trøndelag   fm: Finnmark

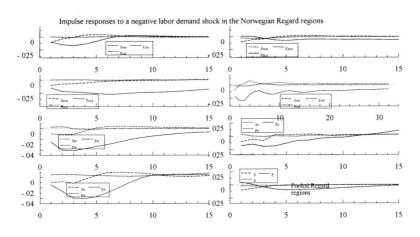

Regions

oa: Oslo & Akershus   w: West
sco: South Coast   c: Central
sce: South Central   n: North
sw: South West

PART III

SOCIAL PRACTICES AND LEGAL FRAMEWORK

CHAPTER 9

Finance, Gender and Structural Change in the European Union[1]

Barbara MACLENNAN

Commercial banks together with selected sections of the non-bank public decide how much money is created and who is to get it, given the interest rate determined by the central bank. But who actually does get it and for what purposes is known only in the vaguest and most general terms. In opening up a line of inquiry into money, finance, and investment, I will consider the culture of banking as it evolves within the law and institutions of the European Union and the framework of the Basle Accord. Within the latter, promulgated in 1988 by OECD bank regulators to be in force at the end of 1992 in advanced industrial countries, new rules have been devised to take effect from 2004. Meanwhile, in the European Union, as part of general financial supervision, the regulation of the commercial banks has been left with the national authorities of Member States, whereas interest rate or monetary policy for the Euro-12 becomes the responsibility of the European Central Bank. The sequence of changes that constitute economic and monetary union is thus only the moving backdrop to recent developments in the business of European banking. I will investigate ways in which access to purchasing power through bank credit, which is more uneven than disparities of income or wealth, might moderate rather than exacerbate these inequalities. This is a conundrum that exercises not only theorists and legislators but also the commercial banks, concerned about their reputation, the possibility of punitive levies and the likelihood of further regulation.

This chapter surveys the prospects for developing a more inclusive political economy through changes in the allocation of bank credit.

[1] I would like to thank Sheila Dow, Roger Hammersland, Ulrike Liebert, Ton Notermans, David Purdy, and the editors of this volume for helpful comments.

Crucial for the implementation of investment decisions that determine future economic outcomes is the availability of finance. In neither the private sector nor the public sector where funds may be raised by borrowing, or, alternatively, may come from undistributed profits or tax revenue respectively, do women have much influence on investment decisions. Conversely, in community associations where they may have more influence, no finance for investment is obtainable. Bank loans together with the issue of shares or bonds constitute the principal sources of funds for investment. I will argue that there is some potential for modifying the commodification of social life and for redressing the gender imbalance in power to influence the future, by reallocating bank credit to bring about structural change.

The argument that follows is divided into three main parts. In the first part, I outline the structural characteristics of a mixed economy drawing attention to conventions of national income accounting that weight the different sectors unequally. I regard gender as intrinsic to economic and social structure, cutting across and coexisting with the distinct social relations of production that obtain within the diverse sectors. In the second part, surveying some of the laws and cultural practices that restrict the distribution of money in the form of bank credit, I use the term "relationship banking" to describe credit procedures involving personal encounter that are in the course of being superseded, as western banking culture is transformed. Like other custom and practice which excludes women from economic and political power, banking practice reproduces gender socially and culturally as a hierarchical relation. Thus, the chapter is organised around three distinct types of social relationship, abjuring the methodological individualism and aggregation of mainstream economics. Reviewing post-war political economy in the final part of the chapter, I assess the prospects for changing the balance in favour of those with least economic and political power.

Changing Economic and Social Structure

Though the meaning has evidently altered through the years, economists have never been very precise in their definitions of "structural" when referring to structural change, structural adjustment, structural unemployment, structural impediments to job creation, or structural reform. My intention is to contest the meanings of terms such as structural change and structural adjustment implied by mainstream economic theory and by the policy recommendations of international institutions such as the IMF, the World Bank, and the OECD. Instead of analysing employment within the interpretative framework of the labour market or using a concept related to its "structural" features, the rate of unemployment supposedly necessary to keep inflation from changing, NAIRU[2], I shall pursue a more Keynesian line of analysis that identifies money, finance and investment as determining employment. But whereas Keynes, as a short-term remedy, postulated the most useless kind of activity – digging holes in the ground and filling them up again[3] – to indicate that, in a crisis of unemployment, and thus, a crisis of income distribution, it does not matter what people do in exchange for income, I would assert the importance, for human wellbeing and for the evolution of the culture, of what people create, what they do, and with whom they do it. This is the economic and social structure as elaborated below.

In the longer run, Keynes anticipated some socialisation of investment without being very specific about what that would mean. It is this potential not only for employment creation but also for a range of broader economic and social objectives that I intend to explore with a view to promoting structural change in the economy, by facilitating enterprise that is not-for-profit relative to business-sector enterprise, hitherto privileged by the banks' credit creation. Profits are not a necessary prerequisite of loan repayment. What is envisaged are projects that are socially desirable and, at the same time, viable in the sense of affording the means to repay the loans needed to finance them from revenue received for the services they offer or the goods they sell supplemented, if necessary, from other sources. Where there is enthusiastic support for an undertaking, revenue from charging for a facility may be augmented by less orthodox fundraising.

I focus on social relationship to analyse the structural characteristics of a mixed economy. The definition of capital not as a factory full of machines but rather as a particular type of relationship, namely, that between those who own or control and those who do not own but need access to the means of production, is to be found in Marx's *Capital*. Later, the separation of ownership and control and the invention of limited liability was analysed by Berle and Means[4] and other American institutional economists in the 1930s. Ownership again became an issue more recently in the former communist countries, during the period when, in the advanced industrial economies, privatisation of public enterprises had become more of an axiom than an analytical question. Whether conducted by individual entrepreneurs, by public companies with limited liability, or by multinational corporations, a great deal of the dynamic of social change comes from the convulsive expansion of capitalist commodity production. Restructuring, permeating and inter-

---

[2]   Ton Notermans gives a critical account of the concept in this volume.
[3]   *Cf.* Keynes, 1936, p.129.
[4]   Berle and Means, 1933.

acting with patriarchal gender relations, capitalism sets the tone of much of economic, social and political life. But patriarchy too, like other kinds of subordination or oppression, can foster resistance and lead to change. I therefore regard gender relations as being not only intrinsic to social structure but also transformative.

The household or domestic economy[5], the public sector, voluntary organisations, partnerships, co-operatives, family businesses, artisan and peasant production as well as different types of capitalist production are all linked together in reproducing an ever-changing economic and social structure through time. Social relations within the domestic economy, though they may in some respects come to resemble them, are distinguishable from capitalist relations of production: physical and emotional bonds are closer and more intense; food is produced to be eaten not for profit; no wages are received for the work done; the ownership of the means of production is different. Likewise, social relations within the public sector are qualitatively distinct though similar in some respects to capitalist relations: they too are hierarchical; but there is a different configuration of personal ambition vying with the ethos of public service and the norms of capitalist efficiency. The same goes for voluntary organisations, co-operatives, partnerships, family businesses, artisan and peasant production. Partly because the differences are quite subtle and partly because of differences among national or regional cultures, it is difficult to go beyond ostensive definition and (using the authority of Wittgenstein) claim nevertheless that it is thus possible in all cultures to differentiate the social relations that characterise each mode of production that is articulated to the others in the economic and social structure.

Despite this diversity, present conventions of national income accounting[6] take production in capitalist enterprise as the norm and, relative to that, underestimate or give no value at all to what is done in different social settings. For example, the value ascribed to chicken soup and nursing care provided within a capitalist enterprise, such as a private nursing home, would comprise the cost of materials, wages and profits; in the public sector it would include only the cost of materials and wages; in the domestic economy just the cost of materials; and, if provided on a peasant small-holding, nothing at all would be recorded. Thus the value of goods and services appearing in the national accounts depends on the ownership of property and on the nature of the social relations existing between the persons involved in their production and

---

[5] The current convention in economics is to refer to the national economy as the domestic economy but I use the term in its original sense.

[6] *Cf.* Moore, 1994.

delivery. As Pigou noted long ago, even if the same services are provided as before, the national income falls when a housekeeper marries her employer[7]. Structural changes appear as changes in magnitudes. What is called growth can be described instead as the expansion of commodity production. Impressive growth rates in the UK since 1992 coexist with chaotic privatised transport systems, the longest working hours for men, the highest level of child poverty in Europe[8] and, arguably, the worst quality of life. The data are changed in the games that business accountants play with the tax authorities. To take advantage of the lowest corporation tax in Europe, multinational corporations assign low values to imports into Ireland and high values to output thus inflating Irish GDP. As Richard Douthwaite remarks: "GNP is a measure of the volume of trading going on in a country which has no necessary relation to the quality of life"[9]. The more self-sufficient people are, the lower their GNP will appear to be, at a given level of consumption. National income does not give a good measure of economic welfare. Furthermore, comparison of national economies is vitiated in so far as their economic and social structures differ.

The values recorded in the national accounts cannot, therefore, measure the relative importance of the different modes of production in any national economy. It may be estimated in any number of ways giving very different results. If we have to use numerical values for the proportions accounted for by the different sectors, some indication can be given by the number of hours worked in each sector or, better, just the time in people's lives spent within each social setting. In orthodox economics, the household is regarded as owning resources which it hires out in the market, buying consumption goods, financial services, and other assets with the proceeds. It is not a site of production, of procreation, or creativity but primarily a site of consumption. Taking a different view, I prioritise the household or domestic economy over the other modes of production because it is within this social setting that new people are created and nurtured and have their first formative experience of life, with decisive consequences for their future and the relationships that will constitute their society.

But since the domestic economy does not exist in isolation, the issue arises of how the other sectors can contribute to the work and care that are undertaken in it? To simplify consideration of economic and social structures in Europe, while recognising that family businesses are significant in the national economy of Italy, as is peasant production in

---

[7]   Or, as A. C. Pigou puts it, "If a man marries his housekeeper", 1st edition, 1920, 4th edition, 1932, p. 33.

[8]   UNICEF Report, 2000.

[9]   Douthwaite, 1993, pp. 9 and 17.

Greece, Spain, Portugal and Ireland, I will, for the purposes of this chapter, refer to only four sectors of the economy: the business sector, the public sector, the voluntary sector and the household sector. Economic policies are to be judged primarily by reference to what is beneficial to the domestic economy over what is conducive to growth of Gross Domestic Product.

The conventions of measuring and counting are not arbitrary in the sense of accidental for they derive from the state's need for revenue[10]. They are arbitrary, however, in the sense that they represent certain perspectives, at least to the partial exclusion of others. At a time when women were being encouraged to give up their wartime jobs, return to the home and dress in Christian Dior's more "feminine" fashions, statistician Richard Stone (awarded the Nobel Prize in 1984) prevailed over his colleague Ragnar Frisch to have domestic production omitted from the measurement of national income. This established the post-war order for all United Nations' countries. More frequently differences of view are played out behind the scenes, modification in formerly-accepted practice being signalled only in the publication of supplementary data or in the appearance of footnotes to indicate that the figures are no longer comparable with the series previously published. An instance of the former is the recent publication of estimates for domestic production by the British Office of National Statistics. The practice of doing a gender audit of government budgets is also quite new and does not yet appear regularly in published sources. Only when the institutional power structure changes and the armies of accountants, tax inspectors, and statisticians, following conventions to produce the data, are given different rules to follow, can the statistics needed to pursue feminist arguments on a comprehensive scale be produced[11]. And so, there is a circularity involved here. Until the power relations within society (those same power relations that generate data) have been transformed and the social subordination of women has ended, what is needed from those with some influence and a commitment in favour of wider access to public policy-formation is an acceptance, as legitimate, of forms of argument that do not depend on data fabricated within the institutional power structure[12]. Given the power of numbers, the lack of statistics to clinch any argument, cannot be regarded as innocuous but rather as an absence suggestive of dis-empowerment and requiring investigation. Consequently, as well as calculation of supplementary data and con-

---

[10] The early accounts in William Petty's *Political Arithmetic,* written 1676, published 1690, were linked to wars being fought both within and outside England.
[11] See Waring, 1989.
[12] See Fajertag and Pochet (eds.), 2000, p. 37 and *passim.*

struction of alternative data, changes in the norms of argument are required.

The Culture of Banking – Law, Custom and Practice, Financial Deregulation, Technological Change

"Relationship banking", partly for reasons of political economy and partly driven by technological change, is a practice that is being supplanted. In the wake of the 1998 financial crises, use of this term to describe custom and practice in the previously much-admired Asian Tiger economies, increased in frequency but acquired the pejorative overtones of Orientalism. Condemned as the "crony capitalism" held to be responsible for the crises, this explanation was preferred over the alternative which attributed the trouble to financial deregulation and the removal of prudential controls, as demanded by international financial organisations following free market precepts. The trend away from "relationship banking" as the basis for allocating credit is being reinforced by the substitution of computerised information data for face-to-face meeting. Loans made on the basis of credit-scoring by computer, reduce banks' labour costs. Some types of discrimination practised at a personal level may be eliminated and individuals unable to get credit in their locality can access a wider market and may be able to get it through the internet. But, if by wider access to credit is meant lending to those who do not currently meet the conditions set by the financial institutions, then, unless differences in banking cultures are very significant, computerised credit scoring does not help. Investment requires decisions to be taken in the present, the outcome of which will only be known in the future. For this, computerised information which necessarily relates to the past is not very useful and does instead generally reinforce the prevailing banking culture which follows the biblical injunction: "to him that hath shall be given[13]". The culture of banking has been affected by changes in law, custom and practice, financial deregulation, technological innovation, the expectation of European economic and monetary union and the beginnings of its realisation. Because, as already mentioned, financial supervision is being left with national authorities, however, changes in the business of banking are only indirectly related to the sequence of changes that constitute economic and monetary union.

The issue, in this chapter, is whether some developments could be steered towards widening access to finance. Banking cultures and regulatory practices outside the European Union might also suggest policies with the same objective. The Grameen Bank of Bangladesh, for

---

[13] *Gospel according to St. Matthew*, chapter 25, verse 29.

instance, offering loans to women without collateral since 1983, has relied on social relationship to ensure repayment. It has been a model for other experiments in the extension of credit, including *l'Association pour le Droit à l'Initiative Economique,* part of an anti-poverty programme running from 1994 to 1998, supported by the European Union, and still operative[14]. This is certainly a programme worth maintaining though its scope, limited as it is to micro-credit, *i.e.* small loans to individuals, is circumscribed. I am proposing a different, but engagingly simple, adaptation of Grameen's banking practice[15] to fit with western culture: instead of small loans, make large loans! Bank credit, refused to women as individuals because of the disproportionately high administrative costs of monitoring small loans, could, if directed to substantial loans for social investment, benefit communities and redress somewhat the imbalance of power to influence the future.

While investment decisions taken in the present are the most important determinants of future outcomes, finance is necessary to put them into effect. Members of community organisations are usually all too familiar with the needs, problems and deficiencies of their own locality. Its capacities may require more political action and energy to bring into existence. From the awareness forced upon them by their quotidian experience, which may differ markedly from that of men in their community, women have ideas about what is needed to improve everyday life in their locality, whether it be building a child-care centre, erecting housing to meet specific needs, establishing a food-processing cooperative, constructing a swimming pool, or opening a cafe. Local projects of this kind would offer stable employment, less subject to the vagaries of trade than the decisions of multinational corporations. Non-profit groups already provide a significant proportion of jobs in all European countries. The social investment proposed is intended to moderate the cultures in which we live through structural change, by altering the balance between the sector of profit-seeking enterprise and other sectors of a mixed economy so as to counterbalance the commodification of social life.

European Union

Borrowing to invest is oriented to the future and, in the process of cultural transformation, credit allocation is of the greatest consequence. The Stability and Growth Pact, committing euro-insiders to stability programmes, also binds the Member States which are euro-outsiders – Denmark, Sweden and Britain – to convergence programmes. The

---

[14] See Nowak, 1994.
[15] See Bernasek and Stanfield, 1997.

ceiling of three percent of GDP, imposed on public borrowing, in origin a rough average of the proportion of public investment in the Member States, but applied across the board, regardless of the size of the existing public sectors, imposes a kind of credit rationing on the public sector, leaving to the sentiment of the market and to the predilections of the commercial banks the allocation of credit they are disposed to exercise in the private sector. The finance of public investment is thereby constrained where infrastructure is lacking in less mature national economies, where large public sectors need to maintain a large capital stock and in those economies where public investment has been neglected, as it has been in the UK, for example, over the last two decades. Are there to be no new schools and hospitals? Are old schools and hospitals to be allowed to crumble, or will kindergarten and nursing homes for the elderly be forced into the private sector? No corresponding limits on borrowing are specified either for business activities or for personal loans and credit cards that sustain private consumption. Now, whereas for the level of the interest rate and aggregate demand it may not seem to matter whether expenditure is on services provided in the public sector, on investment goods or on commodities for consumption, it does matter for the kind of culture that is reproduced. And this, the Stability and Growth Pact seems to have prejudged with limits on public sector borrowing for investment that do not apply to private sector borrowing. Whereas some human motivations, qualities, and relationships are to be valorised and sanctified by credit, others are to be left to their own devices or to wither on the vine.

Features of our cultures are reproduced through financial institutions: some reinforced by the provision of credit while others are weakened, etiolated and impaired by denial. According to the rational choice model of economics, the gender differential in bank lending is due to a difference in preferences between women and men. Men are more prepared to take risks; women, alleged to be more risk-averse, do not ask for loans. This does not take account of the law nor of more insidious custom and practice. It does not pay attention to the ways in which the life-situations of women differ from those of men nor to the ways in which risk may be socially constructed[16]. It also draws a veil over why banks, in their pursuit of profit, take on such a high degree of risk that, over the centuries, state regulation has been necessary to protect the public from the repercussions of bank failure and the loss of their money. It would seem that somehow the banks have missed the opportunity to reduce their exposure to risk by lending to women.

---

[16] For how risk is socially constructed, see Bernasek, 2000.

Envisage the conventions of lending and borrowing as costume drama and imagine a scenario in which a young woman seeks a loan. An historical perspective is required so that some particulars may be treated as belonging to the past. For example, the Napoleonic *Code Civil* widely established in Europe affirmed the state's interest in familial order by delegating all authority to male heads of household and, in Italy, women were barred from contracting debts or writing cheques without their spouses' consent until repeal in 1919[17]. Outside the purview of the Napoleonic Code, a married woman in England could offer no collateral for a loan since, until the Married Women's Property Act was passed in 1882, her wealth was owned by her husband. These disabilities did not only affect married women. In Manchester, in the early 1970s, one of those mutual societies, fondly lamented on the Left in the 1990s when transformed into profit-seeking banks with stock exchange quotation, required me to get a male colleague, a lecturer like myself in the university's economics department, to act as guarantor, countersigning the contract for the loan needed to buy my house. This would become unlawful under the British Sex Discrimination Act of 1976. Against custom and practice, however, the law does not necessarily provide a remedy.

The European Commission's attempts to introduce legislation going beyond equal pay, as laid down by Article 119 of the Treaty of Rome, have typically been contested by the Council of Ministers. Only the efforts of the European Women's Lobby during the 1996 Intergovern-mental Conference brought some discrimination outside the place of employment within the provisions of the Amsterdam Treaty. Thus, since 1997, equal opportunity has become one of the four pillars of employment policy in the European Union but there is still no European legislation to prevent discriminatory treatment in access to credit.

At the same time as the "liberal" definition of equal opportunity to mean equal treatment (which involved, for example, treating pregnancy as illness) was challenged in the Treaty of Amsterdam, a declaration appended to the Treaty exempted public credit institutions from "liberalisation"[18]. It maintained the restriction on assets in which such

---

[17] See de Grazia, 1991, p.19.

[18] European Union Treaty of Amsterdam: "37. *Declaration on public credit institutions in Germany* The Conference notes the Commission's opinion to the effect that the Community's existing competition rules allow services of general economic interest provided by public credit institutions existing in Germany and the facilities granted to them to compensate for the costs connected with such services to be taken into account in full. In this context, the way in which Germany enables local authorities to carry out their task of making available in their regions a comprehensive and efficient financial infrastructure is a matter for the organisation of that Member State.

banks in Germany (and Austria) can invest. This can be construed as favourable treatment of state banks to compensate them for the costs of providing "services of general economic interest" because, with their relatively large holdings of public debt against which, according to the capital adequacy requirements of the Basle Committee on Banking Supervision, no capital need be held, they are able to economise on capital as compared to their private competitors. Critics of the declaration claim that since the functions of issuing government debt and printing money have now been separated, government debt in national currency is no longer automatically free of default risk because governments joining EMU lose their monetary sovereignty, the right to print money to pay off national currency debt. They propose, therefore, that the Basle large exposure directive which prevents banks from lending more than twenty-five percent of their capital to a single borrower should, therefore, be extended to public debt. Using related arguments, the Banking Federation of the European Union, the lobbying organisation of the commercial banks, has lodged a complaint with the European Commission regarding the public guarantees from which three named German banks, in this category, benefit[19]. The Federation claims that the high (triple A) credit rating granted to such banks, 22 German and 4 Austrian, as compared to only 5 private banks, 2 Dutch and 3 French, enables the former to borrow at low cost on the international capital market thus distorting competition. It is just this distortion not the banks' existence *per se* that is being called into question, stresses the

---

Such facilities may not adversely affect the conditions of competition to an extent beyond that required in order to perform these particular tasks and which is contrary to the interests of the Community.

The Conference recalls that the European Council has invited the Commission to examine whether similar cases exist in the other Member States, to apply as appropriate the same standards on similar cases and to inform the Council in its ECOFIN formation." p.138.

Arnold, 1999, p. 22 renders this as "The declaration on public credit institutions in the Treaty of Amsterdam approves of the favourable treatment of state banks as a compensation for the provision of services of general interest, such as an efficient financial infrastructure". He converts "general economic interest" into the less specific "general interest" and omits from "comprehensive and efficient financial infrastructure" the crucial word "comprehensive". Having made these rather significant modifications, he rhetorically asks "But aren't private banks equally (or even better) equipped to provide such services?" and concludes that the "Treaty of Amsterdam thus constitutes an unfortunate setback in the process of creating competitive conditions in European banking".

[19]   The complaint, lodged on 21 December 1999, was aimed specifically at the *Westdeutsche Landesbank* (WestLB), the *Stadtsparkasse Koeln* and the *Westdeutsche Immobilienbank*. See *Bulletin Quotidien Europe*, 28 July 2000, pp. 8-9.

Banking Federation's secretary general[20]. In short, to anyone favouring private enterprise and "a level playing field", the declaration appended to the Treaty of Amsterdam represents a setback in the process of creating so-called "competitive" conditions in European banking. But it also raises the interesting question of whether private-enterprise banks are disposed to provide all-inclusive services of general economic interest to match the constitutional obligation of local authorities in Germany to make available, through the *Sparkassen*, a comprehensive and efficient financial infrastructure. There is manifold evidence that commercial bankers themselves, as well as legislators and theorists, are conscious of shortcomings.

A Social Contract with Commercial Banks

Contemporary confidence in banks owes as much to the state's response to bank failures in the past as to the banks' mode of conducting their business operations. Most private banks were deprived of the power to issue their own notes, *i.e.* print money, which they did to excess during periods of brisk trade in the nineteenth century. The paper they now deal out carries the state's imprimatur: it is the exception rather than the rule for banknotes to display the name of a bank other than the state bank or at least the one that handles the government's finance[21]. If the European Union is "becoming more state-like and federal in nature", does it matter that there is no precedent for such a large amount of currency that is not connected to a state[22]?

The visible face of money is, anyway, only a fraction of deposits, the predominant component of the money stock. And deposits are numbers that barely see the light of day in the bank accounts of individuals, organisations, businesses, and government agencies. Behind the computer screens, the numbers being added and subtracted flicker back and forth. This is money[23]. In the extraordinary system that allows commercial banks' lending activity to be "the fulcrum for money creation"[24],

---

[20] The complaint is about the distortion of competition by the *Anstaltslast* and the *Gewährsträgerhaftung*, not about the existence of the *Sparkassen* and *Landesbanken*, emphasised secretary general, Nikolaus Bomcke.
[21] Scottish banknotes are an exception and credit cards, used to carry out an increasing volume of day-to-day transactions, likewise bear only the name of a company.
[22] *Cf.* Mazey and Richardson, 1993, p. 3, and Padoa-Schioppa, 1999, p. 2.
[23] The numbers, in each of the Euro-12 countries, will be multiplied by a different known factor of less than one and so will be lower in every case. Italian lire are counted in thousands, millions or milliards and, although the conversion factor, rather dauntingly, is .001936, a capuccino conveniently will cost just one euro instead of 2000 lire.
[24] Dymski *et al.,* 1993, p. 217.

loans may be used to purchase bonds or derivatives, to speculate on commodity or foreign currency markets, spot or forward, to buy shares which may deliver the ownership of one company into the hands of another. To purchase a material asset, a loan agreement for, say, £30,000 when used one day to buy a motor vehicle becomes a deposit the next day in the account of the seller who, in anticipation of the sale, may either have been granted a loan or used an earlier payment to add to the account of the motor manufacturing company. The latter, likewise, either using credit or earlier payments adds, to its workforce's bank accounts, already augmented in some cases by bank loans, figures for their wages, a percentage of which will be siphoned off as tax revenue to add more numbers, representing their salaries, to the bank accounts of university staff, likewise the beneficiaries of personal loans. More notional, but with the same potential to be activated as money, are credit lines offered by banks as inducements to companies to buy for a fee other financial services. Unused loan commitments can exceed actual loans[25].

The polity already goes beyond the European Union. To manage an increasingly internationalised system, in which financial innovations increase risk due to more distant business relationships between debtor and creditor, the Basle Accord devised capital adequacy standards. For certain approved banks these standards are now to be replaced by their own credit-rating systems of assessing default risk so that they are not tempted to take risks for which the capital required by the Accord is lower than they themselves would estimate. But regulation lags behind banking "a creative industry always finding new ways of taking risks and rarely penalised"[26]. "[D]eposit insurance, the regulation of capital adequacy and large exposures"[27], and attempts to improve licensing and supervisory standards "to minimise the threat of contagion from insolvent to solvent institutions"[28] assist in maintaining depositors' confidence. Deposit guarantees are double-edged, however, in relieving banks from the sole responsibility for looking after their customers' deposits. They contribute to what economists call "moral hazard", the inveterate tendency of the banks to take on too high a degree of risk. Should the worst happen, to avert a crisis of illiquidity which would result from bank failure that could spread through the inter-linked financial sector inducing loss of confidence, panic and a collapse in

---

[25] At the end of September 2000, American banks had a record amount of unused loan commitments of $4.3 trillion compared with total loans of $3.8 trillion. *The Economist*, 13-19 January, 2001, p. 78.

[26] *The Economist*, 19-27 January 2001, p. 16,

[27] Padoa-Schioppa, 1999, p. 23.

[28] Padoa-Schioppa, 1999, p. 23.

demand for commodities for both consumption and investment, the state steps in to put together a package of guarantees, if the commercial banks and other financial institutions fail to do this collectively. Altogether, the banknotes, the guarantee of deposits and rescue by the state in case of failure, constitute a public resource and boost public confidence to the benefit of commercial banks' business.

What should be asked of the banks in return? The most common demand relates to means of payment. The banks do not welcome the costs of administering small accounts for people on low income who will not be in the market to purchase additional financial services. But commercial bank deposits are the predominant component of the money stock. Anyone without a bank account, to make or receive payments, has to forget about e-commerce and handle cash which is more inconvenient and expensive. This issue is presently a matter of dispute and negotiation between the commercial banks and the British government which wants to cut its own administrative costs of paying social benefits to precisely those poor people – the majority women – who do not have bank accounts. At the same time, however, the banks jealously guard their right to accept deposits from all and sundry and are opposed to such rights for post offices or credit unions, because deposits constitute the financial capital with which they make their profits.

As already mentioned above, the present arrangement for the Euro-12 transfers responsibility for monetary policy to the ECB while leaving responsibility for banking supervision with the national authorities. Although in most of the Member States the central banks were responsible for both policies, there are precedents for separate institutions in Germany, as well as in the UK and Japan. For the geographical areas covered by monetary policy and bank supervision not to coincide is, however, without precedent. Tommaso Padoa-Schioppa, referring presumably to himself, claims that the drafters of the Maastricht Treaty understood "the anomaly of the double separation"[29], geographical and functional, and saw the potential difficulties arising from it. For example, the recent bank merger wave, having taken place not so much across borders as within national boundaries, has created entities which might well be considered by national authorities to be "too-big-to-fail" but could be viewed quite differently by the ECB. The latter might favour non-intervention in a case where the ramifications of failure in the wider context of the euro-zone would not be too far-reaching. In the event of the interaction between the Euro-system and national supervisory authorities not working effectively, Article 105(6) of the Maastricht Treaty provides for specific supervisory tasks to be entrusted

---

[29] Padoa-Schioppa, 1999, p.7.

to the ECB. What is more the ECB must be consulted on any draft of EU or national legislation regarding banking supervision and, on its own initiative, can provide advice on the scope and implementation of EU legislation.

Legislative Proposals

The imperative to reduce costs to meet competition in a single financial market leads to closure of bank branches and reduction in personnel, leaving rural areas and impoverished urban areas without banking services. But rumbles of discontent in Europe, varying with the diversity of banking practices and institutions in the different Member States, have not reached the level of political protest that resulted in the electoral success of the social credit party in 1930s Canada or in the US banking laws of the mid-1970s. In the 1930s, radical ideas for the reform of banking were put forward by the Social Credit Party which won a provincial election in Alberta. But its plan to give an equal increment of purchasing power to everyone through the allocation of credit by the state was declared unconstitutional. This would have replaced the normal system of money creation through the allocation of credit by commercial banks which, as the customary witticism has it, distribute additional spending power to those who don't need it while denying it to those who do, thus exacerbating inequalities of income and wealth. Nor do the social and political conditions which generated the Equal Credit Opportunities Act, 1974, the Home Mortgage Disclosure Act, 1975, and the Community Reinvestment Act, 1977, in the US, exist in Europe today. These were enacted against the practice of the banks "redlining" the run-down inner cities, to cut the costs of processing loan applications, and so refusing finance to black people still living in these areas, evacuated by whites. Though distribution of credit is perverse, in the sense of aggravating inequalities of income and wealth, the issue has, as yet, a fairly low political profile in Europe. But it may be that the legacy of neo-liberalism together with the squeeze on public expenditure demanded by the convergence criteria have so reduced expectations of the public sector in some Member States that more demands will henceforth be directed to the private sector, as in the US, where expectations of the public sector are low[30].

Although judged not to have been very effective in the American context because of poor enforcement, the laws themselves, the revisions to which they have been subject, and the perceived deficiencies in the

---

[30] American legislation not only requires banks to lend to the communities from which they take deposits, so as to counteract their preferred traditional value system, but also requires banks withdrawing from a locality to set up a credit union.

way they have been implemented suggest lines of inquiry that might be followed by the European Commission currently assessing the appropriateness for Europe of a Community Reinvestment Act (CRA). This research, however, instead of being undertaken in the Directorate General for Economic and Financial Affairs, or in the Directorate General for Employment and Social Affairs, or even in the Directorate General for Regional Policy, has been shunted for dubious reasons into the Directorate General for Health and Consumer Protection.

It is neither possible nor necessary to decide on the priority of striving for further European harmonisation, embarking on reform of national regulations or allowing banks to respond to pressure and criticism by self-regulation. It might seem wise to build on the diversity that exists while seeking to adapt good practice from scrutiny of other countries, both within and outside the European Union. The drawback of this approach is that competition among the national systems, exploiting the incompleteness of the regulatory framework, could provoke further deregulation. And so, without aiming for full harmonisation and "a level playing field", some benchmarks for European-wide supervision, to accompany national and regional efforts to spread finance more widely, are desirable. In what looks like an attempt to avert unwelcome regulation, European banks are promoting a concept of "corporate citizenship" to imply responsibility for the whole community including its disadvantaged members; but, for the present, this seems to be more of a public relations exercise than a substantial plan[31]. In the different Member States, diverse arrangements include the French option of direct action to ensure access to financial services via state intervention. The Irish government has, in the past, used the threat of taxation to negotiate with the banks. Outside the eurozone, Sweden has pursued public-private partnerships. The UK government was said to be considering the American model, in which CRA compliance is a precondition for merger approval, but has rejected the recommendation of the Cruickshank report (2000) that all bank take-overs be referred to the competition commission which might have scrutinised such compliance[32]. Though the hazard of an unpredictable levy as was visited

---

[31] A voluntary code of practice adopted by the Association of German Banks has been proposed as a Europe-wide guideline for 2002. At the first European Business convention on Corporate Social Responsibility, in November 2000, the Commission welcomed a Voluntary European Charter on a Minimum Level of Banking Services for All.

[32] In the United States, community associations have been able to challenge merger and acquisition applications by banks on the grounds of inadequate CRA performance. "In hundreds of cases such challenges have resulted in agreements between banks and community groups," Dymski *et al.* (eds.), 1993, p. 237.

upon the banks, in 1991, by an avenging UK government and apprehension of a windfall tax, in the summer of 2000 when they announced record profits, may have been expected to favour negotiated agreements, these have not been realised because of lack of political pressure.

European banks could be required to adjust the tension between commercial confidentiality and democratic accountability in favour of the latter. In some Member States, the Directive on the "participation of workers in the conduct of firms" could in principle open the way for bank employees to monitor lending policy and become the agents of accountability though their membership of supervisory boards is coming under pressure in the financial markets that want to give primacy to shareholders interest (after the directors have awarded themselves share options). The American Home Mortgage Disclosure Act of 1975 obliges banks to indicate the districts in which mortgages on housing have been granted so that their discrimination against ethnic minority communities can be checked. If banks do not inform the public about the enterprises to which they give the privilege of access to credit, and thus command over resources, they could instead be required to demonstrate that loans for community purposes constitute some agreed proportion of total lending. To avoid confrontation with the conjoined business lobbies, UNICE and SME, the Financial Services Institute of Hamburg, *Institut für Finanzdienstleistungen,* suggests alliance with small and medium-sized enterprises to require banks to lend to the communities from which they take deposits.

Changes in Banking Business

Though Europe has been the centre of merger activity, cross-border bank mergers with the exception of some French, German and Dutch cases have not, as already mentioned, been very common. The facilitation of mergers rendered by fixed exchange rates then monetary union, through elimination of exchange-rate variation, seems to have been less decisive than the sweet imperatives of a large market. Britain outside the eurozone became, by way of mergers and acquisitions, the world's biggest exporter of capital in 1999, overtaking the US[33]. But an interesting side effect of the merger of the Deutsche Bank and Bankers Trust, for example, is that the European bank's operation in America becomes subject to the regulatory laws that, in Europe, the banking Federation is trying to thwart.

---

[33]   Data from UNCTAD.

The surge in eurobond issue by corporations following the fixing of exchange rates in December 1998, in contrast to the mergers which were, in a sense, anticipated, took most people by surprise. With many of their corporate customers borrowing directly from the financial markets, banks in continental Europe (as opposed to those in the UK which typically do not provide much financial capital to business) may find themselves looking for different types of borrower and may welcome new categories of low-risk, low-return social investment. Will this change make the banks more willing to finance community investment? Though the spare lending capacity may not be found in localities or cultures conducive to flourishing voluntary associations and the latter may not exist where the need for social investment is most urgent, just one or two favourable conjunctions of finance and enthusiasm could set an example to be followed, when the stories of their success are told. Where there is no spare lending capacity, if credit is allocated to social investment, funds would no longer be available to less socially desirable uses and the attitude of bankers becomes even more crucial. Forces acting in a contrary direction, however, cannot be disregarded. Banks are moving farther into operations with low cost, high risk, and high returns, which, even with the greater incidence of bad debts typical of larger banks, will, after these have been written off, still be more profitable. "Under competitive pressure from other banking systems whose emphasis is much more on maintaining liquidity, the German banks are rapidly expanding into securities-related areas, and locating activity increasingly in London as the European financial (as opposed to economic) centre." Even so, were a community reinvestment act established to familiarise the concept, it is not beyond the bounds of possibility to envisage banks securitising social investments for sale to pension funds, trade unions and other asset holders who support such schemes[34]. And the ending of stock market euphoria may favour more balanced portfolios with low risk[35].

The business of banking is changing. The income of western banks and other financial institutions comes increasingly from fees and less from interest, converging rather surprisingly with Islamic banking which prohibits usury but permits charging for other services rendered. One such source of bank income, however, foreign currency exchange within

---

[34] Two thirds of fund managers expect demand for funds that take account of environmental, social and ethical issues to increase, according to a survey by Deloitte & Touche, January 2001. The Bolivian BancoSol has issued 5 million dollars worth of bonds backed by its microloan portfolio, 2 million of which were bought by foreigners.

[35] The shortage on the stock exchange of less risky gilts is mentioned in *The Economist*, 20-26 January 2001, p. 76.

the eurozone, will disappear on the euro's introduction in 2002. This together with the continuing pressure for profitability may again induce them "to seek more revenue from unfamiliar business or highly risky geographical areas"[36]. Are there prospects of limiting such risky behaviour in favour of low-risk low-return long-term investment to enhance the quality of life in the localities where people live?

Social Investment and Credit Guarantees

There is a brief reference in the Delors report[37] to "more effective structural and regional policies", but neither there nor in debate on the Stability and Growth Pact has the issue figured largely. Countries which have entered into monetary union require means, other than exchange-rate changes, of addressing problems of lack of demand from within the eurozone because financial integration by attracting funds out of less prosperous regions could, as Sheila Dow points out, exacerbate disparities[38]. While the fall in the value of the euro boosted demand for eurozone goods from outside, the reduction of cross-border transaction costs is likely to increase the volume of trade inside[39]. Now that the project for monetary union is under way, extension of finance for social investment to change the pattern of output and employment should be given serious attention.

Local knowledge is required to specify the kind of social investment for which finance is needed. Though it is not possible to generalise, it is safe to presume that, in some parts of the European Union, there is insufficient provision of nurseries for child-care and a lack of certain kinds of housing. Youth clubs and sports clubs, woodland groves and safe play areas for children in cities are widely lacking. To be more specific in regard to three localities with which I am familiar: destitute young people in inner cities need housing, ideally, to be built by themselves to meet their own requirements; housing is also needed by people with low income in rural areas, as the better-off, in escaping to the countryside either for short breaks in a second home or for retirement, push up house prices beyond the means of the rural poor. Where there is shortage of places, nurseries for children below school

---

[36] Padoa-Schioppa, 1999, p. 11.
[37] Delors Report, para 52. *Cf.* Goodhart, 1989, p. 10.
[38] See Dow, 1994, pp. 158-161.
[39] Balance of payments data, within the eurozone, become extinct, having perhaps produced more heat than light, but, in January 2000, for the first time, balance of trade figures for the regions were produced by the British Office of National Statistics.

age are needed, even in the salubrious Mugnone valley where loans to finance this, and a swimming-pool, could soon be repaid.

In financing social investment, banks would need to make some realistic assessment of its viability just as they do for the finance of business investment. Substantial loans do not entail disproportionately high administrative costs for the banks, one of the disincentives to extending small loans to the poor [micro-credit]. The problem of security of repayment could be managed in a number of ways, according to circumstance. Some modifications may be needed in the laws regarding liability for debt in associations, co-operatives, trusts etc. In the event of difficulty in servicing a loan, debt can be rescheduled. Though not being advocated as a general rule, credit guarantees would be possible for social investment in areas already designated under Objectives 1 and 2 of the European Structural Funds. Some commercial bank loans are already guaranteed by the European Investment Bank[40].

Over two centuries after Adam Smith argued against special measures for privileging exports as advocated by "mercantilist" writers, government export credit guarantees are still widespread in Europe. Negotiation about limiting this sort of credit to effect a "level playing field" slipped off the agenda of a recent EU meeting. Now the issue of credit guarantees, at least for arms exports, has been passed to the OECD. In Britain the export credit guarantee department has, most controversially, granted credit guarantees for the export of arms to regimes engaged in violent repression or aggressive war. Construction companies building dams abroad with dubious environmental and ethnic consequences have been among other favoured applicants for such guarantees. On occasion, arms sales have been scandalously linked to dam projects in one gigantic destructive package. When the plans of trade unionists in arms-related industry to use their skills for other purposes are only a memory[41], shareholders and executives in the arms and construction industries with predominantly male employment, continue to be the beneficiaries of publicly-funded export credit guarantees which, in turn, constitute a high proportion of third world debt.

Export credit is not the only type of lending guaranteed by the state. In the UK, an executive arm of the Department of Education and Employment, the government-owned student loan company (SLC), sub-

---

[40] The business lobbies are likely to be more united in protest against any fixed proportion of credit going to non-profit organisations than they are over unfair competition resulting from the different export credit guarantee arrangements in different Member States.

[41] See Purdy, 1988, pp. 123ff., for the story of the shop stewards' plan in the 1970s to convert Lucas Aerospace from production of military hardware to production of socially necessary goods.

contracts, to a private enterprise, data-processing which is done over-night in India and Sri Lanka, the transactions costs of foreign exchange in this global division of labour being easily offset by lower wages in Asia. British banks refused to take on this lending but where banks co-operate, as in the US, student loans are another instance, altogether more benign, of lending that is guaranteed. Abolition or mere reform of export credit guarantees would release funds to guarantee some loans for social investment to contribute to diversity in economic and social structure.

Towards an Inclusive Political Economy?

Does history suggest whether a more balanced determination of resource use can be expected from the tendency for corporatist struc-tures in Europe to be extended to wider networks[42], the post-war settle-ment having failed to deliver an inclusive political economy? Acquies-cence in that settlement, partly due to a presumed difference in the wartime heroism and suffering of men and women and partly due to unequal opportunities for collective political discussion, permitted the re-establishment of a civilian order which involved structural upheaval in the use of resources and distribution of income. It was not just munitions and aircraft production that were run down, in the public sector, British Restaurants and nurseries for children also were closed. Though some instances of debarment of women from political and economic life were removed (with the liberation of France in 1944, women got the vote; and in the UK teachers, but not civil servants, who married were allowed to remain in their positions) national tripartite bargaining, generally did not succeed in developing an inclusive politi-cal economy[43]. A degree of consensus was maintained only while trade unionists' appetite for private consumption was held in check by fears for the future and memories of 1930s and wartime deprivation. When apprehension that the post-war boom would end in slump, as it had before, gave way to confidence among both employers and employed that "full employment" could, and would, be maintained, money-wage increases triggered wage-price spirals or eroded profits, investment fell and the reduction in demand for business loans induced banks to look for customers where little was known about economic conditions. In due course, the failing consensus was matched by financial turbulence.

---

[42] See Fajertag and Pochet (eds.), 2000.
[43] The links between Keynes's theory, aggregate demand management, and national tripartite bargaining are quite loose though, if export demand is set aside, then there would indeed be three main components to aggregate demand among which investment is the crucial dynamic force.

When the reduction in the cost of oil[44], which had sustained growth, was reversed by OPEC's decision in December 1973, signalling an adjustment in the balance of global power, it generated economic problems and a political challenge which social democrats failed to meet[45]. Outside the ranks of organised labour pursuing their sectional interests in male-dominated trade unions, there was growing disillusion with corporatist means of controlling income distribution and resource use. One indication that they had lost credibility among the wider populace is the disparity between women's and men's support for social democratic parties committed to such policies[46]. This forced Mitterrand, in the years running up to the 1981 French presidential election, to make a calculated and comprehensive effort to gain women's vote. Against the political trend, he won the day *with "les trois quarts des smicards sont des smicardes"* proclaiming his awareness that the majority of those on the minimum wage were women and that it should be raised[47].

One possibility of delivering on the rhetoric of solidarity failed to get off the ground. In the attempts to reduce working hours in France and Germany, no heed was paid to the gender division of labour or to the redistribution of paid and unpaid work. In Italy, without trade union support, the "hours in the city" campaign was waged primarily by women[48]. The Netherlands, by contrast, with a consistently high proportion of women ministers and parliamentary representation and the largest network of feminist economists in Europe, can be cited as a model of solidarity in gender politics, exhibiting "the Calvinist culture of moderation[49]". Elsewhere, the flow of funds out of currencies where governments attempted to tackle unemployment with social democratic solutions was interpreted as demonstrating the impossibility, in the newly "liberalised" financial markets, of Keynesianism in one country. As a response to this, the idea of Keynesianism in Europe provided some part of the impulse towards economic and monetary union. But more generally, failure to agree on distribution of income carried through into the 1980s in different redistributive endeavours. The price of failure was paid disproportionately by the fall in income of those who successively became unemployed: first, men in heavy industries, then,

---

[44] Oil prices, fixed in dollars, fell in terms of other currencies as the value of the dollar fell with a decisive drop in 1971, largely as a result of the cumulative outflow required to fund the American war against communism in Vietnam.

[45] Instead of a moderate general price rise equitably reducing real wages, profits, rent (income from property) and pensions to effect the necessary re-distribution of income from oil-importing to oil-exporting countries, there was a rise in unemployment.

[46] For long runs of voting behaviour, see Crouch, 1999, pp. 320-325.

[47] Quoted in Jenson and Sineau, 1995, p. 134.

[48] See Belloni, 1999.

[49] Quotation from Notermans, 2000, p. 15.

young men unable to enter them, later, women in the public sector, and, finally, young women seem to be the ones that have paid the highest price of all in the pattern of unemployment that has emerged while those still in employment continue to prosper albeit with less security than before. Reversion to an older mode of economic management deprived trade unions of power and continuing unemployment brought back labour discipline. Neoliberalism, however, also defaulted on its rhetoric as regards employment. In due course, the shortfall in women's support for the British Labour Party narrowed from the mid-1970s maximum of twelve percent to a difference of just two percent in 1997 for the party reconstituted as New Labour. By this time, electorates across Europe had voted in favour of giving social democrats another chance to manage their substantially transformed economies, economies in which unemployment was still a problem.

Belief in the ingenuity and adaptability of business is quite compatible with social democracy. If there is incongruity it is rather with neoliberalism and the politics of the Third Way which continues concessions to business in a manner that suggests lack of appreciation of these qualities. A new policy of *laissez faire*, combined with resistance to the commodification of all social relations, would let entrepreneurs get on with the business at which they excel and use their ingenuity to adapt to social priorities without, as at present, special credit, grants, subsidies, or tax breaks. Neo-liberals although vocal regarding "unfair" competition from the public sector, as in the case of the German and Austrian banks already mentioned, rarely object to special concessions for business, beyond requiring "a level playing field", which prompts one to wonder what game – golf, basket-ball or some unnamed other – is being played.

The want of adequate representation among the social partners negotiating over how directives will operate within the EU and participating with national governments and the ECB in the twice-yearly "macroeconomic dialogue" instituted at Koeln in 1999 is one of the most visible signs of the democratic deficit. Whereas political parties, periodically having to face elections in which women's votes count, have devised various ways of addressing women's interests or women's representation, in the case of France going as far as to rewrite part of the constitution, trade unions, while induced to offset falling membership by accepting part-time workers, have not seen gender representation as a means of establishing their legitimacy or regaining lost power. The ETUC's political agenda and the provisions it makes to avoid replicating the kind of token female representation typical of national labour movements fail to allay suspicions of misogyny. And the way in which other pressure groups and citizens' alliances might influence the use of resources is unclear. The list of parties to the Irish agreement, *Programme for Prosperity and Fairness,* 2000, gives one pause to wonder whether inclusion of the Construction Industry Federation (CIF) and the Irish Farmers' Association (IFA) will redress the gender imbalance in negotiation[50]. There is a danger that the proliferation of groups included in social dialogue will not only make outcomes more a matter of chance but will also, in rendering it more difficult to navigate the channels of power, reproduce and exacerbate existing imbalances.

In considering the structural characteristics of a mixed economy I have placed particular emphasis on gender and on the distribution of finance as determining the use of resources. To modify the existing inequalities, I am proposing that grassroots organisations should have access to bank credit. For this reason, women, particularly those involved in community associations, must ask for bank loans to finance the investment needed in their communities and must monitor banking regulation which, both nationally and at the level of the European Union, may be in the process of setting some standards for community reinvestment, including social investment. With an historical approach towards the future, the links in a sequence of possibilities are bound to be fragile as compared to the strict deductive chain of inference linking premise to policy recommendation in a utopian blueprint or a model that makes no allowance for contingency. But the proposals have robust enough roots in present discontents to influence possible futures. Social investment would give some substance to the concept of "corporate citizenship" with which the banks are currently trying to improve their image. Their expertise in business funding could be adapted to assess the viability of projects to be located near their branches, allowing bank employees to develop their knowledge of the district in which they work and perhaps to become committed to its regeneration and beautification.

Finally, with less than token female representation in a European institution reproducing part of the culture in a very small way, I take as given but leave unexamined the reasons for gender domination and subordination.

---

[50] The full list comprises the Irish Creamery Milk Suppliers' Association (ICMSA), the Irish Co-operative Organisation Society Ltd. (ICOS) Macra na Feirme, the Irish National Organisation of the Unemployed (INOU), Congress Centres for the Unemployed, The Community Platform 1, Conference of Religious of Ireland (CORI), National Womens' Council of Ireland (NWCI), National Youth Council of Ireland (NYCI), Society of Saint Vincent de Paul, Protestant Aid, Small Firms' Association (SFA), Irish Exporters' Association (IEA), Irish Tourist Confederation (ITIC) and Chambers of Commerce of Ireland (CCI).

CHAPTER 10

Constructing EMU:
Euro-Scepticism, and the Emerging
European Public Space[1]

Ulrike LIEBERT

The European single currency is not only a technical matter
facilitating economic exchanges but also as a political symbol with
relevance to citizens' everyday lives: "A currency produces global
values of a society and at the same time is its expression[2]". As Murray
Edelman noted, political symbols – such as flags or political terms like
"unemployment" – are icons of mass culture that involve language and
rituals, touch the experiences of people, and carry "a range of diverse,
often conflicting meanings that are integral aspects of specific material
and social situations[3]". In this respect, national currencies have come to
represent a multitude of everyday lives' frustrations and expectations.
For instance regarding the German Mark, Jürgen Habermas has coined
"DM-nationalism" as a term to describe how Germans of the Federal
Republic in the aftermath of the Second World War have replaced
obsolete national pride with a "substitute consciousness" based on their
"libidinous occupation" of the *Deutsche Mark*[4]. Embodying ideas of
stability and well-being, the *Mark* has infused Germans with a sense of
security and trust, much in contrast to the former *Reichsmark* or a
currency, such as the Italian Lira, which is seen as unstable and weak.

In the dynamics of European integration, the project founded on the
Maastricht Treaty to launch the *euro* as the single currency of twelve
Member States in 2002, will certainly mark the most visible move

---

[1]   My thanks for valuable comments on earlier drafts of this chapter go to Bo Stråth and
      the members of the project group at the European University Institute, Florence,
      especially to Amy Verdun and Barbara MacLennan; as well as to Sid Tarrow, Antje
      Wiener, Uwe Puetter, and Milena Sunnus.
[2]   European Commission, "Working Group on the Euro" no year, p. 3
[3]   Edelman, 1988, p. 8
[4]   Jürgen Habermas, DIE ZEIT, 30.3.1990

toward an "ever closer Union", thus far. However, although it is certain that from that year on, citizens in the "eurozone"[5] will use the *euro* on a daily basis, it is less certain whether it will become a political symbol of European union, enhance European consciousness, a European identity and solidarity, as some of the most ambitious supporters of EMU hope[6].

We might expect difficulties in materialising such visions for several reasons: First, the launch of the single currency occurred in the aftermath of Maastricht, when the "permissive consensus" of mass publics' support for elite driven supranational integration policies had been deeply eroded in EU-Member States.[7] Second, the legitimacy of EMU is contested on most different principles and norms, from scepticism about abandoning a stable national currency, to opposition against building the European Union around a Central Bank[8]. And, ultimately, even many of those political analysts and elites supporting the single currency, rationalise it through the lens of "European nationalisms", taking for granted, hence, the conception of the EU as a political space fragmented by national identities, where citizens hardly communicate across national borders, rarely understand their neighbour's languages, differ in their memories of the past, and diverge on the norms and values they hold. The dilemma is obvious: how could, under these conditions of diverging norms and values, the *euro* ever become a symbol of European unity, let alone a European identity? As Amy Verdun and Thomas Christiansen argued, EMU suffers from "dilemmas of legitimacy" insofar as it "rests on the creation of a set of powerful institutions with direct and executive authority in an area of policy-making", while their establishment "precedes the emergence of a political community in which such decisions, or, more significantly, the procedures for the taking of such decisions, can be grounded"[9].

If we adopt a social constructivist perspective to the study of European monetary integration, crucial aspects of the process of institutionalising EMU-governance are opened up, namely the role that discourses, communicative interaction and ideas play in the framing of collective understandings, in the formation of attitudes and behaviour, and in the

---

[5] Greece bcame the twelfth euro-member in January 2001
[6] The Euro-MP Daniel Cohn-Bendit and Olivier Duhamel see the *euro* as a common measure, common instrument and political symbol for a European consciousness, a European Identity and Political Union; *cf.* Cohn-Bendit and Duhamel, 1998, pp. 96, 165 and 257.
[7] Eurobarometer 43, 1995, p. xi, Niedermayer, 1995.
[8] Fischer, 1997.
[9] Verdun and Christiansen, 2000, p. 162

transformation of norms that can be considered as constitutive for a political community[10].

Thomas Risse *et al.*, in their comparative analysis of elite political discourses on the *euro*, have advanced such an analysis of the social construction of EMU. They found that EMU, despite major drawbacks since 1992, only survived because German, French and British policy-makers backed it with a "common vision of European integration", but who, in order to legitimate EMU *vis-à-vis* their electorates, used symbols of national identity as well as constructions of "European domestic interests" as powerful tools in domestic discourses[11]. What the authors leave open is how to account for the fragility of public support and the intense politicisation of the issue of EMU in mass publics. One might argue that precisely the frame of "European nationalism", when adopted by domestic pro-EMU elites, might be conducive to scepticism and opposition against the *euro*, and, hence, promote *euro*-scepticism[12]. I will argue that an elite-centred approach, limited to the domestic level, and excluding mass publics, will miss an important mechanism involved in the social and political process of constructing the *euro*.

Adopting social constructivism as an analytical framework allows it to study mass public attitudes as an expression of – competing or hegemonic, supranational or domestic – political discourses. In their discourses, governing elites as well as opposition groups, frame the *euro* as a public object in ways to produce meanings, to attract feelings, to be valued, or to be judged on normative grounds, within or across national boundaries. The empirical question is then to identify the alternative frames that make the *euro* either become a political symbol of European unity, of collective identity, and social solidarity, or – by contrast – a scapegoat and symbol of European centralism and fraud, forced social and cultural homogeneity? For answering these questions EMU is explored as a contested public territory of domestic, transnational and supranational struggles about meanings. The tool-kit used for this study links the quantitative analysis of European public opinion data to the qualitative analysis of discursive "framing", both inspired by the "constructivist turn" in EU-integration studies. While the former is useful for exploring cross- and intra-national variations in the distribu-

---

[10]   Christiansen *et al.*, p. 540ff; see also Jepperson *et al.*, 1996, Risse and Wiener, 1999, Checkel, 2000 and Kohler-Koch, 2000

[11]   Risse *et al.*, 1999, p. 175ff.

[12]   "*Euro*-scepticism" is used here as a sub-specie of "Euroscepticism", conceived of to encompass "contingent or qualified opposition", as well as "outright and unqualified opposition" to European integration, in the face of "an on-going *de facto* process" of integration, promoted at the institutional level by supranational elites, but restricted to the issue of European monetary unification; see Taggart, 1998, p. 366.

tion of preferences in mass public attitudes, the analysis of discursive frames provides a framework for studying the construction and change of normatively based attitudes.

In this chapter, I will argue that the complex process of the social construction of EMU can be better understood:

- first, if the comparative analysis of public support for EMU is matched by an analysis of *euro*-scepticism; with a particular focus not only on cross-national variation, but also on inner-national differences – in particular, elite-mass disparities, and gender gaps – in order to capture domestic differences involved in the construction of EMU;

- second, if quantitative opinion analysis is linked to the qualitative study of political discourses about EMU, to explore ideas, feelings, and values projected on the *euro* more in-depthly;

- third, discourse analysis includes domestic as well as supranational communication, to better understand resonance and interactions between both levels in the social construction of EMU.

In my conclusion I will describe the passage into this stage of European monetary integration as a unique experiment, because, under the given constraints of the Euro-polity, EMU is the most salient European issue so far with the potential to turn the EU into a sphere of publics.

Patterns and Dynamics of *Euro*-Scepticism (1993-2000)

During the ratification of the Maastricht Treaty of the European Union, one of the crucial premises on which the "The European Would-be Polity" had rested, crumbled: the assumption of mass public "permissive consensus"[13]. Conventional wisdom since the beginning of the seventies had been that national leaders could "presumably call upon whatever reservoirs of support and solidarity exist within their polity to allow discretion to public authorities in the exercise of their governing responsibilities"[14]. In this view, public support for the EC could be conceived as a generalised and "passive condition" for elite action, and publics did neither impede nor activate "system growth and change" in European integration[15]. After 1990, the "erosion of the permissive consensus"[16] became problematic. First, public support for the EU decreased by nearly one third. Second, the new mass public Euro-

---

[13] Lindberg and Scheingold, 1970.
[14] Lindberg and Scheingold, 1970, pp. 121 and 130
[15] Lindberg and Scheingold, 1970, p. 121.
[16] Reif, 1992.

scepticism was marked by a new gender gap[17]. Third, contentious movement activists mobilised mass constituencies to vote negatively in a series of domestic referenda on the EU, namely four times in Denmark (1992, 1993, 1998 and 2000), and once in France (1993), as well as once also in Austria, Sweden, Norway and Finland (1994). This transformation of mass public attitudes indicated a shift of European integration from a neo-functionalist or inter-governmental elite driven project to a contested, politicised process of Europeanisation. This shift also affected EMU, given that the Single Currency soon turned into a hot issue of public debate in many Member States.

In the language of official EMU-documents, Member States are classified in two groups: the "Ins", consisting of those who fulfilled the convergence criteria and whom the European Council, at its May 1998 meeting, accepted for the third stage of EMU beginning, on 1 January 1999; the remaining ones who either did not meet the requirements regarding debt, inflation and budget discipline, were named "Pre-Ins[18]". However, if one substitutes official convergence criteria by indicators for the legitimacy which EMU enjoys, measured by mass public support for EMU and by *euro-s*cepticism, a new classification emerges. For this purpose, in the following I will explore three different aspects of the legitimacy of EMU: elite-mass disparities; gender gaps; and the polarisation of the issue of the *euro* over time, all of which are covered by Eurobarometer survey data[19].

Out of Touch?
EMU Views of Top Decision-Makers and Publics

Elite-mass disparities in public attitudes toward EMU have been explored by a study conducted by EOS Gallup Europe[20] in 1996. Then, in the EU-15, 85% of top decision makers supported the single

---

[17] Liebert, 1997 and 1999, Nelsen and Guth, 2000.

[18] "Pre-Ins" was the common label for a diversity of Member States who did either not fulfil the criteria (Greece until 2000) or who opted out (UK), who opted against (Denmark) or who did not yet opt for joining EMU (Sweden).

[19] Since 1973, the European Commission mass public opinion surveys in EC/EU Member States provide, thus far, the most valuable source for quantitative comparative data and public opinion analyses on Europe. Since 1993, the item "public support for the *euro*" was included regularly in surveys, such as "Eurobarometer", "Europinion special", and the "Continuous Tracking Service", and there was also conducted a special survey on EMU, in 1999.

[20] EOS Gallup Europe: "The European Union. A View from the Top. Top Decision Makers and the European Union", is based on a 1996 survey among 22,729 holders of high office, in five sectors: elected politicians; civil servants; industry; media; cultural/intellectuals, from fifteen Member States.

currency, compared to only 53% of the general public[21]. Hence, a gap of 32% between elites and publics in their views on EMU was found, which varied considerably across Member States: On the one hand, the country where elites were most out of touch with mass publics on the issue of EMU was Germany: here, support scores between elites (90%) and general publics (40%) differed by fifty percentage points. On the other hand, Italian elites appeared to represent mass public preferences relatively best: the gap between elites (88%) and mass public support (78%) was only at ten percentage points (see Table 1).

In their mass-elite gaps on the issue of EMU, the three most patently euro-sceptic Member States – Sweden, Denmark and the UK – differed considerably. While a majority of the Danish elite (74%) and of the Swedish elite (64%) favoured the single currency, they clearly departed from their general publics, with 38% and 37% of differences. By contrast, British top decision makers in their attitudes tended to be more in touch with mass public preferences – the gap here was only twenty-six percentage points.

One would assume that top decision-makers from industry favoured EMU more than any other elite sector across Member States. However, this was not at all the case. In Germany, civil servants were the strongest supporters of EMU. In Italy, support by cultural elites was nearly as strong as by industry. Among the Member States that did not join EMU, the picture was not less complex. In the UK, civil servants were also most in favour of EMU, with industry and the media least so. Both, in Sweden and Denmark, industry was most strongly in favour. But while in Sweden, cultural elites were the protagonists of *euro*-scepticism, and politicians followed them at some distance, in Denmark the reverse was true: here, politicians were much less in favour of EMU than cultural elites[22].

---

[21] Eurobarometer surveys on the item of EMU are based on the question asked to respondents whether they are for or against the following statement: "There has to be one single currency, the euro, replacing the (National Currency) and all other national currencies of the Member States of the European Union".

[22] EOS Gallup Europe 1996, p. 42

Table 1: EMU from Top and from Below, 1996

Member state	TDM	Public	Gap
EU 15	85	53	32
Germany	90	40	50
Belgium	98	53	45
Austria	78	34	44
Denmark	74	36	38
Sweden	64	27	37
Finland	68	35	33
Spain	95	62	33
France	90	59	31
Portugal	83	52	31
Luxembourg	93	63	30
Greece	92	64	28
UK	60	34	26
NL	91	66	25
Ireland	89	66	23
Italy	88	78	10

Source: EOS Gallup Europe 1996; p. 40/41

Note: numbers in percent indicate the proportion of respondents who indicated to agree with the opinion that there had to be one single currency, the euro, replacing the national currencies

Women and Euro-Scepticism

Explorations of the gender gap in public attitudes toward European integration have expanded traditional approaches to European public opinion analysis by integrating gender differences into their research design[23]. Using Eurobarometer studies from the 1980s and 1990s, it was found that women's support for the EU in most EU-Member States is lower than men's, that female *euro*-scepticism in a number of them is stronger than male *euro*-scepticism; that in a few cases these gender gaps have narrowed over time, while in others they have expanded

---

[23]   Liebert, 1999; Nelsen and Guth, 2000

277

further[24]; and it was further suggested that gendered public attitudes were a decisive factor for the Intergovernmental Conference of 1996-7 to incorporate gender equality provisions in the Treaty reform[25]. The question is whether the findings of gendered patterns of EU-support will also hold for attitudes towards EMU. In the following, I will draw on Eurobarometer analyses to support the claim that this, in fact, is the case.

In 1996, the gender gap in public *euro*-opposition across the EU-15 was at five percentage points, within four Member States, where gender disparities were more than just significant: in Denmark (20%); in Sweden (13%); in Finland (11%); and in the Netherlands (10%). By contrast, in the UK, Ireland, Greece, Spain and Italy, gender gaps in opposition to EMU were nearly non-existing. Germany was the only case where male opposition was stronger than the female one, exceeding it by six percentage points (see Table 2).

The special report on "European public opinion on the Single Currency" documented a gender gap in public attitudes towards the *euro*, with more men supporting it (1998: 65%) than women (1998: 56%), and less men opposing the Euro (1998: 27%) than women (1998: 30%[26]). An examination of Standard Eurobarometer data from Spring 1996 and Spring 1998 shows that this gender gap had been increasing by ten percent in this period. In 1998, the sole exception among Member States were Finland and Germany, where male opposition was stronger, and Italy, where both were at the same level (1998: 6%) (see Table 2). Between 1998 and 2000, gender gaps in public *euro*-support increased in most Member States, except Belgium and Greece. Gender gaps were above ten percent in Denmark, Finland and Sweden, they were lower than ten percent in the Netherlands, Germany, Austria, and Portugal, while in the UK, Ireland, Spain, France and even Italy they reached a significant level. In this context, Sweden appeared as one of the most peculiar cases, given that in 1996-1998, the level of public support for EMU had significantly increased both among men and women, while gender disparities had widened further. With regard to Swedish *euro*-opposition, its overall level dropped by five percent, but with the gender gap remaining at thirteen percent (see Table 2).

---

24 Although gender gaps in EU support have tended to diminish over time, in Denmark, Sweden and the UK they have increased during the past decade; *cf.* Liebert, 1999.

25 Liebert, 1999.

26 See European Commission "European Public Opinion on the Single Currency", 1999, pp. 45-47

Table 2: Gender Gaps in Euro-Scepticism, 1996-1998

Member State	1996 male	female	1998 male	female
DEN	55,7	75,1	41,2	50,3
FIN	61,1	72,8	48,9	45,9
SWE	50	63,4	45,1	58,2
UK	59,7	59,8	34,8	37,4
GER-E	47,8	51,3	19,7	18,5
GER-W	54,3	48,8	32,4	30,6
AUS	40,5	47,3	25,9	27,3
EU	**35,7**	**40,9**	**28,2**	**35,6**
FRA	27,8	35,1	14,7	21,2
BEL	27,2	33,9	23,7	27,4
LUX	27,1	32,1	8,3	12,1
NET	21,6	31,3	9,6	18,6
POR	21,4	27,9	11,1	19,5
GRE	19,6	20,6	14,7	23,4
SPA	20,6	20,6	10,9	15,6
IRE	19,8	17,6	16,9	17,8
ITA	12,3	12	6,3	6,3

Source: EB 49/Spring 1996 and EB 51/Spring 1998

Note: figures in percent indicate the proportion of those male or female respondents who were against the opinion there has to be one single currency, the euro, replacing the national currencies

Domestic divisions of public attitudes toward EMU, hence, include disparities between elite views and mass public opinion, on one hand, and gender differences, on the other hand. The Report on "Top-Decision-Makers", and the Special Report by the European Commission on Public opinion, are the best data sources available so far to describe how these two dimensions of domestic patterns of differentiation – and potential politicisation and conflict – combine and how they vary in cross-national comparison. Regarding these variations, Member States fall into four groups: (1) gender differences and elite-mass divides are both most pronounced in five Member States: Denmark, Sweden, Finland, Austria, and Belgium; (2) on the contrary, disparities in both dimensions have been relatively minor in Italy, the UK, Greece, Ireland, and Luxembourg, (3) elite-mass gaps were largest, with gender gaps being minor or absent, in Germany and Spain, and finally (4) in the

Netherlands, France and Portugal, gender gaps have been significant, with elite-mass disparities being relatively smaller.

If the patterns of public opinion can be classified along these two dimensions, the question to be addressed in the next section is whether we can also distinguish between different dynamics of public attitudes towards EMU across Member States. If after Maastricht, mass public opinion on the issue of EMU has left behind its earlier "permissive consensus", and if patterns of domestic public opinion fall in so different clusters, we should also expect differences in the dynamics of how public opinion evolves: whether there is increasing polarisation or rather a trend toward homogeneity.

Polarisation of Public Attitudes towards EMU?

It can be seen as a success for European elites in promoting EMU that public support increased between 1993 and 2000 from 52%, by 8%. However, one should not ignore that while *support* for the *euro* remained fragile, *euro*-sceptic attitudes expanded, and that this was the case not only for *euro*-outsiders, but also for a majority of *euro*-insiders.

First, since the issue of EMU was included in regular EB-surveys in 1993, they reveal a cyclical pattern in the dynamics of public acceptance of the *euro*: while from 1993 to 1997, the level of support shrank to 47%, only, after the "Euro-11" had been officially established, did it expand again, to 68% in 1999. After having moved into the third phase of introducing the *euro*, citizens of the *euro*-zone, while still holding their national currencies in their hands, apparently turned sceptic again, and support faltered, by 10% (58% in 2000).

Furthermore, Member States show quite different patterns of how levels of mass public *euro*-support, on one hand, and *euro*-scepticism, on the other hand relate to each other. In 2000, *euro*-supporters enjoyed a majority in nine Member States, with Italy (81%), Belgium (76%) and Spain (75%) leading the hegemonic camp, where *euro*-sceptics commanded the support of no more than between 14% and 21%. *Euro*-sceptics were in the majority in four Member States: in the UK (61%), Sweden (54%), and Denmark (51%). In the three remaining Member States – Austria, Finland and Germany – neither of the camps reached a majority[27], but public opinion remained polarised. Between 1998 and 2000, only three out of fifteen member governments were confronted with stable (Greece) or even receding (Belgium) *euro*-scepticism. By contrast, the UK and Germany both witnessed increases of *euro*-sceptics, by 25% and 20%, respectively.

---

[27]   Eurobarometer 53, Spring 2000, p. 46

Concluding, we can say that in six Member States, EMU suffers from legitimacy deficits. This applied in 2000 not only to three of the four *euro*-outsiders, UK, Sweden and Denmark, but also to the three "euro-11" members, Austria, Finland and Germany; in all of them, support for EMU remained under the threshold of fifty percent. Although in some cases the share of sympathisers increased, all six saw the proportion of *euro*-sceptics grow between 1998 and 2000 (see Table 3). A process of growing politicisation can be assumed to be in course, hence, particularly in those Member States where *euro*-scepticism rises, and especially when accompanied by a trend towards polarisation, with a drop of public support for the *euro*.

Table 3: Dynamics of Public Attitudes towards EMU, 1998-2000

Level of *euro*-support* in 2000	Stable or decreasing *euro*-scepticism* 1998-2000 (percent)	Increasing *euro*-scepticism* 1998-2000 (percent)
Above 50%	GRE (0) BEL (-5)	NET (+13) FRA (+11) IRE (+5) ITA (+8) POR (+7) SPA (+5) EU (+1)
Below 50%		*UK (+25) GER (+20) AUS (+11) DEN (+5) SWE (+3) FIN (+1)*

Source: Own calculations, based on EB 51/1998 and 53/2000

(*) Figures for "support" indicate the proportion of those respondents who agreed with the opinion that there had to be one single currency, the euro, replacing national currencies; figures for "euro-scepticism" indicate the proportion of those who were against it.

During the two years after the official launch of the *euro*, public attitudes remained polarised in Denmark, Sweden and Finland; and divisions became deeper in the UK, Germany, and Austria. On the other hand, in Italy where mass publics with their "permissive consensus" on European integration had provided continuous support to their domestic elites, especially during the hardships of fiscal adjustments under the convergence criteria discipline, *euro*-scepticism grew moderately (by 8%) only after 1999, while support remained at a high level.

The question is how these complex patterns and diverse trends in public attitudes towards EMU can be explained.

Explaining Public Euro-Scepticism: Quantitative Evidence

Quantitative opinion analyses have sought to identify the sources of citizens support for EMU, by focusing on national interest and identity as well as on domestic gender differences. Regarding national identity and interests, Anderson and Kaltenthaler suggest that EU-monetary policy is more an "issue full of symbolism regarding the future of the nation-state", than an object of individual cost-benefit calculations[28]. This observation holds for most Member States, where *euro*-scepticism is associated not primarily with cost-benefit calculated expectations, but rather with the expectation to lose national sovereignty. However, with respect to this general claim, Germany is the most prominent exception. Following survey data, Germans are highly prone to "material calculations" and intensely susceptible to the costs of EMU: negative expectations are concerned primarily with economic growth and employment opportunities[29]. To explain this German idiosyncrasy[30], an assessment of effective domestic impacts of EMU appears of little help. As a comparison of Italy and Germany, with their contrasting levels of *euro*-scepticism, shows, such differences do not correspond to the effective hardships resulting from the strength of state fiscal discipline and restructuring policies in both cases. Italian political elites who were empowered by Maastricht, in their attempt to correct the "misfit" between Italian public finances and EMU-requirements, adopted more drastic measures of consolidation and expenditure cuts than most other Member States, including Germany[31]. Contrary to all "rational" expectations, public *euro*-scepticism in Italy remained at an extremely low, and *euro*-support at an extraordinarily high level. The Italian case suggests therefore to conceive of public attitudes towards the *euro* not as an effect of domestic consequences of EMU, but rather as a facilitating resource for or as a constraint on government action in response to

---

[28] Anderson and Kaltenthaler, 1998, p. 24f., in an analysis based on EB 42, found that satisfaction with EU-institutions and materialism explained EMU-support, while national pride, domestic political satisfaction and post-materialism explained its lack, and egocentric, self-interest based calculations did not matter.

[29] See Europinion special, January 1999, B34; *cf.* also Cautrès and Reynié, 2000.

[30] *Cf.* Huffschmid, 1998.

[31] Sbragia, 2000.

monetary union. Hence, although comparative quantitative analysis cannot explain ideosyncrasies such as the German or Italian, it is indispensable to identify them.

The same applies to comparative gender gap studies based on quantitative data. Regarding the gender gap in EU-support, quantitative approaches have advanced explanations based on socio-demographic characteristics; utilitarian motives; political ideology; gender differentiated values; and the institutional context, namely of the democratic and the welfare state. Nelson and Guth, in their test of a large range of such alternative explanations, provide three important insights into why women tend to be more sceptical of European integration than men[32]: Women, in their assessments of the EU, indicate influence by a number of factors different from those which influence men. Second, contrary to traditional expectations on the one hand, and to feminist expectations on the other, neither "women's values", such as religion, nor the "woman-friendliness" of the welfare state they live in, are capable of explaining variations in women's attitudes towards the EU. Third, and most importantly, the authors demonstrate that much of the gender gap variance is due to "national idiosyncrasies", and that for understanding which national traditions matter, "we need further exploration"[33].

For understanding patterns and dynamics of public opinion involved in the social construction of EMU, quantitative approaches to public attitudes are hence indispensable for identifying contrasting cases. But in the context of the diversity of domestic economic and social structures and political institutions in EU-Member States, it is dubious whether it is reasonable to look for a single set of causes or motivations to explain *euro*-scepticism and to develop theories that are valid and can be generalised across the EU. Quantitative studies based on culturally unspecific questionnaires conceal the fundamental ambiguities of diverse meanings and language terms that are constructed to measure variables. For examining these ambiguities with their more deep-seated motivational bases, qualitative in-depth studies are needed to complement quantitative analyses.

In the next section, I will adopt such a qualitative approach to explore the patterns and dynamics of "idiosyncratic" cases more in detail. For this purpose, I will compare political discourses on EMU, by focusing on the most contrasting cases, identified above: Denmark and

---

[32] Among these "women specific" factors, with a positive relation to their pro-European attitudes, Nelson and Guth identify "knowledge about the EU", "educational resources", and number of children; while they find "ideology" to work differently for both genders; Nelsen and Guth, 2000, pp. 279-282.

[33] Nelsen and Guth, 2000, p. 286

Sweden, Germany, France, Italy and the UK. The comparative approach to political discourses on EMU in these Member States rests on a distinction between different types of "frames" for constructing the *euro*.

Euro-Sceptic Discourses in the Social Construction of EMU

Seen as a process of social construction, the introduction of the single currency into the fragmented polity of the EU could have been expected to provoke mass politicisation. Precisely because of the need to explore "national idiosyncrasies" that show up in the politicisation processes on the issue of EMU, I suggest here the adoption of a qualitative, interpretative framework for examining discursive strategies. This framework is based on a distinction between different types of cognitive and normative frames that are used in public discourses. A public discourse is conceived here as "the sum of political actors' public accounts of the polity's purposes, goals, and ideals, while its function is to explain political events, to justify political actions, to develop political identities, to reshape and, or reinterpret political history, and, all in all, to frame the national political discussion"[34]. I will further distinguish between five particular discursive strategies to frame the domestic discussion of the issue of EMU: Europe-nationalist frames; traditional cultural-nationalist frames; social-nationalist frames; social-constructive frames; and feminist frames. These strategies shall be characterised by the particular frames on which they rely, and which are based on more general rhetoric devices: ideas about whether and how EMU will impact on people's social practices; ideological constructions of collective identities and expectations about how these will be affected by monetary union; and evaluations whether the norms on which EMU is based will collide with certain normative principles that are taken for granted.

To illustrate these particular discursive strategies and how they shape frameworks of meaning for making EMU intelligible to domestic publics, I will draw on empirical evidence from Member States and illustrate (1) the "Europe-nationalist" framework by German debates; (2) the "cultural nationalist" framework by examples from Britain; (3) the "social nationalist" framework by examples from Sweden and Denmark; (4) the "euro-constructive" framework by the French discourse; (5) and the "feminist frameworks" in transnational European debates. At the same time, this framework will serve to explore more indepthly these most "idiosyncratic" cases with regard to patterns of

---

[34] Schmidt, 1998, p. 3ff.

public attitudes towards EMU that quantitative analysis has helped to identify.

The "Europe-Nationalist" Frame and the German Debate

In their attempts to persuade domestic publics that monetary union and the ensuing domestic changes are, both, empirically desirable and normatively acceptable, political elites have used a variety of ideas, languages and frameworks. Discursive frameworks that argue for European Union because of national interests have been depicted as "Europe-nationalist", as they emphasise not only the inevitability but also the necessity of European integration, by claiming that this was in the best national interests: by serving domestic preferences, and because of being basically shaped by domestic interests[35]. To succeed so convincingly, and to help effectively to change a country's policy paradigm, elites must reconstruct the dominant discourse and change its underlying belief structures, by building at the same time on old understandings, while creating something new[36].

Amy Verdun and Thomas Christiansen have pointed to the dangers of output-oriented strategies for legitimating EMU in terms of anticipated positive economic effects of the single currency[37]. In the perspective of self-denominated "Euro-constructivists" (see below), such as Daniel Cohn-Bendit and Oliver Duhamel, this strategy is further handicapped by its Europe-nationalist rhetoric, stressing national interests and expectations that, in the short or long run, could be frustrated – thus, Euro-nationalism would ultimately feed into Euroscepticism.

By no means exclusive in this respect[38], the case of the Federal Republic of Germany may illustrate the paradoxical effect of Europe-nationalist frames. In their attempts to persuade Germans concerned about a weak and inflationary common currency, Europe-nationalists had vowed the *euro* would be *"Stark wie die Mark"*[39], as sound as the DM, due to two devices: the fiscal and budgetary discipline imposed by the Stability and Growth Pact on "weak currency" countries, and through the European Central Bank that would follow the model of the

---

[35] *Cf.* Moss and Michie (eds.), 2000; on Italy and the UK, see Talani, 2000.

[36] Vivien Schmidt has developed this "dynamic capacity of a discourse to change a country's policy paradigm", see Schmidt, 1998.

[37] Verdun and Christiansen, 2000, p. 178

[38] For instance, Jacques Chirac is said to have claimed in public that he constructed Europe "because France could be the best in doing this"; quoted from Cohn-Bendit and Duhamel, 1998, p. 101.

[39] German Ministry of Finance: *Stark wie die Mark*, Bonn, April 1992;

"politically independent" German Bundesbank[40]. Later on, when facing the devaluation of the *euro*, the Europe-nationalist argumentation had to switch to claims about the benefits which even a weak single currency was supposed to bring to "exporting Germany" as well as to its labour market[41]. Paradoxically, this line of argument would imply that if the *euro* regained strength, economic growth rates would have to be expected to decline, and unemployment to increase once more. With their contradictory arguments in favour of EMU, German Europe-nationalists unwillingly fed into *euro*-sceptic arguments: with Finance Minister Theo Waigel's insisting critique of Italy and other "non-mature" and "less-disciplined" Member States[42]; and with the government slogan "strong as the mark" coupled with an emphasis on German export interests. For the left-wing opposition, EMU was framed ambiguously, as an "as much anti-imperialist as imperialist project of a new type": constrained by insufficient measures of consolidation; as a substitute for a political union that enhances EU-interventionism within Member States and abroad, with a "mutual control of national interests", imposing sanctions on those who in their national interest "allow themselves too many debts", and supported by a European Social Democracy that has abandoned "its image as a spokesman of the Social"[43].

In view of these ambiguities of a nationalist pro-*euro* discourse, mass public *euro*-scepticism expanded in Germany, paradoxically after EU Member States, under the pressure of the German ministry of finance and in order to appease German anxieties, had adopted the Stability and Growth Pact: between 1998 and 2000, German *euro*-scepticism increased by twenty percent. Of all member peoples, Germans confessed to be most concerned about the issues of national economic growth and

---

[40] Ironically, with this line of argument, instances where the German Bundesbank also compromised were removed, for example in 1990, in setting the conversion rate for the East- and West-German currency union, where the electoral logic of the German party government counted, despite economic concerns, as the ultimate "raison d'etat": see Busch, 1991. On the other hand, the Economist noted that the DM, since 1996, had turned into the "world's weakest currency", *The Economist*, 11 April 1998, p. 25

[41] "Zeitpunkte: Das neue Geld. Was uns der Euro bringt"; Zeitmagazin, 2/1998; Christoph Zöpel, "Der schwache Euro ist gut", in *Die Zeit*, 14 September 2000.

[42] "The stability of EMU has to be secured against finance political defections (Fehlverhalten) of some. For this purpose, the membership criteria and the institutional safeguards of the Treaty have to be articulated and operationalised", Press Communication of the Federal Ministry for Finance, Bonn, 10 November 1995; in: *Deutsche Bundesbank, Auszüge*, No. 77, 13 November 1995. I owe this quote to Uwe Puetter, doctoral student at Belfast University.

[43] Gegenstandpunkte, 2000, p. 145

of employment perspectives[44]. Ultimately, following conventional German wisdom, growth as well as employment would be both negatively correlated with a strong DM.

So far, both European-nationalists as well as *euro*-critics with their frames have interacted with a German public already sceptical about the *euro,* in constructing, first, high expectations based on nationally calculated costs and benefits, which in one way or another, necessarily had to feed into the fears of negative outcomes. This appears to be a typical dilemma of a pro-*euro* discourse that is constrained by national frames: "Europe is reduced to a necessity, an unavoidable minimal organisation, instead of communicating it as an ideal, an innovation, or a new horizon"[45].

Cultural-Nationalist Frames and the French and British EMU Debates

While Europe-nationalist strategies are based on sometimes quite sophisticated reconstructed frameworks to articulate old domestic and new European frames, cultural-nationalist frameworks revitalise the full symbolic repertoire of traditional unreconstructed nationalism. Their creativity is primarily in how they link empirical evidence to perceptions of threats to national sovereignty, with considerable variations in the level of dramatisation. On one extreme, there are more moderate cultural nationalists who claim that monetary and economic integration would ultimately impose also cultural homogeneity on EU-Member States. The *euro* is, hence, constructed as a symbol for "unification from above" which would leave no space for heterogeneity, difference and cultural particularity. On the other extreme, there are cold warriors such as Martin Feldstein, former foreign advisor to Ronald Reagan, in an article against the *euro,* who invented the most threatening scenario of EMU: "The American Civil War shows that a formal political Union cannot impede an inner-European war. But even if one cannot know exactly whether the conflicts (which will derive from the introduction of the *euro*) will be conducive to a war, this is a possibility too real to discard it"[46].

---

[44] Regarding the effects of EMU on economic and job growth, 72% respectively 65% held pessimistic views; see Commission, Special Report, 1999.

[45] Cohn-Bendit and Duhamel, 1988, pin a large range of such ideals on the horizon of EMU: the *euro* as an instrument for dismantling national borders, and a unique measure advancing social and cultural integration; ultimately, as a symbol of European unification, consciousness and identity, See, especially, p. 101ff.

[46] Feldstein, 1992, pp. 19-22 and Cohn-Bendit and Duhamel, 1998, p. 160.

Between both extremes is where cultural essentialists locate themselves. For instance, French anthropologist, Emanuel Todd, predicted at the end of 1998, shortly before the official launch of the *euro*, EMU would not survive longer than 2005. In his view, EMU was based "on the false premise that European societies are similar and their various components are prone to convergence and harmonisation. It refuses to take into account the very real and inflexible cultural, traditional, ethical and linguistic differences"; therefore "the whole thing will founder, the great myth will be debunked, and we will all rush back to create our national currencies and economies, the euro will be gone by 2005, or I eat my hat"[47].

Following Eurobarometer-data, nationalist frames would have been relatively most successful in Swedish, British and Danish public debates, where relatively the largest proportions of mass publics ground their *euro*-sceptic attitudes on national identities and the perception that the sovereignty of the nation state was under threat from the EU[48]. A closer scrutiny of the Swedish as well as of the Danish EMU-debates provides evidence that a quantitative account conceals profound differences between the discursive frames used in Nordic debates, and compared to British and French unreconstructed nationalist discourses. In the Nordic countries, frames are mixed, with ethnic-national identity being of minor importance, while "social-nationalist" frames can be found up-front.

Social-Nationalist Frames and the Swedish and Danish EMU Debates

To Swedes, who are deeply split on whether or not to join EMU, the "loss of national sovereignty" refers to the "Swedish model of society", and its future in a uniting Europe. In particular, emphasis is placed on the "communal vision" of politics on which this model is constructed

---

[47] Todd, 1997, p. 32. In his book "*L'illusion economique. Essai sur la stagnation des societies developpées*", Todd further developed his argument based on national identities: contrary to national socio-cultural diversities, the Maastricht project with its combination of commercial openness and "monetary mysticism" pursued the aim of defining "a new, larger and more powerful nation of Europe" and that it was driven by a continental European and authoritarian strategy of "monetary fusion" from above, as Germany had already experienced it in its economic history several times (Todd, 1998, pp. 195-218).

[48] Asked why they feared EMU, 49% of all respondents across EU-Member States pointed to a "loss of national identity", in the UK it were 64% (compared to 30% not), and in Sweden 54% (compared to 41% not), contrasting most with Italy, where the smallest proportion of respondents (21%) shared such nationalist concerns, and 67% did not; see Eurobarometer Special Report, 1999.

and which a Swedish trade union newspaper described as the "soul" of the Social Democratic Party[49]. In this sense, Swedish social-nationalist frames rest essentially on social democratic norms and the complementary fears of losing social and political rights. A particular topic of Swedish Euro-scepticism is the perceived insecurity deriving from the Single Market and European regulations which allow alcohol and drugs to sweep over the Swedish border[50].

Unlike Sweden, which did not get an official opt-out clause from EMU and where the debate has been contained in the party political arena, in Denmark, the issue of EMU has provoked the most extensive and open public debates in the EU, thus far. Here, "nationalist" and "democratic" frames appear to be in competition and at the same time allied: In the referendum campaign on EMU, in September 2000[51], anti-EMU leftist and right wing forces struggled on contradictory meanings of the "no" which a majority of Danes had voted for. The Socialist People's Party, on one hand, interpreted this victory according to its slogan "No to the *euro*, enhance the international solidarity", and, in alliance with the "group for a Europe of democracies and differences", called for an inversion of the trend towards a European federal state, in which the *euro* would serve as a motor, and for the launch of a new European debate[52]. On the other hand, the right wing populist Danish People's Party called for a "no" for the sake of national identity. *Euro*-opponents could build a successful alliance by constructing the *euro* as a motor for a "European super state", built on neo-liberal principles of less state and more market. This construct was an umbrella that equally served right-wing populists, for their nationalist and protectionist anti-immigration appeals, and also leftist and feminist forces, who were advocates of the successful Danish model of a welfare state. State investment programmes since the beginning of the 1990s helped to build a social security net, with low unemployment, and generous public infrastructures, benefiting especially women and working parents. Hence, the idea that a combination of a transfer of state competencies to Brussels and Frankfurt, with an increasing number of EU-immigrants,

---

[49] Reuters News Service, Swedish Social Democrats split over EMU decision, 7 March 2000.

[50] Reuters News Service, Swedish Social Democrats split over EMU decision, 7 March 2000.

[51] In the series of six European referenda held in Denmark since 1972, the government and EU elites lost this last one most dramatically, against 53.1% of "no", and with a high participation of 87.7%

[52] Agence Europe: Hohe Beteiligung beim Referendum über den Euro, Argumente dafür und dagegen; 29 September 2000.

would undermine this national system, found much popularity with a nationalist alliance of left as well as right-wing forces[53].

"Euro-Constructive" Frames and the French EMU Debate

"Euro-constructive" frameworks share with "social-nationalist" frameworks a basically critical approach towards the neo-liberal conception of EMU. But differing from principled leftist critiques of the global capitalist economy, they take a pragmatic view and see opportunities for curing the shortcomings of a neo-liberal philosophy by strengthening the social dimension of the EU. Thus, the French Communists have described their supportive position in favour of the *euro* as "euroconstructive": "Precisely because we are convinced of the necessity of a European Union and of the possibility to change it through intervention, we define ourselves without complexes as euroconstructive"[54]. More principled leftist *euro*-sceptics argue, on the one hand, that the convergence criteria, and namely the three percent tap on the budget deficit, would undermine social security systems. On the other hand, the intensification of economic competition is depicted as a threat to national economies, conducive to the growth of unemployment, and, as a consequence of greater labour market flexibility, to larger wage disparities. With respect to the issue of employment, *euro*-constructivists such as Daniel Cohn-Bendit, are sceptical, too. However, instead of rejecting EMU, they rather stress the need for active employment programmes. Their view is that the effect of EMU on employment will vary, depending on sector, Member State and region; but that, as a baseline, the Amsterdam Treaty provision on the coordination of national employment strategies is insufficient[55].

Gendered Frames, the Nordic Debate and Transnational Controversy

"Gendered" discursive frameworks for EMU use "gender" as an explicit analytical category, and thus depart from the majority of political discourses that rely on implicit normative assumptions on appropriate or "natural" gender roles. Some authors contend that all political discourses on the EU and on EMU are gendered, even if not explicitly so, social practices and institutions within which EMU is

---

[53] *Die Tageszeitung*, 30 September 2000, p. 13
[54] Secretary of the PCF, Robert Hue, in *L'Humanité*, 15 December 1997, cited in Cohn-Bendit and Duhamel, 1998, p. 81
[55] Cohn-Bendit and Duhamel, 1998, p. 27ff.

embedded are shaped by gender relations[56]. Here, I will limit my analysis to explicitly gendered discourses, only, and, hence, explore the social construction of EMU through the lens which feminist analysts have developed. Depending on the situated knowledge they draw on, their discursive frames may build on ideas about the impacts of EMU, regarding gender specific interests and gender relations. Feminist discourses that import gender into the constructions of EMU and of the EU more generally[57], may draw on different cognitive frames, ideas and norms, but they all emphasise differential meanings of EMU for women, men or their relations.

For the Danish case, Chiara Bertone has demonstrated that "gender" since the 1970s was a "hidden dimension" in the Danish EC-debate, but that the notion of a "women's voting block" against the EU during the 1990s was paralleled by deliberate attempts to construct a specific women's perspective; despite deep disagreements on its contents, these attempts were successful in creating space for gender perspectives in public debates[58]. Although not in all Member States such spaces for women's publics or opportunities for women's groups, activists or scholars exist to them same degree to participate in domestic EC-debates, in recent years a transnational feminist dialogue has developed on issues related to the EU.

In domestic and transnational debates about the EU and EMU, feminist and gender frames have emphasised at least five major ideas. First, the idea that labour market liberalisation in the EC had gender biased unequal effects, and that it was questionable whether EC gender equality policy was capable of correcting them. For instance, Anette Borchorst argued that EC regulations magnified differences between women: "the highly monetarist character of the political and economic union [...] reinforces a dualism between workers with secure full-time jobs and workers outside or partly attached to the labour market. This dualism is heavily structured along gender lines"[59].

Second, they have pointed to the more specific negative effects of EMU-policies on Nordic "women-friendly" welfare states, and their opportunities for women's employment and wage equality. In particular, feminist interpretations of EMU have emphasised the negative implications of the stability pact and of the convergence criteria for women, depicting them as driving forces for national savings packages and welfare retrenchment policies. They point to several critical facts: that after

---

[56] See Barbara MacLennan's chapter in this book.
[57] See a discussion in Shaw, 2000.
[58] Bertone, 1998, p. 108ff.
[59] Borchorst, 1994, p. 40

Sweden's entry in the EU, women experienced reductions in the level of parental leave payments from 90% to 75% of their income; that the Swedish labour market is gendered, with women finding work primarily in the public sector; and that economically vulnerable groups have hence either suffered from income reductions or are threatened by the expectation of unemployment[60].

Third, supporters of a critical view of EMU as a predominantly market driven and market expansion project, and a threat to domestic social welfare systems, do not share the same view of the effects of EC-gender equality policy. The case of unequal pay of a Swedish midwife which was presented in 2000 to the European Court of Justice, indicated that women's economic citizenship even in a Member State with advanced gender equality, such as Sweden, was constrained by gender segregated labour markets, and, hence, might benefit from EU jurisdiction[61]. Others, like Brigitte Young or Susanne Schunter-Kleemann, would admit that the EU did not exclude measures for combating labour market inequalities between men and women, but they would insist that these should not be overrated *vis-à-vis* the progressive commodification of women. Reflecting the marginality of gender frames in the German EMU-debate, Susanne Schunter-Kleemann argued that equal opportunity policies of the EC constituted "a small and relatively insignificant niche, isolated from the "big power game" that determines the overall economic and political setting"[62]. Sylvia Walby, from a British perspective claimed on the contrary that *vis-à-vis* EMU EC-equality law should not be undervalued as a means to enhance working women's rights, in the private as well as the public sector[63].

Fourth, normative reflections on EMU that are informed by a gender framework, see the EU-gender policy approach as fundamentally ambiguous: on one hand as too excessively oriented towards the market and women's employability, and, on the other hand, as still supporting an outmoded notion of maternalism[64]. From the Nordic perspective, "maternity protection" that is the core concern of the 1992-EC pregnant workers directive, is seen as "outmoded" and as an indicator of a dominant trend in the EU toward the male breadwinner – female care taker model[65]. EMU and the pressure it creates for a social and political

---

[60]   Ingrid Hedström, EU-correspondent of Dagens Nyheter, in an interview conducted by Milena Sunnus, doctoral student at Bremen, in April 2000 in Stockholm; for similar arguments, see Twaddle 1997, p. 189ff.
[61]   For a critical discussion, see Hobson, 2000, p. 85ff.
[62]   Schunter-Kleemann, 1997.
[63]   Young, 2000 and Walby, 1999.
[64]   Shaw, 2000.
[65]   Hobson, 1999 and Shaw, 2000.

union is seen as a motor promoting this trend towards a social policy harmonisation, based on a German type insurance model, and not the Danish model of a tax financed welfare system[66]. These critical reflections on the impact of the EU on gender equality indicate that norms of a just and legitimate social order are still contested across the different gender worlds of the European Union. Although Northern enlargement in 1995 has made welfare and gender regimes within the EU more varied than ever before, precisely this diversity is perceived to be under threat from EMU. In the aftermath of Maastricht, Anette Borchorst wondered whether it would be the conservative or the liberal welfare regime model that was going to win the race, at the expense of the social democratic regime[67]. The view that EC law did not attempt to strengthen the family should be corrected, at least in part, because the EU adopted a "parental leave directive" in 1996, and inscribed the principle of "gender mainstreaming" into the Amsterdam Treaty in 1997[68]. However, Nordic feminists continue to see EC law as a "logical trap" by which women are caught, given the negative position of the European Court of Justice regarding domestic affirmative action measures which, by adopting quotas in favour of women, seek to increase the share of women in certain labour market sectors[69]. It is rather uncertain, hence, whether these ambiguous developments will encourage *euro*-sceptical feminists to transform their normative frames and critical ideas, or whether they will rather enhance nationally situated discourses and the fragmentation of the European space.

Finally, only in some instances could more pragmatically gendered frames also be found, for example in the British debate. Quite unimpressed by more fundamental feminist concerns, gender sensitive politicians brought "gender-constructive" frames into the EMU-debate, to counter women's *euro*-scepticism by responding to their special practical interests *vis-à-vis* EMU. For instance, the British Guardian reported a "startling gender split on monetary union"[70], a few days after the start of the third phase and the introduction of the *euro* in the eleven members of *euro*-Land, with the "Anti-Euros" having a 32-point lead among women, compared to a lead of only twelve points among men.

---

[66] *Cf.* Abrahamson and Borchorst, 2000.
[67] Borchorst, 1994, p. 38
[68] Gender equality policy in the EU in 2001 includes nine directives, more than one hundred ECJ decisions, anti-discrimination principles inscribed into the Amsterdam Treaty, policies for combatting trafficking in women, as well as "gender mainstreaming" to be generalised to all policies of the EU. *Cf.* Rossilli, 2000 and Hantrais, 2000.
[69] Lundström, 1997, pp. 74ff. and Hobson, 2000, p. 85.
[70] *The Guardian*, 7 January 1999, p. 6.

293

The explanation neither pointed to the popularity of the *euro*-sceptic "heroine" Margaret Thatcher, to the conventional wisdom of female conservatism, nor to "residual monarchism" among British women. Why did British women not like the *euro*, then? *The Guardian* argued that the failure consisted of not casting the language of the debate so that women could see the advantages to themselves and their families: Far more women than men fear the *euro* would mean higher interest and mortgage rates (47% of women, 35% of men), and that it would be bad for the British economy (41% to 31%). Quoting Claire Ward, a Labour MP, "enthusiasts [...] bored on about macroeconomics, (while) the assertions of the sceptics have concentrated on the home life of the British voter and gone largely unchallenged". By contrast, women needed to be shown, by the transparency of the *euro*, that "a basket of goods from a British supermarket is more expensive here than elsewhere"; and that if Brits had the same rates as in *euro*-countries, this would mean 70% off the average mortgages. A Labour party's former Women's Officer, having pioneered focus groups before the 1997 elections, reported that "women responded best to everyday implications": "A lot of men like to think they understand the economic 'big picture', even when they don't really, and women want to know what impact decisions will have on their own accounts at the end of the week[71]".

Compared to the conditions under which the Werner Plan was drafted in 1970, gendered *euro*-scepticism indicates that the premises for a paradigm of social rationality beyond 2002 have changed. Women's labour market activity rates and traditional gender orders have been transformed since the 1970s, when the Werner Plan was debated. As a consequence, gender questions have taken on new meanings that need to be reflected in any attempt to renew the connection between the monetary issue of a political economy and a "Social Europe". First, from multiple European gender perspectives, "Social Europe" should not compete with national welfare states, especially in Nordic Member States, where they have institutionalised "women power" and high levels of gender equality[72]. Neither would a return to the traditional "male breadwinner family" ideology be accepted in Nordic Member States, nor the imposition of an egalitarian "dual breadwinner" norm in Continental Europe. Second, in the perspective of structural long-term mass unemployment, an exclusive or predominant focus on labour markets by linking social entitlements to individual achievements in paid employment, appears anachronistic; and neither would, from the

---

[71] *The Guardian*, 7 January 1999, p. 6.
[72] Hernes, 1987 and Borchorst, 1999, pp. 161ff.

perspective of gendered notions of justice, the "basic income guarantee" appear satisfying. Third, recent developments in EC gender policy have started to extend the labour market focus towards reconciling work and care for all individuals with care responsibilities, without falling back into traditional ideologies of gendered divisions of labour, are on the agenda. Feminist welfare analysts have developed the idea of re-evaluating, and at the same time "degendering" care, thus enhancing women's economic freedom.[73]

Supranational Frameworks
for Constructing Public Support for the *Euro*

The step-wise introduction of the single currency is arguably the first time in the history of European integration indicating that more than a European "issue community" began to emerge. The contours of a European public space became visible at a progressively accelerating pace[74]. At first in 1992, in the campaigns for the first Danish Maastricht referendum, the *euro* became salient as a European issue in a single domestic debate; other domestic publics followed becoming sensitised to the issue at different points in time. In a second step, in 1995, when faced with acute legitimacy problems of EMU[75], supranational elites launched the most extensive and costly information and mass communication campaign ever conducted, since the inception of the EC, to be extended until – at least – 2002[76]. At a third stage, on 1 January 1999, when the *euro* was officially launched, domestic debates on EMU had synchronised at a cross-national scale. At a fourth and so far final stage, in September 2000, during the Danish referendum campaign on EMU, transnational communication across the Danish boundaries began

---

[73] Feminist political theorist Joan Tronto has suggested to redesign social citizenship rights such that individual social entitlements should primarily derive from *socially valuable care activities* and not (or only in a second place) from earned income and labour market performances; *cf.* Hirschmann and Liebert, 2001.

[74] Analyses of the transformation of domestic public spaces suggest the emergence of transnational "issue communities" around European policy-making; see Klaus Eder, 2000.

[75] *Cf.* Verdun, 1999, p. 212.

[76] These communication and information campaigns were developed to accompany the implementation stage of EMU until at least 2002, when national currencies will be substituted by the *euro.* For that purpose, the Commission contracted groups of experts to define the conceptual terrain on which *euro*-campaigns were based; see European Commission, Euro-Papers, several numbers and years.

295

to develop, with media transmissions of Danish debates into other Member State publics[77].

Despite the embryonic condition of the European public space that is emerging around the issue of the *euro*, the paradox of EMU consists of the asymmetries it creates for the Euro-Polity, as long as EMU lacks a political union, and political unity is not grounded on democratised institutions[78]. Under the conditions of EMU resting on an independent ECB, and on intergovernmental institutions, such as ECOFIN, with weak competencies of the European Parliament and the Commission, supranational communication campaigners were not autonomous. If they had wanted to bring the EU closer to its citizens[79], they were certainly restrained, on one hand, by national governments as well as by the ECB. But supranational elites were also dependent, on the other hand, on the legacy of the peculiar organisational culture of the proper Commission. Different from the Werner Plan language, in the negotiation of the Maastricht Treaty (1989-1991), a technocratic frame had come to prevail in the crafting of the formal framework for EMU, where tripartite *Euro*-corporatism was abandoned and replaced by a neo-liberal discourse about EMU, as a way to institutionalise a liberal market economy and to cope with global competition[80]. Michel Cini has shown that under Jacques Santer as President of the Commission, this discourse of technocracy, elitism, and neo-functionalism continued to prevail, while its re-articulation and the integration of accountability, representation, and new government ideas for legitimising EMU proved quite difficult[81]. The Commission therefore restrained its role to specifically targeted actions towards enterprises and the general public. While the

---

[77] For instance, the *Berliner Zeitung* headlined that Danes gave "a democratic, no nationalist No" (30 September 2000, p. 6), while the *Süddeutsche Zeitung* calculated "the Price of the Danish No" (30 September 2000). For *The Scotsman*, "the Danish rejection of the *euro* was significant for the Scottish political debate" and for "fighting for an alternative vision of Europe" (30 September 2000, p. 3). The Austrian Minister of Finance showed sympathy with the decision of Danes which he saw as a consequence of the sanctions against Austria – as an expression of the "fear of a super-Europe", *Die Presse*, 30 September 2000.

[78] Philippe Schmitter suggests as a solution to the "embarrassing" issue of nondemocratic, but autonomous institutions such as the European Central Bank, to establish a permanent oversight function within the committee structure of the European Parliament; *cf.* Schmitter, 2000, pp. 87-8. However, other Member States than Germany have remained reluctant so far towards "superimposing a political union on the single currency", *cf. The Economist*: "Ever closer union?" 11 April 1998, p. 25.

[79] Schlesinger and Kevin, 2000, p. 206ff.

[80] See Stråth and Magnusson in this volume and Verdun, 2000, p. 2f.

[81] Cini, 2000.

main task of reaching the general public remained a prerogative of Member State governments, the Commission contributed to preparing publics for the *euro* by measures to stabilise citizen expectations[82]. An analysis of the language which prevails in the Commission's public information and communication campaigns on EMU, and in particular in those associated with mobilising help for "vulnerable groups" – such as women, or blind people – shows that the technocratic style typical of the Commission's organisational culture continued to prevail. A Commission Dossier framed women as "vulnerable groups", in the need to know "a variety of things but in particular they need to understand prices and values of the euro and become acquainted with the look of notes and coins". These frames obviously fail to resonate with the gendered patterns of public opinion, and the gender frames which *euro*-sceptic discourses have articulated. Talking about the "need of women", responsiveness is suggested. But in order to reassure female publics of the benefits of the single currency, acquaintance with the look of notes will hardly be sufficient. By renouncing to a more responsive policy language, as well as to a language richer of political symbolisms[83], Commission public relations experts forewent appeals that would have touched the real world experiences of their target publics. By "out-sourcing" the task of building public support for the common currency to commercial agencies, supranational elites could not convert mass public indifference, let alone mass public *euro*-scepticism into more stable support. To the extent to which these communication campaigns for the Euro were conducted like advertisement spots, based on beliefs that the social construction of the *euro* could be made from scratch, independently from cultural, normative and institutional foundations, the symbolic politics of monetary union did not resonate with *euro*-sceptic discourse and those constituencies' concerns reflected by it.

In contrast with the Commission, the European Parliament developed a more responsive language, in particular from a gender perspective. In its resolution on the "Commission Communication on Mainstreaming" in 1998, the EP claimed that "women's position and situation in society should be taken more into consideration when advancing policies to support the internal market, and not least policies to support EMU". All necessary steps should be taken to ensure that EMU and fiscal consolidation had a positive impact on equality between women and men. An effort was needed to ensure that the establishment of a single market that "boosts growth, competitiveness and employment" is not hampered by inflexibility caused by the entrenched patterns of job

---

[82] Reich, 2000.
[83] *Cf.* "Commission Staff Working Paper"; "Euro Made Easy Programme" etc.

segregation in the labour market. Dedicated measures should be taken to speed up the desegregation process, in particular promoting diversity and the full use of women's capacities and potential in management positions and decision-making in the public and private sectors. In view of the demographic changes associated with the ageing of the population in Europe, the future labour supply would become increasingly important. As women were increasingly equal to – or even better qualified than – men, this would increase the pool of qualified labour supply and could enhance the smooth functioning of the Single Market[84].

Hence, despite its limited role in EMU-policy, the EP, and particularly the Women's Rights Committee, used its prerogative *vis-à-vis* the Commission, to promote an innovative policy idea: to apply the procedure of gender impact assessments to all EMU-supporting policies. The principle of "gender mainstreaming" could thus serve as a general supranational policy device that would not ignore locally specific differences in gender relations, but rather require systematic comparative research to integrate them into policy-making.

Conclusion and Further Perspectives

In this chapter, I have described how, after Maastricht and the end of the permissive consensus, EMU can be studied as a complex process of social construction, involving social practices, ideologies and identities and norms. For an analysis of European monetary integration, I have suggested distinguishing three distinct dimensions that are involved in this process: patterns and dynamics of public (elite and mass) attitudes towards the issue of EMU; different types of domestic discourses; and supranational communication strategies with mass publics and specific "target groups".

My intention was to demonstrate that the analysis of three dimensions of the communications involved in the construction of EMU is a necessary condition for assessing the legitimacy problems that invest the *euro* as a political symbol, with a multitude of different and contradictory meanings: from peace to war, from a European identity to a neo-imperialist project, from social justice and solidarity to domination. In this framework, one can assess EU-communication strategies for building public support, identify those domestic discourses that resonate with patterns of public attitudes and behaviours, describe how legitimacy gaps widen or narrow over time, and show how similar

---

[84] COM 1998, 122 final; Rubery/Smith: *The Future of European Labor Supply*, European Work and Employment Research Center, Manchester School of Management, UMIST, November 1997

discursive and practical devices function differently in different contexts, depending on specific cultural and institutional connotations[85]. More particularly, three findings shall be highlighted. First, supranational discursive frames which the Commission employed in its mass public and targeted communication campaigns on EMU were less responsive and symbolically "thin", and that this was the case because they rested, among others, on a social psychological conception developed by a group of experts contracted by the Commission[86]. Second, it was found that the Commission campaigns started in 1999 for targeting "women as a vulnerable group", which, because of their contents, can be expected to have little effect on gender gaps especially in Nordic contexts where feminist frames prevail in EMU-debates. As the third, and possibly most important result, it was noted that despite multiple *euro*-sceptic discourses, and despite the relative lack of responsiveness of supranational communication campaigns, the issue of EMU has turned the EU gradually into a sphere of publics that interact across national boundaries. To explain these dynamics, *euro*-scepticism, although an expression of different ideas and collective identities and shaped by contrasting norms, paradoxically has served as a crucial mechanisms in this process: by stimulating interest in a variety of issues linked to EMU, and by promoting transnational communication about these issues. Whether, as a consequence of transnational communicative interactions, sticky domestic norms will change, depends not at least on the further evolution of dialogical public spheres in "a Europe of multiple voices"[87].

Any attempt to address the dilemma of legitimation of EMU needs communicatively to integrate *euro*-scepticism, and for that purpose would require arenas for communication and institutionalised channels of access for public constituencies to transmit more actively and successfully their concerns to EU-policy makers. It would require to incorporate into the "currency of ideas" (Kathleen R. McNamara) that currently promotes EMU also some ideas relevant to public interests of European civil society. Among these ideas, gender frames have not yet lost public interest, as some modernisation theorists expected. As Anette Borchorst pointed out, "women and men perceive issues surrounding

---

[85] *Info Frauen Europas*, November December 1998, No. 83, Brussels, p. 4

[86] DG XXIV commissioned an interdisciplinary group of psychologists, economists, lawyers, and sociologists from France, the UK, Italy, Belgium, Germany, Spain, and the Netherlands to produce a number of reports, as the basis for a comprehensive "Information Programme for the European Citizen" on the single currency. Given the psychological perspective, these did not take socio-economic, identity-based or normative concerns seriously into account.

[87] Nanz, 2000.

European integration differently – women are in general more sceptical than men. The full implications of these gender disparities need to be analysed with a view to adjusting Community policies. The equal support of women and men respectively should be a yard stick for assessing the success of European integration". From the perspective of gendered *euro*-scepticisms in the EU, the legitimacy of EMU would, hence, not only depend on matching it with a political union, but more specifically on embedding it in developing European public space.

CHAPTER 11

EMU and the Shift from a "Social Policy" Agenda to an "Employment Policy" Agenda in European Labour Law

Diamond ASHIAGBOR[1]

This chapter examines the interaction between EMU and the European Union (EU) employment strategy, in particular, the importance of EMU as a catalyst in the development of the EU's social and employment policy in the years following the Treaty on European Union in 1992, up to the inauguration of a new employment policy in the Treaty of Amsterdam. In analysing the EU's discourse on labour market regulation, it is arguable that a shift has occurred in the EU's position on the "labour market flexibility" debate: that the EU institutions are more readily accepting of the orthodoxy that labour market regulation and labour market institutions are a major cause of unemployment within EU countries and that a deregulatory approach, which emphasises greater "flexibility" in labour markets, is the key to solving Europe's unemployment ills, along with macroeconomic stability, restrictive fiscal policy and wage restraint. As the EU's employment strategy has matured, this increased emphasis on employment policy has come to displace discourses around social policy. This change in emphasis has important implications for EMU since it signals a re-orientation from an approach to labour market regulation which had as its core a strong concept of employment *protection* and high labour standards, to an approach which prioritises employment *creation*, and minimises the role of social policy, since social policy is seen as potentially increasing the regulatory burden.

---

[1] I am grateful to Karl Klare, Philippe Pochet, Silvana Sciarra and the participants of two seminars at the European University Institute, Florence for their helpful comments. However, any remaining errors or omissions are my own.

Conceptualising Unemployment: A "European" Problem

High unemployment in (some) EU Member States is seen as creating a problem for the EU as a whole, since high levels of employment, competitiveness and social cohesion are all key goals of the Union[2]; goals which would be threatened by mass unemployment. Nevertheless, it has taken some time for Member States to agree to transfer competence over employment policy to the EU institutions, instead preferring national solutions. Even then, the actual competence of the central EU institutions over employment policy is limited to a monitoring or "benchmarking" capacity, rather than a more pro-active role in implementing a centralised labour market policy, or attempting to generate employment through Europe-wide programmes of expenditure.

How, then, did (un)employment come to be seen as a problem for which a European-level solution was most appropriate[3]? After all, is it correct to talk of such a phenomenon as an EU unemployment problem, in view of the fact that "the variation in unemployment in 1996 between the highest, Spain, and the lowest, Luxembourg, was nineteen percent, and the average rate of difference between the three countries with the highest and the lowest unemployment was around twelve percent"[4]. The diversity in levels and in the duration of unemployment is often downplayed or ignored in the desire to present unemployment across EU countries as a problem with a common cause (over-regulation, leading to rigid labour markets) and thus a common solution (deregulation and labour market flexibility). Indeed, Stephen Nickell cautions against overstating the similarities between (un)employment trends in EU Member States in order to provide a suitable contrast with the US "employment miracle"[5]. Although there is no consensus on the relative

---

[2] Article 2 of the TEU reads: "The Union shall set itself the following objectives – to promote economic and social progress and a high level of employment and to achieve balanced and sustainable development, in particular through the creation of an area without internal frontiers, through the strengthening of economic and monetary cohesion and through the establishment of economic and monetary union".

   In addition, Article 2 of the EC Treaty reads: 'The Community shall have as its task [...] to promote throughout the Community a harmonious, balanced and sustainable development of economic activities, a high level of employment and of social protection, equality between men and women, sustainable and non-inflationary growth, a high degree of competitiveness and convergence of economic performance, a high level of protection and improvement of the quality of the environment, the raising of the standard of living and quality of life, and economic and social cohesion and solidarity among Member States".

[3] For early discussions on a possible European level employment policy, see the Cecchini Report of 1988, on the completion of the internal market: Cecchini, 1988.

[4] Symes, 1998, p. 6.

[5] Nickell, 1997, p. 55.

importance of the various underlying causes for the trend increase in the European unemployment rate since the 1970s, a growing orthodoxy explains differences in post-war unemployment levels between developed countries, in part, as a result of differences in labour market regulation:

> Perhaps the most prevalent or "dominant" view is that the current unsatisfactory situation in European labour markets is a result of the interaction of labour market rigidities and a series of adverse shocks since the early 1970s[6].

The OECD *Jobs Study*[7] provided detailed empirical and analytical support for the thesis that, whilst there was "no single recipe for full-employment[8]", nevertheless, Europe's unemployment problem should be addressed by a combination of structural reforms and judicious[9] macroeconomic management.

As Pierson *et al.* point out, the view of unemployment which informed the European Commission's 1993 White Paper[10] is that, "although it spreads across the continent, European unemployment is not one discrete challenge, but many separate and simultaneous ones"[11]. However, it is also clear that the dominant perspective amongst commentators is that there is a peculiarly *European* problem, which demands a *European Union* solution; a problem possibly related to that feared disease of "Eurosclerosis"[12], with its particular "take" on the role of labour market "rigidities" in creating unemployment. If one accepts the argument that labour market rigidities are at the root of unemployment[13], then it would certainly make sense to consider European countries as having a common problem, arising from the similarity in the patterns of labour market regulation and institutions, at least as compared with the more lightly regulated US market. Furthermore, as

---

6 IMF, 1999, pp. 91-92.
7 Organisation for Economic Co-operation and Development, 1994.
8 Organisation for Economic Co-operation and Development, 1994, p. 41.
9 IMF, 1999, p.109.
10 Commission of the European Communities (hereinafter CEC) White Paper on *Growth, Competitiveness and Employment: The Challenges and Ways Forward into the 21st Century*, COM (93) 700 final (Luxembourg, Office for Official Publications of the EC (hereinafter OOPEC) 1993).
11 Pierson *et al.*, 1998, p. 5. Also, see Elmeskov, 1998: "There may not be much which is particularly European about the unemployment problem in Europe".
12 Giersch, 1985.
13 Siebert, 1997.

Richard Jackman argues, it may be that the creation of the EC in itself contributed to the growth of unemployment in the Member States[14].

The European Commission's 1993 White Paper, however, evidenced doubts that the high levels of unemployment could be categorised as a peculiarly European phenomenon:

> The difference between the unemployment rates currently experienced in the major economic areas in the world – 11% of the civilian labour force in the Community against rates of about 7% and 2.5% in the United States and Japan respectively – has given rise to questions about the existence of a *specific European unemployment problem*[15].

But this is countered by the observation that:

> An examination of the Community's past performance and a comparison with the other major areas, however, suggest that no hasty negative conclusions should be drawn[16].

So, *on the one hand*, there was concern not to overplay the view of unemployment as a peculiarly "European" problem, as this might appear to endorse the view that "rigidities" lay at the heart of unemployment in EU countries which had pursued what might be called the "European social model":

> [The White Paper] recognises the need for more efficient labour market and associated policies. It also recognises that the market alone cannot solve the employment, unemployment and associated social problems faced by the Community [...] This means significant changes, but it does not simply mean a deregulation of Europe's labour markets. Rather, it implies an updated, rational and simplified system of regulation and incentives which will promote employment creation, without putting the burden of change on those already in a weak position in the labour market[17].

On the other hand, political expediency required *some* common effort to combat unemployment if greater market integration was to occur. In particular, although Member States had failed to include employment within the convergence criteria for monetary union, it was inescapable that if they did not individually take action at the national level to combat such high levels of unemployment, they would face difficulty meeting criteria such as public expenditure targets. As markets of all types converge within the EU, it becomes clear that huge disparities in labour market performance across Member States are incompatible with increased integration, both economically and politically, since the need

---

[14]   Jackman, 1998, p. 60.
[15]   CEC, 1993, *White Paper on Growth*, p. 40, emphasis added.
[16]   CEC, 1993, *White Paper on Growth*, p. 40, emphasis added.
[17]   CEC, 1993, *White Paper on Growth*, p. 123.

to "create more jobs for our citizens"[18] is almost as important as "strengthening the Union's democratic legitimacy"[19] in the push to make the Union more acceptable to its citizens.

In addition, the absence of any reference to employment in the Maastricht Treaty (the Treaty on European Union, TEU) was criticised during the national debates in the run-up to its ratification[20]. It appeared as though the EU, as a polity, cared little about unemployment[21] at a time of high unemployment and fiscal rectitude. However, this is not to say that the convergence criteria which were eventually agreed upon did not, in actual fact, have a profound effect on Member States' employment and social policies[22]. Certainly, many EU countries were experiencing increased unemployment, as governments sought to meet the monetary and fiscal criteria for monetary union, placing further constraints on public expenditure[23]. The importance of such domestic political pressures in the development of an overarching EU employment strategy is not to be underestimated. Pierson *et al.*, for example, argue that "[i]n such a context, whether these two processes – unemployment and convergence – were causally related became less important than whether they were linked in public perceptions"[24]. High European unemployment became an important political issue partly *because* it came to be linked with popular support for monetary integration.

The Shift from a "Social Policy" Agenda to an "Employment Policy" Agenda

Social policy at EU level has always been under-developed, in particular, lacking a clear Treaty basis. The fragmented nature of the legal base, or competence, for social policy law led to years of stagnation in this area. At the time of the original Treaties, however, the prevailing wisdom was that the goal of market integration did not require harmonisation of Member States' social policy. According to the report produced by the International

---

[18] European Council Meeting on 9 and 10 December 1994 in Essen, Presidency Conclusions; Press Release, Brussels, 9 December 1994, No. 00300/94.

[19] European Council Meeting on 9 and 10 December 1994 in Essen, Presidency Conclusions; Press Release, Brussels, 9 December 1994, No. 00300/94.

[20] Laursen and Vanhoonacker, 1994.

[21] CEC, *The Amsterdam Treaty: A Comprehensive Guide* (Luxembourg: OOPEC, 1998.

[22] Barrell *et al.*, 1996 and Teague, 1999.

[23] Teague, 1999, p. 167.

[24] Pierson *et al.*, 1998, p. 7.

Labour Organisation's Committee of Experts in 1956 (the Ohlin Report)[25], it was not necessary, in creating a single market, for national systems of labour and social law to be harmonised. The theory of comparative advantage which underpinned the Report held that differences in levels of social protection or labour law or wage costs between states engaged in international trade did not, in themselves, pose a serious obstacle to competition or efficiency because these differences broadly reflected differences in productivity[26]. The conclusions of the Ohlin Report, which had been commissioned by the prospective Member States[27], were substantially adopted by the inter-governmental Spaak Report of 1956[28], on which the Treaty of Rome was based. The goal of economic liberalisation at the centre of the putative Community was thus founded on the idea that: competition does not necessarily require a complete harmonisation of the different elements in costs; indeed, it is only on the basis of certain differences – such as wage differences due to differences in productivity – that trade and competition can develop. [...] In addition, wage and interest rates tend to level up in a common market – a process which is hastened by the free circulation of the factors of production. This is a consequence rather than a condition of the common market's operation[29].

The social policy which *did* develop was one which was, on the whole, justified on market integrationist grounds: the incremental development of a framework of basic minimum standards was justified as a protection against destructive downwards competition, to provide "a bulwark against using low social standards as an instrument of unfair competition, and protection against reducing social standards to gain competitiveness"[30]. Legislative activity in the area of social policy developed at a faster pace in the early 1990s, given impetus by the availability of qualified majority voting under Article 118a of the EC Treaty, and inspired by the acceptance by eleven of the then twelve Member States of the Charter of Fundamental Rights for Workers in

---

25 International Labour Organisation *Social Aspects of Economic Co-operation: Report of a Group of Experts*, Studies and Reports, New Series, No. 46, (ILO, 1956); summarised as International Labour Office, "Social Aspects of Economic Co-operation" (1956) 74 *International Labour Review* 99 (the Ohlin Report).

26 Deakin, 1996, p. 66.

27 Davies, 1992, pp. 318-319.

28 Comité Intergouvernemental Créé par la Conférence de Messine, *Rapport des Chefs de Délégation aux Ministres des Affaires Etrangères* (Brussels, 1956), the "Spaak Report", summarised in English in Political and Economic Planning, *Planning* No. 405 (1956).

29 Comité Intergouvernemental Créé par la Conférence de Messine, *Rapport des Chefs de Délégation aux Ministres des Affaires Etrangères* (Brussels, 1956), the "Spaak Report", summarised in English in Political and Economic Planning, *Planning* No. 405 (1956), at 233.

30 CEC, 1993, *White Paper on Growth*, p. 5.

1989[31]. Whilst the EU's competence in the area of *social* policy has undoubtedly grown from what was envisaged by the Treaty of Rome, *employment* policy remained the preserve of Member States, with the exception of small areas such as vocational training[32]. This reluctance to hand over competence in employment matters was exemplified by the negotiations in the Intergovernmental Conference prior to the 1992 Treaty on European Union. More recently, however, in particular since the Essen European Councilin 1994, there has been a shift from an emphasis on social policy to employment policy[33], albeit that the social policy which had existed was mostly an employment-related social policy[34].

We have witnessed a move away from legislative proposals on social law, first, towards coordination of Member States' social policy, and more recently towards coordination of Member States' employment policies. Having gained a clear competence to legislate on social policy following the TEU through the inclusion of the Protocol and Agreement on Social Policy in the Maastricht Treaty (a competence which was further confirmed through the introduction of a new Title on Social Policy by the Treaty of Amsterdam) the EU institutions, and in particular the Commission, seem to be shying away from making new social policy proposals which would, it was feared, increase the regulatory burden. For example, the Commission's 1994 White Paper on European Social Policy stated:

> Given that the solid base of European social legislation has already been achieved, the Commission considers that there is not a need for a wide-ranging programme of new legislative proposals in the coming period[35].

Further, in the 1997 Green Paper on *Partnership for a New Organisation of Work*[36], the Commission envisaged the need to move "from rigid and compulsory systems of statutory regulations to more open and flexible legal frameworks"[37]. The preference seems to be to leave regulation of the social field to agreements between the social partners, which are seen as being somehow less interventionist.

---

[31] Szyszczak, 1995.

[32] Freedland, 1996.

[33] Barnard and Deakin, 1999.

[34] Freedland, 1996, p. 277.

[35] CEC, *White Paper on European Social Policy: A Way Forward for the Union* (Luxembourg, OOPEC, 1994) COM (94) 333 final of 27 July 1994, p. 5.

[36] CEC, *Green Paper: Partnership for a New Organisation of Work* (Luxembourg, OOPEC, 1997) COM (97) 128 final.

[37] CEC, *Green Paper: Partnership for a New Organisation of Work* (Luxembourg, OOPEC, 1997) COM (97), para 44.

One very useful framework of analysis which can help one understand the origins (and possible future direction) of the EU employment strategy, is that offered by Mark Freedland[38]. He posits a distinction between EC economic regulation supported by an economic policy discourse and EC social regulation supported by a social policy discourse[39], although "EC employment policy measures are informed by economic policy as well as by social policy"[40]. Freedland argues that the *White Paper on Growth, Competitiveness and Employment* and the *Green Paper on Social Policy*[41] "conform very exactly to [this] dichotomy between economic and social policy"[42]. The employment strategy can be seen as an arena within which these tensions are being debated. The question becomes whether this economic efficiency/employment policy discourse can be reconciled with the social justice/social policy discourse. One argument runs that the Union "should set itself the purely economic goal of market liberalisation, and that social policy, in so far as it is incompatible with this approach, should be marginalised"[43].

Freedland identifies three discourses or policy agendas currently competing for dominance of the EU labour law agenda:

- a social policy agenda which provides a continuation of the policy discourse of the 1970s and 1980s, stressing social dialogue, the role of the social partners, and ideas in respect of representation at the workplace;

- an employment policy agenda which redefines priorities as the creation and maintenance of high levels of employment; this agenda re-orientates the discourse towards macroeconomic ideas of competitiveness; and

- a human and equality rights agenda, focusing on rights, for example as encapsulated in the fundamental rights charter. This agenda provides one possible way to recapture the ground lost in the move to the employment policy agenda.

Freedland is right to note that "social policy" as it was conceived consisted almost entirely of employment issues; but I would argue that it is still useful to think in terms of a decided shift towards a more specific "employment policy", because what we are observing is a move away

---

[38] Paper given at a conference at the European University Institute, Florence, 11-12 February 2000; see also, Freedland, 1996.
[39] Freedland, 1996, p. 286.
[40] Freedland, 1996, p. 291.
[41] CEC, Green Paper on *European Social Policy: Options for the Union* (Luxembourg, OOPEC, 1993) COM (93) 551 of 17 November 1993.
[42] Freedland, 1996, p. 297.
[43] Barnard and Deakin, p. 359.

from social *law* and *legislative* initiatives, towards *soft law*, or rather *polices* aimed at employment creation, which for the most part eschew legislation. Perhaps it would be simpler and more accurate to talk of a move from employment law to employment policy. And in this context, the second of the above agendas seems to be in the ascendancy in the policy discourse of the EU institutions, connecting employment policy with EMU, and thus having a "knock-on" effect on the direction of future labour market regulation.

The Green and White Papers on Social Policy

The 1993 Green Paper defines social policy as including the "the full range of policies in the social sphere including labour market policies"[44]. However, it seems true to say that Community social policy has almost always been an *employment-related* social policy[45]. When describing the width of coverage of Community social policy, the Commission in fact reveals that it is quite narrowly focused on employment-related issues:

> Community social policy has covered a wide range of areas, these include equality of opportunity, health and safety matters, employment and labour law matters, issues of social protection and social security, as well as action focused on specific points such as poverty and the role of the disabled[46].

This list of issues considered central to the Union's fledgling social policy reveals a *protectionist* bias; with the exception of separate sub-discourse on poverty and social exclusion, the emphasis seems squarely on protecting those in employment rather than employment-generation. A major step towards the realisation of a European employment policy came in 1993; first with the Commission's Employment Framework Initiative, which set out the basis of a concerted strategy for employment and second, with the "Growth" White Paper[47], which developed that employment strategy in the wider economic, industrial and social context of the Union. This strategy was then endorsed by the Brussels European Council in December 1993[48]. As a precursor to the Essen criteria, the Brussels European Council identified seven areas for action by Member States, in response to the suggestions for combating un-employment and improving employment contained in the "Growth" White paper:

---

[44]   CEC, 1993, *Green* Paper, p. 6.
[45]   Freedland, 1996.
[46]   CEC, 1993, *Green Paper*, p. 9.
[47]   For the sake of brevity, the 1993 White Paper will be referred to as such, but this is not to understate the importance of the other goals of "competitiveness" and "employment".
[48]   CEC, 1994, *White Paper on European Social Policy*, p. 9.

- improving education and training systems, especially continuing training;
- improving flexibility within enterprises and within the labour market;
- the reorganisation of work at enterprise level;
- targeted reductions in the indirect costs of labour (statutory contributions), particularly of less skilled work;
- better use of public funds set aside for combating unemployment;
- specific measures concerning young people without adequate training;
- developing employment in connection with new requirements[49].

However, by the time of the Essen Council, two (related) things had occurred: the White Paper on Social Policy, had appeared, wholeheartedly adopting the "employment policy" agenda of the "Growth" White Paper – and its concomitant downplaying of a Community legislative agenda. Secondly, the Commission's strategy to create 15 million jobs in fifteen years, at a cost of 400 billion ECU[50] had failed to gain acceptance by Member States:

> Member State Finance Ministers resisted those measures which required substantial expenditure [...] and the Council itself rejected the idea of an ambitious and costly initiative. Hence the measures agreed at the Essen summit were far more modest[51].

Could one describe this expansionist agenda (ultimately thwarted) as an example of the Commission's "Keynesian" aspirations, which was reigned in by the Essen Council? The Growth Initiative can be read as one of the Commission's "Keynesian" solutions which was so loathed, and ultimately squashed, by Member States reluctant to hand over significant budgetary independence to the EU institutions to tackle unemployment from the centre:

> There can be no doubt that the causes and consequences of high and rising unemployment in Europe represent the single most serious challenge facing Member States today [...] There is general agreement that the main solution to the problem will come from increased growth. In this regard, a number of measures are already in hand, including in particular, the Growth Initiative agreed at the Edinburgh European Council and reinforced at the Copenhagen Council. However, there is also a growing recognition that growth alone will not be enough [...] *It is clear that many of the policy*

---

[49] CEC, 1994, *White Paper on European Social Policy*.
[50] The European Currency Unit; the ECU rate was determined against a basket of currencies of the Member States.
[51] Goetschy, 1999.

levers which will have to be pulled are, and will continue to be, a matter of exclusive Member State competence[52].

This sentiment was reiterated – and in fact strengthened – at a later date: as Commission President, Jacques Santer, pointed out, at the time of the Stability and Growth Pact at the Amsterdam European Council in 1997[53], "our generation will neither see economic government nor political government in Europe"[54]. Furthermore, he added: "We do not wish to have a Keynesian policy and to launch major programmes"[55].

The White Paper on Growth, Competitiveness and Employment

Although the Green Paper was ostensibly about *social* policy, an important by-product of it was the Community-Wide Framework for Employment, proposed by the Commission in May 1993, and adopted by the Social Affairs Council of June 1993. Further evidence of "employment policy" displacing "social policy" came with the "Growth" White Paper, which placed employment policy firmly within the context of wider economic integration and monetary union:

> We must [...] place our thinking within a macroeconomic reference framework for both economic and monetary convergence which will increase the opportunities available to our economies.[56]

By the time of the "Growth" White Paper, the emphasis had very much switched to employment generation. The explanations for European unemployment put forward by the White Paper were that Member States were gravely affected by the oil price shocks of the 1970s[57], resulting in a fall in investment and a rapid growth of inflation. In particular, that "inflation had arisen largely because of rising wages, hence encouraging the introduction of labour saving technology, which resulted in fewer jobs being generated from economic growth"[58]. The White Paper did not advocate a "quick fix" to the EU's unemployment problems, but rather a combination of macroeconomic and structural measures[59]. Of the latter, three main areas for action are identified: first,

---

[52]   CEC, 1993, *Green Paper*, pp. 40-41; emphasis added.
[53]   Resolution of the European Council on the Stability and Growth Pact. Amsterdam 17 June 1997, OJ C 236, 2 August 1997, p. 1; Council Regulation (EC) No. 1466/97 of 7 July 1997 on the strengthening of the surveillance of budgetary positions and the surveillance and co-ordination of economic policies, OJ L 209, 2 August 1997, p. 1.
[54]   See *Agence Europe*, No. 6993 (n.s.) Thursday 12 June 1997, p. 2.
[55]   See *Agence Europe*, No. 6993 (n.s.) Thursday 12 June 1997, p. 6.
[56]   CEC, 1993, *White Paper on Growth*, p. 12.
[57]   CEC, 1993, *White Paper on Growth*, pp. 40-43; see also Symes, 1998, p. 30.
[58]   Symes, 1998, p. 30.
[59]   CEC, 1993, *White Paper on Growth*, p. 48.

greater flexibility in the economy as a whole, and in the regulatory framework in particular, which should become more "enterprise-friendly"; secondly, the creation of an efficient labour market able to respond to new competitive situations; and thirdly an open international environment[60].

In order to create more jobs, the White Paper therefore recommended investing at least 400 ECU billion in large scale transport, telecommunications and environmental projects. It is interesting to note the explicitness with which such job creation schemes are advocated; the White Paper contains clear commitments – targets, even – which do not appear in subsequent policy pronouncements and certainly do not form part of the Luxembourg Process[61]. For example,

> The European Union should set itself the target of creating 15 million jobs by the end of the century[62].

> For all the countries of the Union, it is essential to reduce the cost of unskilled and semi-skilled labour by an amount equivalent to 1 or 2 points of GNP by the year 2000[63].

Areas in which the White Paper envisaged such job creation occurring included employment in what would become a new (or revitalised) "social economy"[64]. Further hopes were pinned on the above-mentioned "trans-European networks"[65] which cover developments in information technology, transport and energy. With regard to transport, the White Paper leant very heavily on Article 129b EC[66] (now Article 154 EC) to advocate renewed infrastructural investment, argued as necessary in itself, and also for its job-creation potential. Following on from the Commission White Paper, the 1994 European Council in

---

[60] CEC, 1993, *White Paper on Growth*, p. 50.

[61] The only real "target" which survived the process from the White Paper to Amsterdam is that in respect of youth unemployment.

[62] CEC, 1993, *White Paper on Growth*, p. 11; further elaborated at p. 43.

[63] CEC, 1993, *White Paper on Growth*, p. 18.

[64] CEC, 1993, *White Paper on Growth*, pp. 19-20; suggested sources of new jobs in the social economy include improvements in the quality of life, such as the renovation of old housing, and local services such as home help for the elderly and disabled.

[65] CEC, 1993, *White Paper on Growth*, Chapter 3.

[66] Article 154(1) "To help achieve the objectives referred to in Articles 14 and 158 [respectively: the completion of the internal market as an area without frontiers by 1993; and economic and social cohesion] and to enable citizens of the Union, economic operators and regional and local communities to derive full benefit from the setting-up of an area without internal frontiers, the Community shall contribute to the establishment of trans-European networks in the areas of transport, telecommunications and energy infrastructures".

Essen[67] launched an "integrated employment strategy", which adopted, for the first time at European level, short- and medium-term policy on employment, in addition to initiating an annual process of Commission monitoring of Member States' employment policies which was to be codified at Amsterdam. The Essen Council identified five priority areas for action by Member States:

- promoting investment in vocational training;

- increasing employment through periods of growth (an end to the peculiar European phenomenon of "job-less growth");

- reducing non-wage labour costs;

- improving the effectiveness of labour market policy;

- improving measures to help groups at risk of exclusion from the labour market.

Further stimulus to the employment creation agenda was given by the Florence European Council in June 1996, which, in accordance with the Confidence Pact for Employment[68] proposed by the Commission, exhorted Member States to adopt a series of initiatives to improve job generation programmes. Whilst not legally binding, the Confidence Pact anticipated the Amsterdam employment guidelines as an instance of the use of "soft law" measures, which nevertheless placed informal pressure on Member States to coordinate their employment policies. There then followed the Dublin European Council in 13-14 December 1996, which further endorsed the proposal in the Confidence Pact for a commitment by all the social and economic "agents" to play their full part in employment matters, and urged swift action on the projects for territorial employment pacts.

Ultimately, however, the Commission's proposals for infrastructure and public works programmes, were blocked by Member States[69], who refused to sanction the necessary centralisation of expenditure and competence for employment policy which this would have necessitated[70]. The European Council meeting at Essen failed to reach agreement to endorse this proposed expansion of public investment to increase jobs. Why? One possible explanation:

---

[67] European Council, Meeting on 9-10 December 1994 in Essen, SN 300/64.

[68] CEC *Action for Employment in Europe: A Confidence Pact*, Luxembourg, OOPEC, 1996) CSE (96) 1 final.

[69] In particular, by finance ministers.

[70] "In total some ECU 400 billion of investments in the transport and energy trans-European networks will be required in the next 15 years, of which some ECU 220 billion by 1999". CEC, *White Paper on Growth*, p. 32.

In contrast to the macroeconomic policy recommended in the Delors report [the "Growth" White Paper], the OECD (1994)[71] sees a stable macroeconomic framework, with control of inflation as its central aim, and a reduction in public sector deficits, again in order to establish low inflation, as the primary requisite in the European economy. Expansionary fiscal policy is viewed as unacceptable since it could increase inflation and damage the growth confidence within the private sector. Wage flexibility is viewed as essential for competitive advantage, and minimum wages are considered to be a form of social policy which, in most circumstances, results in decreases in employment[72].

In order to achieve the target set by the Commission, of creating at least 15 million jobs by the year 2000, it would prove vital to tackle the employment intensity of growth[73]. Although there had been some (albeit modest) growth in EU economies the poor job content of such growth was a problem which was much lamented in the literature.

Although the two texts (the Commission's White Paper and the OECD's *Jobs Study*) do not directly "speak to" each other, one can see a number of interactions and parallels between the two. The White Paper, followed almost immediately by the Essen European Council which was to lead eventually to the Luxembourg Process with its annual guidelines and monitoring of national employment policy, finds echoes with the OECD Jobs Strategy[74], which also led to its own "active, detailed and multilateral monitoring"[75] of proposed reforms, and "peer review" *i.e.* multilateral surveillance of countries by one another[76].

However, what is more fundamental is the differing policy choices which these two papers represented. The OECD *Jobs Study* route to combating unemployment was through increasing the employment intensity of growth, via structural reform and the pursuit of stringent macroeconomic framework. The Delors route, on the other hand, would have necessitated expansionary fiscal policy, and whilst acknowledging the necessity of structural reform, was loath to equate such reform with outright deregulation, if by that was meant an abandoning of traditional social settlements which valued a high level of social transfers and social inclusion. Both papers acknowledged the importance of tackling the employment intensiveness of growth, in particular, this would be

[71] OECD, *Jobs Study: Facts, Analysis and Strategies*, Paris, OECD, 1994.

[72] Symes, 1995, pp. 191-192.

[73] "The *employment intensity* is the relationship between the rate of growth of an economy and its rate of employment creation," CEC, 1993, *White Paper on Growth*, p. 43; emphasis in the original.

[74] CEC, 1993, *White Paper on Growth*, note 67.

[75] OECD, 1994, *OECD Jobs Study: Implementing the Strategy*, p. 3.

[76] OECD, 1994, *OECD Jobs Study: Implementing the Strategy*, p. 4.

essential in order to achieve the target set by the Commission, of creating at least 15 million jobs by the year 2000.

Ultimately, in refusing to endorse the Commission's more expansionary vision, Member States would appear to be preferring the OECD's more restrictive view of macroeconomic policy. However, I would contend that Member States were, at the time of the Essen European Council, acting more to reject the expansionary fiscal policy of the Delors' White Paper, and its concomitant increase in competence for the central EU institutions in the area of macroeconomic policy, than to endorse the sort of thinking which was behind the parts of the *Jobs Study* which advocated greatly increased wage flexibility and diminished social policy interventions. One could argue that the approach of the Member States at this time was to steer a middle route (not to be confused with a Third Way) between the austerity of the OECD's approach and the ambitions of a Delors Commission which, unlike its successor, *could* envisage a form of "economic government". As Barnard and Deakin put it:

> For a while in the mid-1990s there was an active debate about whether to use centralised expenditure to stimulate demand through investments in infrastructure and public works. This received some impetus from the publication of the 1993 White Paper, Growth, Competitiveness and Employment, but the Member States refused to countenance a significant increase in the Commission's budget and the idea faded away[77].

The form which the later EU employment strategy took was, in part, dictated by Member States' reactions to the expansionary proposals of the White Paper. Member States' rejection of the supply side measures advocated by the White Paper led, ultimately, to a policy based on centralised coordination of employment policies, rather than a more distinctly European employment policy[78].

The White Paper and Deregulation: The US as a Comparator

> [T]he Community's economy, with the exception of the period 1986-90, has always been characterised by low employment creation [...] and the origin of its problems go back to the beginning of the 1970s, when it proved unable to increase its rate of job creation to match the increase in the number of people seeking employment. By contrast, the USA has been able to respond

---

[77] Barnard and Deakin, 1999, p. 356.
[78] Barnard and Deakin, 1999, p. 356. "[A]ny programme with even a whiff of Keynesian expansion [was] immediately shot down": Teague, 1999, p. 37.

to an even larger increase in the number of people looking for jobs with a strong increase in employment creation[79].

The comparison between increasing unemployment in EU countries and the US "employment miracle"[80] has often proved irresistible. However, what is very clear from an examination of the institutional discourse in respect of the US "employment miracle" is that there is some caution expressed, certainly in the early 1990s, over following too closely the American model, at least with regard to the measures to increase the employment intensity of growth. The path to higher employment creation should not, it would seem, be at the expense of increasing wage inequality or major downward wage mobility, beyond what would be acceptable to European "civil society" in terms of political economy. It is worth noting the following:

> An increase in the employment intensity of Community growth to match the US performance would require the implementation, on a large scale, of measures increasing the willingness of employers to hire workers and in particular:
>
> (i) a considerable downward widening of the scale of wage costs in order to reintegrate those market activities which at present are priced out of it;
>
> (ii) a reduction in all other costs associated with taking on or maintaining labour, eg social security rules.[81]

Instead of this path of modest growth and very high employment intensity, an alternative, that of a more modest increase in the employment intensity of growth with a stronger rate of growth is seen as preferable:

> An increase in the employment intensity of growth of the order of magnitude of the one envisaged in this second scenario, while not being easy to achieve, would not require the drastic measures needed to reach the performance of the USA. *In addition it could be achieved with the consensus of most of those concerned.*[82]

This is just one example of the unwillingness, at that moment in time, of the EU institutions to advocate adoption of the US model of labour market regulation. Matching US performance was to be achieved though methods other than those used in the US, for reasons of political economy and out of respect for the desire which existed in most

---

[79] CEC, 1993, *White Paper on Growth*, pp. 41-42.

[80] Houseman, 1995; and the special issue of the *Comparative Labor Law and Policy Journal*, 1998, Vol. 19.

[81] CEC, 1993, *White Paper on Growth*, p. 45.

[82] CEC, 1993, *White Paper on Growth*, p. 46; emphasis added.

Member States, to protect social solidarity and avoid increased inequality.

In particular, this approach is spelt out more clearly in the section of the White Paper entitled "Turning Growth into Jobs"[83]. Given the need for both sustained economic growth and a more employment intensive pattern of growth, the White Paper recognises "the need for more efficient labour markets", whilst also noting that "the market alone cannot solve unemployment". The strategies suggested to boost the employment-intensiveness of growth involve measures to make labour markets more flexible, to tackle such problems as the inadequate match of labour supply to the needs of the market (what could be labelled "mismatch unemployment") and those caused by over-protection of "insiders" at the expense of "outsiders"[84], *e.g.* social protection schemes which protect those already in work, acting as an obstacle to recruitment[85]. However, it is clear that for the Commission at least, increased flexibility is not to be seen as synonymous with deregulation: flexibility requires a "remodelled, rational and simplified system of regulation, not simply deregulation of Europe's labour markets"[86].

If one compares the approach adopted by the White Paper in particular, and the Commission in general, it is quite different from the solution to the EU's unemployment ills proposed by international organisations such as the OECD. It is perhaps unrealistic, however, to expect individual Member States to adopt the sort of wholesale deregulation advocated by the OECD:

> The desire to maintain gains in social welfare through wage rates and working conditions, which have been made in Europe in the last fifty years, are not easily abandoned. Throughout most of Europe deregulation of the labour market is socially and politically unacceptable [...] To ignore the strong commitment of most European countries to the protection of workers' rights and social equity within the labour market is unrealistic.[87]

This much can be seen from the reluctance of most Member States even to engage in modernisation of their regulatory regimes as demanded by the Employment Guidelines, even though the thrust of the Guidelines, whilst pushing flexibility, is by no means automatically deregulatory.

---

[83] CEC, 1993, *White Paper on Growth*, Chapter 8, pp. 123-135.
[84] See Lindbeck and Snower, 1989.
[85] CEC, 1993, *White Paper on Growth*, p. 124.
[86] CEC, 1993, *White Paper on Growth*, p. 123.
[87] Symes, 1995, p. 192.

The Maastricht IGC and Competence over Employment Policy

Most European countries are currently entering a recession, yet they have signed up to the Maastricht Treaty which requires a degree of fiscal contraction[88].

As mentioned above, the Maastricht Treaty on European Union dealt extensively with social policy, in giving it a firm treaty base for the first time. A great deal has been written about these developments[89]. However, what is more pertinent in this context is how social law and social policy and employment issues were kept so clearly separate from the debate on monetary union, and excluded from the convergence criteria.

Following the ratification of the TEU, combating unemployment and encouraging non-inflationary growth became central aims of the newly-formed European Union[90]. Nevertheless, a moot point during the Intergovernmental Conference leading up to the TEU was whether or not to include employment *targets* within the convergence criteria which Member States had to respect if they wanted to participate in Economic and Monetary Union[91]. Ultimately, however, the anxiety of most Member States to retain their competence in the area of employment policy, led to the exclusion of this policy area from the convergence criteria[92]. The Delors Committee Report[93], which was responsible for determining much of the future content of EMU[94], had envisaged EMU

---

[88] Barrell, *et al.*, 1994, pp. 39-40.

[89] See, for example, Bercusson, 1992, p. 177; Fitzpatrick, 1992, p. 199; Szyszczak, 1995, No. 1.

[90] The Treaty of Amsterdam subsequently amended Article 2 EC again, but following the TEU, it stated that the Union's tasks included "promotion of sustainable and non-inflationary growth respecting a high level of employment and social protection". See also Barnard, 1995, p. 65.

[91] To ensure that the sustainable convergence required for the achievement of EMU came about, the TEU set five convergence criteria which needed to be met by each Member State before it could take part in the third stage of EMU. Checks on whether the criteria are being met were to be carried out on the basis of reports by the Commission and the European Monetary Institute.

[92] The convergence criteria are referred to in Article 121 of the EC Treaty and set out in Protocol 21 annexed to the Treaty.

[93] Committee for the Study of Economic and Monetary Union (The Delors Committee), *Report on Economic and Monetary Union in the Community* (Luxembourg, OOPEC, 1989), Annex I, p. 39. Much of the discussion of the Report is taken from Snyder, 1999.

[94] The recommendations of the Delors Committee formed the basis for the EMU provisions of the TEU, inserted into the EC Treaty as Articles 2, 4, 8 and Title VII EC (formerly Articles 2, 3a(2), 4a and Title VI, prior to the Treaty of Amsterdam).

as a three-part process, involving (a) closer coordination of Member States' economic and monetary policies, (b) the establishment of a European Central Bank, and (c) the replacement of national currencies by a single European currency[95]. Furthermore, as Snyder points out[96], the thinking at the time was that wage flexibility and labour mobility were essential to avoid differences in competitiveness between different regions and countries. This perspective is interesting in being so very much at odds with the "comparative advantage" approach, which had dominated the Treaty of Rome, tolerating the absence of a "level playing field" in labour costs between Member States[97]. Now it appeared that the reality of a common currency required common market countries to behave more like an entity with a common labour market, if EMU was to work.

Given the TEU's explicit goal of combating unemployment, plus the new commitment to monetary union, the reluctance to confer competence over employment policy to the EU level requires some explanation. Clearly the path taken by national employment policies was not insignificant to the success of EMU, especially in view of the need for a coordinated Europe-wide macroeconomic policy and fiscal policy. Why were Member States not willing to surrender control over employment policy even though employment policy is, arguably, such a fundamental part of macroeconomic policy?

One explanation for the absence of social, employment or industrial policy issues from the EMU negotiating agenda, and ultimately from the EMU convergence criteria, is the way in which the institutional characteristics of the EMU negotiations narrowed down the agenda. The EMU negotiations have been described as a "core executive" activity[98], involving almost exclusively Member States' finance and foreign ministries, heads of state or government, central bank officials and the EC Monetary Committee. Even the Commission was displaced from its normal central role in agenda-shaping[99], and furthermore,

> [s]ectoral interests were very much excluded from the EMU negotiations. Employers' organisations, trade unions, and industrial and banking associations were not incorporated in the process, either at national or EC levels[100].

---

[95] Snyder, 1999, p. 431.

[96] Snyder, 1999, p. 432.

[97] International Labour Office, "Social Aspects of European Economic Co-operation", 1956, 74 *International Labour Review* 99; see also Deakin, 1996.

[98] Dyson and Featherstone, 1999, pp. 13-15 and 754-756.

[99] Dyson and Featherstone, 1999, p. 755.

[100] Dyson and Featherstone, 1999, p. 14.

The convergence criteria were thus restricted to the more "technocratic" issues, on which it was, apparently, easier to reach consensus. As Dyson and Featherstone point out:

> The EMU negotiations were concluded successfully precisely because certain highly contentious issues, which were rooted in conflicts of basic political belief, were factored out of the bargaining.[101]

A further explanation for the absence of social and employment issues from the Maastricht agenda is that this was as an(other) example of what Salais labels "social nationalism" (see Robert Salais in this volume). It was not until 1993 and 1994, following the European Council meetings in Brussels and Essen, respectively and the Commission's Green and White Papers on Social Policy, that the Union seemed prepared or able to stake a claim for a more clearly *European* employment policy – or at least the coordination of *national* employment policy at European level.

Although, as discussed above, the European Council meeting at Essen failed to sanction the Commission's proposed expansion of public investment to increase jobs, it nevertheless marked a significant juncture in the development of EU employment policy[102]. The Essen Council endorsed the employment policy agenda of the Delors White Paper; what it did not do, however, was to consent to a major allocation of competence over employment policy to the Commission. Instead, it could be argued that having "discovered" employment policy as a matter of concern for the EU as a whole, the Essen Council marked the beginning of a process whereby political initiative was shifted from the Community institutions to the Member States, acting within the parameters set by the European Council[103]. As the Presidency Conclusions stated:

> The European Council urges the Member States to transpose these recommendations[104] in their individual policies into a multiannual programme having regard to the specific features of their economic and social situation.[105]

---

[101] Dyson and Featherstone, 1999, p. 756
[102] See Sciarra, 1999.
[103] Kenner, 1999, p. 34.
[104] The Essen recommendations/criteria were (1) promoting investment in vocational training; (2) increasing employment through periods of growth; (3) reducing non-wage labour costs; (4) improving the effectiveness of labour market policy; and (5) improving measures to help groups at risk of exclusion from the labour market.
[105] European Council Meeting on 9 and 10 December 1994 in Essen, Presidency Conclusions; Press Release, Brussels, 9 December 1994, Nr 00300/94.

These policy recommendations, or guidelines, on employment were to be part of an annual process of Commission monitoring of Member States' employment policies. With this came a concomitant change of emphasis from legislative harmonisation to the use of "soft law"; the emphasis was now to be on coordination rather than harmonisation, through the use of guidelines rather than legislative instruments.

Employment policy and economic policy were to become more closely coordinated through early, rather vague and non-binding, initiatives such as the Confidence Pact for Employment[106], leading eventually to the sort of "Reinforced Economic Policy Co-operation"[107] which placed employment right at the heart of a successful monetary union, with the Resolution on growth and employment[108], and the Employment Title itself.

The Emergence of a Fully Fledged Employment Policy

By way of conclusion, is it possible to say – following the insertion of a Title on employment into the EC Treaty by the Treaty of Amsterdam – that the EU now has a "fully fledged" employment policy, which is not parasitical on its social policy? There are two preliminary observations to make here. *First*, the Member States' rejection of the Commission's proposed supply side measures has proved to be a major obstacle to the full realisation of a specifically *European* employment policy. Instead, the process begun at Essen has led to a Luxembourg process based on centralised coordination of *national* employment policies[109]. As a result, I would argue, the Union's employment policy is still very much a circumscribed policy; a core element of employment policy still remains largely national, and as Barnard and Deakin describe, facilitative rather than prescriptive[110].

Secondly, the need to find an effective employment strategy to reduce unemployment and to offset the potentially adverse effects of EMU on jobs has been hindered, it seems, by unresolved tensions, by "the continuing differences between those pressing for greater labour market deregulation and those advocating an increase in expansionist macro-level intervention"[111]. The possibility of reconciling existing or

---

[106] CEC, *Action for Employment in Europe: A Confidence Pact* (Luxembourg, OOPEC, 1996) CSE (96) 1 final.

[107] See the Council website at http://ue.eu.int/en/summ.htm.

[108] Resolution of the European Council on Growth and Employment, Amsterdam 16 June 1997, OJ C 236, 2 August 1997, 3.

[109] Barnard and Deakin, 1999, p. 356 and Teague, 1999, p. 37.

[110] Barnard and Deakin, 1999, p. 358.

[111] Towers and Terry, 1997, p. 274.

restructured models of social protection with employment growth is a difficult question which has, to some extent, being avoided in policy discourse in the years following the Amsterdam Treaty, until the Lisbon European Council took up the issue of social protection and brought it into the foreground of debates on employment[112].

In considering the status of EU employment policy, it is important to remember that the employment policy measures put in place by the Treaty of Amsterdam almost entirely take the form of soft law[113]. The Amsterdam Treaty introduced a new Title on Employment (Title VIII) into the EC Treaty, together with the Title on Economic and Monetary Policy (Title VII), the combined effect of which is a strategy to promote employment based on the coordination of Member States' macro-economic policies and structural reforms. The core of the new employment strategy, set out in Articles 125 to 130 EC, is a new power vested in the Union, *supplementary* to that of the Member States, to promulgate common guidelines similar to those adopted at the Essen Council. The annual procedure for the creation of employment guidelines begins with the adoption by the European Council of conclusions on the employment situation in the Union, on the basis of a joint annual report prepared by the Council and the Commission (Article 128); these conclusions enable the Commission to propose employment policy guidelines, which must be consistent with the economic guidelines established under Article 99(2) for monetary union. The Council then adopts these employment guidelines by qualified majority after consulting the European Parliament, the Economic and Social Committee, the Committee of the Regions and the Employment Committee (Article 128(2)). The second strand of the employment strategy involves action by Member States, which are obliged to report annually, in National Action Plans for Employment, on measures taken to implement employment Policy in accordance with the Broad Economic Policy Guidelines (Article 128(3)).

This procedure, for the production of annual employment guidelines, is modelled closely on the convergence arrangements for national economic policies, with two exceptions: first, the common employment guidelines do not advocate measures to harmonise national provisions, although they do have an indirect impact on Member States' policy. *Second*, in contrast to the provisions on EMU, Title VIII does not

---

[112] European Council in Lisbon, 23 and 24 March 2000, Presidency Conclusions, Brussels Press Release, SN 100/00; see also European Council Meeting in Santa Maria de Fiera, 19 and 20 June 2000, Brussels Press Release, SN 200/00.
[113] See Sciarra, 2000.

prescribe any macroeconomic objectives to be achieved, along the lines of the economic convergence criteria[114].

The first set of Employment Guidelines, formally adopted by a resolution of the Council in December 1997[115], centre around four "pillars" – improving employability, developing entrepreneurship, encouraging adaptability in businesses and their employees, and strengthening the policies for equal opportunities – which are further elaborated through nineteen Guidelines[116]. Although the "pillars" and guidelines have a clear Treaty basis, in Title VIII and Article 128, they can be seen as examples of "soft law" in that they are not produced in the form of legally binding instruments, such as directives or regulations, which the EU institutions have at their disposal. Nevertheless, these guidelines have important implications for policy and law-making within Member States.

The EC Treaty is careful to spell out that legislation and regulation is still a matter for Member States. Article 127 states that the Community shall encourage cooperation and complement Member State action to promote employment, but nevertheless, Member States' competences must be respected. In addition, Article 129 states that measures taken by the Council to promote employment "shall not include harmonisation of the laws and regulations of the Member States". Further, in contrast to the situation where a Member State acts inconsistently with the economic policy guidelines, there are no real sanctions which can be imposed on a Member State which fails to comply with the employment guidelines.

Thus, in place of the sort of harmonising legislation which was the hallmark of the Union's increased competence in the area of social policy, the new employment strategy is marked by coordination rather than convergence[117], with use made of "benchmarking"[118], rather than targets as such. The legal obligations to which the Employment Title may give rise are still far from clear[119]. As Silvana Sciarra observes:

---

[114] See CEC, *The Amsterdam Treaty: A Comprehensive Guide* (Luxembourg, OOPEC, 1998).

[115] The 1998 Employment Guidelines, Council Resolution of 15 December 1997, available at: http://europa.eu.int/comm/dg05/empl&esf/docs/guideen.htm.

[116] The latest version of the annual employment guidelines are contained in CEC, *The Employment Guidelines for 2001: Proposal for a Council Decision on Guidelines for Member States' Employment Policies for the Year 2001* (Luxembourg, OOPEC, 2000).

[117] See Biagi, 1998.

[118] See Tronti, 1999.

[119] Sciarra, 1999, p. 157.

"Employability" has no precise legal standing as a word, but is the policy side of a new and peculiar legal command addressed to Member States. So are "entrepreneurship, adaptability and equal opportunities" – all difficult criteria to be translated into binding norms and yet the essence of a "co-ordinated strategy for employment".[120]

This increased use of "soft law" and governance by means of guidelines has run parallel to what I have argued has been a more general shift from social law to employment policy. There have, of course, been exceptions, in that the focus on a discourse of employment creation has not entirely silenced social policy/social law discourse. One important exception, illustrating Mark Freedland's analysis of the co-existence of competing policy agendas, is the social dialogue process which, in the period since the Treaty of Amsterdam, has produced three directives, on Parental Leave[121], Part-Time Work[122] and Fixed-Term Work[123].

Furthermore, one should not underestimate the impact which such soft law measures are having on Member States' employment strategies and regulatory polices toward the labour market. For example, benchmarking of employment policies may be useful not only as a procedure by which Member States can measure and compare the operation of their labour markets; it can also be a means by which the worse performing countries can improve their employment performance, in part, through adopting examples of best practice[124]. In addition, although the Employment Strategy in general, and in particular the annual guidelines and Commission monitoring of Member States' employment policies, do not *directly* affect Member States' regulatory systems, nevertheless, there has been indirect pressure for change[125].

The *de facto* bringing of employment questions into EMU has occurred in a rather narrow manner; narrow because it has been almost

---

[120] Sciarra, 1999, p. 165.

[121] Council Directive 96/34/EC of 3 June 1996 on the framework agreement on parental leave concluded by UNICE, CEEP and the ETUC, amended by Council Directive 97/75/EC of 15 December 1997, Official Journal (OJ) L 145, 19 June 1996 and OJ L 10, 16 January 1998.

[122] Council Directive 97/81/EC of 15 December 1997 concerning the framework agreement on part-time working concluded by UNICE, CEEP and the ETUC, amended by Council Directive 98/23/EC of 7 April 1998, OJ L 14, 20 January 1998 and OJ L 131, 5 May 1998.

[123] Council Directive 99/70/EC of 28 June 1999 concerning the framework agreement on fixed-term work concluded by UNICE, CEEP and the ETUC, OJ L 175, 10 July 1999.

[124] See Tronti, 1999.

[125] See Weiss, 1998.

entirely divorced from the traditional social policy concerns which used to dominate this policy area before the shift to a focus on employment creation. Thus, for example, whilst at a purely formal level – in the amended EC Treaty – there is a clear connection between Title VII on Economic and Monetary Policy and Title VIII on Employment, there is no interaction between economic and employment policy, and Title XI on Social Policy, Education, Vocational Training and Youth. The provisions of the Social Policy Title on, for example, social security and social protection of workers, or social dialogue between management and labour, are presented almost in a vacuum, unrelated to questions of employment creation or macroeconomic policy. In this context, therefore, the importance if the Lisbon European Council cannot be overstated. The key achievement of the Lisbon meeting was to integrate all the various "processes"[126] arising out of the Employment Strategy, and to provide, for the first time since Amsterdam, a positive and unambiguous link between social, employment and economic issues[127]. Lisbon differed from other post-Amsterdam summits, in placing the renewal of the "European social model" at the heart of an integrated economic and employment strategy. The language used, that of "full employment" (in contrast to the reference to "high levels of employment" in the Treaty of Amsterdam) and "modernising and improving social protection", indicate a political willingness once again to prioritise social policy. It remains to be seen, however, to what extent the renewed emphasis on social policy since Lisbon will be translated into a return to the use of "hard law" mechanisms.

---

[126] Previous European Council meetings at Luxembourg (20-21 November 1997), Cardiff (15-16 June 1998) and Cologne (3-4 June 1999) each spawned a new "process" to describe the implementation of the employment strategy, and its relation to structural reform and economic policy.

[127] See the follow-up Commission document, CEC, *Communication from the Commission to the Council, the European Parliament, the Economic and Social Committee and the Committee of the Regions, Social Policy Agenda*, Brussels, 28 June 2000, COM(2000) 379 Final.

PART IV

FUTURE PROSPECTS

CHAPTER 12

The Werner Plan
as a Blueprint for EMU?

Ton NOTERMANS

The Economic and Monetary Union (EMU) agreed upon in Maastricht in December 1991 in many ways reflects the culmination of the decline of Keynesian policies which set in during the early 1970s[1]. The Keynesian conception of the need for activist economic policies to stabilise an otherwise inherently unstable economy (see Chapter 3 by David Purdy in this volume) implied a design of policy-making institutions which allowed for a high degree of discretion and flexibility and, in theory at least, for democratic control of the choices made by policy making institutions. The need for flexibility and discretion emerged from the assumption of cyclical economic instability requiring frequent adjustment of policies. The requirement of democratic control in turn resulted from the recognition of clear trade-offs in macroeconomic management – most famously the alleged trade-off between employment and inflation as expressed in the so-called Philips Curve – implying that only democratically accounted bodies could effect legitimate choices.

The design of the core institutions of EMU, namely the European System of Central Banks (ESCB) and the Stability and Growth Pact (SGP), in contrast, was dominated by a concern to reduce discretion and remove macroeconomic policy decisions from the arena of (partisan) politics. Based on the theoretical view that monetary policies in the longer run only affect the price level (cf. the chapters by Sheila C. Dow and Roger Hammersland in this volume) and that democratic governments have incentives to pursue destabilising policies, the ECB was designed at Maastricht as one of the world's most independent and least accountable central banks[2]. The SGP, designed at the Dublin and Amsterdam summits of 1996 and 1997 in turn imposed tight constraints on aggregate fiscal management of the Member States, limiting the

---

[1]   Thanks to Barbara MacLennan for comments.
[2]   De Haan and Eijfinger, 2000, pp. 397, 404-405.

permissible budget deficit to three percent of GDP. Although these constraints do allow for some countercyclical fiscal spending for those states who manage to maintain their budget close to balance or in surplus in normal times, and although the SGP allows for larger deficits under exceptional circumstances, the imposition of statutory limits by means of an international treaty on fiscal management betrays a policy philosophy which is fundamentally critical of the Keynesian concepts of the post-war period.

Institution building is frequently thought of as a way to give permanence to policies irrespective of the change in political hue of governments[3]. Yet, economic history teaches that the idea of creating policy institutions which will provide for optimal choices under all conditions in the future is fundamentally naïve[4]. The design of EMU was informed by the problems of escalating inflation and budget deficits so characteristic of the 1970s and 1980s. At the beginning of the twenty-first century, however, the European economy displays rather different traits than one or two decades ago; inflation has been conquered whereas the unemployment problem seems intractable, budget deficits have been successfully contained giving way to sizeable surpluses in some countries, the Conservative and Christian Democratic statesmen who designed EMU largely have had to vacate their seats to social democratic colleagues, and popular support for European integration is at an all time low. In this new environment the institutional set-up of EMU may no longer be optimal[5].

This chapter asks if the economic and political changes that have occurred since Maastricht are such as to call for a redesign of the central institutions of EMU. Can the promise of the economic viability of a specific European Model of Society in a global economy be fulfilled within the given institutional framework or does that framework contain an inherent "neo-liberal" orientation and hence a pre-programmed conflict between the political demise of neo-liberal strategies and their institutionally based persistence? The main questions concerning the appropriateness of the present institutional design revolve around the issues of monetary policy strategy, the role of fiscal policies in stimulating more employment and the need for tighter coordination between fiscal and monetary policies.

Given that disinflation has brought durable unemployment in its wake, the conviction that tight money is neutral in the longer run is

---

[3]   March and Olsen, 1995, p. 29.

[4]   Jonung, 1999.

[5]   Wyplosz, 1999.

increasingly shaken[6]. If, however, there are good indications for assigning the ECB a co-responsibility for output, the present policy philosophy would require revisions. Similarly, as Keynesian are wont to argue, if deficit spending plays a crucial role in stabilising output and stimulating growth, the SPG would seem overly restrictive. Finally, if both fiscal and monetary policies have real effects a different mode of coordination of the two might be desirable.

In view of the receding support for the theoretical orthodoxy on which the present EMU is built, it may be asked if the older Werner Plan with its clear Keynesian traits may provide a better institutional framework for macroeconomic management in the twenty-first century. This paper argues that the resurrection of the Werner Plan would seem neither advisable nor likely. The constraints on fiscal and economic policy-making introduced by the TEU may prove valuable institutional safeguards against inflationary problems in a situation where the capacity for European tripartite bargaining, which the Werner Plan implicitly seemed to assume, do not, and probably will not exist in the near future. However, the unaccountable nature of the ECB together with its insistence that it is not involved in any trade-offs between output and inflation are argued to be obstacles to the legitimacy of economic integration and prosperity.

The structure of the chapter is as follows. Section two briefly reviews the institutional set-up of EMU. Section three outlines the pressures for change in economic management. Section four argues that there are indeed good indications that Europe's unemployment problem is closely related to the monetary policy pursued. Section five argues that European level Keynesianism would not seem advisable given that there is no good evidence that such strategies ever worked successfully in the longer run, even during the so-called post-1945 "Golden Age" (*cf.* Chapter 3 by David Purdy). Moreover, the Golden Age strategies of subordinating the Central Bank to overall economic management hinged on the strong institutional ability to contain wage growth under full employment; a condition which no longer exists in the same form. Section six concludes by arguing that economic prosperity and political stability may probably be best served by a central bank which does remain somewhat at a remove from the political process in order to prevent inflationary and budgetary pressures, but which at the same time is made to clearly recognise and debate the short- and long-term effects of monetary management on economic activity.

---

[6] Ball, 1996, Collignon, 1998a and b, Dow in this volume, Friedman, 1995, Iversen, 1998, Modigliani 1997, Notermans, 2000, Ostrup, 2000 and Tobin 1980. As yet, however, there is no clear consensus as to why money is not neutral in the long run.

The Set-Up of EMU

Historically European governments have given rather different answers to the question of how independent the central bank should be from political interference. The general pattern seems to be that in times of substantial inflation the political will to grant the central bank independence increases strongly whereas in times of durable unemployment and depression the tables are turned[7]. If we confine ourselves to the developments in Western Europe during the twentieth century, two full circles can be discerned. With the beginning of the first World War central banks lost political independence in order for governments to be able to mobilise the economy for warfare. During the first years after the armistice this pattern continued as governments sought to counteract possible social unrest by the pursuit of a policy of growth and unemployment. Yet the massive inflation that developed after 1918 – turning into hyperinflation in Austria and Germany – soon led to a change of course. The general understanding – shared by almost all west European governments – was that the governments' recourse to the central bank's printing press had been the main cause of inflation. The central bank's independence, which came to be re-established since the early twenties, generally took the form of linking the national currency to gold. Under the gold standard, so the theory went, money creation would be constrained by the amount of gold reserves, a variable generally not under the control of governments. Moreover, adherence to the gold standard would eliminate discretion from monetary management as overly expansionary policies would threaten a depreciation of the currency and *vice versa*.

The tight monetary polices required to re-establish the parity with gold effectively ended inflation but also heralded a period of mass-unemployment. With the beginning of the 1930s the stagnation of the 1920s gave way to the downward spiral of deflation, contraction and the even higher unemployment of the Great Depression. The Great Depression marked the beginning of the end of central bank independence. Starting in September 1931, West European governments successively abandoned the Gold Standard. Instead of being orientated to maintaining the parity, monetary policies were now to be oriented towards the domestic goals of growth and full-employment, which also implied that the governments should be able to have the last say instead of the central banks[8]. After 1945 this new philosophy was reflected in the nationalisation of a large number of central banks. As the unemployment of the 1930s gave way to full employment of the post-1945 period all countries

---

[7] Kindleberger, 1985, p. 41.
[8] Temin, 1989.

had to contend with rising inflationary pressures. Yet, instead of increasing central bank independence the preferred solution consisted of a greater reliance on negotiated wage moderation to contain inflation so as to allow monetary policies to maintain a relatively relaxed course. The obvious exception to this pattern was Germany where the Bundesbank enjoyed great independence and the so-called principle of *Tarifautonomie* – jealously defended by the trade unions – prevented any sort of incomes policies. The German experience would come to inform much of the institutional design of the EMU. On closer examination, however, the deviating pattern of Germany during the long post-war boom may have been more a matter of form than substance as the room created by a fairly high capacity for wage moderation was exploited by the Bundesbank to pursue growth oriented policies similar to those in other countries[9].

Rising trade union militancy since the late 1960s, increasing inflationary pressures, and two oil price shocks, eventually brought this post-war constellation to an end in favour of a policy assignment in which monetary management freed itself from the responsibility for growth and employment and again came to give overriding priority to price stability.

The Maastricht Treaty continued this trend towards greater central bank independence, as the ECB it created is probably the most independent central bank ever. Article 7 of protocol No. 18 of the Treaty of Amsterdam grants the ECB full instrument independence[10]. The instrument independence is complemented by article 21.1 (protocol 18) which forbids the ECB from lending to public authorities, thus closing a possible loophole through which the latter may have acquired some direct influence over monetary policies.

Similar to the statutes of the pre-EMU Bundesbank, which in many instances have served as a blueprint for the TEU, the ECB is also granted a considerable degree of goal independence. Article 2 states:

[...] the primary objective of the ESCB shall be to maintain price stability. Without prejudice to the objective of price stability, it shall support the general economic policies in the Community with a view to contributing to

---

9   Holtfrerich, 1998.
10 "When exercising the powers and carrying out the tasks and duties conferred upon them by this Treaty and this Statute, neither the ECB, nor a national central bank, nor any member of their decision making bodies shall seek or take instructions from Community institutions or bodies, from any government of a Member State or from any other body. The Community institutions and bodies and the governments of the Member States undertake to respect this principle and not to seek to influence the members of the decision making bodies of the ECB or of the national central banks in the performance of their tasks."

the achievement of the objectives of the Community as laid down in Article 2 (ex Article 2) of this Treaty.

Since the treaty nowhere specified how price stability is to be interpreted, it was left to the ECB to develop its own interpretation. According to the ECB price stability means "a year-on-year increase in the Harmonised Index of Consumer Prices (HICP) of the euro area below two percent." Price stability "is to be maintained over the medium term"[11].

The six members of the ECB's Executive Board are nominated for a non-renewable term of eight years "by common accord of the governments of the Member States at the level of the Heads of State or Government" (Article 11.2, protocol 18). Approval of the European parliament for appointments is not required; it merely needs to be consulted. Nevertheless, the EP has used its right of consultation to conduct in-depth interviews with the nominees for the board. The Governing Council, which is the ECB's central policy-making institution, consists of the six members of the executive board plus the governors of the national central banks participating in EMU (Article 10 protocol 18). With the exception of Finland where parliament holds the right of nomination, the Member State governments appoint NCB governors. However, in order to participate in the single currency the Treaty stipulates that NCBs must be fully independent. Moreover, the statutes and the treaties do not provide for the possibility of dismissing (individual members of) the policy making bodies of the ECB in case the Council, EP, and/or Commission judges the ECB not to have fulfilled its mandate. Dismissal of individual members instead is solely linked to individual inability to perform the relevant function properly (article 11.4 and 14.2, protocol 18).

In terms of independence, the ECB may look similar to the Bundesbank, but *de facto* it enjoys a much greater degree of independence[12], because the latter's statutes could be changed by a simple parliamentary majority. Despite its formal independence, the Bundesbank was hence constrained in its actions by the need to maintain a sufficient basis of support amongst either the government or the public. The ECB protocol in contrast is an international treaty, which can only be changed by unanimous consent of the contracting parties[13].

---

[11] ECB, 1999, pp. 46-47.

[12] Tavelli, Tullio and Spinelli, 1998, p. 343, however, rank the ECB on a shared first place with the Bundesbank.

[13] Article 41 of protocol 18 does provide for a simplified amendment procedure to some articles of the ECB statutes, either by a qualified majority of the Council or an unanimous Council and after having obtained the consent of the EP. None of the

In theory the independence of the monetary authority including the prohibition of lending to public authorities should be sufficient to guarantee price stability, at least to the extent that expansion of the money supply is a necessary and sufficient condition for inflation. Nevertheless, the TEU has instituted formal constraints on the fiscal management of the Member States as an integral part of monetary union. Also in the case of independent NCB's a need for coordination of fiscal and monetary policies has generally been recognised, based on two main arguments. First, even though inflation is considered a monetary phenomenon[14], this is seen to hold true in the long run. In the short run threats to price stability may arise from other sources than undue monetary expansion, and excessive budget deficits is considered one of the most important sources[15]. Secondly, unlike Ulysses, political authorities can only tie one hand to the mast, because they must necessarily retain the right to change or amend the provisions governing the independence of the monetary authority. Widespread policy conflict between the central bank and the political authorities is thus likely to undermine the credibility of the latter. Accordingly, to strengthen the commitment to price stability the independence of the monetary authority needs to be complemented with a provision requiring the political authorities to conduct fiscal policy in a way which, if it does not support it, at least does not run counter to the policies of the bank.

Notwithstanding the generally recognised need for coordination of fiscal and monetary management it was rather uncommon for states to have statutory limits on budget deficits. That the EU nevertheless has such limits in the form of the SGP is mainly due to two factors. First, due to the decentralised nature of fiscal policy-making in the EU some countries thought it necessary to include upper limits on budget deficits in the design for EMU in order to prevent free-riding. Because it removes the threat of exchange rate crisis, so the reasoning went, EMU may increase the incentives of national governments to run excessive deficits. Excessive deficits, however, may be inflationary and hence threaten the stability of the common currency. Admittedly, governments

---

articles which can be thus amended concern the objectives, the independence and the functioning of the decision making bodies of the ECB.

[14] ECB, 1999, p. 47.

[15] Put somewhat differently, the theoretical argument involved here seems to employ a somewhat arbitrary switch between a long and short-term perspective in order to justify asymmetric coordination. That money is supposedly neutral in the *long-run* is used as a justification for the central bank rejecting to co-ordinate its policies with the government. That money is not neutral in the *short-run* instead is used as a justification for the government subordinating fiscal management to the goals of the central bank.

running excessive deficits would in the extreme cases face bankruptcy. Yet, since it is widely considered to be both politically and economically unfeasible for other Member States not to intervene in such a case, the threat of bankruptcy is held not to create sufficiently strong incentives for prudent fiscal management.

The German insistence on institutional safeguards against suspected "southern European profligacy", however, could not provide a sufficient political base for the pact. Admittedly, an EMU without Germany would have been unthinkable. Yet, German politicians would have found it impossible to insist on an SGP if this would have implied the failure of the EMU project. Agreement on a SGP proved possible because the German fear of free-riding dovetailed with the desire of many politicians to tie their hands by creating an external constraint on fiscal management[16]. Spending cuts are hardly ever popular. However, the growing budget deficits of the 1980s placed an increasing burden on debt service and, in the view of many politicians, had become an obstacle to economic recovery. By linking the issue of fiscal austerity, at least in those countries where the public was broadly favourable, to European integration, national policy-makers sought to reduce domestic political opposition against their preferred policies.

The Stability and Growth Pact is contained in two council regulations, namely Regulation (EC) No. 1466/97 of 7 July 1997 and Regulation (EC) No. 1467/97 of 7 July 1997, and the Amsterdam European Council Resolution on the Stability and Growth Pact of 17 June 1997. Regulation 1466/97 aims at strengthening the surveillance of especially fiscal policies by requiring EMU Member States to submit annual "stability programmes" and authorising the council to issue recommendation to individual Member States concerning the required measures in order to reach the medium-term objective of "budgetary positions close to balance or in surplus". The core of the Stability and Growth Pact, however, consists of regulation 1467/97 which details the measures to be taken in case an EMU Member State incurs an excessive deficit.

The imposition of penalties is not automatic but to be decided by the Council of Ministers and by qualified majority voting. More concretely, Regulation 1467/97 resolved that sanctions could be suspended in case of exceptional circumstances. Exceptional circumstances are said to be present when excessive deficits result from "an unusual event outside the control of the relevant Member State and which has a major impact on the financial position of general government or when resulting from a severe economic downturn". (Article 2). A severe downturn is defined

---

[16] Buti *et al.*, 1998, pp. 86-87.

as an annual fall of real GDP of at least two percent. In case of a fall of real GDP smaller than two percent the Council may nevertheless decide that exceptional circumstances calling for a suspension of sanctions were present, after having considered further evidence "in particular on the abruptness of the downturn or on the accumulated loss of output relative to past trends". Furthermore, in the Amsterdam Council resolution on the Stability and Growth Pact Member States have committed themselves "not to invoke the benefit of Article 2 paragraph 3 of the Council Regulation on speeding up and clarifying the excessive deficit procedure unless they are in severe recession; in evaluating whether the economic downturn is severe, the Member States will, as a rule, take as a reference point an annual fall in real GDP of at least 0.75 percent".

In practice, this implies that: (1) Sanction will be automatically suspended in case of a annual fall of GDP of at least two percent; (2) Sanctions may be suspended if GDP fell by between 0.75% and 2% but exceptional circumstances prevailed; or (3) if exceptional events outside the control of the Member State have occurred. Because the wording of the Amsterdam resolution does not unequivocally rule out the possibility of appealing to article 2 paragraph 3 of the excessive deficit procedure, the clause concerning events outside the control of the Member States in practice most likely will mean that the imposition of sanctions will always be a matter of bargaining within the Council.

Sanctions consist of an annual interest-free deposit up to a maximum of 0.5 percent of GDP. If the excessive deficit has not been corrected within two years the deposit will become a fine which will be distributed amongst the EMU members that are not running excessive deficits according to their share in the total GDP of these Member States.

However, there is widespread doubt whether the Stability and Growth Pact will be a workable instrument[17]. Unlike monetary policy, fiscal management traditionally has been at the core of partisan debates. Attempts by the EU to impose policy changes from above are likely to be intensely conflictual. Unless the imposition of fines coincides with a particular domestic political constellation in which it will help create a majority for those advocating fiscal contraction, it may prove a very unwieldy instrument, also because the pact was not part of the original TEU and is seen by many governments as imposed by Germany but not strictly necessary for the proper functioning of EMU.

---

[17] Wessels, 1998, p. 403 f.

From the EMU to the Werner Plan?

Both in economic and political terms the first two years of the Euro have been surprisingly smooth. The transition to the single currency did not give rise to any speculative pressures nor did the ECB feel tempted, as some feared, to establish its reputation by pursing an excessively tight policy. Instead the introduction of the Euro coincided with a noticeable economic upswing and a concomitant fall in unemployment rates whereas inflation figures, especially when purged of the effects of the oil price rise, remained very modest. Largely due to the favorable economic developments, the single currency and its institutions have not become the focus of any serious political controversy. Admittedly, the ECB at times has been exposed to harsh criticism from professional economists[18], who occasionally have been joined by an European Parliament (EP) lamenting its limited influence on the ECB and the opaqueness of the latter's decision-making[19]. Yet, such criticism has not provoked an audible echo amongst policymakers. Apart from some remarks by Italy's minister of labour, Cesare Salvi[20], Oskar Lafontaine remained a lone voice with his early attacks on the ECB. Also the attempt, especially by some German critics to interpret the weakness of the euro versus the dollar as proof that the ECB is not seriously committed to stability has remained without followers. Nevertheless it would seem too early to conclude that Euroland has found a durable political and institutional equilibrium. The environment of the early twenty-first century in many ways is dissimilar to the environment of the 1980s which largely inspired the institutional set-up of EMU. Accordingly, clear pressures for change can be identified.

The most conspicuous change concerns the spectacular resurgence of social democracy to the position of dominant political force in Europe[21]. Whereas social democratic heads of state were vastly outnumbered by their Conservative and Christian Democratic colleagues when the monetary union was negotiated at Maastricht, the tables had been turned by the time the single currency was introduced. However, EMU has not been subjected to the clash which the historical sequence of events might suggest, between an allegedly neo-liberal institutional design and the centre-left outlook of the politicians having to operate with this design. After the inflationary excess of the 1970s and the spiralling

---

[18] Buiter, p. 1999, Bini, Smaghi and Gros, 2000; Favero *et al.*, 2000.
[19] Huhne, 2000 and Pries, 1997.
[20] "It is unacceptable that the only body that makes decisions in Europe is the ECB, which follows an ultra-monetarist theory and acts with superficiality and improvisations." Quoted in *Financial Times, 18 October 2000.*
[21] Cuperus and Kandel, 1998.

budget deficits of the 1980s the framework of an independent monetary authority committed to price stability and statutory limits on fiscal deficits has generally found favour with social democrats as well. In its Third Way incarnation European social democracy neither attempts to redress the institutional balance in favour of the nation state in order to allow for a renewed national Keynesianism, nor does it aspire to bring about the centralisation and coordination of fiscal and monetary policies required for Keynesianism at the European level. The institutional innovation associated with the re-emergence of social democracy mainly concerns a significantly increased emphasis on transnational policy networks and methods of open, or soft, coordination. The prime examples in the field of economic management concern the annual exercise of compiling the so called Broad Economic Policy Guidelines (BEPG) and the Employment Policy Guidelines (EPG)[22].

However, the fact that social democracy has been content to work within the institutional framework designed by its predecessors does not imply continuity in policies. The substantive change concerns first and foremost a stronger emphasis on the need to boost Europe's employment performance and a revaluation of the role of the state. As the spectre of inflation gradually faded from sight during the 1990s but European unemployment remained high, thereby placing significant additional burdens on already strained welfare states and budgets, the previous "neo-liberal" strategy of assigning tight monetary policies to inflation control and expecting a rekindling of growth from labour and product market deregulation increasingly lost appeal. As Jos de Beus[23] has argued, governments, "must deal with local constituencies that are frustrated by globalisation or disappointed with the European Way of embedding global freedoms and risks."

It is this political void which Third Way social democrats successfully filled by means of strategy which on the one hand emphasises the possibility of political choice in a global economy while simultaneously stressing the commitment to a stable macroeconomic framework and to a type of organisation of welfare arrangements and labour markets which aims to enable individuals to take part in the productive process rather than providing passive income support. The core element involves the postulate that a specific European Model of Society which a strong emphasis on fairness, solidarity and equality of opportunity can and should be successfully defended in an era of globalised markets. As Jos de Beus argues in this volume, the Third

---

[22] de Beus in this volume.
[23] de Beus, 2000b, p. 1.

Way entails the assumption that the pursuit of fairness is compatible with the principles of allocative and dynamic efficiency.

The main strategy to bring about this compatibility involves the pursuit of competitiveness though technologically advanced production on the basis of highly skilled labour[24]. Put simply whereas the neo-liberal mantra was allegedly competitiveness by means of downward adjustment of costs, and in particular wage and non-wage labour costs, the Third Way conception is one of a highly dynamic economy whose level of productivity is sufficient to allow for a significant element of collective consumption and decent wages without threatening competitiveness. Such a modernisation of European economies requires a substantial investment in the (continuous) education of the workforce together with a reform of product and labour markets in order to promote the development and dissemination of new technologies and products and to stimulate the inactive to re-enter productive activity.

On the macroeconomic side, Third Way politicians do not contest the basic contention underlying EMU, namely that a monetary strategy oriented primarily towards the pursuit of price stability has benefice affects in terms of growth and employment over the long run. In practice the new political climate in Europe has involved a noticeably stronger emphasis on the depressive effects of tight money, based on the experience that previous periods of sharp monetary disinflation have given rise to rather long-lasting drops, in GDP and employment growth[25]. Overall the macroeconomic rhetoric of the Third Way however, is rather more defensive than is the case for the supply side arguments; its main political purpose being to convince sceptical voters that the spiralling inflation and budget deficits of the 1970s are a thing of the past.

In terms of implementation, Third Way strategists, with the exception of the Labour Party again place high emphasis on consultation with labour market organisations and a wider set of relevant interests in the framework of social pacts, both to reduce the possible political fallout from necessary reforms of welfare states labour markets and fiscal spending, and to increase the effectiveness of such reforms.

Although this triple reorientation in the form of activist leftist supply side policies, moderation of monetary tightness and social concertation has its main political basis in social democracy, it has wider support. The growing dissatisfaction with neo-liberalism has only affected wide strata of the electorate requiring also Conservative and Christian Democratic parties, especially in times of floating voters, to withdraw

---

[24]   European Comission, 2000.
[25]   Cameron, 1999, pp. 31-33 and Dyson, 1999.

from their close association with liberalism in order to again re-emphasise older concepts of social solidarity. For example, the Spanish Conservatives have managed to successfully depose the SPOE from government by a Third Way type of platform which exploited the socialists' close association with neo-liberalism. Similarly, the German CDU seeks to wind itself out of the post-Kohl malaise by rediscovering elements of traditional social Catholicism. Although the Third Way's rhetorical emphasis on the politics of mobilisation[26] would suggest polarisation, the political landscape of Europe in the early twenty-first century rather presents the picture of a reorientation whose essence is shared by all the mainstream parties and whose political viability hence would seem less vulnerable to social democratic electoral performance.

The problem of viability instead revolves primarily around the question of the compatibility of old institutions and new preferences. Because the politics of administration[27] dominates the implementation of the new programme, Third Way strategists have clearly pinned their hopes for success on legitimacy through performance instead of legitimacy through participation. Moreover, this choice has been made at a time when the popularity of the EU is at an all-time low. Whereas, according to the EU's Eurobarometer surveys[28], in October-November 1998 54 percent of Europeans held a favourable view of integration, by March-April 2000, only a minority of 49 percent thought so[29]. Simultaneously the share of those believing that their home country benefits from EU membership dropped from 49 percent to 47 percent[30].

As became clear with the disappointing outcome of the EP elections of 1999, social democracy may have to convince the electorate of its ability to perform in the short run if it is to maintain its present position. If problems of falling electoral popularity, growing opposition to structural reforms and disappointing economic performance were to come to a head, the combination of an independent ECB, the SGP, soft coordination and benchmarking and the absence of fiscal federalism will not provide an equilibrium solution. In such a constellation, as during the 1930s, it is likely that governments will be pushed towards solving their conundrums by means of macroeconomic stimulation. There are in principle two institutional outcomes of such a strategy. On the one hand popular pressures on national governments to address the problems of

---

26 See de Beus in this volume.
27 See de Beus in this volume.
28 Source: http://europa.eu.int/comm/dg10/epo/eb.html
29 "Generally speaking, do you think that (our country's) membership of the European Union is...? (a good thing/ a bad thing/ neither good nor bad)."
30 "Taking everything into consideration, would you say that (our country) has on balance benefited or not from being a member of the European Union?"

the domestic economy might exert a push towards the re-establishment of the priority of national politics in economic management. The resulting exchange rate system may look much more like the Bretton Woods system in which exchange controls are argued to have produced sufficient isolation of policymaking from external pressures in order for democratic demands on policy-making and exchange rate stability to prosper alongside each other[31].

The alternative outcome might be to try and restore the primacy of the political on the European level, in the sense of an activist, centralised and discretionary form of economic management aimed at institutionalising a "European Model of Society" which rejects the neo-liberal proposition that competitive pressures will require the eventual adoption of an US type model. How such a EU would look like on the macroeconomic level is much less clear. The only historical precursor would seem to be the stillborn Werner Plan of the 1970s with its emphasis on a European fiscal policy authority, the coordination of European wide wage bargaining with fiscal and monetary policies.

Reflecting the already declining Keynesian consensus of the post 1945 period, the plan envisaged a "centre of decision making for economic policy" which essentially implied that fiscal management was to be conducted at the European level[32]. Although inflation was, as it always has been, a major concern for monetary authorities, the required policies to safeguard price stability were primarily interpreted in a Keynesian framework which assigned the process of wage setting the central responsibility for price stability. Hence, the Werner Plan called for a strong role for the social partners. In essence, the Plan envisaged transferring the tripartite negotiated wage setting which was practiced in many of the member countries to the European level.

The Case Against EMU

The independence of the ECB essentially rests on two sets of motivations. First, EMU rests on a theoretical interpretation which regards government intervention in monetary policy making as a destabilising element. Secondly, creation of EU level constraints on policy-making has frequently served the purpose of strengthening the hand of the executive relative to domestic forces. This section deals with the first set of arguments. The second set will be addressed in sections 5 and 6.

---

[31] Eichengreen, 1997.
[32] Dyson, 1994, pp. 79-83.

The ECB clearly bears the marks of the theoretical revolution in monetary economics of the 1970s according to which monetary management in the long-run only affects the price level and not real variables. Simplifying somewhat, inflation solely is a function of the money supply which is controlled by the central bank. Unemployment, in the standard neo-classical analysis is purely a function of the real wage. Most neo-classical analysis will admit that changes in monetary policy will have short-term effects on employment because nominal wages do not adjust instantaneously. In the somewhat longer run monetary management has no effect on economic activity[33] hence justifying the separation of monetary policies from economic management in general.

The presently most widely accepted analysis of the unemployment problem, the so-called Nickell-Jackman-Layard model (NJL), however, retains a less rigid separation between the unemployment and inflation problems. Starting from the somewhat more realistic assumption of imperfect goods and labour markets, the NJL model assumes the firms' price setting to take the form of a mark-up over wage costs. If the mark-up changes with economic activity the resulting Feasible Real Wage (or labour demand curve) may be negatively sloped. But indications are that the variation in mark-up may be small, so for all intents and purposes the curve can be drawn as a straight line.

---

[33] Admittedly ECB Executive Board member Issing (2000) argued that low inflation promotes growth. The theoretical argument for this remains somewhat unclear. Moreover, such an effect is not assumed to occur in the models the ECB itself uses.

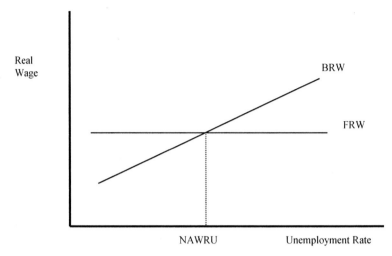

Figure 1: The NJL Analysis

In sharp distinction from the neo-classical view such a horizontal labour supply curve implies that unemployment is not a problem of excessive real wages. The actual level of employment is determined by the intersection of the FRW curve with what NJL call the Bargained Real Wage Curve (or labour supply curve). The bargained real wage curve displays the level of real wages desired by wage earners at different levels of employment. The curve is upward sloping as a higher level of employment will induce a desire for higher real wages. The slope and position of the curve, however, depend on structural features of the labour market, in particular trade unions' strength and militancy, unemployment benefits, minimum wages, and regulations concerning hiring and dismissals. Points on the FRW curve to the right of the intersection with the BRW curve imply escalating inflation as wage earners will try to increase their real wage, and firms pass on higher wage cost into higher prices. Points to the left instead will imply falling inflation or deflation. Only the intersection of both curves – the so called NAWRU (Non-Accelerating Wage Rate of Unemployment) or NAIRU (Non-Accelerating Inflation Rate of Unemployment) is compatible with price stability.

The immediate cause of unemployment hence is the authorities preference for price stability. Indeed as Richard Layard[34] has argued: "The only reason we have unemployment is that governments are using it to contain, or to reduce, inflation". Yet, the solution to the unemployment problem is not to be found in the field of monetary policy. Unless one should be content to live with continuously accelerating inflation the problem can only be solved by means of structural reforms in wage setting resulting in a rightward shift of the BRW curve. Reforms that might accomplish this include shorter duration and less generosity of unemployment benefits, hence increasing the cost of unemployment, reduction of minimum wages etc.

Although the NJL analysis underlies much of the OECD's famous 1994 Job's study and the IMF's analysis, and also has left clearly discernible traces in the EU's Broad Economic Policy Guidelines (BEPG) and Employment Policy Guidelines (EPG), its empirical support is not very strong. The main empirical problem is to identify structural shifts in wage setting which might account for Europe's successive shifts in unemployment. Figure 2 shows the development of unemployment rates in the EU since 1970. Basically unemployment has increased in three consecutive waves, namely during 1964-75, 1979-1983 and in the early 1990s. Although unemployment rates subsequently receded somewhat from the peak of the respective crises, they remained substantially higher after each episode. In the perspective of NAWRU theories this must imply that each of these three periods saw significant structural changes in the process of wage bargaining resulting in a leftward shift of the BRW curve. Yet it is difficult to find the corresponding increase in trade union militancy, more generous provision in terms of minimum wage and unemployment benefits etc. If anything one might in fact argue that especially with the crisis of social democracy and the dominance of right centre governments since the early 1980s structural reforms have gone in a direction which should have lowered the reservation wage and hence shifted the BRW curve to the right instead of the left[35].

---

[34] Layard, 1986, p. 29.
[35] Ball, 1996, Røed, 2000, sec. 2.2, and see also Artis, 1998.

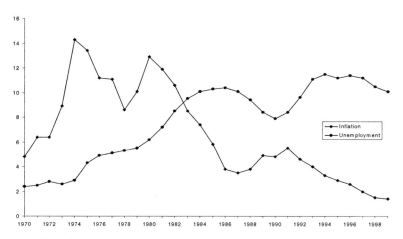

Figure 2: Inflation and Unemployment in the EU (15), 1970-2000

All three episodes of sharply rising unemployment have been characterised by exceptionally tight monetary policies. In 1974 the Bundesbank, soon followed by several other countries, switched to a sharply restrictive stance in order to stamp out inflation. During the second oil price shock such policies were pursued throughout the western world, starting with the FED's turn to ferocious disinflation in the fall of 1978, followed by Britain's Margaret Thatcher in 1979, the Bundesbank in 1980, and French President Mitterrand in 1981-2. The restrictive policies of the early 1990s instead, were not primarily inspired by sharply increasing inflation. Instead the Bundesbank's move to restrictive polices in the wake of German unification was allowed to spread to other European countries given their commitment to the Maastricht criteria of fixed exchange rates and fiscal austerity.

Such a sequence strongly suggests that Europe's unemployment rate, rather than reflecting deep structural features of wage and price setting is strongly influenced by macroeconomic policies. Europe's high unemployment, as compared to, for example the US, is the result of insufficient job creation and not of excessive labour force growth[36]. As Figure 3 shows, both total employment and the total labour force have

---

[36] Cameron, 1999, p. 7 and Collignon, 1998, Ch. 8.

grown significantly more in the US than in the EU(15) since the mid-1970s[37].

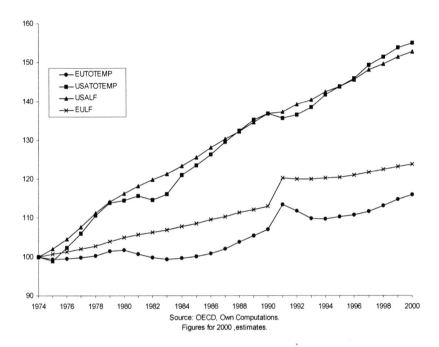

Source: OECD, Own Computations.
Figures for 2000 ,estimates.

**Figure 3: Total Labour Force and Total Employment,
USA and EU (15), 1974-2000** (1974=100)

The empirical evidence that inflation can be reduced with little cost in terms of foregone output is rather weak[38]. Central bank independence and credibility of monetary policy does not seem to reduce the costs of disinflation. Moreover, monetary disinflation has generally stood at the beginning of prolonged periods of low growth and high unemployment[39]. This has been so in the 1970s and 1980s and it was similar during Europe's previous experience with macroeconomic disinflation in the 1920s.

---

37 The jump in European levels in 1991 is due to the inclusion of the former GDR.
38 Micosi and Padoan, 1994; Fischer, 1994 and 1996.
39 Modigliani, 1997.

347

At the same time it is well-known that employment growth shows a strong correlation with GDP growth[40]. GDP Growth and hence employment growth, in turn, is strongly correlated to the investment share, *i.e.* the share of GDP being allocated to investment. Indeed, Colignon[41], Morley[42] and the EU Commission[43] have shown that unemployment and the investment share are strongly inversely correlated. Figure 4 looks at this relation form a slightly different angle, plotting the employment rate[44], which the EU is committed to raise to seventy percent by 2010, and the investment share[45]. Again, the close correlation of the two curves is striking.

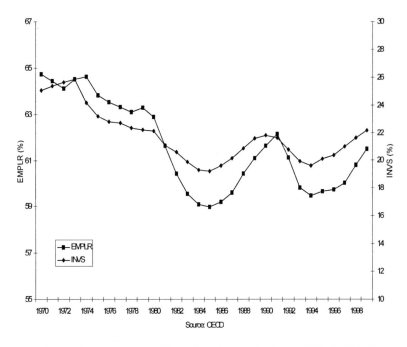

Figure 4: Employment Rate and Investment Share in the EU (15), 1970-2000

[40] Cameron, 1999, pp. 20, 28.

[41] Colignon, 1998.

[42] Morley, 1998.

[43] EU Commission, 1998b.

[44] EMPLR, defined as total employment as a share of the working age population.

[45] INVS, defined as total fixed investment excluding stockbuilding as a share of GDP.

Such evidence together with mounting political opposition to structural reforms that seem to have few effects has again caused doubts to emerge in many quarters concerning the accuracy of the neutrality of money postulate. In contrast to the neo-classical picture which expects full-employment from real wage flexibility at given capacity, the history of employment seems to be not primarily one of the changing relative price of labour but of expanding employment in line with expanding capacity (corrected for productivity growth) and *vice versa*. As was the case in the interwar period when the neutrality of money postulated was adopted to justify disinflation and was abandoned when the combination of tight money and structural reforms proved unable to lead off unemployment, the present phase of low inflation but stagnating growth and employment is again strengthening Keynesian oriented analyses in which monetary management can and does have longer term effects on economic activity currently experience a revival.

The most obvious channel through which monetary policy affects long-term real outcomes is through its influence on investment behaviour and hence on long-term growth and the level of productive capacity. The desired level of capacity private entrepreneurs wish to attain, and accordingly the extent of net (dis)investment, depends critically on the expected rate of growth. Durably higher growth rates will, *ceteris paribus*, imply higher demand for the firm's products and hence the need to durably extend the level of capacity. The overall growth rate of GDP, however, in essence is determined by the sum of private investment decision. It follows that objective factors like current profitability are not sufficient determinants of the level of investment. Indeed if profitability were the core determinants of private investment, Europe's unemployment problem would have been solved already. Deregulation, privatisation, and welfare state reform may very well improve productivity and profitability. However, because they affect in principle all firms in the same way they cannot be a sufficient condition for a growth in aggregate investment. Presently levels of profitability have again become roughly comparable to what they were in the 1950s and 1960s. Investment instead is crucially influenced by expectations about future growth rates. Since growth rates depend on the expectations and accordingly investment decisions of a myriad of independent actors in a market economy, there is no unique, market determined growth rate. Instead expectations concerning growth have an essentially self-fulfilling character; growth indeed being low if the majority of actors expect it to be low and vice versa.

It is on the expectations determining the level of investment, hence the supply side, that the central bank probably has its most decisive impact. It stands in the power of any central bank to terminate an upswing by means of sufficient restriction of credit. Incidental phases of tight policy will, as a rule not affect longer term expectations. Yet, a fundamental change in the policy regime informing central bank behaviour must necessarily have a strong impact on expectations[46]. The long-term nature of Europe's unemployment hence can be interpreted not as the result of primarily structural factors but as the outcome of a downward adjustment of expectations in response to a change in monetary policy regime from the growth oriented outlook of the 1950s and 1960s to the disinflationary outlook since the 1970s[47].

The Case for EMU

At least from a political science point of view, the economic arguments employed to justify the political independence of central banks, would seem rather unconvincing. Inflation in this view results from undue political interference with central banks. By administering a dose of cheap money, politicians can reduce unemployment thereby improving their chances of re-election. The increase in output, however, will only be temporary, the only lasting effect being higher inflation. Freeing the central bank from political influence was hence seen to be economically stabilising and socially optimal. In other words, the dynamics of electoral politics are argued as leading to outcomes which do not in fact reflect the true interest of the voters hence making the independent conduct of monetary policy compatible with the demands of democracy.

Moreover, an independent central bank, so the argument goes, will be able to reduce inflation almost without costs in terms of output because the credibility of the commitment to price stability will induce wage and price setters to quickly adjust to the new nominal framework. Independence and transparency of decision-making, in this perspective are mainly of importance as a means to promote the bank's credibility, *i.e.* to prevent political considerations from invading monetary policy-making. It is questionable, however, whether the political-economic theory on which the ECB is based does, or ever did, provide an accurate account of monetary policy making in Europe.

Apart from the economic objections mentioned above, the main political objection to this view is that it fails to explain why political parties can successfully pursue policies that do not reflect the true interests of the electorate. In this view, the stimulating effects of

---

[46]   Tobin, 1980, p. 19.
[47]   Martin, 2000.

expansionary money arise because inflation reduces real wages. However, since this happens against the wishes of wage earners they will subsequently recover their original wage at which point a higher price level will be the only lasting affect. But, if wage earners are unwilling to trade-off more employment for lower real wages it must remain mysterious why they should choose to reward electorally the party responsible for the short-run boom resulting from surprise inflation[48]. Rather this view should lead to the conclusion that democratic governments have no incentive to engineer surprise inflations because it is not in the interest of the majority of the electorate. Moreover, the independence, which all the national central banks and subsequently the ECB gradually came to enjoy since the 1970s, was granted by governments. Yet, governments according to the standard view have no incentive to do so since it robs them of an instrument for promoting re-election.

The move towards central bank independence, in my view, is best understood, not as an attempt by governments to curtail their own power, but as a commitment technology similar to the external constraint on fiscal deficits of the SGP. The economic crisis of the 1970s and 1980s was not provoked by excessive regulation, welfare states and wages leading to inferior competitiveness but was of a purely macroeconomic nature[49]. The post-war monetary regime that allowed for a stabilisation of positive expectations of growth relied critically on a set of labour market arrangements that successfully contained inflationary pressures despite full employment. The inflationary problems of the 1970s and 1980s were essentially due to the failure of wage setting institutions to provide moderation in a regime in which growth and full employment was essentially assigned to macroeconomic authorities. As labour markets lost the ability for moderation, commitment to the full employment goal was no longer possible. Instead tight monetary policies had to take over the task of stabilising the price level previously played by labour market institutions. Independent central banks hence were a device employed by governments to signal to the labour markets that monetary bail out of excessive wage agreements would no longer be possible, thereby hoping to restore some degree of order in wage bargaining. Put differently, governments did not act against their own best interests but strengthened their hand by making the central bank independent. To be sure, central bank independence was not a necessary device for governments who were willing to take direct responsibility for disinflation, like the one of Margaret Thatcher in Britain. External

---

[48] Leijonhufvud, 1986.
[49] Collignon, 1998.

constraint strategies in the form of independent central banks or fixed exchange rate commitments rather proved attractive for the weaker continental (coalition) governments who at times had strong historical ties with labour[50].

Instead the Keynesian argument for subordinating the ECB to political authorities and for removing the constraints of the SGP rests on different theoretical and historical grounds. It departs from a reading of economic history which attributes the felicitous post-war coexistence of democracy and unparalleled prosperity to the pursuit of Keynesian demand management policies. With ongoing globalisation states are said to have lost their "Keynesian capacity" at some point during the 1970s or 1980s[51]. Handing over the management of monetary policy to an EU-level institution therefore did not imply as such a reduction of the possibility for democratic determination of macroeconomic management. The choice countries faced in actual fact was allegedly between no influence and some influence, however minuscule that may be for small states under a system of simple majority decisions. Because the Euroland economy is much more closed in terms of trade relations than any of its constituent members, EMU might be seen as having recreated the conditions under which democratic politics can again reassert its primacy over macroeconomic management.

However, theoretically this argument rested on treating Consumption and Investment as potentially interchangeable components of aggregate demand implying that a shortfall in investment could easily be compensated for by increased public demand. In practice, such a strategy which intends to replace failing private investment activity with public expansion has been unworkable. Successful economic management, as argued above, has to rest on stimulating instead of replacing private investment activity. Keynesian demand management should be confined to the rather more modest role of mitigating short-term fluctuations or complementing policies aimed at recovering the incentives to invest. Historically, therefore, the role of Keynesianism has been much less essential than commonly assumed.

As Peter Temin[52] has shown in an innovative study of the Great Depression, Keynesian policies were largely absent during that period. Nor was the long post-1945 boom, the alleged high point of social democratic welfare state Keynesianism, characterised by the widespread

---

[50]   Consequently the Labour Government of Tony Blair, in contrast to the Conservatives, held independence of the Bank of England to be a cornerstone of its economic policies.

[51]   Scharpf, 1987.

[52]   Temin, 1989.

use of countercyclical demand management techniques[53]. In fact, such policies were first applied on a widespread scale in the 1970s and the results were not very encouraging[54]. Although in common usage, the term Keynesian social democracy, therefore is somewhat of a misnomer. The role of Keynesianism for the political Left in fact comes close to the role of socialist doctrines pre-1930, which played an important ideological role for maintaining the specificity and coherence of social democratic parties but had only limited value in terms of practical policies.

Moreover, the argument that policy autonomy has been eroded since the 1970s may be less convincing than frequently thought. Capital mobility as such does not erode macroeconomic policy autonomy. As, the policies of larger countries like the US, Japan and Euroland show, under flexible exchange rates capital mobility leaves a quite substantial amount of domestic autonomy[55]. Admittedly, many smaller countries found floating exchange rates extremely difficult to manage. However, this may have been a reflection of a particular labour market constellation and not an inherent trait of flexible rate management. Presently also smaller countries like Sweden and Switzerland, and the UK show that flexible rates may very well be manageable. The UK and Sweden presently belong to the countries with the highest (employment) growth rates whereas Switzerland records unemployment levels substantially below the EU average. The empirical evidence that exchange rate flexibility has negative real effects is weak. Eichengreen and Frieden[56] point out that most studies indicate that "exchange-rate variability and uncertainty have only small effects on trade and investment". Moreover, even if exchange rate flexibility had large real effects, reduction of uncertainty would seem to call for the stabilisation of real effective exchange rates. Given that trade composition and inflation rates differ cross-nationally, stabilisation of real exchange rates calls for nominal exchange rate flexibility. Accordingly, the argument cannot be used in support of arrangements like the EMS or the EMU.

A successful return to the policy practices of the long post-war boom would hence not so much rest on the recreation of a Keynesian policy capacity at the EU-level but would rather hinge on the possibility of returning to the labour market arrangements of that period. Yet, such a turning back of the clock would seem both unfeasible and undesirable.

---

[53] Matthews, 1968, Crafts and Toniolo, 1996, pp. 11-12, Vandenbroucke, 1999, p. 41.
[54] Jonung, 1999 and Notermans, 2000.
[55] Notermans, 1997 and Oatley, 1997.
[56] Eichengreen and Frieden, 1994, p. 7.

Admittedly, at the beginning of the twenty-first century, the labour market constellation is rather different from the 1970s. First, as Stefan Collignon[57] has pointed out much of the inflationary wage pressures of that decade resulted from increased wage indexation and union militancy informed by the desire to protect real wages from increasing price rises. Inflation, in other words, tended to produce institutional and behavioural outcomes conducive to even higher inflation. After more than two decades of disinflation, those pressures, however, seem to have largely disappeared. Secondly, the emergence of so-called social pacts in many European countries has restored, albeit in different forms, a workable compromise between labour market organisations and governments[58]. Third, the last twenty-five years have witnessed at times profound changes in labour market, welfare and trade union legislation, many of which have been conducive to wage moderation[59].

Yet, it seems doubtful that these changes provide a sufficient foundation for European wage bargaining institutions to play the role of major safeguard against inflation assigned to it by the Werner Plan. First, the arrangements of the 1950s and 1960s depended on a degree of deference of the rank and file to both union and party leaderships that is inconceivable with the presently much more diversified and individualistic labour force and electorate. Secondly, trade unions are increasingly less representative of the workforce giving a disproportionate voice to older male workers in regular employment, public sector employees, and in many cases, also to pensioners. Third, the new social pacts have never been tested in periods of tight labour markets. Moreover, in many countries the "national emergency" of having to satisfy the Maastricht criteria drove the partners to the bargaining table. As the present resurgence of labour market conflicts in Italy and the high Irish inflation rate show, there may be at least some doubts whether such pacts can be relied on sufficiently in a setting of high growth under a single currency.

Accordingly, market forces will have to provide for a substantial part of the price discipline formerly provided for by bipartite or tripartite forms of negotiated wage setting. It is in this context that the single currency, economic integration and a substantial part of the neo-liberal legacy of the 1980s will play a crucial role. The elimination of the instrument of devaluation implies that the employment consequences of excessive wage increase in individual Member States will be felt immediately; an effect further strengthened by the increased competition

---

[57] Collignon, 1998.
[58] Rhodes, 2000 a, b.
[59] On Britain see Rhodes, 2000c.

resulting from the single market programme[60]. Finally, more flexible labour markets will play an important role in stabilising any growth regime to the extent that they increase the pressure of the unemployed on the wages of the employed and increase the incentives of the unemployed to enter the labour market.

Put differently, whereas the neo-liberal doctrines of the 1980s interpreted flexibilisation and labour market deregulation as sufficient for rekindling growth, such measures should perform the role of protecting macroeconomic growth strategies from the inflationary trap into which West European societies fell in the 1970s. The market replacing microeconomic policies of the 1950s and 1960s generally were justified by a quest for equality but came at the price of isolating large segments from market pressures, and hence directly contributed to the emergence of high unemployment rates as a mechanism for containing inflation. Indeed, leftist parties especially have developed strongholds in a large and well protected public sector; a sector moreover that frequently was at the forefront of inflationary battles. At a time, however, when the frequently undemocratic process of centralised wage setting with little input from local employers and employees and little concern for local conditions, is a thing of the past, also the Left will have to accept that market forces must play a much larger role in ensuring the compatibility of local autonomy with a growth-oriented policy regime. Contrasting the "undemocratic" EMU with the allegedly democratic regime of the post-war boom overlooks that this regime was founded on a rather undemocratic corporatist form of labour market relations, plus – one might add – an excessive influence of interest organisations on economic policy-making which left parliament with little more to do than rubber stamp decisions. If indeed the removal of class and group privileges is an ideological constant of social democracy[61], then this will also have to apply to the privileges extended to the social democratic clientele of blue collar and public sector workers when protection from market forces becomes an obstacle to full employment.

Similar to an independent ECB, the Stability and Growth Pact may perform the useful role of protecting growth-oriented policies from inflationary pressures. Admittedly, there are no good economic reasons for setting the maximum allowable deficit at three percent of GDP and accumulated debt at 60 percent of GDP. As the examples of Belgium and the US in the 1980s and 1990s show, high deficits are not necessarily inflationary.

---

[60] Cameron, 1999, p. 25 and European Commission, 1998a and Salvati, 1997.
[61] Grundwertekommission, 1999, p. 20.

Nevertheless, the SGP may constrain the growth of public sector wages and employment, providing a partial substitute for market pressures in the private sector and thus may prove a valuable supporting element in a policy of price stability. Finally, within the framework set by EMU, adherence to the SGP may make relaxed monetary policies more likely for three reasons. First, because adherence to the Pact may help convince the ECB that there is little imminent danger of inflation. Second, as argued above, the SGP will be politically difficult to implement, and an appropriately stimulating monetary policy will therefore be crucial to its success[62]. If it involves the danger of driving especially large EMU countries into excessive deficits the ECB may wish to think twice about the political wisdom of monetary restriction. Third, if the ECB were to behave overly excessive the room for counter-cyclical stabilisation which the SGP provides may not be ample enough to satisfy increasing political demands for job creation thus possibly provoking intense political pressures on the ECB.

The Need for an Accountable ECB

In the absence of high overall growth rates, European (social democratic) governments will be forced to seek the solution to the unemployment problem in politically contentious strategies of redistribution of labour – including strategies of real devaluation – and increasing earning inequality. Moreover, low growth rates also reduce the effectiveness of job growth strategies relying on wage differentiation. The demand for the services produced in a low wage sector will depend on the overall growth rate, *i.e.* on the expansion of higher and middle incomes. Put differently the lower the overall growth rate the higher the degree of wage differentiation would need to be in order to have the same employment effect. Finally, to the extent that the ECB, like the Bundesbank, comes to interpret rising growth and falling unemployment as advance indicators of inflation, none of the present strategies practiced by social democrats will have a chance of succeeding. If the ECB sticks to its view that a growth rate of around 2.5 percent is the maximum compatible with price stability, then any strategy for lowering unemployment must fail as long as the macroregime remains unchanged.

Given the economic dislocation caused by high inflation strategies which created unemployment for the sake of price stability were politically feasible in the 1970s and 1980s. The crucial problem, however, is that central bank independence proved an important device for European governments, not due to an inherent inflationary bias of

---

[62] Allsopp and Vines, 1998.

democracy, but due to a peculiar historical situation marked by disintegrating wage-setting institutions. As inflation has been conquered low growth and mass-unemployment has become the major concern for European policy-makers. In this climate, the ECB is being and will continue to be questioned about the broader effects of its policies. Do they support or hinder deficit reduction? Do they obstruct or promote the process of welfare state reform? Do they promote moderation by rewarding wage agreements at or below productivity growth with invest-ment stimulating interest rate policies? It is this new political climate which also explains the European fascination with the US model of a central bank which is statutorily committed to also stimulate output; a fascination, by the way, which is not confined to European social democrats as the recent discussion between President Duisenberg and members of the European Parliament shows[63].

Hiding behind the neutrality of money doctrine may not be a feasible strategy for the ECB. European voters not only expect low inflation but also lower unemployment from EMU[64], an expectation also explicitly fuelled by the Commission[65]. Even an independent central bank cannot afford to systematically neglect the political preferences of society concerning the inevitable (short-run) trade-off between price stability and growth and employment, if it is not to jeopardise its legitimacy. For the ECB, this aspect would even seem more important because it is a new institution that still has to gain the confidence of the European public. On the other hand, one might argue the ECB is in fact less constrained because the threat of changes in central bank legislation which faced all NCB's who were too much at odds with society's preferences is much less potent. Yet, it would seem doubtful that its legal independence would allow the ECB – supposing it were willing to do so – to ignore the problem of legitimacy.

The ECB has started its operations in a period where confidence in European institutions is at an all-time low. Moreover, the ECB itself apparently has not managed to convince the sceptics amongst the EU population of the value of the single currency project. On the contrary, support for the euro has gone down since its inception from 64% in October-November 1998 to 58% in March-April 2000[66]. Moreover, in the three EU members not participating in the single currency the

---

[63] EP, 2000.
[64] Kaltenthaler and Anderson, 2001.
[65] Cameron, 1999, p. 27.
[66] "What is your opinion on each of the following statements? Please tell me for each proposal, whether you are for or against it. There has to be one single currency, the euro, replacing the (national currency) and all other currencies of the Member States of the European Union."

possibility of observing EMU in operation seems to have done nothing to strengthen support. On September 28, 2000, 53.1% of Danish voters rejected EMU membership in a referendum called by the social democratic government. In the UK and Sweden support for the euro in March/April 2000 was considerably lower than in the Eurobarometer survey of October/November 1998 – the last one before the start of the single currency – namely from 36% to 22% in the UK and from 44% to 38% in Sweden[67].

Profound national disaffection with the ECB may hence lead to political pressures for withdrawal, a threat that did not exist for NCBs. Moreover, for many European policy makers, EMU was part of the project of promoting ever-closer political integration. If the ECB, due to excessively tight policies, proves to become an obstacle to further integration and to the popularity of national politicians, it may easily lose support also at EU level. Finally, although Governing Council members do not take directives, national governments have the power of appointment, which may lead to the emergence of national frontlines within the ECB. Irrespective of the power of appointment, it is not unreasonable to assume that Governing Council members are influenced by the preferences, debates and interpretations of their national context. A lack of legitimacy in several national contexts may hence paralyse the ECB.

The ECB, however is singularly ill-equipped to address trade-offs between objectives. A core problem is that the ECB itself has set the objective of 0-2% inflation[68]. Discussing the trade-offs between price stability and output would involve the ECB in an eminently political discussion for which it obviously has no legitimacy. As Otmar Issing[69] himself has remarked: "The more clearly and narrowly the mandate is defined the easier it will also be in a democracy to justify the delegation of powers to an unelected body, since value judgements and trade-offs concerning several unranked objectives should naturally remain the preserve of democratically elected representatives".

In this constellation, the present institutional set-up of the ECB would seem to be an obstacle to an open discussion about European macroeconomic policy priorities. One solution, as proposed by Favero *et al.*[70], would be to remove the goal independence, and have the EP or the Council define a statutory goal for the ECB. With a politically imposed objective the discussion about trade-offs, from the perceptive of the

---

[67] Source: Eurobarometer 50, 53.
[68] Favero *et al.*, 2000.
[69] Issing, 1999, p. 8.
[70] Favero *et al.*, 2000.

ECB, becomes a technical one as it revolves around the question whether and to what extent measures to stimulate output are compatible with the goal. An alternative solution would be, in analogy with the FED, to include the concern for economic activity and employment amongst the objectives, hence forcing the ex ECB to explicitly discuss the trade-offs involved in its choices.

The problem with both solutions is the one familiar from the debate about the EU's democratic deficit; namely, that Europe lacks a demos. To engage the ECB in an open discussion about trade-offs assumes that there is a political majority in Europe for a specific set of policies and that the electorates in Euroland will consider decisions legitimate which have been taken by a majority but possibly against the votes of all the representatives of the respective countries. This obviously is not the case, at least at present. Indeed, as the Danish EMU referendum of 28 September shows, electorates especially in small countries may be willing to forego economic benefits because of the fear of becoming dominated by an EU majority. National elections still are the elections that count in the eyes of the voters – just witness the turnout for the 1999 European Parliament Election (55%). Accordingly, the national parliaments rather than the EP are the institutions which first and foremost are invested with legitimacy in the eyes of the electorate[71]. The Eurobarometer surveys conducted in October-November 1999, for example, show that a more important role for the EP is only supported by 43% of the population. However, the same survey also showed that 52% support joint decision-making in the fight against unemployment[72].

Given the presence of different views and priorities and the absence of a truly European debate, majority decisions may lack legitimacy in some countries with the risk of making monetary management the object of national conflicts. Indeed the peculiar structure of the ECB as an eminently political institution hidden behind a technical façade may have been largely motivated by this lack of a demos. The goal independence of the ECB obviates the need for a political discussion at EU level about goals and de facto delegates this to the ECB. To avoid discussion about trade-offs the ECB itself desperately hides behind the long run neutrality of money doctrine, insisting that only structural reforms in labour markets, welfare states, taxation systems etc., can promote growth and employment. Moreover, the opaque set-up of the two-pillar strategy with its numerous indicators and reference values serves to give the ECB the necessary flexibility to remain in touch with

---

[71] Kielmansegg, 1996.

[72] Unfortunately, Eurobarometer does not inquire about support for joint decision making in fiscal policies.

the priorities of the surrounding society without having to discuss its policies in such terms.

Judging from the first two years of operation, one gets the impression that the ECB, with the best possible intentions, has tried to form opinions about euroland preferences concerning trade-offs between output and exchange rate stability within the framework of low inflation. In practice, it seems well aware that pursuing policies which conflict with the preferences in European society, *e.g.* a hard currency policy with no regard for output, or excessive caution concerning inflation, will not be conducive to gaining the legitimacy in the eyes of governments and the public on which its long-term survival depends. Hence, the relatively relaxed stance it has taken, at least up to mid-2000. But as the partially controversial discussion about the euro/dollar exchange rate has suggested, it is questionable whether such a solution is feasible and desirable as soon as hard choices will have to be made.

In the longer run the legitimacy of the ECB and hence its ability to function satisfactorily may depend on the development of such a demos. Admittedly, the single currency itself has already done much to stimulate a true European-wide debate. Moreover, the present social democratic dominance in Europe, especially since the Lisbon summit, has contributed towards debating and forging *European* priorities for economic management. As yet, however these are but first steps.

CHAPTER 13

Are Third Way Social Democrats Friends or Enemies of European Integration? A Tocquevillean Tale on the Politics of Administration

JOS DE BEUS

Introduction: A Case of Restrained Love of Europe

Are Third Way social democrats friends or enemies of European integration[1]? I will argue that their strategy of joint modernisation "with a smiling face" does not express pan-European civic friendship. Third Way social democracy cannot afford any frivolity in the reconstruction of the nation-state which is, after all, its only remaining bastion. It does not wish to preside over a swift and hazardous completion of a federal state based on European identity, European popular sovereignty and a European constitution. But Third Way politicians and policy makers are not hostile either. They must deal with local constituencies that are frustrated by globalisation or disappointed in the European way of embedding global freedoms and risks. Yet the Third Way does not champion re-nationalisation. It does not share the disbelief in monetary union of American economists and diplomats. Nor does it endorse the common market as the ultimate internationalist ideal. And it does not expect to gain much by sclerosis or indeed a break-up of Europe. Instead, Third Way social democracy attempts to transcend contradictions between friends and enemies of European integration by recasting the conditions of permissive consensus.

[1] I am grateful for the help of Frans Becker, Uwe Becker, Dick Benschop, Laurent Bouvet, Jet Bussemaker, René Cuperus, Michael Dauderstädt, Pieter van Dijk, Daniel Drache, Cees van der Eijk, Richard 't Hart, Anton Hemerijck, Arend Hilhorst, Otto Holman, Kees van Kersbergen, Frédéric Michel, David Miliband, Philippe Pochet, Philip van Praag, Paul Scheffer and the editors of this volume.

The old permissive consensus implied that political parties responded to a public opinion that was not interested in European integration while granting national representatives a wide discretion in order to take supranational measures that would foster common survival and economic growth[2]. The new permissive consensus implies that social democrats – the strongest movement in European politics today notwithstanding the Christian democratic lead of 53 seats in the European Parliament – face a public opinion that is suspicious. The national audience, notably the Danish one with a vengeance, demands fine-tuning in the sense that European regulators should take the affected interests of the broad middle class seriously. Negotiators know that each of them faces specific limits, beyond which European agreements will upset the local state of mind. Hence, the necessity and workability of two-level consensus, that is, consensus within domestic constituencies *and* consensus amongst state elites. Third Way social democrats endorse the ideal of European perpetual peace, the goal of the European knowledge society and the methods of two-level governance – limited use of public force, spreading and sharing of authority, networking by diplomats and other professionals. The expected pay-off is neither the rise of a quasi-national community that allows for good governance from Brussels, nor the formation of European majority rule, but rather accommodation and the rise of a European consensus democracy. This is a mixed order of intergovernmental and communitarian elements. It is also an alternative to American associational democracy, English majoritarian democracy and French republican democracy. It protects and promotes egalitarian policies and results in a broad sense, such as decent jobs for all[3]. To put it more provokingly: the Third Way group of European architects is fulfilling the Christian democratic promise of European universalism after the collapse of Christian democracy. Its image of an enlarged European Union with many and partly rival layers and clusters of cooperation looks like a greater Germany or Holland rather than a greater Britain or France[4].

This is a speculative claim which I will spell out as precisely as I can. First, the Third Way can be seen as a coherent public philosophy which is distinctively progressive and compatible with the tradition of social liberalism and reformism. To see it as the triumph of neo-liberalism or as the exhaustion of ideology does not make much sense – compare with

---

[2] Lindberg and Scheingold, 1970, p. 41 and Hix, 1999, pp. 134-7.
[3] Guéhenno, 1999, pp. 145-193 and Lijphart, 1999, pp. 42-47.
[4] Middlemas, 1995, Scharpf, 1999, Van Parijs, 2000.
I do not side with a specific Nederlandocentric view which implies that any European community will resemble Dutch political tradition. See Heldring, 1965 and de Beus, 1999a, 1999b.

Callaghan (2000). The Third Way discourse in European parties suggests an end of the end of social democracy, the recent era in which social democrats either opposed popular right-wing policies of austerity or took responsibility for such policies without preserving votes[5].

Second, I point at a specific Third Way view of European integration. This view entails both more than functionalism – Monnet's method – and less than federalism. Its terms of agreement entail the offensive answer to the challenge of the American new economy – the opening of public utility, the capital market and corporate governance – and the role of public policy in achieving full employment, updating social rights and combatting social exclusion in an extended market economy. Other points of agreement are expansion of the European sphere of peace and the rule of law through the studied and controlled abolition of Middle Europe, the initiative of heads of state as a mode of democratic guardianship, and new methods for taming rivalry between nation-states and regionalism through open coordination.

Third, I argue that European unification since 1997 neither culminates nor unravels. It proceeds in a constellation of issues, concepts and realignments which is special, in the sense that the old French-German axis is running out of steam and new alliances between large and small Member States surface. Current unification, supervised by, respectively, the Netherlands, Luxembourg, Austria, Great Britain, Germany, Finland, Portugal, France, Sweden and Belgium – the latter two countries acting as Council's Presidents in 2001 – coincides with the convergence of social democratic parties towards Third Way positions with respect to reform. This includes both economic and partly non-economic policies, such as defence and immigration.

Fourth, I will briefly discuss the objections against my account from the viewpoint of comparative political studies. Does it neglect external constraints, opportunism related to various state interests, splits within and between centre-left parties, and contingencies like the Stability Pact after the war in Kosovo, the free fall of Kohl and the strange rise and fall of Lafontaine and Strauss-Kahn[6]? I argue that the comparativist picture of entrenched institutional variety and Third Ways of transformation is incomplete[7].

Fifth, I will turn to the political limits of the Third Way from the viewpoint of democratic internationalism. Both the focus on economic

---

[5] Kitschelt, 1999.

[6] Their brief moment of collaboration concerned the Euro 11 group. See Oskar Lafontaine and Dominique Strauss-Kahn, "Euro dwingt nieuwe verantwoordelijkheden af", *NRC Handelsblad*, 30 January 1999.

[7] Merkel and Thierse in SPD, 1999; see Giddens, 2000, p. 31.

policy – towards full employment – and activated intergovernmentalism – against the extreme right – of left leadership may temporarily solve the perennial problem of clashing political cultures, yet they do not settle European reform, democracy deficit and enlargement[8]. Furthermore, they do not appease the federalist movement, such as Fischer's famous call for a centre of gravity which speeds up political union[9].

The closing section concludes on further research. I try to explain both European and domestic strategies of social democratic modernisers as adaptation to an emergent model of democracy called audience democracy[10].

But before take-off I need to clarify the notion of political primacy. Restoration of political primacy seems to colour the willingness of Third Way social democrats to welcome globalisation and individualisation, and to revise post-war conceptions of citizenship accordingly. Political primacy in the sense of democratic management of the transnational economy, the topic of this entire volume and collective effort of research, is the core of the project of social democratic innovation since the late 1990s. It is also controversial, since conventional wisdom suggests that the private sector is driving change in Europe and that the politics of left-wing governments follows[11].

Politics from Mobilisation toward Management

Democrats tend to question the privileged position of multinational corporations: managers can not and must not rule society. Social democrats like to talk about political renaissance after the winter of neoliberalism. Europe watchers – a third, partly overlapping species – conclude that European integration "after Maastricht" remains a case of high politics. Still, the present significance of the primacy of the political cannot be taken for granted. Surely, the idea itself should never suggest that politics is the sole foundation of social order, that political action is the highest stage of the good life, or that the will of the people may overstep moral and legal constraints, such as basic human rights.

In a broad sense political primacy means that a free and sovereign people determines its own destination by means of a constitutional balance of power between several branches of government that promotes cooperative conflict between political parties for the sake of the public interest and the legitimate rights of citizens. A more narrow view

---

[8] Siedentop, 2000.
[9] Fischer, 2000
[10] Manin, 1997.
[11] Dunn, 2000, *Financial Times*, "Europe Reinvented", 19 January 2001.

of political primacy suggests that representative parties exercise authority and effective control in the government's relations and interactions with powerful corporate actors in the market economy. The broad view stresses the need for a well-ordered political system in an ever closer union of European peoples; the narrow view stresses the need for popular credibility in economic policy coordination.

Today, the dominant social democratic interpretation of European primacy of politics seems to entail some well-considered convictions – compare Padgett and Paterson (1991) on the previous period. First, European commitment does not depend anymore on social democratic conditionality in the sense that social democratic leadership would reject European unity even if it does not perform adequately according to conditions such as full employment. Although European commitment is still weaker than national commitment, it has become more deontological and conventional. New rounds of integration may be optional and should be optional as well from the viewpoint of democratic self-control. Old forms of the *acquis communautaire,* such as the Common Agricultural Policy, may well be obsolete and up for reform. European intervention may be less workable than national intervention in the foreseeable future, thus requiring special attention and justification. Still, the European community of fate is given in the eyes of new generations of social democrats. To put it more concretely: non-membership of the EMU and criticism of the policies of agencies such as the ECB are no longer considered symptoms of basic disagreement and scepticism.

Second, competent management of domestic crises and troubles under the sign of social justice is vital for social democratic parties but also unthinkable without European assistance. Governments wrestle with similar problems with respect to unemployment, poverty, crime, ethnic intolerance, congestion, imbalance of investments in infrastructure, and the erosion of political authority and central control. The obvious priority of such issues does not preclude a European orientation anymore.

Third, the willingness to join European initiatives and projects is connected to precommitment to rules and understandings which block the return to war, aggressive nationalism and protectionism. It is also connected to a European model of society that differs from an American model. Social democrats reject the idea of a market society or private society in general[12]. They support the idea of a property-owning democracy, in which individual and collective property rights are spread and the social function of capitalism is maximised through the regula-

---

[12]   Rawls, 1999, pp. 457-8.

tion, limitation and compensation of market power[13]. A modicum of peaceful rivalry with the United States in the area of science, technology, trade and mass culture is inevitable in this perspective.

Finally, the gulf of electoral victories in the 1990s signals both the necessity and the opportunity of social democratic renovation. On the one hand, voters in many Member States are fed up with neoliberal policies of the centre-right. They want the centre-left to restore the public domain without repeating its mistakes of the 1970s such as mis-management of inflation. On the other hand, simultaneous incumbency and the nearly unanimous support for monetary union and enlargement by social democratic leaders create a window of opportunity for deepening cooperative efforts in economic matters, such as solving Europe's jobs crisis, as well as non-economic matters, such as European citizenship and geopolitics in a wide sense[14].

However, there seem to be two views on the nature of progressive partisan politics in the current European setting. I will call them the politics of mobilisation and the politics of management[15]. Mobilisation implies the introduction of party politics in the European arena, while management implies the insulation of European policy from party politics. According to the first view, social democratic parties should speed up convergence in order to both establish positive integration and a truly European electorate, committed to the progressive values and principles in the European treaties. As the New Right commanded the international combat against bureaucracy, stagflation and moral permissiveness in the long 1960s, so the Third Way tries to command international struggle against unstable and destabilising world markets; the deprivation of millions of outsiders inside and outside of Europe, and the cult of greed and entertainment of the long 1980s. The Third Way is a collective noun for decisive action at the intersection of the national public sphere and the European one. It includes a shift towards the Party of European Socialists (PES); the purification and revival of European Parliament (EP); entrepreneurship of a duly reformed European Commission in the fight against unemployment and, more generally, in the construction of Europe's social union; politicisation of the European Council according to a left-right scheme; the introduction of economic policy coordination, tripartite bargaining and checks and balances in the EMU; an invitation to Europe-wide debate on social democratic proposals about governance and the quality of life; militant humanitarianism and cosmopolitanism; and active confrontation with market funda-

---

[13]   Meade, 1964, 1975.
[14]   Notermans, 2000, pp. 242-249.
[15]   See Cox, 1997, p. 63.

mentalism and the extreme right. In short, the convergence of national economies and policies will be followed by the convergence of democratic politics towards a symmetric Union that not only includes managers, bankers, farmers, and top civil servants but also unions, workers, consumer organisations and political activists[16].

According to the second view, social democratic parties should focus on improvement of management and the output of European consultation and bargaining, rather than on mobilisation and input[17]. There is no escape from prudent pragmatism "from above" in complex and interconnected issues with respect to the liberalisation and re-regulation of markets, experimental reform and re-calibration of welfare states, adaptation of European procedures and budgets, and the preparation of enlargement. On the one hand, national voters give priority to instant protection of their security and standard of living. They seem to support good governance on the basis of professional competence and compromise, rather than participation and contestation in transnational epistemic communities. On the other hand, most governments and vested interests in the Member States prefer minimal rules for market competition and policy competition to grand designs of classical federalism. In this constellation, the middle ground between *laissez faire* and social engineering can only materialise by innovative ideas and methods. Social democracy does not have to fall back on the method of Monnet and a Delorsian overstretch of that method[18]. Nor does it have to rely on the ploys, deals and dialectics of intergovernmentalism[19]. Instead, it should abolish waste and corruption in European programmes; cultivate transnational networks that soften intergovernmentalism; articulate the moral nature of its long-term goal of the robust middle between unity and diversity, and welcome experiments that exploit subsidiarity. Perhaps the best recent illustration of such left-wing politics of policy is the introduction of benchmarking – score-boards, peer pressure, mainstreaming – in employment policy[20].

Both views try to outline an alternative to the European tradition of Keynesianism and corporatism[21]. One might argue that both views are compatible or that the history of social democracy is full of oscillation

[16] Sassoon, 1997a, pp. 755-777, Sassoon, 1997b, Beck, Van der Maesen and Walker 1997, Cuperus and Kandel, 1998, Giddens, 1998, pp. 129-153, Dauderstädt, Gerrits and Márkus, 1999, and Giddens, 2000, pp. 122-162.
[17] Scharpf, 1999, Ferrera, Hemerijck and Rhodes, 2000, Laffan, O'Donnell and Smith, 2000 and Telò, 2000.
[18] Grant, 1994 and Ross, 1995.
[19] Moravcsik, 1998.
[20] Goetschy, 1999 and Pochet and Goetschy, 2000.
[21] Yergin and Stanislaw, 1999, pp. 302-330.

between the bet on civil society and the bet on central government[22]. I will assume, however, that one of these views will be preponderant in the contemporary pursuit of the primacy of politics. Which view, then, is the viable one in case the Third Way discourse prevails not only in Great Britain, but also defines the very momentum of European social democracy and European integration in the new century? As an idealist coming from one of Europe's small countries and founding Member States, I am inclined to assess the dynamics of Europe since 1997 – the victories of Blair and Jospin – from the viewpoint of freedom-as-attainment, that is, the politics of mobilisation. As a realist in political science, however, I would like to examine the Third Way contribution to European integration in terms of freedom-as-routine. Hence the politics of management.

Such politics seems an unintended consequence of pacification[23]. The long European peace discourages active citizenship and class confrontation while encouraging a soft mode of political leadership that maintains an ambitious standard of rights and well-being of the many. As the phrase "politics without enemies" of Third Way thinkers demonstrates, there is no reason to think that the Third Way's correction of neoliberalism can avoid adjustment to the politics of management. Indeed, during the 1990s the gap between the nation-state as site of mobilisation and the European Union as site of management has been closed because of the parties' turn towards "governance", a mode of public policy marked by the limited use of hierarchy – particularly competition policy and public inspection – abundant use of civil society – delegation, market incentives – and strategic use of policy networks and policy cultures[24]. This turn coincided with a turn from mass organisation of loyal members and constituencies to permanent media campaigns for catching floating votes[25].

So the European centre-left's rediscovery of political primacy may very well reveal a Tocquevillean irony. It was Tocqueville who recognised the tranquillity and conservation of the social democratic combination of equal access to political power, absence of legal privileges and high rates of social mobility. He also foresaw the rivalry between American and Russian superpowers. But he could not determine its result, nor could he imagine the liberal coordinates of the perfect state as "an immense and tutelary power, which takes upon itself alone to secure their [the citizens'] gratifications, and to watch over their fate", indeed

---

[22] Dryzek, 1996.
[23] Guéhenno, 1993, 1999, Manin, 1997, Van Doorn, 1996, 1999 and Cooper, 1999.
[24] Mayntz, 1999.
[25] Walter and Dürr, 2000.

as an "absolute, minute, regular, and mild" power[26]. Could this, then, be the notoriously unknown "telos" of social democratic movement and European movement since the end of war? This is the philosophical question which guides the following exploration of the Third Way in Europe.

The Current Renovation of the Left

In general, the Third Way is no new method of electoral campaigning, no ratification of neo-liberalism, and no logarithm for steering clear of the free market and the universal welfare state. It is yet another mixture of liberalism and socialism which allows for social-liberal package deals and alliances. Furthermore, it is the product of protracted party modernisation, legitimisation of governmental decisions, policy learning and exploiting a competitive edge in representative democracy[27]. I will first define the first principles of the Third Way and then try to spell out its main strategies for reform.

The political thought of the Third Way is quite surveyable. It is nicely captured by Plant's phrase of "supply-side citizenship[28]". First, the principle of liberty boils down to personal autonomy and self-reliance in the market economy. This entails submission to the civic rules of moral responsibility and social virtue. The market is updated as a sphere of peaceful and productive expression of individuality and sociability. As political participation and associational life belong to the citizen's repertoire, so do entrepreneurship and releasing human capital. Market participants in civil society do much more than occasional bargain-hunting. They abide by the legal and conventional rules of local concern with contracting parties, decent and honest transaction, joint venture in case of collective interest, and social initiative on the basis of ability to pay.

Second, the principle of equality is reformulated in terms of pluralism and meritocracy. Each member of the political community should enjoy the basic resources and capabilities which are needed to survive and flourish in an advanced market economy. The emphasis here is on standards for the social minimum, health, and schooling, *i.e.* start qualification, employability. Further, there should be equality of opportunity from start to finish, outlined in procedures and plans for anti-discrimination and checks on asymmetric power relations. Finally, the citizen in specific social-economic positions should receive renu-

---

[26] Dahl, 1985, Elster, 1990 and Ankersmit, 1997.
[27] De Beus and Notermans, 2000.
[28] Marshall; 1997, Blair, 1998, Giddens, 1998, 2000 and Gamble and Wright, 1999. See, Plant, 1999.

meration according to desert, while also bearing the costs of failing plans and efforts at her or his own expense. A partly general, partly contextual demarcation of private – collective and individual – responsibilities is called for. However, special projects for inclusion are needed to attain a stable equilibrium between improvement of qualities and circumstances via self-help, private insurance included, social security or public assistance.

Third, the principle of solidarity is translated into reciprocity. Each citizen ought to have access to full communal participation and to social entitlements. This is often connected to a broad concept of work in which family care, volunteering and public service are seen as sensible and profitable activities on a par with conventional formal labour. The flipside of these advantages are obligations to work according to fitness, training, in particular free training at the expense of the taxpayer, expected contribution to public goods, or – slightly more vaguely – promotion of social cohesion. The formula "no right without respon-sibility" means that those willing to share the economic benefits of social cooperation in a wide sense have a corresponding obligation to make, if so able, a personal and relevantly proportional productive contribution to the community in return for these benefits[29]. Government may moralise here in the name of the nation as long as public policy itself is instrumental to "empowerment", that is, the education of each individual citizen towards independence, say, teaching everyone to fish and assign a ration of fish to all of those who never get a perfect command of it. Another requirement for credible moralism is that the government protects an ethos of equal concern and respect via its legislation and administration within the rule of law. A merely punitive approach of the unemployed is prohibited.

Finally, the principle of democratic rationality suggests that this entire pursuit of fairness is compatible with the principles of procedural justice and democratic legitimacy – constitutionalism – but also with the principles of allocative and dynamic efficiency – competitiveness. Third Way thinkers contend that the trade-off between conflicting political goals must be shaped in permanent public deliberation under the sign of civic dialogue, decentralisation, deconcentration, subsidiarity and proper democracy in all contemporary forms of groups and organisations, bringing in all stakeholders. Further, they argue that sound democratic policy which facilitates and stabilises freedom, equality and solidarity for all – the social investment state of Giddens or the active welfare state of Vandenbroucke – makes a substantive net contribution to steady

---

[29] White, 1999, p. 168.

capitalist development, at least a contribution that dominates the neoliberal one.

These principles are supposed to inspire the countervailing power of social democrats against the new right, the new monopolists, such as owners of mass media, and the new conservative internationalism, the so-called Washington consensus. But the Third Way wants to be more ambitious than that. It presents itself as the sole embodiment of left-wing offensiveness, based on principled and practical policies.

First, social democracy should welcome globalisation as the primary mode of economic growth in a regime of economic freedom and value pluralism. The Third Way returns to the old belief in technical and material progress. Its growth policy adds two new dimensions. On the one hand, growth should come from the new technology – computing, internet, biotechnology – and the new business and distributive services. Small and medium-sized firms are first-best here. On the other hand, growth should be qualitative. It minimises ecological degradation, particularly by innovation of methods of production and management. It strikes a balance between private and public goods, toil and leisure, old and new risks, as well as competition and local community. The point of economic growth is the widening and deepening of human freedom and development.

Second, social democracy should restore the weight of full employment and the labour ethic. The goal of employment policies is to be individuality-friendly in a number of ways. Full employment concerns men and women as well as young and old citizens. It entails part-time jobs, as a device to balance contractual obligations to one's employer and family obligations. It may include temporary exit – prolonged learning – and frictional unemployment – unemployment benefits with an efficient replacement rate – as the unintended consequences of upward mobility of the employable worker. It takes the quality of jobs into account, that is, work as a source of self-respect, income and a career – minimum wage, decent labour conditions – as well as the relevant comparisons between the open sector and the sheltered sector, public services included. Last but not least, it is a non-inflationary rate of employment.

Third, social democracy should level basic opportunities, while accepting outcome differences in terms of possession, life-style and prestige. The "celebration of creativity, diversity and excellence"[30] is about individualisation, restricted in a dual sense. Social democrats must abolish extreme differences of income and wealth. On the one hand, poverty should be eliminated with a policy-mix of safety nets, fiscal and

---

[30] Blair and Schröder, 1999.

moral promotion of acceptance of jobs at the proper level of skills, schooling, facilities of child care, sanctions such as workfare, access to social services without the poverty trap, and urban renewal against segregation, ghettos and no-go areas. On the other hand, the super-rich should pay wealth taxes, while exit-options such as living abroad and gated communities, should be discouraged.

Fourth, social democracy should strengthen the public sector in a series of coherent and market-conform reforms which buttress national competitiveness. Public finance entails a structurally balanced budget, lower micro and macro levels of taxation, relative to the recent European past, a shift towards consumption taxes, simple direct taxes and ecological taxes, and, more generally, political control of public expenditure and the tax base. Macroeconomic policy focuses on low interest rates, moderation of wage costs, reduction of labour time, flexible labour markets, investment in the sector of education and the new economy, and public-private partnership in national projects, *i.e.* new transport. Microeconomic policy implies differentiation of the wage structure, an extension of the market scope, privatisation and quasi-markets in the public sector, competition policies, and active labour market policies. Recasting of the welfare state means an innovation of pensions, social security, social assistance, health care, housing, education, and transport which combines universalism and selectivity, while introducing financial incentives to deal with problems of adverse selection, aggregate risk aversion, moral hazard, asymmetric information, natural monopoly, incomplete contracts and externalities. A distinctive element of public sector reform is an overhaul of bureaucracy in the fight against organised crime, the depravation of the urban public domain and family breakdown. Notermans rightly refers to this entire programme as "liberal social democracy", a mixture of restrictive macroeconomics and market-supporting micro-economics (see Notermans in this volume).

Fifth, social democracy should reinforce its commitment to the open society and humanitarian mission via a wide range of campaigns and measures. These include, among other things, rational control of the influx of labour migrants, well-ordered hospitality towards political refugees, incorporation of communities of migrants – language courses, special programmes for migrant employment and migrant entrepreneurship – regulation of global fair trade, development aid on the condition of good governance, participation to peace-keeping operations, and regional stability pacts. A special component here is the attention for public ordering and surveillance of global financial markets.

Finally, social democracy should promote a reform of the political basic structure for the sake of inclusive citizenship and strong democracy. Giddens calls this strategy the "democratising of democracy"[31]. This reform entails, among other things, social pacts, regional autonomy, interactive policy-making, the legal position of ethnic minorities and women, party finance, non-governmental associations, the institutions and practices of representative and direct democracy – accountability, powers of parliament, referenda – and personal liberties and responsibilities.

At the level of principle and rhetoric, the new social democracy seems to prefer political mobilisation to political management. Indeed, the Third Way's proverbial transcendence of crossroads conceals one of the most difficult ideals in political history: to create a democratic republic of citizens in a "great society" (Adam Smith) without borders. Giddens' future Europe is neither the federal state nor the free market zone, but a form of extended multi-level governance which protects and promotes peaceful regionalisation, close cooperation across Europe and the United States, and global control of global problems[32]. Does Giddens really turn Rousseau on his head? Or does he formulate a conception of European citizenship which is unstable, floating somewhere between national fellow-feeling and global humanity[33]?

The Third Way View of Steady European Integration

Some, such as the British commentator Jonathan Eyal, have argued that the Third Way list of principles and strategies is a national agenda, indeed a British one[34]. This is plainly wrong, given the many Third Way practices of continental left government *avant la lettre*, such as in the Netherlands and Denmark, and the resonance of the Third Way in continental public debate. If right, it would have been a grave tactical mistake of New Labour to even think that it can regain European clout by Anglocentrism.

A much more interesting consideration concerns the danger of false Europeanism. The mantra of party meetings is that European unity is a least-cost solution to the international problem of collective action in the spirit of international justice and solidarity. The fact of the matter is that social democratic politicians display sophisticated strategies of defection in the spirit of patriotic self-centeredness, thus reinforcing the cursed inefficiencies. Too many tax expenditures to please foreign investors, too many illegals, too many noisy airports, and so on. For example, the

---

[31] Giddens, 1998, p. 70 and Giddens, 2000, p. 61.
[32] Giddens, 2000a.
[33] Hoffmann, 1998 and Miller, 2000.
[34] Eyal, 1999, 2000; see Marquand, 2000.

book *Aufbruch* (1998), written by the leading Third Way ideologue in Germany, focused on German recovery and did not include one single line on the future of European integration after German reunification[35]. The Third Way does indulge in the mantra, particularly at summits of party leaders, in conferences of the PES and during campaigns for the EP. At the same time, it seems to discourage – sanction is too strong a term here – strategies of unilateralism, like cut-throat fiscal competition. The Third Way view of European integration in the new century is a small set of general commitments to the domestication of state rivalry and national rivalry[36]. I will present it in the same order as the new domestic creed of the Third Way.

First, globalisation requires a decisive European response. It includes consolidation of the EMU and Europe's new currency; elimination of lags and gaps in Europe's informational revolution, such as diffusion of the internet; and strategic inclusion of Eastern Europe. The last of these issues is literally vague at the edges. There is uncertainty and disagreement within and across social democratic parties about the prospect of inclusion of Russia and Turkey. The most important considerations are common security, internal unity of Union policy, constitutional democracy, the European model of society and the *acquis*. These considerations pull in different directions[37]. The other issues are less controversial, although similar vagueness can be noted with respect to the moment of entry to monetary union of the United Kingdom and Sweden, American-European arrangements about trade policy and monetary policy – Lafontaine's challenge – and the compromise between Anglo-American and continental modes of corporate governance – the place of shareholders, capital markets, trade unions and councils of employees.

Second, Europe's unemployment problem requires special coordination of macroeconomic policy and employment policy[38]. The Third Way does not suggest an immediate revision of the Stability and Growth Pact. Instead, it promotes a pragmatic reading of formal rules for stabilisation plus a procedure of benchmarking that produces common self-binding within the constraints of national diversity and the mixed

---

[35] Hombach, 1998.
[36] There is a specific research dilemma here. Either you rely on PES-sources – like proposals of the socialist EP faction – which are empty. Or you rely on official government sources from Member States where social democrats are in power, knowing that these sources reveal national interests and priorities of the state apparatus. Reliable sources like the controversial Blair-Schröder document (June 1999) are rare.
[37] Attali, 1997, 2000.
[38] Mulgan *et al.*, 2000.

European order, particularly negotiated conversion of Commission guidelines into national plans of action, Council recommendations and public audits.

Third, Europe's egalitarian alternative concerns not only the growth of employment but also (i) an implicit agreement not to fall back on social dumping, (ii) policy harmonisation and convergence on the basis of the Amsterdam protocol on social policy, the United Kingdom included, and (iii) application of benchmarking to the area of poverty reduction – twenty million less poor people[39]. Although the Third Way could vindicate concrete proposals with respect to minimal expenditure on social protection and the accessibility of public services, such proposals still have not reached the European stage of agenda-setting and choice[40]. The idea of a Social Union of core states is recurrent, but opposite to the Third Way's idea of the widest possible membership.

Fourth, modernisation of the public sector in Europe's Member States requires tax harmonisation, as well as close cooperation and division of labour in the special area of defence – a rapid reaction force. The Third Way is rather reluctant in widening the budget limit of the European Union and introducing a European fiscal tool. The accession of countries like Poland warrants revision of the Common Agricultural Policy and the funds for regional restructuring and cohesion, rather than more direct European intervention.

Fifth, true European power and responsibility require a broadening of the agenda beyond the Single Market project of liberalisation, privatisation, and competition policies. This agenda concerns European justice, migration, world trade, African development, and global environment. European interparty dialogue has been missing or failing here in the past. Each party sticks to its favourite complaints and demands. As far as I can tell, the Third Way's contribution remains nil here.

Finally, the constitution of Europe needs some breakthroughs with regard to the accountability of the central bank, the social dialogue, the quality of European Parliament, the balance of power between this parliament, the Council of Ministers and the European Commission, the size, national weights and voting procedures of the Commission in an expanded Union, the authority of foreign policy, variable geometry, and the relationship with ordinary citizens. The Third Way is particularly strong in taking stock of all dilemmas and options here. So far, it has not made one single authoritative proposal with some public appeal or force.

---

[39] Vandenbroucke, 2000.
[40] Bussemaker, 1999, Scharpf, 1999; and Van Lancker, 2000.

What should we conclude from this broad survey of the Third Way vision of Europe? The SPD is critical:

A first cursory survey does show that, apart from employment policy and a somewhat less rigidly monetarist approach of monetary policy, the perceived space for social democratic intervention is smaller than the seldom explicitly stated but often mentioned reference to the "necessity of a European coordination of policy" suggests. Hence, it does not come as a surprise that such a European space is still not sufficiently explored from the viewpoint of social democracy, neither in most social democratic manifestos nor in recent joined memoranda and white papers. Here we envisage a crucial need for programs and actions for social democratic parties and governments alike[41].

Others concur with this negative assessment, which seems to point at a European social democracy deficit[42]. Such scepticism is confirmed by the PS contribution to the Socialist International. This long-expected answer to the Blair-Schröder document is more interventionist, but it is also old wine and rather trivial where European integration is concerned.

However, this entire assessment seems to follow naturally from the premise of the European politics of mobilisation. From the viewpoint of the politics of management, it is hard to deny that the Third Way has an explicit vision on the future of the nation-state in the European Union as well as on the need for intergovernmental activism based on Third Way consensus of policy-makers, civil servants and experts. The advantages of European political consultation are similar to the well-known advantages of national economic consultation: stability of institutions, action according to long-term goals, binding agreements, mutual under-standing of inconvenient facts, and common responses to commonly defined problems[43]. I will now turn to the practical impact of social democrats on the European front.

After Amsterdam: Third Way as European Middle

Although 1997 was the year of the Treaty of Amsterdam, it was also the year in which a new generation of social democratic leaders came to power in the largest Member States. Schröder's surprising triumph a year later only confirmed the transfer of power from the right to the left in most Member States. The period between 1997 and 2000 shows

---

[41] SPD, 1999, p. 17.
[42] Robinson, 1998, Becker, Cuperus and Kalma, 1999, Becker and Cuperus, 2000, and Dauderstädt, 2000a and 2000b
[43] According to Visser, quoted in Pochet, 1999, p. 26.

neither stagnation – such as the late 1960s and 1970s – nor innovation – such as the 1980s and early 1990s – but ongoing accumulation based on the complex yet familiar pattern of domino dynamics – more countries – and disequilibrium dynamics – more sectors[44]. For example, the workload of the European Parliament today is three times the volume of legislation at the height of the internal market programme[45]. Clearly, someone has to play the lead of Sisyphus, as Hoffmann demonstrated so brilliantly[46]. In this particular period it is the revisionist-of-revisionism's turn.

The period itself is brief. Yet it covers interesting developments and, occasionally, exciting events. I call to mind the provisions on common combat against unemployment in the Amsterdam Treaty (articles 125-130) and the guidelines for employment policy in 1997; the first-round admission of countries to EMU, the appointment of the first central bank's president and the establishment of the Euro 11 Council in 1998; the dismissal of the Santer Commission by the EP, the dialogue on macroeconomic policy between ministers, commissioners, social partners and the ECB as well as the revival of the Standing Committee on Employment, the precarious results of the social democratic parties in the European elections, the Stability Pact for the Balkans, and the final decisions on the medium-term union budget, migration policies and enlargement in 1999; and, finally, the bilateral boycott of Austria by fourteen Member States, the Intergovernmental Conference on Institutional Reform, the Lisbon agreements on the New Economy as well as the Nice agreements on the distribution of power between large and small countries in 2000.

I will not discuss all these changes in full detail. In order to determine the social democratic influence and nature of the current round of integration, it is sufficient to concentrate on a pair of dimensions, namely the general substance of recent European policies and the general procedural quality of European decision-making.

Substantive European integration entails the following areas:

- recognition of employment as a distinct goal of European policies in the integrated market economy of Europe, such as an employment rate of minimally 70% in 2010[47];

---

[44] Emerson, 1998, pp. 38-43.
[45] *Financial Times*, 7 March 2000.
[46] Hoffmann, 1995.
[47] Scharpf, 1999, pp. 158-160.

- prudent interest rate manipulation by the ECB, that is, preservation of price stability and, occasionally, little stimulative boosts[48];
- continued macroeconomic convergence within the framework of the Stability and Growth Pact, resulting in extended membership;
- consolidation of public expenditure and taxation at lower levels of national social equilibrium within new European rules against tax cuts which would increase the public deficit, inflation, the public debt – in particular, unsustainable finance of public pensions) and inefficient welfare systems[49];
- coordination of national macroeconomic policies for the sake of reduced gross costs of unskilled and low paid labour as well as enhanced incentives of labour training;
- speeding up the expansion of information technology and communication technology by 2010 – internet in schools, basic public services, European networks, European research, small firms;
- recognition of the special place of public services – equality of treatment, quality, and continuity in electricity, post, broadcasting, heath care, and so on – in European competition policies[50];
- continued social policy coordination, such as health and safety regulation, social rights of non-national residents, participation of the United Kingdom, and anti-discrimination[51];
- coordination of active labour market policies, targeted at employability of workers as well as the reduction of youth unemployment, structural unemployment, and under-employment in the service sector;
- consolidation of European Works Councils;
- formation of a European Rapid Reaction Corps in 2003, deployed during humanitarian crises on European territory in cooperation with NATO;
- accession of Eastern European countries as a new element of both the European mission and united integration; and
- politicisation of European identity, especially the principles of personal liberty, non-discrimination, protection of minorities, the

---

[48] Cameron, 2000, p. 33.
[49] *Financial Times*, 22 May 2000.
[50] Scharpf, 1999, pp. 161-169.
[51] Ferrera, Hemerijck and Rhodes, 2000, ch. 4.

378

rule of law, liberal democracy and market freedoms, as in the Haider controversy.

The procedural dimension to recent European policy-making entails the introduction of benchmarking in social policy, consultation and broad guidelines in macroeconomic policy, the extension of dialogue between representatives of state, capital and labour, and the intensification of summit diplomacy with regard to social protection in a broad sense – poverty, education, and so on. The compromise of Nice (December 2000) adds a number of reforms of the Union's political system to the list: limitation of the size of the European Commission and rotation of commissioners after 2005; updating the voting weight and procedural blocking power of larger Member States in the European Council, extension of qualified majority rule, facilitation of enhanced cooperation between subsets of Member States, and expansion of the European Parliament's size.

It is obvious that a number of long-standing demands of the Left do not appear in this survey of European initiatives. I simply refer here to harmonisation of fiscal policies, pension policies, migration policies, energy policies, development and aid programmes, and, last but not least, proposals for a quasi-national European constitution. Nevertheless, the quality of the fit between the Third Way vision of Europe and recent European integration seems reasonably strong[52].

First, the emergent European view of Third Way social democrats does surface in the performance of European authorities (discourses, plans). Second, European projects and methods since the late 1990s are partly, yet significantly, different from the ones in the 1980s, in the sense that today negative integration gets reinforced by positive integration. This transformation of European neoliberalism cannot be fully understood without taking specific social democratic commitments and concerns into account: parties matter. Third, ideas about the national optimal policy-mix and the optimal facilitating and constraining role of supranational policies do converge. The former includes rule-bound macroeconomic stabilisation in a setting of opened and liberalised markets; consensual wage moderation and wage differentiation; modes of taxation and social transfers that are employment friendly and dynamically efficient; legalisation of basic rights of flexible workers, and unorthodox methods of tackling poverty and social exclusion[53].

Prominent scholars such as Scharpf, Streeck and Rhodes note that the current European regime does not satisfy the old requirements of

---

[52] This is also the outcome of recent academic studies of sector experts, like Goetschy and Kenner, as well as by partisan sector studies, such as Leadbeater, 2000.

[53] Ferrera, Hemerijck and Rhodes, 2000, ch. 3.

European Keynesianism, corporatism and well-ordered social and political union. This observation reinforces my point that the ongoing modification of neo-liberalism does not serve the goal of a European welfare state but boils down to soft coordination of a partly open-ended restoration of welfare states at the national level, marked as they are by specific weaknesses: French youth unemployment, British poverty, German and Dutch inactivity, and so on. The role of de-politicisation in this process of coordination is constituent rather than incidental[54]. This time, conventional European pragmatism and the usual spill-over of overlapping new views of public policy from the level of national elites to the level of European elites go in tandem with a basic change in political culture – compare Green-Pedersen, Hemerijck, Van Kersbergen (2000). On the one hand, most Member States, including the United Kingdom and France, turn to consensual institutions and practices rather than majoritarian ones. Such institutions and practices support joint responsibility between political agencies in government and in civil society as well as divided responsibility[55]. On the other hand, most Member States recognise the structural consensual nature of European institutions and practices, such as broad coalition-making. European integration operates through diffusion of power rather than concentration of power[56].

Third Ways, or the Objections from the Point of View of Comparative Political Science

Comparative political scientists may criticise my analysis by questioning the empirical adequacy and determinacy of the concept of Third Way.

A first objection is that it does not discuss the relevant counterfactual. What if Major, Juppé, Kohl/Schaüble and other European conservatives had still been in charge since 1997? Would not the European logic of interdependency and the force of internationalisation have prompted a similar change of the policy-mix? In some areas, such as European foreign policy, defence policy and trade policy, this might well have occurred. But in the crucial area of economic and social policy the objection seems less plausible. In some cases, such as Spain, one can indeed argue that the success of the conservative party and its Third Way platform illustrate the counterfactual. Reasoning must be a bit dialectical here. By their overshooting towards neoliberalism in the period 1982-1996, the Spanish social democrats paved the way for an

---

[54]   Ferrera, Hemerijck, Rhodes, 2000, p. 84.
[55]   Lijphart, 1999, pp. 1-6.
[56]   Lijphart, 1999, pp. 42-47; compare Maclay, 2000

effective conservative response in terms of a Third Way social contract. In other cases, such as in the United Kingdom, the conservative party was too divided and constrained to invent a more relaxed and generous view of European integration[57].

A second objection raises the issue of opportunism, driven by divergent state interests and producer interests. Opportunism – instead of principle – either explains the Third Way road to Europe or it causes the coming dilution of the Third Way coalition of Member States. This objection seems to make sense in a number of cases, such as Schröder's silent abandonment of the Blair-Schröder document after a series of local election defeats, Blair's wavering with respect to British entry in EMU, the resilience of state subsidies to leading national firms, the inability to overhaul agricultural policy, and the inability to formulate a credible strategy of enlargement with the proper set of extra outlays, internal reforms and final dates. It is hard to deny the role of opportunism, defined as relentless and concealed pursuit of self-interest. On the one hand, no social democratic project for Europe will succeed if it neglects vital interests of the affected countries, especially the protection of unskilled compatriots in trans-European labour markets. On the other hand, opportunism may easily undermine the present early stage of positive integration. The objection itself is, of course, a general one. I see no special reason for thinking that Third Way social democrats are more opportunistic than other European politicians. It has been argued that Jospin and Schröder differ from Mitterand and Kohl. They do not see European integration as a moral cause and a matter of war or peace. Perhaps so. Yet such a line between older and younger leaders seems to arise in all European political movements.

A third objection points at division and the risk of schism in centre left parties. In particular the French social democrats do not give up their view of state planning, nor can they do so in the French setting of coalition politics and public sector syndicalism. More generally, many social democrats, even the Dutch, have aired criticism of the Blair-Schröder document. This objection is obvious. If social democrats fail to overcome national difference, then the Third Way in the European Union will collapse, while leaving behind nothing else than international convergence toward supply-side policies. But will they fail? The practical distance seems much less than the rhetorical distance, even in the French case – privatisation. The role of the rank and file in European social democratic parties is much reduced: the age of schism seems

---

[57] de Beus and Notermans, 2000 and Young, 1999.

gone. Further, there are no major Left parties waiting in the wings to capture the pivotal position of social democrats[58].

A final objection brings in the role of luck. What if the present rate of economic growth decreases, the monetary authorities cannot define a unified and credible approach, scandals of corruption spread, or Christian democrats recover? The best answer to this objection is, of course, that political scientists or strategists can neither bank on luck nor eliminate it.

Fischer's Response, or the Lim⸱⸱s from the Point of View of European Politics

Third Way politicians are prone to postpone public debate on European political order and to bypass the whole issue of "effectiveness versus legitimacy". They either welcome soft convergence by means of benchmarks or accept the gradual strengthening of the European Council at the expense of the European Commission. The preparation of internal reform in Nice has been old-fashioned, that is, bureaucratic, secret and dominated by concerns about national prestige. Fischer, the German Minister of Foreign Affairs and leader of the German Greens, responded forcefully to this practice. He offered a new federalist design with a vanguard of Member States, a written constitution, a directly elected European president, and bicameralism – a House of national members of parliament and a Senate, directly elected. Similar proposals were made by Third Way academics, such as Beck, but never by prominent Third Way social democrats.

Indeed, the social democratic response to Fischer's proposal has been lukewarm and national throughout. The French questioned Fischer's integrity and consistency. The British proposed a reinforced national base of European representation. The Dutch supported commissioner Verheugen's case for Europe-wide referenda, while also supporting the British case for a new parliament of members of national parliaments[59]. There is to date no authoritative statement of social democratic leaders of government, ministers, parliamentarians and commissioners about the integration of a European bill of rights, enhanced cooperation between subsets of Member States, enlargement, and internal reform. Most leaders of social democratic parties seem to agree on a prominent role of the European Council from the point of view of

---

[58] See on all these issues the special issue of Revue Socialiste 1999, Chambers, 2000, Crowley, 1999 and Desportes and Mauduit, 1999.
[59] Chevènement, Védrine, Blair, 6 October 2000, Blair and Aznar, 13 June 2000 and Melkert, 9 October 2000.

representative democracy. It is unclear whether Schröder's recent call for a formal arrangement of the competences of European, national and regional layers of the executive branch of government modifies this overlapping consensus on the agenda-setting primacy of leaders of national governments.

From a political point of view, then, one may try to argue that Third Way politics and policies represent false democratic internationalism. They are conducive to recession, massive unemployment, a structurally weak exchange rate of the euro *vis-à-vis* the dollar, the dominance of shareholders in European mega-corporations, the frustration of candidate Member States in Eastern Europe, as well as poor countries in Africa, political alienation and strengthening of the extreme right, sclerosis of the European apparatus or a new differentiation between federalist Member States and non-federalist ones.

I will not discuss each of these critical considerations. Some of them sound familiar in the long history of left-wing rejection of reformism as well as the more recent one of stage two of monetary unification. Others are much more specific, both theoretically and empirically[60]. It is sufficient to note that the dominant politics of management pulls social democratic parties into different directions. On the one hand, it makes them extra prudent and alert as to the timely perception of mistakes and endemic failure. If, for example, balanced budgets would vindicate a return to the Galbraithian disequilibrium between public squalor and private wealth, then ministers such as Brown (United Kingdom) and Eichel (Germany) will change their policy-mixes. On the other hand, the new intergovernmentalism of Third Way social democrats cannot provide the constitutional balance and civic commitment which are needed to control the above mentioned dangers of European fragmentation.

Concluding Remarks about Two-Level "Audience Democracy"

This chapter distinguished two views of the primacy of politics, gave an account of Third Way principles and strategies as a coherent and egalitarian programme at the national and European level, constructed a suitable fit between Third Way modernisation and European integration since 1997, and addressed some important objections with regard to the viability of the Third Way approach to European social democracy.

Both the supporters and the opponents of the Third Way agree that the return of social democracy boils down to modernisation as response to major changes of the political environment, in particular, globalisa-

---

[60]   *The Economist*, 2000 and Notermans, 2001.

tion and individualisation. Political scientists discuss the relative weight of external and internal factors. My contribution in this ongoing debate is a specific thesis. Both the Third Way and the progressive activism of European heads of state – guidelines on employment, humanitarian intervention, the boycott of the Haider-coalition in Austria, the new economy, comprehensive membership of Eastern European countries – can be seen as a way of coping with the circumstances of democracy in an era of perpetual peace. The match between national Third Way projects and European equivalents, if any, will follow the two-level avoidance of partisan passion rather than its climax.

Social democracy faces a dual phenomenon, namely steady improvement of steering performance and continuous electoral volatility, as well as recurrent dissatisfaction[61]. Social democrats contributed to the improved record of core states in terms of economic growth, employment and price stability compared to previous decades. Yet the Dutch PvdA gained its first victory rather late, in 1998, the Labour Party got into trouble in by-elections partly because of its leader's goodbye to the state of grace, and the German SPD was defeated in a series of regional elections – only to be broken by the party finance scandal of former Chancellor Kohl and the christian democrats. In the 1999 elections for the European Parliament all social democratic parties lost except for the PS of Jospin, who seems to mix anti-neoliberal rhetoric with pragmatic reform of state capitalism. Further, measures like public burden and expenditure increases and interest rate cuts are implemented by stealth, while other measures like social pacts engender depoliticisation[62]. What is going on?

The Third Way indicates the transition from the mass party of the post-war era to the elite party of today, tied to the state and the public at large rather than to organised interests and distinct constituencies. An élite party is driven by career politicians, media experts, spin doctors and think-tanks in its pursuit of credibility in the eyes of floating voters. Such a party's power to fight rival parties, to lead the nation and to overhaul public policy is more limited than the mass party's power. Electorally, an elite party is more vulnerable than the mass party ever was, which may account for its obsession with internal control.

The context of this change of the party system is pacification. The main features of democracy in the shadow of war were: industrial revolution, emancipation, moral leadership, mobilisation of the working class, overcoming class polarisation, celebration of work and the jobholder, hierarchy as organisational principle, the planning state, na-

---

[61]   Pharr and Putnam, 2000; Bentley *et al.*, 2000
[62]   Rhodes, 2000, p. 180; Ferrera, Hemerijck, Rhodes, 2000, p. 84.

tional solidarity, active citizenship and thick community. Democracy in the light of peace approximates a different ideal type. Its features are: informational revolution, globalisation of production and communication, possession of rights, consensual leadership, governance of the interests of the middle classes, including most employees, containment of poverty and segregation, celebration of shopping and the consumer, bargaining and deliberation as the dual principle of organisation, the facilitating of state (soft law), national security, voter sovereignty – the citizen as client – and thin community. As Elster put it: "modern societies are safer and bleaker than their traditional counterparts. They are safer because fewer threats are made and carried out, and bleaker because fewer promises are made and kept. People are less violent, but also less helpful and cooperative. In addition bonds of altruism and solidarity may also be weaker"[63].

How must this trend be assessed from the viewpoint of progressive conscience and conviction? Will the Third Way interpretation of the idea of citizenship and the role of the state boil down to a new primacy of politics, a triumph of socialism, or a final acceptance of the primacy of economics and law, a triumph of liberalism? According to authors like Katz and Mair, leaders of established "people parties" have become divorced from internal principals – members, activists – and external principles – voters. They share common interests in maintaining their monopoly of representation and consequently undercut competition through "cartellisation". Cartel parties marginalise, overwhelm or coopt challengers[64]. This view makes sense of the recent wave of corruption scandals, which affect social democrats until this very day, *i.e.* Mandelson, Schleusser, Strauss-Kahn. Yet it overrates the harmony of parties and party coalitions and underrates the dynamics of regular partisan competition. For instance, it is hard to see French cohabitation or the alliance of the German social democrats and Greens as an intended or functional cartel.

According to Kitschelt, the disappearance of a radical socialist alternative to capitalism as well as the eroding acceptance of patronage politics have made party leaders more dependent of the real success and quality of their leadership and programmes, while also making them more sensitive to voter desires. Difficult trade-offs become routine[65]. This view seems more plausible, although it neglects the dangers of hollowing out party associations – chequebook membership, lack of debate – and osmosis of state bureaucracy and party oligarchy.

---

[63]   Elster, 1989, p. 284.
[64]   Katz and Mair, 1995 and Mair 1999, 2000.
[65]   Kitschelt, 2000.

According to Hobsbawm, the Third Way is the continuation of political markets by other means. The very triumph of inclusive consumer society engenders the decline of social participation, collective action and the public sphere; selection of pseudo statesmen; depoliticisation of the young, and minority rule in the oldest democracies: "I fear that the more politics is depoliticised and privatised, the more the democratic process will be eroded. Politics is becoming something run by minorities and, as in Italy, it ends up being perceived as not very relevant to the real lives of people. This is not a good thing for the Left, or for public life"[66]. This view rightly assumes a link between social and political participation, between republicanism and social democracy (active citizenship), and between reflexive modernisation and individualisation, for instance, the rise of television and the transformation of parties into campaign machines[67]. However, Hobsbawm fails to explain why non-English speaking activists should accept an ongoing European self-colonisation with respect to American leadership in politics. Nor does he show why the Third Way mixture of politics of mobilisation – renewal of ideology – and politics of administration – governance without enemies – must be a halfway house.

We need to study the new politics as a stable system with logic and consequences of its own. We need to explain why social democrats are forced to follow certain rules of the game and at the same time to correct its deficiencies with respect to proper representation, effective provision of public goods and distributive justice. This is not the paper to analyse that new system or to solve the general conundrum of political stability *and* discontent in most durable democracies. Our contribution is the following speculation about four rules of the game in well-pacified democracy.

First, the going concern of elite parties is mass protection rather than mass mobilisation and mass experiment. The electorate is accustomed to a high and stable standard of law, to the internal plurality and partial incompatibility of legitimate public goals, and to the complexity and partial inertia of public policy and social order. It loathes meddlesome government, it restricts total mobilisation to periods of national threat, and it permits only local experiments subject to the rule of law and freedom of science. The conservative nature of mass protection makes it unlikely that radicals will get elected or that reformist government will realise a unified vision of the future, social ideal or grand design.

Second, partisan government does not rule in an interplay with the legislative and judicial branches but rather with all political powers, that

---

[66] Hobsbawm, 2000, p. 116.
[67] Bennett, 1998; Putnam, 2000.

is, with the civil service, organised interests, mass media and public opinion. Politicians belong to professional factions of eligible managers of the state apparatus. Voters belong to an audience of spectators who monitor the personality and style of leadership: applauding, booing, creating waves of alertness. Interactive democracy alias direct communication between government and public dominates the older mechanisms of direct democracy and parliamentary democracy[68]. Old parties do have some options in attracting new electoral constituencies without scrapping old ones. But they cannot afford to loose electoral control. Hence, the formation of sophisticated campaign teams and the resigned acceptance of the massive exit of ordinary party members,

Third, intractable conflicts – if any – are solved by means of consensus. Even majoritarian democracies converge towards practices such as broadening the public domain – joint responsibility, proportional group benefits – and dividing the public scope – veto rights, group autonomy. The conventional wisdom that majority rule is the only viable device for effective and fair decisions dies out[69].

Finally, cases of sclerosis generate small crises. Politics does not simplify social choice anymore. It wrestles constantly with the complexity of issues due to the plurality of stable ways-out, contingency, the significance of timing, and the pattern-preserving force of previous success. In the new democratic governance there is no place left for traditional crisis in the sense of an apocalyptic moment of basic purification of society in the face of decline and anarchy. There remains, however, the danger of stagnation in settings of rough equality of power and institutionalised veto. This is pre-empted by massive diffusion of reflexive consciousness of potential or recurrent frictions and difficulties, leading to the agonising kind of self-critique and reappraisal which is needed for timely recognition and solution of new social and constitutional problems[70]. We may add here that the 1980s debate on post-socialism illustrates this function of a "sense of crises" rather well.

Third Way coalitions seem to play this particular game of audience democracy at both the national and the European level. They manage the business of all stakeholders instead of serving the vanguard's cause. They define publicness in terms of mass media coverage. They cultivate the art of wheeling and dealing. Certain feats of arms come to mind here, such as Clinton's balanced budget, Blair's devolution, Jospin's labour time reduction and Schröder's tax reform. And they thrive on occasional crises.

---

[68] Manin, 1997.
[69] Bellamy, 1999 and Lijphart, 1999.
[70] March and Olsen, 1995, Scharpf, 1997 and Pierson, 2000.

All this gathers a lot of opposition, indifference and hate as well. Partly this is the ritual reaction to social democratic authority and its propensity of crisis management, partly this is a novel phenomenon that indicates a lack of habituation to domestic democratic peace – France, Germany, United Kingdom. The Netherlands is one of the few European countries where social democrats cultivate the art of politics as administration. But even in this particular case older notions about political primacy survive and a major part of the social democratic constituency continues to demand a prominent role of national government in the economy, a constitutional framework of European politics as well as a strong voice of ordinary members in party organisation.

CHAPTER 14

Welfare Reform, Social Citizenship and European Integration

David PURDY

Throughout Europe, governments are redesigning their welfare and social security systems in response to domestic and global pressures. The focus of reform varies from country to country: retirement pensions in Italy, disability benefits in the Netherlands, welfare-to-work and family policies in the UK. But a common concern is the need to promote or accommodate greater labour market flexibility, whether with respect to wages, hiring and firing, working hours or working practices. My aim in this chapter is to examine these developments in the light of two rather different concerns: the ideal of social citizenship, once celebrated as the proud achievement of the original welfare state and still, I suggest, a potent source of ethical and political inspiration; and the process of European integration which, because of the unique character of the European Union as a confederation of semi-sovereign nation-states, forms a crucial front in the struggle to build a viable system of global economic governance.

In the first section, after briefly analysing the social relations of work in contemporary capitalist societies, I describe the Anglo-Saxon approach to work-welfare reform, which is widely admired as a response to "welfare dependency". In the second section, I review the concept of citizenship, noting the ways in which modern citizenship differs from its ancient and medieval predecessors, and examine the proposition that the social dimension of citizenship associated with national welfare states is threatened by the emergence of a global economy. In the third section, I consider the national and European strategies that might be adopted to counter this threat, and argue that the so-called "logic of globalisation" is, in fact, the institutionalisation, on a supranational scale, of neo-liberal ideology and is by no means beyond the scope of political control. At the same time, in the final section, I criticise "realist" accounts of the relationship between welfare reform and global constraints for their lack of social vision and suggest a

pragmatic "middle way" between orthodox welfare-to-work programmes, on the one hand, and Utopian proposals for a universal Basic Income, on the other.

From Welfare to Work via the Third Way

In the world – or worlds – of welfare capitalism, as in all civilisa-
tions, the work involved in reproducing human society – from day to
day, from year to year, or across the generations – takes a variety of
social forms: paid employment, on a full-time or part-time, permanent or
temporary basis; self-employment, whether as a fee-earning contractor,
working proprietor or cooperative partner; unpaid domestic or voluntary
work; and non-monetised forms of production such as subsistence
farming and local exchange and trading systems (LETS). The social
product too consists of a variety of different kinds of things: marketed
commodities, public goods, net additions to (or subtractions from) the
stock of "social and environmental capital", and human beings themselves, both as biological organisms and as social individuals. At the
very least, therefore, in analysing the economy, we need to distinguish
between the *business sector*, in which profit-seeking firms employ
waged labour to produce commodities; *the public sector*, in which
government and other public agencies employ waged labour to provide
public goods; the *household sector*, in which individuals and members
of families or other cohabiting groups provision and care for themselves
and each other on an unpaid basis; and the *voluntary sector*, in which a
plethora of membership organisations, charitable bodies and community
associations employ both paid and unpaid staff to cater to social needs
that are either not met at all, or not met so well, by commercial
enterprise or the state. Note also that just as the last three sectors purchase commodities from the business sector for use in their respective
spheres, so the production of commodities and the accumulation of
capital depend on the productive, redistributive and regulatory activities
of the state, on the procreative, caregiving and socialising activities of
households, and on the networks of trust, reciprocity, cooperation and
fellowship built up and maintained through the activities of the voluntary sector.

Notwithstanding all this diversity, contemporary public policy
towards work, is mainly concerned with promoting employment in the
"mainstream" economy, whether by creating more jobs, improving the
efficiency of the labour market or increasing the supply of suitably
trained and motivated workers. These concerns will, of course, normally
impinge on the "marginal" sectors of the economy. For example, the
institution of paid parental leave or the provision of subsidies for third-
party childcare will ease the conflict between parenthood and employ-

ment. Similarly, contributory social insurance schemes may accord recognition to unpaid caring or voluntary work. Nevertheless, given that almost everyone is unavoidably preoccupied with getting and spending, even when, in doing so, they "waste their powers", paid work tends to take precedence over unpaid contributions to the common good. Furthermore, in the past decade, employment policy has been recast in ways that reinforce the dependence of non-propertied households on the labour market. Wrestling with mounting welfare bills and anxious to avoid putting up taxes or increasing budget deficits, governments have sought to reduce the generosity of income-maintenance for claimants of conventional working age, by lowering benefit replacement ratios, tightening eligibility rules and introducing "activist" benefit regimes aimed at curbing welfare dependency and reconnecting the workless classes with the labour market.

The recommodification of the labour market has been pursued with particular zeal in the US and the UK, whose work-welfare arrangements are now held out as a model which countries with higher rates of unemployment, lower rates of labour force participation and lesser rates of job creation would be well advised to emulate. Steering a middle course between the social costs of excessive market deregulation and the economic costs of excessive social protection, advocates of the Anglo-Saxon Third Way commend four basic precepts: macroeconomic stability, labour market flexibility, fiscal prudence and work-welfare activism. In conditions of free trade and mobile capital, they argue, the only way for governments to maintain business and financial confidence is to balance their (current) budgets – at least over the course of the cycle – to borrow only for investment, to limit the ratio of public debt to GDP and to hold down both the tax burden in general and the rates of personal and corporate income tax in particular. With the scope for stimulating aggregate demand thus constrained, the best hope for tackling the backlog of long-term unemployment and social exclusion inherited from two decades of monetary stringency, slow growth and economic restructuring, is to loosen up the institutions of the labour market and help or "encourage" those who would otherwise have difficulty supporting themselves through paid employment, to acquire the requisite skills, experience and attitudes. Accordingly, the objectives of Third Way employment policy are to maximise labour force participation, to enhance the employability of disadvantaged groups, to promote investment in "human capital", to transform education at all levels into training, and to inculcate the habits of self-reliance, hard work and thrift.

The favoured tool for pursuing these goals is some form of targeted "welfare-to-work" programme. In the UK, for example, the New Labour

Government's New Deal is aimed at six distinct groups: the young unemployed, aged 18-24; able-bodied adults, aged 25-49 who have been unemployed for two years or more; adults, aged 50 and over who have been unemployed for six months or more; jobless lone parents; non-employed partners of the long-term unemployed; and people of working age with disabilities or illnesses that do not debar them from working. As a condition of obtaining and retaining entitlement to benefit, claimants in all these categories are required to attend their local job centre for interview, assessment and counselling about the opportunities and pathways available to them. In the case of the first two groups, once this initial phase of the programme is complete, claimants are also required to participate in one or other employment-related activities, choosing from the array on offer according to their needs, capacities and preferences. In the other cases, participation beyond the counselling stage remains voluntary. The precise options open to New Deal participants vary according to programme. In the case of young people, for example, they include subsidised employment (normally with a private employer), work with a voluntary organisation, enrolment in a local environmental task-force and remedial education or basic training. All these options are limited to six months except for the last, which extends over a year.

Four other features of the New Deal are worth noting. First, programmes are generously funded by a new, earmarked "windfall tax" levied on the profits of privatised public utilities, an astute arrangement that minimised taxpayer resistance and enabled the government to detach the New Deal from the regular procedure for planning public expenditure. Second, programmes are administered by the Employment Service, a public agency, though in some areas management has been contracted out to private firms in order to facilitate comparisons of service performance. Third, great emphasis is laid on the need to co-ordinate the work of different government departments concerned with social exclusion, and to develop partnerships, particularly at the local level, between the public sector, private employers and voluntary bodies. Fourth, strenuous efforts are being made to overcome barriers to employment– such as homelessness, transport costs, drug abuse and lack of affordable childcare – and, likewise, to build bridges to employment, chiefly through the introduction of various state-financed, but employer-administered tax credits which, taken in conjunction with a newly established national minimum wage, are designed to "make work pay".

To date, the New Deal has generally been welcomed as an improvement on the similar, but less well funded, coordinated, focused and prioritised initiatives undertaken by previous Conservative governments. Predictably, it has also been given credit for bringing down unemployment, though much of the UK's recent success on this front is probably due to the prolonged expansion enjoyed by the British economy since the pound was devalued in 1992, after being ejected from the ERM. Both overall and long-term unemployment rates were falling steadily *before* the New Deal began, casting doubt on the conventional view that most contemporary unemployment is *structural* in character and suggesting that few people are so unemployable that a strong and sustained period of economic growth will not pick them up. Conversely, supply-side measures on their own are unlikely to make much impression in depressed regions and areas where the demand for labour is weak and unemployment remains high even when the national economy as a whole is buoyant. Critics of the New Deal also complain that the service sector jobs which programme participants are most likely to enter, are largely part-time, frequently temporary and mostly low paid, offering little security of tenure or prospect of advancement.

Whatever the force of these criticisms, in the present context the important point about the New Deal is that it reinforces the already pre-eminent role of paid work and commodified production in social life, crowding out activity in the household and voluntary sectors of the economy and putting at risk the development of children, the well-being of adults, the cohesion of communities and the vitality of civil society. To cite just a few relevant indicators: in the UK, where working time is now largely deregulated and where average *annual* hours of work are already the highest in the EU, the *weekly* hours, inclusive of overtime, worked by both full-time and part-time employees, male and female alike, actually rose during the 1990s, despite the belated implementation of the EU Working Time Directive[1]. The intensity of paid work has also risen, along with the proportion of employees working irregular or anti-social hours. Taken together, these developments have elicited wide-spread concern about the "parenting deficit", the weakening of family bonds and the slump in the birth rate. Similarly, notwithstanding the widely recognised importance of "social capital" in sustaining social cohesion and enhancing economic performance, the supply of unpaid volunteers to serve as school governors, political activists and com-munity, sports or youth club organisers is dwindling, while large parts of the voluntary sector are being co-opted as agents of public policy and transformed into market contractors, including even some of its most informal parts, such as the "grandmaternal social services" on which many working mothers have traditionally relied for auxiliary childcare.

Of course, the Third Way extends to other branches of the welfare state besides social security and the labour market. But I have singled

---

[1]   See Harkness, 1999, p. 93

out this area of policy, partly because welfare-to-work programmes are already being touted as a model for the rest of Europe, and partly because I want to compare them with other proposals for recasting the work-income nexus which seek to relax – rather than intensify – pressure to participate in the labour market, to offer people more – not less – freedom in deciding what to do with their lives and how much of their time to devote to paid work, and to revive the institution of social citizenship as an essential source of social cohesion in a capitalist society. I shall return to both these points later. For the moment, in order to prepare the ground, I want to explain why prevailing forms of social citizenship are generally less universal, egalitarian and robust than their civil and political counterparts, and why even these imperfect social achievements are now being eroded or threatened by the processes of globalisation and European integration.

Citizenship, Nations and the Welfare State: The Challenge of Globalisation

Citizenship is a socio-legal status which confers certain duties and rights on those who share it. It is framed by specific public institutions and enacted through cultural practices which accord special – indeed, *sacred* – value to certain norms of social identity and the common good. The precise scope and character of the citizen body, the substantive content of citizens' duties and rights, the institutions which give shape to citizenship and the practices which nurture it, all vary greatly from one epoch and culture to another. Using these variables, Table 1 below provides a genealogy of citizenship in the West, from its origins in the city-states of ancient Greece to the present day. Inevitably, the classification offered is highly schematic. Its purpose is to highlight different historical models of citizenship and to illuminate the problems of revitalising the *social* dimension of citizenship in an age when social policy, already hemmed in by globalisation – or as Mishra (1999) calls it, "neo-liberalism writ large" – is no longer entirely determined by sovereign nation-states, but at least on a range of issues, is the subject of ongoing and complex negotiation within a transnational and multi-levelled system of governance.

Following Riesenberg (1992), Table 1 demarcates modern citizenship from its pre-modern forerunners. In the city-states of classical antiquity and medieval Italy, citizenship was an exclusive and hierarchical status, tied to military service and participation in public affairs, evoking intense local loyalty and serving to maintain social cohesion in the face of endemic warfare with rival states. Under the *Pax Romana*, the citizen body remained narrow in scope and privileged in character, but the military and political demands on citizens diminished, along with the associated rewards, in favour of a less heroic, more subaltern and more juridified way of life, though vestiges of classical republican practice survived at municipal level in the interstices of imperial rule. In the nation-states of the modern world, by contrast, citizenship becomes an inclusive status, at least in a normative sense: in the long run, all denizens of the national territory tend to become citizens, though a good deal of cross-national variation is evident in the treatment of resident aliens and second-generation immigrants[2]. National citizenship is also egalitarian in the sense that it is a single status with no internal gradations. These two features impart a powerful democratic logic to the politics of nation-states, slowly extending not only the scope of the demos, but the range of the political agenda, and expanding opportunities for political actors – elites, parties, pressure groups and movements – to challenge and change the distribution of resources and power. Furthermore, although war and preparations for war continue to play a prominent role in the life of nations, the institutions and culture of modern citizenship are also shaped by economic rivalry between nation-states, interacting with competition between capitalist enterprises. The mobilisation of entire national populations in pursuit of military and economic goals, coupled with the idea of the nation as a cultural community, bound together by ties of language, mores, character, and history, creates ample scope for political actors. inspired by collectivist ideologies of varying hues, to forge connections between national success (however defined) and social solidarity.

---

[2]   See Brubaker, 1990.

David Purdy

Table I: A Genealogy of Western Citizenship

Historical model	Scope and character	Socio-legal status/ Substantive content	
		Duties/virtues	*Rights/rewards*
ancient/ medieval city state	exclusive and hierarchical	military service political service jury service	public honour personal growth economic benefits
Roman Empire	exclusive and hierarchical	taxpaying	legal privilege
sovereign nation-state	inclusive and egalitarian	working voting taxpaying	civil rights political freedom social entitlements
contemporary European Union	inclusive and egalitarian	[unsettled and contested]	

Historical model	Public institutions	Cultural practices	
		Social identity	*Common good*
ancient/ medieval city state	citizen army citizen assembly jury system	civic communitarian	military security social cohesion
Roman Empire	imperial law municipal self-government	Romanized cosmopolitan	military security social order
sovereign nation-state	rule of law market economy liberal democracy welfare state	national-popular	military security cultural integrity social solidarity economic success
contemporary European Union	multi-tiered governance	post-national, multi-cultural	market integration + some form of social protection

This was the matrix from which welfare states emerged, taking different paths and assuming different forms in different nations, depending on local historical and cultural conditions. To characterise the kind of society that came into being as welfare states grew to maturity, T. H. Marshall (1963) coined the term "welfare-capitalism". He also called it the "hyphenated society" to emphasise that it was a hybrid shaped by contrary pressures: the disequalising logic of the market and the egalitarian logic of citizenship. Under capitalism, market forces continually throw up winners and losers, but in a state where all denizens are citizens, and all citizens enjoy extensive social rights, the resulting inequalities are somewhat attenuated, and those that remain, Marshall thought, would be legitimised, blunting the edge of class conflict and strengthening social stability.

Generalising from British experience, Marshall argued that the (modern) status of citizenship had evolved in three successive, but overlapping stages, beginning in the seventeenth and eighteenth centuries with the rise of capitalism, continuing in the nineteenth and early twentieth centuries with the development of democracy, and culminating in the twentieth century with the growth of the welfare state. During the first stage, the rising bourgeoisie secured what Marshall called the civil rights of citizenship, comprising both the classic liberal freedoms – of thought, conscience, expression, movement, assembly and association – and the "possessive individualist" freedoms of contract and security of property; during the second, the rights to stand for public office and to vote in elections for national and local government were gradually extended to the entire national population; during the third, a range of social entitlements was established, including free education and health care, affordable housing and a guaranteed minimum income. Though Marshall chose to concentrate on *rights* rather than *duties*, it was implicit in his conception of citizenship as a national institution with profound social consequences, that besides obeying the law, good citizens would participate in elections, contribute – according to their abilities – to the work that keeps society going, and contribute – according to their means – to the tax costs of running the state.

Though widely accepted and highly influential during the golden age of the welfare state, this account of social citizenship has since fallen from grace. Marshall has been taken to task for his Anglocentric and teleological view of history; for ignoring non-class social divisions, especially those of gender, ethnicity and race; for offering an idealised view of the post-war welfare state that gives a false or misleading impression of the extent to which, in practice, social entitlements were either available on the same terms to all citizens, as the term "social citizenship" implies, or really did serve to countervail market inequality and cultivate social solidarity, as Marshall maintained; for failing to appreciate that the egalitarian logic of citizenship is just as likely to provoke conflict as to curb it; and for neglecting the difference – of degree, if not of kind – between civil and political rights, on the one hand, and social rights, on the other, the protection of the former absorbing a relatively modest proportion of GDP, at any rate in law-abiding states, the provision of the latter absorbing anything between 30 and 60% of GDP, if social transfers are included, or between 15 and 25% if they are left out.

All these criticisms are valid. What they show, however, is that Marshall's account of actually existing welfare-capitalism was flawed: they do not impugn the concept of social citizenship as a *normative ideal*. To be sure, the precise shape and scale of social citizenship are controversial and even the notion that citizenship *has* a social dimension by no means commands universal assent. Nevertheless, while there are, or have been, societies whose citizens enjoy rights without welfare (the US, Japan, Singapore), as well as others whose citizens enjoy welfare without rights (the former socialist states), in Western Europe the *principle* of social citizenship is widely accepted. Here, most people would agree that without at least *some* form of collectively guaranteed access to "primary goods" – the material and cultural prerequisites for pursuing *any* version of the human good –whatever degree of equality citizens enjoy in the civil and political spheres is largely bogus. As Anatole France famously observed: "The law in its majesty permits rich and poor alike to beg in the streets, to sleep under bridges and to eat at the Ritz". And as R. H. Tawney rather more trenchantly added: "Freedom for the pike is tyranny for the minnows". Nor do social entitlements benefit only individuals: institutions that bind individuals together into a (national) community of fate make it easier for society as a whole to cope with difference, diversity, division and conflict in a context of material scarcity. It is, therefore, not surprising that for all their imperfections and despite two decades of retrenchment, the core institutions of the welfare state retain an impressive degree of public support in all Western countries. In this sense, as Mishra (1999) argues, if there is a winner in the contest between *laissez faire* capitalism, state socialism and welfare-capitalism, it is the last, for neither of the others can match its overall record of combining economic growth and general prosperity with political democracy and social justice.

The question is whether this record can be maintained. For Europe's welfare states face an unprecedented combination of challenges. Not only are they having to contend, on the domestic front, with rising age-dependency ratios, increasing health costs, high rates of unemployment or "inactivity", the continued decline of employment in manufacturing and the rise of the service economy, the advent of flexible labour markets, changing gender roles and the growing diversity of family and household forms; they are having to do so under a set of external constraints which severely limit their room for manoeuvre, and in an ideological climate which is still overshadowed by neo-liberal antipathy to collectivism in all its forms. No social institution can be preserved in aspic and welfare states would have had to adjust to the cumulative effects of economic and social change even if national economies had not become more exposed to international competition even if financial markets had not been deregulated, even if foreign direct investment had not grown in scale and even if the EU had not introduced the single market programme or embarked on the road to EMU. As it is, the effect of these developments has been to institutionalise neo-liberal ideology and politics, giving them a sharp global edge in the battle over the future of the welfare state and tipping the scales against the electoral and interest group forces which have hitherto managed to defend it.

The modalities of power in the new global order are well known. As pointed out earlier, financial deregulation has curtailed the ability of national governments to pursue full (or fuller) employment by managing aggregate demand. It has also strengthened the hand of those forces within each state pressing for the central bank to be given operational independence and for public finance to be hedged about by predetermined rules and commitments. As well as reining back the state, a regime of this kind weakens the bargaining power of organised labour, for if monetary discipline, the threat of unemployment and labour market deregulation can be relied on to contain wage inflation and secure worker compliance, there is no need for tripartite corporatism and consensus politics, and the classic social democratic strategy for maintaining full employment, high public spending and progressive taxation is undermined. At the same time, the freedom which capital now enjoys to move rapidly and without hindrance across national boundaries makes it harder for centre-left governments to maintain high rates of corporate taxation, payroll taxes and personal income tax. This, in turn, lowers the threshold of tax tolerance, squeezes public consumption, encourages the middle class to defect from the welfare state and damages the framework of social solidarity. And to make matters worse, the premium attached to international competitiveness increases the risk of social dumping, threatening a downward spiral of wages, working conditions and social expenditure.

It is, of course, important to distinguish between the *logic* of globalisation and what actually happens. As Hirst and Thompson (1999) argue, the issue is how domestic governments and their allies respond to all these pressures and what scope exists in the present international environment to reform and protect the welfare state, rather than allowing it to die. The next section explores these issues, with particular reference to the European Union and the current balance between national and supranational social policy.

Recasting the Welfare State: National and European Strategies

While globalisation has undoubtedly reduced national policy autonomy compared with the golden age of the welfare state, some European governments have nevertheless managed to maintain high levels of welfare spending, while improving the performance of the national economy and bringing down unemployment. Hirst and Thompson (1999) cite Denmark and the Netherlands as notable examples. In both cases the crucial factors seem to have been the willingness of employers to accept the need for *some* degree of social protection and to engage in social dialogue, the willingness of trade unions to accept flexible working arrangements both to safeguard their own institutional survival and in the interests of wider social solidarity, and the willingness of coalition governments with small majorities to threaten and cajole the unions into breaking with the past. Likewise, both countries have reformed their work-welfare systems, using active pressure rather than punitive sanctions to deter welfare dependency. As a result, labour force participation rates are high (or rising), long-term unemployment is low and the unemployed are not marginalised. More generally, disposable incomes are much less unequally distributed than in the UK or US and there are excellent public services which most citizens use, regardless of income or occupation. Thus, neither country has allowed a gulf to open up between those who pay for the welfare state and those who benefit from it, in contrast to the exclusionary Anglo-Saxon welfare states where taxpayers have come to regard selective or means-tested social security programmes as a pure, unproductive burden.

In a similar vein, Rhodes (1998) argues that while globalisation inhibits welfare *spending*, national governments retain control over the *design* of welfare policy. Hence, given that untrammelled market freedom produces social dislocation, there is still a role for purposive state intervention to secure an acceptable balance between the interests of employers in not being over-regulated and overtaxed, the interests of employees in not being exploited or insecure and the interests of non-employees in not being humiliated, poverty-stricken or excluded. "The next century", he maintains, will still be the era of nation-states in charge of disciplining and taming the markets [even if] the contours of this involvement are largely unknown." Rhodes goes on to commend what he calls "competitive corporatist" social pacts as a way of reconciling international market pressure with national social solidarity, citing as examples recent negotiations over pension reform in Italy, over working time in the Netherlands and over pay restraint, social security and job training in Ireland. To be sure, such "national productivity coalitions" may yield important advantages to domestic and multi-national capital, but they are, he insists, preferable to "unilateral neo-liberalism".

The arguments and evidence cited by these writers seem decisive against the view that the Anglo-Saxon version of the Third Way represents the *only possible* response to globalisation. Yet they need to be treated with caution. As Hirst and Thompson themselves point out, the Danish and Dutch cases contain many path-dependent features and cannot be taken as models which other countries may emulate. Rather, they are *possible worlds* whose existence demonstrates that provided they are suitably refurbished, high-spending welfare states can survive in an internationalised economy. There are, moreover, dangers in a *generalised* strategy of competitive corporatism, especially in circum-stances where the prospect of sustained economic expansion is precluded by an unduly restrictive European monetary policy[3]. If growth is sluggish and every state is striving to keep ahead of the game, with no supranational rules to keep competition within bounds, each may end up having to work harder simply to stay in the same place, and countries that start to fall behind may resort to social dumping, holding back "progressive" states and creating an atmosphere of mutual mistrust which could lead to economic warfare.

This is a particular risk under the current EMU regime which removes the option of devaluation as a remedy for competitive weakness and leaves national governments with only two alternatives, both much harder to implement and slower to take effect. One is to seek EU regional assistance, though under existing arrangements this is not really intended for entire national economies and is far too limited in scale. The other option is to strive to reduce unit labour costs. This can work, but only in certain conditions: *either* workers and employers must be willing and able to collaborate in restraining wages and raising productivity; *or* workers must be too weak and disorganised to prevent employers restoring profitability at their expense. In between these extremes, where workers are strong enough to resist employer imposi-tions, but not strong or disciplined enough to practise successful class collaboration, the most probable outcome is class stalemate and the

---

[3]   On the need for the ECB to pursue a relaxed monetary policy and the conditions that make it safe to do so, see Notermans, this volume.

national economy will languish. Admittedly, in these circumstances, devaluation would not work either, except as a temporary safety valve, but under EMU even that is precluded, and with rising unemployment disrupting the fiscal balances, free marketeers will demand welfare cutbacks, while their collectivist opponents press for protectionist controls. Whichever camp prevails, the cohesion of the EU as a whole will suffer.

Mishra (1999) is surely right to insist that standards of social protection must not become part of a competitive game, but must be part of the *rules* of the game. The problem is how to achieve this result. Hitherto, efforts to create an EU-wide system of social protection have been bedevilled by disparities of economic development and differences of policy regime among Member States, by conflicts of ideology and interest over the proper scope of social policy, and by intergovernmental disputes over the proper division of responsibilities and powers between national and supranational levels of policy-making. Yet the EU could, in principle, enact and enforce a social code both to regulate competitive relations among existing Member States and to prevent established citizenship regimes from being undermined by the admission of new Member States with inferior social standards. A possible way forward is outlined by Scharpf (1997) who proposes a European agreement on standards of social and environmental protection with a novel twist: to accommodate economic disparities among Member States and to ensure that levels of protection rise in line with economic growth, standards would be graduated according to per capita GDP. In particular, taking the proportion of GDP that each state devotes to (some agreed definition of) welfare spending, plotting it against national per capita GDP and determining the resulting regression line, Member States would set an upward sloping lower bound so that it passed through or close to the position of the lowest outlier. National governments would retain control over the balance and design of social programmes, but would agree to refrain from welfare cutbacks that caused their spending ratios to fall below the threshold.

Such an agreement would, of course, mean abandoning any hope of transforming the EU into a federal welfare state, with substantial administrative and revenue-raising powers of its own. But this has always been a Utopian idea and will not become any less so as the EU is enlarged to include the former socialist states of Eastern Europe and a heterogeneous group of states in the Mediterranean basin, all of them much poorer than existing members. By contrast, a system of graduated benchmarking would bring candidate states into the framework of social regulation at an early stage. Admittedly, to date social dumping has been more of a threat than a reality, but that is no reason not to take it seriously, for a pact precluding mutually ruinous competition would bring immediate gains in reassuring the public about the future of the welfare state and the purpose of welfare reform, at negligible cost in terms of resources expended or options foreclosed. Mishra (1999) goes further and suggests that such a system could be extended to all OECD countries and, eventually, to every country in the world. For the rich, industrialised states, basic social standards might consist of universal education and health care, income-maintenance programmes designed to keep the incidence of household poverty as close as possible to zero, a combination of in-kind services, cash transfers and parental leave designed to give all parents of pre-school age children a genuine choice between staying at home or participating in the labour market, and a parallel system of publicly provided or financed care for severely disabled or frail elderly adults. The corresponding requirements for the poorest countries of Asia and sub-Saharan Africa might amount to little more than primary health care, basic sanitation, safe drinking water and adequate nutrition.

Interestingly, in the present context, Mishra calls for a conceptual re-orientation of social policy from social *rights* to social *standards*, arguing – *inter alia* – that the language of rights is largely Western in origin and is alien to the non-Western world, yet recognising that what is valuable about the concept of social citizenship is its concern with the maintenance of social cohesion and its attachment to universal provision and balanced development as key aspirations. This is a useful corrective to a narrowly Eurocentric perspective, which could have some surprising repercussions. As things stand, the USA, one of the richest countries in the world, would certainly fall below the relevant health care and household poverty thresholds. In the context of an ongoing global debate about standards of social protection, involving governments, experts and non-government organisations, it is perhaps not too fanciful to imagine a transnational coalition of rich and poor states joining forces with American trade unions and social movements to help bring that country's backward welfare state into line with international norms.

A commitment to variable welfare thresholds, coupled with an imaginative and outward-looking approach to global economic management would also help in reforming EMU. In principle, a currency union need not entail any specific fiscal and financial regime. Like the original decision to proceed to EMU agreed at Maastricht, the Stability and Growth Pact adopted at the Dublin Summit in December 1996 was a thoroughly political construct. It was pushed through by Germany as a way of keeping up pressure on national governments to pursue tight fiscal and monetary policies, and accepted by other Member States, including those which had opted out of the single currency, mainly because the project of European integration had become so closely bound up with EMU that to court failure, or even loss of momentum, was to put at risk the degree of intergovernmental cooperation and supranational pooling of sovereignty that had already been achieved. Yet like the Maastricht convergence criteria before them, the rules of the Pact lack any sound theoretical justification and could easily do a lot of harm. The least defensible and most mischievous of these is the provision authorising the Council of Ministers to impose financial penalties on Member States with budget deficits in excess of three percent of GDP, except when the deficit is due to a natural disaster or to a recession in which GDP falls by more than two percent (a rare occurrence). As MacLennan points out[4], this rule takes no account of variations in the size and recent history of the public sector in different countries and imposes an arbitrary ceiling on borrowing to finance public investment, unmatched by any comparable limits on the scale of borrowing by the private sector. If, moreover, the rule were strictly enforced, governments could easily end up running *pro-pro-cyclical* fiscal policies, with the attendant risk of exacerbating economic fluctuations. Both for this reason and because a decision to impose penalties requires a two-thirds majority in the Council of Ministers, the rule is unlikely to be invoked. Its main function is to symbolise the EU's commitment to neo-liberal orthodoxy and to stiffen the resolve of national governments to face down domestic opposition to fiscal retrenchment.

In many ways it would have been better if EMU had been approached at a more gradual, evolutionary pace, with less emphasis on nominal macroeconomic variables and more on convergence in the real economy. However, given that the project long ago passed the point of no return, the issue now is how to make the best of it. To correct the deflationary bias built into the eurozone's current monetary regime, to ease pressure on national public finances and to recover ideological ground from neo-liberalism, two reforms are required: first the ECB's responsibility to prevent the annual rate of price inflation in the eurozone from *rising above* two percent needs to be balanced by a corresponding duty to prevent it from *falling below* two percent or, to be more realistic, to keep it as close as possible to the centre of a predetermined target range; second, as Eichengreen (1997) argues, the "three percent budget deficit" rule needs to be replaced by a "full employment budget" rule so as to relegitimise the use of automatic fiscal stabilisers. Coupled with a commitment to introduce graduated welfare benchmarks as part of a more general move towards global economic

---

[4] See MacLennan, this volume.

regulation, these steps would do much to create a warmer climate for national social policy.

Welfare Reform and Social Vision

And yet, a warmer economic climate will not, of itself, bring forth a new vision of Social Europe. The measures just outlined are essentially defensive: they seek to ease constraints on national policy, but offer no positive conception of the welfare state in a post-national, multicultural world. The same applies to "competitive corporatism" which, as its proponents seem almost pleased to admit, is a matter of making realistic adjustments within narrow margins of manoeuvre. This is not an idea to set the pulses racing. For one thing, recasting the welfare state in an era when the collapse of communism, the demise of social democracy and the development of globalisation have all but eliminated serious opposition to free market capitalism, is hardly going to arouse the same hope or elicit the same energy as the original project of constructing welfare states in an age when collectivist ideologies were still in the ascendant and the world had just emerged from three decades of war, revolution and economic turmoil. This conjunctural weakness is compounded by conceptual conservatism. Advocates of social pacts still think of them as grand, tripartite bargains between organised labour, organised capital and national governments. But contemporary capitalism is marked by *multiple, intersecting* lines of social division which include gender, race, ethnicity and (dis)ability as well as property ownership, knowledge and skills; and contemporary culture is irreversibly pluralistic, with nations in decline as imagined communities and a variety of social identities and moral outlooks competing for popular allegiance.

Of course, in countries where there is an established practice of social dialogue and the social partners are willing to cooperate for the common good, it makes sense to demand social concessions in return for helping to regain or retain national competitiveness and business profitability. But this does not foreclose debate about the long-term goals of social policy. In the light of the previous argument, three central themes suggest themselves as guiding stars to help pragmatic reformers keep wider horizons in view, even if the stars themselves are destined to remain forever out of reach: these are personal autonomy, social solidarity and structural pluralism.

People are autonomous to the extent that they can think for themselves, make their own choices and have the capabilities, resources, time and opportunities to shape their lives in accordance with their innermost values and beliefs. This ideal should not be confused with self-reliance. To varying degrees at various times, we all depend on others, some of whom are known to us, most of whom are not. Or to put the same point in another way: as we saw in Section 1, what is required to keep society going, bind it together and enable it to flourish is not just the production of commodities and the provision of public goods, but the development of social capital, the enhancement of the environment and the reproduction of human beings themselves, not as "bare, forked animals", but as thinking, feeling moral agents equipped with an extended repertoire of values, ideas, knowledge, habits, abilities and skills. Understood as an aspiration rather than as an achievement, the concept of social citizenship combines these perspectives – that of the individual person and that of society as whole – inspiring fresh efforts to build a social framework which supports people as they develop their gifts and pursue their life's work and which they, in turn, are willing to support with their intelligence, energy and loyalty.

To show what all this implies for public policy and to explain what is meant by "structural pluralism", the third of the long-term goals enumerated above, I want to return to the subject of work-welfare reform with which I began. My discussion is framed with the UK in mind because this is the country I know best, but it is intended to illustrate the benefits of connecting two kinds of discourse which are usually kept apart: speculation about possible worlds and debate about the art of the possible. I fully agree that thought experiments and political projects are two quite different things. But what I hope to demonstrate is that if you want to change the world, even by only a little, it helps to think the unthinkable!

To clarify the issues at stake, Table 2 sets out four alternative work-welfare regimes. The first two rows summarise, respectively, the traditional UK system of income-maintenance for unemployed workers and the welfare-to-work system that was described in Section 1. The third and fourth rows outline two alternative and as yet untried proposals for reforming the work-income nexus.

The traditional system was an essentially *passive* arrangement. Its main purpose was to deliver insurance-based or means-tested social security benefits to male breadwinners during what were expected to be short, albeit indefinite, periods of unemployment. As a rule, in order to obtain and retain benefit entitlement, claimants merely had to show that they were: (a) out of work; (b) capable of work; and (c) available for work. To keep families above the poverty line, benefits included supplements for financial dependants. Hence, in order to preserve work incentives, it was necessary either to institute a national minimum wage at a rate which offered a sufficient premium over out-of-work benefit payments or, if wages were left unregulated, to provide means-tested *in-work* benefits for low paid family breadwinners.

Welfare-to-work programmes, by contrast, are *active* policies targeted on specific groups of jobless benefit claimants. Their aim, as we have seen, is to curb welfare dependency and promote social inclusion by increasing the supply of suitably qualified and motivated workers available for employment, particularly in the business sector. Participants may be offered temporary work opportunities in the voluntary sector or in some form of community service. But options of this kind are usually regarded by all concerned as inferior substitutes for "real" jobs with private employers, serving at best as temporary stepping stones into mainstream employment. There is no provision or inducement for jobless citizens to contribute to the social good in *unwaged* or *non-commodified* ways, not simply as a short-term, last resort, but as a regular and preferred option. The programme described in Table 2 as "Participation Income" or "Liberal Workfare" is intended to make good this deficiency.

Table 2: The Work-Welfare Interface: Four Models of Public Policy

Programme	Coverage	Work Requirements	Participation		Associated Measures
			Duration	*Character*	
Traditional out-of-work income-maintenance	unemployed claimants (insured and uninsured)	capacity and availability for work	indefinite	protective social entitlement	demand management public sector job creation regional/retraining policy minimum wage or in-work low pay supplements
Welfare-to-work programmes	targeted groups of jobless claimants	participation in job-related activities	short-term	compulsory labour supply activation	overcoming barriers/ building bridges to mainstream employment
Participation Income/ Liberal Workfare	all jobless citizens	participation in publicly approved activities	indefinite	voluntary labour supply activation	creating work opportunities in the social economy
Citizen's Basic Income	all citizens	none	lifelong	emancipatory social entitlement	???

What is envisaged is an arrangement whereby anyone without a job is entitled to a regular allowance from the state on a scale at least equivalent to the prevailing national minimum wage, provided only that they undertake to participate for an agreed number of hours per week or per month in any one of a wide range of publicly approved activities or projects in the social economy. In effect, the state would act as paymaster, though not employer, of last resort, thereby securing the right to work without compromising the contributory principle that benefits should be earned, not issued as free handouts. Various procedures could be used to decide which activities and projects should be subsidised in this way – competitive bids to local authorities or development agencies, local referenda or even selection by lot – though care would be needed to ensure that projects were well managed, gave value for money and offered no threat to existing jobs in the mainstream economy.

Besides being entirely voluntary, "Liberal Workfare" might actually be better at combating social exclusion and kindling the spirit of community than conventional welfare-to-work programmes. Voluntary organisations are not motivated by the pursuit of profit, though, of course, they must balance their books. They cater to needs which other sectors miss entirely or meet less effectively. They are well placed to channel public support towards disadvantaged groups who are excluded from mainstream employment. And being free from the relentless pressure to compete and expand that drives capitalist enterprise, they are more committed to the communities they serve and the places they inhabit. On the other hand, the scope for creating work opportunities in the social economy depends on whether finance can be raised to sustain them, whether through borrowing to cover capital costs[5] or through taxation to cover recurrent costs, and this is subject to fiscal and ideological constraints. Cyclical swings in budget balances and the grip of financial orthodoxy inhibit the use of public funds to subsidise voluntary activity no less than they inhibit direct job creation in the public sector, though projects which are locally organised and community-oriented might be more popular with taxpayers and voters than traditional forms of public sector employment.

"Liberal Workfare" lies half-way between welfare-to-work and an even more liberal system generally known nowadays as *Citizen's Income* (CI). This has attracted considerable attention in recent years from activists and academics alike. It refers to a recurrent social transfer, financed out of taxation and provided on a lifelong basis to every individual citizen, each in his or her own right, with no means test and

---

[5] On the scope and prospects for reallocating credit towards the finance of social investment, see MacLennan, this volume.

no work requirement. Thus defined, CI is not tied to some pre-determined standard of subsistence: it could be paid on any (feasible) scale, from a purely token amount to the highest level that can be permanently sustained. Nor need CI stand alone: it could easily be combined with other types of social transfer, though most proponents see it as a way of revitalising the social dimension of citizenship which would, if feasible, overcome the defects of the old welfare state. They look forward, therefore, to the day when CI forms the centrepiece of social security. Clearly, this could happen only if it were paid on a scale at least equivalent to the standard of subsistence inscribed in *current* benefit scales, thereby making it possible to phase out most existing benefits without plunging anyone into poverty. Such a system has come to be known as *Citizen's Basic Income* (CBI) and there is, by now, an extensive literature seeking to justify the idea in principle and to design a viable model[6].

Given the dominant mores and values of our society, CBI – however justified, organised and financed – is likely to remain a utopian dream. For it to become feasible, two formidable obstacles would have to be overcome. One is the so-called "free-rider" problem that would arise if some people claimed their CBI entitlement without contributing to the work that makes it possible. The seriousness of this problem would depend on how many otherwise fit and capable adults opted to withdraw from work in the mainstream economy, what else they chose to do instead and what their fellow-citizens thought about their behaviour. The second barrier lies in the heavy financial cost of BI, even after allowing for savings from phasing out redundant social security programmes. And both these problems are compounded by the fact that we cannot be sure how people would allocate their time and what they would do with their lives once paid work had ceased to be a matter of sheer economic necessity or legal compulsion: the only way to find out is to try it!

But even if, for the time being, Citizen's Basic Income is neither socially acceptable, economically viable nor politically feasible, as an *idea* it has two great merits: it links the debate about the future of work with the debate about the future of citizenship, forcing us to ask searching questions about what counts as work and what citizenship entails; and it offers an alternative to the "compete and grow, work and spend" culture that dominates our world, holding out the vision of a society in which "wage slavery" has been abolished and everyone is genuinely free to pursue the kinds of work and the ways of life that suit them best, not because they are superabundantly rich, but because *as*

---

[6]   See Purdy, 1994 and Van Parijs, 1995.

citizens they are prepared to pay the requisite costs: both the "psychic" costs (if any) of supporting "free riders", and the more tangible, albeit – from *our* standpoint – unknowable, fiscal costs of supporting each other.

CHAPTER 15

Filling the Gap between Macroeconomic Policy and Situated Approaches to Employment. A Hidden Agenda for Europe[1]?

Robert SALAIS

Firms and workers in Europe are more and more aware that European countries are experiencing a new type of economic development which is quickly expanding – even in mature industries and standard requirements of skills – and is proving to be durable. This type of development began more than ten years ago with the ongoing dissemination of information technologies and with the surge of a new wave of innovation. Innovation now is permanent and more and more founded upon knowledge, theoretical and practical. New objects of attention and new claims have emerged. As new economic possibilities become apparent for both sides of industries, negative restructuring of activities and the cutting of jobs are increasingly intolerable for workers. They call for greater security to cope with the mutation of work, flexibility requirements and the prospect of mobility. Firms are looking less for subsidies than for structural policies and legal reforms allowing them to improve their competitiveness. As a consequence the need for new conceptions of economic and social policy for employment and for the construction of Europe is more and more urgent. All of this is comfortably labelled as the features of a knowledge-based society. Although this is primarily a slogan brandished upon the political scene and which merely reveals the backwardness of politicians who lag behind the transformation of the European economy, the notion is useful when rigorously reformulated.

This contribution is divided into three sections. The first one explains that in a knowledge-based economy the building of institutions and of mutual expectations between actors has precedence over the

---

[1] The English writing of this contribution has been revised by Marguerite Morley.

413

design of policies to be undertaken by States. Thus, to provide a framework of security, Europe must leave room for initiatives coming from intermediate levels and organisations; it has to guide and consolidate these initiatives in an appropriate subsidiary way. This is what we call a situated approach. The second section is historical, based on European archives[2]. It shows that an irreplaceable opportunity to take such an approach to employment and social issues was missed in 1991, during the Intergovernmental Conference on Political Union which prepared the revision of the Treaty. The diagnosis is that the failure was due, not to the pressures of market liberalism, but to the resurgence of a sort of social nationalism. Then follow some questions which are discussed in the third section. Ten years on, what are the outlines of the European landscape in these matters? Is it still possible to escape a future in which the European project risks dissolution in a market zone with States competing in social dumping?

Several studies have been made of the dramatic 1991 events, notably by George Ross (1995), Martin Rhodes (1995), Gerda Falkner (1998) and Ken Endo (1999)[3]. Except for Ross, they did not have access to original material. They mainly viewed the political process as a bargaining between rational actors – the Commission and the governments – using purely strategic arguments. Though extremely valuable and informative, they did not address the central point, that is how external factors – for instance national specificity – are reformulated in arguments internal to the process of discussion. Priority must be given to the exchanged arguments and to what they express, precisely because they had a practical meaning when pronounced. Every participant in the preparatory meetings for which we had minutes knew – and he knew that others knew – that they had to reach a final effective common outcome, a wording of the future Maastricht Treaty on the social field. Thus, every argument made sense in relation to the expected content of the final outcome. That is the reason why it has been extremely important to have access to the minutes of these meetings. Without these minutes, there is the risk of absolving the negotiators of their political responsibility, as Rhodes did for instance, and wrongly attributing the failure mainly to the social actors (unions and employers) even though they did not participate. The state of social dialogue in European countries and the diversity of its rules are certainly deplorable, but played no role as such. By the contrary, at their meeting of 31 October

---

[2]   We thank the *Secrétariat Général de l'Union Européenne* for authorising access to these archives and the *Archives Historiques des Communautés Européennes* (Florence) for its welcome. Philippe Pochet and Jonathan Zeitlin made helpful comments.

[3]   Ross, 1995, Rhodes, 1995, Falkner, 1998 and Endo, 1999.

1991 the ETUC, UNICE and CEEP reached an agreement to strengthen the role of social partners in the Treaty and proposed an ultimate wording of Articles 118.4, 118a and 118b[4] which is very close to the one retained for the Social Protocol. In some way one could say that social actors helped governments to save face on the social dimension issue.

Institutions and Mutual Expectations take precedence over the Design of Policies in a Knowledge-Based Economy

A knowledge-based economy is able, by definition, to produce – in competitive conditions based on price and quality – a wide range of products and services which are *conceived as permanently evolving* under a continuous process of innovation[5]. Creation of knowledge occurs in the course of work activities; and it emphasises the need for new qualities of work, notably that of reflexivity. Without understanding what you are doing, where it comes from and what it is connected to – ends, values, common goods etc. – knowledge cannot be produced, nor accumulated. This means that the transformation of work in these directions is central for the development of a knowledge-based economy.

Knowledge is not Information

It is essential to understand that knowledge is different from information. Information is standardised. It can be marketed as such. Information can also be directly managed by the administrative and statistical apparatus of the State. In order to be implemented, standard macroeconomic policies – that are substantive and discretionary – require the circulation of information. Knowledge is not standardised. It cannot be marketed, nor be the basis for State intervention. Knowledge has to be produced within processes of work activities of a certain type[6]. In these, work must be conceived as reflexive action, constructed coordination and innovation-seeking. These processes occur among specific populations of actors – producers like firms, workers, researchers, etc; and users like buyers, consumers etc. – who share the same conventions and beliefs in connection to a product. Only the actors involved can

---

[4] See Tables 1 and 2.

[5] See Storper and Salais, 1997, and Sabel and Zeitlin, 1997.

[6] B. Lundvall distinguishes three types of knowledge: the "know what", that is general knowledge which can be easily transformed in standardised information; the "know why" which refers to organisations and to their objectives; and the "know how" whose full meaning is only apparent when using it in production. Continuous processes of innovation rely heavily on this third form. See Lundvall, 1995.

efficiently exploit the knowledge created because they alone have the capability to do so.

Thus, knowledge exists on the markets only when it is directly incorporated into products and services. This incorporation takes the form of norms and standards of quality which help producers and users to deal with products adequately and efficiently. Knowledge thus is the basis for defining the future quality of products or services. To be effective the corresponding codes and variables must be defined jointly by producers and users in order to meet their interests and to bridge their divergences. No market can exist without this form of agreement on the quality of what is exchanged: what is its utility and for whom? What are its necessary technical specifications? These characteristics are equally central for the labour markets. When established, norms and standards become the conventions which create the market for the corresponding product, service or type of work. Only at this moment can information using the existing codes and variables begin to circulate between actors; its meaning is the same for everybody; thus exchanges can happen on the market with security and efficiency. But we must be aware that information is rarely stabilised for a long time, because the root of competition is the changing of the rules.

In fact, in a knowledge-based economy with permanent processes of innovation, competition is not primarily about prices; it is first and foremost about quality. Winners are those who create the norms and standards – or who can impose modification of the existing ones – to which future products and services must conform. They are winners because they define the rules of the market and thus they define the new work capabilities required. This process is of a double nature. Firstly, it is uncertain: its outcome is unpredictable. Secondly, it requires the initiative and voluntary commitment of a lot of actors. Even if they rely on past knowledge incorporated in public norms and agencies, only those who participate in the making of a new product – or service – *know* what this product is and how to define its norms and the types of work needed or to modify existing standards.

The Location of Economic Action

Alfred Marshall and Friedrich Hayek would have immediately understood the notion of location of action. They would not have fallen into a fallacious opposition between macro and micro, or between the State and the market. Unfortunately, the spontaneous misunderstanding of social sciences today, too often, is that location refers to micro (as opposed to macro). Those who support these claims have never entered the doors of a firm or thought about the ways in which problems come to an entrepreneur, are formulated and solved. Nor they have espoused the habits and world views of a worker. For practical men[7] a firm only exists if it belongs to a real world composed of people, of other firms to sell to and buy from, of things to do and products or services to produce etc. Thus a firm belongs first to a territory, secondly to an industry, thirdly to a network of firms (horizontally or vertically linked, depending on contracts, financial links, joint-ventures etc.). Within its territory, its workers reside; bank agencies and financial services are located; municipalities and regional authorities are in charge of infrastructure and structural policies (such as training and apprenticeship schemes); public administrations apply regulations. Within its industry, are situated practical knowledge, professional skills and habits, research activities, rules of behaviour, common values, all of which constitute the basis for mutual expectations and for the conclusion of contracts. Within its network, the firm finds markets, new claims about the design of its products, conflicts of power and of domination via the formation of prices and standards. When a worker has to choose a new job or decide to be mobile, get training or not, his choice is also situated in a territory, an industry, a profession, a network of sociability and so on. These intermediary spaces of action provide him or her with knowledge, resources and expectations, which are not purely individual, but collectively shaped and created. Contrary to a widespread and erroneous view, even large firms are less preoccupied with the pure mobility of capital than with optimising the financial profitability they can extract by relying on these productive spaces and on the geographic diversity of their human and physical resources. More and more, multinational firms try to exploit these "situated" and specific collective resources and structures.

Neither Market Decentralisation, nor Keynesian Policies, but Coordination at Intermediary Levels

In the field of public action, two primary preoccupations are introduced: to provide actors with a framework of security for their expectations; to leave room to intermediate levels of voluntary coordination between economic actors. The first concern is connected with the problem of actors having to deal with uncertainty, the second one with the proper establishment of norms and standards regarding quality of products, services and types of work. The two are linked by a common feature: the *location* of knowledge and of action.

Public action must start from the premise that for adequate knowledge to be produced it must be situated, that is, it must be grounded in

---

[7]   We borrow this notion from Keynes who assigned great importance to it. For instance, Chapter 12 of Keynes, 1936.

concrete situations. The same applies for work to be efficient. This profoundly modifies the standard view of economic policy, in a way that most politicians and civil servants have not yet perceived. The State no longer possesses general information adequate for external pre-defined substantive action. For the State ignores what is relevant in situations where it would like to impose the satisfaction of some general interest or common good (such as the level of employment, the fight against poverty, and so on). Achievement of the common good must advance *through* the voluntary commitment and autonomous action of people in these situations. The only way to achieve this is to offer *rules* that could serve as accepted references for private actions. *The State must make politics, not only policies.* The stakes are *institutional, not strictly political.* That means that the primary role devoted to the State is to organise in a proper way the collective deliberation conducing to rules of coordination which could be shared and consistent with the achievement of the common good.

One must be aware that neither market decentralisation, nor standard macroeconomic policies can provide the necessary security. And they cannot alone establish adequate standards and norms of quality. The reasons for this are simple. Markets can function only when their rules are stabilised and when information can circulate. But market rules and relevant information are always threatened in a knowledge-based economy by newcomers and innovators trying to impose new definitions of quality. Thus markets could never be efficient in the way standard theory assumes. Nevertheless market ideology is right when emphasising the role of autonomy and free initiative. Macroeconomic policies work only if people can form favourable expectations about the future. In case of uncertainty, and this is the case, they do not work. Nevertheless Keynes was right when he insisted on the necessity of a collective framework allowing practical people to form expectations. But economic policy must abandon the aim of influencing the course of events by substantial and discretionary means.

State action relates to the rules – that is to institutions understood as a set of revisable rules – that serve as a framework of reference for private expectations and actions. At bottom, for these rules to be efficient they must be debated and made public. They leave room for interpretation in action, for innovation, for acquisition of knowledge. Thus actors must participate in their elaboration in conjunction with public authorities. And the most reasonable appropriate levels of elaboration seem to be the intermediary ones: industry, trade, territory, industrial group, especially for quality rules regarding products and work. For the tension between generality of knowledge and its necessary revision can be best managed at these levels. As there are conflicting interests, the active presence of public authorities is required to oblige participants to integrate the common good in their search for solutions.

Building a Framework of Security at the European Level

For the European countries Europe as such is now the place where knowledge-based innovation is developing and where the corresponding products, services and types of work are being defined. Economic integration obliges Europe to play the main role for building the type of institutional framework we are discussing. The challenge is double and risky. The evidence is that the conventions of coordination and the intermediary levels mentioned above have a strong and longstanding national dimension, in social and work questions above all, but also for product quality and definition. And they differ among European countries – and probably regions – due to specific historical processes and social foundations. The European principles of mutual recognition and of free circulation reveal some awareness of this diversity of conventions. But the construction of Europe adds a new dimension: conventions must evolve in order to be compatible with it. Thus the European process must be defined as a process of creation of rules by mutual agreement. This is probably the only possible workable definition. The challenge which Europe is facing for providing security in a knowledge-based economy is that these rules are special. They should be designed for favouring the shifting of national conventions toward their mutual compatibility within a unified European space. This shifting cannot be imposed, it can only be guided by mutually agreed rules. It must remain under the control of collective actors organised at intermediary levels – industries, professions, territories, groups etc. – for the reasons developed above: the fact that they and only they possess the practical knowledge about products, their markets and the types and skills of the work they need for their making.

Europe has two types of instruments at its disposal for this purpose: macro policies, especially monetary policy plus financial regulations, and the establishment of common standards in the various fields of economic and social activities. Both require transformation to deal with the challenges posed by a knowledge-based economy, and new relationships between them. Europe has already experimented with types of process close to what we have discussed above. For instance, since 1985 Europe has developed a "new approach" for establishing norms of quality for products: security for consumers and workers, protection of the environment etc. In this approach, European authorities define only basic requirements to be satisfied by producers. Professions and sectors with the help of national administrations and experts have the responsibility to voluntarily achieve an agreement on common norms which satisfy the basic requirements. European authorities can control the process and harden basic requirements. Improving quality appears to be the key for mastering competition on internal and global markets; it indirectly requires investments in human capital[8].

In what follows, we will focus only on social and employment issues. Are there new objects of European attention in this field? If so, how are they dealt with? Do they incorporate some of the requirements we have argued for above? Since 1997 employment guidelines and attention paid to social protection are objects of this type. But the construction of Europe is a long-term historical process with some strong moments, and maybe turning points. What is occurring now can only be understood in the light of past events. The "social dimension" of Europe has truly existed for fewer than ten years. But it exists in a form different – and in my view qualitatively differently – from that advocated by its promoters. What lessons about its characteristics and difficulties can we learn from analysis of the process that will be useful to us today? In the next section we will turn our attention to the 1991 IGC on Political Union that implemented the "social dimension" of the Treaty.

New Objects in Employment and Social Issues and the Lost Opportunity of the 1991 IGC

In the domain of employment and social affairs, practical people – employers, workers, experts etc. – do not identify the new objects as connected to "employment" or to "social issues", but use the vocabulary of transformation of work. This shift is very important because it prefigures what we discussed above. The difference between the two is the following one. *Employment is the subject for policy design. Work is the subject for building institutions and mutual expectations.*

Europe and the Move from "Employment" to a "Work" Focus

As in the past, the objective of full employment remains important. But the "employment" focus is too marked by its origins – the post-war macro-Keynesian policies – and its long decline over the last twenty-five years, to be useful today. These policies progressively degenerated into a social treatment of unemployment. They provided a soft way to cut

---

[8] See "Industrial policy in an open and competitive environment. Guidelines for a Community approach", COM(90) 556 final, 16 November 1990. The issues are extensively studied in Kessous, 1997. The process for defining and improving norms of quality for products has well worked, though some problems now occur, probably due to dogmatic liberal conceptions in European competition policies.

jobs and restructure industries[9], notably by facilitating early retirement for workers under 60 or 55 years of age (as in France and in Germany, for instance, in the coal and iron industries). But they are unable to cope with the creation of new activities, new firms or with the necessary reallocation of skills. Furthermore they gave rise to a dynamic of permanent restructuring and downsizing in which social standards and labour law rules are seen as impeding adjustment. In this view, clearly economic concerns are separated from and opposed to social concerns; the latter have only the status of a cost to be minimised.

According to a "work" focus, public action has to leave the way open to processes which locally recalibrate and reorganise state support and delivery of resources in favour of people at work or looking for work. This leads to a reconfiguration of the collective space in which public action is designed: new objects, additional actors, new identities and capabilities; new rules of the game. It defines new collective stakes. The state's role is no longer to achieve substantive and discretionary macro policies; it is to help to provide actors with a set of rules they can use as a reference for "situated" coordination[10].

The problem for Europe is to make its way along the path leading to this reconfiguration. The first trial to deal with was the writing of a new section of the European Treaty, "the social dimension". This happened at the IGC on Political Union in 1991 under the Delors presidency of the European Commission. This historical moment is of great interest for our purpose. The challenge was to arrive at an agreement between the governments, and between the governments and the Commission, on two issues: the role Europe could play in social affairs *and* a new conception of public action. Retrospective evidence is that the agreement sought was about politics and not just about policies – the central point which interests us here.

This first trial was a failure. As we will see, the Commission had some intuition of the nature of the new objects involved and of the problems they pose for standard macroeconomic approaches. The list it drew up of the "deep-set trends common to all the Member States" is typical. It mentioned: the internationalisation of economies; keeping costs under control and seeking greater flexibility; the increase of the proportion of labour force accounted for by the tertiary sector and by women; training, both initial and continuing; the changing of the mix of

---

[9]   Note that this reasoning is durably incorporated into the European landscape, at least since the CECA Treaty and the restructuring of coal and steel industries during the 1970s. One must never forget that the Rome Treaty is in continuity with the CECA Treaty.

[10] More is said in Supiot, 1999.

qualifications required; geographical and occupational mobility; alteration and diversification of workers' aspirations and new areas of convergence between them and the needs of firms[11]. These objects clearly belong to a "work" focus as we defined above. But it turned out that only a minority of governments were aware of the changing of the social landscape. For the most part they continued to consider employment and social issues as a matter for central global policy and for policy remuneration[12].

The "Social Dimension" in the 1991 IGC

The concern for the "social dimension" referred to Articles 117 to 121. With help from the Commission, we have had access to the minutes of most of the preparatory meetings dealing with it[13] on one side, of the personal representatives at the IGC and, on the other side, at Ministerial level. So we have been able to follow the whole process from the first proposals made by the Commission (with its explanatory memorandum) to the final drafts[14] elaborated by the Luxembourg and the Netherlands presidencies of Europe and adopted by the governments. We had at our disposal the various counter-proposals made by the governments in these meetings, and the minutes of the discussions. The arguments exchanged help us understand the stakes and the political strategies. Annexes 1 and 2 compare the first and the final wordings of Articles 118 and 118b.

The Commission invoked two reasons for its proposal: "a concern for effectiveness – to ensure that the economic and the social actually do move ahead in step"; and "the desire to secure consistency and balance within the Treaty itself by ensuring that a fundamental area such as the social field is not treated any differently from other fields". These concerns were not addressed, and ultimately are still not met today. Nevertheless they were and remain essential for the success of Europe (notably its acceptance by the Europeans). Due to this damaging and irretrievable delay there is a greater probability that market ideology has

---

[11] Source: "Initial Contribution by the Commission to the IGC on Political Union", SEC(91) 500, 15 May 1991, pp. 81-82.

[12] It should be recalled that, in parallel, other bodies of the Commission were still looking for structural policies (public expenses, public works etc.) to maximise employment, which had a Keynesian flavour.

[13] Our selection of meetings comes from Ross, 1995.

[14] There were several drafts coming from the Commission and the presidencies along the whole process. The "Initial Contribution by the Commission", quoted above (note 10), has been written after the discussion of the Luxembourg Non-paper of 30 April 1991 at the 17th meeting of personal representatives on 6 May 19991. It integrated some reactions on this non-paper coming from the representatives.

irreversibly invaded the social and labour market issues. We will focus on two points. Firstly, was the conception of the Delors Commission in line with the type of economic policy we believe a knowledge-based economy needs (the provision of a security framework; the primary role of intermediary levels and institutions)? Secondly, we assert that the failure was not the outcome of some British economic liberalism or pressure from employers, but was the result of an upsurge of social nationalism (around which a kind of second-best consensus emerged among a large majority of governments).

In 1991 was the Delors Commission in line with the Needs of a Knowledge-Based Economy?

Two factors must be considered: 1. the common good proposed; 2. the role for intermediary levels. For both, the Commission's proposal was headed in the right direction. This of course does not mean that, in 1991 and the years before, the Commission was aware of the needs of a knowledge-based economy. The language was about new technologies and the main ambition was to enforce the role of the European level and of social dialogue in the social field. But the arguments deployed are significant.

In setting European social standards under a "work" approach, the role of state authorities is to determine and publicise the common good toward which collective deliberation and action should be directed. It is also to indicate some of the rules that could be used to attain this common good. This was precisely the purpose of Article 117 for the Commission; it was dropped from the final version. Let us first compare the two versions of Article 117[15].

> *First Draft*: The Union's objectives shall be to improve living and working conditions, to guarantee fair social protection, to encourage the social dialogue between management and labour, to develop human resources and to combat social marginalisation.
>
> These objectives should be pursued through the completion of internal market and Economic and Monetary Union. They shall also be implemented through structural policies, the adoption of common rules and through agreements concluded between management and labour.
>
> In pursuing these objectives, the Union shall have regard to the competitiveness of companies and the diversity of national practices, especially in the area of contractual relations.

---

[15] It became Article 1 of the Social Protocol (not signed by the UK and Ireland) of the Maastricht Treaty.

Final version: The Community and the Member States have as their objectives the promotion of employment, improved living and working conditions, proper social protection, dialogue between management and labour, the development of human resources with a view to lasting high employment and the combating of exclusion. To this end the Community and the Member States shall implement measures which take in account of the diverse forms of national practices, in particular in the field of contractual relations, and the need to maintain the competitiveness of the Community economy.

It is extraordinary to observe in retrospect how the changing of only a few words and expressions and the suppression of some others was enough to completely modify the approach which defines the common good in social issues.

According to the objects listed (see above) the first draft is much closer to a "work" approach than to an "employment" one. The memorandum emphasises that "the circumstances in which social policy is conducted have changed considerably and deep-set trends *common to all the Member States* have become apparent". These features of newness and commonality justify a specific role for the Community: "to provide the appropriate framework for the shared and balanced control of change while also helping to consolidate and improve the European social model". In the Explanatory Memorandum appended to its draft, the Secretary qualified the social objectives as "sacrosanct" and stated that "social policy is inseparable from economic policy". He added in his comments the objective "to ensure a high level of employment" which is not found in the draft, but without the insistence of the final version (where "employment" can be found twice). We will come later to one of the major differences between the two versions, the Union being replaced by "the Community and the Member States". The draft insists that the way for pursuing the social objectives is "through the completion of internal market and EMU". It means that a dynamic and tight link between social and economic objectives of the Union is sought, each being favoured by the advancement of the others. This is essential to ensure an upward process of growth.

The positive link between social and economic issues disappears from the final version. The same is true for the list of instruments (structural policies, common rules and agreements between social partners) replaced by a vague mention of "measures". The final version reinforces the mention of "the diversity of national practices" and of "competitiveness" in a sense which means that potentially the pursuit of social objectives is hostile to them. It comes back to the old "employment" approach, a purely social one which fundamentally considers that employment and social objectives are costly, but must be announced for reasons of political necessity.

The Commission's first draft emphasises the role of intermediary levels, organisations and institutions in the establishment of European social standards (Articles 118, 118b and 119). The final version weakens this role, coming back to a traditional architecture dominated by States (Articles 2, 3 and 4) (see tables 1 and 2).

The mission of endeavouring to develop the "social dialogue" is firmly attributed to the Commission by Article 118b in the perspective of "[framework] agreements applying through a trade or industry at European level"[16]. Both the transnational and intermediary characteristics of the new objects are thus pointed out. It is suggested that they could be treated through agreements, but without forgetting the other instruments listed in Article 118. Article 118b underscores that "at the request of the parties concerned, agreements may be the subject [...] of a decision taken by the Council [...], and addressed to the Member States so as to make them mandatory for the duration of their validity". From Article 118, par. 3, the Commission is provided with the initiative "to consult on the possibility of attaining the objectives [...] through framework agreements". And, importantly, Article 118, par. 4 opens the way to the Commission to be directly assisted by the social partners "acting as a management committee[17]" in cases where laws are not to be implemented by the Member States. Finally, as the memorandum stressed, the main instrument for establishing European standards and for improving them would have been the Community Charter of the Fundamental Social Rights for Workers (adopted at the end of 1989) and social dialogue the main motor[18]. To this end "the Council and the European Parliament, acting on a proposal from the Commission, in accordance with the co-decision procedure, [...] shall adopt, by the means of law, minimum requirements applicable in each Member State" (Article 118, par. 2). A common social law would have been possible, starting from minimum provisions, later improved via a range of instruments within which priority, but not exclusivity, would have been

---

16 This was what Ross, 1995, p. 150, calls the "Commission's 'negotiate or we'll legislate' clause".

17 The Belgian representative proposed in the discussions the creation of a "Comité européen du Travail". See below.

18 "Inspiration [for the wording] has been drawn from three sources: certain provisions of the Community Charter of the Fundamental Social Rights of Workers; the Commission opinion on Political Union; the results of the social dialogue, chiefly in the form of joint opinions on the introduction of new technologies, the organisation of work and the adaptability of the labour market", (*cf.* "Initial Contribution by the Commission to the IGC on Political Union", SEC(91) 500, 15 May 1991, p. 86.

given to social dialogue and agreements. The memorandum notes that, though there has been in Europe a move to decentralise social bargaining, in practice one is witnessing "a new interplay between levels of negotiation" in which "in several Member States central government has intervened, using a variety of methods". Thus the proposal intends to freely use all forms of intermediary levels and actors to whom the role of proposing common rules is assigned before their endorsement by the Union: trade, industry, firm, Member State; the whole for the best development of a European framework, depending on the initiatives taken, in which domain and by whom. It would have implicated, not all the domains of law, but the new objects listed above for which Community action could have added value. The new objects accessible to the Union are defined in European vocabulary by Article 118, par. 1 – note the decisive area "living and working conditions, so as to ensure the protection of basic rights of workers". But it is evident that all the European framework would have progressively exercised an incentive to modify national law and industrial relations, while respecting the autonomy of decision and of negotiation of the actors involved.

The emphasis put on the role of intermediary levels is often understood in political sciences as an appeal to corporatism[19]. This is a double misunderstanding. Firstly, it is confusing the search for an explanation with the only description of an institutional mechanism. Secondly it misunderstood the principle of subsidiarity, confusing it, some times with a liberal principle of decentralisation of collective choices or, on other times, with a hierarchical distribution of competencies. Doing that is replicating and re-enforcing the same confusions that a majority of governments made during the Maastricht process (see, below). It could have been true that, in the mass production regime of growth before the 1980s, a simple macro-institutionalised bargaining scheme was efficient to cope with global variables. But this time is over. In part I, I argued that, in an economic growth marked with uncertainty, the appeal to intermediary levels – under some conditions of common goods achievements – is presumably, if there is one, the only efficient and fair way to define social and quality of work standards. This is already the case for hygiene and security standards at European level. It means that analysis of bargaining procedures can never be isolated from the objects at stake and that it requires a precise assessment of their operation and of their outcomes for workers and firms in their daily activities. As the memorandum explained, the principle of subsidiarity must be understood as the reference guiding collective action towards a European common good. It is neither decentralisation, nor hierarchy. In

---

[19] See, among others, Falkner, 1998.

a given situation of action it allows to determine the respective roles of the different actors involved at different levels in that action. Each actor is required to discover by itself his most efficient way to act and to freely coordinate his action with the actions of others. The premise is that there is agreement on the common good pursued. Due to its anchorage in continental tradition of thought (notably, but not only[20], in its Christian side), it is not surprising that most of the Anglo-Saxon political philosophy has the greatest difficulties in grasping with the meaning of subsidiarity. It is equally true that, starting from the opposite side, the French tradition of State intervention shares the same difficulties.

Almost all the new objects disappeared in the final version (Article 2, par. 1): "living conditions" and its linkage to "working conditions", "participation", "so as to ensure the protection of the basic rights" – thus the relation with the Social Charter – "basic and vocational training", "levels of skills", "the functioning of the labour markets" are excluded. To this is added "the integration of persons excluded" – equality between men and women being treated in the draft in a special article. The list of items excluded from qualified majority is more detailed. The excluded items are separated into two parts: those which can be treated, but which require unanimity; those completely excluded. Explicit reference to the Commission is reduced. The exclusion of "life" cuts the links between work, leisure and home life that are important for working people and for their relatives. It leaves room for employers to take unilateral measures without any acknowledgement of workers' possibilities and wants; for instance, to reorganise work activities, hours and schedules, without any consideration either of the constraints they put on people, or, reciprocally of their specific needs. According to flexibility requirements, it is one of the major regressions.

The "conditions of life and work" were of great importance for the Commission. Their improvement figured in Article 117 as one of the objectives of the Community and in Article 118 as a domain belonging to qualified majority. Present in the first proposals[21], they were attacked first by the UK which "considered that the notion of conditions of life is too vague, like those of adequate social protection and fight against exclusion". This criticism was approved by the Netherlands and, in the following discussion of Article 118, accepted by the Belgian and French

---

[20]   See, for instance, Millon-Delsol, 1992.

[21]   In a proposal by the Commission for the 15th meeting of the personal representatives of 24 April 1991 (SEC(91) 864, Annex II) and in the Luxembourg non-paper of 29 April 1991 (SEC(91) 957, Annex 1) which served as a basis for discussion in the 17th meeting of the personal representatives of 6 May 1991 (*idem*).

representatives. Followed by Ireland and later by Spain, the UK pleaded for substituting a reference to employment in Article 117 to these objectives[22]. Consequently, the Luxembourg presidency abandoned the "conditions of life", but the Commission advocated – without success – its reintroduction, during the following fifthing at ministerial level in 13-14 May 1991. It stated that "the introduction of conditions *of life* allows establishing a link between work and private life" and, in relation, referred to "paragraphs 7 to 9 of the Social Charter" These paragraphs state that the achievement of the internal market must lead to an improvement of conditions of life and work of the workers within the European Community, by the bias of an approximation of these conditions. Among these conditions are mentioned: working time and its adjustments and all forms of employment other than open-ended contracts[23], procedures for collective redundancies and those regarding bankruptcies, for every worker residing in the European Community, a right of annual paid leave and to a weekly rest period; and a right to his conditions of employment stipulated in contract of employment (by law or collective agreement)[24].

The abandonment of the attempt to institute benchmarks concerning basic rights in the field of life and work renders impossible, as one's observes later, any ambitious process of establishing and improving social standards within Europe. This benchmarking would have forced policy makers to pay more attention to the diversity of situations – thus to localise their operation – and to create more collective solidarity. Exclusion of skills and training distanced the construction of Europe from the priority of policies of human capital development – now invoked in the Lisbon summit of March 2000. It is difficult to guess what the Commission would have undertaken in "the functioning of labour markets", probably on the issues of atypical forms of employment. The procedure of social dialogue is more formal, but its autonomy and efficiency restricted. Most notably the support of possible European

---

[22] Minutes of the 17th meeting of the personal representatives. Ireland proposed to add "the development and creation of employment" as an objective for the Community.

[23] A draft of the Charter (in English) presented by the Commission speaks of "the organisation and flexibility of working time, particularly by establishing a maximum duration of working time" (COM(89) 471 final, pp. 9-10). Of course the purpose for the Commission was not to organise and develop flexibility, but to provide workers with rights and guarantees in case of flexibility, everywhere in the Community.

[24] In the same intervention, the Commission suggested – equally without success – other amendments to the text of the Presidency: in Article 118.1 a reference to the notion of participation ("a source of efficiency as it is witnessed by the Japanese system") and to the functioning of the labour market; and in Article 118.6 a reference to the *level* of remunerations (which would have meant that the rate of wages increases belongs to the field of Article 118).

rules on intermediary levels and actors disappears. The Commission now only "promotes the consultation of management and labour at Community level" (Article 3, par. 1) on "the possible directions of the Community action" (*Ibid.*, par. 2) via a complicated procedure. Any mention of participation, albeit limited, of the European Parliament has been suppressed. It would have brought an element of embryonic democratic choice in social issues. Article 120 in the first draft stated that "a law [...] shall define the conditions in which actions to promote the attainment of the objectives set out in Article 117 [...] may be launched in the framework of multiannual programmes". No mention of programmes figures in the final version.

The wording of the Article devoted to the social dialogue varied along the process from April to October. Jacques Delors and the Commission launched a procedure of European social dialogue at Val Duchesse in 1985 and had great ambitions for its role in the building of Europe (as emphasised by its Article 118b – see Annex). The Luxembourg non-paper of 29 April was close to the initial proposal of the Commission. Criticisms came from the UK (see below) and from Germany. Belgium agreed; Spain declared being close to the German position; other delegations were silent. Germany found that "the text mirrored a kind of paternalism" and was opposed to any reference to the Commission. In its proposal, Germany gave primacy to the dialogue between social partners upon the role of the Commission. "This [German] proposal aims at enforcing the role of social partners at European level and at not impeding new developments desired by social partners. The achievement of the social dimension of the internal market cannot be under the sole responsibility of the Community's legislator. In the same meeting, the Commission tried – without success – to obtain an agreement "in admitting the suppression of any mention to trade or industry agreements"[25]. But the Luxembourg presidency comes back to a softer redaction, speaking of "consultation of social partners on the opportunity for a Community action" which was kept in the following versions. The final version of Articles 118.4, 118A and 118B (which figure in Articles 2 to 4 of the Social Protocol) comes from the agreement between social partners of 31 October 1991. This version seems to mix various intermediary proposals coming from the Commission and from the Luxembourg and Netherlands presidencies.

---

[25] The German proposal figures in Annex II, Minutes of the 17th meeting of personal representatives of 6 May 1991.

The Upsurge of Social Nationalism around which a Kind of Second-Best Consensus Emerged among a Large Majority of Governments

It has been often stressed that the emergence of a social Europe was impeded by a *de facto* alliance[26] between the economic liberalism of the British Government and the European organisation of employers (UICE – within which British employers were influential. And that the comprehensible desire for Member States and the Commission to obtain the signature of all favoured the abandonment of most of the Commission's proposal. It is true that the initial proposal was ambitious, as we have seen, and had its own diplomatic difficulties. But it is hard to believe that the negotiators did not know that the British would not sign, whatever the changes. For the British gave multiple warnings. If that was the only reason, except fatigue and bureaucratic complexities[27], nothing kept the eleven countries which had signed the Social Protocol from returning more or less to the initial draft. Nevertheless, except the articles dealing with the social dialogue – which, for most of them, came from the agreement of 31 October 1991 between social partners – the Social Protocol is identical to the version elaborated by the Luxembourg presidency of Europe at the end of its presidency[28]. Even if by this the signers had left the door open to the British, it would have been a sign of purely opportunistic and political attitudes on these issues on the part of governments; thus a neglect of fundamental issues which are not political, but contribute to determining the future of the European economy. Finally, if the whole process had been firmly launched, with clear political messages, employers' organisations would have had no choice but to participate .

Thus something else happened. T' ; minutes of the several meetings convened in preparation for the IGC help us understand what occurred. The meetings discussing the "social dimension" took place mainly from March to June 1991. What is the most striking is the wide range of positions that national representatives took in the meetings[29]. It appears that they were unable or did not make efforts to grasp the new objects, linked to the transformation of work and European economic integra-

---

[26] For this type of argument, see Rhodes, 1995.

[27] Which must not be underestimated, see Ross, 1995.

[28] Compare, for instance, Articles 1 and 2 of the Social Protocol with the Articles 117 and 118 of the project of Treaty diffused by the Luxembourg presidency for the European Council of 28-29 June 1991. See SEC(91) 743/2 of 21 June 1991.

[29] As Ross, 1995, p. 150 remarks, "those who wished to strengthen the EC social dimension (the Belgians, French, Dutch, German, Italians and Danes) disagreed about how much strengthening to do and about decision rules".

tion, that the Commission presented to them, and the role that the Union as such could play in relation to these objects. Nevertheless the issue was far from being new. Attention could have been paid to the works on the social dimension of the internal market, undertaken by the Commission and published in 1988. These works emphasised the need to anticipate and accompany the mutations engendered or accelerated by the achievement of the internal market[30]. On the contrary, the representatives above all expressed their national conceptions and social thoughts while ostensibly discussing the draft set of Articles or proposing new redaction. Thus two huge problems arose. The first one was, on the part of national social administrations, the absence of any serious thinking about the necessity of a European framework to deal with the transformation of work and European economic integration. The second one was a complete misunderstanding of the principle of subsidiarity along which the Community has been designed to act, manifested by all the states, except Belgium, Italy and, probably, Germany.

We will begin with the least surprising positions which did not change during the process. Ireland and above all the United Kingdom were the most hostile. The UK expressed "reluctance against any extension of the Community competence in this domain[31]", the reason invoked being "the importance of national traditions". For the UK representative, this meant that "the question of industrial relations has always been a difficult problem" in his country since 1945. He could not abandon the decentralisation of these relations, which would be jeopardised if Community measures were applied in that domain[32]. He stated that "the diversity of social systems allows the less rich countries to have at their disposal a competitive advantage that must be kept" and that "the level of social protection depends on the level of economic development". It is difficult to make a better plea in favour of social dumping, that the Commission proposed to combat with the implementation of the Charter of Fundamental Social Rights! After having first excluded any European social policy– the motive being "the deep roots

---

[30] Stress was put on globalisation, the restructuring of European industries (with a reperage of "sensible industries"), the "introduction of new technologies – information and communication technologies – modifying the mode of work and necessitating adapted training" etc. (in *Social Europe,* special issue, 1988, part 2). See equally COM(90) 556 final, on industrial policy which emphasises a "permanent need for structural adjustment" and the "acceptation of a high rhythm of structural adjustment", pp. 2-4.

[31] Minutes of the 7th meeting of personal representatives on 1 March 1991, SEC(91) 419. More than pure nationalism, the British expressed a kind of "liberalism in one country" position.

[32] Fifth meeting at Ministerial level on 13-14 May 1991, SEC(91) 962.

national social policies have in each Member State"[33], Germany raised the stakes, suggesting[34] a "social Union" which would have covered all the domains of social policies, and in which decisions would have been made by a "special qualified majority"[35]. No other country supported the German position, the debate contrasting status quo with some extension of the domain of social policy. More surprisingly, the French initial proposal in March was non-constructive; reverting to the existing Treaty, it intended to limit the action of the Commission (Article 118) "to the mission of promoting close collaboration between the Member States in the social field", by studies, opinions and the organisation of consultations. The only concession was the suppression of the limited list which previously figured in the text[36]. Later the French supported the Commission's efforts during the meetings, but the reduction of scope had already been made by the Luxembourg presidency. The Danish were the most "social Europeans", reinforcing the draft of the Commission in some points. For instance they suggested adding the "need to promote equal opportunities in education and in further education and follow-up training" (Article 117). In Article 118, "the Community shall have the dual task of adopting a common policy and promoting close cooperation between Member States in the social field, particularly in matters relating to employment, fundamental labour and social rights and social security". In the list of matters, they add joint decision-making and that "the statutory and contractual rights of workers in a Member State are observed where foreign labour is used" and in Article 118b they suggest that the social dialogue "may furthermore encourage the introduction of labour and social rights" with appropriate proposals from the Commission[37].

Due to their deep-rooted Social-Christian traditions (a spirit they share with the Commission's draft), the Italians and the Belgians[38] were the closest to the European dynamics envisaged. Italy made the connection with the field of "economic and social cohesion" which, otherwise, is the object of another part of the Treaty, also to be revised and

---

[33] Minutes of the 1 March 1991 meeting.

[34] Minutes of the 6 May 1991 meeting.

[35] That is higher (66) than the usual one.

[36] Concession counterbalanced by the vagueness of the social field by itself. Minutes of the 12th meeting of personal representatives on 25-26 March 1991, SEC(91) 631, annex XXIII.

[37] *Ibidem*, annex XXII.

[38] Thus it is not necessary to suppose, as Falkner, p. 95 did, that there could have been some strategic agreement between the Commission and the Belgian government to push Belgians to test some ideas before the Commission put them on the table. Community of political philosophy is enough to arrive at the same proposals.

discussed (Articles 130, and 130a to 130d). This connection is legitimate, but likewise reveals the constitutive ambiguity of this field of the Community's action (see below the discussion of Spain's contribution). The Italian contribution considered that all the global economic and social transformations underway "oblige the Community and the Member States to adopt a strategy to face these new realities. The main objective of this strategy shall be the economic and social cohesion, whose achievement must guide the macroeconomic policy of the Community[39]. For elaborating and putting in operation the main economic choices, the institutions of the Community would be helped by the cooperation of an organism representative of the social partners (which could stem from a reform of the European Economic and Social Council), for social policy is one of the pillars of the cohesion. Finally it stated that "Italy which has already intervened in the past in favour of a concrete application of the Social Charter emphasises again that the social dimension should not be limited to avoiding the eventual negative consequences of the Internal Market, but should become an autonomous means of intervention for the Commission". The Belgian delegation noted the quasi-blockage of an efficient Community social policy; it called for an enlargement of the Community's competencies in the social field and for the adoption of the rule of qualified majority – as in the economic field, a difference of treatment being unjustifiable. To favour the emergence of a "law obtained by collective agreement"[40], the Belgian delegation proposed that the social partners play a greater role. A permanent organism, the "Comité Européen du Travail", would be in charge of the elaboration of a body of European social legislation. It would be composed of employers' and workers' representatives, chosen by their organisations and would have had a "quasi-legislative" role[41]. This probably clarifies what the Commission was looking for when referring to "a consultation body" (Article 118 par. 3 and 4).

While agreeing with the Commission's proposal, Spain parlayed its vote by calling for a reform and a substantial increase in European structural funds. Barring this, Spain threatened not to sign the Treaty[42].

---

[39] Contribution dated 19 February 1991. Minutes of the 13th meeting of the personal representatives on 11 April 1991, SEC(91) 777, annex VII.

[40] In French, "*droit conventionnel*".

[41] Note dated 25 January 1991, *ibidem*, annex III. See also Annex III, Minutes of the 7th meeting of personal representatives 1 March 1991, SEC(91) 419. Falkner, p. 95, provided details from a copy she possessed.

[42] During the discussion of the cohesion Articles, the representative of Spain "underlines the very importance of this question for its delegation and indicates that it will not sign the Treaty if the cohesion is not solved" (Minutes of the 12th meeting of personal representatives of 25-26 March 1991, SEC(91) 631, p. 11).

Less ably than Italy, Spain tried to mix "social dimension" and "economic and social cohesion" (ESC). The Spanish position was specified in a note linked to the debates about the Articles 130 and following (devoted to ESC)[43]. The Spanish emphasised some past misunderstandings which proved to be very costly for the four countries which ranked far below the average GDP per capita for the European community (Spain, Greece, Ireland and Portugal). The objective of ESC is too often identified with the Structural Funds although it should have been taken into account by all the common policies and the Internal Market. For Spain, this is not a question of trade-off between the operation of the structural funds and the costs of the process of convergence toward the euro for the poor countries. The structural funds are not equitable; they are profitable for the richer countries – a diagnosis made by several reports. Thus the Spanish asked for two reforms: a new progressive tax applying the principle of relative prosperity; a compensation fund among countries aimed at promoting the formation of physical and human capital in priority in the less favoured regions. These proposals were refused, for they faced the opposition of the rich countries, Germany in particular, whose contribution to the European budget was high and in competition with the future costs of German unification[44].

As we noted before, one of the spectacular changes made to Article 117 is the replacement of "Union" by "Community and the Member States". Most of the countries differentiated two levels, the level of the Community and their level. They saw them as competing primarily for the distribution of social competencies as if, when a competency is provided to the Community it is removed from the national jurisdiction. Thus the majority of them defended what they saw as private prerogatives and interests threatened by the Commission. Inversely they appreciated Community action in social issues when it provided additional resources without any strings attached. Many other clues point in the same direction. At the beginning of the final version of Article 118, the Community "supports" first and "complements" after; it was the reverse in the draft. The concern is not "the action of the Member States", but their "activities" – which refer to actions pre-defined by the States. In a new article (Article 3 of the Social Protocol), the Commission is asked to "encourage co-operation between Member States and facilitate their co-ordination in all social policy fields under the Agreement". The concerns vis-à-vis the Commission seem to impede its

---

[43] Minutes of the 12th meeting of personal representatives of 25-26 March 1991, SEC(91) 631, Annex XIX.

[44] Nevertheless Ireland, Portugal, Italy and Greece supported the Spanish proposals. Minutes of the 5th meeting at ministerial level.

capacity for "active regulation"[45], that is its capacity to circumvent the texts via widened and unanticipated interpretation leading to new fields of action.

The authors of the Memorandum appended to the Commission's draft were of course perfectly aware that new powers for the Commission would result from the wording of Article 118. For all decisions in the areas listed could be taken, not by unanimity between Member States, but by qualified majority. This extends the latitude of the Commission as it disposes of a right to initiate proposals and as it could be supported by social actors – "management and labour" – when they came to an agreement. But this was not the point. Under the subsidiarity principle, power is not sought out for its own sake. The objective assigned to the Commission is only to look for new ways and new capacities for acting at the Union level in the social field, the construction of Europe being considered as a global and collective process in which all actors are involved. Effective actions and texts[46] from the Commission were perfectly clear, intellectually speaking. Its memorandum reminds the national delegations that the application of the principle of subsidiarity – with due regard for the specific nature of social matters – "lies not so much in choosing between social issues, distinguishing those for which Community jurisdiction is recognised, as in suggesting what, in the light of the needs identified and the potential value added by Community action, is the most appropriate in each case – harmonisation, co-ordination, convergence, cooperation etc.". It reiterates that the Social Charter states that the completion of the Internal Market is "the most effective means of creating employment and ensuring maximum well-being"[47]. The evidence is that these arguments were not understood for what they were. A majority of delegations continued to debate as if the issue was to distinguish between Community and national jurisdictions, and made no effort to perceive the needs for European action as such. They remained mired in a downgraded version of subsidiarity, a purely hierarchical one opposing two levels, the Community and the States. We can suspect that this downgraded version could have later disseminated.

---

[45] An expression of Rhodes, 1995.
[46] See, for instance, "The principle of subsidiarity", SEC(92) 1990 final.
[47] Remember that this close link with the Internal Market (that is, with economic issues) was cut in the final version of Article 117.

How to Overcome Social Nationalism and to Re-Launch the Dynamics of Europe in Social Affairs

As the Commission was aware, any durable lag in the implementation of Europe-wide structures in social issues created a greater risk for social dumping. In 1997 an important initiative was undertaken, *i.e.* guidelines for employment. Did these offer an alternative to the opportunity lost in 1991? Or would it be necessary to launch what could be called a hidden agenda, that is an agenda free from political strategies and what should this agenda be?

A Greater Risk for a Downward Competition between National Social Models?

The economic and social arguments developed by the Commission's memorandum sound perfectly valid[48]. They suggest a clear intuition of the nature of the changing of the economy which accelerated during the 1990s. They underscore by contrast the dangers that Europe faces for not having extended the scope of its action in this area. These can be summed up as follows:

–   Completion of the internal market and economic integration emphasise the transnational nature of problems, such as the protection of workers' rights in the case of transborder operations[49]; information – consultation and participation[50], obstacles to mobility within the Community. Steps must be taken to ensure that the internal market develops without any distortion of competition

–   The call to establish and build Europe upon a platform of fundamental rights shared by all Member States. The enforcement of the Community Charter of Fundamental Social Rights voices two ambitions: to proclaim an European identity and to combat social dumping. Otherwise employment relocation could be used as blackmail to undermine national social policies.

–   Constructive – that is "consistent with the requirements of completing the single market and with the fundamental rights"- diversity of national systems, cultures and practices is "something to be exploited". But this view focused mainly on the possibility it offers for a process of exchange of good practices

---

[48]   Remember the other texts from the Commission we quoted above which developed the same arguments, based on detailed economic studies and statistics.

[49]   Company mergers, takeover bids, bankruptcies, collective redundancies.

[50]   Industrial democracy and/or financial participation of employees in transnational businesses.

and learning from them, not on local productive specialisation which could be equally "exploited" by Europe.

- The autonomy of both sides of industry has to be firmly recognised and given support through the elaboration of laws. Application of the principle of subsidiarity is double, between Community action and national (or infra-national) action; between legislation and collective bargaining. It does not mean the disappearance of legal backing, but the focusing of European legislation on framework agreements and minimal common requirements.

Whatever the causes (explicit intention or by-product of a specific political conjuncture) of this reassessment of national sovereignty on employment and social affairs, it left room for competition between national social models. It acted as a signal that the restructuring of European industry could go forward without any European regulation or restriction. The blockage of social Europe has been evident since 1991. The directive on European Work Councils, launched in 1980 and accepted only in 1994 – too late to have any influence on the re-structuring process until now – is the exception. Even today there is still no European legal status for firms (an option which as been debated for more than twenty years[51]) and no directive on information and consultation of workers, though the draft has been ready since 1996. At Nice IGC (December 2000), governments agreed on a Charter of Fundamental Rights. But, like the Community Charter of Fundamental Social Rights of Workers – adopted on 8-9 December 1989 – it has not been implemented in the Treaty and, in many respects, it seems less ambitious than the 1989 Charter. In ten years only three agreements have been concluded between social partners at the European level (parental leave, part-time work, fixed-termed contracts). There is no explicit social dialogue at territorial level and although social dialogue has been developed at industry level, it has not yet resulted in agree-ments. Dialogue has been developed for the preparation of further Euro-pean opinions, recommendations or directives for which the initiative belongs to the Commission. Some extension has been sought in the direction of civil society and non-governmental organisations. The whole is not negligible. But, subsequent to the rigid procedures defined in the Treaty, the whole process remains under the control of the Com-mission, for the most part a kind of technocratic appendix to it, though

---

[51] An agreement has been achieved in Nice, December 2000, on a European status for firms. It remains to see what will be the possibilities offered. Remind that the blockage was about the participation of workers and their representatives to the heading instances of the firm. "Participation" was one of the concepts which disappeared in 1991 from the draft of the Commission for Article 118.

the ETUC did its best to create collective mobilisation at the European level. Ironically the restraints imposed to the initial draft for the operation of European social dialogue converted it in a quasi neo-corporatist institution at European level without power. Finally it looked like its wrong interpretation popularised by political theorists of the 1970s, though this was not part of Delors' intention.

Could the Employment Process Engaged in 1997 be a New Start?

The launch of the employment process proves that the promoters of the integration of "the social dimension" have not left the battlefield. But lost opportunities are lost opportunities. The employment process could not start from the same point of departure. Several possible paths had been closed. This has a cost, even for this new process. The most evident is that it has been necessary to revert to an "employment" focus and to accept the constraints that ensue: the predominance of national governments and administrations; the resurgence of a political con-ception – to the detriment of an institutional one; the slow degeneration of horizontal subsidiarity and of the primacy of collective autonomy for building social Europe. The room left to active and extended social dialogue and to local democracy on economic and social choices in that process of construction is really very narrow, if it even still exists.

European employment policy, following the Luxembourg (1997) summit, has been developed along two lines: macroeconomic policy and the guidelines for employment. These two directions are conflicting. A macroeconomic approach for employment is reaffirmed. Economic policies are linked to the defence of the Euro and to an imperative of wage moderation. The view is that the level of employment is only a by-product of macroeconomic growth; and that employment policies have to accompany the necessary industrial restructuring. Once again we find the old reasoning. The guidelines reason in terms of "activation" for labour markets, which creates additional problems.

It is nevertheless true that the employment guidelines – with a title that refers to an attempt to guide national policies toward common Euro-pean goals – the same spirit as before in a new strategic context – have other goals. They attempt to promote human capital in European labour markets – via enhancing employability, adaptability, eliminating dis-crimination and fostering spirit of enterprise – and to introduce elements of social dialogue. But as macro views dominate, the main prospect offered to labour market reform is suppressing the barriers to wage and mobility adjustment that social and law rules constitute. As historical experience demonstrates, the objective of an "employment" approach is quantitative. Policies must maximise the number of jobs, whatever they are. In that context it will prove extremely difficult for the employment guidelines to support a process for the development of employment and social standards in Europe.

Is a Hidden Agenda still Conceivable for Europe in these Matters?

If nothing happens, the way is open for the deregulation, or more accurately for a re-regulation of European labour markets in the tradition of economic liberalism, during the next years. In his vigorous statement on the logic of European integration, Wolfgang Streeck[52] pointed to an "elective affinity between nationalism and liberalism". The reason invoked is that "negative integration through removal of barriers to trade and mobility is easier for sovereign countries to agree than positive integration through the building of common institutions". Our study of the Maastricht process relative to the social dimension of Europe brings clear evidence in favour of Streeck's statement. The outcome of nationalism on employment and social affairs is downward market pressures within Europe. Governments are obliged to engage in competitive adaptation they cannot control. Anticipation is needed and this necessitates the building of a European security net by law and collective agreements.

The openness to liberal regulation of labour markets would be far from the initial aims of the Delors presidency of Europe in 1991; but the outcomes of past experiences are not encouraging. This statement might seem extravagant when looking at the political European landscape where left-leaning governments are in the majority and may have increasing room to manoeuvre thanks to economic recovery. But as, unlike Social-Christian parties, they are historically inclined toward an "employment" focus, the decreasing of the number of people registered as unemployed is enough for these governments to expect political benefits. As the British example shows[53], the quality of jobs does not matter if quantity is obtained, whatever the means used. This is the reason why the European objective to maximise the rate of employment and of participation to labour market is ambiguous and insufficient. The focus on quality of employment required in the Social Agenda accepted in Nice IGC is important. It reintroduces a piece of "work" focus within the dominant "employment" focus.

---

[52]   Streeck, 1998. See also Streeck, 1995.
[53]   Remember that in the Maastricht process, the British and Irish governments were those who pleaded to replace the objective of improving life and work conditions by the promotion of employment (see, above, part II).

Nevertheless the lessening of economic threats linked to unemployment could offer opportunities for collective action. Other opportunities are related to the role work capabilities play in a knowledge-based economy. Studies on territory economic specialisation indicate that a "positive economic integration" is expanding through the negative integration pointed by Streeck. The single market creates new opportunities for innovation, products and work competencies which could be used as a basis for improving economic competition quality and not only in price. For instance the Airbus 380 (that will compete with the Jumbo) would not have been possible without the joint progress of the internal market, European economic integration and territorial capabilities. This could offer a support for improving standards among European economies. New standards of work and of social protection can be created, progressing in continuity with the old ones. Thus it seems unnecessary to be so desperate as Streeck is, or seems to be. The reform of European politics of competition in that direction must be advocated. And it remains totally true that intermediary levels and organisations and social dialogue are irreplaceable for providing these standards adequately. If not, as we can already see, precariousness will extend with its cortege of social exclusion. It will hinder the speed and efficiency of a recovery founded upon knowledge. Here is, if any, a hidden agenda for Europe.

This is a hidden agenda because it could not be political. European governments and politicians only learned from the collapse of Keynesian policies to be more cautious in their promises regarding employment. But they remain bogged down in searching for the benefits obtained in national political markets when unemployment falls – although they have no real responsibility for that fall in the new economic context. I agree with Jos de Beus – see his contribution in this book – that Third Way social democrats in their diverse variants are searching for a political rhetoric coping with or surfing on transformation of work, knowledge society, new aspirations for equality and individual achievement, civil dialogue and communal participation. In a way, they try to reformulate some core dimensions of Social-Christian thought in terms of modern political liberalism. As such the task is difficult and full of ambiguities. But the question I raised is not about rhetoric, but about effectiveness. Political liberalism is quite different from market economic liberalism. What is at stake in social law and rights demands at European level is to provide people at work and their representatives with *effective* capabilities to voice, to deliberate and to influence economic choices and social standards. In other terms it at least means introducing political liberalism within the field of market operation; and more generally providing people with elements of a European work status. In part I, I have tried to argue that this is part of a

440

joint-process of efficiency and of equity in a knowledge-based economy. There is some doubt about the willingness of Third Way governments to undertake that task. If using de Beus's terms, a politics of mobilisation would be needed where governments which have abandoned direct economic intervention are more inclined to a politics of management. The open method of coordination which is the new European way seems to provide some procedural outcomes – for instance, the acceptance of the Social Agenda in Nice. It remains to prove that substantive outcomes are achievable and that going beyond pure intergovernmental coordination is feasible. Restoration of political primacy is desirable, but with public reassessment of values and common goods. And it needs clarification of the respective roles of all the actors, notably the Commission, the European Parliament and the social actors. The formula used in the Nice Communiqué that the Council "invites" the Commission and the social actors to undertake this and that sounds inadequate.

In our views, the intuition of the founders of Europe in the 1950s remains durably relevant, *i.e.* that Europe is too serious a matter to be left solely to professional politicians and that it would only be possible with the mobilisation of intermediary collective entities. The situation is once again one in which the achievement of an agenda relaunching a social Europe can only be initiated by collective actors in the economy – employers and workers and their organisations – and in civil society – non-profit organisations, mutual societies, local and regional authorities.

What could be the terms of such an agenda? Some general features follow from the preceding analysis. Linking the agenda with practical knowledge and experimentation of the ongoing transformation of work and the economy is essential to its success. Rather than social dialogue at the European level on standard issues too paralysed by formal rigidities[54], it might be better to start from new problems encountered throughout Europe in a given industry, territory, industrial group or network of firms. For instance in transport or environmental industry, or in a cross-border territory, wherever social and employment issues are closely linked to the common European good – *e.g.* security, free circulation, environment, local economic and social development. Focusing the agenda on the capabilities that European law could give to certain actors would be equally essential for favouring the incorporation of knowledge in products, services and work activities. There is potential for new rights of action and of participation in economic choices, for reform of European structural funds in which capability needs – initial education and vocational training, upward mobility in the labour markets, better employability and adaptability – could be

---

[54]   Rigidities that should be loosened in favour of freer initiatives for social partners.

satisfied. Only by providing means for effective freedom can the security needed to face the uncertainties of acting in a knowledge-based economy be ensured. The provision of capabilities should probably focus on those actors in a weaker position in markets and in organisations: small and medium-sized businesses; workers – and among workers the less qualified workers; and all persons threatened by exclusion from normal employment.

Appendix 1:
First Draft by the Commission[55]

It was placed under: TITLE III. THE SOCIAL DIMENSION AND THE DEVELOPMENT OF HUMAN RESOURCES in Chapter 1. Social Provisions.

Article 118

1. In order to attain the objectives set out in Article 117 , the Union shall complement and support the action of the Member States in the following areas:

- the working environment and protection of the health and safety of workers;
- living and working conditions, so as to ensure the protection of basic rights of workers;
- basic and advanced vocational training;
- levels of skills;
- information for and consultation and participation of workers;
- the functioning of the labour market, in so far as this is made possible by economic convergence and the approximation of social practices in the Member States.

2. To this end the Council and the European Parliament, acting on a proposal from the Commission in accordance with the co-decision procedure and after consulting the Economic and Social Committee, shall adopt, by means of laws, minimum requirements applicable to each Member State.

3. Before presenting proposals in accordance with paragraph 2, the Commission shall consult ... on the possibility of attaining the objectives set out in paragraph 1 through framework agreements in accordance with Article 118b. Where the Commission establishes that a framework agreement is possible, it shall take the initiative of initiating the procedure provided for in Article 118b.[56]

---

[55] In "Initial Contribution by the Commission to the IGC on Political Union", SEC(91) 500, 15 May 1991.

[56] The Commission may adjust the proposed provisions of Article 118(3) and 118(b) in the light of:

If such an agreement cannot be reached within a reasonable time, the procedure provided for in paragraph 2 shall apply.

4. Where a law is not to be implemented by the Member States, the Commission shall be assisted by a ...[57] acting as a management committee within the meaning of Article 189b in respect of such implementing regulations as it is to adopt.

A law may, however, in the first instance, leave the responsibility for implementation of all or some of its provisions to management and labour.

5. Provisions adopted pursuant to this Article shall not prevent any Member State from maintaining or introducing more stringent protective measures compatible with the Treaty.

6. This Article shall not apply to measures regarding the harmonisation of social security systems, the right of association or the conditions governing the right to strike, nor to provisions regarding access to employment for nationals of non-member countries.

Measures in these areas shall be adopted in accordance with the procedure provided for in Article 235.

Article 118b

1. The Commission shall endeavour to develop the dialogue between management and labour at European level which could, if the two sides consider it as desirable, lead to relations based on agreements, including [framework] agreements applying throughout a trade or industry at European level.

2. At the request of the parties concerned, [framework] agreements may be the subject of a Commission recommendation or of a decision taken by the Council, acting by a qualified majority on a proposal from the Commission after consulting the European Parliament and the Economic and Social Committee and addressed to the Member States so as to make them mandatory for the duration of their validity.

    –   the outcome of discussions in the ad hoc Group on Social Dialogue;
    –   the involvement in the procedure of a consultation body, the nature of which remains to be determined.

[57]   A consultation organ of a type to be determined.

Appendix 2:
Agreement

On social policy concluded between the Member States of the European Community with the exception of the United Kingdom of Great Britain and Northern Ireland

Article 2

1. With a view to achieving the objectives of Article 1, the Community shall support and complement the activities of the Member States in the following fields:

 – improvement in particular of the working environment to protect workers' health and safety;
 – working conditions;
 – the information and consultation of workers;
 – equality between men and women with regard to labour market opportunities and treatment at work;
 – the integration of persons excluded from the labour market, without prejudice to Article 127 of the Treaty establishing the European Community.

2. To this end, the Council may adopt, by means of directives, minimum requirements for gradual implementation, having regard to the conditions and technical rules obtaining in each of the Member States. Such directives shall avoid imposing administrative, financial and legal constraints in a way which will hold back the creation and development of small and medium-sized undertakings.

The Council shall act in accordance with the procedure referred to in Article 189c of the Treaty after consulting the Economic and Social Committee.

3. However the Council shall act unanimously on a proposal from the Commission, after consulting the European Parliament and the Economic and Social Committee, in the following areas:

 – social security and social protection of workers;
 – protection of workers where their employment contract is terminated;
 – representation and collective defence of the interest of workers and employers, including co-determination, subject to paragraph 6;
 – conditions of employment for third-country nationals legally residing in Community territory;
 – financial contributions for promotion of employment and job-creation without prejudice to the provision relating to Social Fund.

4. A Member State may entrust management and labour, at their joint request, with the implementation of directives adopted pursuant to paragraphs 2 and 3.

In this case, it shall ensure that, no later than the date on which a directive must be transposed in accordance with Article 189, management and labour have introduced the necessary measures by agreement, the Member will be required to take any necessary measure enabling it at any time to be in a positions to guarantee the results imposed by that directive.

5. The provisions adopted pursuant to this Article shall not prevent any Member from maintaining or introducing more stringent protective measures compatible with the Treaty.

6. The provision of this Article shall not apply to pay, the right of association, the right to strike, the right to impose lock-outs.

Article 3

1. The Commission shall have the task of promoting the consultation of management and labour at Community level and shall take any relevant measure to facilitate their dialogue by ensuring balanced support for the parties.

2. To this end, before submitting proposals in the social policy field, the Commission shall consult management and labour on the possible direction of Community action.

3. If, after such consultation, the Commission considers Community action advisable, it shall consult management and labour on the content of the envisaged proposal. Management and labour shall forward to the Commission an opinion or, where appropriate, a recommendation.

4. On the occasion of such consultation, management and labour may inform the Commission of their wish to initiate the process, provided for in Article 4. The duration of the procedure shall not excess nine months, unless the management and labour concerned and the Commission decide jointly to extend it;

Article 4

1. Should management and labour so desire, the dialogue between them at Community level may lead to contractual relations, including agreements.

2. Agreements concluded at Community level shall be implemented either in accordance with the procedures and practices specific to management and labour and the Member States or, in matters covered by Article 2, at the joint request of the signatory parties, by a Council decision on a proposal from the Commission.

The Council shall act by qualified majority, except where the agreement in question contains one or more provisions relating to one of the areas referred to in Article 2(3), in which case it shall act unanimously.

Article 5

With a view to achieving the objectives of Article 1 and without prejudice to the other provisions of the Treaty, the Commission shall encourage cooperation between the Member States and facilitate the coordination of their action in social policy fields under this Agreement.

Postscript

Lars MAGNUSSON and Bo STRÅTH

What remains of this book can be regarded as a reflection on the future prospects of the European integration based on the historical map that we have drawn in this volume. This reflection takes the form of a postscript rather than a conclusion. With the EMU-project at the very centre of attention, we pose the questions: What is the European dimension today? Is such a thing as a European model conceivable? What elements would it contain?

We discern a situation where EMU has lead to an increased and intensified integration in several sectors. Social issues have returned once again during the 1990s, not least in response to popular protests after Maastricht (the referendums in France and Denmark). Hence, the social dimension as well as the labour market strategy (the Luxembourg process) can be regarded as instruments to recreate lost legitimacy. The security political field is another example of intensified integration. Immigration politics is a third example. At the same time as the internal frontiers disappear in the EU, the external frontiers became more obvious (Schengen).

The image of Europe as an economic tiger full of dynamic and expansionist power is perhaps uncontroversial as a political goal. Much of the same can be said regarding the goal of becoming the world-leading knowledge based society and economy in ten years' time (Lisbon). Certainly, the Stability and Growth Pact within the framework of EMU could be seen as the political instrument of such a virile European economy. Hence, growth and structural change, higher competence and life-long learning no doubt have a European dimension and can be seen as the key element of an imagined European model.

But for what purposes should the economy be strong? Is there anything more about a European model than becoming a leading knowledge-based society (or societies)? This is certainly the most important issue for the future of Europe. What seems clear against the backdrop of these two questions is that in the history of Europe the connection between economic growth and social welfare has deep historical roots and from this entanglement there has been a connection to the political.

447

Social protest and the responses to social protest have been important not to say constitutive elements of the European nation states during the last two centuries. These dynamics for a better society out of social conflict became the basis for public responsibility for welfare and solidarity. This kind of dynamics is particular European in comparison with, for instance, economies like those in the US and Japan. How could it be translated from its nation-state entrenchment into a European dimension and projected into a European future?

There is a need for a Europe with a social face and for a Europe with a human face. In this volume, for example, Barbara MacLennan, David Purdy and Robert Salais develop ideas of how this face could look like in their chapters. They define a kind of social citizenship, which no doubt is a different kind of citizenship than its usual connection to ethnicity. A Europe with a social and a human face must go beyond ethnic (and religious) definitions of political belonging. Citizens rights should not only be defined in political terms but also in social ones. How does the Europe of the future guarantee certain social rights to all its citizens, *i.e.* all human beings who live there? What does this problem mean in the light of the enlargement of the European Union? Fears of excessive migration in the future from the candidate countries has led to proposals for different levels of European citizenship. However, if free migration is only allowed for some citizens of Europe, what does this say of European citizenship in general?

An issue here is whether the trend during the 1990s of power migration from the Commission to the Member State Governments and from harmonisation towards soft law, bench-marking and subsidiarity is the best way to cope with the question of a European social citizenship. Are minimum level standards the only politically conceivable method or could more ambitious goals, based on a strong economy, be imagined? The problem seems less important possibly at a time when most governments pursue some kind of social democratic politics, but what would happen with another kind of European leaders? Is the transformation from institutional and regulative power to politics something to be regretted in this context? Is it wise to erode the European dimension in the institutional setting, based on a strong Commission, which guarantees a certain continuity? Is a European United Nations what we want in the long run?

This question becomes ever more urgent in the framework of growing strains between France and Germany. These two countries, or rather the specific interrelationships between them, have constituted the motor of European integration ever since the early 1950s. This motor stutters considerably as Burgess and Stråth discuss in their chapter. Leading German politicians suggest repeatedly a more federal Europe;

the answer from France is a Europe of the nations as during the time of De Gaulle. The strains come from the issue of the control of the European money. How to lubricate the motor?

These are all questions for the future that emerge out of this book. We can only raise the questions. The answers we do not know, but we think that it is important to get the questions right before we go for the answers.

The question of the implications of a strong European economy goes also in a direction other than the social. Should a European economic tiger also be a military tiger? Should Europe pass and remain silent in the face of the recurrence of genocide on the European continent? Is the role as vice-sheriff under the hegemony of American rule satisfying in a long-term perspective? Or should Europe have military power to intervene in Kosovo and elsewhere? To such questions the answers regarding European strength are less clear and more controversial than they are concerning the economy.

They became even more problematic when they are connected to the question of how a European tiger should behave as a guardian of its borders. What is Schengen going to mean – not in terms of the internal borders between the Member States, but in relation to the world outside? With what strength should immigrants be met? Are they welcome or not? If they are so should we also treat them as such in our labour market or do we only want to see them entrenched in specific low-wage pockets where nobody else wants to be?

At the moment when the editing of this volume is coming to a close we experience a Europe where the main problem seems to be agriculture. Sadly enough all efforts in this context are now focused on solving acute problems (BSE, foot and mouth disease etc.) rather than on the long-running problems of European agricultural policy. That this sector needs reform is without any doubt – especially due to the enlargement process. This problem triggers national rivalry on subsidies and difficulties in agreeing on a formula for a European policy. It is not too difficult to imagine how such a situation could spread into the social field in the form of national competition about standards in welfare and labour markets which could lead to social dumping, tax evasion and similar phenomena. It is urgent to prevent such development of an vicious circle and instead generate a positive virtuous circle.

Three alternative scenarios (in political implementation they may overlap) for the connections between the economic and the social stand out at the beginning of the twenty-first century:

- A European adjustment to the US American neoliberal model where the social is seen as subordinated to the economy and where social problems are thought to be solved automatically through an economy that becomes strong through less state intervention. This approach was particularly articulated in the 1980s but seems to have passed its best days by now, even if it still has adherents, especially in the UK.

- A social Europe governed through political rule-setting. This approach is divided into two alternative views on the road to the goal: (1) rule harmonisation and a strong Commission, an approach which has adherents in Germany in particular; (2) rule coordination through bench-marking and "open coordination" or agreements on minimum standards among the governments. This approach has adherents in particular in Scandinavia and France.

- A national welfare order as it emerged in the 1930s and lasted until the 1970s should be reactivated. This approach has adherents in particular in Scandinavia and the UK.

In the face of this crossroads situation, the most important question is the one we raised above: what constitutes the European identity for the future? And what role can EMU play – in the context of a wider European political economy – in order to develop an order which builds both on economic growth and social justice.

Bibliography

Abrahamson, P. and Borchorst, A., 2000, "Penge er ikke alt – om EU og den Danske Verlfaerdsstaat" (Money is not all – About the EU and the Danish Welfare State), in *Danmark og Oemu'en. Politiske Aspekter*, Aarhus: Radet for Europaeisk Politik systime.

Agell, J. and Lundborg, P., 1999, "Survey evidence on wage rigidity and unemployment: Sweden in the 1990s", *Working Paper No. 12*, Department of Economics, Uppsala University.

Akyüz, Y., 1995, "Taming International Finance", in Michie, J. and Smith, J. G. (eds.), *Managing the Global Economy*, Oxford: Oxford University Press.

Alesina, A., and Summers, I., 1993, "Central Bank Independence and Macroeconomic Performance: Some Comparative Evidence", in *Journal of Money, Credit and Banking*, 25.

Allsopp, C. and Vines, D., 1998, "The Assessment: Macroeconomic Policy After EMU", in *Oxford Review of Economic Policy*, 14 (3).

Anderson, C. J., and Kaltenthaler, K. C., 1998, "The sources of citizen support for European policy authority: the case of monetary policy", *Paper presented for APSAS Annual Meeting*, 3-6 Sept.

Anderson, P., 1996a, "The Europe to Come", in *London Review of Books,* 25 Jan.

Anderson, P., 1996b, "Under the Sign of the Interim", in *London Review of Books*, 4 Jan.

Ankersmit, F.R., 1997, *Aesthetic Politics*, Stanford: University Press.

Apel, E., 1998, European Monetary Integration, 1958-2002, London: Routledge.

Archibugi, D., Held, D., and Köhler, M. (eds.), 1998, *Re-Imagining Political Community*, Cambridge: Polity Press.

Ardener, E. P. M. and Molyneux, P., 1994, *Changes in Western European Banking*, London: Routledge.

Arnold, I. J. M., 1999, *The Third Leg of the Stool: financial stability as a prerequisite of EMU*, London, LSE Financial Markets Group, Special Paper Series.

Arthur, W. B., 1988, "Self-reinforcing mechanisms in economics", in Anderson, P. W., K. J. Arrow and D. Pines (eds.), *The Economy as an Evolving Complex System*, Redwood City, California: Addison-Wesley.

Artis, M., 1994, *Stage Two: Feasible transitions to EMU*, London: Centre for Economic Policy Research.

Artis, M., 1998, "The Unemployment Problem", in *Oxford Review of Economic Policy,* 14 (3).

Ashworth, W., 1987, *A Short History of the International Economy since 1850*, Essex: Longman.

Attali, J., 1997, "A Continental Architecture", in Gowan, P. and Anderson, P. (eds.), *The Question of Europe*, London: Verso.

Attali, J., 1999, *Europe 2000*, Brussels: Report for the European Commission.

Baer, G. and Padoa-Schioppa, T., 1989, "The Werner Report Revisited", in *Collection of Papers Annexed to the Report on Economic and Monetary Union* (Delors Report).

Balassa, B., 1961, *The Theory of Economic Integration*, London: Allen and Unwin.

Balassa, B. (ed.), 1975, *European Economic Integration*, Amsterdam and Oxford: North-Holland and American Elsevier.

Ball, L., 1996, "Disinflation and the NAIRU", *NBER Working Paper*, No. 5520.

Baran, P. and Sweezy, P., 1966, *Monopoly Capital*, New York: Monthly Review Press.

Barnard, C., 1995 [1999], *EC Employment Law*, Chichester: Wiley.

Barnard, C. and Deakin, S., 1999, "A year of living dangerously? EC social rights, employment policy, and EMU", in Towers, B. and Terry, M. (eds.), 1998, *Industrial Relations Journal European Annual Review 1998*, Oxford: Blackwell.

Barnes, I., 1996, "Monetary integration and the 1995 Nordic Enlargement", in Miles, L. (ed.), 1996, *The European Union and the Nordic Countries*, London and New York: Routledge.

Barrell, R., Caporale, G.M. and Sefton, J., 1994, "Prospects for European Unemployment", in Michie, J. and Smith, J. G. (eds.), *Unemployment in Europe*, London: Academic Press.

Barrell, R., Morgan, J. and Pain, N., 1996, "The Impact of the Maastricht Fiscal Criteria on Employment in Europe", *EUI Working Paper*, RSC No. 96/61.

Basevi, G. *et al.*, 1975, "'The All Saints' Day Manifesto and EMU", in *The Economist*, London, 1 November 1975. [Reprinted in: Fratianni, M. and Peeters, T., (eds.), 1978, *One Money for Europe*, London: Macmillan.]

Beck, W., Van der Maesen, L. and Walker, A. (eds.), 1997, *The Social Quality of Europe*, Bristol: Policy Press.

Becker, F., Cuperus, R. and Kalma, P., 1999a, "Memorandum Derde Weg", *Paper*, Amsterdam: Wiardi Beckman Stichting, March.

Becker, F. and Cuperus, R., 1999b, "Als ideeën reizen. Memorandum Derde Weg II", *Paper*, Amsterdam: Wiardi Beckman Stichting, December.

Bellamy, R., 1999, *Liberalism and Pluralism*, London: Routledge.

Belloni, M. C., "A woman-friendly city: policies on the organisation of time in Italian cities", in Hufton, O. and Kravaritou, Y. (eds.), 1999, *Gender and the Use of Time*, The Hague: Kluwer Law International.

Benassi, M., 1999, "Women's earnings in the E.U.: 28% less than men's", in *Statistics in focus. Population and social conditions, Theme 3 – 6/1999*, Luxembourg: Eurostat.

Bennett, W. L., 1998, "The Uncivic Culture", in *Political Science and Politics*, 31.

Bentley, T. *et al.*, 2000, *Getting to Grips with Depoliticisation*, London: Demos.

Bercusson, B., 1992a, "Maastricht: A Fundamental Change in European Labour Law", in *Industrial Relations Journal*, 1992: 23.

Bercusson, B., 1992b, "The Dynamic of European Labour Law After Maastricht", in *ILJ,* 1992: 23.

Berle A.A.and Means, G. C., 1933, *The Modern Corporation and Private Property,* New York: MacMillan.

Bernasek, A., 2000, "Gender, Risk and Investment: A Feminist Perspective", paper presented at the IAFFE Conference, Istanbul, Aug. 15-17, 2000.

Bernasek, A., and Stanfield, J. R., 1997, "The Grameen Bank as Progressive Institutional Adjustment", in *Journal of Economic Issues.*

Berthold, N. *et al.,* 1999, "Real wage rigidities, accommodative policies, and the functioning of EMU", in *Weltwirtscaftliches Archiv,* 135.

Bertone, C., 1998, "Constructing a women's perspective on the European Union: the Danish debate", in *NORA,* vol. 6, No. 2.

Biagi, M., 1998, "The Implementation of the Amsterdam Treaty with Regard to Employment: Co-ordination or Convergence?", in *International Journal of Comparative Labour Law and Industrial Relations,* 14: 4.

Bini Smaghi, L. and Gros, D., 2000, *Open Issues in European Central Banking,* London: Macmillan.

Blair, T., 1998, *The Third Way,* London: Fabian Society.

Blair, T., 2000, "Prime Minister's Speech to the Polish Stock Exchange", Warsaw, 6 October.

Blair, T. and Aznar, J., 2000, "Europe bolstered by a single currency", in *Financial Times,* 13 June.

Blair, T. and Schröder, G., 1999, *The Third Way die Neue Mitte,* London and Berlin, June.

Blanchard, O. and Katz, L., 1992, "Regional evolutions", *Brookings Papers on Economic Activity,* No. 1.

Borchorst, A., 1994, "Welfare state regimes, women and the EC", in D. Sainsbury (ed.), *Gendering Welfare Regimes,* London: Sage.

Borchorst, A., 1999, "Gender Differences and the Discourse on Gender and the EU in Denmark", first draft of a paper prepared for U. Liebert (ed.), *Gender Politics and Europeanisation: Transforming National Public Spheres* (forthcoming P.I.E.-Peter Lang).

Borchorst, A., 1999a, "Institutionalised Gender Equality", in Bergqvist, C. *et al.* (eds.), *Equal Democracies? Gender and Politics in the Nordic Countries,* Scandinavian University Press.

Bordo, M. D., Simard, D. and White, E. N., 1995, "France and the Bretton Woods International Monetary System, 1960-8", in: Reis, J. (ed.), *International Monetary System in Historical Perspective,* London: MacMillan.

Brandt, W., 1976, *Begegnungen und Einsichten 1960-75,* Hamburg: Hoffman and Campe.

Brothwell, J., 1988, "The 'General Theory' After FiftyYears: Why we are not all Keynesians Now", in Hillard, J. (ed.), 1998, *J. M. Keynes in Retrospect,* Cheltenham: Edward Elgar.

Brubaker, D., 1990, "Immigration, Citizenship and the Nation-State in France and Germany: A Comparative Historical Analysis", *International Sociology* 5 (4).

Buiter, W.H., 1992, "Moeten wij ons zorgen maken over de budgettaire voodoo van Maastricht?", in *Economisch Statistische Berichten*, Mar. 1992.

Buiter, W. H., 1999, "Alice in Euroland," in *CEPR Policy Paper* No. 1.

Bulletin Quotidien Europe, 28 July 2000.

Burgess, J. P., 2001, "What's so European About the European Union?", in *Culture and Rationality: European Frameworks of Norwegian Identity*, Oslo: Norwegian Academic Press.

Burgess, J. P., and Tunander, O., 2000, *European Security Identities: Contested Understandings of EU and NATO*, Oslo: Prio.

Busch, A., 1991, "Die deutsch-deutsche Währungsunion: Politisches Votum trotz ökonomischer Bedenken," in Liebert, U. and Merkel, W. (eds.), *Die Politik zur deutschen Einheit. Probleme, Strategien, Kontroversen*, Opladen: Leske + Budrich.

Bussemaker, J., 1999, *Het sociale Europa*, Amsterdam: Partij van de Arbeid.

Buti, M., Franco, D. and Ongena, H., 1998, "Fiscal Discipline and Flexibility in EMU: The Implementation of the Stability and Growth Pact," in *Oxford Review of Economic Policy*, 14 (3).

Callaghan, J., 2000, *The Retreat of Social Democracy*, Manchester: University Press.

Calmfors, L. and A. Forslund, 1990, "Wage formation in Sweden", in Calmfors, L. (ed.), *Wage formation and macroeconomic policies in the Nordic countries*, Stockholm: SNS Förlag.

Calmfors, L., et al., 1997, *EMU: A Swedish perspective*, Dordrecht: Kluwer academic publishers (revised version of the Calmfors report).

Cameron, D., 1999, "Unemployment, Job Creation and EMU," in Bermeo, N. (ed.), *Unemployment in the New Europe*, Cambridge: Cambridge University Press [previously a paper at Yale University, Department of Political Science, 15 December].

Canals, J., 1997, *Universal Banking*, Oxford: Oxford University Press.

Caporaso, J., Cowles, M. and Risse, T. (eds.), 2000, *Europeanisation and Domestic Change*, Ithaca, N.Y.: Cornell University Press.

Cautrès, B. and Reynié, D., 2000, *L'opinion européenne*, Paris: Presses de Sciences Po.

CEC, 1990, "One Market, One Money: An Evaluation of the Potential Benefits and Costs of Forming an Economic and Monetary Union", in *European Economy*, No. 44. Oct.

CEC, 1993a, *European Social Policy: Options for the Union*, Green Paper, COM (93) 551, 17 Nov. 1993, Luxembourg: OOPEC.

CEC, 1993b, *Growth, Competitiveness and Employment: The Challenges and Ways Forward into the 21st Century*, White Paper, COM (93), Luxembourg: OOPEC.

CEC, 1994, *European Social Policy: A Way Forward for the Union*, White Paper, COM (94) Luxembourg: OOPEC.

CEC, 1996, *Action for Employment in Europe: A Confidence Pact*, Luxembourg: OOPEC, 1996 CSE (96).

CEC, 1997, *Green Paper: Partnership for a New Organisation of Work*, COM (97), Luxembourg: OOPEC.

CEC, 1998, Progress report from the Commission on the follow-up of the Communication: "Incorporating equal opportunities for women and men into all Community policies and activities", COM 1998, Brussels.

CEC, 1998, *The Amsterdam Treaty: A Comprehensive Guide*, Luxembourg: OOPEC.

CEC, 2000, *Communication from the Commission to the Council, the European Parliament, the Economic and Social Committee and the Committee of the Regions, Social Policy Agenda*, 28 Jun. 2000, COM (2000), Brussels.

CEC, 2000, *The Employment Guidelines for 2001: Proposal for a Council Decision on Guidelines for Member States' Employment Policies for the Year 2001*, Luxembourg: OOPEC.

Cecchini, P., 1988, *The European Challenge 1992, The Benefits of a Single Market*, Gower: London.

Centre for Economic Policy Research, *European Economic perspectives*, Centre for Economic Policy Research, No. 21, Feb. 1999.

Chambers, G., 2000, "European Social Democracy in the 21st Century", *Working Paper* 1/2000, London: Friedricht Ebert Stiftung.

Checkel, J. T., 2000, "Bridging the Rational-Choice/Constructivist Gap? Theorizing Social Interaction in European Institutions", *ARENA Working Papers* WP 00/11.

Chick, V., 1986, *The Evolution of the Banking System and the Theory of Saving, Investment and Interest*, Economies et Sociétés: série Monnaie et Production 3.

Chick, V., 1992, *Selected Essays of Victoria Chick*, London: Macmillan.

Chick, V., 1993, "The Evolution of the Banking System and the Theory of Monetary Policy", in Frowen, S. (ed.), *Monetary Theory and Monetary Policy: New Tracks for the 1990s*, London: Macmillan.

Chick, V., 1998, *Big Banks, Small Business and the Regions in Bankers' Europe*, London: University College London mimeo.

Chick, V. and Dow, S. C., 1988, *A Post-Keynesian Perspective on Banking and Regional Development*, in Arestis, P. (ed.), 1988, *Post Keynesian Monetary Economics*, Cheltenham: Elgar.

Chick, V. and Dow, S. C., 1997, "Competition and the Future of the European Banking and Financial System", in Cohen, A. J., Hagemann, H. and Smithin, J. (eds.), *Money, Financial Institutions and Macaroeconomics*, Boston: Kluwer.

Christiansen, T., Jorgensen, K. E. and Wiener, A., 1999, "The social construction of Europe", in *Journal of European Public Policy*, 6: 4, Special Issue.

Cini, M., 2000, *Organisational Culture and Reform: The case of the European Union under Jacques Santer*, European University Institute, Working Paper

Coats, A. W. (ed.), 1999, *The Development of Economics in Western Europe since 1945*, London: Routledge.

455

Coffey, P. and Presley, J. R., 1971, *European Monetary Integration,* London: Macmillan.

Cohen, G. and Wenninger, J., 1994, *The Relationship between the Fed Funds Rate and Economic Activity,* Federal Reserve Bank of New York: Research Paper No. 9406.

Cohen, S. D., 1977, *International Monetary Reform, 1964-69,* NY: MacMillan.

Cohn-Bendit, D., and Duhamel, O. (in co-operation with Thierry Vissol), 1998, "Euro für alle. Das Währungswörterbuch"; Cologne: Dumont, in *French: Petit Dictionnaire de l'Euro*; Paris: Seuil.

Collignon, S., 1998a, *In Search of Monetary Stability: From Bretton Woods to Sustainable EMU,* Mimeo, Paris: AMUE.

Collignon, S., 1998b, *Does the Central Bank Set the Natural Rate of Unemployment?* Mimeo, Paris: AMUE.

Comité Intergouvernemental Créé par la Conférence de Messine, *Rapport des Chefs de Délégation aux Minstres des Affaires Etrangères,* Brussels, 1956: The "Spaak Report", summarized in English in "Political and Economic Planning", *Planning,* No. 405 (1956).

Commission of the EEC, 1970, "A plan for the phased establishment of an economic and monetary union", Commission of the EEC, *Bulletin of the EC,* Supplement 3; COM (70) 300, 4 March, Brussels.

Commission of the European Commission, 1998, Progress report from the Commission on the follow-up of the Communication: "Incorporating equal opportunities for women and men into all Community policies and activities", COM 1998, 1222 final.

Committee for the Study of Economic and Monetary Union (The Delors Committee), 1989, *Report on Economic and Monetary Union in the Community,* Luxembourg: OOPEC.

Cooper, J., 1999, "The Long Peace", in *Prospekt,* 40, April.

Cox, R., 1997, "Democracy in Hard Times", in McGrew, A. (ed.), 1997, *The Transformation of Democracy?,* London: Polity Press/Open University Press.

Crafts, N. and Toniolo, G., 1996, "Postwar Growth: An Overview," in Crafts, N. and Toniolo, G. (eds.), *Economic Growth In Europe Since 1945,* Cambridge: Cambridge University Press.

Craig, P. and De Búrca, G. (eds.), 1999, *The Evolution of EU Law,* Oxford: Oxford UP.

Crocker, K. J., 1996, "Regulatory issues with Vertically Disintegrated Public Utilities: A Transaction Cost Analysis", in Groenewegen, J. (ed.), 1996, *Transaction Costs and Beyond,* Boston, Dordrecht: Kluwer Academic Press.

Crockett, A., 1994, "The role of convergence in the process of EMU", in Steinherr, A. (ed.), 1994, *30 years of European monetary integration from the Werner Plan to EMU,* London and New York: Longman.

Crouch, C., 1999, *Social Change in Western Europe,* NY, Oxford University Press.

Crouch, C. (ed.), 2000, *After the Euro. Shaping institutions for Governance in the wake of European Monetary Union,* Oxford: Oxford University Press.

Crowley, J., 1999, *Sans épines, la rose*, Paris: La Découverte.

Cukierman, A., 1992, *Central Bank Strategy: Credibility and Independence*, Cambridge, Mass.: MIT Press.

Cuperus, R. and Kandel, J. (eds.), 1998, *European Social Democracy: Transformation in Progress*, Bonn-Amsterdam: Friedrich Ebert Stiftung-Wiardi Beckman Stichting.

Cuperus, R., Duffek, K. and Kandel, J. (eds.), 2000, *Multiple Third Ways*, Amsterdam: Wiardi Beckman Stichting.

Dahl, R. A., 1985, *A Preface to Economic Democracy*, Berkeley: University of California Press.

Dauderstädt, M, 2000a, "A Social Democratic European Policy", *Background Paper* for the Eurokolleg Seminar, Bonn: Friedrich Ebert Stiftung, 15-16 June.

Dauderstädt, M., 2000b, "Wege, Umwege und Dirtte Wege zu einem sozialen und demokratischen Europa", in *Eurokolleg* 44, Bonn: Friedrich Ebert Stiftung.

Dauderstädt, M., Gerrits, A. and Márkus, G. G., 1999, *Troubled Transition, Social Democracy in East Central Europe*, Amsterdam: Friedrich Ebert Stiftung-Wiardi Beckman Stichting.

David, P. A., 1985, "Clio and the Economics of QWERTY", in *American Economic Review*, 75.

David, P. A., 1994, "Why are Institutions the 'Carriers of History'?: Path Dependence and the Evolution of Conventions, Organisations and Institutions", in *Structural Change and Economic Dynamics*, Vol. 5, No. 2.

Davidson, P., 1972, *Money and the Real World*, London: Macmillan.

Davidson, P., 1992, "Would Keynes be a New Keynesian?", in *Eastern Economic Journal*, 18 (4).

Davidson, P., 1994, *Post Keynesian Macroeconomic Theory*, Cheltenham: Elgar.

Davies, P., 1992, "The Emergence of European Labour Law", in McCarthy, W., (ed.), *Legal Intervention in Industrial Relations: Gains and Losses*, Oxford: Blackwell.

de Beus, J., 1969, "Memorandum from the Commission to the Council on the Coordination of Economic Policies and Monetary Cooperation within the Community", in *Bulletin of the EEC*, COM (69) 150, Supplement 3.

de Beus, J., 1970, "Commission Memorandum to the Council on the Preparation of a Plan for the Phased Establishment of an Economic and Monetary Union", in *Bulletin of the EEC*, Supplement 3, 4 March

de Beus, J., 1973, "Communication of the Commission to the Council on the Progress Achieved in the First Stage of Economic and Monetary Union, on the Allocation of Powers and Responsibilities among the Community Institutions and the Member States Essential to the Proper Functioning of Economic and Monetary Union, and on the Measures to be taken in the Second Stage of Economic and Monetary Union", in COM (73) 570 def. *Bulletin of the EC*, Supplement 5, Brussels, 19 April 1973.

de Beus, J., 1990a, *Economic and Monetary Union*, SEC (90), Brussels, 21 Aug. 1990.

de Beus, J., 1990b, "One Market, One Money", in *European Economy*, 44, Oct.

de Beus, J., 1993a, (European Commission), "The Economics of Community Public Finance", in *European Economy*, 5.

de Beus, J., 1993b, (European Commission), "Stable – Sound Finances. Community Public Finance in the Perspective of EMU", in *European Economy*, 53.

de Beus, J., 1999a, "Die politische Kultur der Niederlande im Zeitalter der Globalisierung", in Karpf, E., Kiesel, D. and Wittmeier, M. (eds.), *Partizipation und politische Bildung in Europa*, Frankfurt am Main: Haag & Herchen Verlag.

de Beus, J., 1999b, "The Politics of Consensual Well-being", in Kelly, G. (ed.), *The New European Left*, London: Fabian Society.

de Beus, J., 2000, "EMU and the European Model of Society – The Dutch Case", in Ross, G. and Martin, A. (eds.), 2000, *EMU and the European Model of Society*, New York: Bergham Books.

de Beus, J. and Notermans, T., 2000, "Een taxatie van de Derde Weg", in *Beleid and Maatschappij 2000*.

de Bondt, G. J., 1999, "Banks and Monetary transmisison in Europe: Empirical Evidence", in *Banca Nazionale del Lavoro Quarterly Review*, No. 209 (June*)*.

De Gaulle, C., 1969, *Discours et Messages, 1962-5*, Paris.

De Gaulle, C., 1987, *Lettres, Notes, et Carnets, 1964-66*, Paris.

De Grazia, V., 1991, *How Fascism Ruled Women, Italy 1922-1945*, Berkeley: Univ. of California Press.

De Haan, J. and Eijfinger, S. C. W., 2000, "The Democratic Accountability of the European Central Bank: A Comment on Two Fairly-Tales," in *Journal of Common Market Studies*, 38 (3).

De Nederlandsche Bank, 1973, *Report for the Year 1972*. Amsterdam.

De Nederlandsche Bank, 1974, *Report for the Year 1973*. Amsterdam.

Deakin, S., 1996, "Labour Law as Market Regulation: The Economic Foundations of European Social Policy", in Davies, P. *et al.* (eds.) *European Community Labour Law: Principles and Perspectives, Liber Amicorum Lord Wedderburn*, Oxford: Clarendon Press.

Decressin, J. and Fatas, A., 1995, "Regional and Labour Market Dynamics in Europe", in *European Economic Review*, 39.

Delors Report, 1989, *Report on Economic and Monetary Union in the European Community*, (Committee for the Study of Economic and Monetary Union) Luxembourg: OOPEC.

Desportes, G. and Mauduit, L. 1999, *La Gauche Imaginaire*, Paris: Grasset.

Devine, P., 1988, *Democracy and Economic Planning*, Cambridge: Polity.

Dhotier, P. and Kapur, I., 1996, "Towards a market economy: Structures of Governance", International Monetary Fund working paper, No. 11.

Dixit, A. K., 1996, *The Making of Economic Policy: A Transaction-Cost Perspective*, Cambridge, Massachusetts, London, England: The MIT Press.

Dølvik, J. E., 2000, *Economic and Monetary Union: Implications for Industrial Relations and Collective Bargaining in Europe*, paper for the Twelfth International Conference of Europeanists: "Europe 2020", Council for European Studies, Chicago 30 March/1 April, 2000

Douthwaite, R., 1993, *The Growth Illusion, how economic growth has enriched the few, impoverished the many and endangered the planet*, Tulsa, Council Oak Books.

Dow, J. C. R., 1964, *The Management of the British Economy 1945-1960*, London: Cambridge University Press/National Institute for Economic and Social Research.

Dow, S. C., 1994, "European Monetary Integration and the Distribution of Credit Availability", in Corbridge, S., Thrift, N. and Martin, R. (eds.), 1994, *Money, Power and Space*, Oxford: Blackwell.

Dow, S. C., 1999, "Stages of Banking Development and the Spatial Development of Financial Systems", in Martin, R. (ed.), 1999, *Money and the Space Economy*, London: Wiley.

Dow, S. C. and Hillard, J. (eds.), 1995, *Keynes, Knowledge and Uncertainty*, Cheltenham: Edward Elgar.

Dow, S. C. and Smithin, J., 1992, "Free Banking in Scotland, 1695-1845", in *Scottish Journal of Political Economy*, 39 (4).

Drake, H., 2000, *Jacques Delors: Perspectives on a European Leader*, London and New York: Routledge.

Dryzek, J. S., 1996, "Political Inclusion and the Dynamics of Democratization", in *American Political Science Review*, 90.

Dugger, W. M., 1993, "Transaction Cost Economics and the State", in Pitelis, C. (ed.), *Transaction Costs, Market and Hierarchies*, Oxford, UK, and Cambridge, US: Blackwell.

Dunn, J., 2000, *The Cunning of Unreason*, London: Harper and Collins.

Dymski G., Epstein G., Pollin R. (eds.), 1993, *Transforming the US Financial System, Equity and Efficiency for the 21st Century*, Armonk: Sharpe.

Dyson K, 1994, *Elusive Union. The Process of Economic and Monetary Union in Europe*, London and New York: Longman.

Dyson, K., 1999, "Benign or Malevolent Leviathan? Social Democratic Governments in a Neo-Liberal Euro Area" in *The Political Quarterly*, 70 (2).

Dyson, K., 2000, *The Politics of the Euro-Zone. Stability or Breakdown?*, Oxford: Oxford University Press.

Dyson, K. and Featherstone, K., 1999, *The Road to Maastricht. Negotiating Economic and Monetary Union*, Oxford: Oxford University Press.

Eatwell, J., Milgate, M. and Newman, P. (eds.), 1987, *The New Palgrave: A Dictionary of Economics*, London: Macmillan.

ECB, 1999, *Monthly Bulletin*. Jan. 1999.

Edelman, M., 1988, *Constructing the Political Spectacle*, Chicago and London: The University of Chicago Press.

Eder, K., 2000, "Zur Transformation nationalstaatlicher Öffentlichkeit in Europa. Von der Sprachgemeinschaft zur issuespezifischen Kommunikationsgemeinschaft", in *Berliner Journal für Soziologie, 3*.

Eichengreen, B., 1992, *Golden fetters: The Gold Standard and the Great Depression, 1919-1939,* Oxford: Oxford UP.

Eichengreen, B., 1993, "Labor markets and European monetary unification", in Masson, P. and Taylor, M., (eds.), *Policy issues in the operation of currency areas,* Cambridge: Cambridge University Press.

Eichengreen, B., 1996, *Globalizing Capital. A History of the International Monetary System,* Princeton, New Jersey: Princeton University Press.

Eichengreen, B., 1998, *European Monetary Unification. Theory, Practice, and Analysis,* Cambridge, Massachusetts, London, England: The MIT Press, 1997 (second printing 1998).

Eichengreen, B. and Frieden, J., 1994, "The Political Economy of Monetary Unification: an Analytical Introduction," in Eichengreen B. and Frieden, J. (eds.), *The Political Economy of European Monetary Unification,* Boulder: Westview Press.

Eichengreen, R., 1997, "Saving Europe's Automatic Stabilisers", in *National Institute Economic Review,* 159 (January).

Elmeskov, J., 1998, "The Unemployment Problem in Europe: Lessons From Implementing the OECD Jobs Strategy", *EUI Working Paper* RSC No. 98/24.

Elmeskov, J., 1993, "High and Persistent Unemployment: Assessment of the problem and its Causes", *OECD Economics Department Working Paper.*

Elster, J., 1989, *The Cement of Society,* Cambridge: University Press.

Elster, J., 1990, *Desires and Opportunities,* Deventer: Van Loghum Slaterus, Duijker Lecture.

Emerson, M., 1998, *Redrawing the Map of Europe,* London: MacMillan Press.

Emerson, M. *et al,* 1992, *One market, one money,* Oxford: Oxford University Press.

Emminger, O., 1976, "Deutsche Geld- und Währungspolitik im Spannungsfeld zwischen innerem und äußerem Gleichgewicht, 1948-75", in Deutsche Bundesbank (ed.), 1976, *Währung und Wirtschaft in Deutschland, 1876-1975,* Frankfurt: Deutsche Bundesbank.

Endo, K., 1999, *The Presidency of the European Commission under Jacques Delors. The Politics of Shared Leadership,* London, MacMillan.

EOS Gallup Europe, 1996, *The European Union "A View from the Top". Top Decision Makers and the European Union,* 1996.

EP, 2000, *Hearing before the Committee on Economic and Monetary Affairs of the European Parliament.* ECB, 20 Jun. 2000.

Europäische Kommission, *Texte zum Euro. Servet/Collicelli/Burgoyne/Reich: Zusammenfassung der für die Arbeitsgruppe Euro bei der DG XXIV der E.K erstellten Beiträge über die psychosoziologischen Aspekte des Übergangs zum Euro,* No. 29. (no year).

European Commission, 1973, "Declaration on European Identity," in *General Report of the European Commission,* Brussels: European Commission.

European Commission, DGII, 1998a, *Growth and Employment in the Stability-Oriented Framework of EMU,* Brussels: EU.

European Commission, 1998b, *Employment in Europe 1998,* Brussels: EU.

European Commission, 1999, *Economic policy in EMU: A study by the European Commission Services*, New York: Oxford University Press Inc.

European Commission, 1999a, *European Public Opinion on the single currency. Special edition,* January 1999 (by Daphne Ahrendt).

European Commission, 2000, *Employment in Europe 2000,* Brussels: EU.

European Commission, *Europinion special,* various volumes and years.

European Commission, *Integral text of the final communiqué of the conference of the heads of sate or governments on 1 and 2 December 1969 at The Hague* (Hague Communiqué).

European Commission, *Standard Eurobarometer,* Nos. 49, 51, 53.

European Commission: "Euro Papers" Series, Working Group on the "euro"; DG XXIV (no year) *European Economic Review* 38, 1021-1039.

Eyal, J., 1999, "De Derde Weg brokkelt langzaam af", in *NRC Handelsblad,* 22 Nov.

Eyal, J., 2000, "Blair heeft in 1000 dagen zijn glansrol zelf verspeeld", in *NRC Handelsblad,* 27 Jan.

Fajertag G. and Pochet P. (eds.), 2000, *Social Pacts in Europe – New Dynamics,* Brussels, ETUI.

Falkner, G., 1998, *EU Social Policy in the 1990s. Towards a corporatist policy community,* London: Routledge.

Favero, C., Freitas, X., Persson, T. and Wyplosz, C, 2000, *One Money, Many Countries. Monitoring the European Central Bank* 2, London: CEPR.

Fell, J. P. C., 1996, *The role of short rates and foreign long rates in the determination of longterm Interest rates,* EMI Staff Paper No. 4.

Ferrera, M., Hemerijck, A. and Rhodes, M., 2000, *The Future of Social Europe,* Oeiras: Celta.

Fischer, A. M., 1996, "Central Bank Independence and Sacrifice Ratios" in *Open Economies Review,* 7.

Fischer, J., 2000, "From Confederacy to Federation – Thoughts on the Finality of European Integration", Berlin: Humboldt University, 12 May.

Fischer, J., 2000, "Vom Staatenverbund zur Föderation – Gedanken über die Finalität der europäischen Integration", Rede in der Humboldt-Universität in Berlin, 12. May.

Fischer, S., 1994, "Modern Central Banking," in Capie, F. *et al,* 1994, *The Future of Central Banking,* Cambridge: Cambridge University Press.

Fitzpatrick, B., 1992, "Community Social Law After Maastricht", *ILJ,* 21.

Foden, D. and Magnusson, L. (eds.), 1999, *Entrepreneurship in the European Employment Strategy,* Brussels: ETUI.

Foden, D. and Magnusson, L. (eds.), 2000, Contested territory. *Entrepreneurship in the European Employment Strategy,* Brussels: ETUI.

Fredriksson, P., 1995, "The dynamics of regional labor markets and active labor market policy: Swedish evidence", *Working Paper* No. 20, Economics Department, University of Uppsala.

Freedland, M., 1996a, "Employment Policy", in Davies, P. *et al.* (eds.), 1996, *European Community Labour Law: Principles and Perspectives, Liber Amicorum Lord Wedderburn*, Oxford: Clarendon Press.

Freedland, M., 1996b, "Vocational Training in EC Law And Policy – Education, Employment or Welfare?", *ILJ*, 25.

Friedman, B., 1995, "Does Monetary Policy Affect Real Economic Activity?: Why Do we Still Ask this Question?", in *NBER Working Paper*, No. 5212.

Friedman, M., 1968, "The Role of Monetary Policy", in *American Economic Review, 1968.*

Gamble, A. and Wright, T. (eds.), 1999, *The New Social Democracy*, Oxford: Blackwell Publishers.

Gardener, E. P. M. and Molyneux, P., 1994, *Changes in Western European Banking*, London: Routledge.

Gardener, E. P. M., 1993, *Capital adequacy and large exposure standards*, Bangor: University College of North Wales.

Garrett, G. (1993), "The Politics of Maastricht", *in Economics and Politics* 5(2).

Gavin, F. and Mahan, E., 2000, "Hegemony or Vulnerability? Giscard, Ball, and the 1962 Gold Standstill Proposal", in *Journal of European Integration History*, 2/2000.

Gegenstandpunkt, 2000, "Europa 2000-Zwischenbilanz eines (anti)imperialistischen Projekts neuen Typs (I): Von der Währungsunion", *Politische Vierteljahresschrift*, 4.

Gerlach, S., 1995, "Adjustable pegs vs. single currencies: How valuable is the option to realign?", in *European Economic Review, 39.*

Giddens, A., 1998, *The Third Way*. Cambridge: Polity Press.

Giddens, A., 2000, *The Third Way and its Critics*, Cambridge: Polity Press.

Giddens, A., 2000a, "A Third Way for the European Union?", *paper.*

Giersch, H., 1985, "Eurosclerosis", *Kiel Discussion Paper* No. 112, 1985, Kiel: Institute for World Economics.

Giersch, H., Paqué, K. and Schieding, H., 1992, *The Fading Miracle. Four Decades of Market Economy in Germany*, Cambridge: Cambridge University Press.

Gilbert, E. and Helleiner, E. (eds.), 1999, *Nation-States and Money*, London: Routledge.

Glyn, A. and Sutcliffe, B., 1972, *British Capitalism, Workers and the Profits Squeeze*, Harmondsworth: Penguin.

Goetschy, J., 1999, "The European Employment Strategy", in *European Journal of Industrial Relations*, 6.

Goldin, C. and Libecap, G. (eds.), 1994, *The Regulated Economy. A Historical Approach to Political Economy*, Chicago, University of Chicago Press.

Goodhart, C., 1989, "The Delors Report, Was Lawson's reaction justifiable?", *Special Paper Series* No. 15, London: LSE Financial Markets Group, May.

Goodhart, C. A. E., 1995, "Financial Globalisation, Derivatives, Volatility and the Challenge for the Policies of Central Banks", *Special Papers* No. 74, London: London School of Economics.

Goodwin, C. D., 1998, "The Patrons of Economics in a Time of Transformation", in Morgan and Rutherford (eds.), 1998, *From Interwar Pluralism to Postwar Neoclassicism*, Durham-London: Duke University Press.

Grant, C., 1994, *Delors*, London: Nicholas Brealey Publishing.

Grant, C, 1995, *Delors: Architecte de l'Europe*, Paris: Georg Editeur.

Green-Pedersen, C., Hemerijck, A. and Van Kersbergen, K., 2000, "Neoliberalism, the 'Third Way' or What?", paper, Nijmegen: Faculty of Policy Sciences, April.

Gros, D. and Thygesen, N., 1998, *European Monetary Integration. From the European Monetary System to Economic and Monetary Union*, London: Longman.

Grundwertekommission beim Parteivorstand der SPD, 1999, *Dritte Wege – Neue Mitte*, Berlin: SPD.

Guéhenno, J., 1993, *La Fin de la Démocratie*, Paris: Flammarion.

Guéhenno, J., 1999, *L'Avenir de la Liberté*, Paris: Flammarion.

Haas, P. M., "Introduction: Epistemic Communities and International Policy Coordination", in *International Organization*, 46.

Habermas, J., 1990, "Der DM-Nationalismus", in *Die Zeit*, 30 Mar. 1990.

Hagtvet, B., 2000, "Verdiuthulingen av sosialdemokratiet", in *Aftenposten* (Oslo), 7 February.

Hammersland, R., 2000a, "Who's in the driving seat in Europe, International Capital markets or the BUBA", Unpublished paper, EUI.

Hammersland, R., 2000b, "Large T small N; A two-step approach to the identification of cointegrating relationships in time series models with a small cross-sectional dimension", Unpublished paper, EUI 2000.

Hampsher-Monk, I. and McKinnon, C. (eds.), 2000, *The Demands of Citizenship*, Dulles (Va.): Continuum.

Hanny, B. and Wessels, W., 1999, "The Monetary Committee of the European Communities: A Significant Though Not Typical Case", in Van Schendelen, R., (ed.), *Do EU Committees Matter? A Case Study Book*, Dartmouth/Aldershot: Robin Pedler.

Hansen, A. W., 1938, *Full Recovery or Stagnation?*, New York: Norton.

Hansen, A. W., 1949, *Monetary Theory and Fiscal Policy*, New York: McGraw-Hill.

Hantrais, L. (ed.), 2000, Gendered Policies in Europe. Reconciling Employment and Family Life, London: MacMillan Press.

Harkness, S., 1999, "Working 9 to 5?" in Gregg, P. and Wadsworth, J. (eds.), *The State of Working Britain*, Manchester: Manchester University Press.

Harrod, R, F., 1939, "An Essay in Dynamic Theory", in *Economic Journal* 49 (March).

Heilbroner, R. and Milberg, W., 1995, *The Crisis of Vision in Modern Economic Thought*, Cambridge: Cambridge University Press.

Heldring, J. L., 1965, "Europe: a 'Greater Holland'?", in *International Spectator*, 14.

463

Helfferich, B. and Kolb, F., 2000, "Multilevel Action Coordination in European Contentious Politics. The case of the European Women's Lobby", in Imig, D. and Tarrow, S. (eds.), *Contentious Europeans: Protest and Politics in an Integrating Europe,* forthcoming.

Helleiner, E., 1994, *States and the Reemergence of Global Finance. From Bretton Woods to the 1990s,* Ithaca: Cornell University Press.

Hernes, H, 1987, *Welfare State and Women Power,* Oslo: Scandinavian University Press.

Hicks, J., 1937, "Mr. Keynes and the Classics: A Suggested Interpretation", in *Econometrica* 5 (April).

Hicks, J., 1974, *The crisis in Keynesian economics,* Oxford: Basil Blackwell.

Hicks, J., 1980, "IS-LM: an Explanation", in *Journal of Post-Keynesian Economics* 3 (2).

Hirschmann, N. and Liebert, U. (eds.), 2000 *Women and Welfare. Theory and Practice in the U.S. and Europe,* Piscataway (NJ): Rutgers University Press.

Hirst, P. and Thompson, G., 1999, *Globalisation in Question* 2/e, Cambridge: Polity.

Hix, S., 1999, *The Political System of the European Union,* London: MacMillan Press.

Hobsbawn, E., 2000, *The New Century,* London: Little Brown.

Hobson, B., 1998, *The Interplay Between Identities and Institutions: The Centrality of Paid Work and Swedish Women"s Mobilization in Periods of Welfare State Expansion and Retrenchment,* Paper presented at the Conference on Women in Japan and Sweden: Work and Family in Two Welfare Regimes, Stockholm, September 14.

Hobson, B., 1999, "Economic Citizenship: Reflecting Gender through the European Union Policy Mirror", paper presented at the Conference on Equality, Democracy and the Welfare State: Europe and America. Institute for International Studies, Stanford University, 10-11 May 1999.

Hoffmann, S., 1995, *The European Sisyphus,* Boulder (Col.): Westview Press.

Hoffmann, S., 1998, *World Disorders,* Lanham (Mrd.): Rowman and Littlefield Publishers.

Holden, S. and Vikøren, B., 1994, "Interest rates in the Nordic countries: Evidence based on devaluation expectations", in *Scandinavian Journal of Economics* 96 (1).

Holden, S., 1998, "Wage drift and the relevance of centralised wage setting" in *Scandinavian Journal of Economics,* 100 (4).

Holden, S., 2000, "Monetary regime and the co-ordination of wage setting", Memorandum No. 1, Department of Economics, University of Oslo.

Holden, S., 2001. "Monetary policy and nominal rigidities", Mimeo, Department of Economics, University of Oslo.

Holtfrerich, C., 1998, "Geldpolitik bei festen Wechselkursen (1948-1970)", in Deutsche Bundesbank (ed.), *Fünfzig Jahre Deutsche Mark.* München: C. H. Beck.

Hombach, B., 1998, *Aufbruch*, Munich: Econ Verlag.

Honkapohja, S. and Pikkarainen, P., 1992, "Country characteristics and the choice of exchange rate regime: Are mini-skirts followed by maxis?", in *Bank of Finland Discussion papers*, No. 36.

Houseman, S. N., "Job Growth and the Quality of Jobs in the US Economy", in *Labour: Review of Labour Economics and Industrial Relations* (IIRA) S93-S124.

Huffschmid, J., 2000, "Hoist with its own petard: consequences of the single currency for Germany", in Moss, B. H. and Michie, J. (eds.), 2000, *The single European currency in national perspective. A Community in crisis?*, London: Macmillan.

Hufton, O. and Kravaritou, Y. (eds.), 1999, *Gender and the Use of Time*, The Hague: Kluwer.

Huhne, C., 1999, *Report on the annual report for 1998 of the European Central Bank*, European Parliament, Session Document A5-0035/1999, Committee on Economic and Monetary Affairs.

Hurd, I, 1999, "Legitimacy and Authority in International Politics", in *International Organization*, 2/1999.

Imig, D.Tarrow, S. (eds.), 2000, *Contentious Europeans: Protest and Politics in an Integrating Europe*, forthcoming

Institut De Gaulle (ed.), 1992, *De Gaulle en son Siècle III*, Paris: Institut De Gaulle.

International Labour Organisation, 1956, *Social Aspects of Economic Co-operation: Report of a Group of Experts*, Studies and Reports, New Series, No. 46, (ILO, 1956); summarized as International Labour Office, "Social Aspects of Economic Co-operation" (1956) 74 *International Labour Review:* 99 (the Ohlin Report).

International Monetary Fund, 1999, *World Economic Outlook*, Washington, IMF.

Isachsen, A. and Røste, O., 1999, *Euroen og den norske kronens skjebne*, Bergen: Fagbokforlaget.

Issing, O., 1999, "The Eurosystem: Transparent and Accountable. Or: 'Willem in Euroland'", in *CEPR Policy Paper No. 2*.

Issing, O., 2000, *How to Promote Growth in the Euro Area: The Contribution of Monetary Policy*, Brussels: 12 May 2000, Conference of the National Bank of Belgium.

Italianer, A., 1993, "Mastering Maastricht: EMU Issues and How They were Settled", in Gretschmann, K. (ed.), 1993, *Economic and Monetary Union: Implications for National Policy-Makers*, Maastricht: European Institute of Public Administration Press.

Iversen, T., 1998, "Wage Bargaining, Central Bank Independence, and the Real Effects of Money", in *International Organization*, 52 (3).

Iversen, T. and Pontusson, J., 2000, "Comparative Political Economy: A Northern European Perspective", in Iversen, T. and Pontusson, J. and Soskice, D. (eds.), *Unions, Employers, and Central Banks. Macroeconomic Coordination and Institutional Change in Social Market Economies*, Cambridge: Cambridge University Jackman, R., 1998, "The Impact of the European Union on

Unemployment and Unemployment Policy", in Hine, D. and Kassim, H. (eds.), *Beyond the Market: The EU and National Social Policy*, London: Routledge.

James, H., 1995, "The IMF and the Creation of the Bretton Woods System, 1944-58", in Eichengreen, B. (ed.), *Europe's Postwar Recovery*, Cambridge: Cambridge UP.

Jenson, J. and Sineau, M., 1995, *Mitterrand et les Francaises, Un rendez-vous manqué*, Paris: Presses de FNSP.

Jenson, J., 1996, "Introduction: Some Consequences of Economic and Political Restructuring and Readjustment", in *Social Politics*, Spring, 1996.

Jepperson, R. L., Wendt, A. and Katzenstein, P. J., 1996, "Norms, Identity, and Culture in National Security", in Katzenstein, P. J. (ed.), *The Culture of National Security. Norms and Identity in World Politics*, New York: Columbia University Press.

Jimeno, J. and Bentolila, S., 1998, "Regional unemployment persistence (Spain, 1976-1994)", in *Labour Economics*, 5 (1).

Johansen, S., 1988, "Statistical analysis of cointegrating vectors", *Journal of Economic Dynamics and Control*, 12.

Jonung, L., 1993, "Kreditregleringarnas uppgång och fall", in Werin, L. (ed), *Från räntegreglering till inflationsnorm*, Stockholm: SNS.

Jonung, L., 1999, "Med backspegeln som kompass. Om stabiliseringspolitiken som läroprocess", in *Rapport till Expertgruppen för studier i offentlig ekonomi*, Ds 1999: 9 (with a summary in English), Finansdepartementet, Stockholm.

Juselius, K, and Gennari, E., 2000, "European Integration and Monetary Transmission Mechanisms. The case of Italy", Unpublished paper, European University Institute.

Juselius, K., 1992, "Domestic and foreign effects on prices in an open economy. The case of Denmark", in *Journal of Economic Policy Modeling*: 14.

Juselius, K., 1996, "An empirical analysis of the changing role of the German Bundesbank after 1983", in *Oxford Bulletin of Economics and Statistics*, 58.

Juselius, K., 1998a, "Changing monetary transmission mechanisms within the EU", in *Empirical Economics*, 23.

Juselius, K., 1998b, "A structured VAR under changing monetary policy", in *Journal of Business and Economics Statistics, 1998*.

Juselius, K. and MacDonald, R., 2000, *International Parity Relationships between Germany and the United States: A Joint Modelling Approach*, Copenhagen: University of Copenhagen.

Juselius, K. and Toro, J., 1998, "The econometric analysis of money demand in a period of rapid growth. The Case of Spain", Unpublished report at the European University Institute.

Kalecki, M., 1943, "Political Aspects of Full Employment", in *Political Quarterly* 14 (4).

Kaltenthaler, K. C. and Anderson, C. J., 2001, "Europeans and Their Money: Explaining Public Support for the Common European Currency", in *European Journal of Political Research* (forthcoming).

Kaplan, J. and Schleiminger, G., 1989, *The European Payments Union – Financial Diplomacy in the 1950s*, Oxford: Oxford UP.

Katz, R. S. and Mair, P., 1995, "Changing Models of Party Organization and Party Democracy", in *Party Politics*, 1.

Keesing's Contemporary Archives, 1968, *The Arab-Israeli conflict: the 1967 campaign*, Bristol: Keesing's Publications.

Kenen, P., 1969, "The theory of optimum currency areas: An eclectic view", in Mundell. R., and Swoboda, A. (eds.), *Monetary problems of the international economy*, Chicago: University of Chicago Press.

Kenen, P. B., 1995, *Economic and Monetary Union in Europe. Moving Beyond Maastricht*, Cambridge: Cambridge University Press.

Kenner, J., 1999, "The EC Employment Title and the 'Third Way': Making Soft Law Work?", *International Journal of Comparative Labour Law and Industrial Relations*, 15: 1.

Kessous, E., 1997, *Le marché et la sécurité. La prévention des risques et la normalisation des qualités dans le marché unique européen*, Thèse d'économie, Paris: EHESS.

Keynes, J. M., 1936, *The General Theory of Employment, Interest and Money*, MacMillan, London [1973 reprinted in *The Collected Writings of J. M. Keynes*. Vol. VII, London: MacMillan].

Keynes, J. M., 1937, "The General Theory of Employment", in *Quarterly Journal of Economics*, February.

Keynes, M. (ed.), 1975, *Essays on John Maynard Keynes*, Cambridge: Cambridge University Press.

Kielmansegg, P. G., 1996, "Integration und Demokratie", in Jachtenfuchs, M. and Kohler-Koch, B. (eds.), 1996, *Europäische Integration*, Opladen: Leske and Budrich.

Kindleberger, C. P., 1985, "Keynesianism versus Monetarism in Eighteenth Century France", in Kindleberger, C. P., 1985, *Keynesianism vs. Monetarism and Other Essays in Financial History*, London: George Allen and Unwin.

Kitschelt, H., 1999, "European Social Democracy between Political Economy and Electoral Competition", in Kitschelt, H. *et al.* (eds.) *Continuity and Change in Contemporary Capitalism*, Cambridge: University Press.

Kitschelt, H., 2000, "Citizens, Politicians and Party Cartellization", in *European Journal of Political Research*, 37-2, Mar.

Kitschelt, H., Lange, P., Marks, G. and Stephens, J. D. (eds.), 2000, *Continuity and Change in Contemporary Capitalism*, Cambridge: Cambridge University Press.

Kohler-Koch, B., 2000, "Framing: the bottleneck of constructing legitimate institutions", in *Journal of European Public Policy* 7: 4, October.

Krause, L. B. and Salant, W. S. (eds.), 1973, *European Monetary Unification and its Meaning for the United States*, Washington: Brookings.

Krueger, A. O., 1996, "The Political Economy of Control: American Sugar", in Alston, L. J. *et al.* (eds.), *Empirical Studies in Institutional Change*, Cambridge University Press: Cambridge.

Kruse, D. C., 1980, *Monetary Integration in Western Europe: EMU, EMS and Beyond*, London and Boston: Butterworth.

Laffan, B., O'Donnell, R. and Smith, M., 2000, *Europe's Experimental Union*, London: Routledge.

Lafontaine, O. and Strauss-Kahn, D., 1999, "Euro dwingt nieuwe verantwoordelijkheden af", in *NRC Handelsblad*, 30 January.

Lange, P., 1993, "Maastricht and the Social Protocol: Why Did They Do It?", in *Politics and Society*, 21.

Laursen, F. and Vanhoonacker, S. (eds.), 1994, *The Ratification of the Maastricht Treaty: Issues, Debates and Future Implications*, Maastricht: Martinus Nijhoff.

Layard, R., 1986, *How to Beat Unemployment*, Oxford: Oxford University Press.

Leadbeater, C., 2000, *The New Economy: The European Model*, Brussels: Report for the European Commission.

Leaman, J., 1988, *The Political Economy of West Germany, 1945-85. An Introduction*, Houndmills, Basingstoke: Macmillan.

Lee, W. and Prasad, E. S., 1994, "Changes in the Relationship between the Long Term Interest Rate and its Determinants", IMF Working Paper No. 94/124.

Leijonhufvd, A., 1968, *On Keynesian Economics and the Economics of Keynes*, Oxford: Oxford University Press.

Leijonhufvud, A., 1986, "Comment on Barros' paper", in Campbell, C. and Dougan, W. (eds.), *Alternative Monetary Regimes*, Baltimore: Johns Hopkins University Press.

Liebert, U., 1997, "The Gendering of Euro-Scepticism: Public Discourses and Support to the EU in Cross-National Comparison", Cornell University, Institute for European Studies, *Working Paper* No. 97.2, Ithaca NY.

Liebert, U., 1999, "Gender politics in the European Union. The return of the public", in *European Societies*, Vol. I, No. 2.

Liebert, U., Sifft, S. and Sunnus, M., 2000, "Europeanization and the Gendering of National Public Discourses: Great Britain and Sweden in Comparative Perspective", paper prepared for Workshop of the German Research Foundation (DFG), Berlin, 10-11 May.

Lijphart, A., 1999, *Patterns of Democracy*, New Haven (Conn.): Yale University Press.

Lindbeck, A. and Snower, D., 1989, *The Insider-Outsider Theory of Employment and Unemployment*, Cambridge: MIT.

Lindberg, L. N. and Scheingold, S. A., 1970, *Europe's Would Be Polity*, Englewood Cliffs (NJ): Prentice-Hall.

Locher, B. and Prügl, E. 2000, "Feminism and Constructivism: Worlds apart or sharing the middle ground?", in *International Studies Quarterly*, 2000.

Loedel, P. H., 1999, *Deutsche Mark Politics: Germany in the European Monetary System*, Oxford: Oxford University Press.

Ludlow, P., 1982, *The Making of the European Monetary System: A Case Study of the Politics of the European Community*, London: Butterworth Scientific.

Lundborg, P., 1991, "Determinants of migration in the nordic labor market" in *Scandinavian Journal of Economics*, 93 (3).

Lundström, Karin, 1997, "Women caught in a logical trap in EC law: An analysis of the use of quotas in the case of Kalanke", in *Statsvetenskaplig Tidskrift*, 100/1.

Lundvall, B., 1995, "The Learning Economy. Challenges to Economic Theory and Policy", in *EAEPE Conference*, Copenhagen, November.

MacDougall Report (Commission of the European Communities), 1977, *Report of the Study Group on the Role of Public Finance in European Integration*, vols. 1 and 2. Brussels, Doc II/10/77, April.

Maclay, M., 2000, "A Mission for Britain", in *Prospect*, 50, March.

Magnifico, G., 1973, *European monetary unification*, London: Macmillan.

Magnusson, L, and Ottosson, J., 1996, "Transaction Costs and Institutional Change", in Groenewegen, J., (ed.), *Transaction Costs and Beyond*, Boston, Dordrecht: Kluwer Academic Press.

Magnusson, L. and Ottosson, J. (eds.), 1997, *Evolutionary Economics and Path Dependence*, Cheltenham: Edward Elgar.

Magnusson, L. and Ottosson, J., 2000, "State intervention and the role of history-state and private actors in Swedish network industries", in *Review of Political Economy*, vol. 12, No. 2.

Magnusson, L., 2000, *Den tredje industriella revolutionen*, Stockholm: Prisma.

Mair, P., 1999, "Political Parties and Democracy: What Sort of Future?", paper delivered at the Associazione Crs/Democratici di Sinistra, Rome, 24 June.

Mair, P., 2000, "Partyless Democracy", in *New Left Review*, 2-2.

Majocchi, A. and Rey, M., 1993, "A Special Financial Support Scheme in Economic and Monetary Union: Need and Nature", in *European Economy*, 5.

Manin, B., 1997, *The Principles of Representative Government*. Cambridge: University Press.

March, J. G. and Olsen, J. P., 1995, *Democratic Governance*, New York: The Free Press.

Marcussen, M., 2000, *Ideas and Elites: The Social Construction of Economic and Monetary Union*, Aalborg: Aalborg University Press.

Marcussen, M. and Roscher, K., 2000, "The Social Construction of 'Europe': Life-Cycles of Nation-State Identities in France, Germany and Great Britain", in Stråth, B. (ed.), *Europe and the Other and Europe as the Other*, Brussels: PIE-Peter Lang.

Marjolin, R. et al., 1975, *Report of the Study Group Economic and Monetary Union 1980* (The "Marjolin Report"), Commission of the European Communities, Brussels, Doc II/675/3/74, 8 March 1975.

Marquand, D., 2000, "De Derde Weg voorbij", in *Socialisme and Democratie*, 57.

Marsh, D., 1992, *The Bundesbank*, London: William Heinemann Ltd.

Marshall, T. H., 1963, "Citizenship and Social Class" (original 1950), in *Sociology at the Crossroads*, London: Heinemann.

Marshall, W. (ed.), *Building the Bridge*, Lanham (Mrd.): Rowman and Littlefield Publishers.

Martin, A., 2000, *Social Pacts, Unemployment, and EMU Macroeconomic Policy*, Harvard University, Center for European Studies (mimeo).

Matthews, R. G. O., 1968, "Why has Britain Had Full Employment Since the War?", in *The Economic Journal*, No. 311, Vol. LXXVIII.

Mauro, P. and Spilimbergo. A., 1999, "How do the skilled and unskilled respond to regional shocks? The case of Spain", in *International Monetary Fund Staff Papers*, 46 (1).

Mayntz, R. 1999, "Nieuwe uitdagingen voor de Governance Theory", in *Beleid and Maatschappij*, 26.

Mazey, S. and Richardson J., 1993, *Lobbying in the European Community*, Oxford: Oxford UP.

McDowell, L., 1991, "Life without father and Ford: the new gender order of post-Fordism", in *Trans. Inst. Br. Geogr.* 16.

McGrew, A. (ed.), 1997, *The Transformation of Democracy?*, London: Polity Press/Open University Press.

McKinnon, R. I., 1993, "The Rules of the Game: International Money in Historical Perspective", in *Journal of Economic Literature* 31, March.

McNamara, K. R., 1998, *The Currency of Ideas: Monetary Politics in the European Union*, Ithaca: Cornell University Press.

Meade, J. E., 1964, *Efficiency, Equality and the Ownership of Property*, London: George Allen and Unwin.

Meade, J. E., 1975, *The Intelligent Radical's Guide to Economic Policy*, London: Allen and Unwin.

Melkert, A., 2000, "Regeringsleiders moeten agenda EU meer bepalen", in *NRC Handesblad*, 9 October.

Micossi, S. and Padoan, P. C., 1994, "Italy in the EMS: After Crisis Salvation?", in Johnson, C. and Collignon, S. (eds.), *The Monetary Economics of Europe*, London: Pinter.

Middlemas, K., 1995, *Orchestrating Europe*, London: Fontana Press.

Milgate, M., 1987, "Keynes's 'General Theory'", in Eatwell, J. *et al.* (eds.), 1987, *The Bew Palgrave: A Dictionary of Economics, Vol. 3*, London: MacMillan.

Miller, D., 2000, *Citizenship and National Identity*, Cambridge: Polity Press.

Millon-Delsol, C., 1992, *L'Etat subsidiaire*, Paris: Presses Universitaires de France.

Milward, A. S., 1994, *The European Rescue of the Nation State*, London: Routledge.

Minkkinen, P. and Patomäki, H., 1997, "Introduction: The Politics of Economic and Monetary Union", in Minkkinen, P. and Patomäki, H. (eds.), 1997, *The Politics of Economic and Monetary Union*, Boston, Dordrecht and London: Kluwer.

Mirowski, P (ed.), 1994, *Natural Images in Economic Thought: Markets Read in Tooth and Claw*, Cambridge: Cambridge UP.

Mishra, R., 1999, *Globalisation and the Welfare State*, Cheltenham, UK: Edward Elgar.

Mitchell, D. and Garrett, G., 1996, "Women and Welfare State in the Era of Global Markets", in *Social Politics*, Summer/Fall.

Modigliani, F., 1997, "The Shameful Rate of Unemployment in the EMS: Causes and Cures", in Collignon, S. (ed.), *European Monetary Policy*, London: Pinter.

Moravcsik, A., 1998, *The Choice for Europe*, Ithaca (NY): Cornell University Press.

Morgan, M. S. and Rutherford, M, 1998, "American Economics: The Character of the Transformation", in Morgan, M. S. and Rutherford, M. (eds.), *From Interwar Pluralism to Postwar Neoclassicism* Durham and London: Duke University Press.

Morley, J., 1998, "Unemployment in the EU," in Morley, J. and Storm, J. A. (eds.), *Unemployment in Europe – The policy Change*. Discussion paper 73, London: Royal Institute of International Affairs.

Moss, B. H. and Michie, J. (eds.), 2000, *The single European currency in national perspective. A Community in crisis?*, London: Macmillan.

Mulgan, G. *et al.*, 2000, *Achieving Full Employment*, London: IPPR Policy Network.

Mundell, R., 1961, "A theory of optimum currency areas", in *American Economic Review*, 51.

Nau, N., 1990, *The Myth of America's Decline*, New York: Oxford UP.

Newman, M., 1996, *Democracy, Sovereignty and the European Union*, London: Hurst and Company.

Nickell S. J, Layard, R. and Jackman R., 1991, *Unemployment: macroeconomic performance and the labour market*, Oxford: Oxford UP.

Nickell, S., 1997, "Unemployment and Labor Market Rigidities: Europe versus North America", in *Journal of Economic Perspectives*, 1997.

Niethammer, L., 2000, *Kollektive Identitaet: heimliche Quellen einer unheimlichen Konjunktur*, Reinbek: Rowohlt.

North, D. C., 1990, *Institutions, Institutional Change and Economic Performance*, Cambridge: Cambridge University Press.

Notermans, T., 1997, "Social Democracy and External Constraints", in Cox, K. R. (eds.), *Spaces of Globalization*, New York: Guilford Press.

Notermans, T., 1999, "Policy Continuity, Policy Change, and the Political Power of Economic Ideas", in *Acta Politica*, 1999/3.

Notermans, T., 2000, "Social Democratic policies under the single currency", unpublished paper, June 2000.

Notermans, T., 2000a, *Money, Markets, and the State*, Cambridge: Cambridge University Press.

Notermans, T., 2001, "Social Democratic Policies Under The Single Currency", this volume.

Notermans, Ton (ed.), 2001, *Social Democracy and Monetary Union*, New York: Bergahn Books.

Nowak, M., 1994, *La Banquière de l'espoir*, Paris: Albin Michel.

Oatley, T., 1997, *Monetary Politics. Exchange Rate Cooperation in the European Union*, Ann Arbor: The University of Michigan Press.

Obstfeld, M., 1994, "The logic of currency crises", in *Cahiers Economiques*, Banque de France.

Obstfeld, M. and Peri, G., 1998, "Regional non-adjustment and fiscal policy", in *Economic Policy*, No. 26.

Obstfeldt, M. and Rogoff, K., 1994, "The mirage of fixed exchange rates", in *Journal of Economic Perspectives* 9 (4).

Odell, J. S., 1982, *US International Monetary Policy. Markets, Power, and Ideas as Sources of Changes,* Princeton: Princeton UP.

OECD, 1994, *The OECD Jobs Study: Evidence and Explanations and Facts, Analysis, Strategies,* Paris: OECD.

Olsen, J. P., 2001, "Reforming European Institutions of Governance", ARENA, Oslo Working Paper No. 7, Feb.

Olson, M., 2000, *Power and prosperity: outgrowing communist and capitalist dictatorships,* New York, Basic Books.

Ostrup, F., 2000, *Money and the Natural Rate of Unemployment,* Cambridge: Cambridge University Press.

Overturf, S. F., 1997, *Money and European Union*, New York: St. Martin's Press.

Padgett, S. and Paterson, 1991, W. E., *A History of Social Democracy in Postwar Europe*, London: Longman.

Padoa-Schioppa, T, 1999, *EMU and Banking Supervision*, LSE Financial Markets Group, special paper No. 112.

Parti Socialiste, 1999, *Towards a More Just World*, Contribution to the Conference of the Socialist International, Paris, 8-10 November.

Pasinetti, L., 1999, "J. M. Keynes's 'Revolution'", in Pasinetti, L. and Schefold, B. (eds.), 1999, *The Impact of Keynes on Economics in the Twentieth Century,* Cheltenham: Edward Elgar.

Passerini, L. (ed.), 2000, *Images of Europe*, Florence: European University Institute.

Patomäki, H., 1997, "Legitimation Problems of the European Union", in Minkkinen, P. and Patomäki, H., (eds.), 1997, *The Politics of Economic and Monetary Union*, Boston/Dordrecht/London: Kluwer.

Pekkarainen, J., 1989, "Keynesianism and the Scandinavian models of economic policy", in Hall, P. (ed.), *The political power of economic ideas*, Princeton, New Jersey: Princeton University Press.

Pekkarinen, J., 2001, "Finnish social democrats and EMU", in Notermans, T. (ed.), *Social Democrats and Monetary Union*, New York: Berghahn Press.

Pettit, P., 1987, "Towards a Social Democratic Theory of the State", in *Political Studies*, 35.

Petty, W., (1690), *Political Arithmetic* (written 1676).

Pharr, S. J. and Putnam, R.D. (eds.), 2000, *Disaffected Democracies*, Princeton (NJ): University Press.

Phillips, A. W., 1958, "The Relation between Unemployment and the Rate of Change of Money Wage Rates in the United Kingdom 1861-1957", in *Economica*, 25 (Nov.).

Pierson, C., Forster, A. and Jones, E., 1998, "The Politics of Europe: (Un)employment Ambivalence", in Towers, B. and Terry, M. (eds.), *Industrial Relations Journal: European Annual Review 1997*, Oxford: Blackwell.

Pierson, P., 2000, "Increasing Returns, Path Dependency and the Study of Politics", in *American Political Science Review*, 94.

Pigou, A. C., 1920, *The Economics of Welfare*, London: MacMillan.

Plant, R., 1999, "De Derde Weg", in *Socialisme and Democratie* 56.

Pochet, P. 1998, "The Social Consequences of EMU: An Overview of National Debates", in Pochet, P. and Vanhercke, B. (eds.), *Social Challenges of Economic and Monetary Union*, Brussels: European Interuniversity Press (PIE-Peter Lang).

Pochet, P. and Goetschy, J., 2000, "Het Europese werkgelegenheidsbeleid", in *Belgisch Tijdschrift voor Sociale Zekerheid, 2000*.

Pochet, P., 1999, "Monetary Union and Collective Bargaining in Europe: an Overview", in Pochet, P. (ed.), *Monetary Union and Collective Bargaining in Europe*, Brussels: P.I.E.-Peter Lang.

Pochet, P., 2000, "Subsidiarité, gouvernance et politique sociale", in Delpérée (ed.), *Le principe de subsidiarité*, Brussels: Bruylant.

Pries, K., 1997, "Von Greenspan lernen – Parlamentarier möchten beim Euro mitreden", in *Frankfurter Rundschau*, 23 September 1997.

Purdy, D., 1988, *Social Power and the Labour Market*, London: MacMillan.

Purdy, D., 1994, "Citizenship, Basic Income and the State", in *New Left Review*, 208 (November-December).

Putnam, R. D., 2000, *Bowling Alone*, New York: Simon and Schuster.

Radaelli, C. M., 1995, "The Role of Knowledge in the Policy Process", in *Journal of European Public Policy*, 2 (2).

Radaelli, C. M., 1996, "Fiscal federalism as a catalyst for policy development? In search of a framework for European direct tax harmonisation", in *Journal of European Public Policy*, 3 (3).

Rawls, J., 1999, *A Theory of Justice* (Revised Edition), Cambridge (Mass.): The Belknap Press of Harvard UP.

Reich, N., 2000, *Stabilising Citizen and Consumer Expectations by Legal Means When Introducing the Euro in the Participating Member States*, University of Bremen, manuscript.

Reuten, G. *et al.* (eds.), 1998, *De Prijs van de Euro. De Gevaren van de Europese Monetaire Unie*, Amsterdam: Van Gennep.

Revue Socialiste, 1999, *Socialisme européen: vers une nouvelle voie*, 3, September.

Rhodes, M., 1995, "A Regulatory Conundrum: Industrial Relations and the Social Dimension", in Leibfreid, S., and Pierson, P. (eds.), 1995, *European Social Policy. Between Fragmentation and Integration*, Washington: The Brookings Institution.

Rhodes, M., 1998, "Defending the Social Contract: the EU between global constraints and domestic imperatives", in Hine, D. and Kassim, H. (eds.), *Beyond the Market: the EU and National Social Policy*, London: Routledge.

Rhodes, M., 2000a, "Globalisation, Welfare States and Employment: Is There a European 'Third Way'?", in Bermeo, N. (ed.), *Unemployment in the New Europe*, Cambridge: Cambridge University Press.

Rhodes, M., 2000b, "The Political Economy of Social Pacts: "Competitive Corporatism" and European Welfare Reform", in Pierson, P. (ed.), *The New Politics of the Welfare State*, Oxford: Oxford University Press.

Rhodes, M., 2000c, "Desperately Seeking a Solution: Social Democracy, Thatcherism and the "Third Way" in British Welfare," in Ferrara, M. and Rhodes, M. (eds.), *Recasting European Welfare States*. Special issue of *West European Politics*.

Riesenberg, P., 1992, *Citizenship in the Western Tradition*, Chapel Hill and London: University of North Carolina Press.

Risse, T., 1999, "To Euro or Not to Euro? The EMU and Identity Politics in the European Union", in *European Journal of International Relations*, Vol. 5 (2).

Robinson, J., 1962, Review of "Money, Trade and Economic Growth" by H. G. Johnson, in *Economic Journal*, 72 (Sept.).

Robinson, J., 1975, "What has become of the Keynesian Revolution?" in Keynes, M. (ed.), 1975, 1975, *Essays on John Maynard Keynes*, Cambridge: Cambridge University Press.

Robinson, P., 1998, "Britain's Labour Government", *Working Papers II*, Bonn/Amsterdam: Friedrich Ebert Stiftun' /Wiardi Beckman Stichting.

Rødseth, A. and Nymoen, R., 1999, "Noidic wage formation and unemployment seven years later", *Memorandum No. 10*, Oslo: Department of Economics, University of Oslo.

Røed, K., 2000, "Arbeidsledighet, Stabiliseringspolitikk og Lønnsdannelse – Er Kollektiv Lønnsmoderasjon en Farbar Vei Mot Lav Arbeidsledighet?", in NOU 2000: 21, *En Strategi for Sysselsetting og Verdiskaping*, Oslo: Finans-departementet.

Rosenthal, G., 1975, *The Men Behind the Decisions: Cases in European Policy-Making*, Lexington, Mass., Toronto and London: Lexington Books, D.C Heath.

Ross, G., 1995, *Jacques Delors and European Integration*, Cambridge: Polity Press.

Røste, O., 1998, "Tysklands valg av ØMU", in *Internasjonal Politikk*, 56 (2).

Røste, O., 2000, "Hva bestemmer utformingen av valutaområder? Om betydningen av tillit mellom partnerne i valutaunioner", in *Internasjonal Politikk* 58 (3).

Rowthorn, R., 1974, "Neo-Classicism, Neo-Ricardianism and Marxism", in *New Left Review*, 86.

Rowthorn, R., 1980, "Money, Conflict and Inflation" in *Capitalism, Inflation and Conflict*, London: Verso.

Ruggie, J., 1982, "International Regimes, Transactions, and Change. Embedded Liberalism in the Post-war Economic Order", in *International Organization*, 36/1982.

Rymes, T. K., 1989, *Keynes's Lectures 1932-1935: Notes of a Representative Student*, Ann Arbor: University of Michigan Press.

Sabel, C., and Zeitlin, J. (eds.), 1997, *World of Possibilities*, Cambridge: Cambridge University Press.

Salant, W. S., 1989, "The Spread of Keynesian Doctrines and Practices in the United States", in Hall, P. (ed.), 1989, *The Political Power of Economic Ideas*, Princeton, NJ: Princeton University Press.

Salvati, M. 1997, "Moneta Unica, Rivoluzione Copernicana", *Il Mulino*, XLZVI (369).

Samuelson, P. A., 1955, *Economics* (3/e), New York: McGraw-Hill.

Sandholtz, W., 1993a), "Choosing Union: Monetary Politics and Maastricht", in *International Organization*, 47 (1).

Sassoon, D., 1997a, *One Hundred Years of Socialism*, London: Fontana Press.

Sassoon, D. (ed.), 1997b, *Looking Left*, London: I. B. Tauris.

Sbragia, A., 2000, "Italy pays for Europe: Political leadership, political choice, and institutional adaptation", in Caporaso, J., Cowles, M. and Risse, T. (eds.), 2000, *Europeanisation and Domestic Change*, Ithaca, N.Y., Cornell University Press.

Scharpf, F., 1987, *Sozialdemokratische Krisenpolitik in Europa*, Frankfurt am Main: Campus.

Scharpf, F., 1997, *Games Real Actors Play*, Boulder (Colo.): Westview Press.

Scharpf, F. W., 1997, "Economic integration, democracy and the welfare state", in *Journal of European Public Policy* 4 (1).

Scharpf, F., 1999, *Governing in Europe*, Oxford: University Press.

Schiller, R. J., 1979, "The Volatility of Longterm Interest Rates and Expectations Models of the Term Structure", in *Journal of Political Economy*, 87.

Schmidt, V. A., 2000, "The role of values and discourse in welfare state reform: the politics of successful adjustment", paper prepared for the Council for European Studies Conference, Chicago, March 30-April 2.

Sciarra, S., 1999, "The Employment Title in the Amsterdam Treaty: A Multi-Language Legal Discourse", in O'Keefe, D. and Twomey, P. (eds.), *Legal Issues of the Amsterdam Treaty*, Oxford: Hart Publishing.

Sciarra, S., 2000, "Integration Through Coordination: The Employment Title in the Amsterdam Treaty", *Columbia Journal of European Law*, 6: 2.

Setterfield, M., 1993, "A Model of Institutional Hysteresis", in *Journal of Economic Issues*, Vol. XXVII, No. 3, September.

Shackle, G. L. S., 1967, *The Years of High Theory*, Cambridge: Cambridge University Press.

Shaw, J., 2000, "Importing Gender: Feminist Analyses of EU Law", First Draft in preparation for the *Journal of European Public Policy*, special issue on Women, Power and Public Policy, Vol. 7.

Siebert, H., 1997, "Labor Market Rigidities: At the Root of Unemployment in Europe", in *Journal of Economic Perspectives*, 11:3.

Siedentop, L., 2000, *Democracy in Europe*, London: Allen Lane.

Simmons, B. A. (2000), "The Internationalization of Capital", in Kitschelt, H., Lange, P., Marks, G. and Stephens, J. D. (eds.), *Continuity and Change in Contemporary Capitalism*, Cambridge: Cambridge University Press.

Skidelsky, R., 1977, *The End of the Keynesian Era: Essays on the Disintegration of the Keynesian Political Economy*, New York: Holmes and Merier.

Skidelsky, R., 1995, "Keynes for Today", in Dow, S. and Hillard, J. (eds.), 1995, *Keynes, Knowledge and Uncertainty*, Cheltenham: Edward Elgar.

Skidelsky, R., 1999, "The Conditions for a Reinstatement of Keynesian Policy", in Pasinetti, L. and Schefold, B. (eds.), 1999, *The Impact of Keynes on Economics in the Twentieth Century*, Cheltenham: Edward Elgar.

Skidelsky, R., 2000, *John Maynard Keynes: Fighting For Britain 1937-1946*, Basingstoke: Macmillan.

Smith, A., 1759, *The Theory of Moral Sentiments*, [(ed.) D. D. Raphael and A. L. Macfie] Oxford: Calendon Press.

Snyder, F., 1999, "EMU Revisited: Are We Making a Constitution? What Constitution Are We Making?", in Craig, P. and de Búrca, G. (eds.), *The Evolution of EU Law*, Oxford: OUP.

Solow, R., 1990, *The labor market as a social institution*, Cambridge, MA.: Basil Blackwell.

Soltwedel, R., Dhose, D. and Krieger-Boden, C., 2000, "EMU challenges European labor markets", in *International Monetary Fund Working Paper* No. 131.

SPD, Grundwertekommission beim Parteivorstand, 1999, *Dritte Wege – Neue Mitte*, Berlin, September.

Sraffa, P., 1960, *The Production of Commodities by Means of Commodities*, Cambridge: Cambridge University Press.

Stambøl, L. *et al.* 1999. "Regional arbeidsmarkedsmobilitet i nordiske land: bruttostrømsanalyser og etterspørselsbetraktninger i de regionale arbeidsmarkedene", Copenhagen: Nordic Council of Ministers.

Steedman, I.., 1981, *Marx After Sraffa*, London: Verso.

Steindl, J., 1952, *Maturity and Stagnation in American Capitalism* New York: Monthly Review Press.

Steinherr, A. (ed.), 1994, *30 years of European monetary integration from the Werner Plan to EMU*, London and New York: Longman.

Storper, M., and Salais, R., 1997, *Worlds of Production. The Action Frameworks of the Economy*, Cambridge MA.: Harvard University Press.

Strange, S., 1985, "Interpretations of a Decade", in Tsoukalis, L. (ed.), *The Political Economy of International Money*, London: Sage.

Strange, S., 1986, *Casino Capitalism*, Oxford: Blackwell.

Stråth, B., 1987, *The Politics of De-Industrialisation: The Contraction of the West European Shipbuilding Industry*, London: Croom Helm.

Stråth, B., 1996, *The Organisation of Labour Markets: Modernity, Culture and Governance in Germany, Sweden, Britain and Japan*, London: Routledge.

Stråth, B., 2000a, "The Concept of Work in the Construction of Community" in Stråth, B. (ed.), 2000, *After Full Employment. European Discourses on Work and Flexibility*, Brussels: PIE-Peter Lang.

Stråth, B. and Wagner, P., 2000b, "After Full Employment: Theoretical and Political implications", in Stråth, B. (ed.), *After Full Employment. European Discourses on Work and Flexibility*, Brussels: PIE-Peter Lang.

Stråth, B., 2000c, "The Contours of a European Political Economy: From the Werner Plan to the EMU", in Stråth, B. (ed.), *After Full Employment*, Brussels: P.I.E-Peter Lang.

Stråth, B., 2000d, "After Full Employment and the Breakdown of Conventions of Social Responsibility", in Stråth, B. (ed.), *After Full Employment. European Discourses on Work and Flexibility*, Brussels: PIE-Peter Lang.

Streeck, W., 1995, "From Market Making to State Building? Reflections on the Political Economy of European Social Policy", in Leibfried, S. and Pierson, P., *European Social Policy. Between Fragmentation and Integration*, Washington: The Brookings Institution.

Streeck, W., 1998, "The Internationalisation of Industrial Relations in Europe: Prospects and Problems", *Working Paper*, Max Planck Institute, Cologne.

Sumner, M.T. and Zis, G. (eds.), 1982, *European Monetary Union. Progress and Prospects*, London: Macmillan.

Supiot, A. (ed.), 1999, *Au-delà de l'emploi. Transformations du travail et devenir du droit du travail en Europe*, Paris: Flammarion.

Svensson, E.O. and Gerlach, S., 1999, "Money and Inflation in the Euro Area: A case for Monetary Indicators?", Unpublished paper, BIS and SU.

Symes, V., 1995, *Unemployment in Europe: Problems and Policies* London: Routledge.

Symes, V., 1998, *Unemployment and Employment Policies in the EU*, London: Kogan Page.

Szász, A., 1999, *The Road to European Monetary Union*, London: Macmillan.

Szyszczak, E., 1995, "Future Directions in European Union Social Policy Law", in *ILJ*, 24: 19.

Taggart, P., 1998, "A touchstone of dissent: Euroscepticism in contemporary Western European party systems", in *European Journal of Political Research*, 33.

Talani, L. S., 2000, *Betting for and against EMU. Who wins and who loses in Italy and in the UK from the process of European monetary integration*, Ashgate: Aldershot.

Tanzi, V., 1997, "The changing role of the state in the economy: A historical perspective", International Monetary Fund working paper, No. 114.

Tarshis, L., 1987, "Keynesian Revolution" in Eatwell, J., Milgate, M. and Newman, P. (eds.), 1987, *The New Palgrave: A Dictionary of Economics*, London: Macmillan.

Tavelli, H. *et al.*, 1998, "The Evolution of European Central Bank Independence: An Updating of the Masciandaro and Spinelli Index", in *Scottish Journal of Political Economy*, 45 (3).

Teague, P., 1999, "Reshaping Employment Regimes in Europe: Policy Shifts Alongside Boundary Change", in *Journal of Public Policy*, 19: 1.

Telò, M., 2000, "The European Dimension of the Third Way", Cuperus, R., Duffek, K. and Kandel, J. (eds.), 2000, *Multiple Third Ways*, Amsterdam: Wiardi Beckman Stichting.

Temin, P., 1989, *Lessons from the Great Depression*, Cambridge: The MIT Press.

The Economist, 13-19 January 2001.

The Economist, 2000, *A Survey of European Business*, April 29.

Tobin, J., 1972, "Inflation and unemployment", in *American Economic Review*, 62.

Tobin, J., 1980, *Asset Accumulation and Economic Activity*, Chicago: The University of Chicago Press.

Todd, E., 1998, "L'utopie monétaire", in Todd, E., *L'illusion économique. Essai sur la stagnation des societés développées*, Paris: Gallimard.

Toro, J. and Juselius, K., 1999, *The effect of joining the EMS: monetary transmission mechanisms in Spain*, Copenhagen: University of Copenhagen.

Towers, B. and Terry, M. (eds.), *Industrial Relations Journal: European Annual Review 1997*, Oxford: Blackwell

Triffin, R., 1960, *Gold and the Dollar Crisis*, New Haven: Yale UP.

Tronti, L., 1999, "Benchmarking Employment Performance and Labour Market Policies: The Results of the Research Project", in *Transfer: European Review of Labour and Research*, 5.

Tsoukalis, L., 1977, *The Politics and Economics of European Monetary Integration*, London: Allen and Unwin.

Ungerer, H., 1997, A Concise History of European Monetary Integration. From EPU to EMU, Westport Connecticut/London: Quorum.

Van Doorn, J., 1996, "De opmars van het consumentisme en de marginalisering van de politiek", in *Liberaal Reveil*, 37, October.

Van Doorn, J., 1999, "Socialisme als intermezzo", in *HP/De Tijd*, 9 July.

Van Lancker, A., 2000, *Report on the New Social Agenda Medium Term*, Strassburg: European Parliament, PES, 12 May.

Van Parijs, P., 1995, *Real Freedom for All*, Oxford: Oxford University Press.

Van Parijs, P., 2000, "Will Europe Become a Greater Belgium?", in Hampsher-Monk, I. and McKinnon, C., 2000, *The demands of citizenship*, New York: Continuum.

Vandenbroucke, F., 1999, "De actieve welvaartsstaat", Amsterdam: Wiardi Beckman Stichting, Den Uyl Lecture.

Vandenbroucke, F., 1999, "European Social Democracy: Convergence, Divisions, and Shared Questions", in Gamble, A. and Wright, T. (eds.), *The New Social Democracy*. Oxford: Blackwell.

Verdun, A., 1996, "An 'Asymmetrical' Economic and Monetary Union in the EU: Perceptions of Monetary Authorities and Social Partners", in *Journal of European Integration/Revue d'Integration européenne*, 20 (1) Autumn.

Verdun, A., 1998, "The Institutional Design of EMU: A Democratic Deficit?", in *Journal of Public Policy*, 18 (2).

Verdun, A., 1999, "The Role of the Delors Committee in the Creation of EMU: An Epistemic Community?", in *Journal of European Public Policy*, 6 (2).

Verdun, A., 2000a, European Responses to Globalization and Financial Market Integration: Perceptions of Economic and Monetary Union in Britain, France and Germany, Houndmills: Macmillan/ New York: St. Martin's Press.

Verdun, A., 2000b, "Governing by Committee: The Case of the Monetary Committee", in Christiansen, T. and Kirchner, E. (eds.), *Europe in Change: Committee Governance in the European Union*, Manchester: Manchester University Press.

Verdun, A. and Christiansen, T., 2000, "Policy-making, Institution-building and European Monetary Union: Dilemmas of Legitimacy", in Crouch, C. (ed.), *After the Euro: Shaping Institutions for Governance in the Wake of European Monetary Union*, Oxford: Oxford University Press.

Von Hagen, J. and Hammond, G., 1998, "Regional insurance against asymmetric shocks: An empirical study for the European community", in *The Manchester School*, 66.

Wallace, H. and Wallace, W. (eds.), 2000, *Policy-making in the European Union*, 4th edition, Oxford: Oxford University Press.

Walsh, J. I., 2000, *European Monetary Integration and Domestic Politics. Britain, Frances, and Italy*, London: Lynne Rienner.

Walter, F. and Dürr, T., 2000, *Die Heimatlosigkeit der Macht*. Berlin: Alexander Fest Verlag.

Waring, M., 1989, *If Women Counted: new feminist economics*, London, Macmillan.

Weiler, J. H. H., 1999, *The Constitution of Europe*, Cambridge: University Press.

Weir, M. and Skocpol, T., 1985, "State Structures and the Possibilities for 'Keynesian' Responses to the Great Depression in Sweden, Britain, and the United States", in Evans, P. *et al.* (eds.), *Bringing the State Back In*, New York: Cambridge University Press.

Weiss, M., 1998, "The Future Role of the European Union in Social Policy", in Engels, C. and Weiss, M. (eds.), *Labour Law and Industrial Relations at the Turn of the Century: Liber Amicorum in Honour of Roger Blainpain*, The Hague, Kluwer Law International.

Werner Report, 1970, Werner, P., *et al.*, *Report to the Council and the Commission on the realization by stages of economic and monetary union in the Community*, Brussels: European Commission.

Wessels, W. 1998, "Institutionen und Verfahren des WWU Systems: Politikwissenschaftliche Spekulationen", in Ceasar, R. and Scharrer, H. (eds.), *Die Europäische Wirtschafts- und Währungsunion: Regionale und Globale Herausforderungen*, Bonn: Europa Union Verlag.

White, S., 1999, "Rights and Responsibilities", in Gamble, A. and Wright, A., 1999, *The New Social Democracy*, Oxford: Blackwell.

Williamson, O. E., 1996, *The Mechanisms of Governance*, Oxford: Oxford University Press.

Wilson, J. Q., 1989, *Bureaucracy. What government agencies do and why they do it*, New York: Basic Books.

Wyplosz, C., 1999, *Economic Policy Coordination in EMU: Strategies and Institutions*, Paper presented at the German-French Economic Forum, Bonn, 12 January.

Yergin, D. and Stanislaw, J., 1999, *The Commanding Heights*, New York: Simon and Schuster.

Young, B., 2000, "Disciplinary Neoliberalism in the European Union and Gender Politics", in *New Political Economy*, Vol. 5, No. 1.

Young, H., 1999, *The Blessed Plot*, London: Papermac.

Zimmermann, H., 1999, "Franz-Josef Strauß und der deutsch-amerikanische Währungskonflikt", in *Vierteljahreshefte für Zeitgeschichte*, 1/1999.

Zimmermann, H., 2001a, *Money and Security. Troops and Monetary Policy in Germany's Relations to the United Kingdom and the U.S., 1950-71*, Cambridge: Cambridge UP.

Zimmermann, H, 2001b, "Who paid for America's War? The Vietnam War and the International Monetary System", in Gardner , L. C. *et al.* (eds.), *Vietnam in an International Perspective,* Cambridge: Cambridge UP.

Notes on Contributors

Diamond Ashiagbor, BA (Hons) Oxford, was formerly a Lecturer in Law and Research Assistant at the University of Hull, UK and is currently a doctoral researcher at the European University Institute, Florence. Her doctoral research concerns the legal and economic underpinnings of the EU employment strategy. Her research interests are in labour law, legal and economic theories of labour market regulation, and European Union Law (in particular the interaction between social law and economic law). Her publications include articles on EU law and labour law.

J. Peter Burgess is Associate Professor at Volda College, Senior Researcher at the International Peace Research Institute, Oslo, and Visiting Fellow at the Robert Schuman Centre for Advanced Studies, European University Institute, Florence. He has published several works on European culture, politics and identity. His most recent book is *Culture and Rationality: European Frameworks of Norwegian Identity* (Oslo: Norwegian Academic Press, 2001).

Jos de Beus is professor of political theory at the Department of Political Science, Faculty of Social and Behavioural Sciences of the University of Amsterdam. de Beus is preparing a monograph on the globalization of social democracy.

Sheila C. Dow is Professor of Economics at the University of Stirling in Scotland. Her research interests lie in the fields of monetary theory, regional finance and the history and methodology of economic thought. She has published widely in all of these areas, including *Money and the Economic Process* (Elgar, 1993) and *The Methodology of Macroeconomic Thought* (Elgar, 1996).

Roger Hammersland graduated Cand. Oecon, from University of Oslo in 1993. He served as a staff economist in the research department of the Central Bank of Norway from 1993 and is currently a Ph.D. student at the European University Institute, Florence.

Ulrike Liebert is Professor of Comparative Politics at Bremen University, Jean Monnet Chair of Centre for European Studies. She took her Ph.D. at the European University Institute in 1983. She has also had teaching and research activities at the Universidad Autonoma de

Barcelona, University of Heidelberg, and at the Cornell University. Her most recent book, with Nancy Hirschmann, eds., *Women and Welfare. Theory and Practice in the United States and Europe*, Rutgers University Press 2001. She is currently director of a research project on Europeanization, gender politics, and domestic public spheres since 1999.

Barbara MacLennan is a Visiting Fellow at the European University Institute, Florence. Previously, she was assistant lecturer in economics at the University of York and lecturer in economics at the University of Manchester, England. Her research uses the masculine discipline of economics as a foil to develop an analysis of economic and social processes.

Lars Magnusson is the chair of the Department of Economic History, Uppsala University, Sweden, and the National Institute of Working Life, Sweden.

Ton Notermans has studied political science at the University of Amsterdam, the Freie Universität Berlin and MIT. He is currently a Jean Monnet Fellow at the Robert Schuman Centre of the European University Institute. Recent publications include *Money Markets and the State*, Cambridge University Press, 2000, and (editor) *Social Democrats and Monetary Union*, Berghan Press, 2001.

Jan Ottosson is Assistant Professor at the Department of Economic History, Uppsala University, Sweden, and National Institute of Working Life, Sweden.

David Purdy is head of the Department of Applied Social Sciences at the University of Manchester, to which he moved in 1993 after twenty-five years of active service in the ongoing war between political economy and mainstream economics. His publications include *Social Power and the Labour Market* (1988) and his current research ranges over the fields of welfare reform, employment policy, citizenship theory and comparative social policy.

Ole Bjørn Røste is a researcher at the Norwegian School of Management in Sandvika, on leave from the Central Bank of Norway where he has served as a staff member since 1986. In 1995-96 he was a visiting scholar at the University of California, Berkeley.

Robert Salais is Director of the CNRS-labelled research centre "Institutions et Dynamiques Historiques de l'Economie" at the Ecole Normale Supérieure de Cachan. His research focuses on institutional economics, especially on labour markets and welfare. He is one of the founders of the French school of *"Economie des conventions"*, which is now quickly developing at international level. Among his recent works are: *Worlds of Production. The Action Frameworks of the Economy*,

Cambridge MA, Harvard University Press, 1997 (with Michael Storper); *Governance, Industry and Labour Markets in Britain and France,* London, Routledge, 1998 (editor with Noel Whiteside); *Beyond Employment. The Transformation of Work and the Future of Labour Law in Europe,* Oxford, Oxford University Press, to be published 2001 (co-editor with Alain Supiot and others).

Bo Stråth is Professor of Contemporary History in the Department of History and Civilisation/Robert Schuman Centre at the European University Institute Florence. He has published widely on labour market organisation. His research focuses comparatively on processes of modernity in Northern and Western Europe.

Amy Verdun is Associate Professor at the Department of Political Science and Director of the European Studies Programme at the University of Victoria, B.C. Canada. She is the author of *European Responses to Globalization and Financial Market Integration: Perceptions of Economic and Monetary Union in Britain, France and Germany* (MacMillan, 2000) and *Strange Power* (Ashgate, 200). She has also published various articles and book chapters on various aspects of European monetary integration, including on the issue of legitimacy and democracy, the role of experts and the theories of integration.

Hubert Zimmermann is Assistant Professor for International Relations at the Ruhr-Universität, Bochum. He has published on transatlantic relations and European integration. His *Money and Security. Troops and Monetary Policy in Germany's Relations to the United States and Britain, 1950-71* is published by Cambridge University Press in 2001.

Index

A

Action Plan for the Second Stage (1962), 58
Andriessen Frans, 82
Ansiaux H., 75

B

Banks, 18, 19, 41, 78, 181, 182, 185, 191, 194, 197, 198, 262, 264
Barre Plan (1969), 66
Barre Raymond, 65, 66, 74
BIS, 183, 185
Blessing Karl-Heinz, 58, 61
Boyer Miguel, 82
Brandt Willy, 50, 63, 64, 67, 68, 69, 70
Bretton Woods, 27, 37, 49, 50, 51, 52, 53, 56, 57, 58, 62, 63, 65, 67, 70, 71, 74, 80, 125, 126, 129, 133, 134, 140, 141, 146, 148, 158, 164, 165, 183, 342
Brouwers G., 75
Budget stability, 30, 173
Bundesbank, 36, 58, 65, 67, 70, 81, 82, 85, 158, 166, 168, 193, 214, 286, 333, 334, 346, 356

C

Centre of Decision for Economic Policy (CDEP), 78, 342
Citizen's Income, 44, 409
Clappier B., 75
Cold War, 32, 33, 49, 52, 53, 55, 63, 86, 108
Collective wage bargaining, 213
Common Agricultural Policy (CAP), 16, 66, 67, 68, 74, 80, 86, 87, 90, 166, 365, 375
Competition, 39, 42, 44, 45, 84, 90, 95, 104, 106, 113, 119, 131, 159,
164, 182, 185, 186, 187, 190, 191, 224, 256, 257, 258, 261, 262, 266, 269, 289, 290, 296, 306, 354, 367, 368, 371, 372, 374, 375, 378, 385, 395, 399, 401, 403, 416, 420, 434, 436, 437, 440, 449
Competitive corporatism, 44, 401, 405
Conditions of Life, 427, 428
Connally John, 62, 63
Convergence, 21, 35, 70, 76, 84, 88, 89, 136, 137, 149, 150, 165, 174, 183, 186, 189, 193, 194, 197, 209, 291, 302, 305, 311, 318, 322, 323, 363, 375, 378, 381, 422
Convergence criteria, 25, 38, 41, 59, 93, 94, 131, 151, 152, 154, 159, 163, 164, 172, 173, 176, 189, 275, 282, 290, 304, 305, 318, 319, 320, 323, 404
Fiscal convergence, 88, 189
Customs' Union, 74, 75, 86, 87, 90

D

De Gaulle Charles, 32, 33, 36, 56, 57, 59, 61, 62, 65, 66, 70, 140, 154, 159, 449
Delors Jacques, 29, 34, 82, 146, 147, 149, 150, 154, 155, 159, 167, 169, 421, 429, 438, 439
Delors Committee, 19, 83, 88, 150, 163, 168, 170, 318
Delors Report, 38, 73, 74, 82, 83, 84, 85, 86, 87, 89, 91, 92, 94, 95, 96, 126, 127, 131, 142, 147, 148, 149, 150, 168, 169, 265
Democratic deficit, 269, 359

"Work & Society"

The series "Work & Society" analyses the development of employment and social policies, as well as the strategies of the different social actors, both at national and European levels. It puts forward a multi-disciplinary approach – political, sociological, economic, legal and historical – in a bid for dialogue and complementarity. The series is not confined to the social field *stricto sensu*, but also aims to illustrate the indirect social impacts of economic and monetary policies. It endeavours to clarify social developments, from a comparative and a historical perspective, thus portraying the process of convergence and divergence in the diverse national societal contexts. The manner in which European integration impacts on employment and social policies constitutes the backbone of the analyses.

Series Editor: Philippe POCHET, Director of the Observatoire social européen (Brussels) and Digest Editor of the Journal of European Social Policy.

Series Titles

No.34– *Building Social Europe through the Open Method of Co-ordination*, Caroline DE LA PORTE & Philippe POCHET (eds.), SALTSA–Observatoire social européen (2002), 319 p., ISBN 90-5201-984-3.

No.33– *Des marchés du travail équitables ?*, Christian BESSY, François EYMARD-DUVERNAY, Guillemette DE LARQUIER & Emmanuelle MARCHAL (eds.), Centre d'Études de l'Emploi, (2001), 308 p., ISBN 90-5201-960-6.

No.32– *Trade Unions in Europe: Meeting the Challenge*, Deborah FOSTER & Peter SCOTT (eds.), forthcoming, ca. 250 p., ISBN 90-5201-959-2.

No.31– *Health and Safety in Small Enterprises. European Strategies for Managing Improvement*, David WALTERS, SALTSA (2001), 404 p., ISBN 90-5201-952-5.

No.30– *Europe – One Labour Market?*, Lars MAGNUSSON & Jan OTTOSSON (eds.), SALTSA (2002), 306 p., ISBN 90-5201-949-5.

No.29– *From the Werner Plan to the EMU. In Search of a Political Economy for Europe*, Lars MAGNUSSON & Bo STRÅTH (eds.), SALTSA (2001), 526 p., ISBN 90-5201-948-7.

N°28– *Discriminations et marché du travail. Liberté et égalité dans les rapports d'emploi*, Olivier DE SCHUTTER (2001), 234 p., ISBN 90-5201-941-X.

No.27– *At Your Service? Comparative Perspectives on Employment and Labour Relations in the European Private Sector Services*, Jon Erik DØLVIK (ed.), SALTSA (2001), 556 p., ISBN 90-5201-940-1.

N°26– *La nouvelle dynamique des pactes sociaux*, Giuseppe FAJERTAG & Philippe POCHET (dir.), Observatoire social européen–Institut syndical européen (2001), 436 p., ISBN 90-5201-927-4.

No.25– *After Full Employment. European Discourses on Work and Flexibility*, Bo STRÅTH (ed.) (2000), 302 p., ISBN 90-5201-925-8.

N°24– *L'Europe syndicale au quotidien. La représentation des salariés dans les entreprises en France, Allemagne, Grande-Bretagne et Italie*, Christian DUFOUR et Adelheid HEGE, IRES (2002), 256 p., ISBN 90-5201-918-5.

N°23– *Union monétaire et négociations collectives en Europe*, Philippe POCHET (ed.), SALTSA–Observatoire social européen (1999), 284 p., ISBN 90-5201-916-9.

No.22– *Monetary Union and Collective Bargaining in Europe*, Philippe POCHET (ed.), SALTSA–Observatoire social européen (1999), 284 p., ISBN 90-5201-915-0.

No.21– *The Regulation of Working Time in the European Union (Gender Approach) – La réglementation du temps de travail en Europe (Perspective selon le genre)*, Yota KRAVARITOU (ed.), European University Institute, (1999), 504 p., ISBN 90-5201-903-7.

N°20– *Wégimont ou le château des relations humaines. Une expérience de formation psychosociologique à la gestion*, Marcel BOLLE DE BAL, (1998), 353 p., ISBN 90-5201-811-1.

No.19– *De sociale knelpunten van de Economische en Monetaire Unie*, Philippe POCHET & Bart VANHERCKE (eds.), Observatoire social européen, (1998), 194 p., ISBN 90-5201-807-3.

No.18– *Social Challenges of Economic and Monetary Union*, Philippe POCHET & Bart VANHERCKE (eds.), Observatoire social européen, (1998), 172 p., ISBN 90-5201-806-5.

N°17– *Les enjeux sociaux de l'Union économique et monétaire*, Philippe POCHET & Bart VANHERCKE (eds.), Observatoire social européen (2e éd. 1999), 185 p., ISBN 90-5201-805-7.